During the 1970s over a quarter of a million Jews left the Soviet Union. It is doubtful if this mass emigration, which was mainly to Israel, would have been possible without the extensive groundwork of the previous two decades. In this important new study of Soviet Jewry, Yaacov Ro'i examines the cultural, social, political and international context of the movement for Soviet Jewish emigration from the establishment of the State of Israel to the outbreak of the Six Day War.

*The struggle for Soviet Jewish emigration 1948–1967* opens with a discussion of the lives of Soviet Jews, which is based upon a range of personal interviews. Yaacov Ro'i explores how Jewish self-awareness arose both as a product of the Holocaust and as a result of the founding of the State of Israel. Jewish identity was further fostered by popular antisemitism and Soviet policy and local groups developed in clandestine or semi-clandestine conditions to sustain Jewish cultural interests.

The author continues by analyzing the campaign conducted in the West by individual organizations and governments on behalf of Soviet Jewish rights as a whole and emigration in particular. The Israeli government mobilized Jewish and non-Jewish public opinion and support and the presence of the Israeli embassy in Moscow gave confidence and inspiration to Soviet Jews. By 1967, as Ro'i convincingly argues, Soviet Jewish efforts to maintain even a minimal Jewish existence seemed doomed to constant frustration in a steadfastly antisemitic system, and most nationalistically minded Jews accepted that the only way of fulfilling their aspirations was to emigrate to Israel.

# THE STRUGGLE FOR SOVIET JEWISH EMIGRATION 1948–1967

**Soviet and East European Studies**



*Series list continues at the end of the book*

# THE STRUGGLE FOR SOVIET JEWISH EMIGRATION 1948–1967

YAACOV RO'I

Associate Professor of Russian History
at Tel Aviv University

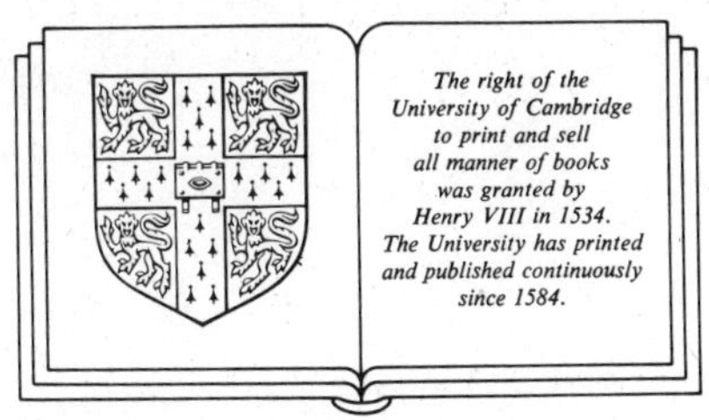


CAMBRIDGE UNIVERSITY PRESS

Cambridge
New York   Port Chester
Melbourne   Sydney

Published by the Press Syndicate of the University of Cambridge
The Pitt Building, Trumpington Street, Cambridge CB2 1RP
40 West 20th Street, New York, NY 10011, USA
10 Stamford Road, Oakleigh, Melbourne 3166, Australia



First published 1991

Printed in Great Britain at the University Press, Cambridge


*British Library cataloguing in publication data*
Ro'i, Yaacov
The struggle for Soviet Jewish emigration 1948–1967. –
(Soviet and East European Studies; 75)
1. Soviet Union. Jews. Emigration, history
I. Title        II. Series
304.8'0947

*Library of Congress cataloguing in publication data*
Ro'i , Yaacov
The struggle for Soviet Jewish emigration 1948–1967/Yaacov Ro'i.
   p.   cm. – (Soviet and East European Studies: 75)
Includes bibliographical references.
ISBN 0 521 39084 2
1. Jews – Soviet Union – History – 1917–
2. Jews – Soviet Union – Migrations.
3. Jews – Soviet Union – Persecutions – Public opinion.
4. Soviet Union – Emigration and immigration.
5. Soviet Union – Ethnic relations.
I. Title.        II. Series.
DS135.R92R63 1990
947'.004924 – dc20   89–70825   CIP

ISBN 0 521 39084 2 hardback

CE

# Contents

## PART II                                                          87



## PART III

Yad leShaul
To the memory of Shaul Avigur

# Preface

A work of this nature seems to require some methodological explanation since it has not been possible to adhere strictly to the rules of historical writing in its preparation. This is because the task of combining in a single volume the history of the struggle for Soviet Jewish *aliya* or emigration to Israel both inside and outside the Soviet Union presented a formidable challenge in terms of both content and methodology which dictated *a priori* some rather than unusual rules. For example, although I strove to maintain a balance between the struggle of the Soviet Jews themselves and the support they received from the outside world, the considerable documentation for the latter – which was largely a public struggle – and the very meager documented information available on the former, which was unorganized, uninstitutionalized and largely clandestine, resulted in my having to use material that is totally different in both genre and quantity.

The sparceness of reliable material on the activities of the Soviet Jews has necessitated the inclusion of numerous stories and incidents for which testimonies could be found. I am aware that, despite my best efforts, the ones I have included may not recount the exploits of all, perhaps not even some of the central, heroes of the struggle. I also realize that the written and oral personal reminiscences on which I have had to rely are not necessarily exact. Nonetheless, I am convinced that the events described herein are representative in that they reflect what happened not only to the people mentioned, but also to those concerning whose activities I was not able to find substantiation or detailed evidence either because they disappeared in the camps or remained in the Soviet Union. Of the latter category, only those whose deeds have already been published are named in this work.

On the purely technical level, generally accepted rules of transliteration have been used, with one major exception: the Russian *miagkii znak*, the soft sign usually rendered ', has been omitted in the names of people and places to make for easier reading. With regard to names, as many Soviet Jews hebraicized their names after emigrating to Israel, Russian Jewish names have been transliterated from the Russian when describing the activities of a Soviet Jew inside the USSR , and from the Hebrew after that person settled in Israel.

# Acknowledgments

This volume has been prepared with the assistance of the Society for Research on Jewish Communities and The Centre for Research and Documentation of East European Jewry, both of the Hebrew University of Jerusalem. Without their generous aid this research would have been impossible, and I should first like to thank these two institutions and their respective staffs. In particular, I owe a major debt to the late Professor Shmuel Ettinger, who headed both institutions for the greater part of the period in which my work on this project was conducted and was always ready to give of his time and to offer assistance and encouragement.

I have dedicated this volume to the memory of the late Shaul Avigur as the person who initiated and orchestrated so much of the struggle for the emigration of Soviet Jewry to Israel. I am also personally indebted to him because the original idea for the project which has resulted in this book came from him and it was his urging and interest which set the project in motion.

A further round of thanks is due to the large number of private individuals who agreed to be interviewed by me in Israel, the U.S. and elsewhere. Many of these also made a great effort to provide me with documentation, that substantiated and complemented their memories. Because of the very nature of the struggle which this book documents, its heroes, specifically those who carried on the battle inside the Soviet Union, were unable for obvious reasons to keep diaries or other records of their activities. Many of the activists who have since emigrated have become my friends and I regard it as one of the rewards of my research that I was thus able to become acquainted with them. The same applies to many of those dedicated people who took up the struggle on behalf of Soviet Jewry in the West.

A considerable portion of the research for Part II of this volume was carried out in the United States. I wish to express my gratitude to the

Kennan Institute for Advanced Russian Studies at the Woodrow Wilson International Center for Scholars, Washington, D.C., from whom I received a visiting grant for the purpose of implementing this particular part of the project.

I also want to thank those who helped me at various stages of my work: Liova Lak, Haya Nezer, Michaela Gepshtein, the late Mordecai Naishtat, Vera Yedidya, Yeshayahu Averbukh and Dr. Yossi Goldstein; Professors Ted Friedgut and Mordecai Altshuler, who were always ready to provide me with details and bibliographical guidance; and most of all Ester Zeitlin, who typed up the original manuscript (most of it twice) despite its virtual undecipherability, Philippa Shimrat, who did some very conscientious style-editing, and Norma Schneider, who took upon herself the unenviable task of cutting the manuscript down to size.

Finally, I must thank my wife for the incredible patience with which she indulges my insatiable craving for writing long books.

# Glossary

| | |
|---|---|
| *agitprop* | CPSU Central Committee department for agitation and propaganda |
| *aliya* | immigration to Israel |
| *briha* | escape or rescue operation organized from Palestine by the Hagana to help Jews in Central and Eastern Europe reach Palestine at the end of World War II |
| *dvadtsatka* | the twenty "initiators" who, according to Soviet law, had to register religious institutions (churches, synagogues, mosques) with the authorities and were responsible for their activities |
| *hatikva* | the Israeli national anthem (prior to 1948 the anthem of the World Zionist Organization) |
| *kaddish* | prayer for the departed |
| Komsomol | the Young Communist League or CPSU youth organization |
| Kol Zion lagola | Israeli broadcast service to the Jewish diaspora |
| *minyan* | ten men or quorum without whom, according to Jewish law, no public prayer can be held |
| *vyzov* | affidavit supplied by a relative of a Soviet citizen resident abroad inviting the latter to join his family and guaranteeing his welfare |
| *yishuv* | the Jewish settlement in Palestine prior to Israel's establishment in 1948 |

# Abbreviations

| | |
|---|---|
| ADL | Anti-Defamation League |
| AJA | Anglo-Jewish Association |
| AJC | American Jewish Committee |
| AJCSJ | American Jewish Conference on Soviet Jewry |
| AJC FAD | American Jewish Committee, Foreign Affairs Division |
| ASSR | Autonomous Soviet Socialist Republic |
| CBJO | Coordinating Board of Jewish Organizations |
| CIO | Congress of Industrial Organizations |
| COJO | Conference of Jewish Organizations |
| CP | Communist Party |
| CPA | Communist Party of Australia |
| CPSU | Communist Party of the Soviet Union |
| CR | *Congressional Record* |
| CRDEEJ | Centre for Research and Documentation of East European Jewry |
| CRIF | Conseil représentatif des juifs en France |
| CZA | Central Zionist Archive |
| DP | Displaced Persons |
| ECAJ | Executive Council of Australian Jewry |
| ECOSOC | U.N. Economic and Social Council |
| FRG | Federal Republic of Germany |
| FRUS | *Foreign Relations of the United States* |
| GA OR | United Nations General Assembly Official Records |
| H. CON. RES. | U.S. House of Representatives Concurrent Resolution |
| H. RES | U.S. House of Representatives Resolution |
| HIAS | Hebrew Immigrant Aid Society |
| IDF | Israel Defence Forces |

| | |
|---|---|
| JAFC | Jewish Anti-Fascist Committee |
| JC | *Jewish Chronicle* |
| JDC | American Jewish Joint Distribution Committee |
| JEE | *Jews in Eastern Europe* |
| JP | *Jerusalem Post* |
| JTA | *Jewish Telegraphic Agency Daily News Bulletin* |
| MGB | Ministenstvo gosudarstvennoi bezopasnosti (Ministry of State Security) |
| M.K. | Member of Knesset |
| MVD | Ministerstvo vnutrennykh del (Ministry of the Interior; USSR) |
| NAACP | National Association for the Advancement of Colored People |
| NCRAC | National Community Relations Advisory Council |
| NGO | Non-governmental organizations |
| NYHT | *New York Herald Tribune* |
| NYT | *New York Times* |
| OVIR | Otdel vnutrennykh i inostrannykh registratsii (Department for domestic and foreign registration; Soviet Ministry of the Interior) |
| PCF | Parti communiste français |
| PCI | Partito comunista italiano |
| PRO | Public Record Office |
| PZO | Prisoners of Zion Organization |
| RCA | Rabbinical Council of America |
| RSFSR | Russian Soviet Federative Socialist Republic |
| S. RES. | U.S. Senate Resolution |
| SCA | Synagogue Council of America |
| SHWD | Shwadron Collection, Dayan Center, Tel Aviv University |
| SSR | Soviet Socialist Republic |
| SSSJ | Student Struggle for Soviet Jewry |
| SWB | BBC Summary of World Broadcasts |
| UJA | United Jewish Appeal |
| WFDY | World Federation of Democratic Youth |
| WJC | World Jewish Congress |
| WUJS | World Union of Jewish Students |
| WZO | World Zionist Organization |
| ZOA | Zionist Organization of America |

# Introduction

It is historical fact that over one quarter of a million Jews left the Soviet Union between 1971 and 1979. This development, which today is known to all, was totally unexpected – indeed, would probably have seemed impossible to any student of Soviet affairs at the beginning of the 1970s. In order to understand the developments of the seventies, one must look to the early stages of the struggle for Soviet Jewish emigration which are much less well known.

The period begins with the establishment of the State of Israel in 1948, certainly the most important event in the postwar international arena for those Soviet Jews who had retained any Jewish consciousness or orientation after thirty years of Soviet rule, especially since Israeli and Zionist leaders saw Israel's right and obligation to serve as a haven for oppressed Jews the world over as its *raison d'être*.[1] It ends with the outbreak of the Six Day War, when the Soviet Union – which had been the first country in the world to afford Israel *de jure* recognition – severed diplomatic relations with the Jewish state; the combination of these two events (the war and the cutting of relations) catapulted the Jewish national movement into a new stage of development and activity.

The main purpose of this book is to show how those Jews whose Judaism and Jewish leanings were reinvigorated, or even initially stimulated, by the establishment of the Jewish state, sought to give vent to their Jewishness within a closed and largely antagonistic environment. I shall also try to explain why these Jews came to view emigration as their only chance for survival as Jews and how they sought to prepare the ground for the implementation of their aspirations. And, as it is impossible to detach the struggle to emigrate from its physical and political context, I shall mention Soviet domestic and international trends and events when this seems called for, without, however, attempting an in-depth analysis of similarities between the

Jewish national "movement" (insofar as this term can be used in the Soviet context in these years) and that of other national or "dissident" movements which sought rather to change the Soviet system; this would have broadened the scope of the book to unmanageable proportions.

Although only 7,000 Jews emigrated to Israel during the nineteen years covered, the significance of this study extends beyond the epic of a few thousand Jews' defiance of the rules of conduct laid down by a seemingly omnipotent regime.[2] For the emigration of the 1970s could not have taken place without the many years of preparation that allowed the masses who emigrated in that decade to take advantage of the confluence of favorable domestic and international circumstances of that decade.

I have concentrated on *aliya* in my discussion of the Soviet Jewish struggle for emigration, even though a large percentage of those who emigrated in later years have settled outside Israel. I have done this deliberately because, in the years in question, the vast majority of Jews who sought to leave the Soviet Union did so with the specific intention of going to Israel and because it is my contention that only those Jews whose struggle has a positive content – that is the search for their Jewish roots and the desire to live in the Jewish state – have the motivation and stamina to maintain a protracted and risk-filled struggle. I would suggest that any other orientation of necessity precludes the formation of the kind of movement that has any chance of success, whether in the face of heavy-handed KGB repression or against the far more sophisticated manipulations of an apparently liberal regime that, in my opinion and the opinion of many former refuseniks, have tended to be no less intent on keeping the main body of its Jews in the Soviet Union.

While it is true that during our period and, indeed, even in the seventies, the majority of Soviet Jews either tried to hide their Jewishness or gave it no expression, estimates of those who would have at least contemplated emigration given propitious conditions ran from half a million to a million. Questions regarding how far such numbers in fact reflected Soviet Jewish reality at any given time or how many of those contemplating emigration even considered making *aliya* to Israel do not gainsay the legitimacy of our topic, especially since the struggle to leave the Soviet Union will presumably be a recurrent, if not a permanent and ongoing, feature of Soviet Jewish existence as long as significant numbers of Jews remain in that country.

It is a given that the *sine qua non* for the struggle for Soviet Jewry's emigration must always be its own actions. For, if Soviet Jews have neither the desire to emigrate nor the belief that emigration is feasible, or if they are not prepared to fight and take the risks involved in achieving this, no group or movement outside the Soviet Union can conduct a struggle on their behalf. However, Soviet Jews do not and cannot constitute a meaningful political force in the Soviet context and therefore rely on the State of Israel and Jewish and other Western liberal individuals and organizations for encouragement and inter-cessions on their behalf. Since assurances of Jewish solidarity, news of demonstrations or direct contact with foreigners interested in their plight, give Soviet Jewry the moral boost which enables them to persist in their struggle, the development of the connection between the movement inside and outside the USSR is a fundamental part of our story whatever the evaluation of the selective importance of the efforts conducted inside and outside the USSR.

The first major event, then, in the story of the post-World War II struggle for Soviet Jewish emigration was the establishment of the State of Israel in May 1948. While people inside the Soviet Union did not dare talk openly of emigration at this stage, a considerable number of Soviet Jews were brave enough, even then, to openly identify with the new Jewish state. Not only did 2,000 Jews gather spontaneously at Moscow's main synagogue on the first Sunday after the state's establishment to celebrate informally,[3] but many thousands attended when – in July – the same synagogue held an official service to mark the event. And, when the first Israeli envoy, Golda Meyerson (later Meir), appeared in the Soviet capital, tens of thousands came to the synagogue on the Jewish High Holy Days to welcome her. Indeed, during the same period, when the new Jewish state was being attacked by its Arab neighbors, young Jews throughout the Soviet Union were applying to government offices and to the Jewish Anti-Fascist Committee for permission to go and fight in Israel's War of Independence.

The bravado – for it was nothing short of that – that the Jews displayed in the year of 1948 both in welcoming the Israeli diplomats and in applying to fight in Israel, can be explained on two levels. First, there was the revival of Jewish consciousness as a result of the Holocaust, the fact that large numbers of the local population had collaborated with the Nazi invaders, and the official antisemitism that began to pervade the Soviet establishment in the mid-1940s. On top of this was the excitement that enveloped large sectors of the Soviet

Jewish population when Israel was established, which, ironically, was encouraged by the Soviet government's support of the Jewish state.

But, after their initial euphoria, the Jews were soon to be disillusioned. Many of those who attended the 1948 High Holy Day demonstrations of support for Israel at Moscow's Choral Synagogue, as well as most of those who volunteered to fight in Israel's War of Independence seem to have been arrested between October 1948 and summer 1950. Throughout the country, too, participants in groups that had formed to learn or talk Hebrew and to discuss the Israeli events they had been able to hear about on foreign (British, American and Israeli) broadcasts, were also imprisoned.

The "black years" of Soviet Jewry – from late 1948 through spring 1953, when Stalin died – culminated in the "Doctors' Plot" of January 1953. It was during these years, the bleakest from the point of view of Jewish nationalist activity,[4] that the camps began to receive large numbers of Jewish prisoners. Yet, even in these years, there were small clandestine groups in various parts of the country for whom Israel's establishment and military achievements during its War of Independence provided sufficient stimulus to keep them going. In the period that followed the Great Patriotic War against Nazi Germany, Israel's military prowess was a value in itself both for older Jews who had been members of Zionist movements in their younger days and for many young people, mostly students, who sought their roots in a country where, on the one hand, there was no longer any Jewish culture and, on the other, they were unable to escape their Jewishness.

The first small-scale emigration to Israel began in the early Khrushchev years. About one thousand Jews left the Soviet Union between 1954 and the outbreak of the Sinai War in October 1956. All of these had close relatives in Israel and were allowed to leave within the framework of family reunification. The great majority of these emigrants were elderly people, above the age of sixty, who came from the so-called Western territories, which had been annexed by the USSR during World War II or in its immediate aftermath. (In this same period members of other national minorities – notably Greeks, Germans and Spaniards – were likewise being permitted to return to their homelands.) After this small emigration which came to an abrupt and almost complete halt with the Sinai War, there was no emigration to speak of, with the important exception of that which took place in the framework of the Soviet–Polish repatriation agreement. Some 25,000 Jews left the USSR for Poland between November 1956, when the agreement was worked out in principle, and the end of 1959, when the agreement expired. Over 90 percent of these Jews went on to Israel, which Khrushchev indicated that the Soviet authorities knew would be the case when they allowed them to leave.

It was not, however, until the late 1950s, when the small emigration of elderly people and the Polish repatriation had generated hope, that the idea of emigration began to take hold among broader sections of the Soviet Jewish community. Jews began to appreciate that although conditions were not yet ripe, emigration was not totally unfeasible.

The struggle for emigration was given impetus by three additional factors. First, despite the fact that he allowed a few Jewish artists to appear publicly with Yiddish songs and a handful of Yiddish books to be published, Khrushchev's liberalization had little meaning for the Jews, whose culture as such was not rehabilitated. Secondly, this liberalization did result in the release of Jews from the camps (together with hundreds of thousands, or even millions, of political prisoners). And many of these Jewish prisoners who had learned Hebrew and Jewish history in the camps now became the nucleus of a new movement as they returned to their places of residence throughout the country. Having already experienced arrest, interrogations, prison and camp, they felt they had little to lose and were thus more daring than the average Soviet Jewish citizen. Moreover, their common experience created the mutual trust necessary for the existence and survival of any such movement. For, whereas the Soviet system had always relied upon the fear and mutual distrust that the regime instilled in its citizens to keep them from cooperating with potential fellow thinkers, now Jews in a number of towns were maintaining contact with each other with the ultimate purpose of implementing a common objective. Finally, there was the Moscow Youth Festival of 1957, which brought thousands from all over the country to see the young Israelis visiting the Soviet capital perform and, even more importantly, to talk Hebrew with them and hear about Israel at first hand. The new motivation that this opportunity aroused in the people who came to Moscow and in those they told of what they had seen and heard when they returned to their homes, had an enormous effect on the movement for years to come.

The seven or eight years that preceded the June 1967 war saw intensified activity in the struggle: new Hebrew study groups were formed, a Jewish *samizdat* began to appear, halls were packed when Yiddish singers performed and the synagogues were crowded with youth on the major Jewish festivals. Moreover, people no longer concealed their desire to emigrate. Elie Wiesel, who visited the Soviet Union in fall 1965, wrote of what he saw in the Moscow synagogue and elsewhere in *The Jews of Silence*. And an Israeli diplomat who visited Jewish communities throughout the Soviet Union estimated in the early 1960s that the great majority of the non-Ashkenazi Jews and of the Jews of the Western territories, as well as large numbers of others, would avail themselves of the opportunity to leave for Israel when and if it presented itself.

The final upsurge came toward the end of the sixties. In the tense weeks that preceded the Six Day War large numbers of Soviet Jews realized that their own fate was intimately connected with that of the Jewish state. After Israel's military successes during this war, they were filled with the same pride and satisfaction that had enabled them to straighten their own rather bowed backs at the time of the Israeli War of Independence. The growth of the general dissident movement during this period had attracted many Jewish intellectuals to the Democratic Movement. Disillusioned when that movement failed to make an impact in the wake of the Soviet bloc invasion of Czechoslovakia in 1968, and as the domestic policy of the Brezhnev leadership hardened, these intellectuals now started thinking in terms of emigration. And, as some of the earlier activists began receiving exit permits in 1969, when the Kremlin apparently decided to let them out in order to defuse the movement by getting rid of its most prominent activists, these frustrated intellectuals moved into their place. Nor was the importance of the dissident movement solely in that it trained, as it were, new cadres for the struggle for emigration; it also created an atmosphere that was conducive to the formation of other dissenting currents and developed methods that were adopted and improved upon by the Jewish movement. In 1969 Soviet Jews began appealing to Israeli and other Western statesmen and public figures to help them repatriate to Israel. Copies of similar approaches to the Soviet leadership were smuggled out to the West in order to heighten pressure on the Kremlin. A new chapter in the story of the struggle was opened in 1970 when a group of activists from Riga and Leningrad planned to steal a plane to fly to freedom in order to highlight the desperation of Soviet Jewry, their subsequent trial and harsh sentences catapulting the movement into high gear.

The Soviet Jewry movement in the West started out by pressing for cultural and religious rights for and the cessation of the discriminatory practices against the Soviet Jewish minority. After a first outcry in 1953 as a result of the Doctors' Plot, Western Jewish individuals and organizations did not really return to the fray until 1956. From that time on, however – often at Israeli instigation – there was a spate of visits to the USSR of Jewish and non-Jewish politicians, journalists and public figures to inquire into the lot of Soviet Jewry. This included Jewish members of Western communist parties, not a few of whom left their parties as a result of what they learned on their visits. The shock of these visitors when they learned at first hand of the total liquidation of Soviet Jewish cultural activity, including the actual execution under Stalin of the leading Jewish cultural and other figures, was usually communicated loudly and clearly upon their return home. Thus, from that time on, a large percentage of the Western delegations that visited the Soviet Union raised the Jewish question with whatever level of Soviet officialdom they came into contact. Despite the suave manner in which the Soviets dealt with these queries and criticisms, Moscow did make some, mostly minor, gestures to the Jews, for Khrushchev was intent on achieving "peaceful coexistence" with the West and sought to minimize anti-Soviet pressures on Western governments. (In periods of tension and cold war Moscow is mostly studiously impervious to foreign pressures.)

Apart from the implications that this mounting interest by the West in Soviet Jewish affairs had for the Soviet leadership, the visits of Israelis and Western Jews to the synagogues and to Yiddish artistic performances brought them into contact with local Jews. And, despite the general obstructions to conversation and private meetings, these visits and whatever minimal contacts could be made were of major importance in showing Soviet Jews that they had not been forsaken by the Jewish world outside.

By the 1960s, many leading intellectuals in the West had become interested in the lot of Soviet Jewry. Since this interest, too, was largely brought about directly or obliquely by Israel, it involved the issue of reunification of families between Soviet Jewish citizens and their relatives in the Jewish state. In the U.S. those interested included people who had been, or still were, leaders of the civil rights movement and other well-known figures to the left of center, some of whom later became active in the anti-Vietnam movement, as well as non-Jewish religious figures and a larger spectrum of Jewish artists, scientists and other important personalities. In Western Europe, too, the impressive battery of public figures who identified themselves with the struggle included Bertrand Russell, Umberto Terracini and Daniel Mayer. Parliamentarians were also beginning to evince an interest in the issue. Indeed, the number of entries related to Soviet

Jewry in the U.S. Congressional Record of the early 1960s is truly astonishing. While, again, their main thrust was the lot of Soviet Jews inside the USSR, quite a few referred to the need for reuniting families separated by war or other circumstances over which they had no control. It was thus not surprising when a number of Soviet Jews sought the assistance of Western figures to help them leave the Soviet Union.

The central slogan of the public movement on behalf of Soviet Jewry that came into being in the U.S. in the mid-sixties very soon became "Let My People Go!" By 1964 the main U.S. Jewish organizations organized the first American Jewish Conference on Soviet Jewry in Washington, D.C., and established a body with the same name to keep the momentum going. That year also witnessed the first large public demonstrations that, while not yet the massive Solidarity Day marches of the 1970s, nonetheless garnered impressive support. As the issue became a permanent fixture on the agenda of the relevant U.N. committees, the Soviet U.N. mission became the natural venue of these demonstrations, although some took place at Madison Square Gardens and elsewhere (mostly in New York). And the year before, Justice Arthur Goldberg and Senators Jacob Javits and Abraham Ribicoff had approached President Kennedy to enlist his help on behalf of Soviet Jewry. This was but the first of several similar attempts to mobilize the active sympathy of U.S. presidents in the Soviet Jewry cause.

The activity centered around the Jackson–Vanik amendment in the years 1972–74, which catapulted the struggle in the West for the right of Soviet Jewry to emigrate to the highest level of super-power diplomacy and opened another chapter in our story, thus had a long history behind it. There can be little doubt that the mass support given the endeavor to withhold most-favored nation status from the Soviet Union because it refused to accept the principle of free emigration, not to speak of the success of that endeavor, would have been inconceivable without the prior build-up of a multi-faceted and many-pronged Soviet Jewry movement in the U.S.

*Exit permits for Israel granted to Soviet Jews between 1948 and 1967*

| | |
|---|---|
| 1948–53 | 18[a] |
| 1954 | 53[b] |
| 1955 | 105[b] |
| 1956 | 753 |
| 1957 | 149 |
| 1958 | 12 |
| 1959 | 7 |
| 1960 | 102 |
| 1961 | 128 |
| 1962 | 182 |
| 1963 | 388 |
| 1964 | 539 |
| 1965 | 1,444 |
| 1966 | 1,892 |
| 1967 (January–July) | 1,162 |
| Total | 6,934 |

[a] No annual breakdown for this period.
[b] Data based on Israel Government Statistical Yearbook but otherwise un-confirmed.
*Source:* Alexander, "Immigration to Israel," Table A-1.

Part I

# "If I forget thee, O Jerusalem . . . "

# 1    The euphoria of 1948

## Soviet Jewry in the immediate postwar years

The end of World War II found the Soviet Union in a shambles. True, it emerged victorious from the war, but the victory had been gained at enormous cost. An estimated 22 million civilians and military personnel had been killed, not to speak of the numberless maimed and wounded. A large part of the country had been overrun by the German army, and the devastation that followed in its wake included the siege of Leningrad and the total destruction of many townships and villages. Moreover, whole branches of the economic activity necessary to a normal existence were either out of gear or destroyed since the entire economy had been diverted to the war effort at least since the German invasion of the Soviet Union in June 1941, which marked the beginning of the "Great Fatherland War."

The mood of the country was complex. On the one hand stood the general bereavement, the trauma of a war that had been fought throughout vast areas of the country and the anxiety that resulted from a serious shortage of food and housing as well as from a certain lack of confidence in the efficacy of Soviet power against Germany's modern, highly mechanized war machine. The technological gap in favor of the capitalist West had been experienced personally by Soviet soldiers, who had seen the outside world for themselves as prisoners-of-war, deserters or conquering heroes. On the other hand was the feeling of pride at the USSR's military successes, in turning the tide at Stalingrad in early 1943 and at having pushed the German army back to Berlin, victories which were broadcast by a huge propaganda campaign aimed at boosting civilian morale, restoring faith in the leadership and encouraging hopes for a brighter future.

As the guns quietened down, the Soviet leadership, still headed by General Secretary Generalissimo Josef Stalin, was faced with major assignments in both the domestic and international arenas. The determination and recognition of the Soviet Union's role as a great world power depended on a speedy economic recovery – the guidelines of which Stalin laid down in February 1946 –, on scientific and technological progress and on the consolidation of Soviet power in Eastern Europe to secure the country's exposed Western flank. These tasks called for the entire population to be mobilized behind the leadership. This, in turn, meant reinvigorating the ideological front, which led to the erection of an Iron Curtain aimed at preventing the Soviet citizenry from being contaminated by contact with the outside world and keeping prying Western eyes from discerning the dimensions of the economic catastrophe that might undermine the USSR's claim to the status of great power.

Finally, following as it had upon the Great Purges of the 1930s, the war had called into question some of Stalin's institutional and leadership achievements. The purges he had initiated had caused major damage to the top echelons of the party and the military, and his refusal to recognize the warning signs of the forthcoming German attack in 1941 had left the USSR unprepared for the invasion. However, despite the terrible shortcomings of his personnel policy and the shortsightedness and limitations of not a few of his decisions and positions, his personal status and power remained unquestioned by the populace. Nonetheless, in order to ensure maximum success in reaching the above-mentioned goals in the aftermath of the war, Stalin was forced to reassert his role as leader by attaining a careful equilibrium among the various party and government establishments as well as among the lieutenants and heirs-apparent waiting to take over from the seventy-year-old ruler.

One of the features of the return to "ideological purity" in the immediate postwar years was the emphasis placed upon the role that the Great (Veliko) Russians had played in achieving victory and in constructing the new socialist society. This meant an increasing identification of the terms Soviet and Russian. The Great Russian was both "elder brother" and example to the citizens of the hundred or so other nationalities and ethnic groupings that inhabited the USSR,[1] for he had not betrayed the mother country as had so many Ukrainians, Tatars, Germans and others.[2] Thus, the concessions made to the national minorities and to such ideological diversions as religion in the stress of war had to be gainsaid. Another feature of the ideological campaign was an enhanced "vigilance," the slogan of recurrent ideological campaigns in the USSR. However, the main practical implication of such campaigns – the legitimization of administrative measures against suspected deviationists – inevitably breeds a general atmosphere of apprehensiveness. It is within this broader general context that the situation of the USSR's Jews and the problems connected with their attempts to emigrate to Israel can and must be viewed.

The end of World War II found Soviet Jewry in a particularly traumatic situation. It had suffered tremendous losses in human life, since the majority of the Jewish population of the pre-1939 USSR and the entire population of the areas annexed by the Soviet Union in 1939–40 lived in those parts of the country that had been overrun by the German army. Although as many as could had fled to the interior (the Urals, Central Asia), this did not prevent most of them, too, from losing close family in the Nazi actions. Moreover, young Jewish men in the Soviet armed forces had been wounded and killed in disproportionate numbers because their motivation to fight the Germans caused them to enlist in a higher ratio than other sectors and then to volunteer for vanguard action against the enemy.[3] Although there is still no definitive statistical analysis of Jewish losses in the 1941–45 period, we know that prior to the German invasion the Soviet Jewish population amounted to approximately 5.2 million,[4] while the first postwar census of 1959 accounted for 2,268,000, a loss of almost 3 million. It has been argued that postwar Soviet censuses have tended to underestimate the number of Jews living in the USSR and there is no question that assimilation has resulted from the high rate of mixed marriages in the interwar years; in addition, some 220,000 Jews repatriated to Poland between 1945 and 1947. But most of the rest, apart from negative demographic trends also partly due to the Holocaust, can be accounted for by deaths resulting from the war.

Besides the loss of their closest kith and kin the survivors were besieged with many other problems. The non-Jewish civilian population, particularly in areas that had been under Nazi rule and subjected to Nazi propaganda, was experiencing the arousal of a deep-rooted antisemitism[5] which often took the form of collaborating in Nazi actions and denouncing Jews to the Germans. In Belorussia and the Ukraine Jews who escaped from the ghettos were frequently refused admission into the ranks of the partisans. Large numbers of deserted Jewish homes were looted and sequestrated, so that when Jewish evacuees began returning in 1944 they not only learned the dimensions of the Holocaust and became aware that the Soviet authorities had not made any effort to save Jews, but also found themselves with no place to live in an undisguisedly hostile environment. In the Ukraine there were even instances of anti-Jewish violence and excesses, both in townships which had had large Jewish populations before the war and in the main urban centers with their major Jewish concentrations.

In addition to this social or popular antisemitism, which the Soviet establishment was showing clear signs of condoning and encouraging on both the central and local levels, the authorities themselves initiated anti-Jewish discrimination: whole professions and institutes of higher learning, especially such "sensitive" ones as the party bureaucracy or the foreign service, closed their doors to Jewish applicants, and the higher echelons in particular of certain apparatuses began to be purged.[6] Specific anti-Jewish measures were enhanced by the Great Russian nationalism associated with party Central Committee secretaries Aleksandr Shcherbakov and Andrei Zhdanov and flouted by Stalin at the end of the Great Fatherland War, which had traditional antisemitic connotations.

The interrelationship between popular and official antisemitism in the Soviet Union deserves a study of its own. Suffice it to say here that they fed each other throughout the postwar period: official antisemitism encouraged those segments of the population with such tendencies, while the existence of popular anti-Jewish feelings enabled the authorities to use the Jews whenever they needed a scapegoat, certain that their ploy would fall on fertile ground.

The atmosphere engendered by these trends and manifestations intensified the Jews' feelings of insecurity. Many sought the answer in renewed efforts to assimilate, to integrate into Soviet society, especially through their professions. These people believed or hoped that they would be appreciated by a regime intent on restoring the economy to its prewar level and on repairing the devastation inflicted upon industry and agriculture by the intense war effort and the German occupation. Others, however, including many who before the war had entertained illusions concerning the inevitability, or at least the possibility, of becoming full-fledged Soviet citizens in the new internationalist socialist society, began to see that their Jewish origins predestined them to distinction, differentiation and discrimination. This latter category were now beginning to feel that no attempt to conceal or disguise these origins and that no contribution to the construction of the new life could counteract them or mitigate their position.[7]

The enhanced Jewish consciousness, after a generation of Soviet rule in which the Jews had largely acculturated, seems also to have been stimulated by direct contact with Jewish refugees from Poland and the Western territories – the Baltic countries, Western Ukraine and Western Belorussia, Transcarpathia, Northern Bukovina and Bessarabia – who had lived a very Jewish existence in thriving communities until the outbreak of the war and their annexation by the USSR. Many had been active members of Zionist organizations, and their Zionist orientation struck a chord in Soviet Jews. For although there had not been any Zionist organization in the USSR since the 1920s, enough Soviet Jews had continued to entertain Zionist sympathies for a spark to be set off.[8]

The first chapter of Jewish emigration from the Soviet Union in the period immediately following World War II is not the subject of this volume. However, since the events of these years influenced subsequent developments, we shall deal with them briefly. The years 1945–47 witnessed a considerable Jewish emigration from the USSR, chiefly of those who had been Polish citizens when the eastern parts of Poland were taken over by the Soviet Union in September 1939 (in accordance with the Molotov–Ribbentrop agreement of August 1939). Their number included both inhabitants of these areas and refugees who fled from the territories invaded by Germany in the early period of the war. The reasons for Jews being allowed to leave the USSR in accordance with repatriation agreements between the Polish and Soviet governments[9] were a source of speculation in the West. Some suggested that Moscow wanted them to participate in the construction of the new Poland;[10] others that the Soviet government wished to rid itself of an element whose failure to adjust to the Soviet way of life and to be accepted into Soviet society represented a potential source of trouble.[11] A third version argued that the Kremlin allowed them to leave because it knew they wished to go on to Palestine and hoped that their anticipated departure from Poland to the Western occupation zones of Germany and Austria would put pressure on the Western governments responsible for administering these zones[12] as well as on the international arena as a whole to solve the political future of Palestine by ending British mandatory rule there.[13] Whatever the reasons, the very fact that Jews repatriated to Poland and were moving on from there to Palestine must have given Soviet Jews reason to think that at least some features of the Jewish immigration to Palestine were welcomed by their government.

Simultaneously with the official repatriation of Jews who had been Polish citizens, there was a clandestine emigration, chiefly to Poland, of Jews from the Western areas of the USSR. This movement was part of the *briha* ("escape" in Hebrew) which was organized from Palestine to help Jews from Eastern and Central Europe with Zionist inclinations to join the Jewish *yishuv*. Hundreds if not thousands of Jews were able to leave the Soviet Union in this way in the years between 1944 and 1947. One *briha* activist, Shmuel (Mulka) Yaffe, wrote in October 1945 that in view of the events and trends of the times, large numbers of Soviet Jews would take advantage of any opening to make *aliya*.[14] *Briha* leaders inside the USSR – in Vilnius, Riga, Lvov – had been Zionist activists in Poland and the Western territories before the war. Most of them were arrested in 1946 and given long terms of imprisonment for anti-Soviet activity. Others who remained unmolested for several years met a similar fate later on, even though their activity had terminated with the arrest of their colleagues.[15]

There were also a number of Soviet Jewish soldiers and officers in Eastern or Central Europe who left their units and headed for Italy or the Western occupation zones of Austria or Germany, from where they eventually reached Palestine. One such officer, who had grown up as a Soviet citizen in Belorussia and gone to university there, had never come across "the Jewish question" until the war, when he encountered antisemitism in the Soviet armed forces. This officer first heard about Palestine and the *yishuv*'s struggle to construct a new life there from soldiers of Britain's Jewish Brigade (comprised of Palestinian Jews) and from Zionists in Poland and Romania. In his words, this gave him "the courage to do something for my own people and hence, of necessity, for myself as well."[16]

Instead of subsiding as the Soviet Union struggled to rid itself of the legacies of the war, both official and popular antisemitism increased in the postwar years. Holocaust survivors in the Ukraine had a particularly difficult time; their homes were assaulted physically and marked with swastikas, and their children were taunted.[17] A 1947 U.S. embassy report on discrimination in the USSR opened by noting that embassy personnel constantly heard "stories of discrimination and actual mistreatment by Russians of people of minority groups, especially Jews. For example, it seems clear that the number of Jews admitted to most higher educational institutions is tacitly restricted." Presumably to demonstrate the intensity of antisemitic feeling, the report went on to point out that the children of a Jewish embassy employee had been "threatened and actually physically harmed by anti-Semitic groups."[18] Even Stalin allowed himself to express antisemitic feelings in this period.[19] Late in 1947 the U.S. chargé in Moscow,

Elbridge Durbrow, wrote his secretary of state that Solomon Mikhoels and Itzik Fefer, two leading members of the Jewish Anti-Fascist Committee (JAFC), had shown considerable concern at the "current state of anti-Jewish feeling" and protested to Foreign Minister Molotov against the exclusion of Jews from "positions connected with foreigners, military activities or relations with the masses." In this context, Mikhoels and Fefer had made specific mention of the Ministry of Foreign Affairs, diplomatic and foreign language schools, military academies, work connected with atomic research ("with a few brilliant exceptions"), chairmanships of party and government committees and even "dramatic schools." Molotov was reported to have "promised that some action would eventually be taken when the government considered circumstances more favorable"; a similar statement was said to have been made by Lazar Kaganovich, one of the sources of hope for the Jews as the sole Jewish member of the Politburo.

Meanwhile, the U.S. chargé went on, Soviet Jews had "reacted to this anti-Semitic policy by becoming more conscious of their status and more actively patriotic to their social group." They were "tending to close ranks" and many, including members of the intelligentsia, were showing more interest in emigrating to the Jewish Autonomous Region of Birobidzhan in the Soviet Far East, "despite the reports of the hard conditions of life which emanate from there."[20]

This renewed and strengthened antisemitism, in conjunction with the new Jewish awareness of Soviet Jews, led them to look for avenues other than those proposed by the Jewish "establishment" (the Jewish Anti-Fascist Committee, the few Jewish theaters and the Emes publishing house) which made every effort to base its activities on the terms of reference allowed it by the Soviet authorities.[21] Jews began "closing ranks" by limiting their social contacts to other Jews out of feelings of solidarity, a common fate and a sense of frustration and/or bitterness at their growing rejection by their non-Jewish environment.[22] In a number of cities and small towns around the country small informal groups came together to discuss "the Jewish problem" and the Zionist solution, and to learn or speak Hebrew. As these activities have, naturally, never been documented in any way (except presumably in the archives of the Soviet Ministry of the Interior, the MVD), they have still not been studied satisfactorily. They were usually known only among those actually involved, the individual members of each group trusting only those whose loyalty was certain; even so, many groups fell prey to provocateurs who penetrated their ranks. Most groups did not even know the identity of other groups in their own towns – let alone in other places – unless one of their members had a close friend or relative in these circles. Thus, while members of different groups may have met occasionally, they knew each other as individuals interested in their Jewish origins. Several met, for instance, at Moscow's Lenin Library, where they looked for books on Jewish subjects or materials in Hebrew and where it was possible to obtain publications sent to the USSR from Palestine during the war.[23] It was only much later, while serving prison sentences in the camps, that members of such groups discovered that theirs had not been the only one seeking an alternative life in the historic home of the Jewish people. Only in the camps did they learn that there were similar circles in almost every town in the USSR, usually of five to ten people, and that many of them had also come into existence in 1945 or 1946.

One such group, of ten or twelve high school students from Zhmerinka in the Ukraine, concluded from their Holocaust experiences that Jewish solidarity and Jewish activity were a must if they wished to survive as Jews. Although they first talked of emigrating to Palestine, when they discovered that emigration was not a realistic goal at that time, they decided instead that Jews should organize in self-defense groups. They wrote a number of leaflets to this effect which they distributed in the Zhmerinka synagogue and even in Kiev and Vinnitsa, dropping them into letter-boxes or people's bags in the market place. These young people were members of the Komsomol, and their views were in no way anti-Soviet or even intended as a protest. They were motivated by the "simple" desire for self-preservation.[24] A similar group organized in Briansk to provide self-defense against the increasingly virulent antisemitism that sometimes took the form of physical assault. Members also studied and discussed writings of Zionist thinkers such as Vladimir Jabotinsky and poems by Ilya Ehrenburg and Margarita Aliger (which they read and then passed on to other Jews) and listened to foreign radio broadcasts, notably those of the BBC.[25]

There were similar groups in Moscow, Leningrad, Kiev, Odessa and Lvov as well as in other cities. One Moscow group, of somewhat older Jews who met to talk and write Hebrew, included several figures who had an important impact on the continued existence of Hebrew as a living language in the Soviet Union. Among them were Zvi Pregerzon, known as A. Tsfoni; Moshe Abramzon, known as M. Hiog or Zvi Plotkin; Meir Boazov or Baazov, a leading Georgian Zionist; Aron

Kricheli, formerly director of the Jewish section of the Georgian museum in Tbilisi; and Yitzhak Kogan or Kahanov. Another, apparently much larger Moscow group centered around Nadia Nemirovskaia, who had come to Moscow from Sverdlovsk where she had spent most of the war (she was originally from Kiev). The group's activity focused on Jewish affairs and Jewish history, Nemirovskaia having a number of Jewish books in her possession, including the pre-revolutionary Russian-language *Jewish Encyclopedia*.[26] Another group formed in the Moscow Institute for Foreign Languages of the Soviet armed forces. It was composed of teachers and students mostly from Bessarabia and Bukovina. Their books included Hebrew primers and literature taken from German headquarters in Berlin.[27]

Talk about Palestine was not limited to those who belonged to groups. Jewish students talked extensively about Palestine among themselves. Especially in the months following the Soviet decision to support the establishment of a Jewish state in part of Palestine, students were quoted as saying: "The only thing left for the Jews is to establish a state of their own like all the other nations. After all, we Jews are also a people."[28] The discovery – with the help of the BBC, the Voice of America and broadcasts from Palestine itself to which many Soviet Jews listened[29] – that the Jews of Palestine were conducting an armed struggle against British imperialism in order to attain independence was a major factor in interesting youngsters in Zionism and in eventually bringing them to Zionist convictions. For it must not be forgotten that this was a time, less than three years after the war, when heroism was very much in vogue, when stories were being written about the military exploits of the Soviet soldier in World War II. But these stories dwelt on the Russian or Slav nationality of the war heroes. Although large numbers of Jews had been awarded for heroism, their role in the war was systematically downgraded.[30] Thus, the struggle of the *yishuv* instilled pride in youngsters who were angered by the lack of materials on the Jewish contribution to the Soviet victory over Nazi Germany and smarting from taunts that the Jews had "fought in Tashkent," i.e. thousands of miles from the front.[31] In the winter months of 1947–48, especially on campuses where there were large numbers of Jewish students, Palestine became a central topic of discussion.[32]

The official Soviet position was to ignore the newly awakened Jewish consciousness, although it did not fail to attack Jewish nationalism alongside the nationalist manifestations of other ethnic groupings in the late 1940s, as part of the ideological campaign that came to be associated with Stalin's second-in-command, Andrei Zhdanov, and was known as the *zhdanovshchina*.[33] It is even possible that, at least until 1948, top echelons of the central leadership really were unaware of this phenomenon; their subordinates may have wanted to keep them ignorant of developments that ran counter to Marxist-Leninist theory, which continued to deny the existence of a Jewish nation, even though individual Jews had to be registered as such under Soviet law.[34] Some Soviet leaders may have believed that the Jewish minority identified *en masse* with the Soviet motherland that – according to the official line – had not only given it equal rights and opportunities but had saved mankind as a whole and the Jews in particular from the Nazi danger. It is just as possible that the Kremlin did read the situation accurately, but did not balk at undertaking mass repression when needed especially as the times enabled implementing such repression without any public reference to Jewish national devi-ationism which it was seeking to downplay. Finally, it cannot be excluded that the personal struggles and policy reappraisals going on in the Kremlin during 1948–49 were somehow connected with this issue.[35]

The fact is, however, that although Deputy Foreign Minister Andrei Gromyko declared the historic right of the Jewish people to Palestine (in his speech of 14 May 1947 at the First Special Session of the U.N. General Assembly) and supported Palestinian Jewry's claims to self-determination, the Soviet Union contended that these principles did not apply to the Jews of the Soviet Union and the East European People's Democracies. For, in the People's Democracies the Jewish problem would be automatically resolved through the eradication of fascism and the construction of new communist regimes; and it had already been solved in the USSR. Indeed, Gromyko's statement that Soviet Jews had no direct interest in Palestine[36] denied any possibility of Jewish sympathy for the Zionist solution.

The Soviet authorities were, however, fully aware of the practical difficulties being faced by their Jewish citizenry in the reality of the postwar years, particularly in those areas that had been overrun by the Nazis. This was clearly expressed in the resuscitation of the Jewish Autonomous Region of Birobidzhan as the national home for the Soviet Jewish population and in the much publicized convoys or "echelons" of Jews, notably from the Ukraine, who went there between the years 1946 and 1948.[37] Some party and government levels must also have been aware of continued Zionist tendencies as in addition to those Jews who deserted while serving the Soviet motherland in Eastern and Central Europe, some left or tried to leave, for example, by infiltrating the ranks of Jews being repatriated to Poland; and others, though apparently not very many, were arrested and imprisoned for Zionist inclinations between the early summer of 1947 and the late summer of 1948,[38] even though the pejorative adjective, Zionist, disappeared from the Soviet media, for perhaps the only time in the history of Russian communism during this period. It is interesting that the Soviet establishment did not allow these phenomena to influence the decision to support the establishment of a Jewish state in Palestine.

Whatever may have been the official Soviet position, Soviet Jews were emotionally prepared to identify with the idea of a Jewish state and the Jewish national consciousness that was taking shape and was given full expression through the events of 1948.

### The Soviet Jewish reaction to the establishment of the Jewish state

The U.N. partition resolution of 29 November 1947 calling for the establishment of a Jewish state introduced two new elements into the situation of Soviet Jews and their attitude to Zionism and Palestine. First, it meant that a sovereign Jewish state was to come into being in the historic national home of the Jewish people; secondly, Soviet support for the partition resolution represented a *volte-face* in the official Soviet position on Zionism and its implementation that dated back to the incipient stages of the Bolshevik party.

From this point of view the years 1947–48 comprised a unique period in the history of Soviet Jewry. For the first (and meanwhile the last) time the Soviet authorities supported the national aspirations of the Jewish people in Palestine. The USSR made its sympathies explicit and manifest beginning with Gromyko's announcement in May 1947 that the Jews in Palestine – like the Arabs – had legitimate rights in that country and that the Jewish people had a right to self-determination and to their own state like any other people. This support continued with official Soviet backing of the U.N. partition resolution in November 1947, insistence upon its implementation (December 1947 – May 1948), the immediate *de jure* recognition it accorded the new state in the face of Arab antagonism and the decision to exchange diplomats. When Golda Meyerson arrived in Moscow and presented her credentials as Israel's first envoy to the Soviet Union, she was the focus of sympathetic attention on the part of the Soviet establishment.

The establishment of an independent Jewish state had immeasurable significance for Soviet Jewry. This contradicted Gromyko's categoric statement that Soviet Jewry had no interest in events in Palestine, a statement which, although not published in the Soviet media, apparently reflected the official position. In September 1948 Counselor Mikhail Mukhin of the Soviet legation in Israel told Shmuel Friedman (later Eliashiv), head of the East European Department of the Israel Foreign Ministry, that antisemitism – the main reason for Zionism – had disappeared in the Soviet Union and would soon disappear in all countries with democratic regimes.[39] Not only was this position rampant in Soviet propaganda, it was not restricted to propaganda alone. When Prisoners of Zion, as those arrested for Zionist inclinations or activities were called, pointed out during interrogations that the Soviet Union had itself voted for establishing the State of Israel, the interrogators retorted: "We had our reasons, but what is your connection with Israel?"[40] The plain fact is that official contentions regarding antisemitism notwithstanding, both antisemitism and Zionist convictions lived on in the Soviet Union, the latter in part, indeed, though not solely, as an outcome of antisemitism.

It is surely one of the ironies of history that Soviet support for the establishment of Israel and Soviet policy toward the new state in its first months encouraged Soviet Jews to identify with Israel openly. If Gromyko's statement on Soviet Jewry had been published in the USSR, the Jews might have been warned that their support for the Jewish state did not conform with government policy. As it was, they threw some of the caution acquired during the postwar years to the winds.[41] For no secret was made of Soviet support for partition; it was officially reported in the press and on the air. The Jews heard of it in foreign broadcasts as well. In addition, *Eynikeyt*, the Yiddish paper of the JAFC, was devoting considerable space and attention to the *yishuv* and its attitude was obviously sympathetic.[42] Nobody in the Soviet Union at this time could have believed that this was the uncensored, spontaneous opinion of the Committee or any of its members. And there were other manifestations of official support to encourage the susceptible to enthusiasm. At the Hanukka celebrations in Moscow's Choral Synagogue in December 1947, its rabbi, Shlomo Shlifer, read out a message from Chief Rabbi of Palestine Isaac Herzog declaring that the redemption of the Jewish people had begun.[43] Jewish writers such as Ilya Ehrenburg, Itzik Fefer and Leib Kvitko were writing and talking about the *yishuv*'s struggle for national liberation without being censored. In what was probably his last public appearance – at a

December 1947 literary evening commemorating the thirtieth anniversary of the death of Jewish writer Mendele Moikher Seforim – director of the State Yiddish Theater and chairman of the JAFC Solomon Mikhoels commented that, like the *muzhik* in one of Mendele's stories, the USSR was showing the Jews the way to Palestine.[44] If these men, acquainted as they were with the ambiguities of Soviet Jewish existence after so many years of first-hand experience in the regime's central institutions, were able to give open expression to their feelings for the *yishuv* and its struggle, surely the rank and file of the Jewish population could abandon restraint and give vent to their long-suppressed sentiments!

It was therefore in an atmosphere of hope and elation that several thousand Jews – including young people – assembled spontaneously at the main Moscow synagogue on the weekend following Israel's establishment to share their excitement with each other. They wondered whether Soviet Jews would be able to express their feelings officially, like their brethren in other countries who were holding rallies and sending greetings to the new state. On 15 May, the day the state was established, two young Jews hung a banner on the eastern wall of the synagogue, near the Ark, with the Hebrew inscription "The Jewish People Lives!" An official service was eventually held in the Choral Synagogue in July, with Rabbi Shlifer officiating, in the presence of a representative of the Council for the Affairs of Religious Cults.[45] The synagogue was decorated with flowers and blue and white banners that read "Long live the State of Israel!" and "The Jewish people lives!"[46]

Although no written announcements had been allowed, the service was announced in the synagogue on the previous Sabbath. So many Jews thronged to the event that they overflowed onto the street outside, where the service was relayed by microphone. Worshippers included many of Moscow's best-known Jewish figures, and the atmosphere was one of unbridled exhilaration; people could not believe that they were actually taking part in such a ceremony.

The service opened with a few words by the synagogue's president, who read out a message of greetings to Stalin followed by a message to Chaim Weizmann, first president of the State of Israel. Many applauded when this second message was read out, crying "Long live Weizmann!" The congregation said the Hallel (a prayer recited on festivals), and – in the words of one member of the congregation – the rabbi's sermon combined Zionist fervor with praise and thanks to the Soviet government for helping to establish the new state.[47]

There are eyewitness accounts that the jubilation occasioned by the establishment of Israel was given public expression in other parts of the country as well. In Lvov a special service was also held in the synagogue and here, too, the throng included many young people.[48] In the Ukrainian town of Belaia Tserkov a certain Rabbi Feldman, who had been decorated for his service in the war, had been trying to resuscitate Jewish life by opening a *minyan* (an informal prayer group), starting to teach Jewish law and collecting money to build a synagogue. He purchased a radio so he could listen to broadcasts from Palestine and when the establishment of the State of Israel was announced, Rabbi Feldman and his pupils burst into dance.[49] The Jews in another Ukrainian township thronged around the loudspeakers to hear what was happening as many people did not yet have radios of their own. Although they doubted whether the Jewish state could solve their own problems, they rejoiced that the Jews had finally attained their own center.[50] At a course on an air base near Moscow, twenty Jewish officers gathered to celebrate, and a general named Levin toasted the Jewish state, saying: "Today is a great holiday for us; after two thousand years an independent Jewish state has come into being." This was followed by another toast – to Chaim Weizmann – while *Hatikva*, the Zionist and now the Israeli national anthem, was sung in Russian.[51] Yiddish writer David Hofshteyn was so excited by the news of Israel's establishment that he sent a telegram to the Ukrainian SSR Academy of Sciences proposing that it open a department for the study and research of the Hebrew language.[52]

Often Jews simply came together in private homes to toast the new Jewish state, an act for which many of them later paid dearly. Some sang Hebrew or Jewish songs, including *Hatikva*. In Moscow Zvi Pregerzon composed a Hebrew poem which was read in groups he distributed it to. In the words of one youngster affected by the creation of the Jewish state, young Jewish people were "on fire."[53]

Jews who were already paying the penalty for their Zionist inclinations in the prisons and camps celebrated the establishment of the Jewish state together with other Jewish prisoners. For Prisoners of Zion who heard the news blasted over the loudspeakers in the daily news broadcast the excitement was almost intolerable. One of them, in a camp in the Komi ASSR, heard the announcement and felt reborn:

> Hot tears of joy streamed from my eyes. [The non-Jews] rose from their bunks and spontaneously shook the hands of the Jews and congratulated them . . . We ran at once to the other Jews in the camp to tell them the news and rejoice with them . . . We spoke Yiddish

with much delight, and those who did not know Yiddish endeavoured to speak at least a few words in the language which symbolised their membership of the Jewish people. In honour of the festive occasion each of us produced the little food in his possession and we ... held a feast together. We could not sleep all night long. In our hearts and thoughts we were at the front with our brothers and sisters who had begun a bitter war, rifle in hand, against the invading Arabs.[54]

This euphoria was reinforced as the Soviet media sided with Israel against the Arabs and the British, describing its War of Independence as one of national liberation against British imperialism and international fascism. Soviet Jews naturally took this to mean that their government was supplying the new Jewish state with military aid as well as supporting it in the international arena. And they were, indeed, correct, although they had no means of knowing that the Soviet bloc was providing the *yishuv* with war materiel and giving military training to prospective immigrants from the People's Democracies as well as to officers from the new Jewish state.[55] Soviet Jews wrote letters to friends and relatives in Israel describing their excitement. One letter from Odessa, dated 17 May 1948, expressed joy, but also anxiety regarding "the forces of darkness surrounding you." Another letter, from Kharkov several months later, began: "For us the proclamation of the State of Israel was a sudden voice from heaven." The writer went on to thank God with the traditional Jewish blessing to Him who had "kept us alive and maintained us until this time," and concluded with "the words of the poet [Yehuda Halevi]: 'I am in the West and my heart is in the East'." And a fifteen-year-old girl wrote: "We are all concerned for your well-being and await your victory daily ... The time will come when we shall all celebrate the festival of victory together."[56]

Although there are no statistics, there is ample evidence that enthusiasm for and the sense of personal identification with the new state were widespread, and that wherever Jews came together the creation of the State of Israel and its military successes were the talk of the day. Two Jewish members of a Soviet commercial delegation then in Paris reported this to New Zionist Organization leader Meir Grossman.[57] And Jews who eventually emigrated to Israel have also reported on the emotions of that period. Physicist Mark Azbel believes that there was not a Soviet Jew who failed to be actively concerned about the fate of the young Jewish state. The sensation, he recalls, was

like that of an incurable paralytic who was suddenly told he would yet run. Life had "anti-educated" Jews for too long, raising them as

> internal antisemites, almost ashamed of themselves, of their char-
> acter, of their exterior, accent, almost believing in their own
> inferiority. And suddenly – the Jews fight, and, like David, they are
> victorious. One could straighten up inside: to the cry "You – Yid!"
> one could proudly answer, "No, I am a Jew!"

Azbel, who was then a high school student in Kharkov and the son of assimilated parents, composed three poems in honor of the state's establishment.[58]

There are similar accounts from all over the USSR. Another future emigrant, Veniamin Fain, who was then in the top grade at a Russian-language secondary school in faraway Stalinabad (Dushanbe) in Tadzhikistan, whose pupils were either Russians or Jews, remembers that all the Jewish pupils supported Israel.[59] When the Jews of Samarkand in Uzbekistan heard of the Arab onslaught against Israel, they held a special fast and prayers.[60] A former medical student in Vinnitsa in Ukraine, where some 70 percent of the faculty and 50 percent of the students were Jewish, recalls that the establishment of Israel created such a festive atmosphere that people felt the Soviet authorities would soon allow them to volunteer with the Israel Defense Forces. Jewish students met daily to discuss the news, asking: "Are people already leaving for Israel?" And they took courses in physical training they felt "would be useful in Israel."[61] Israel was the sole topic of discussion in Georgian synagogues, where the Jews still met regularly even on weekdays. (Georgian Jews tended to adhere to Jewish tradition much more strongly than other Soviet Jewish communities.) "Official Soviet support of the Jewish movement in Palestine," one Georgian Jew who was then still a youngster has written, "enabled people to speak about Zionism . . . People who came to the synagogue related what they had heard from various sources" (mainly, it would seem, from foreign radio broadcasts).[62]

It is impossible to estimate the number of nationalistically inclined groups that came into being throughout the USSR or their membership, or survey their activity, which must be seen in the context of the times and not exaggerated. One Moscow activist of the period estimates that there were about twenty groups in that city.[63] Members of groups formed in previous years stepped up their activities when Israel's War of Independence broke out. For, as Nadia Nemirovskaia told members of her group, their activity was their contribution to a war in which their Israeli brethren were being killed by those who opposed the Jewish state; therefore it must not be relinquished no matter how severe their difficulties.[64]

Even Jews in relatively senior positions, who identified with the regime and were associated with it by others, and who were thought to be thoroughly assimilated, were affected by events in Israel. They, too, believed that its creation would enhance the status and influence of Jews within Soviet society. Non-Jews certainly tended to link developments having anything to do with Israel with their Jewish neighbors and colleagues. Thus, a Leningrad Jewish member of the Writers' Union received a telegram from colleagues in Armenia expressing their excitement at the state's establishment.[65]

In line with the Soviet custom of explaining the official position on a broad range of domestic and foreign policy issues to the public as a basic component of the party's agitation and propaganda program, a number of public lectures were held in 1948 to elucidate the Soviet stand on Israel's establishment. The lecturers, inevitably, were properly authorized propagandists. Yet the fact that most of them regurgitated the party line received from the All-Union Society for the Dissemination of Scientific and Political Knowledge, which had been set up in 1947 under the auspices of the Central Committee *agitprop* department, did not keep Soviet Jews from packing the lectures. British correspondent Alexander Werth reported that at one such lecture in Moscow "a Jewish member of the audience asked whether it would be possible for him to go to Palestine. 'A Soviet citizen should be ashamed to ask such a question' was the lecturer's reply." When another lecturer was asked how a Soviet citizen should proceed if he wished to go to Israel, he replied that in the unlikely event that anyone wished to leave the Soviet motherland, he should approach the Foreign Ministry. An occasional lecturer even had pro-Zionist inclinations; Evsei Efman, head technologist of the Institute for Planning Plants and Equipment for the Oil Industry, who had been a member of the Zionist youth organizations Hehalutz and Hashomer Hatsair in his youth, based the talk he gave in his plant on Israeli as well as Soviet brochures he had been given in order to prepare his lecture. Efman also lectured on Israel on work trips to branches of the Institute.[66]

At least one lecture ended in pandemonium when the lecturer, a member of *Pravda*'s editorial staff, repeated the line used by Soviet Jewish orientalist Vladimir Lutskii in an earlier lecture to the effect that Zionism was a tool of British imperialism and that the Jewish state would not solve the Jewish problem, which in any case existed only in imperialist and capitalist countries. The audience responded with questions that were so provocative that the speaker refused to answer them. And when a number of young uniformed officers and soldiers of the Soviet armed forces rose to demand replies, the meeting was disbanded and those attending asked to show identification papers as they exited. At least twenty of them were subsequently arrested, brought to trial in Kuibyshev and given sentences of ten to fifteen years' exile with hard labor.[67]

Despite the fact that the Soviet authorities could hardly be expected to view such a step with equanimity, much less with favor, especially during the cold war, a considerable number of young Jews actually began applying for permission to emigrate to Israel or at least to volunteer to fight there in its war. These applications were addressed to the JAFC and to the ministries of Defense, Foreign Affairs and Internal Affairs.[68] In trying to understand how the thousands who applied[69] had the audacity to take a step that could at best brand them as having dual loyalty, we found that many Jews based their belief that the Soviet government was approving applications to volunteer in Israel's War of Independence on the Kremlin's support of Israel in the media and especially reports of various fascist elements being enlisted into the Arab forces. For had not Soviet citizens taken up the cudgels of proletarian internationalism in Spain and China in the 1930s? Air force officer Ioakhim Shperber even believed that he would be a member of an expeditionary force, including pilots, to be sent to the Middle East as part of Soviet aid to the Jewish state. At a three-week course he was attending when the State of Israel was proclaimed, all the Jewish officers talked of volunteering to fight for Israel.[70] Efim Gusman, who was employed at an airfield in Gomel, requested permission to leave from his commanding officer.[71] The general atmosphere was such, and the belief in the chances of leaving so strong, that a movement was catapulted into being.

Applications to leave were received from all parts of the country, from as far afield as the Tatar ASSR, the Crimea, Siberia, as well as from the RSFSR, Belorussia and the Ukraine.[72] Some of those planning to go tried to convince their friends to apply as well. Leningrad medical student Leonid Rutshtain collected the signatures of fifty people who wanted to fight for Israel.[73] In Lvov a few students planned to gather signatures for a similar petition to the Central Committee. Members of the Komsomol, they claimed it was their duty to participate in the anti-imperialist war of liberation of the long-suffering Jewish people. But their parents dissuaded them from carrying out their plan.[74] Some Jews already in prison also approached the authorities. One of them, Yaacov Liash, originally from Vilnius, was serving a sentence for Jewish nationalist and anti-Soviet activity in a camp in Uzbekistan, where he had been living with his family. After hearing a lecture on why the Kremlin had supported Israel's establishment, Liash wrote to Deputy Foreign Minister Andrei Vyshinskii asking to be released so he could fight the enemies of the USSR.[75] And when a Leningrad Jew who had been arrested early in 1948 heard of the establishment of the state, he asked the prison authorities to release him so he could help the communists in Israel bring the new state closer to the Soviet Union.[76] Indeed, in the early months after Israel's establishment some Soviet Jews were convinced that if the first Knesset elections brought a leftist victory their chances of being allowed to emigrate would be enhanced.[77]

Needless to say, none of the applications was ever answered. Instead they were turned over to the MVD, who used them as evidence when their writers were arrested in the following months and years (many of those "guilty" of Zionist inclinations or "activity" in 1948 were allowed to remain free for considerable periods). Although the extent to which this letter-writing to the authorities was organized is not clear, some evidence suggests that at least in part it may have been instigated by Hebrew writer Zvi Plotkin. For, over a decade later, Plotkin wrote his brother in Israel that "with the establishment of the state, I organized the clandestine movement of writing letters to Stalin and Molotov concerning *aliya* and recognition of the Zionist movement."[78]

A few Jews even attempted to cross the Soviet border illegally, but all of them seem to have been deterred or caught. A member of one such group, of three boys who were still in high school when the state was proclaimed, records that the stories of Jews, some of them former officers of the Soviet armed forces, going to fight in Israel seemed quite plausible at the time. The group discussed various ways of accomplishing this, even the stealing of a plane. In July 1949, by which time they were studying at university, two of them traveled to the Turkish border – which was thought to be less well guarded than the European one – to explore the terrain. They had considered crossing the border at Batumi, but discovered that the coastline was heavily guarded. On the advice of distant relatives who were local residents, the boys returned to Moscow, where they found themselves under police surveillance.[79] After hearing that all those who expressed a wish to volunteer in Israel were being arrested, one potential volunteer, Efim Shperber, was arrested in the act of trying, with a pilot friend, to steal an aircraft at the Turkish frontier.[80]

The belief that there was a real chance to emigrate was held not only in the context of volunteering to fight. The first actual emigrant, Meir Bobrovskii, a disabled war veteran from Fergana in Uzbekistan, told the Israeli legation that the two hundred Jewish families in that town saw him as the vanguard of their own emigration.[81] Within the context of the favorable Soviet stand on the establishment of the Jewish state, a small group formed in the Siberian town of Tomsk to work toward arousing interest in emigrating.[82]

In 1948 Soviet Jews were not alone in believing they would be able to leave. There were also rumors in the West to the effect that the Soviet Union would allow the emigration of elderly people with sons and daughters in Israel and of the few stateless individuals who were eligible for Israeli citizenship according to Soviet criteria.[83] In fact, however, only six Jews seem to have been allowed to leave in the entire period between May 1948 and Stalin's death in March 1953.

### First encounters with representatives of the State of Israel

From the time it was announced in May 1948 that Israel and the USSR had agreed to establish diplomatic relations and exchange diplomatic missions, Soviet Jews awaited the arrival of the first Israeli envoy with great eagerness. During that summer Avigdor Lezerovich wrote to a friend in Israel that he was "awaiting the arrival here [in Moscow] of Golda Meyerson. In her mission lie my fate and the fate of thousands of our people who long for the light of the mother country, for the redemption and freedom of all Jews." And when Mrs. Meyerson arrived in early September, Moscow's Jews exulted with pride and joy. Lezerovich wrote: "Two days ago Golda M. reached Moscow. There is hope."[84] The cordial reception accorded Mrs. Meyerson by the Soviet authorities probably enhanced hopes that Jews would be allowed to emigrate to Israel.[85] The newsreel showing the new minister presenting her credentials was the talk of the day, not only among Jews with nationalist sympathies, but even among the assimilated.[86] Some went to see Mrs. Meyerson at the Yiddish theater, where audience and actors alike greeted her with a standing ovation.[87] Others went to see her at the Choral Synagogue, including many who had never stepped inside a house of worship; they went to see and perhaps exchange a few words with her and her entourage. One group of Jews she met with, obviously with the permission of the authorities, worked at the Stalin Automobile Plant in Moscow which the Israeli minister was taken to see.[88]

On the Jewish New Year and the Day of Atonement thousands of ecstatic Jews abandoned their customary prudence to attend High Holy Day services in the company of the Israeli diplomats; they were simply unable to hold back their emotions and sense of identification with the Jewish state and its War of Independence. The excitement was infectious: even the hesitant, who had come furtively without telling family or friends, became oblivious to risk once they were at the synagogue. Others were so excited by the prospect of meeting Israeli officials in Moscow that they came in groups, giving no thought to the danger this entailed. The demonstrations on these occasions may also have benefited from organizational activity; for example, it seems that Zvi Pregerzon initiated a telephone campaign urging Jews to be there.[89] Those who had no prior knowledge that a demonstration was in the offing came as well. One group of enthusiasts, upon seeing the Israeli delegation leave their hotel (in a car with the Israeli flag) and finding out that they were heading toward the synagogue, rushed off to Moscow's other two synagogues to fetch their fellow Jews.[90] The atmosphere of these demonstrations has been immortalized by a photograph showing Mrs. Meyerson outside the synagogue surrounded by a throng of Jews of all ages.[91] A young man who took a photograph of the Israeli minister on her first visit to the synagogue distributed some fifty copies before realizing that they were becoming the source of a thriving business.[92]

It is extremely difficult to estimate the numbers of those who took part in the demonstrations on the New Year and the Day of Atonement. Estimates by those who were there on the first occasion fluctuate between 10,000 and 20,000. And it must be assumed that for every person present there were dozens of others who would have liked to attend but refrained out of fear for themselves and their families. Certainly the significance of these demonstrations was tremendous, not only for those who took part in them, but also for the even larger number of Jews in both Moscow and the rest of the USSR who were not there. Indeed, while the overwhelming majority of those present were, naturally, Muscovites, many came from other towns and cities. Some of these had made a special trip to the capital because they heard or surmised that the Israeli diplomats would be attending synagogue on the High Holy Days.[93] Through the latter Jews throughout the country heard of the welcome their brethren had given Israel's first minister and her colleagues; and this knowledge made them aware of the extent and intensity of feeling for Israel and enabled them to let their own feelings flow as well.[94]

It should be pointed out here that the demonstrations of October

1948 took place in an atmosphere of fear and repression. Even though the "Black Years" had not yet reached their nadir, the constraints imposed by the *zhdanovshchina* had already spread to a wide range of cultural and academic activities by late summer 1948, and measures such as the June 1947 State Secrets Act had markedly broadened the punitive powers of the administrative organs.[95] Moreover, Soviet Jews were still faced with the official and popular antisemitism that had not subsided since the end of the war.

Just a few weeks before the demonstrations a Soviet officer confided to an American embassy official, in the secluded atmosphere of a boat on the Moscow–Volga Canal, that although all nationalities were officially equal in the Soviet Union, "you can't change human nature." While the officer claimed to have a "nice" Jewish friend, he did not like Jews: during the war, none of them had gone to the front; instead they had grown fat working in the factories, safe beyond the Urals, and selling produce. In a moment of unaccustomed frankness, he added that if the Soviet Union and the U.S. did actually fight the war that the Soviet media were then actively forecasting, the Jews would all side with the Americans.[96] And, finally, as we shall see below, the Soviet Jewish writer Ilya Ehrenburg had warned Soviet Jews to refrain from associating or identifying with the State of Israel less than two weeks before the Jewish New Year.

All sorts of rumors were rampant at the time according to which the Israeli legation in Moscow was interested in the issue of Soviet Jewish emigration. Indeed, since rumor was one of the characteristics of the Soviet regime[97] it is a moot question whether those connected with the Israelis were initiated and spread by the secret police as an act of provocation, intended first to implicate Soviet Jews in "anti-Soviet activity" and eventually to enable the Kremlin to blame the Israeli legation for causing trouble. It has even been suggested that the High Holy Day demonstrations were initiated by the powers-that-be to provoke Jews into exposing themselves and their dreams of emigration.[98] There is even a chance that the rumors were part of the internecine rivalry among the leadership, those who opposed support for Israel because of its domestic implications hoping to undermine its adherents. In any event, rumors that Mrs. Meyerson maintained close relations with Polina Zhemchuzhina, the Jewish wife of Foreign Minister Molotov, and gave her a list of people who wished to go to Israel, and with Jewish scientist Lena Shtern, a former member of the JAFC presidium, were thought to be connected with the exile of the former to Kazakhstan in early 1949 and the arrest of the latter.[99]

While these rumors at first encouraged those seeking to fight in Israel's War of Independence,[100] the arrests and other tribulations that befell the Jews in the winter of 1948–49 lent them new connotations. Golda Meyerson's "activities" were now said to have been responsible for the dissolution of the JAFC and the closing down of its newspaper and of the Yiddish publishing house. She was also blamed for the arrests of many of those who had been in contact with the Israeli mission about going to Israel to fight and of those who had participated in any sort of Zionist activity. Indeed, Soviet rumor-mongering and disinformation had done a brilliant job. In the years that followed it was not uncommon for Soviet Jews to attribute the hardships and persecution they suffered during these months to Golda's "lack of caution."[101] And many Soviet Jews interpreted Mrs. Meyerson's recall to Israel (to take up a ministerial post in Israel's first elected government) as resulting from Soviet government protests against her interference in the domestic affairs of the Soviet Union.[102] Claims to the contrary notwithstanding, however, there is no hard evidence that the Israeli government discussed the broader issue of Soviet Jewry with the Soviet authorities in this period, although Mrs. Meyerson may have raised the question of family reunification in a very general fashion at a meeting with Deputy Foreign Minister Andrei Vyshinskii in January 1949, only to be told that since emigration involved the Jew in question being relieved of his Soviet citizenship, the Soviet authorities would have to deal with each case individually.[103] Certainly, the Israeli envoy did take to the Soviet Union, when she first went in 1948, a list of relatives of Israeli citizens whom the latter were asking to be allowed to join them in Israel. Further lists of a similar nature, mostly, apparently, with some scores of names, were sent to the legation during the remainder of 1948 and most of 1949. Yet few, if any, of these lists were ever shown the Soviet authorities.[104] At the same time, there were some official requests for Soviet assistance in facilitating Jewish emigration from Eastern Europe, particularly from Romania and Hungary. This issue was raised by Israeli Foreign Minister Shertok in a conversation with Vyshinskii at the U.N. in late December 1948, in which the former stressed Israel's need for new immigrants in order to consolidate its existence and by Golda Meyerson at a further meeting with Vyshinskii, who had meanwhile become foreign minister, prior to the termination of her assignment as minister in Moscow.[105]

While Golda Meyerson's mission to the USSR was largely viewed as a mission of goodwill that would promote Soviet understanding of and rapprochement with the new state and its goals, some Israelis did see it as a golden opportunity to bridge the gap with the silent masses of Soviet Jewry. *Palestine Post* editor Gershon Agronsky pointed out that ''Jews are not allowed to leave Russia for Palestine and one of the first tasks of the Israeli Minister to Moscow will be to try to negotiate for facilities which will permit at least those with relatives in Israel to leave.''[106] Israelis of Russian origin were certain that those they had left behind would draw new inspiration and strength from the sight of an Israeli flag flying in the Soviet capital. At a farewell held by Mapai (Israel's Labor Party) prior to the mission's departure, Foreign Minister Moshe Shertok (later Sharett) read out a letter from Odessa, expressing joy at the establishment of the state and the hope that it would bring redemption to the Jewish people: ''we shall come to you to rebuild shoulder to shoulder with you the ruins of our holy land, to fight for our freedom and to sacrifice our lives on its altar. This is not the dream of one individual, but the desire of most of our people here.'' Another speaker at the farewell, Benjamin West, who had maintained close ties with Jews in the Soviet Union since his own departure in 1924, contended that identification with Israel was so great that hundreds of thousands of Soviet Jews in fact considered themselves Israeli citizens. West also expressed the hope that diplomatic relations would eventually lead not only to the liberation of the thousands of Prisoners of Zion but also to ties between the Jews of both countries.[107] Yet the most the Israeli government seems to have done, apart from intervening on behalf of a few families, was to contact synagogue officials and Jewish theaters and libraries in various parts of the USSR.[108]

The above notwithstanding, Jewish volunteers and others who hoped to emigrate did route their requests through the Israeli legation in Moscow. A few actually visited the legation offices in the very early period.[109] A Jewish professor, Grigorii Spivak, who taught at Moscow University, requested the Israeli legation's help in arranging his *aliya* and that of his sister and her family in Gomel, where a small group of seven people were contemplating emigration. Shmaryahu Kanokov of Mogilev asked his sisters in Moscow to approach the Israeli legation with the same request.[110] Some of those who made contact with Israeli diplomats in public places, hoping to bring the plight of Soviet Jewry to their attention, have lived to tell the tale. One of these, Avraham Shtukarevich of Vilnius, who had already been a Prisoner of Zion, met with an Israeli diplomat in Moscow three times in December 1948 after a chance meeting in a Moscow theater. Shtukarevich informed the

Israeli that the Soviet government was taking drastic measures against Jews who had collected money for Israel or had applied to fight with the Israeli army. He also gave the diplomat names of Prisoners of Zion in the hope that they might be freed from prison, even though there seemed little likelihood that the Soviets would let their Jewish citizens go to Israel.[111] Less than two weeks after his last meeting, Shtukarevich was in Lubianka prison, a Prisoner of Zion for the second time.

The great majority of Jews were less daring; they contented themselves with talking about Golda Meyerson and her activities. When it was rumored that she would be attending the main Leningrad synagogue, so many Jews came to see her that people had to be prevented by force from entering.[112]

These repeated manifestations of deep emotional attachment to Israel undoubtedly caused the Soviet authorities real concern. Less than three weeks after the Israeli mission arrived, *Pravda* published Ilya Ehrenburg's famous article denying that there were any ties between Jews living in the Soviet Union and the People's Democracies and those in the capitalist countries and Israel.[113] Whether this warning was prompted by the general euphoria of Soviet Jews at Israel's creation or by their excitement at the Israeli diplomats' arrival in Moscow is not known. We do know, however, that other Jewish writers were also being enlisted to attack the Israeli establishment and Zionism, although these attacks did not yet entail sweeping condemnations of Israel. In the Warsaw Yiddish *Folks-shtime*, for example, Itzik Fefer cautioned against Zionist leaders who were trying to make Israel into an instrument of the U.S. However, even at this late date (fall 1948), Fefer was still stressing that the creation of Israel was welcomed by the entire Soviet public, who found a continuation of "the finest traditions of our people" in the heroism of the Israeli armed forces.[114] The acting editor of *Eynikeyt*, Grigorii Zhits, took issue with "Zionist leaders in Palestine and their supporters and helpers in capitalist countries," who stated "that the State of Israel is the home of every Jew in the world. For us Soviet Jews this sounds strange and unconvincing . . . Zionist chatter will have no influence among Soviet Jews" who loved their socialist motherland.[115]

The winter of 1948–49 saw efforts to prevent contacts between the Israeli diplomats and Soviet Jews. Thus, when the Israelis presented Moscow's Choral Synagogue with a Tora scroll from Tel Aviv's Great Synagogue shortly after the High Holy Day demonstrations, the ceremony was kept secret, with only a few synagogue officials attending.[116]

Once aroused by the events of 1948, Soviet Jews would never be able to return *in toto* to the *status quo ante* in which those who nurtured Zionist inclinations had closeted them with resignation, while the great majority saw in assimilation the only feasible solution to "the Jewish question." Although by late 1948 the Soviet authorities were indicating clearly that from their point of view the Jewish state was an irrelevant phenomenon for Soviet Jewry, for the latter life in a state of their own had become a potential alternative, even if only as a faraway dream that might bring cheer and hope to an existence that was basically drab, despondent and humiliating.

Although the administrative measures taken against the dominant figures of Jewish national culture in late 1948, and the parallel campaign against the assimilated Jewish intelligentsia in early 1949 can be explained in terms of Moscow's Jewish policy and in the context of what was happening in the Soviet domestic arena, the fact that a large number of applications to leave for Israel were addressed to the JAFC as an institution, as well as to individuals connected with it, cannot have endeared the Committee to the Soviet authorities. In a report on the campaign against "homeless cosmopolitans" that had been unleashed during the winter of 1948–49, U.S. Chargé Foy Kohler pointed out that although they may have stemmed from the "ideological housecleaning" launched by Zhdanov in August 1946, attacks against the Jews transcend those against other groupings and had "deep roots in Russian chauvinism with its traditional anti-semitism as well as anti-foreignism." The establishment of the State of Israel, Kohler continued, "has undoubtedly revived [the] attraction [of] Zionism" for Soviet Jewry. Referring to Ehrenburg's *Pravda* article, Kohler insisted that the "pointed direction [of the] present assault constitutes [a] warning that [the] Soviet Jew can have only one loyalty, i.e. [the] Soviet fatherland."[117] If Kohler was correct in his observations, it is no wonder that Soviet Jews who had demonstrated feelings for Israel were being punished for their attachment to a state outside the USSR's borders. For, if the purpose of the Iron Curtain in the cold war period was to seal off the Soviet population from the world outside, every such attachment could only be interpreted as treason.

# 2    Jewish consciousness during the "black years"

### The mood of Soviet Jewry

The trends that characterized the postwar years were intensified during the last years of Stalin's rule and did not for the most part begin to change until his death in March 1953. The economic recovery program began to bear fruit, notably in the spheres of heavy industry and construction: the USSR conducted its first atomic explosion in 1949; a series of hydroelectric stations, canals and irrigation projects were completed, and cities destroyed in the war were rebuilt, monuments not only to bad architectural taste but also to the Kremlin's ambition and drive. The Iron Curtain became virtually impregnable and the camps became filled with prisoners, including large numbers of demobilized soldiers who had served in Eastern or Central Europe in addition to the ex-prisoners-of-war who had been incarcerated upon their return to the Soviet Union. Among others the ever-growing camp population made a significant contribution to the economic momentum.[1]

Although Zhdanov had died in August 1948 and a number of his closest supporters were purged in March 1949 in the Leningrad Affair,[2] the basic tenets of Zhdanov's cultural and ideological policy – which subordinated the arts and sciences to the needs of the state and severely curtailed the scope of minority cultures – continued to dominate the scene.[3]

The enhanced "vigilance" campaign of Stalin's last six months involved economic trials, purges in some of the national republics, a further deterioration in Soviet–U.S. relations (Ambassador George Kennan was declared *persona non grata* in the USSR), and the Doctors' Plot which was "exposed" in January 1953. The Soviet authorities claimed to have discovered a conspiracy by a group of doctors, most of them Jewish, to kill a number of Soviet civilian and military leaders to weaken Soviet security; their plot was said to have been concocted in collaboration with Western and Israeli intelligence and espionage services. Stalin's new target in the leadership was Lavrentii Beriia, as it was he who had been responsible for security when the doctors allegedly killed Central Committee Secretaries Aleksandr Shcherbakov and Zhdanov by falsely diagnosing their illnesses. Beriia, himself a Mingrelian, was generally associated with the cause, as it were, of minority ethnic groupings against the Great Russians.[4]

Although the Kremlin's policy toward the Jews had become increasingly antagonistic as the year 1948 progressed, the USSR's initial support of Israel befuddled the issue. Thus, the clandestine but total elimination of Jewish national culture, its institutions and leading activists toward the end of the year,[5] and the open assault upon assimilated Jewish "cosmopolitans," both in the winter of 1948–49, which introduced the period that has come to be known as the "black years" of Soviet Jewry, came as a double shock.

In the early months of 1949 the anti-cosmopolitan campaign preoccupied the Soviet media as well as party cells and primary organizations throughout the country. In academic institutions and other places where the intelligentsia was employed, the campaign was accompanied by virulent antisemitism and increasing educational and professional discrimination against Jews. At the same time, the regime was quietly conducting a systematic attack on Jews suspected of nationalist tendencies. The victims of this second offensive were the members of the JAFC presidium, Yiddish writers and cultural figures as a whole, and some who were "guilty" of genuine Zionist sympathies. The anti-Jewish policy of Stalin's last years, the witch hunt that accompanied this massive two-pronged anti-Jewish campaign between late 1948 and early 1953 culminated in the Doctors' Plot and the plan to exile the Jewish population of the European part of the USSR to forced labor camps in Siberia and Kazakhstan in the wake of the doctors' trial, a fate from which the Jews were saved by Stalin's demise. The charges against the doctors were published on the fifth anniversary of the murder of Solomon Mikhoels, as they were supposedly connected with his alleged crimes against the state. The plot's implications regarding personnel changes in the Soviet leadership were lost on and irrelevant to the Jews, yet it capped a period of terror the memory of which continued to strike fear in the hearts of Soviet Jews for decades.[6]

In January 1953 Sir David Kelly, an experienced observer of the Soviet scene who had served as British ambassador in Moscow from

1949 to 1951, wrote: "What has gradually made the Soviet rulers revert to anti-Semitism has been the discovery that they had to deal with a national culture which is unique in having no local background and [which] has maintained its identity in every land and milieu independently of the surroundings." This was "an inexplicable phenomenon" to the Soviet leadership which, as materialists, had "no use for inexplicable phenomena" or for a people with such a "long developed technique of national preservation which cannot be fitted into the communist norms ... " The Jews excelled as "virtuosos, lawyers, doctors of medicine, critics, buyers and sellers – whereas the Soviet ideal is the engineer, the manager, or on the artistic plane the producer in blinkers of straight practical plays or novels or paintings to serve strictly practical objectives defined in the Party line." Thus, the Soviet leaders "sensed that the Jewish community represents a human incalculable element which is a potential threat to the whole Sovietic way of life." The result was "an entirely new type of anti-Semitism which can make use of the traditional popular prejudices for its own purposes and at the same time ... provide a scapegoat for repressed feelings and discontent."[7]

However satisfactorily Kelly's explanation may elucidate Soviet policy vis-à-vis the Jews, its main significance lies in its attribution of official Soviet antisemitism to a gut feeling on the part of Soviet leaders, i.e. a certain malaise which almost precluded any attempt to find a rational solution to the Jewish question because it did not emanate from objective analysis. In the face of this virtual declaration of war on them, the Jews, naturally, felt so threatened that they could hardly be expected to see that the Kremlin's behavior was, in some very deep way, based on fear of them.

One of the most difficult consequences of the anti-Jewish campaign was the isolation it forced on the Jews both as a group and as individuals. Not only did they shy away from the hatred of their fellow Soviet citizens; they became increasingly frightened of each other to the point where they were even afraid of meeting to discuss their views for fear that they might fall victim to MVD stooges (which happened to many of the groups mentioned in the first chapter). Hebrew and Yiddish books, the last vestiges of their Jewish past, were hidden, burned or thrown away, as their mere possession was incriminating.[8] The year 1951 even witnessed the revival of the blood libel, according to which Jews were accused of using the blood of a non-Jewish child in the baking of *matzot* (unleavened bread) for Passover.[9]

It was precisely this atmosphere of severe repression that led some Jewish university students and young professionals to start searching for their roots. They were being discriminated against as Jews because they had Jewish names or because their Jewish nationality was registered in their documents; yet they had no idea what their Jewishness really meant. And nowhere in the USSR could they find out: the publication of Yiddish works had ceased entirely in 1948 and Jewish books published before then were becoming harder and harder to find.[10] Nor were there any courses in Jewish history, religion or literature, or in the Hebrew or Yiddish language, even though official Soviet nationalities policy endorsed the propagation of national tongues and cultures, provided they were "socialist in content and national in form." When the last Jewish cultural institution, the Moscow Yiddish State Theater, was closed in fall 1949, the Jews were denied even those bare trappings of cultural life allowed other national groupings, in effect outlawing them from the Soviet "family of nations." True, some synagogues remained, yet they lacked the personalities that might have guided young people, while religion *per se* held no attraction for a generation which had been brought up on the precepts of dialectical materialism and imbued with the contempt of religion that underlay these precepts.

It was therefore not surprising that an increasing number of young Jews began to look beyond the confines of the USSR to find meaning for their Jewishness. Perhaps only a few dared to talk about leaving for Israel, but more began to discuss their position vis-à-vis the Soviet Union and the new Jewish state and to conduct some minimal cultural activities. It was not that any of these Jewish youths, even now, nurtured anti-Soviet feelings: most of them took the revolution, Stalin and the regime for granted. As they viewed it, their sole problem was Soviet antisemitism and the concomitant, increasingly oppressive discrimination.[11]

In 1951 the Moscow correspondent of a Polish newspaper noted that administrative pressures on Soviet Jews were having precisely the opposite effect to that which was sought by the authorities. Instead of renouncing their national culture and assimilating, the Jews were drawing closer together, segregating themselves and beginning to manifest the signs of national expression characteristic of oppressed nations. The correspondent added:

> It is impermissible to deny the natural right of national life to those who are unable to adapt and assimilate, to those who need Jewish culture just as they need air. Jewish culture and its bearers must be

> given equality of right of expression, influence and development . . .
> Undoubtedly the number of those who yearn for Jewish culture
> today is greater than it was before the centers of Jewish culture were
> wiped out. This is the most pungent proof against the theory of
> integration.

The article concluded that the synagogue was the only place in
Moscow where Jews could meet, and that most of those who congre-
gated there, including many young people, were not believers
attending out of religious conviction, but Jews who wanted to meet
their fellows.[12]

Although many knew that people were being arrested for Jewish
activity and some of those involved in Zionist activities knew that they
were under surveillance, there were some brave souls who continued
to meet to discuss and study Jewish history, to debate Jewish issues
and to hear broadcasts from Britain, the U.S. and especially Israel.
Indeed, despite the considerable risk involved, Jews from the Black
Sea to the Baltic made very effort to maintain this sole contact with
Israel and the Jewish world.[13] Many listened at night when reception
was better, even though they ran the risk of drawing the attention of
those with whom they shared communal apartments in which most
Soviet citizens still lived and where privacy was well-nigh impossible.
Jews in the Black Sea port of Poti told crew members of the Israeli ship
*Meir Dizengoff* at anchor there that all the Jews listened to Yiddish
broadcasts from Israel even though they did not come on until
midnight, when listening to the radio inevitably aroused suspicion.
Sometimes a group of friends would take turns listening to minimize
the risk. By the early 1950s Jews in Siberia were also listening to Israeli
broadcasts in Yiddish and Hebrew.[14]

In addition to the younger generation, small groups of older people
who had somehow escaped the arrests of 1948–49 and who now felt
that they must help arouse Soviet Jews from their lethargy were
beginning to form.[15] Although they knew that such activity meant
going against the assimilation dictated by the Soviet authorities, they
felt that circumstances dictated concrete action. Some few even
attempted to contact members of the Israeli legation until the rupture
in diplomatic relations in February 1953 in the wake of the Doctors'
Plot.

The synagogue remained the main place for local Jews to meet the
Israelis. Israeli diplomats who attended services, especially on the
High Holy Days, were passed notes informing them of the worsening
situation. Apart from stories of discrimination and hardship, the notes

told of the continued interest in the State of Israel and its future. Their writers explained their lack of open contact with Israelis as being due to "local conditions," insisting that it did not reflect feelings of estrangement. They also described how antisemitism and discrimination were evoking a new national consciousness in young Jews. On the 1949 Day of Atonement legation secretary Arye Lapid managed a brief chat with some Jews in the courtyard of Moscow's Choral Synagogue. Lapid gave them the legation's phone number, which they wrote down on the lining of their coats. Thus, when Meir Kanevskii heard that the Jews were being evicted from certain places near Moscow, he called Lapid and arranged a meeting at which he gave him a report on the rumored deportations.[16] On the whole, however, by the early summer of 1950, contact between Israeli diplomats and local Jews – whose visits to the Israeli legation had long since ceased – had become rare, superficial and incidental. Most Jews in those years were clearly too afraid.[17]

Although there were severe restrictions on the travel of foreign diplomats,[18] some Israelis did visit towns outside Moscow.[19] Thus, when trade agreements brought Israeli ships with oranges and bananas to Odessa in the early months of 1952 and 1953, the appearance of Israeli naval officers and sailors in the streets and other public places aroused great excitement among local Jews, as did the sight of crates of oranges inscribed "Jaffa." And when the Israelis went to the theater, Jews in the audience were keenly aware of their presence, although only a few had the courage to actually exchange greetings with them. Others, however, including some who worked in the port, could not resist the opportunity of talking about Israel with Israeli seamen. As with Soviet support for the establishment of Israel, the knowledge that the USSR had made trade agreements with the new state may have encouraged them to believe that contact with the Israelis was permissible. Here, too, the Israelis heard that antisemitism was leading young Jews toward a sense of national pride. They wanted to know about Israel, its social, economic and political development, even about the professions most needed there. The seamen were told that Jews in Odessa met to discuss the Jewish question and Israel, to sing Jewish songs and to listen to Kol Zion lagola. They were also told by many that they had wanted to emigrate when Israel was established, but that none had yet succeeded in leaving. Crew members spoke as well to older people who had been members of Zionist organizations and had neither forgotten Hebrew nor their Zionist ideals. One group of Jews even contemplated sending a member to make contact with the Israeli legation in Moscow, and some Jews asked what Israel was doing to help the Jews of the USSR.[20]

Further if indirect evidence of the Soviet Jew's keen interest in Israel and its development, and of the anxiety this aroused among party ideologues and propagandists, may be seen in the articles on the hardships of life in Israel which began to appear in the press in the early 1950s. One such broadside described the introduction of clothing and footwear rationing in Israel, asserting that this signified the failure of Israeli economic policy and that country's approaching bankruptcy; and this was all the result of Israel's ties with the "adventurist policy of American imperialism."[21] The only possible interpretation of these articles is that they were meant to deter Soviet Jews from even thinking about emigrating to Israel.

### The arrests

The two major tendencies that form the background of the large-scale arrests in the "black years" were (1) the mounting official antisemitism, combined with a politico-ideological and administrative atmosphere conducive to repression, and (2) the growing Jewish awareness among the younger generation which led them to identify with their Jewish roots. It is perhaps worth noting here that arrests in this period inevitably involved protracted interrogations and long prison sentences.

The extreme flexibility of the criteria by which the Soviet authorities defined Jewish "nationalist" activity between fall 1948 and March 1953 make it impossible to estimate how many of the thousands of Jews arrested for nationalist activities during this period were any kind of Zionists. We do, however, know that some of them – including Hebrew writers Zvi Plotkin, Zvi Pregerzon, Meir Baazov and those around them – were Zionist activists. As already mentioned, their own direct testimonies and those of people who met them in the camps credit Plotkin and Pregerzon, respectively, with encouraging Jews to request permission to fight in Israel's War of Independence and with gathering Moscow's Jews to welcome Golda Meyerson in the Choral Synagogue. Plotkin had also traveled to other cities after Israel was established in order to organize groups or cells of former Zionist activists.[22] Another was Nadia Nemirovskaia, who was arrested with her husband and son in 1950; all three died in the camps.[23] Yet another was Meir Kanevskii, who was finally arrested in Piatigorsk in early 1953 after going from place to place to escape surveillance ever since his 1949 meeting with Lapid. The list of charges against Kanevskii included: having given money allegedly received from the Joint Distribution Committee (JDC) to Meir Vofsi, one of those accused in the Doctors' Plot; being a leader of a Moscow organization of Zionist nationalists; having spied for the Israeli legation; and having conducted anti-Soviet propaganda. Kanevskii was sentenced to death, but the sentence was commuted to twenty-five years' imprisonment.[24]

The three Moscow students who had considered crossing the border in order to go to Israel and the many who had asked permission to fight in Israel's War of Independence were also arrested. So, too, were the group of seven people in Gomel who had sought to emigrate in 1948 along with their relative in Moscow, Grigorii Spivak, who had contacted the Israelis for help in obtaining permission to emigrate,[25] and, apparently, all those who had contacted the Israeli legation, most of whom had done so with a similar end in view.[26] In Leningrad about forty Jews were arrested in 1950–51 for having sought to emigrate to Palestine via Poland in 1945 immediately after the war ended.[27]

Those arrested in the Western territories also included people who had been involved in attempts to leave the USSR in the aftermath of the war. Mordekhai Shenkar, who went to Lvov in the hope of reaching Poland and stayed on to help other Jews leave within the framework of the *briha*, was arrested in 1949.[28] Jews who had been active Zionists in the interwar period, before these lands were annexed by the Soviet Union, were also arrested. For many of them it was the second time, as they had been arrested when the Soviets took over and had only been released in the second half of the forties. Those rearrested included some who had refrained from any activity that might antagonize the Soviet authorities. One of those arrested in the early 1950s was Binyamin Robinzon, the brother-in-law of Shlomo Gefen who had been arrested in 1946 for his activity in the *briha*. Another, David Iofis, who was saved from arrest in 1941 by an administrative error had been a Betar (a right-wing Zionist youth group) leader before the war; since his return to Riga in 1945 he had restricted his activities to meetings with trusted friends in private homes on Jewish festivals and listening to foreign broadcasts in the intimacy of his home. Yitzhak Hayit, on the other hand, had taught Hebrew in Riga right up to his arrest.[29] Among the few who evaded arrest was Ezra Rusinek, who had been involved in Zionist activities in Libau prior to the war and had moved to Riga in 1947, to Engels (near Saratov) in 1950, and later moved to Taganrog, where he remained until 1963, when he was able to return to Riga.[30]

Members and former members of nationally oriented groups were arrested throughout the country, such arrests often including the whole group, except possibly the provocateur or informer, who was usually a later recruit to the group. This was the case with a group of Lvov high school students, who had banded together to fight antisemitism and anti-Jewish discrimination and called themselves *Soiuz evreiskoi molodezhi* (Union of Jewish Youth) or SEM. Since the ten or eleven group members also tried to learn Yiddish and Jewish history, books on these subjects were found when they were arrested and their homes searched in 1949. Most of them were sentenced to ten years' imprisonment, charged, among others, with having wanted to sever the Crimea from the Soviet Union and create a Jewish state there, although they had never even heard of the suggestion to set up a Jewish autonomous republic in that peninsula.[31] The members of the Zhmerinka group – who had dispersed to universities in Kiev, Leningrad, Lvov, Vinnitsa and Saratov – were also arrested, the first one after he took part in a discussion of the Lvov group about a leaflet calling on Jewish youth to go to Israel.[32] In March 1953, members of the Tomsk group that had been formed in the winter of 1947–48 were arrested after a provocateur planted in their midst testified to their Zionist activities.[33] Also imprisoned during Stalin's last years were many of the Jewish officers who had formed clandestine circles to study Hebrew and discuss Zionist history in the heartland of the RSFSR although again a few, such as Grisha Faigin, managed to escape punishment.[34]

The first Odessa Jews to be arrested for Jewish nationalism – in 1949 – seem to have been four Yiddish writers, two of them poets. The year 1950 brought the arrest of a group of older Odessa Zionists, who had been listening to Kol Zion lagola and had come together to celebrate Israel's establishment in what they supposed to be the privacy of a private home.[35] A group of six Odessa students who came together early in 1949 to protest the anti-Jewish character of the anti-cosmopolitan campaign and to read those books on Jewish history which were still obtainable at the university library were arrested in fall 1950, charged with "forming an anti-Soviet, Jewish, Zionist, bourgeois youth organization." Their activities had included the posting of wall newspapers at the university.[36] After trying but failing to obtain evidence of a connection between the two groups, so they could accuse the older men of influencing the younger generation, the authorities finally conducted the two trials separately. Indeed, there is little evidence of "group" activity among the older men; they seem to have come together as a group only very rarely, although individual members met with some regularity. Nonetheless, the MVD also sought to prove that the former were in touch with the Zhmerinka group. The members of one group of thirteen students that does seem to have established contact with some of the older Zionists were arrested and sentenced to long terms in prison when they initiated debates on the Jewish problem at Komsomol meetings despite the warnings of their elders. The group was even reported to have collected weapons for self-defense and money to purchase a boat.[37] It would seem that Odessa University was "a hotbed of Zionist activity." In the frenzy of the last weeks of the Stalin period, Ukrainian party daily *Pravda Ukrainy* castigated the "Jewish bourgeois-nationalist Zionists" who had been unmasked there, claiming that "hostile writings" by "hirelings of American imperialism" had been secreted in the library of one of its institutes.[38]

Other arrests in this period included three Jews in Rostov who were charged with having gotten together to celebrate the first anniversary of Israel's independence with a toast to the Jewish state and having distributed pictures of Golda Meyerson;[39] a student at the Saratov law institute, who had applied to fight in Israel's War of Independence and was charged with conducting Zionist propaganda among the students;[40] and a group of four secondary school students in Kiev calling themselves *Dva-sun* – an acronym for the second Sabbath of November (1948) when the group was founded – who were charged with meeting to discuss Jewish problems.[41]

Corresponding with relatives and friends abroad and listening to foreign radio stations were also cause for arrest; indeed, in this period the very existence of relatives in a capitalist country was sufficient to indict a Soviet citizen.[42] Thus, while Jews sought out surviving family in the immediate aftermath of the Holocaust and initiated contact through correspondence, by the end of 1948 or, at the latest, by early 1949, the Soviet correspondents were mostly asking relatives to stop writing. Avigdor Lezerovich, for example, was arrested in February 1949 for having corresponded with a childhood friend in Israel and a sole surviving brother in the U.S. Lezerovich was charged with Articles 58–1a, treason and espionage; 58–10, conducting nationalist, anti-Soviet propaganda; and 58–11, anti-Soviet organizational activity,[43] the MVD having in his file copies of the letters and postcards that he had written and received. While Lezerovich did greet the creation of the Jewish state and its successes in its War of Independence with fervor, the charges brought against him were unfounded, for he had little contact with Jews inside the Soviet Union except for an occasional hushed exchange of views, chiefly with elderly Jews whom he met by chance. It was not until he was in camp that he no longer feared sharing his views or speaking Hebrew and Yiddish.[44]

A group of students at the Riazan medical institute who had listened to foreign broadcasts was arrested and accused of entertaining nationalist sympathies.[45] And in Gomel, the father of Efim Gusman was likewise arrested for listening to Kol Zion lagola and for setting up a *minyan* in a private home. The elder Gusman was also charged with collecting money to build a synagogue.[46]

A number of rabbis and Jews connected with synagogues and *minyanim* were arrested at this time, too, some, but by no means all, for Jewish "nationalism." In Leningrad some two hundred orthodox Jews linked with the Habad movement were arrested, along with the city's two rabbis, the aged Rabbi Abram Lubanov and Rabbi Moshe Mordekhai Epshtain. Tried and sentenced in 1951, the rabbis received terms of five and ten years respectively.[47] The Kharkov rabbi was taken from his home and not heard of again after he received an unsolicited information bulletin from the Israeli legation, sent him because he had received Palcor information bulletins from the Jewish Agency for Palestine during and right after the war. The rabbi's arrest served as a pretext for closing the Kharkov synagogue, which was never reopened.[48] Rabbi Feldman of Belaia Tserkov – as well as the worshippers of his synagogue who had reacted enthusiastically when the Jewish state was established – were also arrested. The rabbi had been warned to close the synagogue, stop teaching Jewish law and refrain from propagating Zionism, but he refused because he did not believe that the authorities would touch a Hero of the Soviet Union. He was charged with having procured the money to build the synagogue from illegal sources. Here, too, the synagogue, said to be "a hotbed of economic crime," was closed down.[49]

Some of those punished for Zionism or Jewish nationalism were "guilty" neither of Zionist activity nor even of Zionist views. One Kremlin doctor was sentenced to ten years in exile just for having greeted Mrs. Meyerson in the Choral Synagogue, and workers at Moscow's Stalin Automobile Plant who had participated in the officially sponsored 1948 meeting with Golda were all arrested in 1950–51.[50] When Mikhail Margulis, one of the three boys who had sought to cross the Turkish border, was imprisoned in the Moscow Lubianka from July 1950 to fall 1951, he met Izrail Genopolskii, who had been arrested for selling three volumes of Dubnow's *History of the*

*Jews* in his Moscow bookstore.[51] And a Mogilev metalworker was arrested for adapting a rolling-press to bake *matzot*, while a Kharkov secondary school student received a ten-year sentence for having disseminated Margarita Aliger's poem "Your Victory."[52]

In other words, the definition of Jewish nationalist, Zionist activity, was sufficiently broad to accommodate the slightest sign of interest in either Israel or Jewishness. It covered activities from membership in "Zionist" groupings, the expressed desire to participate in Israel's War of Independence and contact with the Israeli legation, to correspondence with friends or relatives in Israel or the West; disseminating, reading or merely possessing Jewish history books or Hebrew grammars and dictionaries; and even activities connected with Jewish religious practice. It is difficult to know whether any component of the Soviet establishment really believed in "the big Jewish conspiracy," or what Jews in the USSR called *evreiskoe delo* (the Jewish affair). What is certain, however, is that interrogators often sought to build up such a picture. Equally certain, there was enough Jewish empathy with Israel to worry the Kremlin in a period when its leadership was highly paranoid and rampant nationalist activity in the Western Ukraine and Lithuania was being heavily stamped out. Most ex-prisoners agree that Jews accounted for 5 to 7 percent of the 2 to 5 million political prisoners in the camps by early 1953; this means a minimum of 100,000 Jews were in camps, a large number of whom were "sitting" for "Jewish nationalism."

### Inside the camps

It is ironic that the prisons and camps fostered more meaningful Zionist activity than that for which Jews were being arrested. For prisoners charged with treason, espionage and anti-Soviet activity had already sacrificed their freedom, family ties and professional careers. Whereas members of the various Zionist groups had refrained from discussing their group's existence with their fellow Jews, they now could talk relatively freely even with Jews from other cities and of different generations who were arrested for having inclinations similar to their own. They spent the long periods in prison while being interrogated and awaiting sentence and departure for the camps learning or speaking Hebrew and talking about Zionism and Israel in a way that was unthinkable for "free" Soviet citizens. Moreover, ties forged in the camps helped rejuvenate the Jewish national movement in a large number of Soviet cities after the Prisoners of Zion were released and rehabilitated in the mid-1950s.

Members of the Zhmerinka group, who had been arrested in different towns but were all brought to the Kiev prison prior to being tried, learned there about the history of the Jewish people and of the Zionist movement, about the founder of the Zionist movement Theodor Herzl and Zionist socialist thinker Ber Borokhov, from older Zionists, some of whom had been arrested for the second or third time. Some of these older Jews had received their Jewish education prior to 1917 and may even have been members of the Russian Zionist Organization; others were Jews from the annexed territories or even Eastern Europe. They taught the younger prisoners Hebrew and Yiddish, Jewish history and literature, and Jewish and Zionist songs, including the Israeli national anthem. Small groups of Jews in Meir Gelfond's camp in Vorkuta spent the two hours between their evening meal and lockup time walking in what they called the Jewish street, one group learning Hebrew, another a chapter in Jewish history and a third discussing the latest news from Israel. The same seems to have taken place with slight variations in all the camps, the Jewish prisoners in one camp even managing to produce bulletins or leaflets twice a year.

Camp prisoners also learned of news from Israel from Jews who lived outside camp confines and were thus able to listen to Kol Zion lagola, yet worked together with camp inmates. These were usually former prisoners who had finished their terms but remained in the area in order to complete periods of exile.

In addition to being their first Jewish schools, the camps taught Jewish prisoners a lesson in organization and Jewish solidarity. Three young Jews who arrived in Vorkuta at the very end of 1949 were relegated to a camp in which only five of the 3,000 inmates were Jews. The five "old-timers" immediately set out to help the boys adjust to camp life, bringing them bread, seeing to it that they would not be sent to work in the mines, where their chances of survival would be minimal, and arranging for them to write home so their families would receive direct news from them and be able to maintain contact even if they did not know their exact whereabouts. The Jews were one of the better organized national groupings in the camps. The Jewish prisoners soon found out that they had someone who would help them with the medical committees and allocation of work, in the camp hospital, or in providing extra food. They overcame one of the most common problems – sheer hunger – by forming small groups that treated parcels received by any member as communal property to be shared by them all. Sometimes they even created a small fund on the proceeds realized from selling some of the contents of the parcels.

Since it was out of the question to keep money inside the camps, the fund would be transferred to the Jewish ex-prisoners with whom they had daily contact at work. This money was used by the prisoners whenever they deemed it necessary: on one occasion the Jews in a Vorkuta camp bought food for a fellow prisoner who ate only *kosher* food; on another they supplied medicine to a Jew who had fallen sick, and so on.

If we accept that there were 100,000 Jews in the camps in these years, if most of them experienced some sort of Jewish solidarity there, and perhaps owed the retention of their sanity or even their physical survival to Jewish mutual assistance, this constituted a phenomenon that they would not quickly forget. Often it reminded them of their Jewishness, brought them back, as it were, to the fold. In some instances it led to their becoming dedicated Zionists.

The Jewish festivals were a special experience in the camps. Jewish prisoners would somehow find out when they were due, either from an observant Jew in their midst or from hints in letters from home, such as New Year greetings or a warning to be on the lookout for *matzot* that had been sent for the Passover. The prisoners would then celebrate the festival in question as circumstances permitted. Small groups would hold a *seder* on Passover and, if the parcels they had been sent got through, were actually able to celebrate with a small piece of *matza*. As outside the camps, however, Simhat tora was the main religious event, even if its celebration in no way resembled the traditional ceremonies. The camp authorities usually tolerated these activities, perhaps in line with their policy of turning a blind eye to the celebration of national holidays; in Gelfond's camp the Estonians even celebrated Estonian Independence Day.

It is, then, no surprise that a number of former camp inmates maintain that while many Jewish prisoners may have had virtually no Jewish awareness prior to their arrest, every Jew in the camps became something of a Zionist. This tendency was intensified when the Doctors' Plot was "uncovered." The Jewish prisoners had had a growing feeling of impending catastrophe in the months before the Plot was announced, particularly after the Slansky trial in Czechoslovakia in November 1952 in which eleven of the fourteen accused party and government officials were Jews and in which the indictment charged the "conspirators" headed by party secretary-general Rudolf Slansky of being "Trotskyite-Titoist, Zionist, bourgeois-nationalist traitors." Rumors to the effect that special camps were being set up for Jews had reached the camps and some Jewish prisoners talked of making knives to protect themselves from being slaughtered as had happened in the ghettos set up by the Nazis. But, paradoxically perhaps, in this period of a heightened anti-Jewish atmosphere in the country at large, the antisemitism of their fellow prisoners seemed to disappear at this point, so that Jewish prisoners were even receiving encouragement from members of national groupings generally inimical to them such as Ukranians and Germans. Indeed, in the last days before Stalin's death, when Jewish prisoners were more highly organized than they had ever been, the camp authorities began redistributing the Jews to break up groups that had been together too long and whose organization might prove a threat to the regime at this critical moment.[53]

Although the "black years" were indeed calamitous from the point of view of the Soviet Jewish struggle for national existence and ushered in a period of fear and persecution, they were not totally barren. While, on the one hand, less than a score of Jews managed to leave the Soviet Union for Israel with official permission[54] between Israel's establishment in 1948 and the severance of diplomatic relations less than a month before Stalin's death and the ranks of the older generation of Zionists were being systematically diminished by arrest and imprisonment, on the other, the very hardships and deprivation of these years brought new recruits both inside and outside the camps.

The Soviet regime's hostility toward the Jewish population reached its climax in the last two months of Stalin's life when the Doctors' Plot exposed every Jew – Zionist, non-Zionist or anti-Zionist – to persecution. Publication of the Plot was intended only as the first act of a melodrama that was to culminate in the expulsion of the Jews from the main centers of the European USSR as soon as the doctors' trial was over. In this connection, the writer Ilya Ehrenburg told a friend that after the Plot had been announced, the authorities had tried to get him to sign an appeal to be published in *Pravda* over the signature of a number of Jewish scientists and intellectuals to the effect that, since Mikhoels and his companions had been agents of American imperialism, the signatories approved deporting the Jews to remote areas, as the Volga Germans and Crimean Tatars had been deported during World War II on charges of collaborating with Nazi Germany. The person who requested Ehrenburg's signature even told him that Golda Meyerson and her "gang" had turned the Jews into a fifth column, so that only a handful were still loyal to the Soviet Union.[55]

Some sources have suggested that the Soviet authorities planned to use the Doctors' Plot to trigger the "solution" of the USSR's Jewish problem, that they envisaged that the public trial and subsequent execution of prominent Jews would evoke the wrath of the Soviet citizenry to the point where they would carry out their own reckoning with the Jews, and that the Jews would then be sent to special settlements in the north, Siberia or Kazakhstan on the pretext that this would be the only way to "save" them from the angry masses.[56]

But Stalin died before the letter was published in *Pravda*, and before the doctors – or any other Jewish figures – were brought to public trial. He died on 5 March 1953, just three days after *Purim*, the festival celebrating the final frustration of Haman's plans to kill all the Jews in ancient Persia. And with his death a new era began for the Jews of the Soviet Union.

# 3    The "thaw,"[1] 1953–1956

## Unfulfilled hopes and promises

The first concern of Stalin's successors, said the statement they issued almost simultaneously with the announcement of the General Secretary's decease, was to avert "disarray and panic" by ensuring "uninterrupted and correct leadership." Their second concern was to divide power in such a fashion that would – at least on the surface – institutionalize a collective leadership and some sort of equilibrium among themselves. That there was a huge gap between the theory and practice of the new order and that all was not working smoothly became clear when Malenkov resigned from the Secretariat of the Central Committee on 14 March 1953 less than ten days after Stalin died, although he retained his leadership of the government apparatus and his position in the Presidium.[2] Nikita Khrushchev was listed first in the new five-man Secretariat and on 1 September he was officially appointed First Secretary of the party; a further seventeen months passed before the rivalry between him and Malenkov – and between the apparatuses they headed – was finally decided in his favor and that of the party. During this time Lavrentii Beriia had been ousted from the leading junta and executed by his colleagues, ostensibly for threatening their physical security: Beriia had headed the new Ministry of the Interior (MVD), which amalgamated the MVD and the Ministry of State Security (MGB). As we have seen, Beriia, himself a Mingrelian, was associated with a favorable policy toward the USSR's national minorities, which seems also to have been regarded disapprovingly by his Great Russian companions. With his disappearance from the scene, some of the signs propitious to the national minorities, which had been discernible in the first months after Stalin's death, disappeared as well.[3] The infighting notwithstanding, the slogan "collective leadership" was meticulously retained as a reminder that there would not be any return to the "deviations" of Stalinism and his "cult of personality."

The atmosphere generated by the USSR's new leaders entailed a relaxation of tensions, both domestic and international. At home this meant terminating Stalin's recent reign of terror, an amnesty for political prisoners[4] and the disclosure of how those who had initiated the charges against the doctors had violated "socialist legality."[5] The new mood was soon felt in literature and the arts, which in the USSR are always quick to reflect political change. The "liberalization" and de-Stalinization of the new regime reached their zenith in February 1956 when at the Twentieth Party Congress Khrushchev made his famous "Secret Speech" enumerating the late leader's crimes and distortions of Leninism.[6]

The new leaders also sought to rectify some of Stalin's excesses in the field of foreign policy. An American ambassador was again installed; the Korean War was finally ended in June 1953; East–West conferences at the foreign minister and summit levels ushered in the Geneva Spirit;[7] relations with Yugoslavia and Turkey were normalized; and diplomatic ties with Israel were renewed in the wake of the doctors' release. It was only in the People's Democracies of Eastern Europe that the difficulties inherent in "liberalizing" a communist regime bred serious trouble: if the thaw taking place in the Soviet Union was to be reflected in the satellites, they could hardly be expected to continue accepting their subordination to Moscow; and if it was not to be reflected, what justification could be found for making distinctions between different Marxist-Leninist regimes?[8]

The period of "liberalization" that followed Stalin's death was one of great hopes for Soviet Jews, who believed that the Jewish problem in its broad sense now had a chance of being solved. However, it soon became clear that although the traumatic times associated with the deceased ruler had finally passed, the Jews were not to be included in the process of liberalization. Despite a plethora of promises, the concessions granted in the field of Jewish national culture, which had been outlawed under Stalin, were minimal. On the individual level, too, Jews were still being dismissed from their posts, being discriminated against in terms of professional advancement and having difficulty in entering the best institutes of higher learning, where the *numerus clausus* was retained. That Khrushchev found it as hard to conceal his antisemitism as his other personal tastes and inclinations became evident when he omitted all reference to its Jewish aspects from the denunciation of the Doctors' Plot in his Secret Speech.[9]

Side by side with their new hopes Soviet Jews retained their apprehensions. The memory of the terrible fear that had characterized the last months of the Stalin period could not be erased by a "thaw"; nor could the habit of fear. Some Jews did renew correspondence with relatives in Israel, the U.S. and Britain shortly after Stalin's death, and even asked their relatives for food parcels.[10] They still, however, tended to avoid personal contact with foreigners who were beginning to visit the Soviet Union now that the Iron Curtain seemed to be lifting,[11] a caution which seemed unfounded to uninitiated outside observers, but which was still very much in place as we shall see below.

Despite the fact that the six-day work week made going to synagogue on the Sabbath no easy assignment, the synagogue remained the main meeting-place for Jews, especially on major festivals. In addition to causing difficulties at work, synagogue-going also involved the danger of being seen, photographed and followed. Indeed, the continued presence of informers, even in this period of so-called liberalization, could hardly be expected to reassure Jews that the freedom of worship guaranteed by the Soviet constitution applied either to Soviet reality or to themselves.[12] Nor, for many younger and middle-aged Jews who had grown up as atheists, could the synagogue provide a natural – let alone an attractive – outlet for feelings of national identity. Yet, for those who did somehow attend services, it was the one place where they could give vent to their sense of despair. The tears that were shed during the memorial prayer for the dead (*yizkor*) recited on festivals were also tears for the living: for their fear, their repression and the abandonment by so many of their national heritage, culture and faith.

Under the new leadership there were a few minimal concessions to the Jewish religious establishment, such as the publication of the Peace Prayer Book[13] and the opening of a rabbinical seminary or *yeshiva*.[14] Yet, these gestures were virtually meaningless for the average Soviet Jew given the constraints in which they were couched and his or her general world view. Moreover, there was still no way of learning how to pray, for Hebrew, the language of Jewish prayer, was not being taught anywhere in the Soviet Union (except in closed courses for officials of certain government institutions).

The hope that Jewish culture might be revived did not seem unrealistic. Despite the widespread acculturation of the Soviet Jewish population – which had little alternative – there were still a considerable number of older Jews who knew Yiddish and longed for Jewish cultural expression. Indeed, the year 1954 witnessed first the return of an occasional Yiddish folk-song to the Soviet stage and then of "concerts" of Jewish music and song. The large numbers that attended such events, which turned into "happenings" where Jews could mingle with other Jews, evinced their appetite for Jewish culture. These concerts attracted many more of the intelligentsia than the synagogue, including young people who knew no Yiddish. The first time that Jewish songs were included in a program was at a March 1954 concert in Moscow by the Latvian singer Irma Iaunzem. In April of the same year Jewish songs were included in three Moscow concerts given by two Jewish singers, Sidi Tal from Chernovtsy and Anna Guzik from Kiev.[15] The number of performances of Yiddish music and theater grew to the point where, in the summer of 1955, they were attracting the attention of foreign correspondents in Moscow, who reported the "current smash success" of a "troupe of Soviet Jewish entertainers" who were presenting Yiddish "repertory plays" in Moscow's theaters and public parks.[16]

By early fall 1956 Jewish concerts were reported to be taking place as far afield as Siberia and the Ural Mountains with "workers and students" filling concert halls in the cities of Irkutsk, Sverdlovsk, Omsk, Ufa and Cheliabinsk to capacity.[17] One event in particular created a furore. In late June and early July 1956 American Jewish tenor Jan Peerce performed in Moscow, Leningrad and Kiev. His Moscow performance, before an overwhelmingly Jewish audience, included songs in both Yiddish and Hebrew, the first time that anyone had sung in Hebrew in the Soviet Union since the 1920s. The audience went so wild that Peerce sang encores for well over an hour. He also appeared in the synagogue, where he conducted Sabbath morning services as cantor.[18]

Encouraged by indications that the authorities might be willing to condone the revival of Yiddish culture on a par with the cultures of the USSR's other national minorities, a number of Yiddishists began to strive for the renewal of Yiddish publications and the reopening of a Yiddish theater. Indeed, it seems that some high-ranking persons in the decision-making process contemplated or even advocated a decision to this effect in 1956. It is difficult to ascertain whether their motive was a belief that it would serve to reintegrate the Jews into the Soviet comity of nations, or whether it stemmed from an awareness that something had to be done to counter the adverse effect that revelations concerning the liquidation of Jewish culture – as well as of its central figures – in the late Stalin period were having on the Soviet image abroad.[19] Whatever the considerations, there does seem to have been a discussion of the issues at stake. In 1956 the Paris Yiddish Communist daily *Naye prese* published a conversation between special correspondent G. Koenig and Vice-President of the Soviet Writers' Union Foreign Department Boris Isakov. Although he himself was assimilated, and although he knew that there was a school of thought which maintained that Yiddish cultural activity in the USSR was doomed to failure in view of the Jews' cultural assimilation, Isakov acknowledged that there were still large numbers of Jews who were interested in the Yiddish language and literature. He therefore agreed that Yiddish cultural activities and creativity had to be not only tolerated, but even encouraged. Isakov told Koenig that leading non-Jewish figures in the Writers' Union, such as Secretrary Aleksei Surkov, Boris Polevoi and Konstantin Simonov, shared his opinion that Yiddish literature and theater should be provided with the broadest possibilities for development.[20]

The same paper reported another of Koenig's conversations, with Yiddish writer Yosef Kerler, in which Kerler described the great interest of the Jewish masses in their culture and folklore. And this included many young people, to the surprise and embarrassment of their parents.[21]

The hopes and frustrations of the Soviet Jewish writers who were dedicated to renewing Jewish cultural activity in the USSR were revealed at a meeting they held at the Writers' Union with members of the Israeli delegation to the 1957 Youth Festival and a number of Polish (presumably Polish Jewish) journalists. The Soviet writer described their efforts to gain recognition and have their works printed in Yiddish under the criteria laid down by the USSR's nationalities policy. They also told the visitors approximately seventy writers and poets in the Soviet Union still wrote in Yiddish, about Jewish themes. Everyone present agreed that the undeniable national awakening among Soviet Jewry contradicted official Soviet claims that the Jewish masses no longer had any interest in Jewish culture. The Soviet writers went on to report that they had submitted a memorandum to the CPSU Central Committee to the effect that there had been no Yiddish publications since 1949 although Yiddish writers were still functioning as such; but they received no response other than the repeated promise that a Yiddish almanac would be published.[22]

The Israeli delegation to the Festival also met with Soviet Jewish composers. Lev Pulver, for many years musical director of the Moscow Jewish State Theater and one of the main fulcrums of Jewish cultural activity, told the Israelis that there was a group of Jewish composers in the Soviet Union – including young ones – who longed to be able to publish music on Jewish themes. Pulver also said that he knew many Jewish actors who were hoping that efforts to set up a new Jewish theater would soon bear fruit. The authorities had told them that such a theater had not yet been opened because no suitable building could be found and not because of any ideological opposition to such an undertaking.[23]

Another tidbit with which the authorities fed the hopes of those who sought to renew Yiddish culture in 1956 was the formation of a "collective" for Jewish artistic activity in Lithuania, under whose auspices amateur drama groups performed a few plays and concerts in Lithuanian towns in the following years. The initiative came from Jewish violinist Boris (Berl) Cesarkas (or Cheserkii). In May 1956 Cesarkas told the Chairman of the Lithuanian party's *agitprop* department that the Jewish masses might be more receptive to party and government policies if they were propagated among them through arts and media in a language they could understand. To this end, he suggested setting up a Yiddish library, theater and creative art groups and adding Yiddish programs to the broadcasts of Radio Vilnius. He also called for the publication of a Yiddish newspaper or a Yiddish translation of *Tiesa*, the Lithuanian party daily, as well as for political and other literature to be published in that language and the teaching of Yiddish in schools in accordance with the Soviet constitution. Cesarkas strengthened his argument by pointing out that the non-party Jewish masses were beginning to react to anti-Jewish discrimination and the destruction of their national culture by becoming more rather than less Jewish-conscious, and as a result were attending synagogue and contemplating emigration to Israel. He also proposed that the local *profsoiuz* (trade union umbrella organization), which was already sponsoring Lithuanian, Russian and Polish drama groups, organize a Jewish group utilizing people with the requisite background and talent. In fact, members of the Yiddish drama group that had operated in Vilnius between 1946 and 1948 became the nucleus of the new group.[24]

Despite all these, and no doubt many more, discussions, proposals, plans and promises, it eventually became clear that the authorities had no intention of allowing the rebirth of a meaningful, institutionalized Yiddish literature or, for that matter, of any Jewish cultural activity.[25] At one point – since the nationalities policy tied cultural activity in the national language to the territory of the national grouping in question[26] – those involved in the endeavor to create a theater were told that if they really wanted to achieve their purpose they should go to Birobidzhan. In a similar vein, when a group of writers, including Shmuel Halkin (probably the best-known Yiddish writer to survive the Stalin period), suggested that a special section of Jewish writers be set up within the All-Union Writers' Union, Dmitrii Polikarpov of the Central Committee Section of Literature and Arts told them that the only place in which there was a possibility of them developing a distinct Jewish literature and culture was Birobidzhan.[27] From the viewpoint of the vast majority of Jews, however, Birobidzhan was not a viable alternative.

### The State of Israel and its representatives in the Soviet Union

As in 1917, many Jews in 1953 hoped that the new regime's renunciation of anti-Jewish persecution and discrimination would enable them to integrate into a society that had traditionally rejected them. As we have seen, however, World War II and the "black years" had convinced others that there was no future for them in the USSR. This grouping dissociated itself *a priori* from attempts to revive a Soviet Jewish culture, viewing them as a surrender of basic Jewish national rights even according to Soviet doctrine. For, if Marxism-Leninism accepted the right of every national grouping to self-determination – duly watered down in the USSR to a carefully delineated minimal cultural autonomy in the recognized national territory – and if the Jews were denied even this minimal autonomy because of their dispersion, the only option left for nationally minded Jews was emigration to the Jewish state.

By the latter half of 1955 the dead end that faced Jews who wished to live as such in the Soviet Union was becoming apparent. Just as Stalin's treatment of the Jews as potential enemies of the Soviet state served in the event to encourage their search for national expression, so the reluctance of his successors to restore the Jews' national privileges was having a similar effect.[28]

In this period small informal groups in Moscow, Leningrad, Kiev, Odessa, Riga, Vilnius, Lvov and other cities throughout the USSR continued to meet to discuss topics of Jewish interest. Some of them had formed in the early euphoria of the post-Stalin era; others were comprised of men and women whose commitment dated to earlier times: older people who had been Zionists in pre-revolutionary Russia or younger Jews who had grown up in the Western regions, where they had been educated in Jewish schools and members of a variety of Zionist parties. Many of the latter who were still in their early thirties, spoke Yiddish among themselves and even with their children, and still knew Hebrew well. Baltic Jews in particular have pointed out that they needed no outside influence or confrontation with antisemitism to be reminded of their Jewishness; unlike the prewar Soviet Jewish population, they had never been cut off from their roots.[29]

In Moscow two groups of men and women in their fifties and sixties, erstwhile members of Zionist parties before these were outlawed by the Soviet authorities, formed around Shmerl Goberman (Hoberman) and Gitta Landman. The latter, who had been a member of Nadia Nemirovskaia's group, had taken over Nemirovskaia's position after she was arrested. Gitta Landman made her home available for discussions on Jewish issues and celebrations of Jewish festivals. She also became involved in helping Prisoners of Zion after her own son was sentenced to twelve years' imprisonment and exile. This nucleus of older people now developed a periphery of twenty or thirty younger Jews, including their own children and their friends, who had also come to feel that they had no future in the USSR. The entire group might come together just once or twice a year, for instance, on Hanukka or on Israel's Independence Day.[30]

Some groups came into being to discuss the significance and implications of what Jews heard in broadcasts from Israel and to debate the pros and cons of what they comprehended as Israeli policy from their necessarily patchy knowledge. For many of those who knew Hebrew and Yiddish these broadcasts became the axis around which their lives turned and through them they played a central role in bringing information to a public that had no access to Western, let alone Israeli, publications. In the mid and late 1950s Kol Zion lagola could be heard on short-wave throughout most of the Soviet Union, and on the medium wavelength of a regular radio in areas geographically closer to Israel such as the southern Caucasus and the Black Sea coast. Although systematic jamming made Yiddish-language programs virtually inaudible to Soviet audiences by 1954, Israel's Hebrew – and English – broadcasts could still be heard clearly.[31]

Israeli diplomats and visitors to the USSR received requests from Soviet Jews to simplify the Hebrew in these broadcasts so that more people could understand them. Not only had the Hebrew of Soviet Jews become rusty from disuse; it had also become antiquated during the thirty or so years that they had been cut off from the outside world, during which time the Hebrew language had undergone a marked development. Even the Yiddish broadcasts, insofar as they succeeded in bypassing Soviet jamming, presented difficulties to Soviet Yiddish speakers whose language had become less sophisticated for a variety of reasons.

The technical difficulties notwithstanding, Soviet Jewish emigrants from many different walks of life and different parts of the Soviet Union have testified that a considerable number of Jews listened to Israeli broadcasts with some regularity. It was chiefly through Kol Zion lagola, for instance, that they found out that Israelis would be participating in sports events held in the USSR. The size of the Jewish attendance at these events, the fact that Jews came from all over the country to see the Israelis perform, and the crowds that awaited the Israelis at stopovers on the way to Moscow bore witness to the number of Jews who listened to Israeli broadcasts with regularity, even if we subtract those who were indirect beneficiaries of the broadcasts, having received their information through the Jewish grapevine.[32]

In addition to broadcasts, Israel was represented in the Soviet Union by a diplomatic mission that took advantage of the relative relaxation of the post-Stalin period to move about more freely and more extensively than had previously been possible. The severance of diplomatic relations between the Soviet Union and Israel in February 1953 had disturbed many Jews, who viewed relations between the two countries as a reflection of the Kremlin's intentions toward themselves, some of them even holding the (erroneous) belief that these relations guaranteed their own well-being. Therefore, although the resumption of Soviet–Israeli relations five months later, announced in both capitals simultaneously on 21 July 1953,[33] had little significance in the daily lives of the majority of Soviet Jews, it was greeted with joy by the Jews as a whole as an augury of the new post-Stalin era. The comparatively relaxed atmosphere led some Jews, particularly among those committed to a Zionist outlook, to think that they could act more boldly and with less risk than in previous years. For a few, the new period even bred a sense of urgency, a feeling that this was a passing opportunity which must be seized.[34]

The Israeli government was becoming more aware of the latent interest in Israel among broad strata of the Soviet Jewish population. Thus, when its representatives – headed as before by Shmuel Eliashiv – returned to the Soviet Union they immediately broached the question of Soviet Jewish emigration to Israel with the Soviet government.[35] They had also been instructed to establish and maintain contact with the Jewish population and to provide them with material of general Jewish interest. If before they had attended synagogue on major festivals, they now went regularly on the Sabbath as well. Apart from receiving information about how Soviet Jews were faring and spreading information about Israel (which they had done to a lesser extent prior to February 1953), the Israelis now sought the cooperation of local Jews in an effort to broaden this activity. In particular they began trying to make their contacts with Soviet Jewry more routine.

Israelis planned meetings with local Jews whose addresses they had received from relatives or former comrades who had left for Palestine in the twenties or early thirties. Most of the encounters, however, were initiated by Soviet Jews themselves, who took every possible opportunity, including chance meetings in public places and on the transportation system, to talk to the Israeli diplomats. Although some of the meetings were with people the Israelis had known from the 1948–53 period, most of those now seeking contact had not had any previous connection with Israelis.

The circumstances that led to a meeting were not a yardstick of its outcome. Some accidental encounters led to lasting and fruitful contacts, to new avenues and circles for the distribution of Israeli literature. Conversely, the Jews sought out by the Israelis often refused to meet them out of sheer fear, even cutting telephone conversations short. Sometimes Israelis would arrive at the home of a Soviet Jew only to find him so afraid of being seen in the company of foreigners that his anxiety to end the visit as quickly as possible was obvious. There were also occasions when the Israelis found children at home who had no idea that their parents had brothers or sisters in Israel, for this dangerous information had been kept a close secret. Even Jews who sought out the Israelis usually wanted only to get a glimpse of them but were afraid to engage in conversation. Indeed, many of those who came to synagogue on festivals did so with the sole intention of feasting their eyes on the dais where the Israelis were seated.

One visitor to the Soviet Union, who attended the Moscow Choral Synagogue on a number of Sabbaths with the Israelis, has written that despite the obstacles to conversation, "one felt the electric current which joined the large congregation with the Israeli representatives."[36] The very presence of Israelis added a special component to the somewhat surrealistic atmosphere of synagogue services in a militantly atheistic state. The traditional prayers that centered on Zion and on the ingathering of the dispersed and the oppressed took on a particularly poignant significance. The Israelis could almost hear the unuttered plea to the world outside not to forget Soviet Jewry, to help them in their struggle against spiritual destruction. The Soviet Jewish worshipper seemed to be telling the Israelis: Our place is with you. We shall never renounce our right to help build the Jewish national home. We know that we can be saved and redeemed only in our own country.[37]

There is no doubt that meeting Israelis still involved a considerable risk, particularly under the eyes of the ever-vigilant synagogue wardens. From time to time Rabbi Shlifer himself – clearly on instructions from "above" – indicated his displeasure at the synagogue being used as a meeting-place between Israelis and local Jews. It was only natural, then, that Soviet Jews refrained from speaking to the Israelis inside the synagogue. And the fact that the latter were under constant surveillance (even though they were not always conscious of it) daunted many of those with whom they sought to meet in other places as well. For Soviet Jews had not forgotten the rumors that Mrs. Meyerson's "activities" had brought trouble to the Jews. Wherever they traveled, the Israelis heard about what had happened to those who had been included in the lists she had allegedly passed on to the Soviet establishment. (Although details varied from place to place, the purpose of the stories invariably served to deter Jews from contact with Israeli diplomats.)

No matter where they were held, conversations were mostly very brief: expressions of satisfaction at the Israelis' return to Moscow, requests for an Israeli newspaper or other token from Israel, questions about relatives or friends in Israel and – from time to time – direct questions about chances of emigrating. Those prepared to risk longer conversations were more explicit: they wanted more detailed information about the political and economic scene and other aspects of Israeli life, and they were willing to talk about their own situation as Soviet Jews. Above all, they wanted to know that the Israeli government remembered them and was trying to alleviate their situation.

The meaning of such an encounter for a Soviet Jew in the 1950s can hardly be comprehended by Westerners who have not visited the Soviet Union and met Jews there, whether in this or a later period. Soviet Jewish citizens felt that they belonged to the Jewish people, most of whom lived outside the USSR. Even Jews who perceived themselves as an integral part of the Soviet body politic often sensed that they were different from the rest of Soviet citizenry, that in part they also belonged elsewhere. In many cases, they regarded the State of Israel as their national home, their real representative in the international community. And, except for Kol Zion lagola broadcasts, contact with Israelis was the only way they could find out about Israeli reality since the Soviet media either falsified or ignored the Jewish state's dilemmas and achievements. For Jews who could not understand Israeli broadcasts because their only language was Russian, and who never came across any printed material about Israel, meetings with Israelis were the most tangible proof of their living bond with the Jewish people and its national home. (Even if printed materials did reach hundreds, or, as time went on, even thousands, such material was never seen by the great majority of Jews.) This explains why the constant battle between fear and the desire for such contacts tended to result in the victory of the latter.

The new contacts between local Jews and the Israelis quickly bore fruit. The possibility that Israeli diplomats might be able to give them printed materials on Israel or on other topics of Jewish interest such as Jewish history, in Hebrew, Yiddish and, by mid-1955, even in Russian, made these contacts even more meaningful to Soviet Jews. Deprived of access to such literature for many years, the combined apprehension and joy with which they took these materials into their hands betrayed their spiritual hunger. They were particularly anxious to get newspapers, for these not only provided the most up-to-date material and gave the most direct feel of everyday life in Israel; they were also the easiest to pass on from hand to hand, or more usually from pocket to pocket. New groups came into being, made up of those who received newspapers and the further scores that they attracted. Thus, a clandestine newspaper library was set up in Moscow, with all newspapers received catalogued, and records kept of every paper lent and when it was returned.[38]

In addition to newspapers, particularly *Davar* (the daily newspaper of Israel's ruling Mapai party) and *Omer* (a newspaper in simple Hebrew intended primarily for new immigrants), the Israelis also disseminated pamphlets about Israel, some of them prepared specially for Jews in the USSR, with an eye to their requirements, interests and language capabilities.[39] Barukh Vaisman of Kiev has left us an account of his excitement upon coming across "a treasure": a copy of *Davar* that had become so worn from being passed around that some of the print swas illegible, the first issue of the local Ramat Gan newspaper, a clipping from an unidentified paper, and a small booklet in Yiddish containing information for new immigrants to Israel and a map showing the country's development since 1949.[40]

The receipt and dissemination of Israeli literature, and contacts with the Israeli embassy (the legation was raised to embassy status in August 1954) led to new inter-city connections. Some such links, for instance between Gitta Landman in Moscow and Jews in Leningrad and Kiev, had been forged before. But now the Guberman–Landman group found ways to send materials to Dnepropetrovsk in the Ukraine, as well as to Tashkent and Kokand in Uzbekistan.[41] A few trusted Moscow Jews even aided the Israeli diplomats in locating relatives or friends of embassy staff members or of people in Israel who had asked that regards be passed on, often many years after contact had been cut off.[42] The Israelis also initiated contacts with Jews outside Moscow through people who were passing through the capital usually on trips connected with their work (*komandirovka*).

Most important, however, in reaching Jews outside Moscow were the Israelis' own trips, some parts of the country formerly closed to foreigners being opened up to diplomats, foreign delegations and visitors in the immediate post-Stalin period.[43] Although relations between the two countries never became intensive and although many years passed before there was any Israeli tourism to the USSR, members of the embassy staff were now able to make trips to different parts of the country. Whenever possible they traveled in their own car, which flew the Israeli flag and was inscribed with Hebrew letters. This never failed to attract the attention of the local populace, although most Jews were still too afraid to speak to the Israelis openly. These trips, very rare in the first year or two after relations were resumed, became more and more frequent as the decade grew older.[44]

Wherever they went the Israelis attended synagogue if there was one and made a point of being conspicuous in public places such as the theater or opera. They would use local public transport for the same reason. Indeed, many conversations were begun in trains or in the planes which were increasingly being used for domestic travel. An Israeli newspaper, purposely left protruding from a pocket and usually the pretext for starting a conversation, would soon find its way into the hands of a Soviet Jew sitting nearby. Sometimes, as in Moscow, such chance encounters were the first of several meetings, although local Jews quite often failed to appear at subsequent meetings. Either they had been cautioned against this by the authorities or they, or their wives, had second thoughts and decided it would be wiser to skip the appointment. The decision to miss a second, or third, meeting was not the result of paranoia. Throughout the country Jews spotted meeting with Israeli diplomats were summoned to KGB interrogations that sometimes dragged on for years after the meeting had taken place. For instance, a Jew from the Fergana Valley in Central Asia, who performed Jewish religious rites in his town, was so harassed as the result of a chance encounter with the first Israeli diplomat to visit the area in 1954 that he kept away from the synagogue when two other Israelis visited the area ten years later.[45]

Odessa was one of the cities visited frequently by Israeli diplomats, who would come to meet the crews of ships bringing Israeli citrus and bananas. The recurrent visits of these ships, together with the belief that it was less risky to talk to Israeli seamen than to official diplomatic personnel, encouraged more meaningful and lengthier conversations than usual. For example, Jewish port officials in Odessa told Israeli seamen in March 1954 that Jews lived in social segregation, that when the Israeli flag was flown and the Israeli national anthem played at sports events Soviet Jews reached heights of elation, and that young and old alike contrived to listen to Israeli broadcasts, sometimes exchanging views and information afterwards along with such reading matter as they were able to maintain. (The Israelis supplied further materials.) One Jew, who had heard that an elderly Jewish woman had gone to join her relatives in Israel, asked point blank when younger Jews would be able to leave.

The Israelis met two Jewish students at the opera, one of whom told them that he and two friends had been seeking contact with Israel and information on the possibility of emigrating for several years. This student had inherited his interest in the Jewish people from his parents. He had heard about Palestine as a young boy during World War II, when he had been evacuated to Central Asia, where he had the opportunity of speaking with Jews from other countries (presumably Poland and the annexed territories). On returning to Israel, a representative of the Israeli Citrus Board told Prime Minister Sharett that he had paid three visits to the home of Sharett's former Hebrew teacher in Odessa. Although the old man had received Hebrew books and newspapers with tremendous excitement, he burned them after being questioned by the police about his contact with the Israeli.

There is no doubt that the arrival of Israeli ships, carrying Israeli cargoes, was a source of pride to Odessa's Jews, a rarity in an environment characterized by constant humiliation. This was true even for those who did not dare to approach Israelis, but who drew strength from the sight of an Israeli ship and flag. And when those responsible for exporting Israeli citrus contemplated cutting down sales to the USSR because of unloading difficulties and rising prices in

Western Europe, Sharett exerted pressure to prevent this because of the opportunity it offered for contact with Soviet Jews.[46]

Israeli Minister Shmuel Eliashiv visited Kiev and Kharkov, the Ukraine's other large Jewish centers, in spring 1954. He also went to Poltava, where he found the small Jewish population (estimated at 4,000) more fearful of antisemitism – and of contact with the Israelis – than Jews in the larger cities. Diplomats traveling outside Moscow in subsequent years often found that small Jewish communities, particularly in the Ukraine and Belorussia, suffered the most flagrant antisemitism, including physical assault; in some of these towns Jews were even afraid to leave their homes after dark. Their fear could be seen in the somewhat anxious reception given the Israelis by these communities. Indeed, most Jews had moved to larger cities after World War II in order to escape the violent antisemitism of the smaller townships.[47]

Whenever it became known that Israeli diplomats were to attend synagogue in a particular town, crowds would come to see them. On the first of the two Sabbaths on which he visited the Odessa synagogue (in late December 1955 to early January 1956) Ambassador Yosef Avidar (who had succeeded Eliashiv in April 1955) was told by a synagogue member that if the Jews had known of his coming they would have attended in larger numbers: as it was there was a congregation of only about one hundred when Avidar arrived with a group of Israeli sailors then in port. Israeli representatives visiting Leningrad for the Jewish New Year in fall 1955 were showered with requests to pass on greetings to relatives in Israel and with questions about Israeli efforts to redeem their Soviet Jewish brethren: "When will you get us out of here?" These questions were reiterated in Kiev, where Avidar spent the Day of Atonement: "When will we be able to emigrate?"; "How does one get a *vyzov* (the invitation from a relative abroad without which a Soviet citizen could not, at least until the 1980s, file a request to be reunited with his family)?" Some simply asked: "What can I do in Israel if the gates are opened?" A well-known Kiev doctor told Avidar that he had taught his daughters Hebrew in secret and was desperate to emigrate because he could no longer bear life in the USSR.

The approximately 25,000 Jews gathered inside and outside Kiev's sole synagogue for the evening (*Kol nidre*) service were demonstrating their spiritual bond with Jewish tradition and with their own immediate past. The service opened with a commemoration of the Jewish victims of Babii Iar, killed exactly fourteen years earlier, with the entire congregation reciting the memorial *Kaddish*, which is normally said by individuals on the anniversary of the death of close relatives. By attending synagogue they were also identifying with the Jewish state, and many of them paid for this identification when they were duly interrogated by the police in the following weeks.

Barukh Vaisman had since 1951 been secretly writing – in Hebrew – what was to become one of the most detailed and important first-hand accounts of Soviet Jewish life. Vaisman exchanged a few words with Avidar on this same occasion, and was able to give him a section of his manuscript; a previous section had already reached the Israeli embassy through a third party. One of the many dramatic and moving parts of this extraordinary document recounts how, when Vaisman turned on the radio to listen to Kol Zion lagola on a summer evening in 1956, he heard an instalment of his own manuscript; six subsequent programs brought further sections. It was only then that Vaisman knew that his writing had not been in vain, that it had reached its destination and was being used for the purpose for which it had been composed.[48]

Ambassador Avidar found evidence of the intensity of Jewish national consciousness everywhere he went on this and on subsequent tours of the Ukraine and Belorussia. Many of the Jews he encountered, including young people, knew and were prepared to speak Hebrew as well as Yiddish. Wherever he went Jews accosted him and his companions, asking for the newspapers that were protruding from their pockets and for the badges with the candelabrum, the emblem of the State of Israel, that they wore on their coat lapels. "We are all waiting to come to you," a lorry driver told them in Yiddish. "I never believed that I would see an envoy of our state," a young boy said in Russian.[49]

In addition to embassy personnel, a few Israeli delegations visited Moscow for trade talks, symposia or international events. News of their arrival invariably caused excitement among local Jews, even when there was little chance of direct contact.

Israeli participation in international sports events was a major happening for Soviet Jews. There was always a chance – if the Israelis won – that the Israeli flag would be flown and the national anthem played. The first Israeli team to compete in the USSR had taken part in a volleyball championship as early as 1952. And when Israelis took part in the European Basketball Championship held in Moscow in May–June 1953, many Jews from that city and elsewhere came to the Dynamo Stadium to give the Israeli team a standing ovation upon their arrival at the stadium and to encourage them. Although the congregation of the Choral Synagogue was much larger than usual on the Sabbath the Israelis attended services there, there were no attempts to make personal contact. The excitement and tension that the Israelis felt lay beneath the surface and did not burst forth until the championship closing ceremony, when the barrier of fear was suspended for a few moments and a large crowd surrounded them.[50]

The Israeli soccer team that visited Moscow in summer 1956 estimated that about half of the crowd of 80,000 who came to see them play were Jews and that some 3,000 of these had come especially from the provinces. Team members met and talked with Jews from Lvov, Vilnius, Riga, Kiev, Odessa, Kutaisi and Tashkent; one man from Riga told them that 500 Jews had come from that city alone. The Israelis were also told that tickets had sold on the black market for 200 rubles instead of the usual seven. There was a huge banner in the stadium welcoming the Israelis in Hebrew, and when the team left the stadium they found over one thousand Jews waiting to give them a stormy ovation. While many of them hesitated to approach the Israelis directly, others, especially those from outside Moscow, asked them for souvenirs or printed materials or wanted to converse. Those who did speak with the Israelis told them of the prevalence of antisemitism and of their despair over the fact that there was no future for them in the Soviet Union, a despair which had only been magnified by the general liberalization. Sportsmen who brought regards from relatives in Israel visited only three private homes before discovering that they were being followed and then stopped their visits. Again there was much excitement among the 800 people who attended synagogue when the Israelis were there; souvenirs and pamphlets were distributed, and a few Jews held very short conversations with the guests at the end of the service. When the Israelis left the synagogue, many of the local Jews accompanied them to the end of the street and bade them farewell with the Hebrew *shalom* – and tears.[51]

## Soviet Jewish activists: inside and outside the camps

Even though a large number of the Jews who met with Israelis were still too frightened to disclose their new Jewish consciousness and rejected the Zionist solution as not only dangerous for them but unrealistic for the foreseeable future, for many it proved to be a turning point in their lives. A number of them embarked on a virtually new existence that focused upon the receipt of materials from and about Israel, particularly newspapers. As well as giving them a feeling of more tangible connection with the Jewish state, direct contact with Israeli representatives gave them access to far more information about Israel than they could receive from jammed broadcasts in languages they found difficult to understand. These contacts also gave them a more concrete mission: to help broaden interest in, knowledge of and commitment to the Jewish state.

Despite the elation involved in implementing their rendezvous with the Israelis, and to an extent with their fellow Jews as well, the small nucleus of activists soon began to feel a certain frustration. They had to limit those to whom they passed on printed materials or even simply verbal information about events in Israel to old acquaintances or people already known as convinced Zionists. Since fear of informers made them wary of extending their circles to include Jews whose inclinations were either unknown or ambivalent, they were "preaching to the converted." This frustration was compounded by the awareness that their concealed goal – emigration to Israel – stood an extremely poor chance of being realized.

The experience of the Moscow groups that centered around Shmerl Goberman and Gitta Landman illustrates this dilemma. After a single chance encounter with a member of the Israeli legation staff in 1952, Goberman renewed contact when the Israelis returned to Moscow in late 1953. At first the group felt their lives were indeed being imbued with new meaning, yet after a year or so the necessarily limited nature of their activity led to disappointment and embitterment. However, neither their sentiments nor the surveillance to which they were being increasingly subjected affected their activity or purposefulness, for most of them knew from the beginning that they were taking a risk. In the words of Gitta Landman, applying the precepts of her erstwhile mentor, Nadia Nemirovskaia: if they wanted to help secure the existence of the Jewish state, the Jews in the USSR must be prepared to endanger themselves within the limitations imposed by the Soviet milieu. If their mission was to spread information about Israel in order to help maintain ties between Soviet Jews and their homeland, then they must fulfil that mission.[52] At times the surveillance was so open that it seemed to have been designed as a mere deterrent. Nevertheless, the group decided to expand activities, until what Goberman has described as their extremely tense, almost unbearable hide-and-seek existence finally ended with a number of arrests in July 1955. Indeed, Soviet Jews had been warning the Israelis that people were being arrested in connection with the newspapers being passed around, even suggesting that the Israelis stop distributing printed materials.

About ninety people were arrested on a single night, chiefly in Moscow but also in other towns, especially Leningrad, on charges of having known about the two Zionist groups and their activities and for having received Israeli newspapers. Hundreds of homes seem to have been searched, and everyone who was found to have Jewish literature was jailed.[53] The *Manchester Guardian*, the first organ to publish this news in the West, stressed that the attack on Jewish culture and the arrests were being made despite the "Spirit of Geneva" being displayed by Soviet leaders in other areas. "This occurs at a time when hopes were high that with the new policy ... Jews too would be permitted freedom to live a full Jewish life." The paper went on to note that the first "mass arrests" of Jews since the Doctors' Plot were causing "considerable anxiety" among Jews.[54] As in 1953, some Jews burned whatever Jewish material they still owned.

Most of those arrested were released within a month, but six activists – Shmerl Goberman and his wife Rahel, Gitta Landman and her husband Moisei, Boris Rotenburg and Basia Sheveleva – were charged with betraying the motherland through espionage (Article 58-1a), possession of nationalist literature for the purpose of conducting anti-Soviet propaganda (Article 58-10) and anti-Soviet organizational activity (Article 58-11). News that the six were being brought to trial in February–March 1956 brought relatives and acquaintances to the street outside the court as Goberman and his colleagues were conducted from the prison to the court and again after they had been sentenced; the sentences ranged from three to ten years' imprisonment.

During their interrogation the activists discovered that the police had been recording all of Goberman's telephone conversations, both at home and at work, and had bugged his appartment. They also found out that the KGB had very bulky and detailed files covering their activities for many years. Goberman was asked about meetings and conversations that went back as far as his previous arrest in 1926. As usual, the interrogators made constant reference to the files of others, leaving the prisoners to guess how freely they could talk without fear of incriminating their nearest kin or colleagues. For the accused had no way of knowing whether the interrogators' implication that those being referred to were behind bars was really true, or whether his tiredness, weakness and hunger were being taken advantage of in order to implicate persons other than himself.

During the trial the defendants vigorously denied that they had been engaged in any form of counterrevolutionary activity, arguing that as Jews they had simply sought a means of identification with the Jewish state and information concerning it. They insisted that these activities were in no way anti-Soviet, that Israeli broadcasts and newspapers contained no propaganda against the USSR and that they had imparted no information that could damage the Soviet state in their conversations with Israeli diplomats. And when an "expert" testified before the court to the effect that the Israeli press that had been propagated was anti-Soviet, Goberman asked the court for proof of this contention – which was not forthcoming. None of the accused denied the possession of Israeli newspapers (a total of 120 newspapers had been found in their respective apartments). Yet they were adamant that their interest in Israel had nothing to do with the nature of its political regime, pointing out that, although Lenin had said that there was no Jewish nation and that the Jews must therefore assimilate into the new society created by the October Revolution, Marxism-Leninism had always maintained that small nations had the right of self-determination. Moreover, the USSR had been one of the first states to support the establishment of the Jewish state and to recognize its existence.[55]

Just about one month after the Jews who had maintained the closest contact with the Israeli embassy were arrested, the Soviet Foreign Ministry informed Ambassador Avidar that embassy staff members Nehemia Levanon, Moshe Kehat and Moshe Sella were being expelled from the USSR. The diplomats were charged with conducting activities hostile to the Soviet Union, with forming ties with criminal elements and using them to gather information of a provocative and espionage nature, and with the underground dissemination of materials prohibited in the USSR. This although meetings between Israeli embassy personnel and Soviet Jews were limited to discussions of Israeli life and events, had no connection whatsoever with espionage or provocation and did not in any way deviate from accepted diplomatic practice or custom.[56]

The arrests in Moscow and elsewhere notwithstanding, Jewish activists continued to seek opportunities to see, if not to actually speak with, Israeli embassy personnel. Therefore, the staff that remained continued to appear in public, even increasing their travels throughout the country. They did, however, change their tactics: they now made a point of doing everything overtly, of conducting all their meetings in public places, as they realized there was little or no chance of beating the KGB at its own game.

The arrests of summer 1955 were a reminder that Jewish nationalist activity was frowned upon even in periods of "liberalization." Although people were returning from the camps, these were still far from depleted, and the areas in their immediate vicinity continued to serve as places of exile. Indeed, the camps remained a major arena for Jewish activity during the "thaw," their inmates continuing to discuss topics of Jewish interest, to study Jewish history and Hebrew and to celebrate the Jewish festivals.[57] Some of them even kept Hebrew diaries or composed Hebrew songs and poems.[58]

After the uprisings that shook the camp system from summer 1953 well into 1954, the whole atmosphere in the camps became more lax. The uprisings, initiated by prisoner-miners in the northern part of the Vorkuta coal basin, were organized by resistance groups or cells that already existed throughout the camps to act as a nucleus for launching any major action. Although the uprisings were eventually repressed ruthlessly, the unprecedentedly mild reaction to the first stages of the strike seemed to reflect the indecision and lack of self-confidence of the new regime.[59] By virtue of the improvements that were introduced in the camps, contact between them became easier and cooperative activities more extensive. It was therefore only natural that members of the different national minorities took advantage of the relative lenience to strengthen ties between their own nationals and to have as many as possible concentrated in a single camp. Even when this was not possible, information could be exchanged and mutual assistance extended because prisoners were able to leave their camps for a day or two to visit neighboring (and even more distant) camps.[60]

The authorities tended to keep political prisoners on the move, presumably – at least partly – to prevent those charged with the same offense from creating cells of potential dissident activity.[61] However, when Goberman arrived in camp in June 1956, he did meet people who had been charged with offenses similar to the ones of which he was accused. In October 1957, moreover, two Jews from Leningrad arrived in his camp, one of whom had been connected with the activities of his group and had even served as a witness at their trial. Others, from Kiev, who were charged under the same articles, included Barukh Vaisman and Hirsh Remenik, who had belonged to Vaisman's circle, as well as members of Progress and Tikva, a small group of Jewish students who had been arrested in 1956 after having been active for some years, although their orientation was not pro-Zionist.[62] It was in this period that Prisoners of Zion, believing that they would soon be freed, made their first attempts to establish contact with Jews outside the camps who shared their views and aspirations.

It appears that millions of political prisoners were released in 1954–55. While at first most of them were not rehabilitated but sent to places of exile, by 1955 ex-prisoners were being rehabilitated and granted permission to return to their places of residence. Many of these devoted themselves to reconstructing their private lives, both family and professional. Their spouses and children had often suffered greatly while they were in prison, for in addition to the terrible fear and uncertainty in which they had lived, the spouses of political prisoners were usually dismissed from their jobs and had to eke out an existence as best they could. The monthly parcels they were allowed to send the prisoners were a further strain on their meager resources. Fania, the wife of David Iofis, was dismissed from her job as a schoolteacher immediately upon her husband's arrest. She did not find any other employment for a whole year, during which she and her two small children lived on the proceeds of whatever household goods she was able to sell. Even then the only job she could get was as a low-level insurance clerk. Furthermore, the families of prisoners also suffered social ostracism. Several families of Prisoners of Zion have recorded that former friends would cross the street in order to avoid them.[63]

In view of their own sufferings and the strain their imprisonment had caused their families, some former prisoners were simply afraid to do anything that might jeopardize their freedom again. There were, however, many ex-Prisoners of Zion who, emboldened rather than broken by their experiences and feeling they had nothing further to lose, sensed the need to do everything in their power to try and achieve what they felt was inevitable: getting the Soviet state, which had rejected its Jewish citizens, to let them leave for their own national home. In the words of one of them, Meir Gelfond, "a national-Zionist ideology predominated among the Jewish prisoners in Soviet camps," and, now, in the second half of the fifties, "groups of such people who shared a common past, a common ideology, and common hopes for the future, were formed in various Soviet cities."[64] The new groups began in settlement cities such as Karaganda, Vorkuta, Norilsk and Omsk where many of the ex-prisoners settled after their release since they were not allowed to reside in Moscow or the capital cities of the union republics. In Karaganda some fifty ex-prisoners formed a group based in the home of an old Zionist who had moved there voluntarily in the late 1930s to escape arrest. Every night he listened to Kol Zion lagola and then phoned group members to pass on what he had heard. When they met in his home on Sabbath he filled in details.[65] Groups such as these also came into being in the main Jewish centers (Moscow, Leningrad, Kiev, Odessa) and in the nationally minded Jewish cities of Georgia, Lithuania and Latvia. Made up of, or at least initiated by, ex-Prisoners of Zion, these groups maintained ties forged in the camps with Prisoners of Zion from other cities, thereby creating new contacts between different places. According to one group member from Odessa, these connections were the outcome of the confidence bred by shared camp experience. They were implemented under strict security measures: as far as possible information was transferred by word of mouth, and there was a special code for introducing reliable fellow believers to ex-camp inmates in another town.[66]

In the main centers activities were carried out by new people as well, after those of the earlier groups had ended with the arrests of summer 1955. As in the earlier period, small groups mushroomed in institutes of higher learning in both the larger cities and the periphery. New activists and ex-prisoners alike initiated ties with the Israeli embassy, from which they received up-to-date information on what was going on in Israel, particularly during the Sinai War. And, as before, they received printed materials to read, discuss with their immediate group and disseminate among the larger network formed around each such nucleus. The Podolskii family of Moscow made contact with embassy personnel through their son Boris, who was still a high school student when he approached Israeli diplomats in the Choral Synagogue on Simhat Tora in October 1955. Boris told them that his parents were both teachers and that his mother, Dora, had studied Yiddish at the Faculty for Yiddish Language and Literature in Moscow's Pedagogical Institute in the thirties and wanted to meet the Israelis despite the dangers involved.

During her first such meeting Dora Podolskii pointed out that Soviet Jews had learned to disbelieve everything they read or heard about Israel in the Soviet media and that they longed to know the truth: "We belong to the intelligentsia but wander around blindly as though we were illiterates." Soviet Jews were worried that their children who were growing or had grown up totally cut off from a Jewish milieu or Jewish culture, would soon have little reason to remain Jews. The only way that this could be averted was for the Jews to leave *en masse* for Israel, as she, her husband and their son were planning to do. At a subsequent meeting she asked for material to study Hebrew and a

Jewish history book, which was passed to her at a concert of Jewish music. In the course of time the Podolskiis received newspapers, periodicals, a Russian-language Jewish calendar, *Elef millim* (a Hebrew textbook), Pevsner's Russian–Hebrew dictionary and a collection of Yiddish poems, all of them at prearranged meetings in theaters or even in the street.[67]

In Vilnius nationally minded Jews in their thirties began coming together in small groups to discuss ways to combat assimilation among the younger generation. They made New Year cards based on cards received from Israel, spinning tops (*trendels*) for Hanukka and, at the time of the Sinai War, even managed to collect some money for an "Israeli defense fund."[68] In Alma-Ata, capital of the Kazakh SSR, David Khavkin, a young Moscow Jew who had been sent there to work after he concluded his studies,[69] was taking a group of ten to fifteen youngsters for weekly picnics. In the safety of the open air, the young Muscovite held discussions on topics of Jewish interest, which he had been reading about for the past five or even seven years.[70]

One of Riga's leading activists was Yosef Shnaider. In spring 1955 Shnaider's uncle in Israel sent him a parcel which included portraits of Zionist leaders, among them Chaim Weizmann, Israel's first president. Just before May Day, Shnaider, whose photographic studio was right in the middle of Riga, took the portrait of Lenin out of his studio window and replaced it with that of Weizmann. Another parcel from Israel contained the texts and notes of Israeli songs, especially military marches, which Shnaider and his friends copied out in the Cyrillic alphabet and mimeographed.

Shnaider also organized Hebrew lessons for groups of three, each group unaware that theirs was not the only one. And, from some time in 1955 until he was arrested in 1957, he, Yosef Gold and journalist Grisha Neiberg put out a monthly newssheet called *Iton* based on news they heard on Kol Zion lagola or other foreign stations. Since they had no Yiddish (or Hebrew) typewriter *Iton* was typed in Russian. Four copies were typed, which were duplicated until there were about twenty. These were then distributed – personally – mostly outside Latvia. When he traveled to Moscow to see the Israeli soccer team in July 1956, Shnaider took photos throughout the match. Later he circulated copies of the photos and a program containing pictures of the Israeli team. Also in 1956, Shnaider produced 500 copies of a greetings card for the Jewish New Year with a photomontage of an IDF armored unit. Shnaider and his collaborator, Yura Kogan, distributed the cards by inserting one in each prayer book in the synagogue on the eve of the New Year; they even saw that some of the cards reached Moscow, Leningrad and Minsk.

Shnaider also took upon himself to send to those heads of Jewish congregations who signed the *Izvestiia* letter condemning Israel for its part in the "triple aggression" against Egypt, the replies of Jews abroad, among others that of the writer Shalom Asch. Shnaider had attended a special training course in marksmanship in the regular army, in which he served until 1952; now he trained Jewish marksmen for a defense force in the event that Jews were attacked physically; in the environment of violent antisemitism and constant provocations in which the Jews lived, he considered this essential. Shnaider and his commando unit, as he called it, patroled the synagogue area and precincts on festivals.[71]

### The beginnings of family reunification

The period that began with the return of the Israeli legation to Moscow and ended with the Sinai Campaign (December 1953 – November 1956) presaged a new era for the Jewish national movement. It was the first time that Soviet Jews were in uninterrupted contact with Israeli representatives in Moscow. These years also witnessed the first trickle of emigration to Israel: 53 visas were issued in 1954; 106 in 1955; and 753 in 1956.[72]

At this time all emigration from the Soviet Union, no matter the emigrants' nationality, was being conducted under the dual umbrella of repatriation and family reunification. National minorities such as the Germans and Spaniards were also benefiting from repatriation schemes, that were a concomitant of the "liberalization" that was in effect during this period.[73] Even now, however, the word "emigration" was not mentioned; for "liberalization" did not in any way imply that the Soviet establishment recognized the principle of freedom of movement for its citizens. What Moscow was prepared at this stage to condone was the repatriation of foreign nationals whom exigency had brought to the USSR. The Kremlin was also prepared to consider the reunification of Soviet citizens with relatives from whom they had been separated by the war and the upheavals and political instability that had occurred in Eastern Europe in recent years. Yet, while certain Soviet officials viewed this development with apparent favor – for instance, Soviet Ambassador to Budapest Iurii Andropov told his Israeli counterpart, Katriel Katz, that the reunification of families separated by World War II was a positive step[74] – the fact that every case was judged on an individual basis rendered the outcome for each Jew seeking emigration highly uncertain. Nonetheless, any movement toward emigration, however minor, meant that a crack had appeared in a hitherto impregnable barrier. And if there was a light at the end of the tunnel, even if a dim one, it was worth maintaining the struggle.[75]

Virtually all those who emigrated in this period were pensioners reuniting with their children in Israel. Occasionally, women in their thirties and forties (presumably widows or divorcees) were allowed to leave with their children. Although most of these emigrants came from the Western territories, some of them were from other places, even from Frunze, Alma-Ata, Samarkand and Tashkent, towns on the periphery of the pre-World War II Soviet Union. It was not long before the Jewish grapevine had spread the existence of this small and selective emigration to the point where it became an open secret. This news was supplemented from time to time by Israeli broadcasts that told of Soviet Jewish emigrants who had managed to reach Israel.[76] (There was no hint of Jewish emigration in the Soviet media.) In short, although not many were able to emigrate between 1953 and 1956, thousands probably applied and tens of thousands closely followed what was happening to the applicants. Here it should be pointed out that in the USSR and perhaps in all communist societies, countries that do not allow open options as is the case in the free world, there is a strong tendency to "follow the leader." Moreover, the success even of a few was an important factor in reducing the Jews' fears of resubmitting applications, even after they had been turned down several times.[77] For instance, many of the Riga Jews who were finally able to leave the USSR between 1965 and 1967 had started applying for permission to leave as long as ten years earlier.

The beginning trickle of emigration provided the background for the questions which confronted Israel diplomats wherever they went in the Soviet Union, questions concerning procedure – how a *vyzov* could be obtained – as well as more general inquiries: Why are only old people being allowed to leave? When will younger people be permitted to go? When will it become possible for those without any close relatives in Israel to repatriate?

There were still Jews who were so anxious to go to Israel that they entertained ideas of trying to cross the border illegally, either by sea from the Baltic area or Odessa, or through Poland or Romania. After hearing rumors that it was possible to leave via Afghanistan, one group of Jews from Kiev actually contemplated leaving that way.[78]

However, those who were more realistic took the road of asking relatives in Israel to send *vyzovy*. Ultimately, however, many who received such documents were afraid to submit applications to the authorities because friends had warned them of the obstacles and dangers facing those who submitted papers to leave. They were told that they would be harassed by the police, might even be charged with anti-sovietism, and ran the risk of ending up in the camps.

Most of those who decided to file requests were refused, with no indication why A was allowed to leave and B turned down. However, feeling that they had nothing more to lose, many Jews resolved to persist. Refusals did not mean that the struggle to leave had ended, but simply that the process of applying had to be started over from scratch. Indeed, Yosef Shnaider, who filed his first application in 1955, put in six requests before he was arrested for pro-Zionist activities in April 1957.[79] As selection for emigration seemed completely arbitrary, there were no criteria that might have enabled the Israeli government to negotiate for the emigration of any specific category of Jews. The only thing most Jews knew or believed was that although applications were made locally, the ultimate decision in each case was taken by Moscow, and that the large number of refusals stemmed from the desire to discourage applicants. From the viewpoint of Soviet logic it is certainly easier to understand the refusal to allow Jews to leave and the obstacles placed in the path of those who were trying to do so than the occasional gesture of leniency, especially in view of the tremendous resonance of the very small trickle of emigration. The reasons in favor of emigration were probably connected with considerations of international politics, especially the Arab–Israeli conflict, rather than with the Soviet Jewish situation.[80] Nor does there seem any reason to believe that agreements stipulating the emigration of people from other national groupings in this period were the result of Soviet domestic considerations; they certainly did not stem either from "nationalist" inclinations or pressures from the various groupings themselves.

### The Sinai War

The trickle of emigration that had begun in early 1954, had increased in 1955 and grew even more in the first ten months of 1956, came to an abrupt halt when the Sinai War broke out at the end of October. This would seem to imply that whatever emigration the Soviet leaders had allowed was intended to persuade Israel, and perhaps the Western powers as well, that the USSR's stake in the area was matched by an ability to exert influence on both sides of the Arab–Israeli conflict. For the Kremlin was anxious to show that it was a suitable, if not necessary, partner to the arbitration process.[81]

In addition to signalling the end of the first period of emigration, the Sinai War had a profound effect on Soviet Jewry. Throughout 1956, as the Arab–Israeli situation deteriorated, Jews kept voicing their growing concern for Israel's security to Israeli diplomats. If war breaks out, one Kiev Jew said, Jews will swarm to the Israeli embassy to register as volunteers. However, despite the unquestioned identification with Israel on the part of large numbers of Jews this did not come about. The blatantly anti-Israel tone of Soviet reports on the "triple aggression" resounded among the Soviet public, who were enlisted to demonstrate against Britain, France and Israel in places of work and in schools.[82] Those mobilized included Jews carrying signs with Yiddish slogans, as well as Jewish public figures, and the rabbis and presidents of Jewish communities, who were obliged to sign letters condemning Israel's aggression, which were duly published in the Soviet press. Although many Jews who attended synagogue expressed indignation at what they saw as the rabbis' putting their seal on antisemitism, the same Jews also voiced their reservations when Israeli diplomats refused to sit on the same dais with Rabbi Shlifer on the first Sabbath after the condemnation was published (the Israelis prayed instead in the small side hall where a parallel service was conducted).[83]

In the wake of the Sinai War Soviet Jews again became the focus of undisguised hatred and sometimes even physical violence. They were insulted on buses and trains, and Jewish workers were beaten in factories. When the speaker at one lecture called on Soviet citizens to enlist in the struggle on behalf of "our Arab brothers," an audience member retorted that they could start out by fighting the Jews in the USSR.[84] Jews, whether or not they felt any Jewish identity, were asked: "Why did your people attack the Egyptians?" And when those who did not identify with their Judaism or with Israel retorted that Jews in the Soviet Union were not Israelis, they were told that all Jews were responsible for Jewish deeds, no matter where they take place.[85] In Kiev and other towns in the Ukraine there was a pogrom-like atmosphere reminiscent of the period of the Doctors' Plot. In Riga one Jew was said to have been killed and another severely wounded.[86]

The fear and tension in which the Jews lived during and after the Sinai War put paid to most thoughts of their identifying with Israel openly. Indeed, even those contacts with Israelis which had become routine became fewer out of fear. But committed Jews continued to identify with Israel wholeheartedly, if in silence. The war and the wave of antisemitism that accompanied it even brought some hitherto uncommitted Jews to consolidate ranks; in Riga, for instance, they came to the synagogue to say special prayers for Israel's welfare.

Well aware that they could not rely on the Soviet media for the facts, the Jews monitored foreign radio stations, especially Kol Zion lagola, to learn as much as possible about the war's progress.[87] Thus, the news of Israel's victory spread like wildfire, causing tremendous pride. Jews congratulated each other in the streets and could again hold their heads high. Condemned by their non-Jewish neighbors in any event for Israel's "aggression," they felt that Israel's victories, too, reflected on them, in a sense even belonged to them as well.[88] Many young people became actively interested in Israel and Jewish affairs as a result of the Sinai War.[89] One student from Kiev told a member of the Israeli delegation to the 1957 WFDY festival: "I have come to tell you in the name of a group of Jewish students from Kiev that the Sinai Campaign has enabled us to stand erect, and that we identify with you."[90] It is therefore not surprising that Soviet Jews were bitterly disappointed when Israel withdrew from Sinai and the Gaza Strip only a few months later.[91]

The Jewish "national movement" took a marked step forward during the "thaw" period. Although its open expression – insofar as it is possible to talk of the open expression of a non-establishment movement in the Soviet Union of the fifties – should first and foremost be viewed as the struggle for national cultural expression within the USSR, by this time the number of Soviet Jews whose ultimate goal was emigration to Israel was growing significantly. Upon arriving in Israel one Soviet Jewish emigrant from a town near Moscow (i.e. not from the Western territories) said that if the USSR allowed free emigration most Soviet Jews, even party members, would leave.[92] By the mid-1950s it was no longer a secret that the assimilation of Jews into Soviet society was not the success that the leadership claimed it was. The endemic social and official antisemitism had by no means disappeared, and Jews were discriminated against as a national minority in that they were not allowed the cultural expression permitted other minorities. The few artists who were allowed to perform in Yiddish had to get special permission from the authorities; it was not their institutionalized, recognized right. Further, Jews continued to be discriminated against as individuals in their places of work. They were dismissed from senior administrative, economic and academic positions in the national republics where Khrushchev's policy sought the promotion of members of the titular ethnic groupings. And in the RSFSR itself, Jews were still coming up against quotas in the better universities.

The Jews could not even feel physically safe in a country where there were recurrent indications that the authorities were likely to condone antisemitic outbursts and in which the populace needed very little encouragement to give vent to their basic antisemitism. Indeed, the discrimination during a period of relative liberalism had a much greater psychological impact than that carried out during the undisguised and universal repression of the "black years." In short, de-Stalinization did not lead to the rehabilitation of the Jews as a national grouping, did not reconstitute the Soviet Jewish minority as an integral part of the Soviet family of nations. Not benefiting from the general trend of the time either as a group or as individuals, Jews could no longer attribute their hardships to the paranoia of an ageing tyrant; they had to conclude that the system *per se* did not bode well for them.

Feelings of rejection by their native country naturally led many Jews to look to the State of Israel for the solution to their problems. For, had not the Jewish state been established in the traditional Jewish homeland, and with the help of the international community, including the Soviet Union? And had this not been in recognition, as it were, of the suffering that had culminated in the Holocaust? Of the inability of a nation to exist in dispersion without a national center? Not only did Israel offer the Jews moral support by its mere existence, but it also boasted major achievements that were a further cause of pride and encouragement: in science in general, and agriculture in particular, as well as in such formidable tasks as conquering the desert, absorbing hundreds of thousands of emigrants from countries where they, too, had been a despised and hated minority, not to speak of the 1948 and 1956 military victories over their much more numerous enemies.

There is no doubt that a Jewish national identity existed among Soviet Jews in this period: all evidence points to a growing Jewish consciousness especially among the young, to an increased interest in Jewish national roots, and to a widespread and unhesitating identification with Israel. But this "movement" suffered from all the constraints imposed by a totalitarian, or at least authoritarian, regime. It was forced to lead a surreptitious existence in small autonomous groups or cells and had no broad organization, leadership, press, or any other means to effect the wide dissemination of information or propaganda. It had no funds, and even lacked a clearly defined goal or purpose. Although to a certain extent some of these functions were performed by the Israeli embassy, to which many Jews looked for guidance and moral support as well as for concrete aid such as printed materials, this was not an optimal partnership for either party. For the Israelis were a diplomatic mission representing a sovereign state that had its own coincidence or conflict of interests with the USSR in the Middle East. Any rapport between the two states on bilateral or regional issues now came necessarily to be compounded – not only on the theoretical level but by the Israelis' daily behavior – by an extraneous factor that was simultaneously so significant and so problematic that any normal relationship was virtually precluded. And the establishment and maintenance of direct contact with a foreign state laid the Soviet Jews open to charges of espionage, treason or aiding and abetting a foreign intelligence service. Yet in the circumstances the link between the Israelis and Soviet Jews was perhaps a natural one. The Israelis sought contact with local Jews in line with their definition of Israel as a refuge for Jews suffering persecution and oppression, wherever they might be. And Soviet Jews sought contact with the Jewish world outside, particularly with Israel, as well as any materials that would help them learn their national languages, literature and history and that would inform them about life in the Jewish state. They also sought a source of hope that would provide them with moral and spiritual succor in a basically hostile environment.

Part II

# "Zion, will you not ask after your captive sons?"

# 4     The outside world becomes aware of the problem

### Early rumblings

The question of Soviet Jewish emigration appears to have aroused little interest outside the USSR in the late 1940s. This may have been due to the belief that the Jews identified so strongly with the construction of Soviet society[1] that there was no interest on their part. Or it might be attributable to the Soviet Jewish community's having been cut off from the Jewish world for so long that Western Jews simply did not think very much about their lot. Instead, those who were concerned with aiding Jews concentrated on the Displaced Persons, the Jews of Eastern Europe and those of the Arab countries, whose desperate position was much better known. For Israel it would have been senseless to raise this sensitive issue with Moscow at a time when the Soviet interest was in aiding it to establish and maintain a viable Jewish state in Palestine. This caution on the part of the Israeli leadership, which led it to refrain from any open act of identification with Soviet Jewry, also led the Jewish state to adopt a policy of studied non-alignment between East and West on the grounds that there were large Jewish communities in both camps. It also made the rumors that Mrs. Meyerson had made representations to the Soviet government on behalf of Prisoners of Zion and other Jews who wished to join their relatives in Israel and thus wrought havoc on the Soviet Jewish community all the more poignant.[2]

Despite the official position, however, some Israelis involved in preparing Israel's first diplomatic mission to Moscow did emphasize the need to establish contact with Soviet Jews and help them integrate into world Jewry in both their own eyes and those of Jews everywhere. As we have seen, the hope that the establishment of an Israeli legation in Moscow would signify a breakthrough to Soviet Jewry was expressed at the farewell party held by Mapai on the eve of Golda

Meyerson's departure in August 1948. Although most of the speakers dwelt on the coincidence of interests with the USSR and the significance of Israel's being officially represented in a country likely to become the second great major power of the future, several speakers referred to the implications that an Israeli flag flying in Moscow would have for Soviet Jewry. In the words of the chairman, Zalman Rubashov (later Shazar), then editor of the Mapai daily, *Davar*, and a member of the Constituent Assembly, the potential for a link was there even if Soviet Jews were not able to give expression to their feelings on the subject. The *yishuv* had been seeking a way to reach Soviet Jewry ever since Germany invaded the USSR in 1941.[3] As Shmuel Friedman (later Eliashiv), head of the Foreign Ministry's East European Department, pointed out, now that the State of Israel was going to appear in Moscow openly and officially, it only remained to be hoped that the Israelis would find a way to the "silent masses" awaiting such an encounter.

Although Israel refrained from open discussion of the issue of Soviet Jewish emigration, Israel's first mission to Moscow left for the Soviet Union ready to do what it could to facilitate the beginnings of Soviet Jewish emigration to Israel. Mrs. Meyerson's Counselor, Mordecai Namir, has described the mission's dilemma. While they were well aware that some Jews had remained emotionally attached to the Zionist ideal, the Soviet authorities had consistently refused to either recognize this bond or endorse its expression. Appreciation of this, together with their instructions to refrain from any open act of identification with Soviet Jews in order to retain the USSR's friendly attitude in the international arena, left the Israeli diplomats walking a tightrope.[4] In reply to the letter appointing him the Israeli mission's Immigration Officer in late October 1948 – a month after the High Holy Day demonstrations – Arye Levavi, the legation's First Secretary and Consul, wrote Israeli Minister of Immigration Moshe Shapira that while the Israelis were amazed at the intensity of pro-Israeli feeling among Jews, Soviet policy rendered any chance to achieve emigration extremely slight.[5]

The occasional report that reached the West about how Soviet Jews identified with Israel[6] had almost no impact on Jewish leaders. Even the antisemitic atmosphere engendered by the anti-cosmopolitan campaign, which the Soviets made no effort to keep secret (in contrast to the total silence in which they wrapped their onslaught on the vestiges of Jewish culture)[7] evoked little reaction in the West.[8]

One major exception to this general unawareness was the American

Jewish Committee (AJC), whose Executive Committee authorized its staff to "combat the attempt of reactionary and communistic minded groups alike falsely and viciously to identify Jews and Communists" as early as May 1947. The AJC Library of Jewish Information was asked to set up a project to prepare material for background memoranda on the nature of communism and communist attitudes towards Jewry and the Jewish question, paying special attention to the basic ideological incompatibility of communism and Judaism and including a historical survey of the USSR's position on Zionism.

Among the AJC's most important findings was that the Soviets had not made any systematic attempt either to rescue Jews from German-occupied Polish territory or to evacuate them from Eastern Poland, even after the Nazi invasion. Another conclusion of the AJC project was that, despite russification, the Soviet Jewish population had succeeded in retaining some sense of its Jewish identity and avoiding complete sovietization, and that this, together with the influx of hundreds of thousands of Jewish deportees from Poland who were even less integrated into Soviet society, had increased the antisemitism generated by wartime hardships and Nazi propaganda.[9]

In 1951 the American National Committee of the Jewish Labor Committee demanded that the U.S. State Department investigate the conditions of Jews and other minorities in the USSR, urging that the Voice of America play up the maltreatment of Soviet minorities in its broadcasts to that country.[10]

Israel's official silence on Soviet Jewry was broken in May 1950, when Prime Minister David Ben Gurion called on the Soviet authorities to allow Soviet Jewish emigration. The issue was discussed by Foreign Ministers Moshe Sharett and Andrei Vyshinskii at the United Nations toward the end of that year and again at the end of 1951.[11] In 1951, too, in July and September respectively, Israeli Minister in Moscow Shmuel Eliashiv approached Deputy Foreign Minister Gromyko and Vyshinskii on the question of family reunification, stressing its humanitarian aspect in relation particularly to Jews who had experienced the Holocaust and most of whose closest kin had been killed in the war.[12] By 1950 Israel had little to lose by raising the issue: bilateral relations had cooled off (although Israel was still receiving some Eastern bloc military hardware), and emigration from the People's Democracies had been virtually cut off. Speaking in Haifa in June 1951, Sharett stated that Israel had not forgotten Soviet Jewry and that the time would come when this large Jewish group, the second largest in the world, would be permitted to emigrate.[13]

Although Soviet Jewry occupied a very minor place on the agenda of the Twenty-third World Zionist Congress that same summer, the Congress did call on the Soviet government to allow Jewish emigration and to release Prisoners of Zion, resolving that the Congress "cannot accept the denial of the right of emigration of the Jewish community from the Soviet Union." Political Committee Chairman Shneour Levenberg quoted Sharett as insisting that the plea for *aliya* did not in any way represent Israeli involvement in the cold war. And in his report on *aliya*, Aliya Department head Yitzhak Rafael said that although "we have no real knowledge of the desire for *aliya* among the Jewry of Soviet Russia that has been cut off from us for thirty years ... the hearts of tens of thousands of them beat with us today and were they able to do so they would join their brothers in building the Jewish homeland"; he admitted that "we have not done enough for them."[14]

In February 1952 Ben Gurion read to the Knesset the text of Israel's reply to a Soviet note asking Israel (and other Middle Eastern states) to refrain from joining the Middle East Command or any other military alliance directed against the USSR. After giving the requisite assurance, the Israeli note, handed in to the Soviet Foreign Ministry in early December 1951, pointed out that Israel's cardinal aim was the "return of Jews to their historic homeland." It asked the Soviet Union to enable those Jews living in that country "who wish to do so, to emigrate to Israel" in accordance with Soviet policy that was based on "national equality and the right of self-determination for all nations."[15] While this was certainly not cold war language, it did not represent a realistic diplomatic effort, for there was virtually no opportunity for this to happen within the context of current Soviet policy.

## The Slansky trial and Doctors' Plot arouse world Jewry

The November 1952 Slansky trial in Prague and the subsequent Doctors' Plot were a watershed for Israeli policy. Since Israel's "soft" policy designed to take Soviet sensitivities into account was not leading to any positive results,[16] Israeli leaders made their first recorded attempt to arouse American Jewry on behalf of Soviet (and other East European) Jewry. At the United Jewish Appeal (UJA) annual conference, Jewish Agency for Palestine Treasurer Giora Josephtal and UJA Executive Vice-President Joseph Schwartz declared that American Jewry, in conjunction with the State of Israel, must play the dominant role in procuring "the release of as many Jews as possible at whatever the cost in money and whatever the risk . . . involved."[17]

The AJC was already planning a public meeting for which it sought co-sponsors among eight or nine Jewish and non-Jewish religious and sectarian organizations. The media were to be invited to hear a resolution comparing Nazi and communist techniques of securing and holding totalitarian control by attacking various groups, principally the Jews, calling for worldwide resistance to communism, and detailing efforts to call the communist rulers to account through the U.S. government, the U.N. and other channels.[18]

In a memorandum summarizing the implications of the Slansky trial, *Commentary* editor Elliot E. Cohen wrote that it "brought opinion leaders to a new stage of clarity on Soviet barbarism and aroused indignation among all layers of American society that provides a solid foundation of broad, popular sentiment on which we can build programs of education and action." Cohen was convinced that the AJC had "unique assets for playing a catalytic role in this situation," since neither Israel, the Jewish Agency nor the World Jewish Congress (WJC) could "as effectively defend either the world Jewish communities or, for that matter, themselves . . . American Jewry would not want Israel to speak as the voice of all Jewry or to represent 'the Jewish people' and . . . Israel understands fully that this cannot and should not be its role, at least not on this issue." Since "the general, non-sectarian and Christian groups will not move without some clear lead . . . from Jewish groups" and "counsel among both Jewish and general groups is almost unanimously of the opinion that in this case the Jews should not go it alone," the AJC's guidance was indispensable to the public movement that the situation required.[19]

An unsigned AJC memorandum of the period stressed that an education program be aimed at the liberal community both to highlight the chasm that separated liberalism in all its nuances from communism and to ensure a maximum impression on the Soviets, who regarded the liberals as a potential human reservoir for front organization activities.[20]

The 13 January 1953 "disclosure" of the Doctors' Plot brought the issue of Soviet Jewry to the public eye with a bang. As early as 15 January, the Israeli Foreign Ministry announced its intention of raising the question of the treatment of Jews behind the Iron Curtain at the U.N. General Assembly in February.[21] On the same day World Zionist Organization (WZO) Chairman Berl Locker called upon the Soviet government to "Let My People Go." And on 18 January the Zionist Organization of America (ZOA) demanded that the two-and-a-half million Jews thought to still be residing in the USSR and the People's Democracies be allowed to leave for Israel. ZOA President Rabbi Irving Miller introduced a unanimously adopted resolution saying that "if the so-called Jewish 'bourgeois elements' and 'cosmopolitans' are undesirable to . . . the Soviet bloc, they should be permitted to emigrate to Israel."[22]

In a Knesset debate on the worsening situation of Soviet Jewry, Meir Argov of Mapai denounced the Soviet authorities' "blood libel" against their Jewish minority and its culture, and called upon the Knesset to mobilize the Jewish people throughout the world to protest the Soviet attempt to incite the 800 million of the communist bloc against the Jews of the USSR. Argov also called for the gates to be opened to let out "these 'spies', the doctors, engineers and Jewish intelligentsia in the USSR" along with the Jewish masses in that country and in Eastern Europe. The ensuing debate was stormy. It concluded with a statement by Sharett, in the name of the government, reminding Knesset members that the government's communiqué in the wake of the Slansky trial had already expressed apprehension regarding the welfare of those Jews who were still isolated from the Jewish nation, a fear that the 13 January accouncement had proved to be justified. Sharett noted that "disclosure" of the "Plot" was clearly intended for domestic consumption, to instil fear in the Jewish communities of the USSR and the bloc countries, and to prepare the population at large for possible anti-Jewish measures.

The government of Israel, said Sharett, could not remain silent during attempts to revile the Jewish people or when any Jewish community was in danger. Having considered friendly relations with the USSR one of the pillars of its foreign policy, it noted with sorrow that the official Soviet line could not help but "arouse the most vigorous resentment and condemnation by the State of Israel and the masses of the Jewish people the world over." The goverment of Israel would continue to fight for "the right of exit and *aliya* to the State of Israel of all Jews who yearn for Zion."[23]

The Jewish world was astir. In the U.S. Jewish Labor Committee Chairman Adolph Held cabled Soviet Ambassador Georgii Zarubin for an interview, a request that an embassy secretary termed "insulting." Undaunted by the snub, Jewish labor leaders picketed the Soviet embassy and marched on the Capitol to confer with congressmen on the situation of the Jews behind the Iron Curtain.[24] The

Rabbinical Council of America (RCA), representing 500 Orthodox communities in the U.S. and Canada, passed a resolution calling on the State Department to raise the question of the anti-Zionist campaign at the U.N. in order to pressure the USSR into permitting Jews to emigrate to Israel.[25] The Synagogue Council of America (SCA), which claimed to represent "the totality of American Jewry through its six national rabbinic and congregational bodies," also urged U.S. leaders to make representations at the U.N. to "dissuade Communist governments from pursuing such terroristic policies."[26]

An emergency meeting of the national board of Hadassah adopted a resolution that likened the antisemitic drive in the USSR to the beginnings of the Nazi campaign, stressing that "complacency, the ally of all foes of freedom and democracy, will never again lull the free world into inaction and indifference."[27] And the AJC stepped up its activities on the issue of communist antisemitism by seeking joint action with other Jewish organizations. As AJC President Jacob Blaustein wrote to the two chairmen of the Jewish Agency Executive, the urgency of the Soviet Jewish problem obligated Jewish organizations in the West to try to "safeguard the security of the Jews behind the Iron Curtain as well as to enable the emigration of those who desire to leave." This program demanded "considerable contact and frequent discussion with the respective governments and moulders of public opinion in various countries."[28]

Western Jewish reaction to the Plot centered on the question of Jewish emigration from the USSR, although it can hardly have seemed a realistic solution at the time. The *New York Times* pointed out that the Soviet authorities had permitted the emigration of only seven Jews since Israel's birth almost five years earlier, perhaps out of the fear that people of other nationalities might demand similar opportunities.[29] A mass meeting at Manhattan Center, sponsored by thirty-one national Jewish organizations, noted that Jews the world over regarded themselves as their "brothers' keepers" and called on the Soviet government to cease its antisemitic activities and permit Jews to emigrate to Israel, which had declared its readiness to welcome "the victims of this new attack on the Jewish people."[30] A few weeks earlier, Israeli ambassador to Poland and Czechoslovakia Aryeh Kubovy, who had been declared *persona non grata* in Czechoslovakia after the Slansky trial, stressed that the Israeli government and the entire Israeli population were saying: "We want every one of these 2,500,000 persons: we are ready to take them . . . Let my people go."[31]

The USSR's new antisemitic campaign drew the attention of non-

Jewish leaders such as President Eisenhower, Secretary of State Dulles and congressional leaders, who reportedly discussed its implications. However, although Eisenhower condemned the anti-Jewish drive,[32] he did not lodge any official protest, ostensibly out of fear that such steps might cause more harm than good by strengthening the Soviet contention that the U.S. and Israel were allied against the USSR. U.N. delegate Henry Cabot Lodge, Jr., contented himself with a general condemnation of the Soviet Union's "persecution of Christians, Muslims and Jews," although he did note that such discrimination "would prove in the end to be totally ineffective because there was an undefeatable quality in human nature which would always resist totalitarian attempts to destroy religious and ethnic freedom."[33] And Secretary of State Dulles was said to have pointed out that, while American expressions of concern for Soviet Jews would not act to deter the Kremlin, it might alienate the Arab world.[34]

A number of senators and representatives did, however, raise the issue, leading both houses of Congress to pass resolutions condemning the crudity and virulence of Soviet antisemitism and calling upon the administration to register official protests in Moscow and at the U.N., especially because the doctors were accused of having been American agents. A number of New York congressmen insisted that the world could not afford to "sit idly by" when confronted with a new version of Hitler's final solution. In the words of congressman Emanuel Celler: when Hitler started his "drive against the Jews" there was "no official censure" on the ground that this was "an internal problem. Let us not make the same mistake again"; the campaign against the Jews was part of "the Soviet offensive against the entire free world and all its values." Moreover, it affected the U.S. because it was intended as "a weapon of the cold war . . . aimed directly at the United States and the principle of collective security," and was being used to "feed Arab hostility against . . . Israel and draw the Arabs as conclusively as possible away from the Western world." As the traditional "torchbearer of freedom and democracy," the U.S. must "continue to be the beacon light in the free world" and bring its "moral weight to bear" against such persecutions.[35] Senator Irving M. Ives and Representative Jacob K. Javits urged Dulles to voice a formal protest at the U.N. "to bring these Soviet outrages to the bar of world opinion to the end that they shall cease."[36]

Three resolutions were passed on this issue by the Senate and the House of Representatives. The first Senate resolution expressed "shock at the reports concerning the persecution of the Jewish people and the revival of anti-Semitism" in the USSR and expected that the U.S. government would "request that prompt steps be taken to remove all causes for the fears . . . concerning the future security" of Soviet Jewry "without delay." The Senate's second resolution condemned the USSR's campaign against Jews and said that all those believing in democracy and human freedom should be made aware of "the striking parallel between the communist anti-Semitic campaign and like practices by other totalitarian movements such as nazism and fascism." The third resolution condemned Soviet persecution of national and religious minorities, including "most recently the increasing persecution of the people of the Jewish faith," and urged the president to lodge a protest at the U.N., so that that body would "take action in opposition to them as may be suitable under the charter."[37] The House version of the third resolution included a clause requesting the president "to urge the Soviet Union and her satellite countries to allow all Jewish persons within their borders who desire to do so to emigrate and to seek refuge and salvation in Israel and other free lands."[38]

A group of one hundred leaders of American "labor organizations, fraternal societies and cultural institutions" sought – unsuccessfully – to hand the Soviet ambassador a memorandum protesting the persecution of Jews in his country and demanding "an objective and nonpartisan investigation through a U.N. commission regarding the conditions of the Jews and other minorities in Soviet Russia."[39] Statements of protest were also issued by many public bodies, leading scientists – notably Albert Einstein and Harold C. Urey – and church and civic leaders.[40]

Reaction to the Doctors' Plot was heard in other countries as well. A number of Latin American governments promised Israel their full support in any U.N. move protesting the Soviet antisemitic campaign. Argentian President Juan B. Peron condemned anti-Jewish attacks in Eastern Europe and called for Israel to be strengthened as the best haven for possible refugees from that region.[41] In Britain fifty-two Labour M.P.s presented a motion in Parliament asking the British government to take action in the U.N. and through other channels to fight the anti-Jewish drive in communist countries.[42] In the Netherlands Parliament the chairmen of all six non-communist parties issued a joint statement denouncing the antisemitism "raging in the Communist-controlled countries."[43] In France Soviet antisemitism was condemned in a special symposium with the participation of statesmen, scientists and literary figures, including former diplomat and well-known poet and playwright Paul Claudel; novelist and art historian André Malraux; former cabinet minister and leader of the French Socialist Party Daniel Mayer; writer and critic Jean Cassin; and scientist and former foreign minister Jacques Soustelle.[44]

Soviet antisemitic moves even drew some consternation from Western communist parties, many of whose leaders where Jewish. Thus, Natalio Berman, leader of the Chilean CP and a member of parliament for many years, resigned from the party. One of Chile's most popular labor leaders, Berman said he could not remain indifferent to Moscow's slander of the Jews.[45]

Alongside the Israeli government's intention of raising the issue of the Soviet persecution of Jews at the U.N., the WZO and the Jewish Agency decided to convene a worldwide conference of Jewish organizations to demonstrate Jewish solidarity against the communist countries' "unprovoked attacks" on their Jews.[46] To be held under the slogan "Let my people go!" – as even non-Zionist organizations now accepted the fact that Israel was prepared to receive the Jews of the USSR – this was to be the first time that a forum representing so many and such diverse Jewish organizations was convened.

In early March WZO Co-chairman Nahum Goldmann said that the conference, representing the Jewry of almost forty countries, would demonstrate Jewish determination to resist the anti-Jewish drive and thereby influence world opinion.[47] A few days before the conference was scheduled to open in Zurich, a mass meeting protesting Soviet Jewish policy and urging worldwide support for the demand that Jews be allowed to emigrate was held in Tel Aviv. At another rally, in New York, Representative Celler called on the U.S. government to induce the Soviet Union "to let the Jews go – go to Israel, the only place where they may be admitted in goodly numbers."[48] When Stalin died on 5 March the Zurich conference was postponed in the hope that the new Soviet leadership would prove more benevolent to the Jews. However, new Soviet regime or not, once the issue of the Soviet Union's treatment of its Jews had been recognized by Western Jewry, it took on a life of its own and could not be dampened. Thus, the UJA planned a country-wide National Freedom Mobilization for the eve of the Passover (the Jewish Festival of Freedom) aimed at giving American Jews " their first opportunity for a nationwide expression of brotherhood with Jews "undergoing Soviet oppression."[49] Israel, too continued to stress the plight of Soviet Jewry. At an Israel Bonds rally in Brooklyn, Labor Minister Golda Meyerson told those present of Israel's economic problems in the context of the need to be "properly prepared to receive many hundreds of thousands of Jews from the countries of the Soviet bloc ... Our reply to the Soviet campaign of slander cannot be made in the form of expressions of indignation and protest ... Our reply must be one of deeds."[50]

Although Mrs. Meyerson had come to New York to denounce the USSR's anti-Jewish policy at the U.N., Moscow's announcement early in April that the doctors had been released and exonerated and its admission that the charges against them had been false led the Israeli government to mitigate its charges. Mrs. Meyerson did, however, point out at the General Assembly First (Political) Committee that "enlightened opinion throughout the world had been moved to indignation" by the "sinister renewal of a doctrine irreconcilable with the cause of peace and friendship among nations," and that Israel would not consider the U.N. "true to its purpose if it failed to take under review so grave a development." Although the Israeli government noted "with satisfaction and relief" that the Soviets had announced publicly that evidence against the doctors had been improperly obtained, "the central question affecting Jewish communities in Eastern Europe remained unanswered." The entire issue had to be viewed within the context of international relations for, "in the history of our people's unparalleled matryrdom," Mrs. Meyerson continued, "we have observed ... that the libel of 'a world Jewish conspiracy' sponsored or tolerated by governments never remained confined to hostile words but invariably degenerated into deadly acts." Finally, Mrs. Meyerson called for the Jewish communities of the Soviet Union and the People's Democracies to be allowed "the normal degree of self-determination both in their communal and cultural life and the freedom to join in the collective efforts of the Jewish people in Israel."[51]

A number of American public figures continued to urge the new Soviet leadership to demonstrate its goodwill by changing its policy toward the Jews. In this connection, Alexander Wiley of Wisconsin, Chairman of the Senate Foreign Relations Committee, said that the USSR could meet President Eisenhower's challenge for sincere good deeds by resuming diplomatic relations with Israel and giving those among its 2.5 million Jews who wished to leave for that country permission to emigrate.[52]

Moscow's resumption of diplomatic relations with Israel in July 1953 led to new Jewish hopes, which were fanned by media reports of Soviet intentions to allow the emigration of those Jews who wished to leave.[53] "Circles close to the Israeli government" stressed that Israel would not be satisfied by declarations of goodwill, but expected deeds that would back them up. In fact, however, Israel's most urgent desire was to reestablish contact with Soviet Jewry; emigration was considered a second step that would have to wait for the more distant future.[54]

As we have seen, the post-Stalin "thaw" brought little benefit to Soviet Jewry beyond abatement of the terrible fear that had been generated by the Doctors' Plot. Although the major campaign in the West against Soviet antisemitism did become somewhat muted after Stalin's death and the release of the doctors, there were still some protests. Resolution Fourteen of the WJC Third Plenary Assembly in August 1953 expressed "the apprehension of the Jewish people" that "the very survival of a distinctive Jewish life" in the Soviet Union was threatened, and recorded the WJC's "most earnest hopes that the opportunity will be accorded to Soviet Jewry, and to establish appropriate institutions through which it could co-operate with the rest of the Jewish people." Welcoming the resumption of diplomatic relations between the USSR and Israel, "the Congress expresses the hope that the Soviet Union will recognize the right of Jewish emigration from its territories to Israel."[55] A *Special Report on Treatment of the Jews by the Soviet*, published by the U.S. Congress in fall 1954, averred that "the official and deliberate policy of communism was aimed directly at forced assimilation of the Jew as the preferred technique for exterminating the Jews as a people, [the] end result sought by the Communists . . . therefore . . . being no different from the end result sought by the Nazis."[56]

In January 1955 the AJC adopted a statement pointing out that "minor concessions to world public opinion" notwithstanding, the new Soviet leadership had neither introduced any "significant changes" in the general "field of human rights" nor "modified their policy" of suppressing Jewish communal and cultural life. The AJC made several demands of the Soviet government, expressing its conviction that "without the restoration of elementary human rights . . . there is no reason to believe that the Soviet government genuinely desires to become a peaceful member of the family of nations."[57]

The call by Western Jewry for Soviet Jews to be allowed to emigrate did not limit such emigration to Israel. In April 1954 Senator Herbert H. Lehman told a UJA dinner that Jews behind the Iron Curtain "need our constant and unremitting efforts" for the lifting of the Curtain "to permit their escape to freedom in Israel and, to the extent possible, in the United States."[58] In November 1954 the B'nai B'rith Board of

Governors called on the UN to urge the Soviet Union to permit its citizens of Jewish faith to emigrate to Israel or "any other land where they can practice their religion."[59] A similar resolution was adopted by the Consultative Conference of Jewish Organizations in London in June 1955.[60]

When the post-Stalin leadership changed the rules in the game of great-power politics, particularly when it introduced the "Geneva Spirit" aimed at reducing tensions in international relations, Moscow became open to Western pressures on a number of foreign and domestic policy issues. One such issue was the right of repatriation or reunification with relatives abroad of national minorities that had been dispersed during World War II, in particular the Polish, German and Jewish populations of the USSR. The advent of the "Geneva Spirit" also invited initiatives and methods of approach to the Kremlin that would have been unthinkable during the cold war, for example, the May 1955 call by the national convention of the Jewish Labor Committee that the free world put the situation of Soviet Jewry on the agenda of the Big Four in Geneva.[61] In this new international climate, the Soviet Jewish problem as a whole, and above all the question of emigration, now became an issue not only in Soviet–Israeli relations but in Soviet–Western relations as well.

### The Israeli government takes up the cudgels

At the same time as mounting antisemitism in the Soviet Union, which culminated in the Doctors' Plot, was rousing public figures and organizations in the West and Israel to action on behalf of Soviet Jewry and its right to emigrate, the Israeli government was organizing a small group to deal with the problem. Some members of this group had been active in organizing the "illegal" immigration of *Aliya Bet*, which circumvented the immigration restrictions imposed by the British mandatory authorities to bring Jews to Palestine. The new group, which like its predecessor was headed by Shaul Avigur, eventually became responsible directly to the prime minister.

The first task Avigur and his colleagues set themselves was to establish direct contact between Israelis and their families in the USSR (as we have seen, virtually all links between Soviet Jews and their relatives in the outside world had ceased as of 1948). Avigur's office soon organized the dispatch to the Soviet Union of various publications, at first in Yiddish and Hebrew and later in Russian, materials aimed at informing Soviet Jews about Israel, Jewish history and Jewish culture.[62]

When diplomatic relations were restored in July 1953 Avigur's office gave the legation staff precise instructions regarding contacts with Soviet Jews: whom it was advisable to meet, how meetings were to be arranged and what it was permissible and desirable to talk about. Similar instructions were issued to all Israelis who visited the USSR: they were to frequent places where Jews were likely to be, making certain, however, that their conversations with local Jews did not veer into any subjects that might be interpreted as anti-Soviet; in order to ensure that neither they nor their local contacts came under the slightest suspicion of criticizing the Soviet regime, it would be best to stay away from the subject entirely. Nor were the Israelis to discuss the situation of Soviet Jewry. They were to restrict conversations to Israel's everyday life, goals and achievements, and even to discuss its problems and failures.[63]

At the same time the Israelis sought to take up the issue of Soviet Jewish emigration with the Soviet government. In late December 1953 Minister Eliashiv raised the question with Deputy Foreign Minister Gromyko, stressing that Israel would see the granting of permission to emigrate to Israel to those Jews who wished to do so as a sign of friendship. Gromyko's reaction was unequivocally negative. He stated categorically that any discussion or negotiation of this problem was out of the question and expressed his surprise that it had even been raised. Individual cases of family reunification, however, would be dealt with in the normal way – through the Soviet Foreign Ministry's Consular Department.[64]

The Israeli legation – and as of August 1954, embassy – in Moscow conducted a number of conversations with the Soviet Foreign Ministry's Consular Department in the ensuing period. These meetings focused chiefly on specific cases and the solution of practical difficulties that were obstructing the smooth handling of some of them.[65] On one occasion, in July 1954, Andrei Vlasov of the Soviet ministry's Consular Department told legation first secretary Y. L. Gideon that the Israelis should see to it that those interested in uniting with their families approached the militia "and eventually we shall succeed in reuniting the families." On another occasion, in October 1954, acting head of the department Aleksandr Aleksandrov agreed that Israeli citizenship be granted to stateless Jews in the USSR in order to enable their emigration to Israel and that the Israeli embassy maintain contact with prospective emigrants to Israel and help them arrange their journey. Of the seventy-one persons who had received emigration permits by February 1955 – of whom forty-three had actually emigrated – only fifteen were under the age of sixty, including two children whose parents were in Israel; most of them came from the Western territories, particularly what had formerly been Bessarabia and Northern Bukovina.[66]

In summer 1955 Avigur and his colleagues broadened the scope of their activities from helping Soviet Jews establish contact with and learn about Israel to arousing the interest of the Jewish and the non-Jewish world outside in the fate of the Soviet Jewish minority. Avigur and Sharett believed that the "thaw" in inter-bloc relations and the "Spirit of Geneva" meant that the Kremlin would be particularly sensitive to Western criticism in the realm of human rights. In this context, influential individuals and groupings in the West were much more likely to be heeded by the Soviet leaders than they had been in the past. Among others, Moscow was now encouraging foreign delegations to visit the Soviet Union, where they met Soviet officials and sometimes even spoke at official functions. This gave an increasing number of foreigners the opportunity to voice their views and ask questions in face-to-face encounters with Soviet figures, including the top echelons. In addition, the process of de-Stalinization and the denunciation of the "personality cult" created ferment throughout the communist camp not only in the bloc but also – and, from the point of view or our theme, more importantly – in the Western communist parties and among fellow travelers. During this period of mounting criticism and doubts, not only was the Kremlin inevitably more vulnerable and more susceptible to external pressure, but communists the world over were seeking yardsticks by which to examine the CPSU's political and ideological integrity.

At a meeting with Avigur and Ben Gurion in August 1955, Sharett expressed his belief that the time was ripe for Israel to press for Soviet Jewish emigration. The Soviets were emitting signals that they would allow their Jews to leave for Israel if Israel refrained from joining the proposed U.S.–Israel security pact. Sharett, who had grave doubts as to the likelihood of such a pact being achieved, considered that this was an ideal constellation to promote *aliya*. According to one source, in fall 1955 the Israelis and Soviets discussed "at the highest level the possibility of further emigration" (in addition to the trickle of elderly people who were being allowed to reunite with relatives in Israel). However, Israel had to agree that it would not take Moscow to task for its attitude toward its Jews, and also that the campaign on behalf of

Soviet Jewry would not appear to have originated in Israel or be aimed at damaging the chances for better East–West understanding.[67]

In October 1955 Sharett sought to explain to Secretary Dulles why Israel's efforts on behalf of Soviet Jewry, which was "in a state of spiritual asphyxiation," meant that Israel would not be able to go ahead with the security pact with Washington. He told the Secretary of State that, while Israel's main reason for maintaining an embassy in Moscow was to encourage Soviet Jews to renew their link with the Jewish people and its state, the main channel for such a link was *aliya*, and Moscow would not make any concession on *aliya* if Israel proceeded with the security pact.[68]

From this period on many new bodies, in a wide range of countries, began to voice protest over the plight of Soviet Jewry and to call for their right to be reunited with their families in the Jewish national state. While Avigur's group was by no means responsible for all activity on behalf of Soviet Jewry, there is considerable evidence to suggest that many of those who were now beginning to evince interest in Soviet Jewry were directly or indirectly influenced by Avigur and his colleagues. It is no accident that the connection is often difficult to document: while there were some within the Israeli establishment who thought that Israel should publicly place itself at the head of the protest movement, they were overruled by those who believed that the Israeli government should confine itself to pulling strings behind the scenes. Two other principles were central to the conduct of the new campaign. First, every effort was to be made to refrain from expressing any anti-Soviet feeling, just as those who made contacts within the USSR were instructed to avoid any criticism of the regime under which the Jews lived. (This did not mean that the Soviet authorities appreciated the effort. From their point of view any indication of dissatisfaction with the Jews' situation or any expression of their desire to achieve further national rights was by definition anti-Soviet.) And, secondly, all possible measures should be taken to avoid the impression that Israel was in any way seeking to upset the international endeavor to reduce inter-bloc tensions.[69]

Avigur's group laid down three goals for the campaign they were spearheading: (1) that Soviet Jews be allowed to decide how they desired to express their Jewishness; (2) that, as members of one and the same nation, they be permitted to establish and maintain contact with Jewish communities in other countries; and (3) that they be allowed to establish contact with the State of Israel and have their right to repatriate to the Jewish state recognized. The first goal – the call for the implementation of national rights for Jews in the domestic context – could not be removed from the agenda even though it often seemed to obfuscate and complicate the main question: recognition of their status as part of the Jewish nation, from which their rights to contacts with the outside Jewish world and to make their home in the Jewish national homeland follow directly.

The plan was to have Israelis or Western Jews raise the Soviet Jewish issue at all meetings with Soviet officials as well as with representatives of other countries who were to be persuaded to raise the problem with the Soviets. This was to be followed by making visiting Soviet delegations aware of the international Jewish community's interest in having the status and situation of their brethren in the USSR improved through addressing questions to them on the subject whenever and wherever possible. In order to pursue the question in the USSR itself, individual Jews and delegations were to visit the Soviet Union as often as possible to meet Jews, gather information on their situation and raise the problem of Soviet Jewry with every Soviet personality or institution they met or visited. Finally, influential non-Jewish public figures were to be mobilized to the cause of Soviet Jewry wherever possible. All these efforts were to be brought to the Western public by the Jewish press as well as by top-ranking non-Jewish journalists, who were to be informed of the issues involved.[70]

Avigur brought into his group Israeli publicist Binyamin Eliav, who had just returned from serving at the Israeli embassy in Buenos Aires, to be responsible for the dissemination of information on the Soviet Jewish problem. Eliav was also to edit the manuscripts then beginning to come out of the Soviet Union which documented the Soviet Jewish dilemma and proved that large numbers of Soviet Jews still had Jewish and sometimes even Zionist inclinations. As Eliav's brief was to bring the plight of Jewish Jewry to the attention of those not generally connected with Israel who might even avoid any activity officially associated with it, as well as to avowed friends, he made certain that the materials he published contained nothing that might cause them to be identified as originating in Israel.[71]

### Harassment of the Soviet leadership

Between the July 1955 Geneva summit and fall 1956 – a period that witnessed the Polish October, the Hungarian revolt and the Sinai War and Suez Campaign – the Soviet leadership was subjected to considerable world pressure on the issue of Soviet Jewry by governments, political parties and delegations, including those from communist parties in other countries. The question of Soviet Jewry was raised whenever sympathetic delegations visited the Soviet Union or Soviet representatives traveled abroad and the questions and answers were reported on by the Western press. As there is considerable evidence that Moscow was not impervious to these pressures, it is reasonable to argue that some, if not all, of the Soviet promises and measures to ease the position of Soviet Jews in this period were intended as a sop to friends and critics outside the USSR.

In the course of summer and fall 1955 the AJC put out two working papers that followed from a resolution passed at its annual meeting that the West be asked to include provisions demanding improvements in the lot of Soviet Jewry whenever negotiations were held with the USSR. Although the demands were not to include "concessions that could not be granted by the Soviet leaders without destroying the tenets of their own system," there could be "no hope for any real improvement" in the Jews' situation without some "relaxation of totalitarian rules and practices." Among the measures the Soviets should be asked to take were:

1. the condemnation of "all manifestations of anti-Semitism, and discrimination against Jews as contrary to the government's policy . . . and correction of such practices wherever they are found";

2. the amnesty of Jews arrested on charges connected with Zionism or Judaism and review of cases of Jews sentenced during Stalin's anti-Jewish campaign;

3. to provide enough synagogues "to satisfy the needs of all those who want to worship" and facilities for religious education and the training of rabbis, allow religious communities to elect their own leadership, enable the unobstructed observance of religious precepts, encourage secular Jewish education by teaching the Hebrew and Yiddish languages and literature as well as granting Yiddish the same status as all other national languages;

4. to facilitate "freer intercourse and friendly relations" between Soviet and other Jews, including tourism in both directions to visit relatives and friends;

5. to allow emigration, as there are "convincing humanitarian reasons for allowing the reunion of torn families, and for allowing people who had lost all their relatives and friends, to recover and rehabilitate themselves among people of their faith and cultural tradition."[72]

In line with the new spate of activity on behalf of Soviet Jewry, a broad spectrum of Western statesmen – including Canadian Foreign Minister Lester Pearson, Speaker of the Finnish Diet Karl A. Fagerholm and the prime ministers and other socialist members of the governments of Denmark, Norway and Sweden – were briefed on the Soviet Jewish situation before visits to the USSR or contacts with high-ranking Soviet officials so they would be prepared to make pertinent inquiries about the Jews' situation in the USSR.[73] Socialist leaders were natural intermediaries at this time because they tended to be friendly to Israel and its leading party, Mapai, and because the Soviet Union was making a conscious effort to court them.

On the whole, Western politicians were sympathetic when confronted with the Soviet Jewish question. Moreover, most of them agreed to maintain the fiction that they were acting entirely on their own initiative out of concern for fundamental humanitarian principles or as representatives of local Jewish opinion. The attempt to involve Third World leaders was much more difficult. For example, Burmese Prime Minister U Nu simply handed the seven pages he had received from Sharett, which explained the Soviet Jewish situation and urged him to speak up on their behalf, directly to the Soviet leaders with whom he was conferring instead of using it as background material. U Nu's blunder showed not only how little many Asian and African leaders knew about problems peculiar to the Jewish diaspora, but also their ignorance of the complexities of Israeli and world Jewish diplomacy vis-à-vis the USSR. And, of course, it confirmed Israel's role in encouraging foreign statesmen to intervene in what CPSU Central Committee member and Deputy Prime Minister Lazar Kaganovich angrily told U Nu was something in which "Israel has no right to intervene." Kaganovich's irritation, however, was evidence that the campaign was getting under the collective skin of the Soviet leadership.[74]

In the CPSU Central Committee Report to the Party's Twentieth Congress in February 1956, Khrushchev postulated the possibility, and indeed desirability, of cooperating with parliamentary factions in the Western democracies, particularly with those groupings that had hitherto been disdainfully dismissed as "right-socialist." Among the socialist parliamentary delegations that visited the Soviet Union in subsequent months was one headed by Acting Secretary General of the French Socialist Party Philippe Commin which visited Moscow in May 1956.[75] Made up of several leading French socialists, the delegation conferred with Chairman of the USSR Supreme Soviet Presidium Anastas Mikoian, First Secretary Khrushchev, Prime Minister

Nikolai Bulganin and Foreign Minster Dmitrii Shepilov. At the first of two meetings with the Soviet leaders, Maurice Deixonne asked about the traces of antisemitism in the USSR,[76] the legal basis of the recent anti-Zionist trials, and whether Soviet Jews were free to go to Israel. Mikoian admitted that the Soviet regime had not yet been able to eradicate the prejudices of "the capitalist era," and that there were perhaps vestiges of antisemitism, along with "probably . . . Zionist currents among the Jews" (and "vestiges of nationalism" in Georgia). He insisted, however, that Zionists were not being prosecuted for Zionist activity but rather for subversion and espionage on behalf of the U.S. or "other anti-Soviet states." He also reiterated the Soviet argument that Jewish cultural institutions had died of their own accord and that were there a demand for Jewish schools, theaters, newspapers, etc., the Soviet leadership would accede to it.

In response to questions about Soviet Jewry, Khrushchev argued that the Jews themselves wanted their children to go to Russian schools because those who did had better career opportunities. He also stated that while the Jews had played a role far beyond their proportion in the population in the first years after the revolution, having too many Jews in key posts would now lead to justified protests from other nationalities who had meanwhile produced their own cadres. With regard to the question of emigration to Israel, he admitted that travel to Israel was "not encouraged," but also said that the Soviet Union had not and would not prevent the emigration of "those who want this. – But there are none: Soviet Jews are in no way interested in emigrating to Israel."[77]

While the evasiveness of the Soviet leaders and their distortion of the facts showed how uneasy they were on the issue of Soviet Jewry, the consistency of their replies was evidence of high-level deliberation on the question. This underlined the need for those who were to question Soviet leaders about the USSR's Jews – especially those willing to intervene on a regular basis – to be kept up to date on developments in the Soviet Jewish saga.

In addition to socialist parties and groupings, Western communist parties became concerned with the issue, perhaps because Jews occupied central positions in many of them, particularly in the English-speaking countries, where communism had only a tenuous hold on the indigenous proletariat. British *Daily Worker* editor J. R. Campbell, who headed a British Communist Party delegation to the USSR in 1956, wrote that the rumors that there were problems in the field of Jewish culture and that well-known Jewish writers and intellectuals had disappeared, together with the revelations at and in the wake of the Twentieth Party Congress, "created consternation and bewilderment in the ranks of Jewish communists in all countries," for whom these disclosures became "an acid test of the extent, if any, to which the Soviet Union had moved away from the path of social-ism."[78] He went on to write that many Jews had joined the party in the belief that the communist "world of tomorrow" would not only bring discrimination to an end but would become the focus of Yiddish secular culture.[79]

Following the Twentieth Party Congress, several Western commun-ist parties launched special investigations into the fate of Soviet Jewish culture. The British and Canadian parties sent delegations to the USSR in 1956 to meet with CPSU ideologues such as presidium member and Central Committee Secretary Mikhail Suslov. But delegation members did not find it easy to learn what had happened or was happening. For example, when they expressed a desire to meet Jewish writers, they "were informed that this was not possible as they were all on holiday," except for Shmuel Halkin, who was "too ill to receive anyone." What they did manage to find out was that the Yiddish section of the Lenin Library had nothing that had been published after 1948 and that the Great Soviet Encyclopedia, which had devoted some 160 columns to the Jews in its first, 1932, edition reduced this to four columns and omitted the biographies of many eminent Jews in its 1952 edition. Frustrated in its official attempts to discover what had really happened during the "black years," the British CP delegation held "private conversations" with Soviet Jews, who told them that "young Jews who might otherwise have become merged with the general population and have forgotten that they were Jews, awoke to a new sense of unity in distress" during Stalin's last years.

While Soviet officialdom was not forthcoming with regard to the past, the British communists had no great difficulty in learning what the CPSU planned for the future: Suslov made it quite clear that the party had no intention of either turning back the clock or making reparations. When the delegation returned to the U.K. it reported that, as official Soviet policy "expects that the Jewish people in the Soviet Union will become completely absorbed," it was considered unnecessary, even "undesirable," to encourage Jewish culture. In reply to the argument that the USSR had large Jewish centers that could serve as bases for Jewish culture, Suslov insisted that such culture was dying in the Soviet Union and that Moscow had no intention of reviving it artificially. And when leading British scientist

Hyman Levy asked whether it was not a Marxist-Leninist axiom that every national culture should be preserved and even nurtured, Suslov retorted that the Jews did not conform to Stalin's 1913 definition of nationhood. Suslov did not, however, refrain from referring to the Jews as a collective when he stressed that they collectively comprised a security threat to the USSR. Levy could not help but discern a deep-rooted antisemitism in Suslov's further statement that while no one would utter a word if Moscow massacred a million Armenians, a hue and cry was immediately set up whenever a hair on the head of a single Jew was hurt.[80]

When Canadian Jewish communist Joseph B. Salsberg asked why the Jewish Anti-Fascist Committee had been dissolved in 1948, he was told it had been permeated by nationalist influences and outlived its usefulness having degenerated into a Jewish mutual aid society. Salsberg's suggestion that a central Jewish organization be established along the lines of the Cultural and Social Association of Polish Jews was rejected on the tired grounds that the USSR's Jews were assimilated; only in Birobidzhan were they entitled to have their own press, theaters and educational institutions. This, together with a two-hour tirade by Khrushchev on the Jews' negative traits, led Salsberg to conclude that Khrushchev's obvious antisemitism reflected "a backward prejudice," smacked of Great Russian chauvinism and "contradicted Marxist thought," and was not in any way mitigated by the Soviet leader's protestations that Jews held many important posts in the Soviet Union and that his own daughter-in-law was Jewish.[81]

Clearly there was a deep chasm between what Khrushchev and Suslov felt about redressing Stalin's liquidation of Jewish culture and what Jewish communists in the West – and even in Poland – viewed as an opportunity to revive Jewish cultural activity.[82]

In July–August 1956 Avigur sent Binyamin Eliav to Latin America to enlist left-wing figures there on behalf of the campaign of Soviet Jewish cultural rights. Eliav was accompanied by José Luis Romero, leader-writer in *La Nación*, the only Argentinian paper not dominated by Peron. Among those they met were Radical Party left-wing leader Arturo Frondizi, who later told Argentina's Jewish press that the USSR should let Jews who wished to go to Israel do so. Eliav also held meetings throughout the continent with leading figures of the socialist left, progressive intellectuals whom the Soviets were known to be courting, as well as with communist party members. In Chile he was able to convince Jewish educator and scientist Alexander Lipzchutz to try and enlist Chilean poet and Lenin Prize holder Pablo Neruda in the struggle for Soviet Jewish rights. In Mexico he told left-wing labor union organizer Lombardo Toledano, a key figure in Soviet activity in Latin America, that their Jewish policy was losing the Soviets their traditional Jewish backing.

Eliav's Latin American tour was successful in that it disturbed Jewish and other communists and progressives to the point where they formed cells within their groups to protest Stalin's liquidation of Jewish culture and Khrushchev's distortion of the facts, and to press for redress. Eliav also won over journalists, who could be relied upon to take up the cudgels whenever needed.[83]

With the help of Judd Teller, secretary of the Presidents' Club of the American Presidents of Major Jewish Organizations, Eliav also met a number of American journalists and editors, including *Life*'s East European expert, *Reporter* founder and editor Max Ascoli, *New York Times* sovietologist Harry Schwartz (who had recently been to the Soviet Union, where he had some moving personal encounters with Jews) and the *Christian Science Monitor* editorial staff.[84]

Harvard professor of Soviet law and international trade Harold J. Berman visited the Soviet Union in 1955 to carry out research and investigate the possibilities of expanding U.S.–Soviet trade, which he linked with "relaxation of tensions and a betterment of relations." In touch with many individuals and companies interested in developing trade with the USSR, Berman hoped to have the opportunity to tell the Soviets that "the taint of antisemitism had helped to assimilate the reputation of the Soviets in the public mind of this country with that of the Nazis." At one of his meetings with WJC and AJC representatives prior to his trip, Maurice Perlzweig of the WJC told Berman that the time was not ripe for "anything like a genuinely representative body" of Soviet Jewry, and that there was no point in discussing the right of emigration with Soviet officials. What Perlzwieg did suggest was that Berman should press for the right to federate existing synagogue groups into a national body and for the resumption of Yiddish publications as well as Jewish publications in the Russian language.[85]

Although the opportunity to raise the Jewish question with Soviet officials never presented itself on Berman's first Soviet trip, he attended the Choral Synagogue on two Sabbaths as well as a concert of Jewish music. He even met twice with Rabbi Shlifer, to whom he brought a personal message from Nahum Goldmann, asking what steps he and others might take in order to establish contact with Soviet Jewry. Shlifer said the Soviet Jews were very eager to establish such contacts and welcomed the idea that a WJC delegation visit the USSR.

He pointed out that despite there being no central Jewish religious body in the USSR, he was the *de facto* leader of believing Jews, and was recognized as such by the authorities and other Jewish congregations. Berman also spoke with Jews who were satisfied with the state of their civil rights in the USSR, and who pointed to the numerous Jews who held positions of distinction and responsibility as evidence that Jews were being treated equally. However, even those generally satisfied with the regime did not deny that there was widespread antisemitism, although they attributed this largely to the influence of Nazi propaganda during World War II.[86]

In 1956 Professor Abraham I. Katsh, Chairman of the Department of Hebrew Studies at New York University, visited the Soviet Union to track down some of the Judaic treasures stored in Soviet repositories, especially in Moscow and Leningrad. When Katsh asked RSFSR Deputy Minister of Education Aleksandr Arsenev whether Soviet children could learn Yiddish and Hebrew, he received a written reply to the effect that "according to Soviet law every parent has the right to place his child in a class in which instruction of all subjects is conducted in his native tongue. This right applies fully to people of Jewish nationality," and such classes would be arranged if there were ten parents who so "wish to educate their children." Among others Katsh showed the document to Rabbi Shlifer.[87]

On the tenth anniversary of the founding of the United Nations, in June 1955, "representatives of Jewish communities in the free world" called upon the Soviet leaders to prove their professions of goodwill by restoring religious, cultural and other freedoms to the Jews, and upon all communist regimes to grant freedom of movement so that East European Jews might emigrate. The *New York Herald Tribune* noted that this appeal was made "to catch the ears" of Foreign Minister Molotov, who was attending the anniversary celebration, and of Bulganin, who was shortly to leave for the Big Four summit meeting in Geneva. At two press conferences in San Francisco Molotov was questioned about Soviet citizens who wished to join their families abroad, with "special reference to Soviet citizens of the Jewish faith who wish to join their families in the State of Israel." He evaded the issue, the first time with a mere "thank you" and then by saying that the question should "be looked into by the appropriate representatives."[88]

In September 1955 American Jewish Labor Committee Chairman Adolph Held sent a note to Molotov at the UN General Assembly in which he asked the Kremlin to break "the wall of silence" surrounding the fate of prominent Jewish writers, as they belied the Soviet government's supposed desire for peaceful coexistence. Upon being asked about the whereabouts of David Bergelson, Itzik Fefer, Peretz Markish and others, Leonid Ilichev, head of the Soviet Foreign Ministry Press Department, who was then a member of the Soviet U.N. delegation, told newspapermen that he knew Markish was in Moscow, because he saw him at the *Pravda* offices.[89] This was over three years after Markish had been executed. It was in response to pressures such as these that Soviet ambassador to the U.S. Georgii Zarubin announced that an American rabbinical delegation would soon leave for the USSR to discuss the writers and other problems with the Soviet leaders.[90]

Khrushchev and Bulganin encountered similar questions when they visited Britain in April 1956. The WJC took the opportunity to submit a communication asking that Jews in the USSR be permitted to resume their Jewish way of life and to reunite with their families in Israel and elsewhere. This document expressed the conviction that the restraints imposed on Soviet Jews did not conform to the principles enunciated in the USSR's constitution, and that their removal would comprise a major contribution to the cause of international peace, goodwill and understanding along the lines Bulganin had laid down in Geneva.[91]

Not able to hide its disappointment that the Soviets had not changed their basic Jewish policy under Khrushchev, the American Jewish Committee considered embarking on direct negotiations with the Soviet authorities to try and ameliorate the situation.[92] The AJC decided that these talks should be held inside the USSR rather than with Soviet representatives abroad (1) because the "substantial Jewish population"in the USSR was "eager and anxious for contact with the Jewish world outside" and the visits of foreign Jews might help their "will to survival," and (2) because, although there was little likelihood of affecting "the actions or attitudes" of the Soviet authorities, such a visit might effect what former American ambassador to Moscow George Kennan called the "long-range possibility" that the monolithic Soviet structure would gradually crack up and lead "toward a regime which coerces its own people and threatens the outside world somewhat less than is at present the case."[93]

During this period the sympathetic Western press published everything connected with Soviet Jewry, not only appeals to Soviet delegations. Thus, as we have seen, the West was informed about the July and August 1955 arrests of Jews in Moscow and "other cities" for possessing Jewish literature. In early fall 1955 Copenhagen's evening newspaper ran a full-page article entitled "The Jews in the USSR," in which the author pointed out that although the new Soviet leadership averred that it wished to "obliterate memories left by" and "demonstrate its rejection of" the policy that had characterized Stalin's last years, the basic conceptions underlying Soviet Jewish policy could not have changed if the Jews were still suffering religious and cultural discrimination. The Danish correspondent went on to say that there was, however, a change in the Jews themselves: the severe shock of the "black years" had brought about a much stronger desire for national self-assertion, and even a trend toward Zionism. He concluded that while "the security of their own situation" was more important to many Jews than "realizing the Zionist creed," the Soviet government's allowing emigration "would be a welcome gesture of conciliation" even for them.[94]

A *New York Times* article based on conversations with Moscow Jews was pessimistic: Yiddish was doomed to disappear as nobody believed that Yiddish schools would be reopened; antisemitism and discrimination were being experienced by Jews in all walks of life, even by those who held good jobs, whose economic situation was satisfactory and who had assimilated and spoke no Yiddish. As a result, many Jews would emigrate if this ever became possible.[95] Among the *Times'* several articles on Soviet Jewish life were stories on the Jews of Minsk and Kishinev,[96] pleas by Western Jewish organizations and public figures to allow Jewish emigration to Israel[97] and reports on the few family reunifications that did take place.[98] While statements could not help those who had been liquidated (the allusion was to the Soviet Jewish cultural figures executed in August 1952) the *Times* pointed out that they might be "of some importance in preventing similar occurrences in the future."[99]

In May 1956 a group of thirty-seven American writers – including such outstanding intellectuals and well-known progressives as Reinhold Niebuhr and Norman Thomas – published a protest against the Soviet Union's attitude toward its Jews. Denouncing "the frightful acts of genocide perpetrated, and apparently still endorsed by the Soviet regime," the writers urged "freedom-loving individuals throughout the world to raise their voices in protest against these acts of brutality and discrimination."

Several months later twenty-six American Jewish union leaders, writers and other public figures called upon Bulganin and Supreme Soviet Chairman Kliment Voroshilov to publish a statement outlining the current position of Soviet Jews and the measures being taken to reinstate Soviet Jewish culture.[100]

The harassment of the Soviet leadership, both behind the scenes and in public, was clearly instrumental in letting the Kremlin know that the Soviet Jewish factor was part and parcel of the USSR's attempts to make inroads in the West and to promote "peaceful coexistence." Western statesmen, political parties and public figures – including prominent left-wingers and known sympathizers of the Soviet Union – had begun to express interest in a problem that Moscow was intent on keeping under the carpet as it tried to show the West its new "liberal" face.

### First contacts between Western and Soviet Jewry

A further component that began to play a role in our story in this period was Jewish tourism. As the Iron Curtain began to lift – even if only slightly – Jewish journalists, academics and public figures traveled to the USSR as often as possible with the dual intention of gathering first-hand information from and bringing encouragement to Soviet Jews, to show them that, although they were physically cut off from their brethren abroad, they were not forgotten by them.

Upon his return from the USSR, one of the early tourists, Chaim Shurer, chief editor of the Mapai daily *Davar*, urged American Jewry "not to forget the Jews in the Soviet Union." He related a number of incidents in which local Jews had been frightened to talk to him or failed to keep appointments. The only place where he had been invited to drink a *lehaim* and talk about Israel was at a *kolkhoz* where he heard five young cart-drivers talking Yiddish. When Shurer was about to leave them, one of the five asked him if he could not perhaps get to Israel in Shurer's trunk.[101] Another early tourist told of the "air of great expectation" among Soviet Jews despite the deep-rooted dislike of them among the general population. A "broad-minded Russian teacher" in Leningrad had not hesitated to tell this tourist that "the solution is for the Jewish people to live in a country of their own."[102] Another traveler to the USSR in those days was HIAS director Chaim Shoshkes, who went as representative of the New York Yiddish *Tog-morgn zhurnal*. Shoshkes, who met the Yiddish writers who had survived the Stalin purges, brought word from the Soviet Union of Writers that the Soviet authorities had promised to revive Yiddish culture in the Soviet Union.[103]

Perhaps the most sensational revelation made by a Western Jewish tourist in this period was that of Leon Crystal of the New York daily *Forverts*. It was Crystal who publicized detailed evidence that Soviet

Yiddish writers and other cultural figures had been executed. The Israeli embassy had received the information, but not wishing it to reach the world from a source that could be traced to them, the Israelis enlisted Crystal, telling him how to plan his trip to the Soviet Union and with whom to meet there so it would appear that he "gleaned" the information on his own initiative. Upon returning from the USSR early in March 1956, Crystal told a press conference that an "unimpeachable source" had given him not only the facts but even the very date of the writers' execution: 12 August 1952. The writers' closest relatives had recently been given this information by the Public Prosecutor in Moscow who expressed the Soviet government's "profound regret" and promised that the victims would be rehabilitated posthumously.[104] Among the articles evoked by Crystal's revelations was the famous one in the Warsaw *Folks-shtime*, "Undzer vetig un undzer treyst,"[105] as well as a host of reports in the Western communist and left-wing press. These articles served to expose Soviet discriminatory policies against Yiddish culture among Western left-wing intellectuals. Thus, when Binyamin Eliav toured Latin America in summer 1956 he found that many progressives had read these materials.[106]

The delegations of American rabbis that visited the Soviet Union in summer 1956 probably had even more effect on Western public opinion at large. In accordance with Ambassador Zarubin's fall 1955 statement that a group of rabbis would be given visas to visit the Soviet Union to study Jewish religious life there, the Rabbinical Council of America announced in mid-May 1956 that the Soviet embassy in Washington had informed the organization that it could send a six-man delegation. This was the first time the Soviets had allowed an official rabbinic delegation to visit the USSR.[107] The fact that the rabbis' visit was preceded by a statement by the Soviet U.N. delegation on freedom of religious worship in the USSR was clear evidence of Soviet sensitivity on this issue. It was also a clear warning to the delegation that the Soviet government would do its utmost to use this visit to show the West that religious freedom did exist in the Soviet Union.

The RCA delegation arrived in Moscow on 22 June and remained there until 4 July. On 24 June delegation leader Rabbi Hollander addressed an excited Sabbath congregation at the Choral Synagogue. Speaking in Yiddish, the rabbi expressed the concern of American Jewry and of Orthodox Jewry in particular for Soviet Jews, who had remained in the country where so many American Jews had originated and where so much American Jewish learning had its roots. He also dwelt on the need for Jews to be proud of their tradition despite external pressures to disparage it.

Besides Moscow, the group visited Leningrad, Kiev, Odessa, Rostov-on-Don and Tbilisi, Kutaisi, Kulashi, Vani and Sukhumi in Georgia. Everywhere they traveled they were given the opportunity to address the congregants in either Yiddish or (in Georgia) Hebrew. Jews lined the streets to welcome them in Georgia, where Rabbi Klaperman, addressed the crowds that had gathered to greet them extemporaneously, right out on the street.[108]

It did not take the rabbis long to appreciate what the Jews with whom they were mingling meant when they warned the guests not to believe what they were being shown and told by their official hosts. Thus, Rabbi Hollander's offer to supply a Hebrew linotype was rejected outright by the Council for the Affairs of Religious Cults, and his proposal to send Jewish religious books had to be "looked into." Upon being told that there was not and had never been any prohibition against giving private or even group Hebrew lessons to children, Hollander asked whether parents who wished to give their children Hebrew lessons could put up notices telling others to approach the rabbi or synagogue board. This question met with the bland retort that the Council did not interfere with what went on inside the synagogues. The rabbis encountered a similar reply when they met Bulganin and Khrushchev at U.S. Ambassador Charles Bohlen's Independence Day reception: when one of them expressed concern at the scarcity of synagogues in the USSR, Bulganin said it was "up to the Jews themselves." Their experiences confirmed reports by other visitors to the Soviet Union on the discrepancies between what they were told by synagogue dignitaries, especially in the presence of the Soviet functionaries who usually accompanied them, and what they heard in their rare private conversations with local Jews. It was only on the latter occasions that they were informed of the hardship of Jewish life, the lack of religious articles and facilities, the desire to go to Israel and the need for intercession on their behalf by Western Jews and the State of Israel.[109]

A second rabbinical delegation, representing the New York Board of Rabbis (which includes Orthodox, Conservative and Reform rabbis) visited the USSR that summer. Upon their return to New York on 12 July, two members of that delegation, Rabbi Morris Kertzer and Rabbi David I. Golovensky, made a "preliminary statement" at a televised press conference in which they said that what they had seen and heard led them "to the melancholy conclusion that Judaism in Russia is seriously threatened with extinction ... While the Soviet regime ... has, in fact, somewhat relaxed some of its repressive measures, its policies continue to restrict and strangle Jewish life. We were shocked to find that institutions of the Jewish religion and the vehicles of expression of Jewish culture had all but vanished, leaving a Judaism that is anemic and moribund." Moscow's 300,000 Jews had only one synagogue and two "auxiliary houses of worship," and Leningrad's 200,000 Jews had only one. The new prayer book, supposedly in the works for two years, was nowhere to be seen, while "the few prayer books in use are torn in shreds." Nor was there any evidence of the promised Jewish institutions "without which Jewish life cannot long endure."

Rabbis Kertzer and Golovensky found only one bleak ray of light: "the still rigorous will for Jewish life," even among those who did not attend synagogue; the passionate desire of many parents to instil "love for God and loyalty to Jewish traditions" in the younger generation and a few indications that things might be taking a turn for the better. "Many said that had we come two years ago, they would not have felt free to talk to us ... We are hopeful that this is the beginning of a trend that will ultimately ... help create the instruments for the restoration and perpetuation of Jewish life." They ended their press conference with the hope that the Jewish authorities would allow more Jewish delegations to visit the USSR and let Soviet Jewish leaders visit Jewish communities outside the Soviet Union.[110]

In more detailed later reports the rabbis noted that, while there might be less fear than there had been, Soviet Jews were by no means free of fear. One Jew in Moscow had come to see them for an entire week, but was too frightened to hand them the note he told them he had come to give them, and not one Jew dared invite them to his home. Of the hundred or so Jews with whom the rabbis discussed emigration, at least sixty expressed the desire to leave the USSR; one wanted to go the the U.S., three or four did not care where they ended up as long as they got out, and all the rest said that Israel was their goal. One worshipper at the Moscow synagogue told the rabbis that despite their excitement at the rabbis' visit the Jews would prefer to be let out, instead of the rabbis being let in. All in all, the rabbis concluded that their visit had been a tremendous first step in establishing a link between Soviet and American Jewry, but warned that this link had to be maintained and strengthened. As one of them said on American television: the Jews had received them as fellow Jews rather than as American tourists.[111]

The New York Board of Rabbis group was given considerable publicity by the American media in general upon their return. The *New York Times* published three articles by Rabbi Kertzer, which were reprinted in forty-two American dailies. The *Journal American* ran a series of ten articles that were also reprinted in a large number of newspapers and later in a volume entitled *The Status of the Jews Behind the Iron Curtain*. One of the rabbis even wrote an article in *Congress Weekly*. The Yiddish *Tog-morgn zhurnal* published articles by several rabbis from both delegations, and *Forverts* – which was simultaneously publishing Barukh Vaisman's letters "To My Brethren in the State of Israel" – published ten articles by Rabbi Israel Mowshowitz. In addition, several of the rabbis appeared on radio and television and were invited to speak about their trip at Jewish and non-Jewish forums. Public interest in the rabbis' revelations led the media to dwell on the subject of Soviet Jewry, and *Life* magazine thought it important enough to warrant a series of photographs on Jewish life in the Soviet Union.

The rabbis sought to improve conditions for Soviet Jews by exploiting the Khrushchev–Bulganin leadership's sensitivity to Western public opinion. "If the lot of our people continues to improve in Russia," they stated, "then we and the world will know that Bulganin and Khrushchev are sincere in this professed determination to make amends for injustices in their own orbit. If otherwise, it will be another tragic farce."[112]

The publicity given the Soviet Jewish problem in the year 1956 brought it before the public eye as never before, giving both the Jewish and non-Jewish public considerable food for thought. In addition, the growing group of political and other public figures in the West who were in contact with the Soviet establishment were being mobilized on behalf of Soviet Jewry by the small office in Israel designed to promote Soviet Jewish struggle for *aliya*. And an increasing number of inevitably more emotionally involved Jewish journalists, rabbis, communist activists, intellectuals and artists, each of whom undertook to help improve the lot of Soviet Jewry in his or her own way, played a major role as well, together with the impressive group of non-Jews (West European politicians, American Protestant clerics and others) who took up the issue.

Khrushchev and his Kremlin colleagues were keenly aware of this broad interest in the Jewish problem of their country on the part of Westerners. Despite their suave manner in dealing with most queries and criticisms, the importance of the Soviet Jewish question in the eyes of so many groupings and individuals in the West can only have strengthened their interest in satisfying at least some of the demands being put to them.

Coming at a time when the Soviet leadership was making an open effort to win over Western public opinion, particularly that of socialists of various ilks, Western intervention was now much more effective than it could have been in the cold war period, when the Kremlin was studiously impervious to foreign influence. Thus, concessions such as the publication – if only in 3,000 copies – of the "Peace Prayer Book," the opening of a *yeshiva* toward the end of 1956 and a few other gestures in the realm of secular Jewish culture, were probably intended in part, or perhaps even primarily, to counter criticism of Moscow's Jewish policy. However, in the more restricted field of the struggle for *aliya*, there is no evidence that foreign pressure bore any fruit at this time. Although emigration was almost always included in the demands put to Moscow, the complex of considerations involved made it the one least conducive to outside influences. Moreover, at least one of the groupings to whose pressure the Kremlin was most sensitive – that of Western communists and fellow travelers – were least adamant on this score, insofar as they raised it all.

The intervention of Western statesmen, professionals, intellectuals, left-wing progressives and others marked a new stage in the struggle on behalf of Soviet Jewry. While the mounting interest of politicians did not, of course, reach the Soviet public, visits by Western Jews who sometimes managed to talk with Soviet Jews in public places, were able to give the latter considerable encouragement in their unremitting endeavor to retain their identity by showing them that their fate was a matter of concern to the free world. This, together with visits from Israeli diplomats now traveling throughout the country and Jewish delegations and tourists from the West who were reaching the main Jewish centers, was beginning to give Soviet Jews the stimulus they needed to take up the struggle themselves. Deprived of any official leadership of their own, the possibility of turning to the Israeli embassy or to a foreign visitor gave them an address, an anchor, a source of inspiration – even if the contact was mostly sporadic and often dangerous. The Soviet Jewish struggle had a new focus. And Soviet Jews had further reason to hope that their situation would improve now that the "black years" were receding and the barrier of the Iron Curtain was being raised, no matter how partially or symbolically.

# 5 The campaign in the West gathers momentum

Although Westerners interested in Soviet Jewry by and large started off by stressing the need for greater religious freedom and more Jewish cultural facilities, invoking emigration mainly for those who had been separated from their families by war, by the end of the 1950s the tide began to turn toward emigration as the only solution for Soviet Jews who wished to live any kind of Jewish life. By now it had become clear that, even under Khrushchev, the Kremlin regarded its Jews as less than full members of the Soviet family of nations and, further, that it had no plans to change either its attitude or its policy. Thus, the late 1950s and early 1960s witnessed a stronger and stronger shift toward insistence on the right to emigrate, even though the Soviet leadership never acknowledged this right. Therefore, despite Moscow's status as a signatory to the Human Rights Convention, which states that "Everyone has the right to leave any country, including his own, and to return to his country,"[1] the struggle for the Soviet Jewish cause centered around Moscow's acceptance – in principle – of the more limited right of families to reunite. Since much of the Jewish population of the U.S. and Israel had originated in Russia, this acceptance seemed to offer a large enough loophole for tens if not hundreds of thousands of Soviet Jews to pass through.[2]

The public and the behind-the-scenes aspects of the campaign both involved a heterogeneous group of Jewish and non-Jewish politicians and private individuals, including an increasing number of tourists to the Soviet Union. The infusion of emotional and practical backing on the part of the West had a profound effect on Soviet Jewry's own efforts to improve their situation, enhancing the possibility of mounting a two-pronged operation with Israel and the West, on the one hand, and Soviet Jews on the other, working together toward a solution to the problem.

### Publicizing the Soviet Jewish plight

In late 1956 and early 1957 the Israeli office responsible for dealing with the Soviet Jewish problem set up a more-or-less permanent unofficial committee to create policy regarding how the campaign was to be conducted in the Western world. In addition to Shaul Avigur and Binyamin Eliav, the committee comprised Nahum Goldmann in his dual capacity as president of the World Jewish Congress (WJC) and the WZO; Israeli Foreign Ministry Assistant Director-General for Jewish Affairs Abraham Harman, who became head of the Jewish Agency Information Department in 1957; and Israeli Foreign Ministry East European Department head Arye Eshel.

One of the group's first decisions was to mobilize associates in Paris, London and New York, the key centers for the dissemination of information. Eliav found Meir Rosenhaupt (later Rosenne) in Paris and Emanuel Litvinoff in London, both of whom agreed to operate under the auspices of the local WJC office. Rosenhaupt was an Israeli doctoral student of international law at the Sorbonne and Litvinoff, who encountered the Jewish problem accidentally when he visited the USSR, had become so intrigued and incensed by what he saw there that he wrote an article entitled "A Visit to a Moscow Synagogue," which had impressed Eliav.[3] In New York where no single Jewish organization has ever been able to speak for the Jewish community as a whole, it was finally decided, in early 1958, to center the work in the person of an Israeli, Uri Frischwasser (later Raanan), who worked directly with Secretary of the Presidents' Club, Judd L. Teller.

The new operation was to concentrate on establishing the Soviet Jewish plight as a moral question and to invoke a commitment to mitigating that plight among Jews and those non-Jews who were known as defenders of human rights and protectors of oppressed minorities – the component of Western public opinion to whose pressures Moscow was most vulnerable. The Soviet Jewish problem was to be kept entirely separate from the cold war in an effort to calm the USSR's fear that its adversaries would exploit Soviet Jewish émigrés, for example, for intelligence purposes. (The corollary of this was Khrushchev's notion that a U.S.–Soviet normalization would result in open borders that would, *inter alia*, allow the departure of all Jews who might wish to leave.)[4] Further, no matter how urgent the need to impress potential advocates of Soviet Jewish emigration, no statement was to be passed on, let alone published, before being examined to remove exaggerations, non-verified allegations or outright fabrications. For the very fact that discrimination against Jews existed in the Soviet Union was sufficient to give their case legitimacy, and spurious arguments could only be counterproductive. Finally, as before, the Israeli connection with this activity was to remain unknown.[5]

The efforts of Eliav and his colleagues brought them considerable success. Whenever Soviet officials traveled outside the USSR, whether for political talks, professional and scientific conferences or even cultural events, they were confronted with the Jewish question as a moral issue that troubled the Western conscience as a whole and that of its intelligentsia and progressive left-wing elements in particular. Similarly, the numerous Western delegations and individuals who traveled to the USSR raised the moral issue with their hosts.

With regard to the message to be conveyed to supporters of the Soviet Jewish cause, events called for an emphasis on cultural rights for Jews inside the USSR. For there was a common awareness that the liberalization promised by Khrushchev was essentially irrelevant to the Jews. And the publication of articles on the liquidation of Soviet Jewish culture – as well as of many contributors to that culture – signified that Western liberals were viewing discrimination against the Jews as a national grouping as the USSR's most blatant wrong against them. The demand for cultural rights was even acceptable to communists and left-wing intellectuals because, although they considered assimilation the ideal solution to the Jewish problem the world over, they were being forced to realize that Soviet antisemitism precluded the successful assimilation of Soviet Jewry. For them the national status for those ethnic groupings that remained distinct in a socialist state was measured in terms of cultural autonomy. The same was true of non-Zionist Jewish organizations such as the WJC, which had sought to bring Soviet Jewry into its orbit by encouraging the establishment of a representative body with which it could have contacts, but which now appreciated that this was anathema to the Soviet system.

The Israelis who moved the wheels of the publicity campaign on the issue believed that from this base they might be able to get left-wing intellectuals and the Jewish organizations to endorse a program for the reunification of families severed by World War II; indeed, both the WJC and Anglo-Jewry's Board of Deputies included such a program in their resolutions on Soviet Jewry.[6] The Israelis also believed that the call for Jewish cultural autonomy within the accepted Soviet criteria for their national minorities would lead inevitably to an opening of the gates. In their view, rather than revive Jewish culture and the Jewish cultural establishment, the Soviets would come to accept emigration as the optimal answer for their own sakes. In this context, Avigur, Eliav and their colleagues continued to play up Soviet concessions on the repatriation of extra-territorial minority groupings such as the Germans, Greeks and Spaniards, even quoting what the Soviets themselves had to say about the reverse repatriation, as it were, of the Armenian diaspora to Soviet Armenia.[7] Just as Bulgaria and Poland had allowed Jewish emigration to Palestine (and later Israel) in the 1940s without bothering to check on these ties, on the assumption that anyone who wished to leave had family connections there, it was hoped that the USSR would waive examination of the family links of every potential emigrant. Thus the line between family reunification and emigration would become more and more blurred, until it was rendered meaningless.[8]

The first step for those concerned with alleviating the plight of Soviet Jewry was to collect and disseminate precise, comprehensive and updated data on the subject. To this end, Litvinoff produced a "newsletter" on Soviet Jewry that was distributed in Britain as a supplement to the *Jewish Observer and Middle East Review*, on which he had worked for seven years.[9] The newsletter quickly came to be used not only by the English-language press, whose Soviet affairs editors and correspondents were attracted by its careful reportage, but also by the Western European, particularly the Dutch and Scandinavian, media.[10] The newsletter's success resulted in a French edition and, somewhat later, in a Spanish one for Latin America.[11]

By September 1959 Litvinoff was able to establish himself independently. He created European Jewish Publications Ltd. to publish the newsletter, now called *Jews in Eastern Europe*.[12] And shortly afterwards he formed the Contemporary Jewish Library to publish an annual collection of Soviet newspaper items on Jewish topics under the name *Evrei i evreiskii narod* (The Jews and the Jewish People; Russian).[13] Together the two publications helped bring the intensity of Soviet anti-semitism home to the Western intelligentsia. In Paris Meir Rosenne set up the Bibliothèque juive contemporaine to provide a link with the French media and intellectual and scientific communities. The Bibliothèque – which was the base for the activities of both Rosenne and Ephraim Tari, who took over in 1961 – put out its own publications. Some of them were translations of what had already appeared in English and others of documents received directly from the USSR.[14]

And in New York, Moshe Decter, managing editor of the left-wing but strongly anti-communist *New Leader*, who had been recruited in 1958, established Jewish Minorities Research.[15] The fastidiousness with which all three operations adhered to bare facts without falling victim to either provocations or sensationalism made them invaluable instruments of persuasion and polemic.[16]

### Western reactions to Soviet Jewish policy

The documentation put out by Litvinoff and Decter contained appeals by Jewish communists and left-wing intellectuals who were becoming disillusioned as they saw the atmosphere surrounding the USSR's Jewish population remaining stagnant despite Soviet promises that there would be changes. Already in September 1957, Chaim Suller, of the communist *Morgn freyheyt*, noted that "not one book has been published in Yiddish. There is not a single Yiddish newspaper, except the one in Birobidzhan ... There is no permanent Yiddish theater. The Jewish cultural conference [which had been promised] was not called. The Yiddish literary journal has not yet appeared." And, Suller went on to write, the Soviet leaders could no longer hide behind the argument that things Yiddish were not in demand because Yiddish concerts were packed and the almost two thousand copies of the Warsaw *Folks-shtime* that came into the Soviet Union were snapped up and read avidly. Nor were "technical difficulties" a convincing excuse, for sufficient time had elapsed for them to have been overcome. "No Socialist and no friend of the Soviet Union can overlook ... or condone" such violation of the fundamental principles of socialism, Suller concluded.[17]

Chaim (Henri) Slovès, member of a three-man French Communist Party delegation that visited the USSR in 1956, called the Soviet contention that Jewish writers had not "applied themselves to [the] revival of that literature" a downright lie; the Soviet Jewish "literary community has never ceased pressing this question inside the Soviet Writers' Union, the only professional body competent to take it up." Slovès also rejected as irrelevant any comparison between the fate of Jewish culture and that of other Soviet nationalities. "The uniqueness of the Jewish tragedy was not only that individual writers and artists were liquidated, but that annihilation was decreed for the culture as such, the language as such, the very alphabet." Even those writers and artists who had survived were still lacking "the very substance and meaning of their existence." The plans and promises of the immediate post-Twentieth Congress period were still "suspended in air."

Although Slovès had been told that Soviet Jewry no longer needed Jewish culture, Soviet Deputy Minister of Culture Aleksandr Danilov had stated that the more than 3,000 Jewish cabaret-theater performances offered in the single year of 1957 had attracted an attendance of 3 million. Indeed, at the performance Slovès attended in Moscow "the hall was packed," particularly with young people, including soldiers and officers, who "sat with open-mouthed delight drinking in every Yiddish word from the stage." At Moscow's Lenin Library, which serviced all the libraries in the country, Slovès had been informed that "requests for Jewish books pour in constantly from scores of towns and cities all over the Soviet Union." In the library's periodical department which received a number of foreign Yiddish newspapers, these had "worn so thin from being read through and handled by so many eager readers that they have become virtually illegible." Slovès found preposterous the idea of solving the growing demand for Jewish books by publishing them in Russian translation. "No one had ever conceived, or dared suggest" that "other nationalities . . . content themselves with Russian translations of works they created in their own languages." Finally, Slovès insisted, the younger generation's interest in things Jewish provided the clearest and most striking demonstration of "the bankruptcy of [the] Soviet integration theory." The fact that "a large segment of Soviet Jewish youth has experienced a profound spiritual revolution in recent years" meant that "both the theory and the policy based on it have produced results that are diametrically opposed to those that were expected."

Slovès concluded by demanding that "progressive Jewish forces throughout the world" continue to put "the question of Jewish culture" to the Soviet authorities, even though there was no certainty of influencing the situation. "We must categorically and openly condemn not merely the murder of Jewish writers and artists . . . not only the present bloodless tragedy of Jewish culture in the Soviet Union . . . but the very premises of the false theory which underlies and seems to justify the tragedy . . . Every ordinary Jew, every friend of progressive Jewish culture, must face himself and rediscover himself through such a declaration of principle."[18]

While the growing evidence of the repression of Jewish culture was almost impossible to ignore, it was harder to document discrimination against individual Jews, especially since there were still relatively large numbers of Jews in the general student body, among "scientific workers" and in the liberal professions and the arts. And perhaps most difficult to convey were the implications of the dual – national and personal – discrimination which humiliated the Jews, making them fearful and uncertain. Even those who were prepared to admit that their situation was less bad in the late 1950s and early 1960s than it had been were usually unwilling to take the risk of holding a lengthy conversation with a foreigner, knowing that everything they did was being noted in their personal files for future use against them. One of the people who analyzed this fear was *Jewish Chronicle* foreign editor Joel Cang, who went to the Soviet Union in 1959. Although the plans to exile the Jews from the large cities in the European parts of the USSR to Birobidzhan – supported by such known antisemites as Minister of Culture Ekaterina Furtseva and CPSU Central Committee Secretary Mikhail Suslov – had been overruled by Khrushchev when Gosplan Chairman Aleksei Kosygin pointed out the disruptive effect it would have on fulfilment of the Seven Year Plan, Jews were convinced that Birobidzhan was being maintained as a Jewish Autonomous Region to show Soviet Jewry that it was ready and waiting to be filled by them whenever it might suit the Kremlin. The Jews also believed that it was only economic considerations which prevented the Kremlin from removing those holding central and senior posts in industry and science, those not so advanced in their professions still being discriminated against job-wise.[19]

The non-Jewish population, equally aware of the Jews' insecure position in Soviet society, interpreted the attitude of the authorities as a green light for them to behave as crassly as they liked toward the Jews without fear of punishment. Since the Jews were at best second-class citizens and perhaps even disloyal to the Soviet Union, non-Jews often felt entitled to insult, humiliate and even physically assault their Jewish neighbors. These antisemitic outbursts were, of course, convenient outlets for the general feelings of frustration, bitterness and hostility harbored by so many Soviet citizens. Nevertheless, local Jews could only conclude that such manifestations of hatred and contempt were based on deep-rooted sentiments.

The atmosphere in which the Jews were living was summarized in an October 1961 report put out by the AJC Foreign Affairs Department. Its author, an anonymous journalist who had visited the USSR several times in recent years, noted that, on his latest visit, he had witnessed "a general spirit of pessimism" among the Jews. Although he had been told on earlier visits that existing anti-Jewish feelings were a "remnant of the past," now "practically everyone" considered them to be "a permanent aspect of Soviet life." *Inter alia*, the Jews had fallen victim to the severe competition between Russians and local nationals in the various republics for many of the better jobs. For, while non-Russians regarded the Jews – who were culturally and linguistically Russian – as pro-Russian, the Russians, having to make concessions in this competition, ceded the positions of the Jews first.

The journalist also noted that, since "the realities of life in the USSR ... do not permit them to forget their Jewishness," Soviet Jews were becoming interested in all its aspects. This was evinced by their growing attendance at the synagogues on Jewish festivals and the importance they attached to the preservation and advancement of Jewish culture.[20]

By the turn of the decade cultural discrimination against the Jews was being overshadowed as the major focus of Western public concern by the growing number of vehement articles against Jews, synagogues, Zionism and Israel in the Soviet media, as well as by increasing instances of physical assault.[21] From the point of view of those striving to prove the existence of a Jewish problem in the USSR the new, openly anti-Jewish line adopted by the media as an antidote to the Jews' growing national awareness demonstrated that the denials by Soviet leaders, officials and foreign-language publications of the continued existence of a Soviet Jewish problem were conscious lies. Nor could Western sympathizers with the Soviet regime continue to deny the prevalence of Soviet antisemitism. Moreover, as newspaper articles and the first Soviet book on Israel[22] described the unsuccessful absorption of immigrants to Israel, especially those coming from the USSR, the Kremlin had openly, albeit indirectly, avowed that some Soviet Jews had emigrated to Israel. As the situation grew manifestly more serious, it was no longer sufficient to dwell solely, or mainly, on cultural discrimination. Avigur's group also sought new methods to increase the involvement and commitment of Western intellectuals, politicians and public opinion and to increment efforts to reinforce the morale of Soviet Jews. It was at this point that Israel initiated Russian-language broadcasts to the USSR and began the systematic distribution of written materials on Judaism and Israel in Russian.

When the mounting campaign against Soviet Jews began to include charges that synagogues were being used for espionage activities, Congressman Abraham Multer of New York condemned this use of antisemitism "for political ends" in the U.S. House of Representatives. Multer recommended that House members read a recent *New York Herald Tribune* editorial that showed how the recent indictment of "Soviet Jewish religious leaders" for "consorting with foreign agents, namely Israeli diplomatic officials" was reminiscent not only of the Stalin period but of the last decades of Tsarism.[23] The trial in question, the October 1961 trial of Gennadii (Gedalia) Pecherskii and his colleagues, was first publicized in the West by *Tribune* reporter Rowland Evans, Jr., who was in Leningrad at the time. Pecherskii and his two colleagues, who were arrested in June, had been convicted for crimes against the Soviet state. Pecherskii, formerly lay chairman of the Leningrad Jewish community, had been "for years . . . the outspoken advocate of Jewish religious life." Demoted to the post of deputy chairman in 1956 as a result of his "stubborn and public battle for Jewish rights," and stripped in 1957 even "of this lesser title and of all official duties," Pecherskii nonetheless "continued his public pressure for reforms." Evans wrote that, although it was impossible to tell whether this trial would be the "harbinger" of a "new and concerted campaign" against the Jews, he had felt "indications of efforts to discourage contact" between "foreign tourists and Jews who attended synagogue."[24]

In its report on the Pecherskii trial, the *Jewish Chronicle* wrote that it demonstrated "once more Soviet determination to . . .isolate the Jews even more completely from any contacts with their coreligionists abroad," and that "the heavy sentences might have been influenced" by the gathering of thousands of Jews outside the Leningrad synagogue on the High Holy Days in September 1961. The paper went on to report that these gatherings had been irritating the Kremlin for several years, because, like the declaration of half a million Jews in the 1959 census that Yiddish was their mother tongue, they "made manifest" their unyielding spirit.[25]

The Kremlin's replacement of lay leaders in a number of Jewish communities, together with the arrests in Leningrad and Moscow, drew an official statement by Israeli Foreign Minister Golda Meir in mid-November 1961. The statement, which came in reply to a motion tabled by Opposition leader Menahem Begin, was followed by a Knesset Committee for Foreign and Security Affairs appeal to the Soviet Union to give "every Jew who wishes the right to leave in order to join his family and his people" in Israel and to grant "the Jewish community . . . the fullest possibilities to develop its national, cultural and religious life without discrimination."[26]

"Incensed and anxious over the jailings," the Rabbinical Council of

America called upon the U.N. to seek the release of the Jewish leaders, stating that "the entire world can only be repelled" by the incarceration of Soviet Jewish religious leaders for "alleged treasonable activity." The *New York Herald Tribune* reported that, while many Jewish organizations had protested these antisemitic acts, only a few had directed their appeals to the U.N. It noted that many of the RCA's congregants were "just a generation or two away from Russia and some . . . bear painful memories of Nazi atrocities." The Conservative United Synagogue of America asked the U.S. government "to inquire into the arrests."[27]

The attacks on Zionism and Israel dwelt on "absurd" demands for emigration to Israel and on the "subversive" activities of Israeli diplomats, who were distributing materials that libeled the Soviet Union.[28] Books were published on these and kindred themes. One of them, published by the USSR Academy of Sciences in 17,000 copies and entitled "The Reactionary Nature of Judaism: A Short Survey of the Origins and Class Character of the Jewish Religion," depicted Judaism as the servant of the rabbis and Zionists, and as losing its hold on the Jewish masses.[29]

One facet of the new offensive which New York Senator Jacob Javits labeled as evoking "a chorus of protests from the free world," was the prohibition against baking *matzot* for the Passover. The first reports of such restrictions had reached the West in 1957, and in 1959 New York Senator Kenneth Keating told the Senate that the baking of *matzot* had been forbidden in Kiev, Kharkov, Odessa, Kuibyshev, Rostov, Kishinev and Lvov.[30] By 1961, it was reported, *matzot* were being baked in only six Soviet cities. And when the ban became total a year later, even the import of *matzot* was forbidden. The ban's renewal in 1963, 1964 and 1965 led to further outcries in both Houses of Congress, to an appeal by the New York Board of Rabbis that the U.N. Commission on Human Rights "direct an urgent appeal to the Soviet Government for the revocation of that ban," and an appeal to the Soviet authorities by Britian's Chief Rabbi Israel Brodie "in the name of Anglo-Jewry," to repeal their decision.[31]

Western public opinion was even more aroused when, in the early sixties, Jews began to be condemned to death for "economic crimes."[32] Although there had been earlier instances in which Jews had been indicted and tried for allegedly having exploited their positions for purposes of embezzlement, giving or extorting bribes, counterfeiting money or conducting currency speculations, it was not until July 1961 that the West heard that the death penalty was being invoked for these offenses. And this even though one of the corner-stones of the USSR's new criminal code was that the death penalty was limited to those found guilty of "high treason, espionage, sabotage, terrorist acts, banditry and premediated murder . . . under aggravated circumstances."[33]

The economic trials aroused the indignation of a broad spectrum of Westerners. On 15 July 1962, British Board of Deputies President Sir Barnett Janner appealed for mitigation of the severe sentences being handed down to Jews for economic offenses and asked the Soviet government to conduct "a campaign of enlightenment against anti-Semitism in the USSR."[34] In April the U.S. National Association for the Advancement of Colored People requested clemency for those sentenced to die for economic offenses. NAACP Chairman S. G. Spollswood wrote to Ambassador Dobrynin that, as "a group which has long suffered the troubles of discrimination and segregation," the association "considers with increasing concern the fate of Soviet Jewry." Spollswood went on to say that "these savage practices represent an unfortunate retrogression in Soviet law as well as new and disturbing indications of anti-Semitic persecution." In May the International League for the Rights of Man sent an appeal to U.N. Secretary General U Thant signed by 223 leading Americans asking him to intercede over the death sentences. In June forty U.S. and Canadian trade union leaders criticized the second-class treatment being meted out to Jews "in every facet of Soviet life," specifically the death sentences for "so-called economic crimes."[35]

A number of international Jewish organizations had also been addressing themselves to Soviet Jewry during this period. At its founding convention in Rome in January 1958, the Conference of Jewish Organizations (COJO) dubbed Soviet suppression of Jewish culture and religion and the refusal to let Jews leave, especially for *aliya* to Israel, "one of the central problems of our generation." Chaired by Nahum Goldmann, COJO comprised the leaders of seven major national organizations – from the United States, Britain, France, Argentina, Canada and Australia – as well as of two international organizations, the WJC and B'nai B'rith.[36]

The August 1959 WJC Plenary Assembly in Stockholm devoted almost a week to the worsening position of Soviet Jewry. Although more cautious than some of those who followed, Nahum Goldmann set the tone of the Assembly when he called for fresh efforts to rectify the situation. The American Jewish Congress's Joachim Prinz was more outspoken; he informed the Assembly that his delegation had prepared a resolution urging that the WJC take all possible steps to bring the Soviet Jewish problem to the attention of the civilized world. The Assembly adopted this resolution as well as two further ones calling on the Soviet authorities to remove all restrictions on Jewish religious practices and cultural self-expression and to accord its Jews "the basic human right of free emigration."[37]

In 1961 the 25th WZO Congress in Jerusalem appealed to the Soviet Union to recognize the right of its Jews to "a Jewish national, religious and cultural life and their right to *aliya* to Israel" and sent greetings of solidarity to Soviet Jewry, which had remained faithful to its national heritage.[38] And a European conference of rabbis and educators under the auspices of the World Council of Synagogues also passed a resolution on Soviet Jewry,[39] as did the Jewish Student Union of France, whose concern eventuated in the general French Student Union calling on the Soviet government to put a halt to its discriminatory policies.[40]

On the whole, the broader attention paid to Soviet Jewry was still a relatively new phenomenon on the Jewish scene in the West. True, the issue came to the fore from time to time, whenever the Soviet Jewish situation took a turn for the worse (the closure of synagogues, the prohibition of *matzot*, outbursts of hooliganism, or waves of arrests and trials), or whenever an event such as Khrushchev's 1959 visit to the U.S. invited upgraded activity. Yet, despite the constant harassment and despite the access Jewish leaders and organizations had to their various governments and the leading personalities in them – especially in the U.S. – neither American nor world Jewry was able to organize enough political effort or pressure to exercise any meaningful constraint on the Soviet leadership. It was only as the 1960s wore on and awareness of the Soviet Jewish plight increased that the concern for Soviet Jewry became a regular feature of Jewish activity in the West.

The clearest evidence that outcries and protests were making their mark was the undisguised anger of Soviet representatives and officials when Westerners questioned them about the zigzags and inconsistencies of Soviet policy vis-à-vis the Jews.[41] On the one hand, Moscow never stopped playing down the Jewish contribution to Soviet society, never stopped arguing that Soviet Jews were acculturated into the dominant Russian culture and sought nought else but total assimilation; on the other hand, public statements and the media, especially but not solely those aimed at foreign consumption, were portraying a quite different picture of Soviet Jews as holding Jewish cultural events of great popularity and success, and maintaining Jewish choirs, drama societies and theaters. The irritation of Soviet personalities at constant Western harping on the Soviet Jewish situation, and discrepancies in the official propaganda line all demonstrated that the louder, the more persistent and the more widely voiced the protest, the greater the success it could be expected to achieve.

### The American Jewish establishment and Khrushchev's "peaceful coexistence"

The stronger Khrushchev's desire for "peaceful coexistence," the greater was the potential of Western public opinion in the struggle for Soviet Jewish rights. The more the Soviets needed the West, and the larger the constituency they sought to mobilize,[42] the better were the chances that the Soviets would bend to pressures to make concessions on behalf of their Jews. The Soviet Jewish question cropped up at all levels of contact, from the President of the United States down.

Khrushchev's September 1959 visit to the U.S. provided the occasion for a major bout of activity. For Eisenhower himself expressed the concern of American Jewry about the position of their brethren in the USSR in his talks with the First Secretary at Camp David. And Secretary of State Christian Herter took the opportunity of telling his counterpart, Andrei Gromyko, of the anxiety felt in the U.S. "with respect to the status of Jews in the U.S.S.R."[43] Chairman of the USSR Supreme Soviet Presidium Anastas Mikoian and First Deputy Chairman of the Council of Ministers Frol Kozlov, who had helped prepare for the visit of the First Secretary when they were in the U.S. in January and July 1959, respectively, had also been asked about Soviet Jewry at every press conference. Mikoian's attempts to prove that there was no antisemitism in the USSR by pointing out that many Soviet leaders were married to Jewesses led to captions in the American press: "Some of Our Best Wives are Jewish."[44]

Both the Israel office and American Jewish organizations had been preparing for the Khrushchev visit for many months. While connections between the two parties were still rather tenuous despite Uri Raanan's being in regular contact with Judd Teller of the Presidents' Conference,[45] their overall goal on the issue of Soviet Jewry was similar: to alleviate the Soviet Jewish position, including recognition and implementation of the right to emigrate, at least for members of split families. Contacts between the Israelis and the American Jewish establishment gradually intensified, not only because of their common humanitarian goal; the Americans came to rely increasingly on the Israelis' updated and detailed information and also to realize from these and their own sources – chiefly American Jewish tourists – that Israel was the goal of most Jews who wanted to leave the Soviet Union.

The American Jewish Committee, the Jewish Labor Committee and some religious and Zionist organizations had been involved with Soviet Jewry for several years.[46] When an AJC delegation met with Mikoian in January 1959 to ask about rumors that the USSR intended resolving to exile Jews to Birobidzhan at its forthcoming Twenty-first Party Congress, it also presented him with a memorandum protesting national and individual anti-Jewish discrimination and dwelling on the implementation of cultural rights. The AJC hoped that Mikoian's statement a few days earlier had been "an earnest of the Soviet Government's preparedness, at long last, to permit the establishment of an adequate system of Jewish . . . cultural facilities." Certainly, this statement, which purported to describe the current situation and which contended that in the USSR "all peoples enjoy . . . freedom for the development of their culture . . . and that includes the Jews," could not be called accurate. The remaining two sections of the AJC memorandum discussed the facilities available for the expression of the Jewish religion and Jewish participation in Soviet public and economic life, two areas in which their status was demonstrably inequitable, assuring Mikoian that interest and concern regarding the fate of Soviet Jewry would continue until these issues were resolved.[47]

AJC leaders encouraged leading personalities to raise the issue of Soviet Jewry in their contacts with Soviet officials, briefing them on the current situation. It was with this in mind that AJC San Francisco executives Harry Winter and S. Marshall Kempner approached Cyril Magnin, member of the San Francisco chapter and Chairman of the San Francisco Board of Port Commissioners, who hosted Kozlov on his visit to that city in July 1959. Made aware that American citizens were very concerned about Soviet antisemitism, Kozlov promised Magnin, who was shortly to lead a San Francisco trade mission to the USSR, that he, personally, would show him that there was no discrimination against the Jews.[48] The AJC also briefed the San Francisco trade delegation prior to its departure, providing it with written material and urging its members to ask pertinent questions of the Soviets.[49] Similarly, on the eve of his departure for the USSR with eight other governors, AJC officials asked Governor Robert Meyner of New Jersey to bring up the treatment of Soviet Jews during his visit.[50]

On the occasion of Kozlov's visit, three prominent Americans – Dr. Donald Harrington, Minister of the New York Community Church; Reverend John Haynes Holmes, Minister Emeritus of the same church; and Norman Thomas – published in the *New York Times* a letter they had sent to Kozlov in which they charged the Soviet Union with anti-Jewish professional and religious discrimination (based on statistical materials) and anti-Jewish propaganda in the media. When Kozlov tried to repudiate these charges, American Jewish Congress President Joachim Prinz labeled Kozlov's refutations unsatisfactory and the Congress publicized tourist photographs of synagogues that had been boarded up and of the derelict condition of Babii Iar. Asked about the suppression of Soviet Jewish culture at a press conference in New York, Kozlov ignored the question, again denying that synagogues were being liquidated. In San Francisco he said that Soviet Jews lived a much better life than Jews in Israel; in New York he said that he had recently seen Jews in Kiev leading a happy life and "bathing in the Dnieper."[51]

Even though he refused to meet with Jewish leaders, Khrushchev was subjected to considerable harassment on the issue of Soviet Jewry. But he, too, always responded with irrelevant comments. When asked to clarify the Jews' status "as regards equality of opportunity" at his first public meeting, at the National Press Club in Washington D.C., the First Secretary replied that "among the persons who took foremost part in the landing of the rocket to the moon the representatives of the Jewish people hold a place of honor. In general, the national problem does not exist in our country . . . Russian Jews, Ukrainians, Turkmens, Uzbeks, Belorussians, Georgians, Armenians . . . all live in peace and close friendship . . . [and] are together marching toward one communism."[52]

Its own endeavors to meet with Khrushchev having proved unsuccessful, the AJC asked several leading Americans who did have meetings with him to broach the problem of Soviet Jewry. One of these, President of the International Union of Electrical, Radio and Machine Workers James B. Carey, was asked to raise the issue of improving the internal Soviet Jewish situation without touching on emigration and to point out that, whereas the Soviets criticized the U.S. for its racial problems, they were themselves practicing "a serious kind of discrimination."[53]

The AJC tended to work alone as its long tradition as an American Jewish defense organization had provided it with the institutional framework and well-oiled machinery necessary for activity within the

American political community. The other leading organizations, however, banded together in an effort to conduct a combined operation to exploit the Khrushchev visit to the utmost. Five Presidents' Conference leaders – Rabbi Irving Miller of the American Zionist Council, Rabbi Joachim Prinz of the American Jewish Congress, Label A. Katz and Maurice Bisgyer of B'nai B'rith and Moses Feuerstein of the Union of Orthodox Jewish Congregations of America – met Eisenhower on the eve of the visit to urge him to raise the Soviet Jewish issue at the summit talks, and indeed received his promise to do so. The president had also received a lengthy report from Rabbi Richard C. Hertz of Detroit, whom his White House Assistant Robert E. Merriam had commissioned to undertake a special mission to the USSR with a view to briefing the president. And former B'nai B'rith President Philip M. Klutznick set up a committee of the leaders of twenty-one Jewish groups to arrange for a meeting with the First Secretary. However, despite the State Department's sympathetic treatment of the Committee's request, the initiative was frustrated by Ambassador Menshikov's failure to address himself to it.[54]

It is possible, as the Soviets intimated on different occasions, that divergences and mutal recriminations within the American Jewish community allowed them to ignore requests to meet a representative American Jewish delegation. As one American magazine pointed out, American Jewry was so divided that it would be no simple task to choose a delegation to meet with Khrushchev.[55] Khrushchev's disregard of their efforts to meet with him notwithstanding, Prinz felt that these led to a substantial gain in the very planning of a common action, including: "a more representative ad hoc committee;" the agreement of every important national organization except the AJC to "subordinate agency interests to the common good"; a joint statement of the Jewish position and memoranda on the status of Soviet Jewry submitted for study by personalities whom Khrushchev did meet; State Department approval of these approaches; and, finally, tacit agreement on the composition of a small delegation in the event of a meeting. Although its representatives helped draft the joint statement and voted for its adoption – including the section dealing with emigration – the AJC did not join the group, consenting to no more than observer status.[56]

In the wake of the Khrushchev visit, AJC Inter-Religious Division head Rabbi Morris N. Kertzer, who had led the 1956 New York Board of Rabbis delegation to the USSR, appeared as a special guest on Bishop James J. Pike's Sunday television show. Discussing the status of religion and minority groups in the Soviet Union, especially that of the Jews, Kertzer refuted Khrushchev's contention of freedom of religion. Although he agreed that some religious groups enjoyed "freedom of worship," this did not include the Jews, who could not learn Hebrew, the language of prayer, or acquire religious articles, and whose rabbis could not even meet with their congregations. Kertzer concluded that, despite Khrushchev's "act of evasion" in not meeting with the Jewish organizations, the thaw in East–West tensions presented an important opportunity for raising these questions because it made the Soviet Union vulnerable to world public opinion.[57]

Prior to Khrushchev's second visit to the U.S. in September 1960 to attend the U.N. General Assembly, the American Jewish community debated the desirability of approaching him on the issue of Soviet Jewry. The doubts resulted from the fact that Washington–Moscow goodwill had largely passed (mainly because of the U–2 incident), from an unwillingness to disclose disunity among the American Jewish organizations and from the fear of becoming identified with the "captive nations" (like the Ukrainians and Lithuanians) whose sponsors sought the overthrow of the Soviet regime. Nonetheless, many felt that American Jewry must demonstrate its feelings toward the Soviet Union,[58] and seventeen major Jewish organizations called on "men of goodwill everywhere" to exercise their influence with the aim of urging a change in Moscow's Jewish policy, sending copies of the statement to every U.N. delegation in New York.[59]

In August 1962, the tenth anniversary of the execution of the leading Jewish cultural and public figures under Stalin, seven leading Jewish organizations called on the Soviet Union to restore to its Jews "the full right to their own cultural life." While nothing could be done for those who had been executed except "public apology and full rehabilitation," the crime against Soviet Jewry could be rectified by reversing the policy.[60]

The AJC, too, continued to be active, seeking meetings with the new Soviet ambassador in Washington, Anatolii Dobrynin, and endeavoring to keep in touch with the U.S. administration. In August 1962 it asked newly appointed ambassador to Moscow Foy D. Kohler to intervene against the mistreatment of Soviet Jews. In May 1963 its representatives met with returning Ambassador Llewellyn Thompson, who was to become President Kennedy's mentor on Soviet affairs. These meetings helped the AJC understand current State Department evaluations and provided a means of communicating its own findings and positions to the administration. The Committee also supplied the U.S. mission to the U.N. with material for speeches on Soviet antisemitism. Among its initiatives was the late 1962 cable that forty-six Christian and Jewish clergy and lay leaders sent to Khrushchev, and its chapters were responsible for many of the locally sponsored advertisements, appeals and cables that helped keep the Soviet Jewish issue before the American public. The Committee also prepared the petition sent to Khrushchev by prominent scholars and clergymen early in 1963 urging that the death penalty be repealed for "economic offenses."[61]

B'nai B'rith in the U.S. had long been involved with the issue of Soviet Jewry under its former president, Philip Klutznick. In 1960 Klutznick, now chairman of that organization's international council, brought Dr. William Korey, the head of the B'nai B'rith Anti-Defamation League (ADL) Washington office and ex-university teacher of Russian history, to New York. Korey's first assignment was to prepare a major document on the issue of emigration, in the context of a study then being conducted by Philippine judge and statesman José D. Ingles for the U.N. Commission on Human Rights Subcommission on the Prevention of Discrimination and Protection of Minorities. This was the first time that the question of the right of emigration was to be raised at an international forum. Korey's main focus of research was the Soviet Union and Eastern Europe, where World War II had cleft a large number of families and where logic called for the reunion of these families, i.e. emigration with the aim of reuniting them. When Korey's findings, submitted in a formal 25-page report on 29 December 1960, were first used by B'nai B'rith Chairman Label Katz at the Subcommission in January 1961, they drew considerable attention. This was augmented when the Soviet delegate sharply attacked Katz, and papers such as the *New York Herald Tribune*, for instance, thereupon wrote major articles on the issues at stake.[62]

### The mobilization of intellectuals, left-wing opinion and public figures

In the summit atmosphere engendered by Camp David, Avigur's office broached the idea of an international conference of Western intellectuals and public figures that would deal solely with Soviet Jewry. For the Israelis felt that, given the increasing contacts between the USSR and the U.S., particularly their scientific, artistic and business communities, such a conference must make an impact on the Kremlin. Although the Khrushchev–Eisenhower summit planned for 1960 never took place due to the new tensions between Moscow and Washington, a conference was held in Paris in September 1960. Officially it was held under the auspices of Nahum Goldmann, who, according to one report on his efforts to convene it, had revised his earlier belief in hush-hush diplomacy after receiving a number of slaps in the face from the Soviets. The conference was attended by over forty intellectuals and politicians from fourteen different countries, while a number of public figures who were unable to attend, although they agreed with the aims of the conference in principle, sent messages of sympathy and support.[63]

Daniel Mayer, Chairman of the French League for the Rights of Mankind opened the conference by noting that it had convened to discuss "one particular right of mankind," the right to culture and freedom of expression, and to demonstrate solidarity with those who were denied it. Pointing out that many people had tried to convince him that the gathering was a cold war weapon against the Soviets,[64] Mayer contended that a meeting at which so many countries and opinions were represented could never be "against anyone, or at the service and at the disposal of anyone." The next speaker, Nahum Goldmann, stressed that the meeting was intended solely to raise and clarify questions connected with the position of Soviet Jewry.

Jewish philosopher Martin Buber then took issue with some of the basic postulates that underlay Soviet Jewish policy, for instance the one that Jews could not be considered an ethnic entity since they had neither a territory nor an autonomous economic life of their own and were therefore in no position to demand either a continued separate existence or maintenance of their cultural values. Buber maintained that the Soviet failure to take the specific traits of Jewish reality into account was historically irrational and destined to miscarry. He was followed by French Jewish leader André Blumel, who contended that the nearly half a million Jews who had given Yiddish as their mother tongue in the 1959 census should be able to express themselves in that language, while the 1.8 million who said they belonged to the Jewish nationality although their mother tongue was no longer Yiddish should have books in Russian dealing with the history and literature of their people.

The broad spectrum of backgrounds represented at the conference came across in the points stressed by different participants. For example, French Catholic writer Jacques Nantet believed that the conference should call for Soviet Jews to be allowed to go to Israel in the context of the rights of every citizen in a democratic country to leave and return to his home country, while Vice-President of the Italian Academy Vincenzo-Arangio Riuz and Norwegian Socialist MP Aase Lionaes thought that it should rather stress the more limited point of family reunification. The latter, who had spent years dealing with the problems of refugees and split families at the U.N., considered that the simple, human problem of the thousands of Jews in the USSR who still found themselves separated from their closest relatives must be addressed without ideological considerations. She found it "inconceivable" that the Soviets could still insist they had received no applications for emigration to Israel given Golda Meir's report to the Knesset in August that the Kremlin had turned down a great number of such requests.[65] Lionaes also failed to understand why these Jews could not enjoy the same elementary human right of family reunification that one thousand other Soviet Jews who had been reunited with their families in different Western countries had benefited from during the past five years. And Italian lawyer Leopoldo Ricardi thought that the request should be for emigration within a specific and limited period, since the indefinite right to leave in order "to go over to what is considered the enemy bloc" would have an adverse effect on the position of those Jews who remained in the USSR.

Among those who traveled to Paris to call the free world's attention to the plight of Soviet Jewry were Professor of Philosophy Jeanne Hersh of Geneva; Léon Lyon-Caen, First Honorary President of the French Supreme Court of Appeal and President of the Mouvement contre le racisme, l'antisémitisme et pour la paix (MRAP), a French front organization; Lionel Trilling; editor of the Dutch *Church and World* Feitse Boerwinkel; and British writers Wolf Mankowitz and Peter Vansittart. Making a strong plea for the revival of conscience in international affairs, Vansittart denigrated Soviet use of the half-truth to "protect" its Jews from the "dangers" of emigrating to Israel.

Finally, the conference heard Joseph Berger-Barzilai, who had recently reached Israel from Poland after having been repatriated from the USSR. Berger-Barzilai had been secretary of the Palestine Communist Party in the 1920s and had headed the Comintern Near Eastern section until 1935, when he was arrested and began twenty-one years of imprisonment in Soviet camps. He pointed out that, although the arbitrary liquidation of Jewish cultural life had been stigmatized as undermining the main principles of Leninism, those who advocated rehabilitating Jewish institutions were marked for national oppression. But, he continued, no direct administrative pressure, or even indirect constraints, could achieve the Jews' assimilation. Meanwhile, Soviet Jewish citizens who wished to have a Jewish cultural life must be allowed to have theaters and schools for their children in Yiddish, and those who did not believe that a full Jewish life could be achieved under Soviet conditions must be allowed to leave for the Jewish national center, Israel. Berger-Barzilai was convinced that in a period when communism was intent on manifesting its moral superiority vis-à-vis the Western world, the CPSU could not fail to heed such a call from people of goodwill devoted to the cause of progress.

In his closing speech Goldmann said that, although he was convinced that Moscow would one day tell its Jews to leave since there was no other solution, all that could be achieved until then was a moderate program for improving the internal Soviet Jewish situation. He did not feel that it was practical to call for anything that would entail changes in the Soviet system, as would demands for freedom of opinion, of religious practice or of emigration. Daniel Meyer then proposed that the conference agree to remain constituted so that it could reconvene from time to time to consider whether its proposals were being carried out. In his own words: "we shall only have any actual pull and influence if we hang Damocles' sword over the heads of our opposite numbers."[66]

Although the statement finally agreed upon was very moderate in tone, the subject, and the composition of the conference participants, gained it impressive coverage in the international media. A new forum had been created, one that was independent of any permanent standing committee or political body, for the sole purpose of monitoring and reporting on the Soviet Union's treatment of its Jewish minority.

The Soviets were obviously concerned with the conference's impact in the West. Their official reaction was represented by Zinovii Sheinis' article accusing Goldmann of conducting a "lying campaign against the Soviet Union" and maintaining that the conference had been supported by the U.S. and the German Federal Republic with the purpose of intensifying the cold war.[67] At the same time, they sought to convince some of the participants that the situation was not what they had been led to believe. Their first move in this direction was to invite Blumel to visit the USSR. Blumel, who took up the invitation at once, was told by the Soviet authorities that they would permit the setting up of a central organization of the various Jewish communities if the Jews themselves asked for this. Mayer, too, was invited by Soviet ambassador to Paris Sergei Vinogradov in December 1960, when the latter finally received Mayer and Nantet, who had been charged with delivering the conference statement to him. On their visits to the Soviet Union, much effort was expended on introducing Blumel and Mayer to Jews who confirmed successful Jewish acculturation and assimilation into their non-Jewish surroundings.[68] Blumel, who was the object of special Soviet attention, was invited to the USSR three more times in 1961. On the first of these visits Minister of Culture Furtseva told him that the Kremlin would react to friendly approaches but not to any kind of pressure: any concessions would be motivated by a desire "to please our friends outside." She noted that the issues involved encroached upon "the general nationalities question," and that privileges for Jews might arouse resentment among the other minorities.

The very fact that Furtseva received Blumel twice within approximately two months is proof that Moscow was troubled over outside reactions to the Soviet Jewish problem. Moreover, the minister's remarks made it clear that the only way to change the situation was for progressives to keep up the pressure on Moscow. Nonetheless, it seems that Blumel was persuaded that conferences should not be held, that pressure should not be applied, and that the only way of achieving anything was through friends like himself. Following his October 1961 visit he told the French–Soviet Friendship Society that antisemitism in the USSR was receding and that there was an improvement in the field of Yiddish culture. In other words, while he remained concerned over the lot of Soviet Jews and convinced of their links to Jewish tradition and to Israel, Blumel's effectiveness to the cause of Soviet Jewry had been largely neutralized by the Soviets.[69]

Goldmann's own position remained ambiguous. On the one hand, in October 1961 he told a press conference in Jerusalem that the Jews might indeed be fearful of requesting a central Jewish organization; on the other, in the same period he stated that while no Jewish life was permitted in the USSR, Jews were not being persecuted there. This ambivalence was an early rumbling of what later developed into a major controversy between Goldmann, the Israeli government and many of the Jewish organizations involved in the struggle on behalf of Soviet Jewry.

The Paris conference was the forerunner of several conferences convened specifically to discuss the Soviet Jewish problem. One such meeting, of approximately thirty-five Italian public figures who had been gathered together by the Italian participants of the Paris conference, was held in March 1961 and received considerable coverage in the Italian press. The prominent Jewish Communist Senator, Umberto Terracini, told the conference that the Jews' difficult situation was the result of their refusal to settle in the Jewish autonomous region and of the fact that all Soviet Jews did not want the same thing: some wanted a national Jewish life in the USSR, others emigration and yet others assimilation. In the wake of the conference the Soviet ambassador in Rome was presented with a resolution requesting "revocation of the Soviet ban against Jewish schools, theaters and newspapers" and calling upon the Soviet government to "repress the publication of anti-Jewish attacks in the press" and to permit Jewish emigration.[70]

Similar conferences were held in Rio de Janeiro and London in fall 1961. The London symposium was convened by Lord Robert Boothby, Richard Crossman, M.P., and Israel Sieff, and was addressed by Emanuel Litvinoff, Wolf Mankowitz, Manès Sperber, M.P.s Sir Leslie Plummer and Marcus Lipton, Soviet specialists Alec Nove, Max Hayward and Jack Miller and the Reverend William W. Simpson, General Secretary of the Council of Christians and Jews. The experts agreed that publication of Evgenii Evtushenko's poem "Babii Iar" brought the problem of antisemitism in the USSR into the open, and that the struggle for Jewish freedom had become part of the general struggle for freedom in the Soviet Union. Crossman, who was unable to attend, sent a message saying that "continued attention and publicity in the West" was the only way to safeguard Soviet Jews from being further mistreated. The Soviet embassy in London received a copy of the symposium's statement deploring the condition of the USSR's Jewish citizens.[71]

While many of those who became involved on behalf of Soviet Jewry demonstrated their commitment by participating in conferences and signing appeals, others became interested after visiting the Soviet Union. Most visitors to the USSR in these years had given little prior thought to the Jewish question. Indeed, if probed on the subject, they would have said that Jews enjoyed full equality of rights and that there was neither discrimination nor antisemitism. Although some travelers received a preliminary briefing from the Israelis or from Jewish organizations in their countries of residence, it was neither possible nor, perhaps, even desirable to brief everyone. For the majority of those who became involved in the issue were aroused by what they themselves witnessed and experienced as they found that their attempts to meet Jews, including relatives they had come especially to see, were systematically frustrated, even in the synagogue. Yet, although Soviet citizens were usually forewarned of the impending arrival of relatives from abroad and cautioned against saying anything that might be interpreted as discontent or slander against the regime, many tourists saw and sensed enough to evoke suspicion and concern.[72]

One of those who returned even more committed than before was Eleanor Roosevelt, who challenged Khrushchev on the subject of Soviet treatment of the Jews during her first visit in 1957, and was not satisfied with his response that many Jews held high rank in the army and elsewhere. After she pressed him on the inability of Soviet Jews to "settle in or even visit Israel," Khrushchev said: "the time will come when everyone who wants to go will be able to go."[73] American Zionist leader Rabbi Abba Hillel Silver also went to the USSR in 1961, apparently under the auspices of pro-Soviet American millionaire Cyrus Eaton. Silver did not succeed in meeting with leading personalities, and when he asked the academicians and officials he did meet why Moscow was not making any effort to win the support and friendship of America's 5 million Jews, he received the usual line to the effect that the Jews had no desire to express any separate cultural life that would return them to a ghetto existence.[74]

A thirty-five member B'nai B'rith delegation, including President Label Katz and his deputy, Maurice Bisgyer, also visited the Soviet Union at this time. Prior to their departure Katz and Bisgyer met with U.S. Ambassador Llewellyn Thompson on one of his home leaves. They were also equipped with letters of recommendation from Mrs. Roosevelt, which "proved to be more than helpful." They were received by the editors of the new Yiddish journal *Sovetish heymland*, Aron Vergelis and Naum Oisland, who told them that the very appearance of their magazine demonstrated that the Soviets could make the changes called for by the Paris conference and other Western intercessions (contradicting what Silver was told). Katz was also received by First Deputy Minister of Culture Aleksei Kuznetsov, who first insisted that the Jews had equal cultural and political rights, then said that the Soviet Union was seeking to establish a uniform Soviet culture rather than create separate cultural frameworks, and completed these inconsistent statements with the information that a new Yiddish journal would soon be appearing in Minsk. The B'nai B'rith delegation visited several synagogues where, despite curt receptions by some of the wardens, they were able to establish contact with worshippers. Deeply impressed by what they had seen, the members came away prepared to join the struggle for Soviet Jewry.[75]

### The U.S. Congress joins the protest

The U.S. *Congressional Record* for the late 1950s and early 1960s evinces the considerable concern with the Soviet Jewish question in the United States during that period. Indeed, it reflects the increased attention that the struggle on behalf of Soviet Jewry began to attract from top-ranking American legislators, especially from the Jews among them and from those who represented traditionally Jewish constituencies.[76]

In 1956 the *Congressional Record* had included just three insertions on Soviet Jews,[77] but by 1958 the issue was beginning to become more central, albeit through the interest of only a handful of congressmen. Thus, in this year the *Record* printed two items on anti-Jewish discrimination, both of them in reaction to Khrushchev's interview with the French *Figaro*, in which he stigmatized the Jews as "individualists" and as lacking the qualities necessary for the construction of Soviet society, because they did not like "collective work and collective discipline," and both, interestingly enough, dwelt on the issue of emigration.[78]

The thrust of the first major statement on the Soviet Jewish issue, made in 1958 by Jacob K. Javits, who had become a senator the year previously and was to play a major role in the struggle for Soviet Jewish rights until his departure from the Senate in 1980, was that emigration was the sole solution. Javits opened his speech by decrying the Kremlin's transgressions against the Jews as individuals and as a people. He then went on to comment that, at a time when the Soviets "speak of summit conferences, of coexistence and good-will, and pose as humanitarians, this dreadful suppression of the Jewish minority must serve as a gauge of their moral integrity and the sincerity of their promises." He quoted a report prepared by the Congress Legislative Reference Service on Soviet treatment of its national minorities which noted that "organized Jewish communal life" no longer existed "in its vital form" and that, "despite all measures compelling them to conform," the Jews were "still spurned by the Soviet Government as 'foreign' and 'suspect'."[79] In other words, being "neither permitted to assimilate nor to maintain themselves as a national group," the Jews were a "people in limbo."

Javits took issue with the "hackneyed argument" used by Soviet representatives that Soviet Jews did not want to go to Israel. The Kremlin, he said, "wish[es] the Free World to believe that Soviet Jews, denied their rights as a group, discriminated against individually, are nonetheless inclined to . . . settle for the status of second-class citizens in the U.S.S.R." The Soviet Union, he pointed out, recognized "the principle of repatriation" and accordingly "encouraged Russians, Ukrainians and Armenians from all parts of the world to resettle in their respective republics within the U.S.S.R." It even "permitted the repatriation to their respective homelands of tens of thousands of Poles, Spaniards, Greeks and so forth. Yet Soviet Jews are denied the right to resettle in Israel." Javits' statement ended with a warning to the Soviets and their satellites that "the world judges not merely by words but by deeds."[80]

Representative Kenneth B. Keating, also of New York, told the House of Representatives about a B'nai B'rith Anti-Defamation League Report[81] that compared "the Communist repression of the Jews to that of the Nazis during Hitler's reign of terror." After reading the ADL report Keating had asked the U.S. Ambassador to the U.N. Henry Cabot Lodge "to spotlight before the whole world the perfidy of the Soviet Union" in regard to human rights. In his letter to Lodge, Keating said that the U.S. should "take the lead in exposing this matter before the world," for this was "another opportunity for the United States to reaffirm its moral and democratic leadership of the Free World."[82]

Another New York Representative, Robert B. Barry, raised the issue of Jewish emigration in the House in April 1959. After making his main point, namely that emigration was the sole possible solution to the Soviet Jewish anomaly, Congressman Barry read a public address by Zionist Revisionist leader Joseph Schechtman into the *Record*, to bring it to "the attention of the Nation." Schechtman's address concluded by contending that, "instead of a long litany of complaints . . . Jewish national bodies must concentrate on a single powerful idea: that the Soviet Union allow those among its Jewish citizens who wish to leave the country, to do so freely." Even though *Izvestiia* recently blasted as "provocative fabrications and badly smelling concoctions all Western reports that Moscow might permit some of its Jews to leave for Israel," this should be comprehended in the context of its desire to keep the friendship of the Arabs; no fundamental reasons for opposing *aliya* had been given. Therefore, "what is needed now and is long overdue is not an intricate set of piled-up grievances and claims, but one single, clear and simple, even primitive, all-embracing postulate, which would offer a radical and uniform solution to the Jewish problem in the Soviet Union, 'Let my people go'."[83]

On the day designated by a U.N. General Assembly resolution to mark the advent of World Refugee Year, New York Congressman Seymour Halpern asked Congress to focus attention on the plight of Soviet Jews, who were "seeking the only means left to them by which they can preserve their basic way of life and retain their ties with the West – emigration." Reiterating Schechtman almost verbatim, Halpern demanded that "wornout phrases, grievances and demands for concessions that would serve to intensify Soviet efforts to reduce the Jews to some sort of conformity with the mass of the population" be discarded. For it was not "worthwhile" to demand the return of a Yiddish press that was communist, and "the lot of the Jews will never be improved until the Soviet Government permits those Jews who wish to leave to emigrate." Referring to the *Izvestiia* article, Halpern pointed out that since Arab countries had allowed their Jews to leave, Moscow "would have no difficulty in countering any Arab protests over the mass emigration of Jews to Israel."

"The time has come to throw off the layers of demands, grievances and claims that have only been ignored and passed over by the Soviet Government. There is a good chance that the formulation of a bold and dramatic plan providing a thorough solution to [Moscow's] unsuccessful efforts to manage its Jewish minority would be accepted by the Soviet rulers ... The next few years will witness one of the most inspiring and heartwarming scenes – that of the departure of hundreds of thousands of Jews from a country of persecution and discrimination to a land of freedom and opportunity. The opportunity is here for the governments and communities of the free world to support and aid in the realization of this goal."[84]

Although the call for Soviet Jewish emigration was not reiterated in the period that followed, the Soviet Jewish situation remained a current item in the *Congressional Record*. Shocked at hearing about the persecution of Soviet Jews in view of Khrushchev's vehement denials of the existence of "such discrimination" during his 1959 visit to the U.S., Representative Alvin M. Bentley of Michigan read a *Life* magazine article by Patricia Blake into the *Record*. Ms. Blake, who had spent two months in the USSR, noted in her article that synagogues had been closed and "prayer-meetings ... raided" in the past months, while newspaper articles attacked Jews as "'thieves' and 'enemies of socialism'. In this climate of official attack," she went on, "hoodlums have felt free to stone and set fire to synagogues [and] Jews have been severely beaten up and even killed." The *Life* correspondent also told of the primitive conditions under which Moscow's very small *yeshiva* functioned, the students poring over "antique volumes ... in nooks under staircases, in corridors, in the basement." One Russian Gentile had told her that if other religions were the opium of the people, Judaism was treated "as if it were poison gas." And a middle-aged teacher in a small town informed her that whereas before the war he had had many Gentile friends, today he was totally shunned, that Stalin had discovered what "fine scapegoats Jews made," first for the horrors of the war and then for "the horrors of peace in the Soviet Union."[85]

Congressman Bentley also read into the *Record* the memorandum that Rabbi Richard C. Hertz of Detroit had prepared and presented to the White House just prior to Khrushchev's visit. Hertz had returned from his summer 1959 visit to the Soviet Union convinced that "the secrecy enshrouding Soviet handling of the Jewish question" had been broken through. He especially wanted to expose "the lack of good faith" of the Soviet leaders in the sphere of their Jewish policy that was "transparently demonstrated" by "the discrepancies and inconsistencies between publicly announced Soviet goals and actual reality," and to point out to Eisenhower that the Soviets' anxiety for "peace and friendship" with Washington made them vulnerable to U.S. expressions of concern at the situation. He therefore presented a list of actions that the U.S. or American organizations could take, and asked the president to "express the moral concern of American Jews over the lot of Soviet Jews" when he met with Khrushchev.[86]

In February 1960 New York Congressman Leonard Farbstein introduced a resolution "That it is the sense of the Congress that the President of the United States should direct the United States delegation to the United Nations to urge the Union of Soviet Socialist Republics to take such steps as may be necessary to restore to the Jewish people residing [there] the full liberties guaranteed them under the Soviet Constitution, including freedom of speech, freedom of expression, and freedom of religion."[87]

Senator Thomas J. Dodd of Connecticut, who had devoted two full days of the Select Committee to Investigate Communist Aggression and Forced Incorporation of the Baltic States into the USSR hearings to Soviet Jewish policy, protested that the West "closes its eyes" to Moscow's persecution of its Jews. Instead of "protests and indignation, we witness demands for increased trade . . . for stepped-up cultural exchange programs, for state visits." Dodd decried the fact that despite "a whole series of studies by scholarly authorities" on the subject, as well as two congressional reports, "the terrifying story of persecution of the Jews under communism has not penetrated the public consciousness of the free world." Checking through "the available documentation," the senator had been appalled by the "totality of Soviet anti-Semitism, by its utter ruthlessness, by its doctrinal and practical similarity to Nazi anti-Semitism," and by how little he himself and his friends knew "about this terrible crime against humanity which has been going on for more than two decades." Labeling former protests ineffective despite the few Soviet concessions, which he attributed to "the furor" that had arisen in the world communist movement, Dodd demanded: "Let us raise our voices against the inhuman persecution of the Jews ... and let us use our offices at every opportunity to persuade the Soviet leaders to grant equality of treatment to their Jewish subjects."[88]

In the same context, Congressman Bentley said that "as long as silence is maintained, the gradual liquidation of Jewry goes on." Bentley was convinced that the Soviet Union was "the source of the strongest anti-Semitic agitation in the world ... promoting anti-Semitism both inside its own borders by a determined program of discrimination against Soviet Jews and outside the Soviet Union by means of propaganda and incitement of emotionally unbalanced individuals to action."[89]

In spring 1961 Kenneth Keating returned to the subject from the floor of the Senate (to which he had been elected in 1958), putting three articles by Rabbi Stuart E. Rosenberg of Toronto into the *Record*. Rosenberg, who visited the Soviet Union "to speak with my fellow Jews and to hear with my own ears what they had to say about their life in the Soviet Union," insisted that the West must expose Soviet hypocricy and cynicism "toward those who cannot defend themselves" by using "every public forum, every legal and just means."[90] Senator Dodd returned to the fray by denouncing the UNESCO *Courier* for omitting any mention of the Soviet Union's persecution of minorities "especially of the Jewish people," from its October 1960 issue dedicated to fighting racism. Dodd, who had taken up the matter with U.S. ambassador to the U.N. James J. Wadsworth, and had sent a copy of his letter to the Secretary of State, had eventually received a reply from Assistant Secretary of State for Congressional Relations Brooks Hays to the effect that UNESCO took the stand that it could not "recognize or report on such persecutions" within Soviet territory since the USSR denied that its minorities were persecuted. Not satisfied with this position, the State Department had informed UNESCO's Director General that the U.S. government did not "consider the formula used by UNESCO for the selection of problems as a valid and reliable one since it is bound to favor closed as opposed to open societies." Dodd added that if UNESCO persisted in this stance, he would suggest that the U.S. withdraw from that body.[91]

Early in 1962 Senator Javits addressed himself from the floor of the Senate to the escalated anti-Jewish campaign in the USSR, demanding loud and ubiquitous protest against Soviet treatment of Jews. He had recently returned from a visit to the USSR, to which he had traveled in his capacity as member of the Foreign Economic Policy Subcommittee of the Senate Joint Economic Committee, and where he had brought up "the state of the Jews and of Jewish life and culture . . . a matter of great interest in the United States and elsewhere in the free world" with all those he met. Javits began his speech by discussing the Soviet leaders' "double standard of thought and action toward Soviet Jews, which places them in a unique and unprecedented category." Yet, despite the Jews' fear, despite Soviet political, religious, cultural, social and professional discrimination, and despite the Kremlin's determination to isolate them from the Jewish world outside, "2,268,000 persons voluntarily declared themselves to be Jews in the January 1959 census." Javits quoted from the Soviet trade union newspaper *Trud* of 19 January 1962 to the effect that "the subversive activity of members of the Israeli embassy against the Soviet Union is conducted with the knowledge of the Israeli government and on the orders of their transoceanic masters." Javits contended that Jews were being linked with foreign agents in the Soviet media in order to "develop and inculcate in the hearts of their countrymen" a sense of hostility toward "a whole group of people on the bare allegation that they are allies, in some way, with foreign powers threatening the security of their own country." In Javits' opinion, the immediate intention of the Leningrad trial of Pecherskii and his colleagues was "to warn Jews that [the USSR] will not tolerate any emigration of Jews to Israel or any pro-Israel agitation toward that end."

Since "the long-range purpose" was "the liquidation of Judaism and Jewish consciousness in the U.S.S.R.," Javits considered that the world should "protest in the most distinct manner, especially bearing in mind the sensitivity of the leaders of the Soviet Union to any charge of anti-Semitism and the pride which they take in the fact that they live in an allegedly classless, unbigoted country." In order that the protest be effective, Javits pleaded for increased contact between the two sides. For example, many members of the USSR Supreme Soviet, who were "regarded as influential people in the Soviet Union," wished to come to the U.S., and Javits believed that "exposure" of such individuals to American society and government processes would operate in favor of the U.S. without jeopardizing American security.

Javits made his appeal to the Senate as a "forum in which ideas of freedom, including protests against its deprivation, and a sense of denunciation of injustice, have always found a great receptivity." He pointed out that although there was no forum to disclose the facts, to draw conclusions or to lodge protest in the USSR itself, except "at the peril of one's liberty and life," he hoped that "because of the unanimous view of the free world and the sense of outrage which it feels," his protest would "break through even the hard shell placed around the Soviet Union by those who hold its destinies."[92]

A month later, Javits told the Senate that the Soviet authorities were not only using the Jews to "warn the people against currency speculation in black markets," but that the "very calculated effort ... to identify Jews as enemies of the Soviet people ... the scattered geographic pattern of the press reports and the careful labeling [and stereotyping] of Jewish principals make it patently clear that Jews are being used as major characters in a Soviet morality play." Referring to a Jewish Minority Research report entitled *Discrimination against Judaism in the Soviet Union*, Javits charged that only with regard to Jews and Judaism "is the theme of subversion, lack of patriotism and disloyalty injected into official antireligious propaganda."[93]

Again calling the attention of the Senate to persecution of Jews in the Soviet Union, Senator Keating urged "the American people and American organizations" to "take more of a stand on this issue." In this respect, he appealed to the U.S. government to "publicly air the facts ... before United Nations Committees and at the General Assembly." Keating was particularly incensed by the "fanatic Russian nationalism" that lay behind the association of Soviet Jewish interest in Israel with virtual treason. In an article in the *New York Times* (8 February 1962), which Keating asked to be inserted in the *Congressional Record*, Harrison Salisbury maintained that antisemitism was being revived in the USSR, attributing this revival to "aggressive official propaganda against the Jewish religion" which blurred "the boundary between anti-religion and anti-Semitism." Komsomol gangs, which had in the past been "thrown into action" against the Russian Orthodox Church and liberal youth groups, were now being "mobilized to intimidate and browbeat Jewish communities." Salisbury also discussed Soviet "hypersensitivity" to the Zionist question, especially when contacts between Jewish communities and Israeli representatives had "rapidly broadened and deepened" with the general liberalization. Although there was "no sign that any of the Israeli activities were anything but perfectly legal," he concluded, "the Soviet security forces and its propaganda affiliates" had publicly accused the Israeli embassy of espionage, and had recently taken administrative measures against people who had "social and cultural contacts with Israeli diplomats."[94]

In February 1962 Congressman Charles A. Buckley of New York submitted a resolution to the House of Representatives requesting that President Kennedy "convey to the Soviet Union an expression of the grave concern" of the American people at "this growing anti-Semitism"; "urge the Soviet Union to allow all Jewish persons . . . who wish to do so to emigrate and to seek refuge and salvation in Israel and other free lands"; and "to take all possible immediate steps . . . to bring before the United Nations and before the bar of world opinion the facts about the cruel mistreatment of Jewish people within the Soviet Union, to the end that such maltreatment shall cease."[95]

Just a few days later Congressman Farbstein submitted a similar, concurrent resolution along with a second one proposing that the U.N. Human Rights Commission "give greater publicity to instances of discrimination and persecution" against Jews so as to "focus world opinion" upon them, since "whatever limitations" the Kremlin had placed on its "current anti-Jewish programs stem directly from fear of adverse world opinion."[96]

The U.S. administration was much less open to the issue of Soviet Jewry. A letter from Javits to Secretary of State Dean Rusk, to "find out what the facts really are" in view of the lessons of "the experience of recent years," elicited a reply from Assistant Secretary Frederick G. Dutton to the effect that the State Department was unable to determine whether the Soviet population's "potential for anti-Semitism" was being used by the authorities for their own ends. Nor was it clear whether "police action" against individual Jews emanated from anti-semitism or from an attempt "to stamp out black marketeering and various forms of speculation." There was no doubt that the Soviets were conducting an anti-religious campaign, but the Department had been "unable to confirm that any synagogues have been closed."

Although the U.S. government was "deeply concerned about oppressive Soviet policies," it was "difficult for our Government to contribute to the direct solution of the problem of minorities" within Soviet territory. Instead Dutton recommended "appropriate publicity in this country on the initiative of religious groups themselves, without any reference to the U.S. Government . . . Private appeals to the Soviet Government on humane grounds would minimize the possibility of confusing the Soviet Jewish problem with cold war issues."[97]

Senator Keating, who corresponded with the State Department on this same issue, received two communications from Dutton which led him to conclude, to his consternation, that the U.S. government had "done nothing or little about this very pressing problem" over recent months. This "confession of inactivity, and perhaps, although I sincerely hope not, even of disinterest on the issue of Soviet anti-Semitism . . . deeply disappointed" the Senator, whose concern over the economic trials, the prohibition on baking *matzot* and the refusal to permit Jewish emigration, combined with his frustration at the administration's failure "to mobilize the pressure of world opinion against these outrages," led him also to approach U.S. ambassador to the U.N. Adlai Stevenson, urging the latter to insist that the U.N. Human Rights Commission hold "an immediate hearing and investigation into these developments."[98]

Javits, too, kept on badgering the State Department until it finally admitted that there was clear evidence of "discriminatory measures against Jews" in higher education, and that "desecration of [Jewish] cemeteries, closing of synagogues, dispersing of prayer meetings, arrest of lay leaders, prohibition of certain religious practices, and so forth, have been well established," and that there were signs of "increased sensitivity to charges of anti-Semitism."[99]

Despite its growing awareness of the severity of the situation, the State Department continued to bear the brunt of congressional criticism for its ineffectiveness and inactivity. In July 1962 Keating told the Senate that, in his view, "the perfect opportunity now exists for the United States to exert some leadership on this very serious problem." Keating urged the administration to instruct the new ambassador to Moscow, Foy Kohler, to place the Jewish situation "high on his agenda of talks with the Russians"; to exert all his influence "to express the vital concern of the American people in this problem and to exercise all the moral suasion possible to bring about some amelioration" of the Soviet Jewish condition. The matter was of "very real concern and importance not only to the millions of American Jews . . . but also to the 180 million Americans of all races and religions who believe in the world of brotherhood, the dignity of man, and the liberties which have given our Nation its enduring strength."[100]

Referring to the recent nomination of Veniamin Dymshits, the sole Soviet Jew to enjoy a senior government position, to the posts of

Chairman of Gosplan and Deputy Premier, Javits stressed that Dymshits' appointment in no way answered the charges that had been leveled in Congress. Javits said that it must not therefore be allowed to divert attention from them; he also pointed out, however, that the appointment was further proof of Soviet sensitivity to accusations of antisemitism, demonstrating that "world opinion is a force that the Soviet rulers must reckon with."[101]

Another Senator who addressed himself to the Soviet Jewish situation was Homer E. Capehart of Indiana, who suggested that just as attitudes to their Jewish minority had been indicators of the "whole nature" of governments in the past, "the current treatment" of Soviet Jews should serve as a yardstick for testing recent Soviet "assertions that they are undergoing a genuine change to a more humanitarian government and open society." Capehart took issue with the Soviet jurist who asked the *New York Times* why being Jewish was such an "aggravating" circumstance that it merited special treatment. The senator from Indiana also considered fallacious Soviet reasoning that "bonds of brotherhood" between Jews "must be political in nature, and . . . imply a special political loyalty to Zionism and the State of Israel," which automatically renders a Jew a "poor security risk and disloyal citizen." He pointed out that the Jews' "special feelings of comradeship . . . never conflicted" with their "civic and political" loyalty to their countries, especially in states where they were treated "equally with anyone else." The Soviets' "xenophobic and unfounded suspicions" were "a reversion to one of the ugliest features of czarist . . . society" and would not be beneficial to the Soviet Union itself.[102]

While protest was not restricted to Congress, or even to the U.S., the attacks on Soviet Jewish policy from the floor of Congress were particularly telling. Soviet reactions, both direct and oblique, left no doubt on this score.

### Direct succor to Soviet Jewry

The two main goals of the struggle in the West on behalf of Soviet Jewry described so far were arousing the West's awareness of the Soviet Jewish plight and voicing protests in order to influence the Kremlin to ameliorate the Jews' position. Yet there was a third plane of action no less important: the effort to strengthen the morale and even the material well-being of Soviet Jews. Western Jews were determined that their Soviet brethren know they would not be left to suffer persecution in isolation from the rest of the Jewish world. In this respect, the dispatch of all kinds of parcels, particularly *matzot*, and of Western Jewish and Israeli tourism to the USSR were of vital importance.

Here, too, the second half of 1957 was in many ways a watershed. The Youth Festival of that year (see chapter 7) showed beyond question that a large number of Jews associated themselves with Israel in one way or another. The various delegations of the previous year had put the entire Soviet Jewish issue squarely in the awareness of Western public opinion. Now, reports about it and the publicity given to the manifestations of identity with Israel by those who returned from the Festival, brought a new urgency and impetus to the campaign in the West. The poignant contact with Soviet Jews, whose almost pathetic belief that Israel could and would help them, in conjunction with the subsequent intensification of attacks on Israel and Jews in the Soviet media, brought home the need for Israel and world Jewry to try to provide the requisite succor.

Tourists from Israel, especially Russian speakers who had gone to Palestine prior to World War I or in the first years after its termination when emigration was still relatively easy, aroused the confidence of the local Jews. Moreover, since they were often permitted to visit towns beyond the normal reach of official delegations and came into contact with strata of the population who did not usually associate with foreigners, they became vehicles of support (as well as of information which might otherwise have remained unknown).[103] Israelis and other Western Jews on professional missions also often had opportunity to meet local Jews whom the Israeli diplomats did not normally encounter, those who were successful in their jobs, had acculturated and felt part of the Soviet establishment. Even among this group there were many who knew a lot about Israel, listened to Israeli broadcasts and could not restrain themselves from letting loose on the subject when they found themselves alone in the presence of Israelis or Western Jews.[104]

Another major aspect of boosting the morale of Soviet Jews was the relaying to the USSR of Israeli and other Western broadcasts, some of them in Yiddish. Just as the preparation of information concerning Soviet Jewry and its dissemination in the West were a prerequisite for a convincing and effective campaign on their behalf in the countries of the free world, so the broadcasting of information about Israel and world Jewry directly to the USSR was an important means of enabling Soviet Jews to feel a living contact with the Jewish world outside and the Jewish state in particular.

Until 1957 Israeli broadcasts to the Soviet Union had been limited to Hebrew, Yiddish and a few West European languages.[105] Even though these languages could be understood by only a relatively select minority, constant requests were received through various channels to include more descriptions of everyday life in Israel and more songs, both secular and religious, to improve conditions of transmission, and to extend the Hebrew broadcasts to more than fifteen minutes a day.[106]

Growing evidence that Jews throughout the Soviet Union were listening to broadcasts from Israel[107] led the Israelis to initiate Russian-language broadcasts in early 1958. Since 1957 Kol Zion lagola had been adding Russian explanations to the Hebrew lessons being broadcast to Eastern Europe with French and English explanations. Aside from giving Soviet Jews the moral backing they so badly needed, these Russian-language broadcasts were designed to bring them into closer touch with Israeli life and reality, in the belief that an up-to-date, intimate knowledge of events and developments in Israel would help reinforce their Jewish identity. It was also hoped that these broadcasts would give them the wherewithal to refute the massive attacks on Israel in the Soviet press both in their own minds and in their conversations with each other.

Despite the obvious need, Russian-language broadcasts got off to a slow start. The first program was broadcast on Israel's Independence Day 1958. It was followed by broadcasts on the fall festivals and other special dates. But it was not until the new decade that there began to be weekly broadcasts every Saturday night. Soon after this was increased to twice weekly (Friday and Saturday evenings), then to four broadcasts a week, and finally, in 1964, to daily programs. Interestingly, the Russian-language broadcasts were not subject to jamming, perhaps because they were not announced in any of the printed programs of Israel's broadcasting services.[108]

In early 1962 a major effort was made to improve the content of these broadcasts, mainly due to the efforts of Yaacov Yankelevich (Yanai), who emigrated to Israel via Poland, where he had been "repatriated" from the Western Ukraine by virtue of a fictitious marriage. After his release from prison camp (where he had been since 1947), and prior to his return to the western part of the country, Yankelevich had spent six months in Omsk, Western Siberia. Both in Omsk and in the western towns of Rovno and Lutsk he had been a dedicated listener to Kol Zion lagola's Hebrew and Yiddish broadcasts. While accepting the basic guideline of all Israeli-initiated communications concerning and addressed to Soviet Jewry, namely that they be strictly factual and informational, Yankelevich thought that a lot more should be done to make the broadcasts more professional and more in tune with the specific needs of their audience. This meant not only that the emphasis be transferred to broadcasting in Russian, but that the timing, frequency, form and content be adapted to the requirements of the Soviet Jewish population. Yankelevich therefore urged that the broadcasts be transmitted daily, even several times a day, and proposed that they be divided into subjects so that listeners could listen to those that interested them. This was especially important to many of the younger Jews who taped the broadcasts, particularly the songs and Hebrew lessons. Finally, Yankelevich pushed for more careful enunciation in the Hebrew and Yiddish broadcasts in order to help overcome difficult listening conditions as well as the lack of enough knowledge of these languages to understand quick or slurred speech.[109]

In addition to the broadcasts, the Israelis were beginning to give thought to the preparation of written materials designed specifically for the needs and tastes of the Soviet Jewish population. The most important of these were dictionaries and Hebrew-language primers for those who sought to learn Hebrew; Jewish calendars; and Russian-language journals and books that would convey to the Soviet Jewish public something of Israel's atmostphere and bring them into direct touch with an authentic version of its problems and achievements, challenges and aspirations.

One of the most urgent needs was for a Hebrew primer intended *a priori* for the use of Soviet Jews, who could not resort to dictionaries, let alone friends or neighbors, when they did not understand something. Aharon Rozen's *Elef millim* (A Thousand Words), the first edition of which had appeared in 1954–55, was in great demand and was supplied whenever possible by Israeli diplomats and visiting delegations. Yet its size presented something of a problem; so, too, did its carefree text. In the early 1960s Shaul Avigur asked Shlomo Kodesh of the Israeli Ministry of Education, who was the author of a number of books for the study of Hebrew, to prepare a primer that would overcome these restrictions. The book had to be small enough to fit into a pocket and must not contain any references to which the Soviet authorities might take exception. It finally appeared in 1963 under the name *Hasafa ha'ivrit* (The Hebrew Language).[110] The first of two parts of L.I. Riklis' *Mori* (My Teacher), a teach-yourself textbook for the study of Hebrew, was translated into Russian and distributed in the Soviet Union at about the same time. Designed for people who knew no Hebrew and little about Judaism, it contained useful hints about Judaism, Israel and great Jewish personalities.[111]

Jewish calendars, which Jews needed in order to know the dates both of Jewish festivals and of the anniversaries of the death of their closest kin when the *kaddish*, the prayer for the departed, is recited, also became a major source of information about Israel. The first calendar in Russian for the use of Soviet Jewry appeared in February 1956 and was followed by a number of calendars in different formats, giving a great deal of information besides the basic data usually provided. The calendar for the year 5720 (1959/60) contained eight pages of the most important dates in Jewish history since the Exodus, a page on Israel's balance of payments, and another with "some statistical information on Israel's development." A calendar-album for the years 5721–24 (1960/1–1963/4) contained pictures of the first Zionist Congress; of Ben Gurion declaring the establishment of the State of Israel; and of Israeli stamps; a map of Israel; the words and music of *Hatikva*; the letters of the Hebrew (and Yiddish) alphabet; and, like most calendars, the prayer for the departed.[112]

An interesting side benefit of the Israeli calendars was that they compelled the Soviet authorities to backtrack on the restrictions they had placed on the production of calendars within the USSR. For years no Jewish calendar had been produced there apart from a few handwritten copies prepared and distributed clandestinely. But once the Israeli calendars with their considerable additional material began to circulate, the major synagogues in Moscow and Leningrad were allowed to put out their own, which contained only the most basic data and were clearly a lesser evil. These calendars were sold in the synagogues and sent to Jewish communities throughout the country.[113]

Toward the end of the 1950s *Vestnik Izrailia*, a monthly Russian-language journal about Israel and world Jewry, began appearing designed especially for Jews in the Soviet Union.[114] Publications such as this were particularly useful in countering the anti-Israel publications that were appearing in the USSR with increasing frequency in the last years of the decade.[115] After nearly four years of existence *Vestnik Izrailia* was replaced by *Shalom*, "a socio-literary journal."[116] As of early 1962 *Ariel*, "a quarterly review of the arts and sciences in Israel," published by the Israeli Foreign Ministry, also began appearing in Russian.[117] All these materials were extremely important in bringing Israel's message to Soviet Jews as of the late 1950s and, as we shall see, throughout the period until 1967.

The struggle on behalf of Soviet Jewry in general and on behalf of its right to emigrate in particular made significant strides in the West in the late 1950s and early 1960s. The issues at stake became clarified, the possibilities for effective action were explored and developed and more numerous and politically significant groupings and individuals became involved.

First and foremost, Soviet sensitivity on the Jewish issue was highlighted. On the theoretical level, there was the manifest contradiction between the Marxist-Leninist doctrine of proletarian internationalism and the equality and brotherhood of nations and actual Soviet Jewish policy. And, on the more practical plane, there was the process of disintegration being undergone by Western communist movements in the wake of the traumatic impact of de-Stalinization and the Twentieth Party Congress, in which the revelations concerning Soviet Jewry played a definite role. As was pointed out, for example, in the special September 1959 issue of *New Leader* dedicated to the Soviet Jewish problem, the Soviets could never admit that their policy toward the Jews was discriminatory, since this would be tantamount to confessing the existence of a sharp clash between Soviet reality, on the one hand, and Marxism-Leninism and their constitution, on the other. It might even cause difficulties in the realm of foreign policy, where Moscow was pressing its claim to be the champion of disadvantaged minorities in both capitialist countries and in the newly independent Third World states, many of which still considered themselves the object of colonialist discrimination. Yet, the facts were so stark and were becoming so well-known that denials seemed increasingly absurd and counterproductive. Indeed, the evasiveness of the regime's spokesmen when faced with questions about Soviet Jewry was a gauge of their dilemma and embarrassment. The foregoing notwithstanding, the Kremlin had proved unable to change either its policy or the tacit assumption on which it was based, namely that the Jews were a potentially or actually disloyal group, despite the obloquy this brought them in the international arena and its boomerang effect on the domestic scene. For the fact was that the Jews were developing a greater Jewish group consciousness and were becoming more rather than less alienated from the regime in reaction to the measures being taken against them.

Secondly, it was becoming clear in the West that despite de-Stalinization Soviet Jews continued to be constrained upon to withhold their demands for greater rights and their protest against their humiliating situation, and therefore it was for their brethren abroad to speak out on their behalf as openly and as frequently as might be politically expedient and not be sidetracked by the tongue-in-cheek statements of First Secretary Khrushchev and his colleagues.

Although many of the people who visited the Soviet Union at this time in one capacity or another returned with a desire to "do something" for the Jews there and others who developed an interest in their plight committed themselves to action on their behalf, there were differences of opinion as to what foreign Jews and other well-wishers could or should do. Yet they all agreed that Soviet Jewry needed the moral support inherent in the knowledge that the Jewish and non-Jewish world outside was acting on their behalf and that Soviet sensitivity to foreign public opinion and pressure provided the opportunity for such activity.

While the struggle of the late 1950s and early 1960s began by demanding cultural expression for the Jews in their own language, as time passed it became increasingly clear that this was not going to happen. The Jews were not only not being given this expression, but were being subjected to growing cultural, religious and social discrimination instead. Thus, by the early 1960s the cry in the West, especially in Jewish circles, was increasingly for the sole alternative: letting Soviet Jews – or at least those of them who wished to – emigrate.

# 6    The outside world takes up the issue: 1963–1967

In the mid-sixties the campaign for Soviet Jewry intensified and began to arouse broad popular support. An umbrella organization was created in the U.S. to deal solely with the Soviet Jewish problem. Public demonstrations began to take place and the focus of the campaign started to move from concern and protest to commitment and action. This was also when the issue of Soviet Jewry began to permeate the international arena, appearing on the U.N. agenda and cropping up in all areas of Soviet–Western relations, including those with some of Moscow's most ardent supporters in the West. The growing consternation at the Soviet Union's treatment of its Jews, and the growing conviction that the only solution for those who wished to live a Jewish life was emigration, led the campaign to shift more pronouncedly in this direction. The effectiveness of this new shift began to be seen in December 1966, when Prime Minister Aleksei Kosygin announced, at a press conference in Paris, that the Soviet authorities would not obstruct its Jews from reuniting with their families abroad.

One sign of the new period was the publication, in January 1963, of an article by Moshe Decter in the prestigious American journal *Foreign Affairs*. In his article, entitled "The Status of the Jews in the Soviet Union," Decter, the director of Jewish Minorities Research, made the point that the severity of the Jewish problem had been delineated in Soviet poet Evgenii Evtushenko's "searing indictment of antisemitism both historically and as a facet of contemporary Soviet society," in his poem "Babii Iar."[1] Decter also pointed out that the isolation of Soviet Jewry and the discrimination it suffered were a frequent leitmotif of the "underground literature that passed from hand to hand among the university and literary youth." But, despite the sensitivity of a few members of the intelligentsia, antisemitism was still rife in the Soviet Union. This antisemitism was, he said, being abetted by media campaigns against the tenets and customs of Judaism, on the one hand, and, on the other, against economic offenders, the majority of whom were Jewish, and who, the Soviets alleged, "flit through the interstices of the economy, cunningly manipulate naive non-Jewish officials, prey upon honest Soviet workers and cheat them of their patrimony." According to Decter, this atmosphere placed the Jews "in an inextricable vise. They are allowed neither to assimilate, nor to live a full Jewish life, nor to emigrate (as many would wish) to Israel or any other place where they might live fully as Jews."[2]

Decter's article had a wide resonance among intellectuals not generally in touch with the problem of Soviet Jewry. In fact, many of those who eventually became active in the struggle credited it with awakening their interest.[3] Yet Decter's piece was far from being the sole catalyst. For, the following period saw a growing awareness of the issues at stake in both the United States and Western Europe, as an increasing number of articles began to appear in the press and in many of the most respected journals and magazines. Some of the pieces were written by Litvinoff, Decter and Korey, who were by now virtually professional propagandists for the Soviet Jewish cause; others were influenced by the information and materials provided by these three men. Of significant impact, too, were articles being written by Western correspondents in Moscow, many of whom had begun to manifest an interest in the situation. And the purport of all these pieces was generally the same: that the position of Soviet Jewry ran counter to Marxist-Leninist doctrine and the guarantees of the Soviet constitution, not to speak of the fine words of Khrushchev and his colleagues, and that the Western world, which had remained unconscionably reticent in the face of Hitler's persecution of Europe's Jews, had the moral obligation to come to their rescue now, before they were exterminated spiritually in the Soviet Union.

The Decter article brought the Soviet Jewish problem to the political and academic community. But the headlines that followed publication of the correspondence between Khrushchev and British philosopher Bertrand Russell on the subject brought it to the population at large, including Soviet citizens, since it was published in both the West and the USSR. At Moscow's request, a letter from Russell to Khrushchev, as well as the latter's reply, appeared in the British press on 25 February 1963 and in *Pravda* and *Izvestiia* several days later. The correspondence had opened with a telegram on the situation of Soviet Jewry sent to the Soviet leader early in 1962 by Russell, French Catholic writer François Mauriac and Martin Buber. When no reply was received, Russell pressed for one in further letters. In the last of these, the one to which Khrushchev answered, Russell wrote that he was "deeply perturbed at the death sentences passed on Jews . . . and the official encouragement of antisemitism which apparently takes place." In his reply Khrushchev expressed his surprise that the execution of criminals who violated socialist legality and morals was being attributed to antisemitism on the basis that there happened to be a large number of Jews among those executed. The punishment for a crime, he assured Russell, was "determined by the nature of that particular crime and . . . has nothing to do with the nationality" of its perpetrator. Although "reactionary propaganda" has also imputed antisemitism "or the encouragement of it" to the Soviet state in the past, "there has not been, nor is there, any policy of antisemitism in the Soviet Union, since the very character of our multi-national, socialist state precludes the possibility of such a policy." The Soviet constitution, the First Secretary went on, "declares that 'any advocacy of racial or national exclusiveness or hatred or contempt is punishable by law'." The USSR had always educated its citizenry "in the spirit of the friendship and brotherhood of all peoples . . . and intolerance of national and racial hostility."[4]

As a number of Western papers were quick to point out, Khrushchev's statement that the USSR had not pursued an antisemitic policy presumably meant that the Kremlin had no intention of redressing the wrongs done to the Jews and their culture during Stalin's last years. And this, in turn, meant that the growing opposition to Moscow's Jewish policy among the Soviet intelligentsia was likely to have little practical impact, especially since Khrushchev had debated with intellectuals and artists on this point on 17 December 1962 and again on 8 March 1963, shortly after his correspondence with Russell was published. Lord Russell indicated his dissatisfaction with the First Secretary's reply in a two-page letter dated 5 March 1963.[5] And when *Izvestiia* published letters signed by four Soviet Jewish citizens on 24 March claiming that Soviet Jews enjoyed individual equality of opportunity, Russell wrote directly to the editor. After waiting ten weeks for *Izvestiia* to publish this letter, Russell finally released its text. Emphasizing his friendship for the Soviet Union, he said that "One of the tests of true friendship is the ability to speak frankly without fear of being taken for an enemy or of being misunderstood." He then expressed his concern at the difficulties Jews were encountering "in the pursuit of their beliefs," as well as at the articles in Soviet journals expressing hostility toward "Jewish people as such." Russell was also troubled by the fact that 60 percent of those receiving the death penalty for economic offenses were Jews. He concluded: "I fervently hope that nothing will take place which obliges us to believe that Jews are receiving unjust treatment in contradiction to the law . . . I cannot too strongly appeal for understanding of the difficulty experienced by those in the West who are working dedicatedly to ease tension, promote peaceful co-existence, and to end the Cold War."[6]

Despite the unsatisfactory nature of Khrushchev's reply to Russell's earlier letter, the very fact that it was published in the USSR, and in the West upon Soviet initiative, demonstrated once again how sensitive Moscow was becoming to pressure on the Jewish question, particularly when voiced by its supporters in the West. It also showed that the Soviet leadership was keenly aware that the Jewish problem was growing to the point where it was affecting Soviet diplomacy. Indeed, Soviet officials frequenting Western capitals in these years were constantly plagued by questions and protests concerning Soviet Jewish policy, often to their visible chagrin. When Gromyko arrived in Sweden in spring 1964, Swedish television broadcast a program on Trofim Kichko's *Judaism without Embellishment*, while Khrushchev's own tour of Scandinavia later that year provoked demonstrations and other manifestations of dissatisfaction with the USSR's Jewish policy. All this led to the obviously preplanned statement on family reunification that Premier Kosygin made when he visited Paris in December 1966. But it was not only in bilateral relations with Western countries that the Soviet Union was being trounced for its policy toward its Jews; the problem was beginning to be raised in major international forums as well.

### The United Nations[7]

The issue of human rights had been a concern of the U.N. since its inception. The Human Rights Commission, affiliated to the Economic and Social Council (ECOSOC), was set up for this purpose, as was the Third (Social and Humanitarian) Committee of the General Assembly. Yet the U.N. lacked any permanent machinery or procedure (whether comprehensive covenants or limited conventions) for considering complaints concerning specific instances of human rights violations.[8]

While in theory any U.N. member state was free to propose questions pertaining to alleged violations, few states were prepared to risk lodging a complaint against a major power for fear of retaliation.

However, despite the technical impracticability and inexpedience of dealing with human rights violations under these circumstances, the U.N. became the main forum for an international campaign against all forms of discrimination – racial, national, religious, social – the African states in particular demonstrating a tendency to use it in order to air their views on the issue of race. In the course of these discussions the U.N. had on several occasions reaffirmed the Universal Declaration of Human Rights. At its Seventeenth Session in 1962 the General Assembly considered a draft declaration and a draft convention on the elimination of all forms of racial discrimination and religious intolerance resulting from manifestations of antisemitism and other forms of racial prejudice and religious intolerance; these became Res. 1780 and 1781 (XVII). At its Eighteenth Session it unanimously adopted a declaration on the Elimination of All Forms of Racial Discrimination (Res. 1904; XVIII), and at its Nineteenth Session a draft convention on the elimination of all forms of religious intolerance was presented. The USSR had voted in favor of the Universal Declaration of Human Rights and the 1960 Declaration on Colonialism, which specified that "all states shall observe faithfully and strictly the provisions of the . . . Universal Declaration of Human Rights," as well as of the 1961 proposal and 1962 reaffirmation regarding the faithful and immediate implementation of all provisions of the Declaration of Colonialism. It also voted in favor of the International Convention on the Elimination of All Forms of Racial Discrimination and of the International Covenant on Civil and Political Rights that was adopted in December 1966. The latter two documents, as well as the Universal Declaration on Human Rights, all make specific mention of the right to leave any country, including one's own.

It was only natural, therefore, for the U.N. to become one of the most important arenas for the struggle on behalf of Soviet Jewry, especially when the Human Rights Commission's Sub-Commission on Prevention of Discrimination and Protection of Minorities provided a special framework for discussing the right of emigration. However, since the offensive at the U.N., as at other forums during this period, interlaced that right with the struggle for cultural and religious rights, it is necessary to look at both issues simultaneously in order to comprehend the development of the struggle for emigration in its true perspective.

Seymour Halpern of the U.S. alluded to the USSR's Jewish policy early in 1960, during a Sub-Commission discussion on Arcot Krishnaswami of India's "Study of Discrimination in the Matter of Religious

Rights and Practices." In the process of taking issue with his Soviet counterpart on Moscow's attitude toward religious practice and belief in general, Halpern suggested that Krishnaswami's report be amplified to include "discrimination in regard to the security of the person," the need for which had been demonstrated by recent antisemitic attacks in various parts of the world.[9]

Among the most important approaches to the various U.N. bodies, officials and delegations were those by the five Jewish non-governmental organizations (NGOs). These five – the Coordinating Board of Jewish Organizations (CBJO), comprising B'nai B'rith and the British and South African Boards of Jewish Deputies; the Consultative Council of Jewish Organizations, consisting of the American Jewish Committee, the Anglo-Jewish Association and the Alliance Israelite Universelle; the World Jewish Congress; the orthodox Agudas Israel World Organization; and the reform World Union for Progressive Judaism – together with over one hundred other NGOs, enjoyed consultative status at the U.N. and participated as observers at the discussions of its various committees and commissions.

In January 1961, following the submission to the Sub-Commission on Prevention of Discrimination and Protection of Minorities of a CBJO report to the effect that the Jews of the USSR were being deprived of outlets for religious, cultural and educational expression,[10] Soviet delegate V. I. Sapozhnikov referred to "the activities of certain American Zionist organizations" which were "circulating vile slanders against the Soviet Union." Sapozhnikov went on to say that in his country "the Jews, like other minorities, enjoyed all social, economic, political and religious freedoms, with no discrimination whatsoever." He also pointed out that, as racism was not confined to antisemitism, his own proposal to the Sub-Commission sought to prohibit all discriminatory racial laws and to combat the propagation of social, national or religious hatred or discrimination as well as the activities of racist organizations which fomented national, social and religious hatred.[11]

The question of the Jews' right to emigrate became a topic of debate in the context of discussions connected with the study on "discrimination in respect of the right of everyone to leave any country, including his own, and to return to his country," for which the Philippine delegate Judge José Ingles had been designated special rapporteur.[12] In the debate on some of the issues at stake, which took place early in 1961 when Ingles submitted his first progress report, Sapozhnikov took exception to information emanating from NGOs and private persons. This was in reaction to the CBJO report of October 1960, prepared by William Korey and used extensively by Ingles, according to which the Soviet Union still appeared "to make a distinction between the absolute right to leave and the specific right to leave for purposes of either the reunion of families or the reunion of ethnic groups." The Soviet delegate was further annoyed by the contention that, while the USSR had quietly allowed the emigration of about one thousand citizens of various nationalities to join relatives abroad in the half year following Vice-President Richard Nixon's appeal to Khrushchev on the subject, those who sought to leave for Israel under family reunification were denied permission to leave.[13]

When Ingles submitted his draft report in January 1962 the Soviet representative immediately brought up the question of the extent to which the right of free movement had to be subordinated to the national law of each country. U.S. delegate Halpern thereupon recalled that the Soviets had already failed to amend the original Universal Declaration of Human Rights to include "in accordance with the laws of the State," because it was generally considered that the right involved was "inherent . . . and could not be subject to national legislation." He also deplored the fact that some "larger Powers" had not yet submitted monographs in reply to the questionnaire circulated on this entire issue.[14]

At the same meeting, French delegate Jean Marcel Bouquin referred to the "unfortunate phenomenon of divided families" which sometimes resulted from "denial of the right to leave one's country." Bouquin expressed his concern that persons belonging to certain minority groups "were not allowed to leave their country if they intended to settle permanently in a country with which they had special ties." Although he noted that this was sometimes due to national security, Bouquin quoted the Ingles draft report to the effect that it was "easy for Governments to interpret and apply such limitations as they wished."[15] Polish delegate Wojciech Ketrzynski was surely elucidating the Soviet viewpoint when he noted that "the State must take action to protect its citizens against mendacious propaganda, a kind of blackmail whose sole purpose was to cause a stampede." Ketrzynski suggested that in order "to protect its nationals from the painful results of disillusionment and, in some cases, of having left without any possibility of returning . . . the State might decide to adopt measures which were discriminatory in nature because . . . the interest of society as a whole was involved."[16]

The Jewish NGOs made important contributions to the discussion;

although the terms of reference of observers and NGOs did not authorize them to mention any member state by name,[17] the reference to the Soviet Union was usually clear. This was the case, for example, when Agudas Israel's Rabbi Isaac Lewin pointed out that the draft report showed "how one of the most essential human rights . . . could be endangered by a national policy which was explained on grounds of national security or public order," and when Ralph Zacklin of the WJC supplemented Bouquin's remarks by noting that the reuniting of families and "the expatriation of a group or community to a country for which they felt a special bond for national, racial or religious or strictly sentimental reasons" were two instances in which denial of the right to leave one's country had "particularly serious consequences of a humanitarian nature."[18] Korey himself welcomed Ingles' proposal that governments be urged to "provide an effective remedy for anyone who believed that his right to leave his country had been violated or destroyed."[19] Although it, too, had a representative with observer status at the Sub-Commission, Israel was still maintaining its policy of silence on the issue of Soviet Jewry.

The entire scenario was virtually repeated at the Eighteenth Session of the Human Rights Commission (March and April 1962). But here, too, although delegates were not formally prevented from mentioning specific countries by name, as were the experts at the Sub-Commission, they usually hesitated to initiate a head-on collision with the Soviet Union, perhaps because the Soviets sought to imply that an open onslaught would be detrimental to Soviet Jews. By now it was becoming clear to at least some of the Israelis that they could not wait for third parties to overcome their oscillation, but must bear the brunt of the attack at the U.N. themselves. The desire to draw the U.N.'s attention to the plight of Soviet Jews had grown to the point where it seemed to outweigh Israel's fears that – in an arena where the Arabs and some African states took every opportunity to attack Israel and Zionism – its very intervention on behalf of Soviet Jewry would arouse irrelevant antagonism that would bring more harm than good to the cause. Yoram Dinstein, Israel's representative at both the Commission and the Sub-Commission, pressed the issue with his superiors at the Israeli Foreign Ministry,[20] insisting that most non-Jews, and certainly those Third World states with no Jewish community of their own, made no distinction between a Jewish organization such as Agudas Israel and the State of Israel. These arguments seem to have prevailed, since, from the following fall, Israeli delegates did begin to speak at various U.N. bodies and affiliated organizations.

Israeli U.N. ambassador Michael Comay took up the cudgels in October 1962 at the General Assembly's Third Committee. He entered the fray in the general debate on "manifestations of racial prejudice and national and religious intolerance" by drawing attention to the cultural and religious discrimination being suffered by "a large section of the Jewish people . . . in a country which officially recognized the identity of each ethnic, national and religious group within its borders, including the Jewish group," and in which the Jews' "helplessness" was "aggravated by the growing trend to find Jewish scapegoats for economic difficulties."[21] Australian delegate Douglas H. White backed Comay, insisting that if the Soviet Union "had difficulty in giving Jews full freedom to practice their religion," the Universal Declaration of Human Rights placed upon it "a moral obligation . . . to permit them to leave the country." Soviet representative T. N. Nikolaeva expressed her astonishment at this "undeserved attack on her country"; and when U.S. delegate Marietta Tree posed further questions to the Soviet delegation on instances of anti-Jewish discrimination, Nikolaeva and Iakov A. Ostrovskii, also of the USSR, countered with remarks on racism and fascist manifestations in the U.S.[22]

When Ingles presented his report in January 1963, he opened by pointing out those Articles from the Universal Declaration of Human Rights that had served as its basis. In addition to Article 13 (2) these were: Article 2, stating that everyone was entitled to the rights set forth in the Declaration without distinction of any kind such as race, color, sex, language, political or other opinion, national or social origin, property, birth or other status; and Article 29, giving everyone wanting to exercise his rights the right to do so subject only to those limitations determined by law for the purpose of securing respect for the rights and freedoms of others and of meeting the just requirements of morality, public order and general welfare in a democratic society. Although interests of state might be interpreted broadly, Ingles depicted the right to leave one's country as a prerequisite for other rights. Thus, someone who was prevented from leaving a country could be similarly prevented from observing the tenets of his religion, from associating with his "kith and kin" and from obtaining the education he desired. In other words, denial of this basic right "frequently gives rise to discrimination in respect of other human rights and fundamental freedoms," and in some cases "may be tantamount to the total deprivation of liberty, if not life itself." The Ingles document concluded with the contention that, when individuals who "belong to a racial, religious or other group which is being singled out for unfair treatment" are denied the right to leave, there is a "spiralling psychological effect" that leads to "a sort of collective claustrophobia."[23]

Ingles' remarks were of a totally general nature in that he did not address himself specifically to the USSR. Yet Soviet delegate Boris Ivanov charged him with having dealt with artificially created problems that were in any case the exclusive concern of sovereign states. Attempts to impose international regulations on governments in this respect might jeopardize the national interest, infringe upon national sovereignty and exacerbate tensions between states. They might encourage groups engaged in provocation against certain countries to induce mass emigration or, alternatively, open the way for the infiltration of subversive elements. Finally, Ivanov accused the Special Rapporteur of violating his injunctions by using material colored by cold war considerations to document his study, specifically information provided by the Coordinating Board of Jewish Organizations.[24]

At the continuing debate on the Ingles report Bouquin reiterated his concern over the incidental treatment accorded the reunification of families, which was also connected with discrimination. Touching on Soviet Jewry more obviously, though without making specific mention of the USSR, Maurice Perlzweig of the WJC said that, although his organization was opposed to the cold war and did not wish its comments to be misinterpreted, it hoped that governments involved in infringing the right of free movement would lift their bans on families wishing to reunite.[25] Taking up the question of whether technically qualified persons should be allowed to leave a country that needed their services, Krishnaswami of India contended that limitations on skilled personnel were only justifiable as a temporary measure.[26]

The Polish and Soviet delegates took strong exception to the question of Jewish emigration to Israel being included under the heading of religion. Apart from objecting to the source of Ingles' information, Ivanov claimed that spending time on Soviet Jewry's efforts to emigrate diverted attention from the dangerous resurgence of Nazism and rise of fascist elements which could harm Jews throughout the whole world. He also insisted that the question was moot as the number of Soviet Jews wishing to emigrate to Israel was decreasing, and that this was due to their satisfaction with life in the Soviet Union and not because they were discriminated against in regard to their right to leave the country[27] – a rare official admission that there were Jews in the Soviet Union who sought to leave. Perhaps no less important was Ivanov's statement that free emigration sometimes had to be restricted to prevent mass emigration, which seemed to allude to a Soviet hope that by enabling selective emigration they could preclude the danger of pressure for mass Jewish emigration.

Peter Calvacoressi of Britain and Morris Abram of the U.S. both disagreed with Ivanov and Ketrzynski. The former said that what mattered was not why Jews were being prevented from leaving, but that they were being prevented. And Abram pointed out that, laws to the contrary notwithstanding,[28] if there were no problem in leaving the USSR there was no reason for the Special Rapporteur never having received the text of the 1959 decree on entering into and departing from the USSR. Finally, Ingles said that the chapter containing the information provided by NGOs had to appear under either "religion" or "race" since it pertained mainly to Jewish groups. And since some members challenged the concept of race on scientific grounds, the only possibility was to present the information under religion.[29]

Following in Comay's footsteps, observer Meir Rosenne of Israel returned to the issue of family reunification, saying it was of the highest importance to his government. After World War II hundreds of thousands of Jews had found a refuge in Palestine (later Israel), which had striven to help them rebuild their family lives. The people of Israel therefore hoped that the principle of the reunion of families would be put into practice in the Soviet Union, so that those wishing to join family members who had already emigrated to Israel from the USSR or other Central and East European countries would be allowed to do so.[30]

Disputing Rosenne's contention that the Jews of the USSR would want to settle in Israel, Ivanov said that Israel had no right to consider Jews everywhere Israeli nationals.[31] Despite Ivanov's strong objection to this notion, however, one source noted that he himself often referred to the Jews' "return" to Israel when he spoke on the subject.[32] Although he never stopped insisting that any Soviet citizen could leave or return to the Soviet Union at will, in the end Ivanov voted against those parts of Ingles' report which he felt contained unwarranted recommendations to sovereign states.[33]

The next time that Israel openly identified with the question of Soviet Jewry at the U.N. was when Israeli delegate Eliezer Yapou raised the problem of Soviet anti-Jewish discrimination at the General Assembly's Third Committee in fall 1963. Speaking, he stressed, out of anxiety at "the fate of the Jewish community in one of the great countries of the world," Yapou pressed for "the study of discrimination in respect of the right of everyone to leave any country, including his own" and for speedy discussion of the Ingles report by the Human Rights Commission. Ostrovskii again voiced an objection, this time maintaining that the Israeli delegation was "obsessed by a problem which existed only in its imagination," and labeling Israel's "efforts" to become the "defender of Jews in other countries" both "tiresome" and "vain."[34]

At the subsequent session of the Sub-Commission on Prevention of Discrimination and Protection of Minorities, in the context of the discussion on the draft convention on the elimination of all forms of racial discrimination, Israel's Joel Barromi called attention to discrimination against the collective rights of nationalities, ethnic groups and communities. He therefore suggested including an article saying that "the spiritual heritage and the cultural values of a group of persons of a particular ethnic origin are entitled to legal protection as such." The need for such an article, he said, had sadly been demonstrated in Sub-Commission debates on a certain Jewish community which had been deprived of its cultural rights. Regretting that the Israeli observer's clear and unambiguous allusions to the USSR forced him to interrupt the work of the Sub-Commission with his reply, Ivanov tried to explain that Soviet law was based on principles different from Western law and that failure to understand this did not justify criticism: no one was entitled to charge the USSR with antisemitism when its constitution stipulated that discrimination based on racial or ethnic origin was punishable by law.[35]

Although Barromi's procedure resulted in Sub-Commission Chairman Herman Santa Cruz expressing the hope that charges against specific member states would not recur, this did not stop CBJO representative Label Katz from pointing out that some states – namely the one in which a Yiddish-speaking community of almost half a million had no means of cultural expression despite the UNESCO Convention against Discrimination in Education recognizing the right of national minorities to carry on educational activities – spoke of equal rights without implementing them. Barromi returned to the theme of Soviet anti-Jewish discrimination when the Sub-Commission turned to a discussion of a draft declaration and convention on the elimination of all forms of religious intolerance. He believed that a declaration of this nature should include provisions protecting freedom of worship and places of worship; freedom to use the language of a religion, to establish and operate religious institutions and to produce religious articles; freedom of education and the freedom to propagate religious ideas; and freedom of movement for religious reasons both within a given country and between countries. Barromi also called for the inclusion of a prohibition against any publication or public event intended to incite hatred against religious groups, for example articles describing the Jewish religion and Jewish ethics as mere worship of money. He concluded by stating that he was confident the general promotion of human rights would lead to bringing the *de facto* treatment of religious minorities into line with their *de jure* status.[36]

The Human Rights Commission, as well, continued to witness discussion and debates on the Soviet Jewish situation. Introducing an American proposal to include an article condemning antisemitism in the draft convention on the elimination of all forms of racial discrimination which the Commission was debating in 1964, U.S. delegate Marietta Tree insisted that "in certain of its aspects" antisemitism was discrimination based on ethnic origin. And when the Soviets proposed a sub-amendment making antisemitism "one in a list of such terms as nazism and genocide," Mrs. Tree opposed the proposal, insisting that antisemitism was being exploited "to turn groups against each other and to deflect attention from the failures of Governments."

Listing the various forms of discrimination to which Soviet Jews were subjected, Israeli Ambassador Comay said in the same forum that there were grounds for fearing that the Soviet Jewish minority was being made "the whipping-boy for general economic difficulties; the overall effect of such measures must be to arouse popular hostility against the Jews and to revive anti-Semitic feelings." Comay went on to say that Judaism was "consistently held up to ridicule, hatred and contempt in the press and in the publications of official printing houses. Citing the Kichko book as an example, Comay noted that the many thousands of copies that had been distributed constituted "a vicious smear against the history, beliefs and moral standards of the Jews and was illustrated by revolting anti-Semitic caricatures."[37]

ECOSOC (the Economic and Social Council) was a further forum in which the issue of Soviet Jewry was raised in the mid-sixties. In 1963 Jonathan Bingham of the U.S., clearly referring to the Soviet imposition of death sentences for economic offenses, suggested that a draft resolution calling on U.N. member states to study the efficacy of the death penalty as a deterrent to crime include a clause to the effect that capital punishment should not be imposed for crimes of a purely economic character.[38] In July 1964, also at ECOSOC, the head of

Israel's permanent delegation to U.N. European headquarters in Geneva, Moshe Bartur, addressed himself to the Soviet Jewish situation more directly when he told the Council that antisemitism was "still acute in some parts of the world, including the country with the largest Jewish community in Europe," where "a systematic attempt was being made . . . to bring about assimilation artificially." Referring to the contention of the government of the "powerful state in question" that this campaign was being conducted in accordance with the Jews' own wishes, Bartur wondered why, then, "Jews who wished to do so were not allowed to leave the country." Soviet delegate Vladimir Bendryshev countered with the by now standard reply that the Soviet Union had no Jewish problem and that those who invented one were "acting on the instruction of others . . . to distract attention from the racial and other forms of discrimination that were being practised . . . in other parts of the world." Bendryshev also insisted that Soviet Jews did not wish to go to Israel, and that those who had already gone wanted to return because of "the hardships they had to face there."[39]

The Sub-Commission on Prevention of Discrimination and Protection of Minorities was the scene of further acrimonious recriminations the following January, when Morris Abram of the U.S. said that, despite the fact that the new society (i.e. the USSR) was supposed to have had perfected human nature to the point where harmony between races and creeds prevailed, it nevertheless enabled the publication of Trofim Kichko's shockingly antisemitic *Judaism without Embellishment*, which had even been condemned by the communist press outside the Soviet Union.[40] After having received no reply to the copy of the book he had sent Ivanov with remarks and questions, Abram could only conclude that human nature could not be transformed by any change in economic system and that an impartial U.N. organ should be authorized to study the situation where necessary. Evgenii Nasinovskii of the USSR said that Abram's remarks attacked and misrepresented the Soviet situation. Since the absence of discrimination there was a fact backed by the force of law, Abram's statement was simply one more attempt to divert attention from the glaring facts of discrimination in the U.S.

At this same session of the Sub-Commission Israeli observer David Marmor pointed out that his government was following the discussion with profound interest because, although hundreds of thousands of Holocaust survivors had come from Eastern Europe to Israel, the Jews in the Soviet Union – where thanks to the valiant struggle against the Nazis and facilities for escape afforded them three out of five million

Jews had survived – were encountering difficulties in their efforts to reunite with their families in Israel. The Israeli government hoped the Sub-Commission would keep the item under review until a satisfactory solution, one in accordance with the Universal Declaration of Human Rights, was reached.[41] Marmor also discussed other aspects of anti-Jewish discrimination in the USSR in the context of efforts by the Sub-Commission, and later by the General Assembly, to promote human rights through eliminating discrimination in respect of employment, occupation and education as well as religious intolerance. Maintaining that Jews in the USSR had very limited opportunities for religious observance and cultural activity and expression, Marmor said that this situation was of concern to the people of Israel as well as to people of progressive and liberal opinion in many other countries.

Soviet representative Nasinovskii expressed his indignation at the Israeli observer's use of the Sub-Commission for insinuations and unfounded attacks against the USSR, where Jews participated freely in all spheres of life, including government service, science and the arts, and where religious persecution did not exist and all religions were treated equally. Moreover, many Jews did not practice their religion, as the number of believers in all faiths was decreasing there as it was in many other countries. Certainly, all religions being equal, no single faith could be privileged, and representatives of the Jewish faith could therefore hardly claim special privileges for their religion. Finally, Nasinovskii concluded, the fact that some hundreds of Jews had left the country for Israel in the past few years proved that individuals were free to choose both where and how to practice their faith.[42]

At the Twenty-first Session of the Human Rights Commission in March 1965 Justice Haim Cohn of the Israeli Supreme Court, who headed the Israeli delegation, insisted that "since the overthrow of Stalin's regime . . . matters had gone from bad to worse" with respect to the Jews. Nasinovskii termed Cohn's "allegations . . . a slanderous misrepresentation of the facts," contending that not one synagogue had been closed by the government, although "over a decade . . . about ten synagogues had discontinued their services because they no longer had any congregations." Nasinovskii's demurral notwithstanding, the Commission approved an Article on the convention for the elimination of all forms of religious intolerance which included Cohn's amendment guaranteeing every religious community the right to write, print and publish religious texts. At the same session it also adopted, for consideration by the forthcoming session of the General

Assembly, Marietta Tree's amendment to the draft convention on the elimination of all forms of racial discrimination which drew specific attention to Soviet antisemitism.[43]

Back in the Third Committee, in October 1965 Ambassador Comay labeled the Soviet proposal to amend the draft convention on the elimination of all forms of racial discrimination so that Zionism would be bracketed together with antisemitism, Nazism and neo-Nazism as forms of racial discrimination, an attempt "so to complicate the work of the Committee as to achieve the elimination from the Convention of any reference to anti-Semitism."[44]

A year later, in 1966, Israeli U.N. delegate Gershon Avner returned to the theme of Soviet Jewry in this same Committee, noting that, because Jewish history was replete with instances of prejudice, discrimination and persecution, Jews the world over were linked not only by bonds of culture and heritage but also by concern about the situation, fate and problems of every Jewish community. Avner expressed the hope that Soviet Jews would be allowed to pursue and develop their religious life and institutions, to develop their press, literature and folklore in their own language, to maintain contact with Jewish communities elsewhere and to reunite with relatives outside the USSR. When Douglas White of Australia supported Avner, as he had supported Ambassador Comay in 1962, both Mrs. V. M. Dmitruk of the Ukrainian SSR and Nasinovskii protested, the latter again taking exception to Israelis considering themselves the spokesmen of Jews everywhere and suggesting that Israel was using the issue of Soviet Jewry to distract attention from discrimination against Arabs in Israel.[45]

Also in 1966, Israeli Foreign Minister Abba Eban raised the Soviet Jewry issue briefly in a speech before the General Assembly plenary. Eban said that "countless families . . . separated and dispersed across different countries and continents . . . still cherish the hope of reunion." Moreover, Jewish communities which had survived the Holocaust had "a natural longing . . . to join together in the expression and further development of the heritage which lies at the root of their identity," and "men of good will and progressive outlook throughout the world" desired Soviet Jewry to have access to that heritage and to make contact with others who share it. In a world in which barriers were falling, the "renewal of contact between kindred communities" would be "a natural corollary of peaceful coexistence."[46]

The Sub-Commission on Prevention of Discrimination and Protection of Minorities witnessed a further Israeli–Soviet altercation on the

Soviet Jewish problem at its 1967 session, when Israeli Sub-Commission member Judge Zeev W. Zeltner addressed himself to Soviet Premier Kosygin's Paris statement on the reunification of families. Although this would be in line with the USSR's "liberal and magnanimous approach" to the problem of minorities as demonstrated in the case of the Armenians, the fact was that the Jews were not enjoying the same rights as the Armenians. Those Jews who wished to perpetuate their people's traditions and cultural heritage were not being given the same encouragement and opportunity as the members of other Soviet national and religious entities. Besides stating that such remarks violated the principles governing the Sub-Commission's work methods, Nasinovskii labeled Zeltner's observations concerning the Soviet Union a slander intended to "poison the air," mislead public opinion and distract attention from Israel's policy toward its Arab population.[47]

Justice Haim Cohn took up the issue again at the Human Rights Commission in March 1967, when he made the point that fundamental human rights were violated whenever human beings were forced "under a system of compulsory moral and political assimilation, to adopt the language, culture and religion – or irreligion – of the majority." A further remark at the same session by U.S. representative Charles H. Silver, on the refusal of certain governments to allow Jews to rejoin relatives in Israel, drew the ire of the USSR's Iakov Ostrovskii, who said that, in view of its own "aggression" in Vietnam, the U.S. had no right to raise questions of discrimination.[48]

Despite the technical and political difficulties that had to be overcome in order for debate on Soviet Jewish policies to be effective at the U.N., the very airing of the issue at this forum seemed beneficial and fruitful. Certainly the atmosphere engendered by the growing tendency to use the U.N. as an arena for expressing views on racial issues was salutary to such discussion. Moreover, the violent reaction of the Soviet delegates to discussion of the Soviet Jewish situation, their denial of the charges against their government in face of proof and documentation and their counter-charges against Western militarism, imperialism, colonialism and Zionism served to enliven the debate and attract the media's attention to the issues at stake. It also brought more Western states, and occasionally even a neutral state, to become interested in the peculiar position of Soviet Jewry.

### Other international forums

While the U.N. was certainly the most important and all-encompassing forum in which the Soviet Jewish problem was aired in the 1960s, it was by no means the only one. The Socialist International, the international communist movement, the Council of Europe and various Western parliaments and parliamentary organizations, as well as the International Commission of Jurists, also became involved. Since Mapai, Israel's Labor party, was then in power, it was only natural that it often took advantage of conventions and institutions in which it participated to voice Israeli concern at the Soviet Jewish situation. It was on these occasions that the Israeli effort to bring the Soviet Jewish plight to left-wing and liberal opinion and groupings showed that it was making its mark and bringing in dividends. True, some governments and leaders had already indicated their inclinations on this issue at the U.N., yet it was thought that their expressions of concern were likely to be more effective in the framework of the bilateral relations with the Soviets maintained by most of them. Moreover, they felt freer to voice their views on this level than at the U.N., where censure of Moscow was liable to lead to a Soviet counterattack that might involve their states in a public fracas with the USSR.

The Israelis sought to have the problem included every time the Socialist International dealt with issues such as social inequality and the residues of colonialism. They urged socialist governments to raise it collectively and individually both in public statements and in their relations with the Soviet Union. Non-ruling socialist parties were urged to demand action on behalf of Soviet Jewry in their parliaments. Thus, at its Eighth Congress, held in Amsterdam in September 1963, Moshe Sharett succeeded in convincing the Political Committee of the International to appeal to the Soviet Union "to join in wiping out any trace of anti-Jewish discrimination" and "to give consideration to the reunification of families ... in Israel and elsewhere." The Israeli delegation was supported in this by British Labour leader Harold Wilson, who told the plenary that, in consequence of his having raised the problem of Soviet Jewry on his last visit to the USSR, a number of the people he had mentioned specifically to the Soviet authorities had been reunited with their relatives in Britain.[49]

In April 1964 the International set up a Socialist Study Group chaired by Alvar Alsterdal, the Swedish author and former editor of the socialist newspaper *Arbetet*. After almost two years of extensive research, in which they had received an abundance of written material directly from the Israelis as well as from Litvinoff, this group issued a well-documented report entitled "The Situation of the Jews in the U.S.S.R." The report contended that anti-Jewish discrimination in the Soviet Union threatened Soviet Jewry's "continued existence" as a nationality and compared anti-Jewish discrimination in the USSR to anti-black discrimination in the U.S., indicating that the governments concerned could earn "the respect of world opinion by a firm and effective stand against discrimination and prejudices." It also provided statistical evidence that there was discrimination against Soviet Jews as a group in the fields of both culture and religion, and as individuals in higher education and in the incidence of economic trials. The Group urged the Soviet authorities to show Jewish families the same sympathy they had shown in allowing Greeks, Spaniards and Poles to return to their countries, and in conducting the resettlement of Armenians, Ukrainians, Russians and Cossacks in the USSR. This would demonstrate that "the principle of postwar migration to reunify families is not in contradiction to Soviet practice." Finally, the report appealed to the Soviet government, "both on grounds of humanitarian principle and for the sake of international understanding, to end discrimination against the Jewish minority and impose proper restraints upon those who have been responsible for it."[50]

The 1966 Congress of the Socialist International unanimously passed a further resolution regretting that Soviet Jews were being deprived of rights granted to other Soviet national groupings and calling on the Soviet government to allow Jews to reunite with their families in Israel and elsewhere. The resolution was presented by Shneour Levenberg of Britain, member of the Socialist International Bureau, and was supported by Mapai Secretary-General Golda Meir.[51] Several months later the Bureau decided to appoint another special "working party" to study the position of Jews in the Soviet Union and present a report with their findings. Chaired by French Socialist Robert Pontillon, the group was composed of seven members from different countries. When the report appeared in June 1967 it stressed that, despite a few "tentative improvements" since 1964, the Jews' overall position had actually deteriorated. Among the points discussed was their very low level of political representation: their prominence in Soviet science, medicine, the arts and to an extent in economic and managerial positions notwithstanding, Jews had been almost entirely eliminated from the senior ranks of the armed forces, the diplomatic service and political life. The report also called "the most urgent single problem of Soviet Jews – that of uniting survivors of families destroyed or dispersed during the Second World War," and maintained that, despite Kosygin's assurances in December 1966, applications for family reunification were discouraged by highly derogatory newspaper articles on conditions in Israel and Soviet Jews who maintained links with that country.[52]

In November 1966 the International Confederation of Free Trade Unions (ICFTU) Executive Board adopted a resolution urging the Soviet authorities "to permit everybody and particularly the members of the Jewish community . . . to enjoy and pursue its own individual culture and religious life," and "to permit those Jews who may wish to do so, to join, whether in Israel or elsewhere, their families." In a letter to Kosygin, sent a few days after the Soviet Premier's Paris statement, ICFTU General Secretary Omer Becu expressed the hope that everything possible would be done to speed up the administrative procedure connected with Jewish emigration.[53] Also in 1966, the Eighth International Congress of Socialist Youth unanimously adopted a resolution deploring "the restrictions imposed by the Government of the U.S.S.R. on the freedom of movement and cultural freedom of [its] Jewish minority." This resolution, which was proposed by a Swiss delegate and seconded by an Indian, also mentioned the reunion of war-separated families.[54]

While socialist parties and leaders were natural allies for Israel's Mapai party, there were differences of opinion among Israelis and Diaspora Jewish leaders about cooperating with communist parties and politicians. Some feared that this might antagonize Western governments and other elements essential to the creation of a broad public opinion consensus. Others, however, thought that the influence of Western communists in Moscow far outweighed these risks. For it could not be disputed that a number of these parties had officially denounced the CPSU's policies toward Soviet Jewry, or that central figures in many of those who had not adopted this as their official party line had either spoken out publicly against Moscow on this score or were known to have informed the relevant CPSU authorities of their reservations directly.

By late 1964 the largest and most important of the Western communist parties, the Italian CP, was making signals that it had grave doubts about the CPSU's policy toward Soviet Jews. Shortly before his death in August 1964, its all-powerful First Secretary, Palmiro Togliatti, was said to have expressed the conviction that the Soviets had to take steps to revise their Jewish policy because there was still a Jewish problem in the USSR. Communist leaders told Italian Jewish activists and their non-Jewish partners in the cause that the PCI was losing no opportunity to make its position clear to the Soviets. PCI leaders raised the issue with Mikhail Suslov when he attended their Eleventh Party Congress in January 1966, although Suslov assured them that what was being done to achieve the "assimilation of the Jews" was "in their own best interest."[55] And, at a ceremony to mark the publication of a book on the Soviet Jewish problem for which he had written the introduction, communist Senator Umberto Terracini sharply criticized Soviet anti-Jewish discrimination, disclosing that the PCI leaders had discussed Soviet Jewry with their Soviet colleagues.[56] Had the Italian CP given the Soviet Jewish struggle open support, it would have been much more difficult for other left-wing and progressive groupings and individuals to contend that this struggle was anti-communist or anti-Soviet. In the final event, however, the PCI never went officially public on the issue.

One communist party that did not hesitate to divulge its critical stance toward Moscow was the British CP, which publicly pledged itself to combat antisemitism and interference with religious worship and facilities wherever they occurred. In a statement issued in January 1966, its executive committee claimed that the party had successfully intervened on behalf of Soviet Jewry on two occasions. And in May 1966 its official organ, the *Morning Star*, informed its readership that British communists "asked their Soviet colleagues to give 'sympathetic consideration' to suggestions for improving the struggle against the remnants of anti-Semitism in the country." A party statement also called for "greater care ... in the conducting of ideological work on religion and nationalism so as to avoid impermissible crudities which have nothing to do with a principled Marxist position."[57]

Prominent among British communists who had not left the party in protest against Soviet anti-Jewish discrimination but had striven from the inside to bring the facts to light was Alec Waterman, a leading member of its Jewish Advisory Committee. Waterman's belief that the international movement could influence the Soviet authorities to redress these injustices was unshakeable. It was due to his efforts that two resolutions calling attention to the Soviet Jewish plight were passed in 1966. He even produced a special memorandum for the party executive explaining why he thought the CPSU would have to act upon these resolutions. At the same time he noted in his memorandum that there was "an attitude of ambivalence and pragmatism, a reluctance ... to come to grips with this problem" within the CPSU.

Among those of its aspects to which Waterman drew attention as demanding effective treatment were: (1) "crude anti-religious propaganda and publications," none of whose "perpetrators" had "ever been brought before a Soviet court," even though the Soviet constitution "proscribed" the spreading of national and race hatred; (2) the "absence of principled, purposeful and consistent propaganda against anti-semitism," which should have been expected since part of the citizenry, particularly "backward sections" in the newly acquired territories, were infected with "deeply embedded" antisemitism, and elsewhere antisemitism persisted as "a hangover" from Tsarist days or from the Nazis in the areas occupied by them in World War II; and (3) forced assimilation, which was in contradiction to Marxist theory. Moreover, even if the "upsurge of interest" in Jewish history, traditions, customs and folklore that followed the Holocaust ran counter to the party line (which contended that Jewish cultural life was in the process of disappearing as a result of the Jews' assimilation), Waterman asked: "should not Marxists adapt this theory to suit the facts, rather than the other way round?"[58]

The Australian CP also became actively and publicly involved in the Soviet Jewish problem. Jewish public figures in Australia, notably Isi Liebler (then Honorary Secretary of the Executive Council of Australian Jewry – ECAJ) who had been mobilized on behalf of Soviet Jewry by Shaul Avigur as early as 1959, were in contact with communist leaders since 1964. Rex Mortimer, editor of the party organ, *Guardian*, was particularly sympathetic. Early in 1965 he and Bernard Taft of the party's Central Committee issued a statement condemning the USSR's Jewish policy. And when Liebler's pamphlet, *Soviet Jewry and Human Rights*, appeared in 1965, Mortimer supported its position publicly, despite its call for the reunification of families. Indeed, when the CPA Political Committee appointed four party members to reply to Liebler's pamphlet, the group (which included Mortimer) published a statement averring that, like every other national minority, Soviet Jews had the right to maintain their own national and cultural identity. They opposed administrative measures to bring about assimilation both in principle and as "self-defeating, since often such an approach keeps national exclusiveness alive."[59]

Both the French and Belgian Communist Parties sent sharply worded criticisms of the Kichko book to the CPSU. However, the Belgians expressed reservations about family reunification, specifically regarding the effectiveness of raising the issue with the Soviets, and the French punctiliously refrained from criticizing Soviet Jewish policy publicly.[60] Swedish CP chairman Carl-Henrik Hermannson, a nationally oriented moderate who rejected the concept of an international communist movement and did not attend its meetings, came out publicly against both the Kichko book and the ban on *matzot*. He said that Soviet Jews were entitled to equal rights and should be allowed to emigrate to Israel if they felt they would be happier there. Norwegian party secretary Reidar Larsen openly condemned the USSR for publishing the Kichko book and for equating Nazism and Zionism at the U.N. Larsen thought that the basis of the USSR's confused and erroneous Jewish policy was antisemitism and the fact that the Jews, alone among the USSR's national minorities, had a strong orientation toward emigration.[61]

In 1966 the American CP congress called for restitution of Jewish cultural rights and termination of the anti-Jewish campaign in the USSR, noting that the liquidation of Jewish culture there had alienated large numbers of Western Jews from the communist front.[62] By early 1967 the party felt so strongly about the Soviet Jewish situation that it decided to hold a conference on the subject but the conference never took place.[63]

The Council of Europe was another international organization that took up the Soviet Jewish issue in this period. It came up in the Council's Consultative Assembly as early as June 1964, when Belgian Premier Theo Lefèvre condemned the Soviet Union's persecution of its Jewish population at a meeting of the European Parliament's Christian Democratic group. In November of that year another Belgian, Senator Joseph-Edmond de Grauw, placed a motion urging member governments to include a call to respect Jewish rights in any discussion with the USSR. The Council's Political Commission assigned Jean Georges Margue of Luxembourg the task of preparing a report to set out the facts and examine whether the issue should go before the Assembly.

Margue's report came up for discussion at the Political Commission on 26 March 1965. It began by pointing out that there were precedents for the Assembly adopting recommendations and resolutions concerning political events or situations in other than member countries, especially when these concerned human rights, moral and legal principles and religious persecution. The rapporteur said that Europe had a special responsibility toward the Jewish people after World War II and that, indeed, the governments of a number of member countries had raised the question directly with the Soviet Union. Margue contended that even though the Political Commission was concerned with the situation of several national and religious groupings in the

USSR, it should limit its discussion to the Jews because the Soviet Union had mitigated its policy toward other groups but not toward the Jews.

Margue opened the debate in the plenary on 3 May by proposing his resolution. French Socialist senator Marius Moutet, Belgian Christian Socialist Anthony E. M. Duynstee and Haim Zadok of Israel also spoke. On 6 May the Assembly unanimously passed a resolution expressing the hope that the Soviet Union would contribute to the improvement of East–West understanding by restoring full cultural and religious rights to the Jews, by acting to prevent antisemitic propaganda, by eliminating judicial discrimination against Jews charged with economic crimes and by allowing Soviet Jews who wished to join their families in other countries, particularly in Israel, to do so. The Assembly also adopted an order instructing "the Working Party on Parliamentary and Public Relations to bring Resolution 295 to the notice of national parliaments with a view to drawing the attention of Governments to the problem of the situation of the Jewish community in the Soviet Union so that they may raise the problem with the Soviet Government."[64]

The most important non-political international body to take up the issue of Soviet Jewry in this period was the International Commission of Jurists, a non-governmental organization with U.N. advisory capacity representing 45,000 judges, lawyers and teachers of law from over one hundred countries. In the summer 1964 issue of its journal the Commission published a "Staff Study" entitled "Economic Crimes in the Soviet Union," which examined "the content and application of recent legislation in the Soviet Union concerning economic crimes and the place of this legislation according to legal theory" as well as "the extent to which the repression of economic crimes is linked with anti-Semitism." Aside from mentioning, *inter alia*, that "a thoroughly disproportionate emphasis is placed on the fact that some defendants are Jewish," the report's authors concluded that "the concentration of law and propaganda on the suppression of economic crimes evidences a serious moral malaise in Soviet society"; "an invidious and sometimes subtle propaganda campaign" had been directed against Jews and against Jews' "supposed general characteristics"; and that the number of Jews receiving death sentences and severe prison terms had been "greatly disproportionate" to their number in the general population. It was "a simple matter to link the picture of the money-grubbing Jew of anti-Semitic fancy with the picture of the arch-villains of capitalist cupidity." The Jews "had been made the scapegoats for the transgressions of those whose guilt it would be dangerous to make public ... Anti-Semitism represents the most dangerous form of racialism in the world," and no "question of expediency can ever justify its use as a political-social or economic weapon."[65]

### The U.S. Congress and administration

While the struggle on behalf of Soviet Jewry was relatively new in the U.N. and other international bodies, it had been debated in the U.S. Congress since the late 1950s. In 1963, however, the Eighty-eighth Congress introduced a new component into its handling of the problem: interaction between the legislature and the executive. Although there had been some correspondence between one or two of the more concerned senators and the State Department on this question in the past, it had led nowhere. But, as Congress became increasingly perturbed at the deteriorating situation of Soviet Jewry, its members were less disposed to accept the State Department's offhand replies to their requests for direct government involvement in the issue.

The central actors in Congress were still Senators Javits, Keating, Scott, Dodd and Ribicoff[66] and Representatives Farbstein and Halpern.[67] But now they were joined by congressmen like Karl E. Mundt of South Dakota and Donald C. Bruce of Indiana, who were neither Jewish nor represented traditionally Jewish areas, but who took up the Soviet Jewish cause in Congress because they felt that the highest legislative body in the world's greatest power endorsing freedom and human rights could not do otherwise. In the words of Senator Keating on the twenty-fifth anniversary of Hitler's *Kristallnacht*, "the preservation of the liberties of all, and of peace itself, depends on the refusal of the civilized world to accept minority group persecution as state practice."[68] Both senators and representatives were harsh in excoriating Soviet racist attitudes toward its own population.[69] Representative Robert Macdonald of Massachusetts said that developing countries, in particular, should be made aware that Soviet claims to be protectors of persecuted minorities were nothing more than a sham in light of its own antisemitic practices, which were nothing less than outright racism.[70]

A number of congressmen sought practical steps. Representatives Farbstein of New York and Hermann Toll of Pennsylvania submitted resolutions calling on Moscow to guarantee human rights, "including the right to persons separated from their families to be reunited with them," and urging the U.S. mission to the U.N. to seek the "early adoption" by the U.N. General Assembly of a resolution condemning "recent manifestations of anti-Semitism" in the USSR.[71]

As 1963 wore on, and the Soviet Jewish situation showed no sign of improving despite worldwide concern and protest, activist senators became impatient. The first indication of the new atmosphere was a speech by Senator Javits in September, in which he indicated "the irony of history" involved in depriving Jews of the right to emigrate from a country from which they had once been "driven out." Stating outright that Soviet Jews "cannot speak for themselves because they live in a closed society where free speech does not exist," Javits said that others had to speak out for them. But since Eisenhower's expression of concern at Camp David had shown that quiet protests had no effect, the only hope "for the captive Jews of the Soviet Union" was to protest "loud and long" in "a great surge of indignation – the determined protests not only of Jews but of all free peoples who treasure the rights of the individual."[72]

Two days later Connecticut Democrat Abraham Ribicoff and sixty-three other senators submitted a resolution calling on the Senate to condemn Soviet religious persecution and demand that the Soviet Union stop executing persons for economic offenses. After it was passed by the Senate, Javits called for "urgent action on the resolution."[73] This was followed up, on the eve of the Jewish New Year, by a call to Ambassador Dobrynin from members of the House Foreign Affairs Committee, asking the USSR to "alleviate the reported conditions affecting Soviet Jewry."[74]

Keating and Javits spearheaded the effort to get the administration officially involved in the struggle for Soviet Jewish rights by continuing their correspondence with the State Department. In October 1963 Keating told the Senate that he was attempting to urge the government to take "a more rigorous defense of human rights," letting it know that there was "increasing dissatisfaction" with its "passive attitude" toward bringing the problem to the U.N. He suggested that the U.S. make its wheat sales to the Soviet Union – over which there was considerable controversy in the Senate[75] – conditional on that wheat being made available for religious celebrations, a clear reference to the Soviet ban on *matzot*.[76]

Justice Arthur Goldberg, who had been President Kennedy's first Secretary of Labor in 1961–62, worked with Senators Javits and Ribicoff to bring the issue of Soviet Jewry before Secretary of State Dean Rusk and the president. After consulting with Binyamin Eliav, who came to the U.S. especially for that purpose, the three decided to stress the necessity for official U.S. government action on behalf of Soviet Jewry: this was an issue for American Jews, who identified with their brethren in the USSR on a group level and who also had family and personal ties with them, as well as for the American public as a whole, who were not prepared to be partners to any form of peaceful coexistence that did not include an improvement in the Soviet Jewish situation. When Goldberg and the two senators met with Secretary Rusk in September, they found him familiar with the problem. But when he proposed that an international committee of leading Jews, rather than State Department officials, seek a meeting with Soviet representatives, they rejected his suggestion outright, claiming that the department's traditionally "sympathetic but cautious" attitude did not suit the situation. They therefore persisted in demanding a high-level unilateral approach on the part of the U.S.

A few days later, when Goldberg and Ribicoff raised the issue with President Kennedy, they discovered that he, too, had a comprehensive knowledge of the problem. Indeed, it had been suggested to him by Counsel to the President Myer Feldman that the revision of his book *A Nation of Immigrants* include a chapter on Soviet restrictions on Jewish emigration. Although Feldman told Goldberg and Ribicoff that Kennedy did not believe he could do anything except through a personal message to Khrushchev or other private, diplomatic channels, the president did call the closing of synagogues a violation of human rights when he spoke before the U.N. General Assembly in September 1963.[77] He had also intended taking up the matter personally with Gromyko, but their meeting turned into a major discussion of East–West tensions. And when President Kennedy was able to raise it, in passing, Gromyko said that, although the matter would be looked into "sympathetically," the Soviet government could not respond to this overture publicly or officially. In the end, Kennedy decided that linking American–Soviet economic relations with policies such as Jewish emigration was likely to do more harm than good. The Departments of State and Agriculture also opposed such a move, although obviously for different reasons.

As Under-Secretary of State for Political Affairs Averell Harriman told the American Jewish Committee at the time, although the U.S. government "opposes the loss of basic freedoms wherever it may occur" and raised these matters informally whenever there is an "appropriate opportunity," exposing the facts to "the spotlight of world opinion" was often more effective than "formal protests in government-to-government communications" because the Soviets resented official protests on matters which they considered to be within their domestic jurisdiction. Nevertheless, Harriman assured his audience, "if it seems likely that a more direct approach will secure useful ends . . . our Government will make it."[78]

On 27 October President Kennedy suggested that Goldberg, Javits and Ribicoff discuss the issue – in his name – with Ambassador Dobrynin, with whom Javits had been meeting regularly since his appointment to the U.S. in early 1962. The president also agreed to send the three Jewish leaders to Moscow as his personal representatives to discuss the situation with Khrushchev. Kennedy's advisor on Soviet affairs, ex-Ambassador Llewellyn Thompson, who arranged the meeting with Dobrynin, told the Soviet ambassador that Kennedy took a personal interest in the issue. But the meeting was less than successful, Dobrynin taking violent exception to every point that was brought up. He denied discrimination in employment and education, the singling out of Jews for prosecution in the economic trials and even the necessity for Jews to register as such when applying for internal passports and other documents. Dobrynin also expressed his opinion that the prominence given the question of Soviet Jewry in the U.S. could only hinder the international harmony his government was seeking. The three Jewish leaders insisted that American Jewry shared the desire for peaceful coexistence, but that all men of goodwill, not only Jews, agreed that Soviet antisemitism was a stumbling-block to its attainment. And American Jews would not keep silent as long as their brethren in the Soviet Union were being deprived of their fundamental rights. To their suggestion that they continue the discussion with Khrushchev in Moscow, Dobrynin replied that Khrushchev would decide whether further meetings would be beneficial after he received Dobrynin's report on the present meeting. The three never heard anything further on the subject.[79]

In November 1963 Goldberg, Javits and Ribicoff met with members of the Conference of Major American Jewish Organizations, suggesting that its leaders try to convince Kennedy that he, personally, was responsible for American intervention on behalf of their coreligionists. Goldberg said that while the trio's confrontation with Dobrynin had demonstrated to the Soviets America's deep concern over the issue, Dobrynin's replies showed that the Jewish community had to change tactics from quiet diplomacy to public protest. But that protest, he went on, must be prudent and be made on the humanitarian plane, without political considerations.

The three leaders not only insisted on cohesive action, but also called for the press to be supplied with a continual flow of materials on Soviet Jewry so the issue would receive sustained treatment. This was particularly important because Dobrynin had indicated the Soviet feeling that American Jewish intercession would eventually weaken because the Jews would not be able to present a united front. To show the Soviets that this was not going to be the case, Goldberg called upon the Jewish organizations to convene a mobilization conference comprising representatives of a broad spectrum of national Jewish agencies and communities.[80]

Kennedy was assassinated the day after the meeting with the Conference took place, and although attempts were made to interest Lyndon B. Johnson in Soviet Jewry, immediate prospects for high-level contact receded as Soviet–U.S. tensions again grew strained in consequence of the situation in Vietnam.

Nor indeed was any feeling of urgency on the issue discernible within the Executive, although the list of those protesting Soviet antisemitism in both Houses of Congress continued to expand and although senators and representatives stepped up criticism of the State Department for its reluctance to involve the government in the struggle on behalf of Soviet Jewry at the highest level. At the second session of the Eighty-eighth Congress, Senators Hubert Humphrey (Minnesota), Harrison Williams (New Jersey) and Philip Hart (Michigan) joined Javits, Keating, Ribicoff and Dodd in condemning Moscow's anti-Jewish discrimination. Although reunification of families and emigration were not raised specifically in this session, Ribicoff did include "the refusal of the right to emigrate" as one of the six components of the Soviet Union's Jewish policy when he asked the Democratic Platform Committee to protest Soviet persecution of the Jewish people in its 1964 election platform.[81] And in the House no less than eleven resolutions, one concurrent resolution and five joint resolutions were submitted in connection with different aspects of the Soviet Jewish question.[82]

In February 1964 Senator Keating informed the Senate that, "in view of the continuing Soviet campaign of anti-Semitism," he had asked the Department of State "for a full report on the subject urging U.S. action to prevent such excesses." He had just received this report, which conceded that "the Jewish community . . . suffers serious hardship" yet denied that there was evidence that Moscow was seeking "to incite the public to acts of anti-Jewish violence." Moreover, the State Department contended once again that U.S. government action "through diplomatic channels" would not be in the best interest of Soviet Jews but was liable to "antagonize" the Soviet government to their detriment. The Soviet authorities had in the past "often accused Soviet Jews of susceptibility to subversive foreign influences and of being agents of foreign states, most particularly of the United States and Israel." The department felt that official American representations "would seem to lend credence" to these charges as well as losing "in effectiveness because of the tendency in many areas to dismiss U.S. moves involving the Soviet Union as motivated primarily by cold war considerations." At the same time, "the U.S. Government can and does support moves designed to bring about an improvement in the lot of Soviet Jewry," whose "fate . . . is of concern to the world community." It was therefore suggested that "serious thought . . . be given to a united appeal of private organizations representing worldwide Jewry and, if possible, other religious groups."[83]

In a speech before the AJC that April, Secretary Rusk assured his audience that the administration would continue to "make known" its interest "in the welfare of religious communities within the Soviet Union and elsewhere."[84] And when President Johnson sent messages to meetings in connection with Soviet Jewry, his remarks had obviously been composed by State Department officials. Thus, in his first message, to a New York conference on Soviet Jewry in October 1964, Johnson followed remarks on his concern with the situation of Soviet Jews by saying that "the official actions available to us must be reinforced by the pressure of an aroused world public opinion . . . The moral judgement of millions of people throughout the world cannot be ignored by any Government."[85]

The official American position in the mid-1960s was almost certainly influenced by the hope that the Soviets would reciprocate by making fewer references in their media and in official statements to the position of black Americans, an issue on which sensitivity ran high although the U.S. government was taking major steps to counter discriminatory practices. As late as spring 1967 a State Department official was reported as saying that an official American démarche would receive the same response in Moscow as the U.S. government would accord a Soviet protest on anti-Negro tendencies in Alabama.[86]

In the House, Congressman Howard W. Robison of New York took the State Department to task for opposing official protests concerning Soviet Jewry, insisting that "no one can predict what reaction would take place within the Soviet Government to an official protest by our

Department of State," whose policy was having "the effect of sweeping [the problem] under the rug."[87]

A month after Senator Ribicoff's September 1963 resolution on the persecution of Soviet Jewry had been the topic of open hearings at the Senate Foreign Relations Committee, Ribicoff raised the issue again in the Senate in a debate on the general amendment of the Foreign Assistance Act of 1961. Asking the Senate to take "an official stand" on the Soviet Jewish problem, which "has flared up recently in virulent form," Ribicoff proposed an amendment for which he had co-sponsors from both parties. The sole source of opposition was Chairman of the Senate Committee on Foreign Relations William Fulbright (of Arkansas), who suggested an alternative amendment condemning religious persecution in general but making no specific mention of either the Soviet Union or its Jews. Fulbright explained that his opposition to Ribicoff's amendment was in line with State Department thinking.[88] Ribicoff, Javits and others reacted strongly to Fulbright's amendment. In Ribicoff's words, if senators representing 184 million people of every religion and faith voted unanimously on his amendment, "it will be a warning to the Soviet Union that the American people are aroused and ... will not sit idly by." Condemning the State Department's ignorance and indifference, the Senator from Connecticut said that it had never been "sympathetic to these problems." When it came to a vote, Fulbright's amendment was rejected and Ribicoff's accepted by all senators present except Fulbright.[89] But the victory was shortlived, as the House–Senate committee preparing Foreign Aid Authorization Bill H.R. 11380 for passage as U.S. law excised the amendment in response to pressures by Fulbright and the State Department.[90]

Despite the deletion of the Ribicoff amendment from the Foreign Assistance Act, Representative Halpern opened the Eighty-ninth Congress in 1965 with a call for "positive steps ... to alleviate the plight of the Jews in Russia." He took the first such step by introducing two resolutions, one condemning the Soviet war against religion and calling upon it to cease its anti-Jewish persecution, the other expressing House support for the efforts to establish antisemitism as an international offense. He was taking this step in the House not because he wished in any way to tie the hands of the executive branch in foreign policy but because his attempts to urge "fresh diplomatic initiatives" on the part of the State Department had met with the by-now standard reply. Halpern took exception to the State Department's opinion that diplomatic action was undesirable and "contrary to the welfare" of Soviet Jewry.[91]

Ribicoff also refused to let up. He reintroduced his resolution in the form of a concurrent resolution, for approval by the Senate and the House, for which he had the *a priori* support of sixty-seven senators. He was seconded by Javits, who was also in favor of U.N. delegate Morris Abram's suggestion that the U.N. Sub-Commission for the Prevention of Discrimination and the Protection of Minorities should examine charges of Soviet antisemitism firsthand, to "make the Kremlin realize how sterile and harmful to its own prestige is its anti-Jewish policy."[92] Of all the resolutions submitted in both the Senate and the House of Representatives in the period under discussion, this was the only one to be adopted by both Houses.[93]

It is worth noting here that the resolution was passed after the State Department had notified Senator Fulbright that it had reversed its position, a development probably influenced by public pressure on the administration.[94] Although it had "no reason to believe" that the resolution would have "any significant beneficial result," the department considered that, now that Moscow itself had taken steps to reduce "the unfavorable publicity it has received," there was "less likelihood" that the resolution would "harm those we seek to help."[95]

Congressmen in both Houses continued to draw attention to the Soviet Jewish issue. Toward the end of 1966 ninety senators expressed their "staunch support of the American Jewish community's protests against the anti-Semitic policies of the Soviet Union" in an advertisement in the *New York Times*.[96] On the occasion of the Passover in spring 1967 Representative Jonathan Bingham of New York released a statement condemning the suppression of Jewish spiritual and cultural life in the USSR. The statement had been signed by 300 members of the House of Representatives from both parties, including Speaker John W. McCormack, Majority Leader Carl Albert and Minority Leader Gerald R. Ford. The signatories hoped that this "expression of strong disapproval" of Soviet anti-Jewish discrimination would "help awaken the sensibilities of the Soviet Government to the world-wide condemnation of its policies in this respect and exert a positive influence for improvement." Referring to Kosygin's December 1966 assertion that "all citizens, including Jews, are free to leave the Soviet Union," the statement noted: "We await translation of these words into deeds."[97]

The spirit of Congress was, then, clearly in favor of continual and loud protest. Its members played an important role in the American Soviet Jewry movement, by giving it a nationwide and official character that must have made its mark on the Soviet authorities. Yet the administration was still generally speaking anxious that the issue remain separate from Soviet–American relations. Although some headway was made here, it was broad government feeling that raising the question would be pointless or even harmful to Soviet–U.S. relations, to its own domestic program concerning the American black community and even to Soviet Jewry.

### The American Jewish Conference on Soviet Jewry

The American Jewish organizations that had been active in the struggle for Soviet Jewry in previous years now began to work in earnest toward American Jewish unity on the issue. The first major appeal for a coordinated nationwide effort seems to have come from Rabbi Abraham Joshua Heschel of the Jewish Theological Seminary of America, who was known as the "conscience" of many American Jews. In a speech before the Conservative Synagogue Council of America in September 1963, Heschel castigated the American Jewish community for its indifference and insufficient forcefulness in dealing with the issue, pointing out that many American Jews were totally unaware of the Soviet Jewish situation. He appealed to the organizations concerned to put aside their differences and set up an *ad hoc* emergency committee aimed at arousing the Jewish community and general public opinion, as well as a small steering committee to devise a specific plan of action.[98]

Many of the organizations had been conducting "quiet diplomacy" for some time. In their meetings with Soviet embassy officials they had generally been careful to show maximum consideration for Soviet feelings. But by fall 1963 it was clear to them that this approach had failed. To use the words of the Synagogue Council's international committee chairman, Rabbi Theodore C. Adams, they had been deceived; rather than improving, the situation of Soviet Jewry was, in fact, deteriorating. Nonetheless, despite their frustration, the organizations were still not convinced that a new organization devoted solely to the cause of Soviet Jewry was necessary. However, they asked Heschel to convene a steering committee comprising himself and the presidents of the Synagogue Council, the Conference of Presidents, the National Community Relations Advisory Council (NCRAC) and the American Jewish Committee.[99]

After some organizational difficulties and internal differences of opinion over approach, Heschel's committee decided to stage a major event protesting the ever-worsening situation of Soviet Jewry. Several months of planning followed, during which workshops were held on national and local "follow-up." And when the American Jewish Conference on Soviet Jewry took place in Washington, D.C. on 5–6 April 1964, 500 representatives from twenty-four American Jewish defence, cultural, Zionist and religious organizations participated. This conference not only had great media impact; it had far-reaching effects on the whole American struggle for Soviet Jewry.

Conference chairman Label Katz opened by noting that the participants had come together "to proclaim moral indignation . . . without political overtones . . . removed from cold war problems . . . to speak for a community of Jews . . . that is trapped in silence . . . to articulate its plight; to appeal, on its behalf for reason and civilized decency; to mobilize, in its support, those for whom freedom of thought and conscience is an ideal to be cherished – and therefore to be shared . . . Jewish consciousness had a survivalist quality," and the conference was "called to order . . . to help the Soviet Jew preserve and make meaningful his Jewish consciousness." Katz insisted that those convened were calling not for a special status for Soviet Jewry but for the equality of status guaranteed all Soviet citizens by law, for the "inalienable human right . . . of the Jew to be Jewish . . . to be . . . himself."[100]

Justice Arthur Goldberg, who also addressed the assembly, commended the meeting as "a virtually unprecedented testimonial to the unity of Jewish opinion on this vital and important subject." Pointing out the value of this type of protest, he said that on the very first day of the conference it had been reported that the CPSU had partially repudiated the Kichko book.[101]

Senator Ribicoff was even more forceful. He began by describing the Soviet Jewish situation as "deprivation, discrimination, de-Judaization." The Soviet regime, he said, sought to destroy Jewish group survival on the assumption that the Jews were an alien people, not indigenous, who did not "belong" and were already disloyal. As a result of the "traditional, irrational prejudice" which determined this postulate, the Jews were being denied the attributes of nationality accorded all other nationalities in the Soviet Union: language, literature, national history, national heroes, customs. They were being subjected to a "unique humiliation," the "psychological and spiritual destructiveness" of which was "shattering." It was not as if *matzot*, phylacteries or religious calendars would constitute any danger to the regime; nor would circumcision or the burial of their dead according to Jewish rite. But, since the regime recognized that "Judaism might still

. . . set Jewish hearts afire," Jewish institutions had been closed down, sacred articles and rites had been taken away, and "fright stalks the synagogues."

In fact, the policy of de-Judaization, of forced assimilation was "throwing many Jews, especially young Jews, back on themselves . . . stiffening their backs." They were resisting in response to oppression.

Yet, while in the face of "the miracle of creative Jewish survival . . . it would be a foolish prophet who would dare to predict the spiritual end of Soviet Jewry . . . it would be even more foolish and dangerous to rely on miracles." Any hope for the future of this Jewry lay in its own "courageous resistance – and in our determination to do everything we can to bolster their existence and their spirit." It was a historical truth that the West, Jews and Gentiles alike, had not done enough to save the Jews of Europe from Nazi Germany. "Their heirs and survivors in the U.S.S.R. bear their claim on the conscience of us all." The plight of Soviet Jewry was surrounded by a "pall of bland indifference, of polite acquiescence . . . If it is thought of at all in the world at large, it is only as an afterthought. Governments are not agitated by it; leaders do not speak up about it. Humanitarian movements do not make of it a rallying cry . . . It has not been a priority at the United Nations . . . It has not become what it must be – a major item on the agenda of the world's conscience." It was therefore essential that the same kind of support garnered by his Senate resolution be evoked by "private and public voices" in the U.S.

Seconding Ribicoff's remarks, and reiterating many of his long-voiced opinions on the subject, Senator Javits said that since Soviet Jews were "helpless, defenseless and without voice . . . we must give them voice . . . rise to their defense . . . cry out for justice . . . give the world no surcease – until the world pays attention." And, to the Soviet Jews themselves, "we must say with a strong, constant, unyielding voice – We have not forgotten or forsaken you, nor will we ever." Javits ended by warning against "the counsels of caution and fear – or of silence – on the part of American Jewry."[102]

Morris B. Abram struck new ground with his contention that Soviet antisemitism derived from the fact that, although the USSR was a powerful state, it sometimes acted as a "frightened and weak" one. This was because, in a closed society that cannot admit to any faults without threatening the entire system, the desire of even a single person to emigrate would be inadmissible. Yet this need not cast aspersions on the Soviet system, for "individuals may have a variety of their own reasons to choose one country over another, such as the reunification of dispersed families." The Soviet view of the individual as "a cog in the great machine of the state" to which "his need for expression, his traditions, his heritage, even his safety may be sacrificed," contrasted sharply with the American stand, which embodies "the Judaeo-Christian view of social justice and individual human worth."

Abram's final point was that the conference "should call upon all religions and all men of good will to cry out against the shame of Soviet anti-Semitism . . . should call upon the newly independent [Asian and African] nations . . . to speak out in the U.N. and in all international forums against the violations of ethnic identity which the Soviet Union is perpetrating." He recommended that non-governmental organizations and academic institutions create an Eleanor Roosevelt Court of Human Rights to "meet across the street from the U.N. perhaps while the U.N. Human Rights Commission is in session" until the U.N. assumed "its obligations under the Charter to protect human rights."[103]

The conference adopted an eighteen-point resolution specifying measures the Soviet authorities must take in order to remedy the wrongs done to the Soviet Jewish community, the final point calling on the Soviets "to make possible on humanitarian grounds [for] Soviet Jews who are members of families separated as a result of the Nazi holocaust to be reunited with their relatives abroad." It also issued a general statement defining as its aim "to mobilize public opinion into a moral force which will save Soviet Jewry from spiritual annihilation. We who are assembled here are bound by the moral imperative of our history, which demands that we speak out on the fate of our brothers in the Soviet Union."[104]

Although many Jewish leaders had been opposed to the creation of yet another American Jewish organization, fearing the creation of a body not controlled by themselves in a field already overcrowded with fundraisers, the American Jewish Conference on Soviet Jewry was voted into existence as an umbrella organization for coordinating all organizational activity on behalf of Soviet Jewry, albeit with no budget, no full-time staff and no permanent quarters, and with its coordinating role closely circumscribed.[105]

Despite the built-in institutional handicaps, the creation of the AJCSJ was a major achievement and, indeed, a turning point in American Jewish treatment of the Soviet Jewry issue. "The leaders of the mass organizations," it has been pointed out, "were now on record as considering the situation of Soviet Jewry sufficiently serious

... to commit the prestige of their organizations to a new body," one designed to intervene on behalf of these Jews "and nothing else."[106] Moreover, as an organization representing almost the entire American Jewish establishment, it could meet with the U.S. government in the name of American Jewry, one of the most cogent reasons for uniting.

Even now, however, certain individuals and groups remained aloof from the umbrella organization, continuing to reject the need for open protest, which had been the basic premise for its formation. Among those who persisted in favoring the covert diplomacy that most of the AJCSJ's founding members had unequivocally repudiated as the sole method of endeavor on behalf of Soviet Jewry were Nahum Goldmann, president of the WJC and the WZO, and the Lubavich Rebbe, head of the *hasidic* Habad movement. Goldmann made repeated efforts to achieve an amelioration of the Soviet Jewish situation through private negotiations with Soviet officials in the U.S. and elsewhere in the West. He never gave up hope that he would be invited to the USSR to discuss the lot of Soviet Jewry with the leadership of that country as the plenipotentiary of Western Jewry. Goldmann's argument, that publicity deterred left-wing sympathizers by making exaggerated comparisons between the USSR and Nazi Germany, eventually led to an open controversy between him and the Israeli government. The apprehensions of the Lubavich and other Orthodox groups, notably Agudas Israel, were based on the fear that the new movement might jeopardize the clandestine links with their followers in the Soviet Union that were being maintained with the apparent connivance of the Soviet authorities. According to one analyst, those who opposed the public protest of a mass movement were afraid that it might be taken over by unreasonable elements that would end up by embarrassing the Western Jewish community. Some even thought that such protest might increase antisemitism in their own countries, others that it might end up by further harming Soviet Jews.[107]

Despite the few, albeit not insignificant, dissenting voices the AJCSJ established direct contact with the U.S. administration. In the immediate aftermath of the founding conference, a delegation of eight presidents of Jewish organizations was invited to the White House, where they met with President Johnson, and to the State Department, where they met with Secretary Rusk.[108]

Another important outcome of the consolidation of the American Jewish effort on behalf of Soviet Jewry was closer cooperation with Israel. When AJCSJ representatives met with U.S. Ambassador to

Moscow Foy Kohler and Assistant Secretary of State for European Affairs William Tyler in December 1964 – a meeting suggested by Tyler in reaction to sharp criticism of the government position on Soviet Jewry, particularly to that of the State Department – the AJCSJ approach was carefully worked out in meetings with Meir Rosenne, now Israeli consul in new York, and Moshe Decter. The AJCSJ delegation proposed that the U.S. government discuss some of the Washington conference's eighteen points in Moscow and acknowledge that, although it would not solve Soviet Jewry's basic problem, emigration was a partial solution which should not be neglected.[109]

The minutes of a March 1965 AJCSJ meeting reveal that the organization sought to use Senator Ribicoff's resolution "as a peg for making an impact nationally and in local communities." Community Action Kits were being prepared for mailing to those communities that had agreed to mobilize the local population on behalf of Soviet Jewry. There were also attempts to hold hearings in both the Senate Foreign Relations Committee and the House Foreign Affairs Committee, with expert witnesses (such as former *New York Times* correspondent Harrison Salisbury) and individuals representing specific segments of public opinion (such as Martin Luther King). And students were being recruited for a systematic picketing of the Soviet embassy in Washington, to join the Jews and non-Jews from Philadelphia who were already traveling to Washington every few days as part of a Philadelphia community action program.[110]

The first major "happening" – sponsored by the AJCSJ-affiliated New York Conference on Soviet Jewry – was a rally in Madison Square Garden in June 1965, which attracted close to 20,000 people. Addressed by a roster of speakers that included New York Mayor Robert Wagner, Robert Kennedy, black trade union leader A. Philip Randolph and veteran socialist leader Norman Thomas, the audience also heard a message from President Johnson. In his speech, AJC President Morris Abram pointed out that the USSR was practicing "ethnic genocide" against its Jewish population. The Soviet Union, Abram argued, could not really be threatened by allowing ritual objects to be made available to Jews, by permitting them to form religious and cultural organizations, or even by according "every Jewish citizen within its territory the right to leave his country temporarily or permanently." Until there was correspondence between what the Soviets practiced and preached regarding discrimination he promised, "We shall protest – we shall march – and we shall overcome."[111]

One of the major aspects of the Madison Square Garden rally was that it marked the opening of a campaign to gather one million signatories to a protest asking President Johnson to exercise his influence with the Kremlin regarding the USSR's Jewish inhabitants.[112] On the eve of the rally the *New York Times* published a letter signed by Soviet Nobel Prize winners, physicist Lev Landau and economist Evsei Liberman, protesting Western fabrications regarding and intrusions into their lives as Jews in the USSR, and calling upon Americans "not to participate in the provocative meeting which will do nothing but harm mutual understanding between our countries" by discussing "a non-existent problem."[113]

In September 1965 the AJCSJ launched a week-long Eternal Light Vigil in Washington, D.C. Attended by 10,000 people from over one hundred communities, as well as by important government officials and clergymen of different faiths, this was the first major public Soviet Jewry demonstration in the American capital. "By kindling a symbolic Eternal Light," the AJCSJ statement on the vigil announced, "American Jewish leaders, joined by men of different races and religions," sought to show that they would protest "until Jews in the USSR are assured the freedom to practice and perpetuate their religion and their culture."[114] Rabbi Seymour J. Cohen of Chicago, President of the Synagogue Council of America and Chairman of the AJCSJ steering committee, told the assembly that as Jews Soviet Jews were "in limbo," lacking "the strength of roots," "the pride of history," the "link to eternity" and "the fellowship of community," and that it was up to American Jews to rescue them from "spiritual death." The fate of the two groups was "intertwined . . . They are bone of our bone, flesh of our flesh . . . We are all part of a covenant people who share a common history, faith, culture, language and tradition . . . The bar of history would not forgive our inaction."

U.S. ambassador to ECOSOC James Roosevelt told those assembled that the problem of Soviet Jewry "properly belongs on the agenda of the U.N." but must also be "on the agenda of the world's conscience." The week's activities included a message from the president, a briefing at the State Department on Jewish life in the Soviet Union and a conference at the White House with Special Assistant to the President for National Security McGeorge Bundy and Special Counsel to the President Lee C. White. A four-man delegation – Bayard Rustin, Theodore Bikel, Rabbi Seymour Cohen and Reverend John Cronin of the National Catholic Welfare Council – tried in vain to present the petition bearing a million signatures to the Soviet embassy.[115] A replica of the demonstration's symbol, the Eternal Light Vigil Torch, continued to remind people of the problem as it circulated throughout the U.S., its arrival in one community after another providing the occasion for speeches and meetings on the plight of Soviet Jewry.[116]

In an interim report issued by the AJCSJ in December 1965, it was noted that, since the Conference's creation less than two years earlier, Moscow's policies and practices vis-à-vis its Jews had been subjected to "a vigorous and increasing program of exposure to public notice," to which the world had responded with "condemnations that the leaders of Russia had not been able to ignore." The report went on to describe the "dénouement" brought about by the Western, especially Western communist, reaction to the Kichko book, the "economic crimes" and the prohibition against *matzot*, mentioning *inter alia* that even *Sovetish heymland* had "evolved into something rather different from what was intended." Moreover, while Kosygin's remarks in Riga on 14 July 1965, that antisemitism was "completely alien to our society ... and contradicts our world outlook," and the *Pravda* editorial of 5 September 1965 on "the friendship of peoples," did not signify a "genuine reversal" of policy, they did reveal that the Soviet leadership was "vulnerable on this issue" and "susceptible to the pressure of world opinion."[117]

At its second biennial conference in April 1966, the AJCSJ issued a Declaration of Rights for Soviet Jewry that concluded with the pledge that "so long as Soviet Jews are cut off from the Jewish people, proscribed from living their lives as Jews, so long will our voices be lifted in protest and indignation."[118] Prior to the formal signing of the declaration in Congress Hall in Philadelphia, where the conference was held, the delegates participated in an open-air meeting addressed by Senator Hugh Scott of Pennsylvania and NAACP Executive Director Roy Wilkins. Scott described the public protestations against Soviet antisemitism as "life insurance" for the Soviet Jews, while Wilkins compared the struggle to eliminate official anti-Jewish discrimination in the USSR to the civil rights struggle of the American Negro.[119] Bishop James Pike told the conference that, although "our concerns should know no national boundaries" when it comes to human rights, "rightists" should not maximize Soviet behavior toward the Jews and "left-wingers" should refrain from minimizing it "because it is Soviet;" Soviet Jewish policy, he stressed, had to be criticized on its own.[120] Finally, sixty-eight senators cosigned a message from Senator Ribicoff supporting the Philadelphia conference.[121] The conference declaration, too, was brought to Jewish communities around the country during the summer of 1966 under the auspices of NCRAC, some of whose representatives were able to persuade their local mayors to announce a Soviet Jewry Day. According to NCRAC Chairman Albert Chernin, this was only one of the instances in which the AJCSJ's NCRAC connection was used to strengthen ties between the umbrella organization and local communities.[122]

The AJCSJ sought to keep the issue of Soviet Jewry in the public eye. On 19 September – the eve of the opening of the U.N. General Assembly – Eternal Light ceremonies were held in forty-seven American cities and Special Assistant to the President Walt Rostow met in Washington with representatives of all the organizations comprising the AJCSJ. The meeting followed a gathering in Lafayette Park at which AJCSJ Chairman Rabbi Israel Miller had told those assembled that not only was "the entire American Jewish community ... united as never before in this common cause," but that "great champions of human rights are adding their voices to ours. Nobel Peace Prize winners. Great international jurists. Militant civil rights advocates. Leaders of the American labor movement. Clergymen of all faiths." And, Miller concluded, there were indications that the Soviet government had taken cognizance of the protests.[123]

The AJCSJ leaders were convinced that the united national effort was having a cumulative impact that increased "the visibility of the issue on the national level and thus reaches the American and foreign decision-makers and opinion-molders."[124] Rabbi Miller organized another nationwide demonstration for Soviet Jewish rights on 11 December 1966, the anniversary of the U.N. Human Rights Declaration, which was given wide media coverage both locally and nationally. The thirty-two simultaneously held meetings were linked by telephone with Nobel Peace Prize winner Reverend Martin Luther King, who spoke from his home in Atlanta. According to King, "the denial of human rights anywhere is a threat to the affirmation of human rights everywhere." If the Soviet government sought "respect for itself in the international community of nations," King said, "the sincere and genuine concern felt by so many people around the world for this problem" should impel it "not only to affect a solution but to do so with deliberate speed. In the meantime," he concluded, "let us continue to make our voices heard and our righteous protests felt."[125]

The AJCSJ lacked teeth. Yet its very establishment and continued existence served to symbolize American Jewish solidarity on the Soviet Jewry issue and to provide the American Jewish community with an instrument for presenting its case for Soviet Jews to the administration, Congress and the media. It also supplied a mechanism for reaching the Jewish rank and file throughout the country. Since American Jewish pressure and activity were a prerequisite for the administration taking up the question directly with Moscow and in international forums, for Congress to debate it and for the media to publicize it, the AJCSJ – which institutionalized methods of exerting pressure and of radiating activity – is an important landmark in our story of the mounting and increasingly meaningful campaign in the West on behalf of Soviet Jewry. Finally, the fact that it enabled cooperation between American Jewry and the Israeli government for channeling the American Jewish struggle for Soviet Jewish rights into a single mainstream enhanced Israel's opportunities for supplying updated information on the Soviet Jewish situation to all concerned. It also enhanced Israel's ability to exert direct leverage on individual American Jewish organizations and to influence the U.S. administration.

## Public opinion and "grass-roots" organizations in the U.S.

While the creation of the AJCSJ was unquestionably a major achievement from the point of view of the Jewish community's ability to exert pressure on or negotiate with the administration on the Soviet Jewish question, many people viewed it principally as a political initiative that reflected the interests of the community's leadership but was out of touch with the rank and file. In the early and mid-1960s, which were the years of major popular political movements in the U.S., first over civil rights and later over Vietnam, it was almost inevitable that activities would develop simultaneously at a lower, local level. This was especially so since the American Jewish commitment to the welfare of Soviet Jewry represented much more than the concern of one influential and flourishing Jewish community for another large but persecuted Jewish community; American Jews at all levels sensed a direct personal link with Jews in a country from which they themselves or their ancestors had come.[126] These activities were not always in absolute conformity with those of the nationwide umbrella organization and sometimes even at obvious variance with them. Intended at first chiefly to galvanize the AJCSJ into more, and more virulent, action, the "grass-root" forces sometimes clashed with it. Enthusiastic over a cause which seemed to them clear-cut and at the same time to require large-scale, persistent and loud remonstrance, they had little patience for the slow and cumbersome workings which characterized the Jewish organizations and often seemed to render the AJCSJ ineffective.

Whether consciously or otherwise, the organized activity of the American Jewish community almost certainly drew its inspiration from the civil rights movement, which had become very dynamic in the early 1960s. Indeed, many Jews were active in that movement; and some of the principal civil rights leaders – both blacks like A. Philip Randolph, Reverend Martin Luther King, Jr. and Bayard Rustin, and whites such as Norman Thomas – became active in the cause of Soviet Jewry, whom they viewed as another discriminated minority.

The major effort to involve public opinion in the struggle for Soviet Jewry often used the same methods as the civil rights movement. In the words of one Soviet Jewry activist, the civil rights movement was important for the Soviet Jewry movement because it legitimized public protests, particularly picketing and sit-downs, as instruments with which the average citizen could identify and elevated ethnic pride, not only among the blacks but also among its Jewish adherents.[127]

The Soviet Jewry movement soon developed its own special features and activities. Some of these emanated as responses to steps initiated by the AJCSJ, others on the initiative of independent fringe groups seeking to motivate "grass-roots" activities, or from the efforts of the dedicated few who were already active on behalf of Soviet Jewry, usually in connection with the Israeli establishment. In some instances these fringe groups not only developed a momentum of their own but even occupied the center of the stage. This was not necessarily because their program was basically different in content from that of the AJCSJ, but because, by definition, they were able to operate without any institutional constraints. As for the Israelis, they seemed at this time to favor both the establishment and activities of local groupings, apparently seeing in the latter a catalyst that would force the heads of the Jewish organizations into further activity.

The first public Soviet Jewry conference in the U.S. was organized by Moshe Decter of Jewish Minorities Research, who brought together approximately one hundred intellectuals and public figures in New York in October 1963 for a day-long conference on the status of Soviet Jews. Decter's sponsors included Justice William O. Douglas, Norman Thomas (commonly dubbed "the conscience of America"), CIO leader Walter Reuther, Martin Luther King, Jr., Bishop James Pike and author Robert Penn Warren. Among the speakers were Pike, Douglas, writers Saul Bellow and Ralph Ellison, British critic and translator of Russian literature Max Hayward and left-wing playwright Arthur

Miller. Miller, who told the conference how the Soviets had tried to dissuade him from participating, protested "the vulgarity, the travesty of human feelings" of so many anti-Jewish articles in the Soviet press, which "appear to prove the existence of a methodical campaign to discredit, to degrade and, it would seem, to obliterate the Jew as a Jew." As he had told a Soviet embassy official, on the whole Jews were good citizens everywhere, and if Moscow were to leave them alone and "make believe it's not a problem," all Soviet Jews would probably enter this category.

The conference adopted an "Appeal of Conscience for the Jews of the Soviet Union," calling on "those in the U.S.S.R. who genuinely desire the eradication of the evils of Stalinism and . . . thirst for truth, justice and decency," as well as on the Soviet authorities, "to act in this matter [of Soviet Jewry] on the basis of their own ideological, constitutional and legal commitments." The conference also set up a standing committee that would be invoked from time to time to sign appeals and petitions.[128]

One initiative of the standing committee was its sponsorship of an Ad Hoc Commission on the Rights of Soviet Jews to inquire into the Soviet Jewry situation. The Commission included Union Theological Seminary President John C. Bennett; Pastor Emeritus of Corpus Christi Church Father George P. Ford, who had a national reputation as a fighter for civil rights and liberties; Emil Mazey of the United Automobile Workers Union; Floyd McCissick, executive director of the Congress of Racial Equality (CORE); Chief U.S. Prosecutor at the Nuremberg trials Telford Taylor; and Lionel Trilling. The Commission held a day of hearings in New York in March 1966. Some of the witnesses – Wiliam Korey, Erich Goldhagen, Max Hayward, Judd L. Teller – were experts on the Soviet Union and Soviet Jewry in particular. Others who had been to the USSR included: Professor William Brickman, who had headed a large delegation in 1960 to study Soviet education; editor of the Jesuit weekly *America* Reverend Thurston Davis, S.J., who had gone there to study religion; novelist Meyer Levin; historian and essayist Maurice Samuel; an anonymous American lady who had lived in the Soviet Union for thirty years; and David W. Weiss (see below). In its "verdict" handed down in December 1966, which it intended handing to U.N. Secretary General U Thant, the Commission stated that "an overwhelmingly persuasive and irrefutable case had been made out. The future of Soviet Jewry is in grave jeopardy . . . cut off from its past, atomised from within, isolated from its brethren abroad, bereft of educational institutions, subjected to a wide range of discriminatory deprivations in culture, religious education, employment and public life" and denied its natural right of group existence and meaningful identity. The Ad Hoc Commission therefore called on the Soviet Union to permit Jews to perpetuate their group life and culture and to allow the emigration of those Jews who wished to create a "new Jewish life for themselves in Israel."

In March 1967 Bayard Rustin reported that the first secretary of the Soviet embassy in Washington had rejected the Commission's findings as part of "a campaign that serves no other purpose than to deliberately distort the image of the Soviet Union in the minds of Americans and to divert their energies and attention from areas really worthy of application."[129]

Although the initiators of these activities did not succeed in making direct contact with the Soviets, it was widely felt that the latter were becoming increasingly sensitive to what one analyst termed the unrelenting criticism of their Jewish policy. In an article that opened by asking whether the USSR would "heed the appeal of world Jewry to 'Let my people go'," this same analyst noted that Moscow was particularly susceptible to criticism by Jewish intellectuals due to their influence on the media and in the academic realm.[130]

By the early 1960s representatives of non-Jewish religious organizations were also protesting anti-Jewish discrimination with something like regularity in their contacts with Soviet officials. Thus, a six-man delegation from the World Council of Churches questioned Soviet officials about Judaism in the USSR during an official visit there in 1962. Delegation head Eugene Carson Blake, former president of the Council, reported that Soviet officials had responded by denying that there was any problem, but promising to look into it anyway.[131] In December 1962 over forty leaders of different faiths sent a telegram to Khrushchev which they published in the *New York Times* and the *Washington Post*. The telegram pointed out that unless the USSR adapted "its behavior" to the universal standard of "freedom of conscience and expression," it must forfeit "the confidence of all peoples." It concluded by insisting that the world demanded deeds proving that the Soviet Union "in truth upholds the rights of minorities and the equal dignity of men."[132]

In July 1964 2,000 Christian clergymen, including cardinals Francis Spellman, Richard Cushing and Joseph G. Ritter, the heads of seven major Protestant denominations, the seven Episcopalian bishops, and presidents of Protestant and Catholic colleges, universities and seminaries, signed a "Letter of Conscience" urging the Kremlin to cease repressive measures against the Jews.[133]

In 1965 an interfaith Appeal to Conscience Foundation was established to press for religious freedom for Soviet Jews. In winter 1965–66 two of its vice-presidents, Thurston N. Davis and Harold A. Bosley, joined Foundation President Rabbi Arthur Schneier in visiting the USSR to investigate the situation at first hand. Although they were promised by an official of the Council of Religious Cults – just as the 1965 rabbinical delegation had been promised by Rabbi Levin – that 10,000 Hebrew prayer books would be printed as soon as technical arrangements could be made, this did not happen. And in summer 1966 the two Christian clergymen asked the Soviet embassy in Washington for permission to send 10,000 Hebrew prayer books to the USSR, explaining that "the situation facing the Jewish community in the Soviet Union cannot remain the sole concern of Jewry, but is a matter of concern to all men, regardless of creed."[134]

The first local Jewish organization on behalf of Soviet Jewry was formed in Cleveland in January 1963 when two scientists and a Reform rabbi set up what was to become the Cleveland Committee on Soviet Anti-Semitism. With the mayor of Cleveland as honorary chairman, and co-chairmen of various backgrounds, the Committee solicited support and sponsorship from other local political, religious and cultural leaders. It produced a booklet, *Soviet Terror against the Soviet Jews*, which was distributed at the 1963 national convention of the Reform Union of American Hebrew Congregations, at which a strong resolution condemning Soviet practices was passed.[135]

After establishing its own credibility, the Cleveland Committee proceeded to help develop "grass-roots organizations in other parts of the country."[136] It endorsed the "Appeal of Conscience" that emanated from the New York conference held in October 1963 and, in November, circulated its own appeal of conscience.[137] Louis Rosenblum, one of the two scientists who founded the Committee, defined as one of his main aims pressuring the major Jewish organizations to initiate national and local efforts on behalf of Soviet Jewry and creating the tools, techniques and tactics that would motivate Jews to form local groups.[138] Within a short period quite a few similar groups came into being, for example in Philadelphia, Boston, San Francisco and Miami, some of them with the assistance of the Cleveland Committee.

The ultimate goal of the Cleveland group, Rosenblum wrote shortly after its foundation, was getting the U.S. government on record as condemning Soviet antisemitic practices and motivating it to press the

Soviet leadership to change its Jewish policy. There was little hope that this protracted and difficult assignment could be accomplished by the existing Jewish community organizations which, with the exception of the Philadelphia Community Relations Council and the Boston Board of Rabbis, had on the whole been "unwilling to accept responsibility."[139]

In line with its goal, the Committee sent a circular to the sponsors of the Conference on the Status of Soviet Jews which stated that "the entire population, local, national and international" should "participate in a sustained, vigorous campaign of protest ... in the spirit of recent vehement condemnations by sixty U.S. Senators, by civic religious leaders of all faiths, and by members of the House of Representatives."[140] It also wrote directly to Khrushchev referring to the appeals concerning Soviet Jewry by men like Bertrand Russell, Linus Pauling, François Mauriac, Guy Mollet and Albert Schweitzer, all of whom had "devoted their lives to the cause of peace," and who knew that "peace and persecution cannot co-exist."[141]

In October 1963, in the context of the proposed U.S.–Soviet wheat deal, the Committee organized the dispatch of a telegram to President Kennedy signed by fifteen clergymen of different faiths and denominations, calling upon him to ensure that "the wheat not be used as an instrument of discrimination against a minority group. Specifically, the Soviet Government should make the wheat available as desired for use as *matzos* which are essential to Jewish Passover observance."[142]

In March 1965 the Cleveland Council (as the Committee had now become) organized a community-wide rally with the Cleveland Jewish Community Federation to protest Soviet antisemitism and issued a circular proclaiming an ongoing program of action that included: "a broad public petition" to the president requesting "his interference on behalf of Soviet Jewry" in his forthcoming talks with the new Soviet leaders; a mass campaign of continuous letters to the Soviet government; an Interfaith Sabbath Pulpit Exchange devoted to prayers for and sermons on Soviet Jews and their religious deprivations; and a public concert of Russian Jewish works "to underscore the Soviet suppression of Jewish culture."[143]

Also in 1965, the Council put out its own *Handbook for Community Action on Soviet Anti-Semitism* and the first issue of *Spotlight*, a newsletter dedicated to clarifying different aspects of the Soviet Jewish question and "reawaken[ing] concern." In its very first issue *Spotlight* criticized the AJCSJ for being ineffective and urged its readers to call on the national headquarters of Jewish organizations to which they belonged to strengthen that group. The inaugural issue also addressed itself to the desirability of evolving nationwide youth programs on Soviet Jewry and praised Congregation Zichron Ephraim, the synagogue across the street from the Soviet mission in New York, for erecting a plaque that could be seen from the mission which read: "Hear The Cry of The Oppressed – the Jewish Community of the Soviet Union."[144]

In 1966 the Cleveland Council submitted "the elements of a program of education and public opinion arousal" to the Planning Committee of the second AJCSJ convention. It also suggested improving the AJCSJ's "administrative structure" by opening three offices in different parts of the country, maintaining a "continuing professional staff" and ensuring a generous budget: a sound administrative apparatus was "essential to any accomplishment whatsoever."

Beginning in November 1963, the Clevelanders endeavored to confront every Soviet group that visited their city. Their first effort at confrontation was with a sixteen-man cultural mission, which, however, refused to meet with them. In March 1965 Cleveland Jewish youth groups asked members of the Moiseev folk dance company to urge their government to stop persecuting Soviet Jews. From 1966 on the Council sought contact with Soviet officials in Washington as well. Thus, two Cleveland teenagers and a rabbi from that city brought First Secretary Anatolii Myshkov a petition from the Greater Cleveland Youth Council on Soviet Antisemitism which he refused to accept.[145]

The Cleveland Committee established contact with a group of like-minded people in Springfield, Mass., in December 1963 after the latter's protests against official antisemitism in the USSR "reached us from many quarters." Herb Caron of Cleveland told the Springfield people that the few communities in which such protests were developing should "share ideas and profit from one another's errors."[146] The Springfield group said they had done "extensive research" and corresponded with "top U.S. officials, national organizations and leaders involved in this critical area," but that the lack of a "united plan of action for American Jewry, or program to involve the average citizen who is vitally and morally affected" meant that there were only "isolated . . . protests at various levels," which were being "largely ignored or refuted" by the Soviets. Although national Jewish leaders had asked them to "wait a little longer for a plan to emerge from the national organizations," they decided to take action on their own. They wrote a letter to the local newspaper, which had "prompted a stirring editorial." Then they visited the editor of the local Jewish newspaper, which had resulted in "more relevant news releases." And a letter to Israeli Ambassador Abe Harman, largely on the subject of Soviet Jewish emigration to Israel, brought Israeli Consul Meir Rosenne to Springfield on "an informative and heartwarming visit."[147]

When Rabbi Daniel Litt of the Cleveland group heard that a similar group was being organized in Lexington, Kentucky, he wrote his colleague there, Rabbi Robert A. Rothman, expressing his pleasure that "yet another community [was] striving for effective protest against the increasing oppression of our Jewish brethren in the Soviet Union," and giving him advice on how to maximize the new group's efforts. Rabbi Litt ended by stating his hope that the forthcoming conference – the founding conference of the AJCSJ – would realize that the time for resolution-making and quiet diplomacy had passed.[148]

In December 1963 a group of New York businessmen formed the American League for Russian Jews under the slogan "Let them live as Jews or leave as Jews." While the League was never a mass organization, it acted as a catalyst,[149] for example, by providing the impetus for the creation of another activist group, the Student Struggle for Soviet Jewry (SSSJ). Those attracted to SSSJ in its initial stages had been or still were active in the civil rights movement. Later on, SSSJ members came from among anti-Vietnam war activists and from those involved in the campus disturbances of the mid and late 1960s.[150]

The motivating force behind SSSJ was Jacob Birnbaum, a newcomer to the U.S. from Britain, who believed that the Jewish establishment should be pressured into taking action from below by the community at large. In 1964 Birnbaum wrote to labor leader David Dubinsky: "We are a recently founded organization of university students from all parts of the United States, who have joined together in a completely non-affiliated, self-supported group to aid Soviet Jewry," a group that refused to "remain silent as did so many of our parents when the Nuremberg laws were being promulgated." Since the founding conference of the AJCSJ several months previously had not resulted in "any real attempt to initiate a grass-roots campaign, we felt that the time for action had arrived, even though we might incur the displeasure of the organizations who claimed to represent the Jewish masses in this matter."[151]

The SSSJ was brought into being three weeks after the founding conference of the AJCSJ at a hastily called meeting at Columbia University in late April 1964, which drew approximately 250 students to hear Morris Brafman of the American League for Russian Jews. The meeting called for a mass demonstration for 1 May at the Soviet U.N. mission. The more than one thousand students who turned up at the demonstration became the first group to take to the streets on behalf of Soviet Jewry. Not relaxing its impetus, the SSSJ organized a fast for later that month.[152]

The Student Struggle spread its message in summer camps and by devising slogans, songs, skits and a variety of "program aids" that would attract young people. It also prepared handbooks on the Soviet Jewish situation that announced forthcoming activities, contained a suggested bibliography on the subject and explained the purpose and value of Western Jewish protest.[153] Believing that, just as New York was the ideal location for mobilizing public opinion, so Washington was the place for enlisting protection for Soviet Jewry, Birnbaum quickly formed connections with senators, congressmen and the State Department.[154] By summer 1964 the SSSJ was urging the Democratic Party National Committee, which had always "enjoyed extensive support from Jews," to include the issue of Soviet Jewry in the presidential election program (as had the Republicans).[155]

But, above all, the SSSJ continued to organize demonstrations. In June 1964 it held an inter-faith demonstration of solidarity in the form of an inter-faith service, which culminated in a week-long fast. Then, in October, students picketed in front of the Lincoln Center, where a Soviet dance group was performing ("We are protesting the bringing of Soviet dancers to this country while the Jews in Russia are not even permitted to buy *matzohs*"). In the same month it initiated a mass rally and march, at which Special Counsel to the President Myer Feldman told the assemblage that President Johnson was in full sympathy with its position.[156]

The SSSJ's "Jericho March" in April 1965 brought out 3,000 demonstrators carrying seven *Tora* scrolls and seven ram's horns. The ram's horn or *shofar*, blown to bring down the walls of Jericho as the Sons of Israel marched around the city seven times, is used today on the High Holy Days to invoke divine mercy. The demonstrators blew it as they encircled the Soviet U.N. mission seven times in the hope that the walls that separated East from West would come down.

The SSSJ followed this with a "Jericho Ride" to Washington on 20 May, to meet with Soviet embassy First Secretary Myshkov and William Stearman of the U.S. State Department. At a meeting with Stearman the week before, Birnbaum had learned that the protest movement in the U.S. was playing a large part in changing State Department thinking on Soviet Jewry. The day in Washington ended with another march with a *shofar* in the vicinity of the Soviet embassy, at which several congressmen heard an "Appeal to Conscience."[157]

The SSSJ's December 1965 Hanukka *Menora* Rally later became an annual event. Its Passover *Geula* (Redemption) march in April 1966, which was preceded by a *Lel shimurim* (Night of Vigil) and in which 15,000, mostly students, took part,[158] also became an institution; in 1967 twenty-four such vigils were organized in eighteen different cities. At the central event in front of the U.N., a religious service, speeches and seminars took place in a huge "freedom tent." The aim of the vigil was "to align ... with Soviet Jews mentally, psychologically and emotionally in the cause of achieving human freedom, justice and personal dignity ... and to develop an ongoing interest, concern and understanding on the part of all people – Jews and non-Jews – in the problem of Soviet Jewry." Speakers included Representatives James Scheuer and Jonathan Bingham; Reverend Charles Thorne of the Protestant Council of the City of New York; Morris Tushewitz, Secretary of the New York City Central Labor Council; and Norman Thomas.[159]

Two days after the vigil, under the heading "A Passover Appeal for Soviet Jewry," the *New York Times* published the full text of a speech made by the U.S. representative to the Human Rights Commission in March 1967 on "implementation of the Declaration Against Racial Discrimination." An advertisement in the *Times*, signed by the Conference on the Status of Soviet Jews, pointed out that although the text did not mention Soviet Jews by name, it clearly referred to them.[160]

The demonstrations, marches and mass meetings that were emerging as a major weapon on behalf of Soviet Jewry took place mostly, but not solely, in New York City. Although some of them were organized by AJCSJ and other bodies, including many from the establishment, the SSSJ was largely responsible for keeping up the pressure to continue this form of protest.

In this period local and grass-roots activists were not generally separatist by inclination. Although they operated autonomously, without any guidance, let alone instructions or prodding, from the establishment AJCSJ, they did seek cooperation with the central organization, whose goals – the arousing of a Western negative public opinion to embarrass the Soviets and thus get concessions for their Jews – were basically the same as their own. The leaders of the Cleveland group made this explicit in a letter they sent to AJCSJ Chairman Rabbi Miller in the wake of the Philadelphia convention. Activists such as these were not alone in criticizing the AJCSJ for its lack of action, undue formalism and acceptance of *diktats* by the U.S.

administration. People like Rabbi Heschel and Elie Wiesel, for instance, were equally frustrated by the institutional considerations of AJCSJ member organizations that kept that body from effectively pursuing its avowed goals.[161]

By the middle of the decade the dispute between those continuing to demand covert diplomacy and the new protest movement was becoming increasingly academic, for the educational campaigns and public relations tactics of the latter had given it an irreversible momentum.[162] The effect of Western public protest, especially from the Left, seemed proven after the Soviets published the Russell–Khrushchev correspondence and withdrew the Kichko book. True, some of the slogans of the "fringe groups" caused disconcertment among a few of the major organizations,[163] and tensions between them persisted, yet on the whole the AJCSJ and the activists were cooperating. Both groups, too, were working in conjunction with the Israeli embassy in Washington and consulate in New York. In June 1967 Nehemia Levanon, who was responsible for Soviet Jewry at the Israeli embassy in Washington, wrote to Jacob Birnbaum praising his "great work" and "the devotion of Jews like you that give the Jewish people strength to face the great challenges of our times."[164]

Now that the major American Jewish organizations had united in the struggle on behalf of Soviet Jewry, the Israelis were pushing the AJCSJ to take a more clearly defined and unequivocal stance with the U.S. government and to step up its efforts to arouse public opinion.[165] In this context, the Israelis welcomed pressure on the Jewish establishment on the part of the grass-root organizations. They also acclaimed the SSSJ slogan "Let My People Go" over appeals for Jewish cultural and religious rights inside the USSR, although the Israelis wanted Jews to be able to leave in order to go to Israel, which was not necessarily the case, even in the mid-sixties, among advocates of Soviet Jewish emigration, Jewish and non-Jewish, in the U.S. At this point, however, the desired destination of Soviet Jewish emigrants was not an issue that needed to be discussed since those who were being allowed to leave, except for those few reuniting with close family in the West, sought to go to Israel.

### Jews and non-Jews in other Western countries in the fight for Soviet Jewish rights

Although the United States was the scene of the most important and extensive activity on behalf of Soviet Jewry, protest at the plight of Soviet Jewry was not unique to the U.S. Moreover, many of the strategies used there were common to the efforts of Jewish organizations and leaders in Western Europe and Latin America, in Canada and Australia, who were making their concern known to the Soviets with marked success through important local and international forums.

### Jewish organizations and activity

Since the late 1950s the WJC had been sporadically involved in trying to influence the Kremlin to lift the restrictions that were preventing Soviet Jewry from preserving its collective religious, communal and cultural identity and from forming organizations within the USSR or having links with fellow Jews outside. It was not until July 1964, however, that a plenary session of the WJC executive called upon the Soviet government to stop all manifestations of antisemitism and to allow Soviet Jewish emigration, or, more specifically, the reunification of families.[166]

In August 1964 the World Conference of Jewish Organizations expressed "deep concern" over the lack of any "fundamental change" in Soviet Jewish policy and called for "moral pressure" on the USSR to persist in the free world until full cultural and religious rights were restored to Soviet Jews. Also in August, the World Council of Synagogues urged the Kremlin to halt discriminatory practices against the Jews and Judaism and to undertake educational efforts aimed at halting antisemitism and all other forms of religious discrimination in the Soviet Union.[167] The Conference of European Rabbis had already submitted a lengthy memorandum to the Soviet ambassador in Italy in March 1964, protesting the "unjust discrimination practised against Judaism by the Soviet authorities . . . that threaten the very survival of Jewish identity."[168] At a meeting of this same forum in Paris in March 1966, the Conference again expressed "deep concern over the plight of Soviet Jewry," noting that the changes that the Soviet authorities had agreed to were "of a token nature" and that Soviet Jews were still being deprived of "the rights to which they are entitled."[169]

In Europe, as in the U.S., students took on a more activist role in the struggle. In spring 1965 the World Union of Jewish Students (WUJS) devoted a four-day seminar in Brussels to the problem. In fall 1965 the WUJS declared the inauguration of a Soviet Jewry Year for Jewish students everywhere and set up work groups in the various European countries and Australia to create umbrella organizations of Jewish youth organizations and general student organizations. The aim was to disseminate authentic information on the Soviet Jewish situation to the public at large and to present petitions to Soviet embassies in the various capitals.[170] The first such petition to be handed over was in Canberra, Australia, in January 1966 where one hundred Jewish students picketed the Soviet embassy.

In late March of the same year a WUJS delegation presented a petition signed by 30,000 students and professors from several European universities to a Soviet embassy official in Paris. In addition to demanding "the destruction of manifestations of antisemitism," the petition called for the reunification of families and "the right of emigration for those Jews who wish to leave . . . in conformity with the Universal Declaration of Human Rights." However, when the official stated that he could not transmit such a message to his government, the WUJS Paris headquarters sent it directly to Kosygin and Chairman of the USSR Supreme Soviet Nikolai Podgornyi. (The same petition was handed in simultaneously to Soviet embassies in The Hague, Stockholm, Brussels, Copenhagen and Berne.)[171] This was followed in May 1966 by a march on the Soviet embassy in London of a thousand British students protesting Soviet antisemitism. The demonstrators' slogans included "Freedom for Soviet Jewry," "Let My People Go," "Let Jews Live or Leave," "Reunite Families Separated by Holocaust," "Jewish Culture for Soviet Jews" and "Lenin Aided Jewish Culture: Was He Wrong?" As in Paris, when the marchers tried to hand embassy officials a petition signed by 5,000 British academics and students, the petition was refused.[172]

Activity at the national level sometimes led to quick positive action on the part of the governments involved. In Australia, for example, the Victoria Jewish Board of Deputies passed a resolution in March 1962 appealing to the Australian government to raise the plight of Soviet Jewry at the U.N. It followed this up by lobbying members of the Australian House of Representatives and Senate, who raised the issue in the House on 3 October 1962 and in the Senate on 20 October. Within days, Australian Minister for External Affairs Sir Garfield Barwick announced that his country's U.N. representative would raise the subject at the U.N., and within a week Australia became the first government besides Israel to formally urge the USSR to extend freedom of emigration to its Jews.[173]

The Executive Council of Australian Jewry (ECAJ) showed a persistent interest in Soviet Jewry. In spring 1964 it published a brochure that incorporated caricatures from the Kichko book, circulating it among students as well as among leftist and communist groupings which had been denying the existence of Soviet antisemitism. The brochure led to mass protest meetings and expressions of serious disquietude at the situation among top echelons of the Australian Communist Party. It was in this context that Prime Minister Sir Robert Menzies told the Australian House of Representatives in April 1964 that the Australian U.N. representative would again raise his government's concern over racial and religious intolerance in the USSR, especially the antisemitic literature being sponsored by the Kremlin.[174] (This policy was upheld by Menzies' successor, Harold Holt, when he told the House in September 1966 that "Australia has played a vital part in urging upon the Soviet Union a policy of religious tolerance and non-discrimination against the Jewish minority" and would continue to keep "fully in mind . . . the welfare of the Jewish people."[175]) In November 1964 the ECAJ called upon "each and every Jew in . . . Australia, collectively and individually, by all means available, to endeavour to arouse Australian and world opinion upon this subject" and asked for "the active help of all who have human dignity and rights at heart."

In the person of Isi Liebler, Chairman of its Public Relations Committee, the Victoria Board of Deputies played a major role in the Soviet Jewry struggle in Australia. Liebler, for example, was instrumental in bringing the issue to the attention of the Australian Communist Party. At the WJC World Executive Congress in Strasbourg in July 1965 he also accused Nahum Goldmann of playing into the hands of the Soviets and their apologists by understating the problem of Soviet Jewry in his public appearances. Liebler's efforts eventually led the ECAJ to circularize all WJC and COJO constituents in February 1967, expressing its non-confidence in Goldmann's "quiet diplomacy" and castigating him for refusing to give emigration top priority. During these years two Jewish members of parliament, Sam Cohen in the Senate and Sidney Einfeld in the House, were likewise active on behalf of Soviet Jewry in Parliament, in the Jewish community and in making representations to the Soviet embassy.[176]

In France a January 1963 conference representing Jewish communities in twenty-five French cities urged the Soviet authorities to put an end to the "tragic survivals of the pre-revolutionary past and to implement the principles of freedom and equality."[177] Two years later the Soviet Jewish question was the main issue at a mass meeting in Paris to commemorate the anniversary of the Warsaw ghetto uprising. The meeting urged Gromyko, who was then in the French capital, to address himself to the question of the reunification of families. A similar approach was made by the Conseil représentatif des juifs en France (CRIF).[178]

In Italy Chief Rabbi of the Jewish community of Rome Elio Toaff and Justice Sergio Piperno of the Rome appelate court sent cables to the U.N. Human Rights Commission and to the Soviet ambassador in Italy protesting the economic trials.[179] Three years later, in 1966, the Union of Italian Jewish Communities passed two resolutions concerning Soviet Jews. One of them, which had been proposed by the Italian Jewish Youth Federation, expressed the hope that Jewish families separated by the war would be allowed to reunite "in Israel or elsewhere."[180]

The Scandinavian Jewish community was galvanized into action in 1964 on the eve of Khrushchev's visit. Copenhagen's Jewish Community Board sent a letter to the Soviet embassy expressing concern over the situation of Soviet Jewry and requesting an opportunity to discuss the matter with Khrushchev, and the Scandinavian Jewish Youth Federation urged the Soviet authorities to allow cultural exchanges between Jews in the USSR and Scandinavia, offering to make all the arrangements necessary to carry out such a program.[181] And on the occasion of the 1965 WUJS "Protest Day of the Jewish Student," Swedish Jewish students – joined by members of the left-wing student organization Clarte and the Liberal Students' Club – picketed the Soviet embassy in Stockholm and handed its staff a petition protesting the USSR's treatment of its Jews.[182]

Chairman of the Foreign Affairs Committee of the Board of Deputies of British Jews Sir Barnett Janner, M.P., said in October 1963 that the Board had "issued many appeals to the Soviet authorities," but despite the lessening of East–West tensions the trend of Soviet anti-Jewish discrimination had actually intensified "in some aspects," and the Board therefore intended initiating a meeting with the Soviet ambassador on this issue.[183] At an Anglo-Jewish Association meeting the following month, the honorary secretary of the Agudas Israel World Organisation moved a resolution calling for the convening of a combined conference of Anglo-Jewish organizations to discuss the Soviet Jewish situation. He pointed out that three Anglo-Jewish organizations had approached the Soviet embassy separately, but had received no reply. AJA President Maurice Edelman, M.P., stated that he had written to the Foreign Secretary asking for such information as might be available "on the particular problem" of the Soviet Jews. Still in November 1963, Janner discussed the Soviet Jewry position with Minister of State at the Foreign Office Peter Thomas.[184]

A special session held under the auspices of the Board of Deputies in May 1965, that represented the first combined effort of Anglo-Jewish organizations to help Soviet Jewry, adopted a resolution condemning "the harsh discrimination" against the Jews being practiced in the USSR. Opening the session, Board President Solomon Teff said that it was essential for the whole community to speak in one voice on the matter. Janner moved that the Jewish and non-Jewish public be enlightened on the issue through pamphlets and "the holding of meetings to publicise the problem." He stressed that the rights being demanded for Soviet Jews were "not only those to which they were entitled as human beings everywhere but to which they are entitled under Soviet law."[185] In February 1966 the Board of Deputies arranged a second meeting of Jewish organizations in Great Britain to discuss Soviet Jewry.[186]

The May 1965 session was followed in June by a meeting of Jewish youth movements, at which a Committee for Russian Jewry was set up to acquaint youth in general with the facts concerning Soviet Jewry.[187] Toward the end of 1966 the Universities' Committee for Soviet Jews announced a program of lectures, seminars and protest meetings to "inform those groups who are not fully aware of the disabilities facing Russian Jews." And Soviet Jewry was the subject of a special plenary session of the 1966 Inter-University Jewish Federation (IUJF) conference in Liverpool.[188]

On the eve of Aleksei Kosygin's February 1967 visit to Britain, all twelve leading Jewish organizations made a joint appeal on behalf of Soviet Jewry together with the community's religious leaders. After a Board of Deputies request to meet with Kosygin was ignored, Board President Teff made another attempt to set up such a meeting when Prime Minister Harold Wilson introduced him to Kosygin at a reception in the latter's honor; but this, too, was turned down. A joint memorandum was therefore sent to Kosygin. The missive pointed out that British Jewry had been "greatly encouraged" by the Soviet prime minister's Paris statement regarding "family reunion in Israel and elsewhere," and that "the full implementation of such a humanitarian policy ... would be greatly appreciated not only by British Jewry but, we feel sure, by British public opinion in general." The memorandum went on to say that, since Soviet Jewry lacked "the essential means" for maintaining their existence as a community, the Soviets should hasten to make "proper provision for Jewish educational and cultural facilities," adequate synagogues and a Jewish communal organization to enable contact with Jewish communities abroad.[189]

Indeed, the largest European demonstration on behalf of Soviet Jewry held in the period in question was probably the one held during Kosygin's London visit. Organized by the Universities' Committee for Soviet Jewry, the protestors comprised 2,200 Jewish and non-Jewish students in addition to communal leaders, rabbis and two Roman Catholic priests. They marched to the Soviet embassy carrying banners reading: "Reunite Divided Families," "Freedom for Soviet Jewry," "Discrimination Stains Soviet Honour" and "Reopen Jewish Schools." Upon reaching the embassy, the marchers handed a third secretary a memorandum calling for the establishment of Jewish sections in all Soviet student organizations to enable contact on "matters of mutual interest and concern." Ever mindful of the need to avoid giving the impression that the demonstration was anti-Soviet in intent, an all-night vigil scheduled for outside the embassy was canceled.[190]

In Canada the All-Canadian Rabbinic Conference organized a day of prayer for the welfare of Soviet Jews which was observed by all Canadian synagogues in May 1964. In January 1965 fifteen Canadian Jewish organizations held a rally for Soviet Jewry in Ottawa. And in May 1966 over 300 leaders of national Jewish organizations held a one-day conference on Soviet Jewry in Montreal, which was attended by a number of non-Jewish public figures, including members of parliament from all three parties. The conference urged the Canadian government to let the Soviet Union know of Canadian Jewry's deep and abiding concern for their Soviet brethren. It also called on the Soviet government, directly, to let the Jews practice and perpetuate their culture and religion, to use "all the means at its disposal to eradicate anti-semitism" and to permit Soviet Jewish families "separated as a result of the Nazi holocaust to be reunited with their relatives abroad." Finally, it was recommended that the Canadian Jewish Congress National Executive Committee, which had sponsored the conference, "immediately study the feasibility of establishing a special national committee, inviting to it representatives of major national, central and local organizations ... to implement the resolutions emerging from the conference and to direct itself to the matter of devising an ongoing programme of action on behalf of Soviet Jews."[191]

In Latin America, Argentina's Jews displayed their concern for Soviet Jewry on 12 August 1963, the eleventh anniversary of Stalin's execution of leading Jewish writers and public figures, by sending a letter to Soviet ambassador Nikolai Alekseev asking that Jews in the USSR be accorded the same treatment given other national groupings.

A similar message was sent to the Soviet ambassador in Mexico by that country's Central Committee of the Jewish community.[192] In October 1966 the Jewish Central Committee of Chile presented a Soviet parliamentary delegation visiting their country with a letter expressing their concern about the situation of Soviet Jews. And in December the same year, the Jewish Central Committee of Mexico appealed to its government to support U.N. attempts to persuade the Soviet Union to treat its Jews fairly and to allow family reunification.[193]

December 1966 saw a spate of Jewish activity the world over. In response to an appeal by Rabbi Israel Miller of the AJCSJ to sign and publish declarations on behalf of Soviet Jewry on or around the anniversary of the U.N. Declaration of Human Rights, which fell during the festival of Hanukka, Jewish communities in some twenty countries issued identical statements in an International Declaration on Soviet Jewry. These statements announced that they would continue their "protests and appeals until the [Soviet] Jewish minority is assured equality of treatment with all other ethnic and national groups in the U.S.S.R." The program they presented to the Soviet government was based on the Philadelphia Declaration of Rights for Soviet Jewry of April 1966. Although the British Board of Deputies did not sign this declaration, it put out a similar statement of its own on 9 December.[194]

### Action by non–Jewish groups and individuals

There was also a profusion of non-Jewish activity throughout the West during this period, some of it initiated – directly or indirectly – by Jewish bodies and leaders and some by the Israelis. In part this activity was the logical result of developments in international forums such as the U.N., the Socialist International and the Council of Europe, which had aroused the awareness and interest of politicians and intellectuals.

The mobilization of liberal intellectual opinion on the issue of Soviet Jewry deliberately set out to be non-sectarian. In September 1963, when Nahum Goldmann gave his second follow-up report to the participants of the 1960 Paris Conference on the Situation of the Jews in the Soviet Union, he proposed "reviving a campaign to mobilize world opinion to bring about a more tolerant Soviet attitude" toward Jews in response to what he called a steady deterioration in the Soviet Jewish position and the dismantling of the Soviet Jewish community. Goldmann added that "a growing number of liberal-minded prominent men, often closely connected with the Soviet Union by ties of friendship and esteem, consider it their duty to express their anxiety to the government of the USSR about a situation which they consider to be incompatible with Soviet principles.''[195]

Just two weeks later, at the beginning of October, a meeting of some 150 Italian intellectuals and politicians, representing all political views except that of the communists, was held in Rome. Convened on the initiative of a committee of Italian public figures headed by the jurist, Professor Vicenzo Arangio-Ruiz, the meeting opened with the reading of a telegram from Bertrand Russell, probably the most prominent and committed of Europe's non-Jewish intellectuals to take up the Soviet Jewry cause. Russell expressed his profound concern at anti-Jewish discrimination in the USSR, which he dubbed both an infringement on human rights and an obstacle to peace. The two main speakers were historian Aldo Garosci and publicist Enzo Tagliacozzo, Garosci telling the meeting that the question of Jewish rights was a measure of the possibility for an East–West reconciliation in the interests of peace and humanity.[196]

In January 1966 a further conference of Italian intellectuals and men of letters was held in Milan. It was organized by the Italian Committee for Soviet Jewry, headed by Ada Sereni, who had been behind most of the activity on behalf of Soviet Jewry since the March 1961 conference of intellectuals, which supplied information to a wide range of institutions and personalities as well as to the media in order to arouse the Italian public and pressure the government. The main speaker at the conference was Daniel Mayer of France, who attributed any concessions and improvement in the situation of Soviet Jewry to external pressures on the Soviet authorities. It was also addressed by Garosci; the president of COMES (Communauté européenne des écrivains), the poet Giuseppi Ungaretti who had visited the USSR twice; and the president of the Italian Jewish community, Justice Sergio Piperno. The conference, which drew considerable space in Italy's leading newspapers, approved a motion urging the Soviet government to start giving Jews civil, political and religious equality.[197]

In Latin America, the only area with a considerable Jewish community which the Soviet Union viewed as belonging strategically to the Third World, non-Jewish intellectual circles had been aware, at least since Binyamin Eliav's 1956 tour of the continent, that Soviet Jewry was in danger of spiritual extinction. Now Israeli Ambassador to Uruguay Arye Eshel, who had headed the Israeli Foreign Ministry's

East European Department during Israel's early efforts to awaken the world to the problem, was instrumental in translating materials on Soviet Jewry into Spanish for dissemination throughout Latin America. Thus the area was ripe for the conference on Soviet Jewry that Benno Weiser (later Varon), who headed the Latin American Section of the Jewish Agency in New York, organized in Rio de Janeiro in September 1963.

Attended by forty-eight intellectuals, mostly non-Jews and mostly progressives, but not communists, the conference was chaired by President of the Brazilian Academy of Letters Austragesilo de Athayde, who had headed his country's delegation to the U.N. in 1948, when the Declaration of Human Rights was framed. Not only did it bring together some of Latin America's most distinguished thinkers, poets and writers, but many others who were not able to be there in person associated themselves with it and its cause by sending messages of sympathy and support. De Athayde himself termed what Soviet Jewry was undergoing genocide, since that concept had been "amplified . . . to include the elimination of the characteristic values of a people, be they religious, cultural or linguistic."

One of the aims of the conference was to decide how best to bring the Soviet Jewish plight to both the universities and the working classes. Among others, it sent a telegram to Khrushchev invoking the Soviet nationalities policy and Article 123 of the Soviet constitution, requesting a more generous application of both toward the USSR's Soviet Jewish minority. Copies of the main resolution were sent to U.N. Secretary U Thant, the U.N. Commission on Human Rights, the President of the U.N. General Assembly and the Organization of American States.[198]

Latin American intellectuals also manifested their concern for Soviet Jewry in national forums. Argentina's Writers' Association sent a letter to Kosygin in 1965 informing him of its "deep concern regarding news known lately about anti-Jewish discrimination," while in February 1966 the Argentine Federation of Journalists sent a message to the International Federation of Journalists in Brussels asking that forum to take a stand on Soviet attempts to eliminate Jewish culture and to urge the Kremlin to halt its efforts to equate Zionism with Nazism and neo-Nazism.

In early January 1966 it was reported that forty-four leading Venezuelan intellectuals had forwarded a letter appealing to the Soviet Union to end discrimination against its Jews to the Soviet ambassador in Mexico. The signatories had examined the question "in a completely unbiased fashion," and had established that there was a wide gap between the equality guaranteed by the Soviet Constitution and the Jews' real position. They were therefore asking the Soviet government to satisfy them that Jews in the USSR were being treated in accord with the Universal Declaration of Human Rights.[199]

In April 1966 over fifty leading Mexican intellectuals published a six-point memorandum requesting the restoration of Soviet Jewish rights, measures to deter antisemitic publications and the consideration "with benevolence" of cases of Jews seeking to reunite with relatives in Israel and elsewhere.[200] In May 1966 a similar conference of some fifty Uruguayan intellectuals signed a petition against racism and national discrimination, with particular reference to the Soviet Jewish situation. Their demands were put to the Soviets in the name of "peaceful mankind."[201] In the same month a two-day conference of Latin American intellectuals was held in Mexico. Attended by university deans and prominent writers from seven countries, the conference dispatched a resolution to Kosygin, U Thant and the Commission on Human Rights, making it clear that although the participants had no interest in furthering the cold war, they nevertheless considered it "the duty of every intellectual to insist on the restoration of Jewish culture . . . and permission to emigrate for purposes of family reunification."[202]

In December 1966 Chile's Association of Writers adopted a resolution calling on the Soviet government to grant equal treatment and "the complete freedom of human rights" to its Jews. The petition was signed by every member except for General Secretary Enrique Bellow, an active member of the Communist Party, although two other communist members, Association President Francisco Coloane and Guillermo Atlas, did append their signatures. The petition emphasized that the Association had always maintained "a progressive position and an active interest in the realization of Socialism," and that it was making its appeal out of friendship for the USSR, as had Bertrand Russell, Linus Pauling, Martin Buber, Max Born, Albert Schweitzer, François Mauriac "and others of universal prestige."[203]

Other similar conferences were held in this period, including one in Paris in October 1964 that was attended by some forty leading leftist political, literary and academic personalities. Among the participants were Daniel Mayer, who chaired the conference; another former minister, Pierre Bloch; Jacques Nantet; Director of the Catholic monthly *l'Esprit* Jean-Marie Domenach; Vice-Chairman of the National Assembly and Chairman of the France–USSR Friendship

Association Raymond Schmittlein; Jewish novelist Albert Memmi; editor of *le Populaire* Gérard Jaquet; and President of the Movement against Racialism and Antisemitism Pierre Paraf. This conference, too, passed a resolution calling for an end to anti-Jewish discrimination in the USSR and for permission for Jews desiring to join relatives abroad to do so.[204]

April 1965 saw a conference in Stockholm devoted to the issue of Soviet Jewry. It was chaired by Uppsala University Rector Professor Torgny Segerstedt, who also headed the organizing committee, and was attended by Swedish Communist Party leader V. Jansen. One of the speakers, Professor Herbert Tingsten, said that, although Soviet antisemitism was practiced under the veil of anti-Zionism, dual loyalty had to be possible wherever Jews lived. Thomas Jefferson had long ago said that anyone who believed in progress had two mother countries, France and his own country of birth. Even though a non-Jew, Tingsten regarded Israel as his second mother country because of its contribution to universal progress. The conference resolution, submitted to the governments of Sweden, Norway and Denmark, to U Thant and the Human Rights Commission, as well as to the Israeli and Soviet embassies in Stockholm, called upon the Soviets to repudiate antisemitism, to give the Jews equal academic, cultural and religious rights and to allow families to be reunited.[205]

The Stockholm conference also received a message from Bertrand Russell, in which he stressed that an improvement in the Soviet Jewish situation "would greatly assist all those seeking coexistence and is of great importance to progressive and liberal opinion throughout the world." Russell went on to say that "the plight of Soviet Jewry demands the sympathy and constructive assistance of all impartial people." In his opinion the reunification of families was "a matter of the greatest urgency" which the Soviet Union was not implementing although it had recognized it in principle.[206]

In Canada a group of over twenty university professors and civic leaders released the text of a letter to the Soviet embassy in Ottawa just prior to Premier Kosygin's visit to that country in October 1966. The letter "urgently" called on the Soviet government "to take steps to end [anti-Jewish] persecution," explaining that "we are concerned by this state of affairs first as human beings. But it also concerns us in its significance for peace and co-existence in the world."[207]

The issue of Soviet Jewry troubled many sectors of the population around the world besides intellectuals. When Khrushchev visited Scandinavia in 1964, the well-known Danish writer Peter Per Rohde sparked off a vociferous press campaign in Denmark's liberal *Information*. And *Jydske Tidende* published an open letter to Khrushchev from Aktiv Frihad, a Danish organization that fought for freedom for all peoples in line with the Declaration of Human Rights. The group based its expression of concern over the Soviet Jewish situation on the report published by the Socialist International Study Group. Several other Danish newspapers reported that national organizations and private citizens, including former Foreign Minister Bjor Kraft, had written Khrushchev urging that Jews be allowed "to travel or emigrate to Israel at will" and that those Jews who chose to stay in the Soviet Union be accorded equal treatment with citizens of other nationalities. All leading papers published the letter to the Soviet embassy from the Congregation of the Mosaic Faith in Denmark, while wide publicity was given the letter Scandinavian Jewish youth had addressed to Khrushchev.

In Sweden, too, Khrushchev's visit occasioned much critical comment on the USSR's practices toward its Jews. The press published the entire text of a letter to Khrushchev from Sweden's Jewish community, and Prime Minister Tage Erlander brought up the Soviet Jewry issue in his meetings with the First Secretary. However, the most persistent criticism came from Norway, despite the Soviet embassy's efforts to "clear up and refute certain misunderstandings" before a letter from the Norwegian Union of Socialist Youth, which had been published throughout the Norwegian press, was "handed over to Premier Khrushchev." (The Union's letter, too, had been based on the Socialist International report.) The statement of another youth organization, the Norwegian Non-Violence Group, 1964, which described Soviet Jewish policy as "spiritual strangulation," was published by the entire Oslo press with the exception of the communist paper. The Norwegian press also reported on the peaceful demonstration objecting to certain aspects of Soviet policy, including anti-Jewish discrimination, which was staged outside the Norwegian National Assembly. Finally, the ruling Labor Party published the Socialist International Study Group report in a special issue of its periodical.[208]

Once aroused, Scandinavian interest in the Soviet Jewish issue persisted. Thus, in February 1965 the Swedish Ecumenical Council sent a letter expressing concern over anti-Jewish discrimination to the Soviet government, the Commission of the Churches on International Affairs, the Israeli embassy and the Chief Rabbi of Stockholm.[209]

Last, but certainly not least, the Soviet Jewry issue was raised in the parliaments of a number of Western countries as well as by statesmen and government spokesmen in their contacts with Soviet officials. In December 1963 the Belgian parliament held a discussion on the Soviet Jewish situation during a foreign policy debate in which Christian Socialist Leo Tindemans called the problem one that cast a shadow on efforts to reduce East–West tensions. Tindemans urged Foreign Minister Paul-Henri Spaak to make clear to the Soviets that, at a time when the world was denouncing the infringement of human rights in Angola and South Africa, the plight of Soviet Jews had to be decried as well.[210] The Belgians became one of the driving forces behind the decision to raise the issue at the Council of Europe in 1964. And Belgian Prime Minister Lefèvre raised the issue in Moscow when he met with Soviet Deputy Premier Konstantin Rudnev.[211]

British Labour leaders – Hugh Gaitskell, Aneurin Bevan and Harold Wilson – had a long record of intercession on behalf of Soviet Jewry. As Labour M.P. Richard H. Crossman said in an April 1964 broadcast, changes in the international situation had rekindled the hope that "external pressure, if fairly and diplomatically applied, can achieve for Russian Jewry a status it had never enjoyed." The urgent need to buy American wheat and British fertilizer factories had made Moscow anxious to "silence criticism" of its treatment of its Jews.[212]

In July 1965, in the wake of the Council of Europe's May 1965 resolution, the British Foreign Secretary was asked a parliamentary question about Soviet Jewry. Minister of State for Foreign Affairs Walter Padley replied that the government had studied the resolution "with interest and sympathy" but, not unlike the U.S. State Department, did not believe that its "offical intervention" would "assist the achievement of the objects which the Consultative Assembly of the Council of Europe has in mind." And when Col. John A. Biggs-Davison, M.P., asked the government what efforts it had made "to carry [the resolution] into effect" in December, the minister said he had nothing to add to his previous statement.[213]

Harold Wilson had raised the issue with both Khrushchev and Kosygin, first as leader of the opposition and later as prime minister, following what he dubbed "very substantial discussions with those who are most concerned in this country and elsewhere." Yet, when he visited Moscow in summer 1966, he refrained from raising the Soviet Jewish question at the highest level because there were so many other pressing issues and because he knew from de Gaulle's recent visit to the USSR (see below) that the Soviets strongly resented any intercession on the situation on the part of foreign governments. In July 1966

Minister of State for Foreign Affairs Eireen White answered questions on "the well-documented list of persecutions" of Soviet Jews put by Sir John Foster and Sir Alec Douglas-Home by reemphasizing that the government had made its "opposition to all forms of racialism, including anti-Semitism" clear at the U.N. and that the Soviets were "aware of our views." Yet, while it was proper to raise the matter internationally, it was improper "to make official bilateral representations to another country on behalf of people in whom we cannot claim a direct interest." Consequently, the issue was not taken up in "the main plenary part of the discussions" during Kosygin's February 1967 visit, although it was among individual questions taken up separately at the foreign minister level. In reply to a question put to him by Sir Ian Orr-Ewing, the prime minister assured the House that the issue had been raised every time Foreign Secretary George Brown and his predecessor met the Soviet government. Wilson must have been attempting to explain the frustrations he and others were experiencing in this context when he told the Commons that "the Soviet Government do not admit some of the statements we have made on this issue and regard it as an internal matter."[214]

In 1966 a large number of M.P.s from all parties signed a motion calling on the British government "to use its good offices to secure for the [Jews] the basic human rights afforded to other Soviet citizens." Sponsored by Sir Barnett Janner and Michael Foot (Labour), Sir Ian Orr-Ewing and Roger Graham-Cooke (Conservative) and Eric Lubbock and Jeremy Thorpe (Liberal), by early 1967 the motion had collected the support of 340 out of a total of 630 M.P.s, more than had endorsed any other motion on record. Thus, when Kosygin visited Britian in February, a delegation of M.P.s presented him with a letter to bring home to him, in the words of *The Times*, "the strength of feeling in the Commons about the treatment of [Soviet] Jews." The letter noted that the House's concern was "based on reports of the conditions of Soviet Jewry from individuals of repute known for their friendship for the Soviet Union and the Soviet cause and from Communist parties."[215]

Other West European parliaments took up the problem after the Council of Europe resolution. Thus, Netherlands Foreign Minister Joseph Luns told the Dutch parliament that he had raised the situation of Soviet Jews, which was "far from flourishing," "cautiously and tactfully" on his 1964 visit to Moscow, the matter requiring discreet handling.[216] In the Norwegian Storting in April 1966 Edvard Hambro deplored the continued prevalence of antisemitism in a modern state, pointing out that taking up the problem was "completely in accord with the social and humanitarian point of view'' of the European Parliament. Following him, Socialist leader Finn Moe, who had been among the rapporteurs to the Council of Europe, demanded that the Western nations raise the problem of Soviet Jewry in all conversations with Soviet leaders. Norway, he pointed out, had in the past made such approaches to Moscow. Mrs. Aase Lionaes, another Socialist member, who had attended the 1960 Paris conference, provided the statistics on which her contentions concerning anti-Jewish discrimination in the Soviet Union were based when she called upon the Soviet government to grant its Jews equal status and permit the reunification of families.[217]

A number of other prominent West European statesmen tried to conduct behind-the-scenes diplomatic activity on behalf of the Soviet Jewry. One such person was Secretary General of the French Socialist Party Guy Mollet, who headed a ten-man Socialist delegation that met with Khrushchev and other CPSU leaders in fall 1963. However, although Mollet intended handing Khrushchev a copy of the resolution adopted at the Amsterdam Congress of the Socialist International a month previously, the First Secretary made it clear that he did not wish to discuss the matter when he told Mollet that Jews enjoyed full equality and that he considered any intervention on their behalf an act designed to perpetuate the cold war. Upon returning home one delegation member said that attempts to discuss Soviet policy toward Jews and Israel were the gloomiest and most unpleasant aspects of the visit.[218] Presumably not a few of those who brought up the Soviet Jewish situation in their contacts with their Soviet counterparts in this period have remained unknown as a result of the very nature of their activity; it may be hoped that their efforts will be revealed in the not too distant future.[219]

In Chile former Secretary of the Latin American parliament Don Carlos Morales addressed himself to the question of Soviet Jewry in the Chamber of Deputies. He called the fact that Soviet Jews were being deprived of certain fundamental rights "an unpleasant reminder of the Stalin era."[220]

Among the non-European countries whose parliaments addressed themselves to the Soviet Jewish problem was Canada. But when opposition leader former Prime Minister John Diefenbaker asked in December 1963 what the Canadian government was doing to ease the situation, Prime Minister Lester B. Pearson replied that the government was refraining from taking any official action lest this provoke further restrictions against Soviet Jews. Nonetheless, in March 1964

Secretary of State for External Affairs Paul Martin revealed that he had made a personal representation on the situation to the Soviet ambassador.[221] And a Canadian parliamentary delegation to the USSR in 1965 also discussed the rights of Soviet Jewry with its hosts.[222] Diefenbaker retained his interest in the subject. At a May 1966 meeting in Montreal he pointed out to those who felt protest was futile that the lack of protest might lead the Kremlin to assume that the free world was not interested in the fate of Soviet Jewry.[223]

### Israel "goes public"

While Jews in other countries sometimes contented themselves with demands for improving Soviet Jewish conditions inside the USSR, the Israeli establishment and public alike were, very naturally, concerned first and foremost with emigration. This difference in emphasis arose mainly because as the official homeland of Jews throughout the world, Israel viewed immigration both as an essential component of its *raison d'être* and as one of the principal guarantees that it would continue to grow, which, given its special geopolitical position, seemed a prerequisite for its continued existence.

The increased public expression of concern for Soviet Jewry reflected changes in government policy as well as a certain atmosphere among the public at large. When the government of Israel had decided in the mid-1950s to be, as it were, the impresario of a worldwide struggle on behalf of Soviet Jewish rights, its leaders resolved to keep the Israeli role in the background out of apprehension that any avowed Israeli connection would inevitably invest the struggle with political connotations that might ultimately cause it harm. As we have seen, however, this had not prevented the Israelis from being the pioneers of the struggle by establishing and maintaining contact with Jewish and non-Jewish public figures and organizations and continually providing them with updated information on the subject.

By the early to mid-1960s the Israelis began to feel that they had nothing to lose by coming out into the open, especially since the Soviets were indicating that they suspected Israel of being behind much of the public outcry and the behind-the-scenes diplomatic intercessions. Moreover, since the Israelis had, through their diplomats in the USSR, gleaned sufficient information to disprove Kremlin claims that Soviet Jews were satisfied with their lot, the time had come for them to expose such claims as the lies they were. Only in this way could the Israelis counter the harm being done by people like André Blumel who had fallen prey to Soviet persuasion and disinformation and were publicizing their new positions, and by those such as Nahum Goldmann, who, although dedicated to alleviating the plight of their brethren in the Soviet Union, were hesitant to be publicly identified with the public struggle. Finally, it was only a matter of time before Israel would have to proclaim its natural role in the campaign. Just as it was axiomatic that Jewish communities and organizations would lead the way, it was unrealistic to expect Western governments to take up the cudgels for Soviet Jewry in international forums while the Jewish state remained silent in the background.

The argument in favor of direct and open Israeli intervention was put before the Israeli Foreign Ministry by Yoram Dinstein, who was a member of Israel's U.N. mission in 1962–63. As an observer at the Sub-Commission for Prevention of Discrimination and Protection of Minorities and at the Commission on Human Rights, Dinstein had been witnessing the frustration of efforts to raise the issue even in those debates that invited such intervention. For, not only were most full members unwilling to risk a confrontation with the USSR, especially on the sub-commission where they sat as experts and not as official representatives of their governments; but the only Jewish non-governmental organizations willing to buck the trend to silence were the CBJO and Agudas Israel, the WJC representative being particularly insistent on opposing anti-Soviet statements.[224]

Once the Israeli government gave the go-ahead, Ambassador Michael Comay lost no time in making his and his government's debut on the subject at the U.N. From 29 October 1962 on the Israelis never let up raising the issue at every forum in which the opportunity arose. From the moment Israel became vocal, moreover, Soviet Jewry became a permanent fixture on the agenda of relevant U.N. bodies. Soviet reactions to this new policy were not mitigated by the fact that the Israelis, in order to forestall accusations of anti-Sovietism or cold-warmongering, presented their case with maximum precision and without demagoguery, exaggeration or reliance on spurious information. On the contrary, in addition to its continuing attacks in connection with the Arab–Israeli conflict (a concomitant of its relationship with the Arab countries), the USSR began to counter Israel's complaints concerning the plight of Soviet Jewry with charges regarding Israel's treatment of its Arab population.[225]

Israel's campaign at the U.N. besmirched the USSR's public image probably more intensively and ubiquitously than any other onslaught to which the Kremlin was subjected in this period, particularly in the realm of its nationalities policy and the contradictions between Soviet theory and practice. This was soon reflected in Soviet–Israeli relations. Just as the Soviets increased both the public and the diplomatic reprimands of the Israeli embassy staff in Moscow in the face of pressures from a growing number of Jews to emigrate to Israel, they parried all Western attacks on their Jewish policy – whether in the press, at demonstrations and conferences or in parliamentary discussion and at the U.N. – by assailing Israel. They contended that Soviet Jews did not want to go to Israel, a capitalist country with dire problems, and that Israel was conducting a massive anti-Soviet propaganda campaign on the issue of Soviet Jewry both for its own ulterior purposes and as a puppet of U.S. imperialism and cold war policies.

Neither increasing Soviet rebuttals nor the obvious absurdity of many of their contentions deterred the Israelis – as they did not deter the more determined challengers on the issue from other countries.[226] Indeed, the vehemence of the Soviet reaction merely served to convince everyone involved in the struggle that their sole chance of achieving results lay in reinforcing their offensive. Perhaps because the Israelis believed that the renewed Soviet–Arab rapprochement[227] rendered their relations with the USSR a lost cause in any event, and perhaps because the decision to go public on behalf of Soviet Jewish *aliya* represented a major commitment, the Israeli government was not deflected by warnings that there would be no improvement in Soviet–Israeli relations as long as Israel regarded Soviet citizens of Jewish origin as its own citizens and sought to incite them to a Zionist orientation against their will. Just a month before Comay raised the issue in the U.N. General Assembly Third Committee, Aleksandr Shchiborin, head of the Near and Middle East Department at the Soviet Foreign Ministry, told Ambassador Yosef Tekoa that Zionism was the main obstacle to good relations between the two countries because the USSR could not accept the idea that Soviet Jews belonged outside the Soviet Union. Similar statements were made by Soviet officials in the years that followed.[228] At a time when the CPSU was preaching the fusion (*slianie*) of its own national minorities into one Soviet people, the Kremlin was not likely to show sympathy to the contention that the solidarity which transcended national boundaries could be felt not only by the working class of different countries but also by national groupings such as the Jewish people. And this despite the fact that Gromyko had dwelt upon the effect of the Holocaust on the survivors when he supported the establishment of the Jewish state in 1947–48.[229]

In the course of the March 1963 foreign policy debate in the Knesset, Haim Landau of the opposition Herut party addressed himself to the Soviet Jewry issue. He insisted that Israel could not remain silent in face of the closing of synagogues, the propaganda being directed against the Jewish religion, Jews being accused of committing espionage and being executed for economic offenses. It was the obligation of Israel – as well as of the Jewish people everywhere, indeed of every free and enlightened human being – to protest the attempt to cut Soviet Jews off from the roots of their national and religious life. Every possible platform should be used for the purpose, and the help of every possible body and individual enlisted in the effort to curtail the Kremlin's campaign of terror against Soviet Jews. Above all, Landau continued, Israel must insist on the right of those Jews who wanted to emigrate to Israel to be allowed to do so.

M.K. Yona Kesseh of Mapai, who also favored speaking out on the situation, called Khrushchev's reply to Bertrand Russell a "smokescreen" that was even more difficult to penetrate than Stalin's Iron Curtain, one that "befogs and befuddles and softens the tragedy and horrors of the Soviet Jewish political and psychological situation." Citing examples of recent anti-Jewish propaganda in Soviet books and newspapers during the past year, Kesseh called upon the Soviet Union to restore equality to its Jews and to accord them recognition as part of a people seeking "to solve the anomaly of its existence" by rebuilding its national home to absorb those who wished to come to it and those whose countries of residence did not really want them.[230]

The growing awareness of the plight of Soviet Jewry on the part of the Israeli public and the need to do something to alleviate its predicament was reflected in the success of a petition organized in 1963 by Ma'oz, the Society for Aid to Soviet Jewry, which had been formed in 1959. The petition had originated with a number of public figures who felt that the Knesset must be pressured into raising the issue as one crucial to the continued existence of the Jewish people and the State of Israel. Under the dual slogan "Let My People Go" and "Thou Shalt Not Stand By as Thy Brother's Blood is Spilt," the petition charged the government with the task of demanding that the Soviet Union open the gates to Jewish emigration, and of arousing the Diaspora to action and directing a worldwide campaign to win support for Soviet Jewish rights. Ma'oz considered other goals, such as the opening of Yiddish schools or the revival of Yiddish culture, "a waste of national energy." It was therefore not surprising when Ma'oz attacked the WJC for opposing a Soviet Jewry Day in Israeli schools, contending that if it did not want to enter the fray on the popular level, it should relinquish the task of protecting Jews from oppression to the WZO and the Israeli government.[231]

During the 1963 and 1964 High Holy Days, Israel's Chief Rabbis Yitzhak Nissim and Yehuda Unterman asked all synagogues to include a supplication on behalf of Soviet Jewry in their prayers.[232]

In July 1964 Ma'oz sponsored a public meeting addressed by Writers' Association President Yehuda Burla, M.K. Yona Kesseh, Rabbi Moshe Neria and Ma'oz Chairman Shabbetai Bet-Zvi. Insisting that the concern for Soviet Jewish rights could not be interpreted as interference in the USSR's domestic affairs, Burla called it a humanitarian issue comparable to the concern for blacks in South Africa. Seconding Burla's contention, Kesseh said that, while the State of Israel aspired to friendship with the USSR, it was not prepared to pay the price of remaining silent, especially since Soviet Jewry was prevented from raising its own voice. The Soviet Union must allow its Jews to identify as Jews and this included the right to be loyal to the land of their fathers without being considered traitors to their country of residence. The meeting adopted a resolution calling upon Jews in Israel and throughout the free world to join hands in the effort to help their Soviet brethren. It also urged the Israeli government and the Knesset to place the Soviet Jewish plight high on their agendas and to employ every political and moral means to attain an opening of the gates for Soviet Jewry. Finally, it called upon the nations and governments of the world, as well as all humanitarian organizations, to support the Jews by demanding that the Soviet government allow them to emigrate.[233]

Also in July 1964, the Ihud Olami (World Union) of Poalei Zion, which centered on Mapai and formed the main core of the World Zionist Labor Movement, unanimously adopted a resolution warning that the Jewish people would never reconcile itself with the attempt to sever its Soviet branch from the main body of the nation and calling upon the Soviet government to let its Jewish citizens observe their national and religious heritage, maintain spiritual ties with the State of Israel and the other Jewish communities and emigrate to Israel where they could join their families and participate in the building of Israeli society.[234]

When the Ma'oz petition reached 100,000 signatures in early 1965, it was submitted to the Knesset. This occasioned a debate on Soviet Jewry initiated by Herut, whose spokesman Arye Ben Eliezer called on the Soviets to let their Jews worship God in their own way, speak their own language and live a national existence, above all by returning to their own people and their own country. Agreeing that the Jewish people in Israel and the diaspora were united in their concern over this issue, Golda Meir pointed out that Prime Minister Levi Eshkol had been stating this loudly and clearly in the Knesset and elsewhere over recent years.[235] Mrs. Meir's remarks led observers to wonder whether they meant that the Israeli government might be going back on its decision to break its silence over Soviet Jewry in order to improve relations with Moscow. However, when Maki (Israeli CP) Secretary-General Shmuel Mikunis claimed that Soviet Jewry had not authorized anyone in Israel to act on its behalf, that the USSR's Jews considered that country their homeland and that the anti-Soviet statements made by Israeli representatives at the U.N. and elsewhere contradicted Israel's avowed wish for friendship with the USSR, the foreign minister returned to the dais and denied that there was any contradiction between Israel's wish for friendly relations with the Soviet Union and its speeches at the U.N. in support of Soviet Jewry. The issue was once again deferred to the Knesset's Committee for Foreign and Security Affairs.[236]

Soviet Jewry continued to be an issue at different forums. Thus, the tenth Mapai conference in February 1965 issued a resolution calling upon the Soviet government and its people to recognize the right of Soviet Jews to emigrate to Israel to reunite with their families. Enabling Soviet Jews to participate in building the Jewish homeland, the resolution continued, "does not stand in contradiction to the Soviet Union's social character and political needs." The resolution also urged Moscow to make its Jews equal to its "other citizens, peoples and cultures."[237]

In May 1965 a conference of one hundred Israeli academics, writers and artists exhorted the Soviet government to give the Jews the right to develop their own national culture, practice their religion, maintain ties with Jews abroad, and emigrate to Israel within the framework of family reunification, and to stop abetting manifestations of animosity or prejudice that were detrimental to the honor of Jews or Judaism.[238] Just a month later Magen (the Defense Association for Help for the Jews of Russia) issued a statement urging the Soviet Union to free Jews arrested for Zionist activity or practicing their religion and to allow emigration to Israel.[239]

Also in 1965, the Israeli leadership and those responsible for maintaining the public campaign for Soviet Jewry met with Nahum Goldmann in an effort to dissuade him from undermining Israel's endeavors. They tried to show him how the quiet diplomacy that he believed to be the key to achieving results had failed and to convince him that what he termed the exaggeration and hysteria of the public campaign (for example, equating the Soviets with the Nazis) were but an ancillary outcome of the public outcry. Goldmann maintained that the Soviet government had no intention of instigating excesses against its Jews and that the USSR was not an antisemitic state, individual Jews not being discriminated against economically or professionally and enjoying civic rights equal to those of other citizens. While he agreed that a Jewish problem existed in the Soviet Union, namely the deprivation of national rights, the denial of "the facilities to maintain their Jewish identity recognized as such under the law" was not, in Goldmann's opinion, a matter to be dealt with by Israel. Rather it must be taken up by diaspora Jewry headed by "personalities and groups whose opinion is very highly respected by the Soviet government" and whose efforts would focus on persuading the Soviets "that it is against their own interests to pursue this policy and thereby antagonize millions of Jews and non-Jews."[240] The Israelis told Goldmann that the unity which had been built up with so much difficulty was now being threatened by the public dissension of someone as influential as he in the Jewish world. But the meeting did not make a dent in Goldmann's oposition to going public with the struggle.[241]

The year 1966 witnessed further attempts to mobilize the Israeli public. Early in the year Eshkol told the Knesset that Soviet Jewry had been severed from the main body of the nation and from the building of the national home for the past fifty years by an external force that ignored "the great humane and universal significance of the Zionist undertaking. We await the day when the Jews of the Soviet Union will be able to contribute to the reconstruction of [Jewish] people in its national home."[242] In another statement, to a press conference that summer, the prime minister refuted the Soviet contention that Israel's concern over Soviet Jewry represented interference in the USSR's domestic affairs. Moscow's own approach to the ingathering of exiles and rebirth of the languages and cultures of other nations, such as the Armenians, showed there was no justification in its interpreting Israel's reaction to Soviet Jewish policy as hostile.[243] Also in summer 1966, the Israeli Ministry of Education and Culture resolved to hold a week of solidarity with Soviet Jewry in all schools throughout the country. And in December of the same year the Public Committee for Soviet Jewry took the occasion of the anniversary of the Universal Declaration of Human Rights to urge Moscow to revise its policy with respect to Soviet Jews in accordance with this declaration. Specifically, it asked that Soviet Jews be allowed to maintain ties with Jews in other countries, that the Soviet authorities act to reduce anti-Jewish prejudice and that Jews be permitted to reunite with families in Israel and elsewhere and to emigrate to Israel even if they had no family there.[244]

In February 1967 a Soviet Jewry Week was organized by the Israeli Executive of the WJC as one in a series of educational programs designed to make the Israeli public more aware of its links with world Jewry. The week was marked by lectures all over the country, newspaper articles, radio programs and other events. The crowds that flocked to hear Golda Meir and member of the Jewish Agency Executive Haim Levanon at the opening ceremony bore testimony to the bond that large numbers of Israelis felt with Soviet Jewry. Those who got there early enough to gain entrance heard Mrs. Meir describe her experiences as Israeli envoy to Moscow, and her statement that anyone who was not willing to assist in helping Soviet Jewry return to the ranks of the Jewish people was in effect excluding himself from that people. She concluded by declaring: "In spite of everything, they will come to us."[245]

The Soviet Jewry Week was preceded by publicity in the press and in schools throughout the country, and the response it evoked reflected the protracted efforts of Binyamin Eliav and his associates to arouse the Israeli public to the plight of Soviet Jews and make it aware of the pro-Israeli orientation of a large section among them. It was largely with this in view that Eliav had begun publishing the smuggled writings of Soviet Jews like Barukh Vaisman, Zvi Plotkin and Zvi Pregerzon (written under the pseudonyms *Yehudi sovieti almoni* – "an anonymous Soviet Jew" –, A. Tsfoni and M. Hiog). To this end, too, Eliav and his group had been maintaining contact with leading Israeli newspapers, particularly *Ma'ariv* and *Davar*, which disseminated a considerable quantity of material concerning the Soviet Jewish situation.[246]

The campaign within Israel was part of the one being conducted in the world outside, to which the Israeli establishment was still directing its main efforts. The Israelis neither wanted their role to weaken that of American Jewry nor believed that this would happen. Nor did they envision their effort as a substitute for the American Jewish one. On the contrary, the Israelis were convinced that the Jewish protest movement the world over must be united in its struggle in order to be effective. Consequently, there was no room for a pluralistic approach, whether that of Nahum Goldmann or, at the other extreme, of

American Jewish fringe groups who tried to initiate independent political activity. What the Israeli establishment saw as its task, however, was the laying down of guidelines for the movement's strategy and the coordinating of tactics used by the Israeli government and the American Jewish organizations, specifically the AJCSJ.[247] Any differences between the Israeli and the American campaign resulted from the greater control that the Israeli office was able to exercise over Israeli public figures and institutions, although even here it was occasionally subjected to pressures from those who sought louder action, on the one hand, or, on the other, more restraint.

### Jewish and Israeli tourism to the USSR as an instrument in the struggle

Tourism to the Soviet Union began to take on meaningful proportions in the early to mid-sixties.[248] The visits showed Soviet Jews that their brethren in Israel and other countries of the free world cared about their fate; they also inspired those who made them to greater efforts on behalf of Soviet Jewry upon their return home. These trips were, in addition, an invaluable source for up-to-date information on Soviet Jewish reality. This was particularly important as returning tourists communicated their impressions of what was happening in the USSR to people who might not otherwise be aware of the situation.

Tourists with some prior knowledge of conditions in the USSR, either from previous trips or because they had been briefed, had heard lectures or had read about the situation, were particularly useful as they had some idea of where to look and what to look for. Thus, Yiddish journalist Chaim Shoshkes, who had been to the Soviet Union in the mid-fifties and returned twice in the early 1960s, not only knew whom he wanted to contact and how to reach them; he also had access to a number of newspapers and journals in the U.S. and other countries which would publish his latest impressions. And when American Jewish publicist Ben Zion Goldberg was invited to the USSR for the commemoration of the fiftieth anniversary of Sholem Alei-chem's death in 1966, he was able to compare what he was seeing with conditions in 1959 as well as with those he had encountered during visits made in 1934 and 1946. What Goldberg saw in 1966 convinced him that the Soviet Jewish situation had worsened; Jews were becoming reconciled to manifestations of antisemitism, and their sense of not belonging was growing. But, he also noted, interest in Israel was increasing and news of protests on their behalf was getting through and providing encouragement.[249]

One American Jewish exchange scholar, Lewis Feuer, a professor of philosophy and social science at the University of California at Berkeley, spent several months in the USSR in 1963. Impelled by what he saw, Feuer wrote an impassioned account of Jewish life in Moscow, Leningrad, Tbilisi and Tashkent, in all of which he had witnessed the Jews' reaction to the Kremlin's policy of "culturocide." Feuer noted not only the Jews' "nervous searching ... wonderment and bewilderment," but also their attempts "to observe vestigial symbols of Jewish identification" and the desire of many of them to emigrate.[250]

Another American Jew, who visited the USSR in fall 1964, said upon his return that he had left for the Soviet Union as a private citizen but returned as an emissary of "hundreds and thousands of Jews." Hearing what Soviet Jews had to say about their lives as Jews in the USSR had made him realize that he must speak, or rather cry out, to the entire American public in their name. For Soviet Jews believed that protests against Soviet antisemitism by the mighty United States would have eventually to be heeded by the powers-that-be in the Kremlin.[251]

Another American whose visit to the USSR turned him into an activist was professor of bacteriology David Weiss, who attended a scientific conference in Sukhumi, Abkhazian ASSR, in May 1965. After spending eighteen days in the Soviet Union, Weiss was so incensed at the situation of its Jews that he presented a statement to the Ad Hoc Commission on the Rights of Soviet Jews. He said that his first encounters with Jews had shocked him to the point where he resolved to speak to as many of them as possible. He had managed to speak with about 150 "of all ages and backgrounds." Many of these were scientists, including people of major repute, who had sought the opportunity to reveal their Jewishness. Although they usually did this clandestinely and furtively, Weiss was convinced that this was clear evidence that they were neither "assimilated" nor "emancipated," but were motivated by "a strong sense of Jewish identity and Jewish concern." In his testimony Weiss stressed the fear of "virtually all Jews" with whom he spoke, "arising from their condition as *Jews*." A religious Jew himself, he tried to break the barrier of fear by convincing those with whom he was speaking of his own commitment to Jewish values. Only when he was successful in this did they feel free enough to ask him to spread the word about their desperate condition and to explain why they were afraid to talk with him, let alone receive a prayer book, inside the synagogue.

Weiss was particularly upset by the brazen lies about the situation presented by Soviet officialdom. This included rabbis and lay leaders of Jewish communities, who persisted in their claims that Jews were living under satisfactory conditions, and Intourist guides who denied the existence of Babii Iar and undertook endless subterfuges to prevent visitors from going there. It was not surprising, therefore, that despite the "virulent, official, ubiquitous and very insidious" antisemitism "the casual visitor" to the USSR often came away feeling that there was no significant official anti-Jewish prejudice.

Because Weiss believed that "immediate alleviation of governmental pressure could still save the cultural existence of the Jewish community," but that a "delay of some years would probably make such a resurrection impossible," he called for "every conceivable pressure" to be "systematically and ceaselessly brought to bear upon the Soviet Government." He also stressed the "extraordinary importance of visits to the Soviet Jewish community by informed, intelligent and committed Jews from the West." For he was convinced that "the ripples of . . . repeated and effective visits will have an enormous impact on the morale of Soviet Jewry."[252]

Briefing individual tourists and delegations continued to be one of the most important tasks of those seeking to promote the cause of Soviet Jewry. It was especially important for visitors to be told to take stories told them by official Jewish figures, whether at the offices of *Sovetish heymland* or in the synagogues, with a grain of salt, for naïve tourists were often persuaded by such people that the Jewish problem had been solved. Tourists also had to be warned to talk to their relatives only in safe places where the latter were not afraid of eavesdropping, to demand permission to visit Babii Iar and other mass graves of Jewish war victims and even to contact the Israeli embassy. Nonetheless, many visitors continued to fall prey to the USSR's well-oiled propaganda machine.[253] The fact that – as in earlier periods – Soviet Jewish citizens who received foreign visitors were warned beforehand by the police to beware of what they told their guests, and that they were subjected to interrogations and pressures immediately after their contact with foreigners, together with the habit of silence that they had acquired over the years, often meant that only a particularly persistent tourist could get at the truth. When London Jewish businessman M. Wilder returned from a 1963 visit to the USSR, he told how in a Moscow synagogue he had been assured that all was well with Soviet Jewry, but that when he met people in the freer atmostphere of Yalta, he had heard a different version of what was really going on in Moscow – for instance that circumcision was virtually impossible in the Soviet capital.[254]

Jewish tourists were made poignantly aware of the fear their visits aroused.[255] But they also came away with stories of a profound emotional interest in the Jewish state even among those whose sole culture was Russian, of gratitude to Ben Gurion for being a charismatic leader, and of the excitement with which Jews met Israelis in chance or planned encounters. Tourists able to converse in Russian were sometimes subjected to extremely sophisticated questioning about Jewish life in the West and, above all, about Israel, concerning which local Jews were often extremely well informed.[256] When violinist Yehudi Menuhin toured the USSR in 1962 he received a number of fan letters in Hebrew. One musician wanted to know if Israel was really as wonderful as he had heard, and a well-known Moscow artist asked Menuhin for a whole list of Hebrew books, including Bible commentaries, Dubnow's *History of the Jews* and literary works.[257]

After WJC Vice-President Israel Goldstein returned from a visit to Moscow, Leningrad, Kiev, Odessa and Yalta in late summer 1963, he told a press conference in Tel Aviv of the fear that the severe punishments meted out on economic charges, including the sale of *matzot*, had generated among Soviet Jews. Going on to analyze the reasons why they persisted in remaining Jews, Goldstein mentioned two negative ones – antisemitism and Russian nationalism – and one positive one, namely the pride and national consciousness that were given content and meaning by the achievements of the State of Israel.[258] And a Russian-speaking agricultural planner who traveled to the USSR in 1963 to meet with colleagues in his field was questioned about Israel with the same urgent enthusiasm wherever he went (Moscow, Leningrad, Minsk, Mogilev – his home town – Kiev and Tbilisi). In his view, the bond linking Soviet Jews to the Jewish national "collective" in Israel was being strengthened rather than weakened by the regime's Jewish policy.[259]

When local Jews heard that Israelis were due to visit their town, the information would spread like wildfire and they would attempt to meet the Israelis despite the risks involved and although the synagogue officials had been forewarned to prevent contact between them and the visitors. Thus, when the S.S. *Jerusalem* brought a group of British and American tourists, many of them Jews, to the Black Sea ports of Odessa, Sochi and Yalta, Jews came to meet relatives or just to see an Israeli ship.[260] Almost every Jewish tourist who returned from the USSR had met someone who expressed the desire to live in Israel.[261] One American Jewish tourist was told that one-third of the country's Jewish population would leave for Israel at once if the gates were opened.[262] American Jewish students who took part in student exchange programs were also impressed by the interest in Jewish affairs and Israel expressed by their Soviet counterparts. Upon his return, one such student told Chaim Shoshkes that he "had never heard such enthusiastic reactions to Israel as I heard among my student friends there, many of them sons of old-time communists . . . You would be surprised how much more than I they knew about Israel and how many heated discussions they held on this issue." Soviet Jews as a whole, and students in particular, he said, took great exception to attacks on Israel in the Soviet media.[263] Another American student, who had given a local student a pamphlet on Israel, was accused of disseminating anti-Soviet literature and threatened with expulsion.[264]

Tourists in the mid-sixties were sometimes given letters to transmit to the U.N. Secretary-General or the Human Rights Commission by Jews who wished to emigrate. Upon his return from synagogue, an American rabbi visiting the Soviet Union in summer 1966 found a handwritten letter in his pocket addressed to the Commission, which he duly presented to its U.S. representative, Morris Abram. The letter, written in English by a young man who sought to leave for Israel with his wife, parents and brother to join relatives there, said that petitions to Kosygin and Brezhnev had "failed to produce any answer." He concluded: "I am convinced, gentlemen, it is you who have the answer. So I am waiting for your HELP."[265]

Among the American rabbis who visited the Soviet Union in the mid-1960s was Israel Miller, president of the Rabbinical Council of America, who had led an RCA delegation to the USSR in 1956. The nine-man delegation he headed in 1965 traveled to Moscow, Leningrad, Kiev and Tbilisi. They were appalled by the wretched condition of the synagogues and other religious facilities, by the paucity of religious weddings and circumcisions, the "vulgarized version" of the Jewish funeral, the ubiquitous synagogue officials who worked for the authorities and the difficult position of the few elderly rabbis valiantly struggling to keep Judaism alive. As in 1956, some of the rabbis were allowed to address the congregation in Moscow's Choral Synagogue to convey the greetings of U.S. Jewry. One delegation member, Rabbi Bernard A. Poupko of Pittsburgh, who was born in the USSR and could therefore converse with his fellow Jews in Russian, had visited the USSR in 1964.

Rabbi Poupko told those assembled that the rabbis wished to express their "deep gratitude to the Soviet government for having joined . . . the United States of America in voting at the United Nations some eighteen years ago for the establishment of the State of Israel." As he "uttered the words 'State of Israel' there was a thunder of applause and shouts of 'Bravo' . . . Rabbi Levin [of the Choral Synagogue] . . . pleaded with them to refrain from applause in the synagogue on the Sabbath . . . Diplomats, journalists and other competent observers assured us that the synagogue had never before witnessed such a sense of excitement, joy and new hope." In Leningrad one young Jewish student asked Rabbi Poupko: "Tell me truthfully, without hiding anything from me, do you and your colleagues sincerely believe that there is a possibility for me and my friends some day to reach the State of Israel and to settle there?", while in Moscow another student told the rabbis of "the deep and personal pride" with which many Jewish students followed whatever news they could glean about developments in Israel.[266]

His first visit had convinced Rabbi Poupko that "personal and tactful negotiations on a higher level" would be more effective than "public manifestations of anger." Upon his return he called on leaders of all faiths throughout the world to appeal to the Soviet authorities "in a spirit of petition and request, rather than protest and criticism, to remove political, social and economic barriers which alienate Jewish citizens from their heritage."[267] After his 1965 visit, however, Poupko returned with a sense of urgency that caused him to retreat from his original position; he and his colleagues found that "everything done abroad on this matter in a responsible and prudent way was of inestimable value."[268] "Time is running out," he told the 1965 convention of the Mizrachi – Hapoel Hamizrachi Zionist Organization. "In between enthusiastic protest meetings, meaningful resolutions and stirring articles . . . our brethren are languishing in a cultural and religious blackout which may ultimately lead towards total extinction in a decade or two." He therefore suggested that fifty rabbis from the free world "seek permission to spend an unspecified length of time in various Russian Jewish communities ministering to the population."[269] On a third visit to the Soviet Union in May 1967 Rabbi Poupko found less fear, a greater readiness to speak out and a more substantive and palpable hope, strengthened by Kosygin's December 1966 statement regarding family reunification. This time he saw for himself how Soviet Jews celebrated Israel's Independence Day near the Israeli embassy in Moscow, participating as best they could in the celebration of the Jewish state that was so near and yet so far.[270]

Perhaps the most famous tourist of this period was Holocaust survivor and author Elie Wiesel, who visited the USSR for the Jewish holidays of fall 1965 and 1966. Having read much material on and having heard the protests about the position of Soviet Jewry, Wiesel felt the time had come for him to see what was going on for himself. In his words: "If the protests were justified, they were in no way strong enough; if not, they had been much too strong." Wiesel went specifically in order to meet with anonymous Jews, who had "never been placed in the Soviet show window." He did not wish to encounter the trite statements of official Jewish and non-Jewish representatives of the regime; nor was he interested in either "political manifestoes" or "worn-out promises."

Arriving in Moscow on the eve of the Day of Atonement in 1965, Wiesel had his first encounter with a Soviet Jew outside the synagogue only a few hours later. In the shadows he could not see the man's face, "a simple Jew with no name and no destiny, a Jew identical to every other Jew in every city throughout that formidable land." In a "choked and fearful" voice his interlocutor quickly whispered "a few tattered sentences" describing the Jews' situation in the Soviet Union. "Finally came a request to remember everything and tell it all. 'There is no time. We are nearing the end ... If I am being watched, I will pay for this conversation. Do not forget.' ... Suddenly he left me in the middle of a sentence, without saying goodbye or waiting for any reaction." In visits to Leningrad, Kiev and Tbilisi, Wiesel had ample further opportunity to witness the fear and suspicion as well as the pride in being Jewish, the indomitable desire to preserve whatever remnants of Jewish communal existence had managed to survive. What impressed him most of all, however, was the look of the Jews; he would never forget their eyes. Nor would he forget their cry for succor, for support from world Jewry that he heard wherever he visited. These Jews could not understand what they viewed as the silence and apathy of the Jews of the free world. Some of them had heard of the demonstrations and marches that were taking place. But this was only a drop in the bucket in the face of what they had to endure. For their government was intent on making them feel cut off from their fellow Jews, and severance from the world Jewish community was even harder for them to bear than rejection by the non-Jewish society that surrounded them. They took the risk of talking with

Jewish tourists in order to hear about the achievements of the Jewish state and the life of Western Jewish communities. Indeed, the thought that a Jewish future was being built in Israel and the West was one of the things that helped them endure.[271]

Wiesel's book, *The Jews of Silence*, which was originally written as a series of articles for the Israeli newspaper *Yedi'ot aharonot*, was first published in the U.S. in 1966. Reviewed in hundreds of newspapers in the West, it had a stirring impact on Jews and non-Jews alike, and its author was interviewed by the media and gave talks about what he had seen in the Soviet Union in the major cities of America. There can be no doubt that the book was a turning point in bringing the plight of Soviet Jewry to Western public opinion.

Other visitors in this period included a Hadassah Women's Organization delegation led by its president, Charlotte Jacobson, in summer 1966[272] and a group of NCRAC officials, led by Al Chernin, who is on record as saying that the visit to the USSR in early 1967 "turned [him] into a Zionist."[273]

One measure of the effectiveness of Jewish tourists, and Israeli tourists in particular, was the frequent attacks in the Soviet media on both the tourists themselves and local Jews who maintained contact with them. (This was in addition to reminders of the dangers of foreign tourism in general, for example, media warnings against anti-Soviet, reactionary and religious literature allegedly being brought into the country by tourists.[274]) On one occasion three Soviet Jews were accused of having provided foreigners with false reports about conditions in the Soviet Union, which were used by Israel for a hostile anti-Soviet campaign, and of accepting "books of dubious content" and religious articles that countered "our Soviet pride."

Foreigners, too, were warned to avoid contact with local Jews, the implication being that the Soviets would break off social and professional links with foreigners who mingled indiscriminately with members of the Soviet public.[275] When an Israeli tourist who had come to visit his relatives in June 1963 was arrested on the charge that he was a deserter from the Soviet armed forces, this was widely interpreted as an attempt to deter such tourism,[276] as were the times when Israeli tourists had their stays in the USSR cut short after being charged with giving foreign anti-propaganda material – usually Israeli newspapers or journals – to Soviet citizens.[277]

## The outcome of Western pressure to help Soviet Jews

By the mid-sixties, with the growth of the protest movement in the U.S. and in other countries of the free world, Soviet Jews began to respond to the concern and interest their plight was arousing. This served, *inter alia*, as additional proof that activities on behalf of Soviet Jews did not, in fact, harm them. Even the earliest tourists, such as the 1956 RCA delegation, reported that the visits showed Soviet Jews that they were not forgotten and were not as isolated as Moscow would have liked them to be.

In 1965 an anonymous eyewitness, who made several trips to the USSR "on cultural and other missions," reported that on a recent visit he had even been able "to discuss . . . the question of the usefulness of public organized pressure," and that those he had questioned on the subject were "unaminous and emphatic in stating that these activities are important and useful, and should be continued." They felt that the public outcry exposed and embarrassed the Soviet government, stimulated the U.S. government to "greater awareness and responsiveness" and played a major role in strengthening "the morale and steadfastness" of Soviet Jews. This same eyewitness reported that the many Jews who relied "on the short-wave radio" for news of Jewish interest, especially on Kol Israel, in whose broadcasts these events played "a prominent part," listened keenly to news about "protests and expressions of sympathy with the plight of Jews in the Soviet Union."[278]

Efforts such as those of Bertrand Russell were particularly effective on two fronts: they both lifted the morale of the Soviet Jews and let the Kremlin know that its friends in the West were watching with concern what was happening to its Jews. In July 1964 Russell released a letter he had sent to *Sovetish heymland*, in which he sought to publicize the fact that his intercessions had evoked a positive response among "several Soviet [Jewish] citizens, including members of the Communist Party." In his press release, Russell included a letter from one Jew (withholding the signature) who said he was writing to Russell "on behalf of a great number of people" who had read Russell's letter to Khrushchev on the discrimination against Jews in the economic trials with "deep sympathy." Although they wanted no more than the rights accorded to Jews in Poland, Romania and Czechoslovakia, it was "impossible and even pointless" for the Jews to put the problem to their government or to "any other responsible organization" themselves.[279]

The Kremlin did not remain silent in the face of Western efforts to alleviate the plight of Soviet Jews. Throughout the world the Soviet representatives who were being harassed over the Jewish problem – top-level government leaders and medium-level officials on official visits as well as embassies in the various capitals – were showing signs of increasing acrimony over the intensity of the appeals and protests. It reached the point where Soviet representatives were devoting considerable parts of or even entire press conferences or interviews to denying anti-Jewish discrimination in the USSR.[280] In an interview with Chicago Council of American–Soviet Friendship Chairman Mandel Ternow, Foreign Minister Gromyko expressed his consternation that, at a time when the future of mankind was looking bright, "Jewish spiritual leaders grasp the dead hand of Adenauer and his revanchists, and Hitler's ex-generals and judges in a bitter end struggle that can only lead to the annihilation of the Jewish people everywhere together with the human race." And Mikhail Menshikov, now Foreign Minister of the RSFSR, who accompanied Gromyko, could not understand why Jewish leaders ignored Soviet statements on the Jewish question. When Menshikov was asked in return why Khrushchev did not reply to statements by Jewish leaders, he said that the First Secretary made his replies to Bertrand Russell instead, because he did "not trust people noted for their hostility to the Soviet Union, no matter what their religion or faith."[281]

In addition to lodging protests with the governments of those active on behalf of Soviet Jewry, denouncing the Israelis and trying to convince Western figures that they were wrong for speaking out on behalf of Soviet Jewry, the Kremlin endeavored to have symposia and conferences on Soviet Jewry canceled wherever they had influence.[282] Moscow also mounted a huge counter-propaganda campaign, using carefully chosen Soviet Jews to deny anti-Jewish discrimination and feelings of dissatisfaction and isolation as Jews. One of the main figures in this effort was Aron Vergelis, editor of *Sovetish heymland*, who dutifully dismissed reports of anti-Jewish discrimination as part of "a political campaign to conceal racist crimes and antisemitism in capitalist countries." Soviet Jews, Vergelis insisted, had left, and would not return to, the old ghetto-like existence; they had replaced medieval beliefs and traditions with materialism and atheism and had become part of the very hub of Soviet life.[283]

Their protests to the effect that claims of Soviet antisemitism were fascist and cold war propaganda notwithstanding, the plain fact is that foreign protest did result in a number of concessions on the part of the

Soviet authorities. For it was almost certainly foreign pressure that led the Kremlin to mitigate its campaign against Jewish "economic criminals," to renew permission to bake *matzot*, to withdraw the Kichko book (and even censure its author), to stop closing synagogues,[284] to provide the Jews of Zhitomir and Minsk with alternative buildings to serve as synagogues after theirs had been closed and to commute Rabbi Gavrilov of Piatigorsk's death sentence to one of fifteen years' imprisonment.[285] As Senator Ribicoff told a Greater Washington Committee on the Plight of Soviet Jewry in 1965, the continued expression of public opinion was beginning to alleviate the position of Soviet Jewry. Although Ribicoff had said on another occasion that the changes brought about by public protest had been "marginal," now he said: "we . . . dare to hope we will succeed."[286]

Further to the concessions already brought about, Western protest also led to promises of or hints at additional concessions in the areas of culture and religion. Rife since the beginning of marked foreign interest in 1956, in the mid-1960s such hints included reports that a model Jewish school and even, perhaps, a network of schools would be opened, that a Jewish journal (in addition to *Sovetish heymland*) would be published in Kiev, that a Yiddish–Russian dictionary was in the works and that Yiddish State theaters (as against amateur groups) would be created in Moscow and Vilnius.[287] However, as the Universities' Committee for Soviet Jewry in Britain pointed out – in reply to an article in *Soviet Weekly* by the London correspondent of Novosti – "future promises . . . have for long been a basic technique of Soviet propaganda when concern is expressed in the West over the situation of Soviet Jews."[288]

Probably the most important Soviet concession during the period in question, and certainly the most important in the field of emigration, was Prime Minister Aleksei Kosygin's statement regarding family reunification at a Paris press conference on 3 December 1966. This statement was made in reply to a question by a United Press International correspondent on whether Kosygin could give separated Jewish families "any hope of meeting, as was done for many Greek and Armenian families." After denouncing such questions and others concerning Soviet antisemitism, which did "not exist" ("in our country the national question is solved in the interests of all nationalities"), as a "cheap means" used to "reach the public," Kosygin said: "We, on our side, shall do all possible for us if some families want to meet or even if some among them would like to leave us, to open for them the road, and this does not raise here, actually, any problem of principles and will not raise any."[289]

Despite his cautious formulation, this was the first time that the Soviet authorities said they would be prepared to even consider the issue of family reunification; Khrushchev had always either denied that there were Jews who wished to emigrate or postponed treatment of the question to an indefinite future, when East–West relations would be less tense. Kosygin's statement, moreover, had not only clearly been prepared beforehand, but was one that seemed to have practical implications. Finally, although the statement was made in Paris, and therefore obviously intended to assuage foreign criticism, unlike previous statements on this issue by Soviet officials, it was also published in the Soviet media, albeit in a slightly mitigated variation.[290] This meant that, in addition to feeling the need to appease the campaign in the West, the Soviet authorities were now trying to mollify domestic Jewish discontent. In other words, the statement seems to have been one of the first official signs of a successful interaction between activism inside and outside the USSR.

The nuance does not, however, appear to have been appreciated at the time. Certainly, the many comments aroused by the statement did not dwell on this aspect of the Soviet promise. Instead they expressed the hope that, in the words of one article, Kosygin's "pledge" would lead to "a complete reversal of traditional Soviet policy."[291] Not surprisingly, there was still considerable skepticism that the family reunification Kosygin spoke of would be implemented in the near or even not-so-near future. As an AJCSJ release put it: "Too often in the past have promises failed to be followed by performance.[292]

Without necessarily watering down our conclusion that Western protest was having an effect, it should also be noted that Kosygin's Paris statement on family reunification was part of a broader development that did not affect Jews only. This can be deduced from the fact that when the Soviet prime minister visited Canada in November 1966, he told Canadian Secretary for External Affairs Paul Martin that steps would be taken to enable Soviet citizens to join relatives in Canada.[293] Indeed, general emigration from the USSR had begun increasing in 1964. While only ten Soviet citizens had received exit permits to join relatives in the U.S. in 1958, by 1966 more than 700 people left from the USSR to the U.S., about half of them for permanent residence and the rest for visits of up to six months. And, whereas in 1964 only thirty-one visas had been granted for persons wishing to go to Britain, there were about 200 in 1966. Further, the figures for Australia, West Germany, Israel and Latin America had risen as well.[294]

Kosygin's Paris statement became the focal point of the appeals by

Jews and non-Jews alike which confronted him when he visited London in February 1967. These included the joint Jewish memorandum released after Kosygin refused to receive a Jewish delegation, the letter presented to him by a delegation of M.P.s on the "continuing difficulties confronting Jews in the U.S.S.R." as well as Bertrand Russell's most recent appeal on this issue, in which the ninety-four-year-old philosopher pointed out that those who applied to emigrate were still encountering "serious obstruction by officials," causing "a great disservice to the reputation of the Soviet Union." Another appeal, by historian and political scientist Sir Denis Brogan and nine other leading British personalities, also occasioned a great deal of press comment. What had happened was that, while British Jews, non-Jewish liberals and a wide range of public figures were still concerned with the cultural and religious rights of Soviet Jews, Kosygin's statement opened the way for more direct calls for emigration within the framework of family reunification.[295] As the *Guardian*, one of Britian's leading newspapers put it: "The chief problem which concerns the three million Jews of the Soviet Union is the purely human one of whole families being split asunder as a result of the war.[296]

Even though little was being done to implement the commitment implied in Kosygin's Paris statement, the statement itself signified Soviet recognition that domestic and foreign protest was no longer restricted to questions of discrimination against Jews as individuals and as a national minority inside the USSR, but had begun to center on the possibility of their leaving the Soviet Union altogether.

Part III

"Shake off the dust and arise from
the mire
Bedeck thee, my people, in festive
attire"

# 7 A first breakthrough: November 1956–December 1959

We have seen the great hopes with which the Jews of the USSR welcomed the post-Stalin period and their subsequent disappointment when they realized that as a collectivity they were not to be included in the process of liberalization, that the Soviet regime seemed neither willing nor able to find a solution to their situation.

The year 1956 seemed to open up new vistas. *Prima facie*, the Jews had no reason to be satisfied with Khrushchev's Secret Speech at the Twentieth Party Congress in February legitimizing de-Stalinization as official Soviet policy. At the same time, as the contents of the speech gradually leaked out – never published inside the Soviet Union, it was read out in whole, or more usually in part, at party *aktivs* throughout the country – people began to feel the possibility of voicing dissent. The atmosphere of protest, that was further galvanized by the events in Poland and Hungary that shook the entire bloc, was characterized by considerable student unrest.[1] The criticism of obsolete policies and dogmas, that had been permitted in belletristics during the "Thaw" period, now spilled over into a more general critique of cultural and other controls. Although Khrushchev's de-Stalinization proved very limited in terms of the freedoms actually granted, once begun, the loosening of the reins proved to be uncontrollable. Moreover, it was accompanied by the breakdown of the Stalinist system of terror, which some analysts consider Khrushchev's main long-term contribution to the development of Soviet domestic politics.[2]

The new atmosphere helped to reduce the fear that had permeated the population in the late Stalin years, making a particular impression on the younger generation which had grown to political maturity after Stalin's death. Even though a substantial movement did not yet develop and all signs of organization were still being nipped in the bud, the small groups of Jews that had been coming together in cities and townships throughout the Soviet Union took on new life.

Moreover, new groups were formed, largely by students stimulated and emboldened by the unrest that was permeating the universities and by ex-camp inmates.

### The "Polish" repatriation

The Soviet Union had stopped issuing visas for emigration to Israel in October 1956 in retribution for Israel's "aggression" toward Egypt,[3] yet a new opportunity for action presented itself toward the end of that year: a new Soviet–Polish repatriation agreement was signed which offered relatively large numbers of Jews the chance to leave the USSR.[4] The agreement was supposed to be strictly limited to the repatriation to Poland of Poles or Jews who had been Polish citizens in September 1939 or the close relatives of such people. But the Soviet authorities seem to have been aware that Israel was the ultimate goal of those Jews who qualified to leave under its terms.[5] And the fact that the repatriation movement to Poland was given official publicity inside the Soviet Union meant – at least to the less timid – that applying to leave the USSR under the agreement was a legitimate procedure. Indeed, for the three or so years of its duration, large numbers of Soviet Jews who did not fall into the categories specified in the agreement sought to take advantage of the opportunity it provided. These were chiefly Jews who resided in the areas most affected by the agreement, i.e. those that had belonged to Poland prior to World War II and were now incorporated into the Lithuanian, Belorussian or Ukrainian SSR.

After the large-scale postwar emigration of their own Jews, at first to the DP camps in Germany and Austria and from 1948 on directly to Israel, had been cut off in 1950, the Poles did not begin reissuing exit permits for Israel until 1956. A first few were issued in October 1955,[6] and the monthly number grew gradually until it reached approximately one hundred in July 1956. These permits were not limited to the old or to those who had close relatives in Israel. Nor did the authorities prevent the emigration of professionals[7] for whom the new People's Democracies had made emigration very difficult in the 1940s.

In June 1956 Polish Premier Josef Cyrankiewicz, replying to a question on the new wave of antisemitism then sweeping Poland,[8] told a conference of Polish newspaper editors that, although no mass emigration was envisaged,[9] his government would allow large numbers of Jews to leave on the basis of individual applications. In August the Polish Interior Minister told the American Jewish journalist Chaim Shoshkes that his country recognized the right of its Jews to emigrate to Israel and that they were free to go there without any limitations.[10] The reason for this was that Poland was then homogenizing its population by allowing the emigration of those who wished to be repatriated, notably of the German minority,[11] and encouraging the return of Poles.[12]

After Cyrankiewicz's statement, crowds flocked to the district passport offices opened to consider emigration requests, and there were lines of Jews at the Israeli consulate in Warsaw.[13] Even those establishment Jewish organizations and Jewish public figures previously known for urging Polish Jews to associate themselves and their future with that of the Polish People's Republic were indicating their endorsement of emigration to Israel as the optimal solution for Poland's Jews.[14] Although in spring 1957 Jewish emigration from Poland was slowed down and some professions were prevented altogether from leaving, in September 1957 a Polish Foreign Ministry official told an Israeli correspondent that every Polish Jew who wished to emigrate would be able to do so.[15]

The opening of Poland's gates for emigration was a major factor in encouraging Jews who had been Polish citizens in September 1939 to return there from the USSR under the new repatriation agreement. The repatriation that had been resumed in driblets in the second half of 1955 was said to have reached 6,000 by October 1956.[16] Although the need for an agreement had apparently been under discussion for some time, the agreement in principle to the repatriation that was eventually to include some 250,000 people was only reached during the negotiations between the Soviet and Polish leadership that concluded the crisis known as the Polish October, which involved the development or evolution of communism in Poland and the Soviet–Polish relationship.[17] Many of the details of procedure seem to have been elaborated only in the following weeks and months, and the document ratifying the agreement was not signed until March 1957,[18] yet the agreement itself was implemented immediately. It was made clear that it was concluded because there were still Poles on Soviet soil who had not availed themselves of the previous agreements: some of them had served at the time in the Soviet armed forces; others had been incarcerated in Soviet prisons and camps; still others had had personal or family reasons.

The preamble to the agreement stipulated that in view of both governments' interest in consolidating Soviet–Polish friendship, it had been agreed that Polish nationals who had been citizens of Poland on the day that Soviet troops had entered Poland (17 September 1939), as well as their children, including those born after that date, their spouses and their parents, even if the latter two categories had not been Polish citizens in 1939 and were not Polish nationals, would be allowed to repatriate once more. Candidates for repatriation were to go to the militia in their places of residence to submit declarations stating their desire to repatriate along with documents confirming their Polish nationality and former Polish citizenship. The agreement also laid down the procedure to be followed between the moment of registration and departure for Poland, including the information that the cases of those who were rejected by the local militia for lack of the necessary documentation or for any other reason would be investigated jointly by the USSR Ministry of Internal Affairs and the Polish government's Representative for Repatriation Affairs at the Polish embassy in Moscow.

Originally to run until 31 December 1958, the agreement was eventually extended to 31 December 1959. While the Soviets were probably interested *a priori* in concluding repatriation as quickly as possible to put an end to its unsettling effect and the problems it threatened to create for their own planned economy, the Poles sought to drag it out in order to ease the impact on their own society. After all, the absorption of a large number of returnees would certainly affect their economy, even though they apparently intended giving them the homes and jobs of the Germans who were being repatriated to Germany (indeed, the repatriates were largely directed to areas where there had been large concentrations of Germans). Yet by early 1959 the Polish government seemed to be hardly less eager than Moscow to terminate the movement. Thus, they ceased insisting on the repatriation of the thousands of Polish citizens whom the Soviet authorities refused to let go for one reason or another. Here it is significant that, while there were still over 700,000 Poles in the USSR and many thousands (if not tens of thousands) were known to have been refused exit permits by the Soviets, only 30,000 Poles were repatriated in 1959 as against 95,000 in 1957 and 87,000 in 1958.

That Polish Jews were eligible to apply for repatriation was specified in the agreement (Ukrainians, Belorussians, Lithuanians and Russian nationals were explicitly excluded). Although a large percentage of the Polish citizens who had repatriated in the previous decade had been Jews, many Polish Jews, too, had not availed themselves of the opportunity. In addition to the considerations that influenced Poles, the Jews recoiled at the very idea of returning to their destroyed homes and to a country that had become the mass graveyard of their families and friends. Nor were they anxious to face either traditional Polish antisemitism or the return of pogroms in the immediate postwar years. Moreover, they could not be certain that moving on to the DP camps (not an ideal destiny even as a temporary transit) would result in their eventually reaching Palestine, which was itself in turmoil in the mid-1940s.

By the second half of the 1950s, however, the situation was totally different. Those who had struck economic and professional roots in the USSR had come to realize that as Jews, and particularly as Polish Jews, they had no future in Soviet society. Moreover, most of those who had not repatriated in the 1940s because they had been serving prison terms had now been released, and those who had been in military service had been demobilized; in any case, the 1957 agreement specified that a candidate for repatriation who was in a camp would be liberated ahead of time or handed over to the Polish authorities, while anyone in military service would be discharged. Finally, the return to Poland was not viewed as negatively now as it had been in the immediate postwar period, and in most cases Poland was a stopover on the way to Israel. Although Israel was still an unknown quantity for Polish Jews, who lived mainly in outlying districts of the USSR where they were able to learn very little about the new Jewish state, the very fact that it existed and that relatives and friends were living there led them to view it as a reasonably safe haven.

By summer 1956 news of the repatriation was spreading in the major Jewish centers of the Western areas. This, together with reports that Polish Jews were again emigrating to Israel, led Jews to begin contemplating their own repatriation.[19] With the agreement of November 1956, i.e., even before the details were published, Jews in cities like Vilnius and Lvov began talking of their personal intentions openly: of when and how they were going to leave the USSR and of their final destination.[20]

It is generally agreed that the Jews were included in the agreement at the insistence of the Polish leadership, even though it had been reported that Gomulka opposed their inclusion in the 1944–45 agreements. While the reasons for this can only be surmised, Warsaw seems to have had an interest in sprucing up its image in the West as a liberal and humane regime receptive to pressures on the part of Polish organizations abroad, especially in the United States.[21] The Poles may also have thought that the Jews would be more likely to read about the possibility of repatriation in the central Soviet press than non-Jewish Poles, and that the vigor with which they would approach local authorities in order to repatriate would make the path easier for non-Jews as well.[22] It has also been suggested that Jews were included as a by-product of the Polish demand that all former inhabitants of what had been Polish territory prior to 17 September 1939, and not solely Polish nationals, should be repatriated. Since the Soviets excluded those nationals who had allegedly provided the reason why those territories were annexed by the USSR in the first place, this left only Poles and Jews.[23]

Given the difficult economic situation in Poland, which the repatriation movement must necessarily exacerbate, and Warsaw's allowing its own Jews to emigrate, the Polish authorities no doubt agreed to the Jews' inclusion in the agreement on the assumption that they would go on to Israel, just as most of them had sought to do in the 1940s. As we shall see below, Khrushchev himself confirmed that the Soviets knew that the Jewish repatriates would not remain in Poland. And, indeed, during the first months of repatriation, Soviet Jews were granted exit visas for Israel almost as soon as they arrived in Warsaw. It was only in March 1957, three weeks before the agreement was finally signed and published, that the Poles began to reject emigration applications on the grounds that, as returning Poles, they must apply for emigration "in the normal way."

The Poles gave no reason for the change in regulations, but it was generally accepted that it was due to Soviet intervention.[24] Khrushchev was reported to have rebuked Polish Foreign Minister Adam Rapacki for allowing Poland to become a transit point for Jewish repatriates and to have noted that Soviet citizens were taking advantage of the repatriation agreement to get to Israel.[25] Moscow may even have demanded that Poland promise to restrict Jewish emigration before signing the agreement. However, although the pace of the repatriates' emigration to Israel was slowed down considerably from this point, according to Deputy Interior Minister Adam Scznek, the Polish government never formally decided to stop their *aliya*.[26]

The Soviet authorities seem to have been an unwilling partner to the Jews' inclusion in the second repatriation. Many repatriates – and some would-be repatriates who emigrated to Israel later on directly from the Soviet Union – tell of the obstacles placed in their path by Soviet officialdom. Aside from scrutinizing the documents of Jews applying for repatriation much more carefully than those of non-Jews, the Soviet preference for candidates with invitations from relatives in Poland also discriminated against the Jews, most of whom had no family left there. The absence of relatives in Poland meant, too, that it was especially difficult for Jews who lacked the necessary papers to procure documentary evidence of citizenship from the relevant Polish local authority; the circumstances of their flight from Poland during the war and the arrest and imprisonment of so many of them in the Soviet Union had left many Jews without Polish papers. The Soviet authorities made it particularly difficult for young people and professionals, as well as for those residing in Siberia and the far north, where there were no Polish representatives authorized to deal with questions of repatriation.[27]

The Soviets were more amenable to the repatriation of Jews from Lithuania and the Western Ukraine, where the large nationalistic Jewish population was hindering efforts to bring these areas into line. Thus, in the early stages, repatriation from Vilnius and Lvov proceeded relatively smoothly. But the Soviets became alarmed when they discovered that the discontented Jews were both more numerical and more scattered than they had thought. By February 1957 the simple form requesting permission to be repatriated to Poland was replaced by a complex questionnaire containing forty-eight questions tracing the applicant's background[28] and there were continuing reports of Soviet pressure on Gomulka to reject Jewish applicants for repatriation.[29]

While Jews comprised 15 percent of all repatriates in 1957, in 1958 and 1959 this figure was only about 5 percent. This may have been the result of a quota, fixed at the outset, according to which the proportion of Jewish repatriates would approximate that of the Jewish population in prewar Poland (i.e. about 10 percent).[30] If so, Soviet obstructionism vis-à-vis Jewish applicants can be understood since 75 percent of all requests to repatriate in the first three months of the agreement's operation came from Jews. Nonetheless, even though Khrushchev knew that the Jews supposedly repatriating to Poland were really headed for Israel, it seems that the slowdown was connected primarily with the Jews' final destination. Otherwise why would Jews who had corresponded with or received *vyzovy* from relatives in Israel, and who applied to emigrate to that country prior to the repatriation agreement, be refused repatriation to Poland even when they had irrefutable proof of their Polish citizenship?[31] Therefore, when Khrushchev told a delegation of American "progressives," who raised the issue of Jewish emigration to Israel with the Soviet leadership in July 1957, that Jews had recently been allowed to leave for Poland even though the Soviet authorities knew that they were going on to Israel,[32] it seems that – as was his wont – the First Secretary was telling only a partial truth in an attempt to have the best of both worlds. For, as we have seen, the Soviets had been making efforts in the preceding months to prevent the emigration from Poland to Israel of repatriates.

The Soviets may also have become apprehensive about what the Jews would tell in the West about developments inside the USSR, as Khrushchev intimated when he told the same delegation that the Soviet Union was not allowing its own Jews to emigrate because it did not want them to fall prey to capitalist attempts to get them to betray the USSR. For it was well known, Khrushchev pointed out, that U.S. Intelligence had made use of Jews who fled from their countries of domicile, and this countered the interests of Soviet security.[33]

It is also possible that the difficulties Jews were encountering in repatriating to Poland and going on to Israel from there were due to what Western commentators called Arab pressure.[34] In this connection, Khrushchev told the American progressives that Israel's "aggressive policy" was one of the reasons for the Kremlin's clampdown.[35] Thus, as Moscow became increasingly apprehensive at the considerable Jewish interest in taking advantage of the repatriation agreement in order to leave the USSR, it may have tried to dampen this enthusiasm by insisting that Poland be the real and not just the fictitious destination.

In the final account, not all those who had the right to repatriate to Poland from the USSR took advantage of the agreement to do so. There are no statistics concerning the number of Polish Jews who stayed behind in the Soviet Union but it must certainly have run into tens of thousands. A large number were would-be repatriates who relinquished their plans due to the obstacles placed in their way, and there were hundreds, if not thousands, of refusals after the requisite documentation had been presented.[36] Finally, there were the additional thousands who never even submitted requests because they lacked the necessary documentation or because they were too afraid to apply.

It has been estimated that approximately 15 percent of the Jews who did succeed in getting to Poland under the repatriation agreement had never been Polish citizens. Some of them went to Poland legally as children, spouses or parents of former Polish citizens. But there is no denying that there were also cases of faked documents[37] and fictitious marriages. One former Prisoner of Zion recalls that "everyone" tried to find a Polish husband or wife in this period. One group that had formed in Vilnius in 1956 endeavored during the years of the Polish repatriation to help match up Jews who had not been Polish citizens with brides or grooms who were eligible to leave for Poland.[38] However, these fictitious marriages often failed to achieve their aim; the "husband" or "wife" was unable to leave the Soviet Union either because the fabrication was discovered or because the Polish "spouse" never sent the necessary documents although receiving a large sum of money for the purpose.[39]

Whatever the numbers, the Polish repatriation movement of 1956–59 played an important role in the unfolding of our story. In addition to providing a framework for Jews to emigrate from the Soviet Union, it spurred other Jews to apply for permission to leave as well. Thus, in the latter half of 1958, when Jews in Chernovtsy and Kishinev heard that *aliya* was beginning from Romania, they approached the Romanian embassy in Moscow with requests to repatriate within the framework of the Soviet–Romanian repatriation agreement that had been signed in 1957. Although these requests were not granted, the repatriation movement was something concrete around which people began to embroider plans for *aliya*. And once the chance of departure appeared to be almost within reach, and *aliya* from communist countries became more than a dream, Jews in the USSR could not go back to living without hope. The Polish repatriation was also significant in that it disclosed many of the components and pressures that influenced the migration policies of Poland and the USSR, as well as something of the interaction between domestic issues and foreign policy needs. For the Polish repatriation demonstrated that Jewish emigration from the Soviet Union could not be dealt with on the operational plane alone, that it also had to take Soviet inter-bloc considerations and Middle Eastern policy into account, along with domestic constraints.

As the first instance of large-scale emigration from the Soviet Union since the State of Israel was established, the Polish repatriation provided a significant case study of the problems of Jewish emigration from that country. It showed that the uncertainty in which the process was shrouded deterred large numbers of Jews, who preferred the inertia of an existence which, with all its unpleasantnesses, was by now a well-known quantity to risking any drastic change for the worse in their personal situation. It also highlighted how the lack of leadership, organization or a guiding hand, that was part of the Soviet Jewish existence, left the Polish – and other – Jews to their own devices. Although the Israeli legation in Warsaw was able to extend an unofficial helping hand to a few former Polish citizens, by transmitting information about the possibility of repatriation to the more remote areas of the USSR, counseling repatriates on what to write to the relatives and friends they had left behind, applying to the Polish authorities in individual cases and seeking to provide Polish husbands or wives for a few otherwise ineligible Jews, the average would-be repatriate knew that he had only himself to rely on. While this may have been a strengthening factor for the determined few, it discouraged the great majority. The result was that in communities where people saw that applications were being approved, many Jews applied for repatriation, while in places where applications were systematically rejected, the majority chose to waive the possibility of leaving, either *a priori* or at an early stage, feeling that they were no match for the sophisticated obstructionism of the Soviet authorities.

Newspaper accounts, personal reminiscences and other materials lead us to conclude that those who were quick to avail themselves of the opportunity to leave for Poland because they had the environmental support to insist on their rights were mostly able to leave. But those who hesitated were much more likely to succumb to what often seemed the arbitrary whims of Soviet officialdom. The latter were also more likely to be influenced by discouraging letters from those who had reached Poland and were enduring hardships and inconvenience while waiting to go on to Israel. Just as there were towns, especially in the interior of the country or in the southern Ukraine, in which all those who asked to leave were refused, there were other towns in which no Polish Jew even asked to repatriate, daunted by what would happen after an approach to the Soviet authorities or by what awaited Jews in Poland. As in the later emigration, the success and contentment of a relative or friend gave others the strength to withstand the trials to which would-be repatriates were subjected at work, in their social milieu and in OVIR – the office at the Ministry of Internal Affairs to which applications for exit permits are submitted – while the failure and dissatisfaction of just one repatriate or applicant for repatriation engendered further failures and disappointments.

All in all, some 25,000 Jews repatriated to Poland, and over 19,000 of these went on to Israel.[40] These were meaningful numbers greatly exceeding the number of emigrants to Israel from the USSR in the 1954–56 period, not to speak of the emigration directly to Israel in the late 1950s after the stoppage following the Sinai War. Moreover, the Polish repatriation had wide ramifications both inside and outside the USSR for years to come. The Soviet authorities found it necessary to attack those who had sought to leave under the agreement, labeling them traitors to the Soviet motherland, well into the sixties. And when

Jews accused of economic crimes in Khrushchev's last years were found to have been connected with the repatriation movement, the Soviet media used this as an additional proof of their turncoat nature.[41] Yet, the significance of the repatriation movement lay not so much in that it indicated the dilemmas, discrepancies and double standards of Soviet emigration policies,[42] as in that it provided Jews contemplating *aliya* with encouragement, hope and food for thought.

### The Sixth World Festival of Youth and Students

Another watershed in the evolution of the struggle for *aliya* was the Sixth World Festival of Youth and Students, which took place in Moscow in late July–early August 1957 under the auspices of the World Federation of Democratic Youth (WFDY).[43] For the delegates included a large number of young Israelis who took advantage of the relatively free atmosphere of the Festival to mingle with local Jews.[44] And more than the Israelis took the initiative in seeking out Jews, the latter sought out the Israelis.

In the unusually exuberant mood of the Festival, tens of thousands of Jews, including many from outside Moscow, came to see the Israeli delegation. The slogan of the Festival, "Peace and Friendship" (*mir i druzhba*), had been brandished from every street corner and in every newspaper for months before the event and the Soviets sought to demonstrate their new liberalism by removing many of the constraints to which Soviet citizens were normally subjected for the course of the Festival. Thus, even the police seemed to be concerned simply with maintaining public order and looking after the personal security of citizens and guests.[45] Both residents of the Soviet Union and foreign participants in the Festival took maximum advantage of the relaxed setting while it lasted. The former were exhilarated by the novel encounter with thousands of youngsters from all over the world[46] and with their various cultures and ideas. They were able to hear "rock and roll" music in Red Square at the end of the procession of Festival participants, to listen to stories about the outside world from primary sources rather than through the agency of Soviet media or publications and to hear about the wonders of Western technology of which they had no previous inkling.[47]

The Soviet authorities played up the Arab and other Third World delegations;[48] the lack of attention given the Israelis in the Soviet media stood in sharp contrast.[49] Local Jews, however, welcomed the Israelis with the same enthusiasm with which they had greeted Golda

Meyerson on her arrival in Moscow almost a decade earlier. The presence in the Soviet capital of such a large group of young Israelis, most of them *sabras* (native Israelis), gave them a tremendous moral boost. The performances of Israeli folk-songs and dances within the framework of the Festival's official events and the many individual and group meetings with Israeli delegates were especially meaningful to younger Jews, who had not been old enough in 1948 to be inspired by the events of that year or to suffer from their consequences.

Forewarned of the growing excitement among the Jewish population by, among others, telephone inquiries to the Festival's organizing committee preceding the arrival of the Israeli delegation,[50] the authorities made every effort to minimize contact between the Israeli delegation and the local population. They began by sabotaging the welcome given the Israelis even before they reached Moscow. After hundreds of Jews in Kishinev and Zhmerinka waited until the small hours of the night to welcome the train carrying the Israeli delegation, the platforms at other stations on the route to Moscow were cordoned off, or the train would stop outside the station.[51] And in the capital local Jews were prevented from greeting the Israelis by a rescheduling of their arrival for the early hours of the morning (four hours before the original schedule).[52]

The subterfuges used to frustrate the efforts of Soviet Jews to see the Israelis included omitting the Israeli delegation from the published list of delegations scheduled to hold public concerts, changing the venue of the Israelis' performances without notice and canceling their final performance on the untrue pretext that the Israelis were ill and unable to perform.[53] Finally, the Israelis' departure was brought forward by twelve hours to prevent the farewell being prepared for their departure.[54] Thus, when crowds of Jews came to Moscow's Kiev Station to see the Israelis off at the originally scheduled hour of departure on the evening of 12 August, they found out that they had been whisked away in the morning.[55]

The Soviet authorities were particularly disturbed by the enthusiasm with which Israeli printed material, especially the Russian-language pamphlet *Israel Youth*, was siezed upon by Soviet Jews. Although the pamphlet contained no political views and had been submitted for review, and although other delegations also gave out printed matter of a similar nature, the Festival authorities prohibited its distribution. This prohibition was then extended to all Israeli materials, including texts of Hebrew and Yiddish songs, the Jewish calendar and even postcards,[56] the Soviets contending that the material being distributed was causing ferment among a section of the population and was, therefore, an attempt at interference in Soviet domestic affairs. Since the injunction was accompanied by a threat that its violation would lead to the expulsion of the Israeli delegation, and since the Israelis believed it important that they remain in order to continue making contacts, they complied.[57]

The Kremlin's efforts notwithstanding, the Israelis were swamped by Soviet Jews from the day of their arrival until the eve of their departure. The ten-mile procession to the opening ceremony at Moscow's Lenin Stadium, in which each delegation traveled in open cars or buses, preceded by a motorcycle carrying its national flag, was welcomed by an estimated 2 million people who thronged the city's streets.[58] The Israelis who traveled in six cars, estimated that about 10 percent of these were Jews, a large number of whom echoed their *shalom*[59] (Hebrew for peace, as well as a word of greeting).

If the official slogan of the Festival was "Peace and Friendship," for the Jews it was "Jews and friendship" or "peace and Jewry," as groups of Jews called out from here and there in the crowd.[60] One Jew simply called out "Bialik, Bialik" (the name of the leading Hebrew poet). Another jumped onto one of the Israeli cars saying that he wanted to spend a few moments on Israeli territory. And an elderly man called out, "I have waited for this day for forty years. This has been the greatest day of my life. *Shalom aleichem!*" Among the oral and written greetings that flooded the Israelis were postcards bearing the hand-written inscriptions: "*Shalom aleichem*" (the traditional Jewish "welcome"); "*Am Yisraeli hai*" (the people of Israel lives); "Long live Israel!"; "*Shema Yisrael*" (Hear O Israel, the opening words of the most important Jewish prayer); "Long live Ben Gurion!"; "Save us!"; "Next year in Jerusalem" (another phrase from the prayer book).[61] The Hebrew, Yiddish and Russian postcards and notes received by the Israelis described Israel as "our homeland, our protector," expressed the hope that Israel would prosper and remain strong and talked of the Soviet Jews' longing for that country. One well-wisher wrote that the time would come when "the Jews of the entire world will be gathered under one sky – the sky of Israel." Another card simply stated: "We love you! Misha, Yankel and millions more."[62]

As usual, Moscow's Choral Synagogue was the scene of meetings with large numbers of Jews on both of the Sabbaths that the delegation spent in Moscow. Although once more many Jews probably refrained from coming to the synagogue out of fear (the Israelis saw photographers on the roofs of neighboring buildings), there were between

2,500 and 3,000 inside the building and a similar number outside on each Sabbath. In the words of one Israeli, the pressure of the crowds made it look like the synagogue walls were ready to collapse. Although the guests were seated on the *bima* (dais) next to the rabbi to prevent conversation with the congregation, the eyes of the congregation were focused on them throughout the entire service. And when some of them were called up to the *Tora*, to read a section of the weekly portion, the congregants milled around them. Finally, when the cantor recited those parts of the prayers that related to Zion and Jerusalem, people wept openly. Mothers asked the Israelis to let their children touch them. People asked from all sides: "Is there still hope?" or "When will the redemption come?" Again there were cries of "Save us!" and "Long live Ben Gurion!"[63]

The delegation's artistic director, Zeev Havatzelet of Kibbutz Bet Alpha, reckoned that 60,000 Soviet Jews saw the Israelis perform, and one delegation member told a reporter that 20,000 Jews attended a single outdoor performance.[64] The indoor performances were all packed to the limit and large numbers of Jews who had not been able to purchase tickets waited outside to catch a glimpse of the Israelis when they left. The first Israeli dance and folk-song performance – which had been postponed and had its venue changed from the Pushkin Theater in the center of town to the Sovetskii Theater in one of the suburbs – began an hour-and-a-half late because some of the participants were unable to make their way through the throng that had heard about the change and rushed there in the (largely vain) effort to get in. Eventually hundreds of militia had to intervene to disperse the crowd.[65]

Each of the Israeli performances turned into a demonstration, with emotions running high on both sides. Greeted with stormy ovations and knowing what their performances meant for their largely Jewish audiences, the Israelis gave of their best. And the Soviet Jews encouraged the Israelis because they wanted them to perform well, viewing their songs and dances as something that belonged to and represented them. Even the cancellation of a performance caused demonstrations of anger on the part of Jews who had waited many hours at the appointed spot. (On one such occasion a professor who had come for the event from Krasnoiarsk in Siberia collapsed and died on the spot.)[66]

Besides the tens of thousands who came to see the Israelis perform, thousands more had the chance to exchange some words with delegation members and hundreds were able to have longer conversations.[67] They came to see the Israelis at their dormitories in the Timiriazev Agricultural Academy, where Jews gathered from the early morning until late at night; at the synagogue; and in the streets of Moscow. On the days when there were no performances the Israelis split up and organized dancing and singing in the city squares. Wherever they were Israelis were stopped and asked questions about life in Israel, more often than not the person taking the initiative being joined by others, until they were surrounded by Jews, all firing questions.[68]

It is worth noting that, while many of the Soviet Jews were well informed about Israel, especially those who listened to Kol Zion lagola, others knew only what they could glean from the Soviet media. When the latter learned some of the reasons behind Israel's domestic and foreign policy, especially the Sinai War, from the visiting Israelis, many of them replaced criticism of Israeli policies with understanding and even support.[69] Young people in particular peppered the Israelis with practical questions about Israel, knowingly endangering their freedom; some of them, in fact, were later arrested as a result of these meetings.[70] Others had their souvenirs confiscated as they left the Israelis or upon mounting the trains that were to take them home.[71] But, as local Jews told the Israelis when the latter pointed out that there were photographers or conspicuous policemen in the vicinity: "We have no choice. We cannot miss this opportunity. We have to meet you."[72]

While some Jews even dared to wear the badges with the *menora* which the Israelis gave them and invited Israelis to their homes,[73] others would talk to them surreptitiously or in dark places, reminding the visitors of what had happened to Jews who had greeted Golda Meyerson, and the results of Golda's alleged "activities."[74] "Who knows how we shall pay for this after you are gone," the Israelis were told more than once.[75] Their caution notwithstanding, many Soviet Jews made no effort to conceal their growing national consciousness and identification with Israel.[76] Not a few of them stated openly that *aliya* was the only possible solution for a Jewish problem that neither a policy of compulsory assimilation on the part of the authorities nor a tendency toward voluntary assimilation on the part of the Jews had been able to solve. Many of these, moreover, believed that their dream of *aliya* would one day be realized.[77]

Jews of all ages, from all walks of life and all parts of the USSR all told the same story: Soviet Jews were the victims of individual discrimination, were deprived of meaningful national group identity, were apprehensive about their future (one Jew attributed the small-ness of the Jewish family to this uncertainty) and were in perpetual search of something that would give meaning to their Jewishness. Although the post-Stalin regime had retreated from the Doctors' Plot, it had not solved the Jewish problem. Lacking any territorial solution in the USSR (except for the fiction of Birobidzhan), the Jews' right to national self-determination within the confines of the socialist mother-land was an empty slogan. Thus, Israel had become the focus of their burning need for national self-determination and a full national life.[78]

What particularly impressed the Israelis and what probably gave the Soviet authorities the greatest cause for concern was the attitude of the young generation, the product of a post-revolutionary upbringing. Hundreds and thousands of young men and women, most of whom knew no Yiddish let alone Hebrew, and who had no knowledge of Jewish history, came to hear about Israel as something they felt belonged to them. When asked, many of them could give no rational explanation for their link with the people, yet they insisted that, as Jews, Israel was the only place for them. They pronounced the name of the country with awe, received souvenirs with reverence as if they were a priceless treasure, applauded the Israeli delegation with a tremendous enthusiasm and listened to stories of the Israeli War of Independence and the Sinai War with obvious pride.[79] The State of Israel and its exploits not only aroused their imagination and strength-ened their spirit, but also spurred them to action. Some of them were studying Hebrew individually or in small underground study groups and requested Hebrew books, dictionaries and grammars in order to improve their knowledge of the language.[80]

One of the groups that met with Israelis comprised eight students at Moscow State University, only one of whom spoke Yiddish (although another four understood a little). Two of them had approached an Israeli delegation member while he was answering questions about Israel in Red Square. When they whispered in his ear that they wanted to meet him separately, the Israeli warned them that such a meeting might harm them. But they insisted and a first meeting with the entire group took place on the streets of Moscow, the students besieging the Israeli with questions about Israel as they walked. At subsequent meetings they told familiar stories of antisemitism, of their sense of suffocation and insecurity, of the lack of respect for individuals in general and Jews in particular.[81]

Many of the young Jews who met with Israelis were from Latvia and Lithuania, where knowledge of Judaism and Israel was still relatively widespread. They could still remember homes and schools in prewar Vilnius, Kaunas and Riga. Quite a few of them spoke a little Yiddish, a few even Hebrew. Although they came in small groups, they said that they needed as much material as possible because they were representing larger circles in their home towns. Their commitment, too, was unambiguous: they had to emigrate; they could no longer bear the feeling of loneliness and alienation that characterized the diaspora in which they found themselves as the result of an arbitrary fate. Meanwhile, they were ready to do what they could.[82] One young man from Riga even came to Moscow in the naïve hope of fictitiously marrying a girl from the Israeli delegation and returning to Israel with her.[83]

Young people came to the Festival from as far away as Siberia, Birobidzhan, Central Asia, Georgia, the Ural Mountains, Belorussia and Moldavia, from the entire length and breadth of the Soviet Union.[84] A youth from Minsk who was given some pamphlets about Israel came again on the following day; he had read the material thoroughly but still had some questions about the absorption of immigrants, the development of Israel's raw materials, Israeli–Arab relations. Like so many others, he was disappointed by the Soviet regime's obvious failure to deal with the Jewish problem and had come to the conclusion that Israel provided the only solution. Were it not for his hope of eventually getting to Israel and participating in its construction and defence, his life would be pointless. Convinced personally of the need for action, he insisted that many Minsk Jews were ready to be organized. He also felt an urgent need to study Hebrew and Jewish history and asked for a book to study Hebrew and a Hebrew–Russian dictionary.[85] After meeting two Israelis outside the dormitory where they resided, another two students from Moscow spent the entire two weeks of the Festival with them. As one of these students, Tina Brodetskaia, reminisces: "Never before the Israelis came had I seen a free Jew, with a proudly erect head, a straight back and a proud look."[86]

Elderly people met the Israelis with hugs, kisses, tears and the need to talk. A few of them were orthodox Jews for whom Israel was the Holy Land and the Israelis holy people. Some, who had been members of Zionist movements in their youth, followed events in Israel with concern, often with the help of Israeli broadcasts, and prayed for the welfare of the Jewish state and its people. Mostly, however, they were assimilated Jews who had made a sincere effort to disappear as Jews and who had brought up their children accordingly. But now, disappointed and despairing, they sought to atone for long years of detachment from the Jewish people by an attachment to the new Jewish state. Many of these older people had more in common with their grandchildren, who were seeking their Jewish roots, than with their children, who were at the height of their professional careers and therefore reluctant to consider the more fundamental problems of their way of life and world view.[87] Yet even some of these, men and women in their forties and fifties, made direct contact with the Israelis despite the risk involved.[88]

The results of meetings with the Israelis were felt for years to come. An American Jew who visited the USSR two years later recounted that Jews spoke to him of their meetings with the Israelis in 1957 as one of the great occasions of their lives. "Golda Meyerson had been a symbol. These youths were the concrete reality."[89] Many Soviet Jews insist that encounters with the Israeli delegation or with the materials they distributed aroused their sense of Jewish identity or even made them Zionists.[90] Eager to obtain more information and publications and to have another opportunity to talk about Israel, some of these made efforts in the following months and years to meet other Israelis, members of the embassy or of other delegations to international events.[91] A few even corresponded with delegation members to maintain the contact.[92]

The Festival was therefore a major factor in the development of Soviet Jewish consciousness, while the Soviet Jews' demonstration of feeling for Israel was a political act of primary significance that brought the Soviet Jewish problem to the attention of all parties concerned inside and outside the USSR. According to one major Western newspaper, the affection with which the Soviet Jews met the Israelis, their interest in Israel and their explicit statement of unhesitating preference for life in Israel over that in the USSR dealt "a staggering blow" to the Soviet claim that its national minorities prospered under communism.[93] And at the very least the coming together of large numbers of Jews from all over the Soviet Union, in an open act of national identity, gave new strength and courage to those who had hitherto kept their feelings about Israel and *aliya* to themselves or shared them only with a small group of trusted friends.

### Jewish "nationalist" activity in the USSR toward the end of the fifties

Although the Youth Festival presented the opportunity for more concentrated Jewish national activity than any other happening

during the second half of the 1950s, such activities were not restricted
to the two weeks of the Festival. Soviet Jews continued to meet with
Israelis and other Western Jews and to receive materials from them.
They also continued to study Hebrew and Jewish history, and to listen
to foreign, and particularly Israeli, broadcasts. They persisted in their
attempts to set up Yiddish drama and choral groups. Above all, they
went on attending synagogue on the Sabbath and the Jewish festivals
as well as such Jewish "concerts" as were given.

The Israelis visiting the Soviet Union in this period came mainly to
attend international events – academic and professional conferences,
exhibitions, sport events – which took place mostly in Moscow and
Leningrad. For although the country had begun to be opened up to
tourism from the West this did not yet include Israel.[94] Thus Professor
Aharon Kachalsky (later Katzir) of the Weizmann Institute attended a
biochemistry conference in February 1957; a delegation of Israeli
architects participated in a professional exhibition following their
conference and Israeli marksmen competed in a tournament in
summer 1958; and an aviation club visited in summer 1959, as did a
group that showed Israeli films at a film festival in Moscow.

The architects, marksmen and fliers had the opportunity to speak
with large numbers of Jews. Many of them came from outside
Moscow, specifically to seek out the Israelis, sometimes even following them to their hotels. As had happened at the Youth Festival, some
of the Israelis were invited to private homes where local Jews could
talk more freely about what they had heard on Israeli broadcasts and
tell them what printed materials they were interested in receiving from
the outside. At the architects' exhibition the Israeli booth was one of
the most popular foreign booths, its exhibits on the construction of
new townships such as Kiryat Gat, Bet Shean and Eilat attracting
particular interest.[95]

No matter where else Israelis and local Jews met, the synagogue
remained the main place of contact both for Israeli delegates to specific
events and for the Israeli embassy staff. The marksmen, for example,
went to Moscow's Choral Synagogue on all the three Sabbaths that
they spent in Moscow. And, as before, the appearance of Israelis
caused such excitement that prayers were interrupted while they were
being seated on the dais. At the end of the service they were embraced
by congregation members who kissed the Shield of David they wore
on their jacket or shirt lapels and arranged further meetings.[96]

Aside from the emigration allowed by the Polish repatriation, the
second half of the fifties witnessed what looked like real progress in

the field of religion. Not only were American rabbinical delegations allowed to visit the USSR in 1956,[97] but in that same year Rabbi Shlifer was part of a three-man delegation that traveled to Paris for the unveiling of a monument in memory of those who died in the Holocaust.[98] Moreover, as noted above, the Peace Prayer Book was finally published in late 1956 and the Kol Yaacov Rabbinical Seminary or *yeshiva* was opened at the Moscow Choral Synagogue in early 1957. But all these auguries came to naught. In the last years of the decade a vigorous anti-religious campaign that was to continue until the end of Khrushchev's rule in 1964 was launched.[99] In its process Jewish religious communities suffered as much as, if not more than, other religious groupings. Synagogues were closed down, the ban on *matzot* was instituted and repressive measures were taken against rabbis, synagogue wardens and ritual slaughterers.[100]

The visits of Israeli diplomats to synagogues throughout the country and the enthusiasm and excitement they aroused, which had long irritated the Soviet authorities, now became a pretext for closing them.[101] Since the synagogues and those who attended them were frequently accused of Zionism and Zionist activity, even in places where Israeli officials had not visited, it can be assumed that both regular synagogue-goers and the *dvadtsatkas* which had to register religious institutions with the authorities viewed the coming of Israelis as a mixed blessing. They may sometimes have actually become reluctant to have Israelis visit them out of fear that their presence might ultimately doom the minimal Jewish communal existence made possible by the synagogue and the conduct of the traditional prayers and ceremonies.

On the whole, however, the Israelis' tours of the country's cities and townships were of great significance for the local Jewish community and they continued without interruption throughout the period of the anti-religious campaign despite the difficulties and embarrassments. In places where there was no synagogue, the Israelis were sometimes able to locate *minyanim*, often maintained in out-of-the-way, ramshackle buildings or in private homes.[102] Here, too, they brought moral encouragement as well as prayer books and other items of religious practice.

The relationship between the Israelis and synagogue officials throughout the country was indeed no simple matter.[103] The Israelis were not required to let officials know in advance when they planned to attend services in any of Moscow's three synagogues. But even here their advent at services did not always pass without instances of unpleasantness. For example, provocateurs sometimes initiated out-bursts against the Israelis apparently intended to cause enough of an uproar to provide a pretext for prohibiting the diplomats from further participation in services. Rabbi Shlifer's successor, Rabbi Yehuda Leib Levin, and his associates often had problems with the authorities over contacts with the Israelis.[104]

Outside Moscow local representatives of the Council for the Affairs of Religious Cults cautioned synagogue officials when Israeli diplo-mats or other Jewish tourists were planning to visit their town,[105] instructing them to isolate the guests and prevent contact between them and their congregants. Above all, rabbis were warned against allowing their congregations to show undue enthusiasm when the visitors arrived, under pain of bearing the consequences if these instructions were not carried out. Thus synagogue officials were often placed in the unenviable position of having to accord a generally cool – and occasionally even hostile – welcome to guests whom they were thrilled to meet and to refuse the gifts they brought because "the synagogue had all it required." However, when the Israelis sought to bypass the officials by giving their gifts to individual worshippers, the officials sometimes demanded them.

When the president of the Lvov community sought to restrain members of the congregation who tried to greet and shake the hands of two Israeli guests in spring 1959, he told the Israelis – who found his behavior difficult to reconcile with his intimate knowledge of Israeli events and his general warmth – that this was what he had to do in order to assure the continued existence of the synagogue. Prior to the Israelis' visit, he explained, he had been summoned to the authorities and told that he was being made responsible for the congregation's conduct. He was also instructed to make note of the gifts brought by the visitors and the names of those who received them. There is ample evidence that the Soviet authorities hoped warnings against close contact with outsiders would limit the information being spread abroad regarding their anti-Jewish discrimination and acts of violence against Jews and Jewish institutions.[106]

Despite increasing signs of repression, the same atmosphere that generated the student unrest of fall 1956 and the ferment of the 1957 Youth Festival continued to bring young Jews to the synagogues on the Jewish festivals, especially in Moscow and Leningrad. Although the Israelis were often the catalyst, they did not create the young people's need to express their Jewish identity. For, while both young and old Jews were still careful to maintain their guard in their everyday lives, the former at least let down their guard in synagogue, where they knew that (except for the ubiquitous informers planted in their midst) they would be meeting others with similar problems and views. Thus, they came in increasing numbers on the Day of Atonement, especially toward the end of the fast, and on the eve of Simhat Tora. Indeed, every time Israeli diplomats who attended Yom Kippur services in Moscow in September 1958 went out for a breath of air, they attracted a crowd of fifty or sixty people, many of whom manifested considerable knowledge of what was going on in Israel.

In Riga in 1959 the crowd who came for the Kol Nidre service on the eve of Yom Kippur was so large that many people had to remain in the street. Although very few of those attending services knew the prayers and five or six people had to share a single usually tattered prayer book, these Jews felt the need to come together on the Holy Day. On the day itself, the synagogue was full throughout the long hours of the service, people coming whenever they could get away from work, and toward evening, when the work and school day had ended, it was packed to overflowing.

Two weeks later, the festival of Simhat Tora was celebrated with unprecedented fervor by thousands of young people in both Moscow and Leningrad. The crowd that sang and danced in the vicinity of Moscow's Choral Synagogue was estimated at 30,000, 70 percent of whom were young people. When the crowd inside the synagogue showed no signs of leaving at 1 a.m., despite the wardens' attempts to disperse it, Rabbi Levin ordered the lights to be switched off. In Leningrad the singing and dancing continued right through the night. And in both cities Israeli embassy officials who attended the festivities were surrounded by people eager to hear about life in Israel.[107]

One group of young Jews used the street outside the Choral Synagogue as a regular meeting-place during the late 1950s. Over a hundred strong, they met every Saturday night to sing Jewish songs in Yiddish, which some of them knew or, more often, in Russian with an occasional Jewish or Hebrew word thrown in. After a synagogue official begged them to disperse lest their activities bring the vengeance of the authorities down on the synagogue, they transferred their rendezvous to a nearby boulevard.[108]

Outside the two main cities Jews were less bold, especially in the smaller, more outlying townships of Belorussia and the Ukraine although there were some significant exceptions. In particular, the yearning for Israel of the Georgian and Bukharan Jews remained undiluted by efforts to bring them to heel. In both Georgia and Central

Asia warnings did not prevent congregations from welcoming Israelis openly. In Tbilisi and Kutaisi, in Tashkent, Bukhara and Samarkand, Jews learned Hebrew and taught it to their children. And when inspectors in Georgia made checks to see that there were no children attending synagogue services, the children were sent outside, only to return as soon as they left. Here, where Jewish life was less impaired by the massive erosion to which it had been subjected in other parts of the Soviet Union, the attachment to Judaism and the Jewish state was inextricably interwoven.[109]

The sporadic cultural happenings, the beginnings of which we have seen above, also acquired increasing importance in the late 1950s. During this period some twenty Yiddish troupes came into being, mostly in the Western territories. The Vilnius drama group, which had formed in late summer 1956, put on its first performance in December of that year: a show based on the first act of Sholom Aleichem's play "The Great Win." This group attracted young people who wanted to come together with other Jews, but since many of them did not have any particular talent to contribute to the group's activities, there was a constant turnover in membership which had the advantage of bringing a wide circle into its sphere of influence. As most of the members knew no Yiddish, they appeared either in dances, in the choir conducted by Shaul Blekherovich, or in the orchestra conducted by Shaul Meerovich.

The hall in which the Vilnius drama group usually performed had only 200 seats, but when the group was ready to perform the whole of "The Great Win" in early 1957, its initiator, Boris Cesarkas, obtained the thousand-seat auditorium of the Lithuanian Opera by promising that all proceeds of the performance would go to the forthcoming Festival of the Lithuanian Komsomol. Although the placards for this performance were prepared by hand (to avoid having to submit them to the censor) and were hung in places such as the windows of hairdressing salons rather than on the usual billboards, there were not enough seats for all those seeking tickets.

The Jews of Vilnius regarded the group as their own. Jewish carpenters, lorry-drivers, printers and others contributed their services without payment and Jewish street vendors made financial contributions to keep the group alive. Among those who helped in other ways was Yiddish writer Yosef Kotliar, who attended rehearsals and made suggestions as how to improve performances.

In addition to the performances themselves, the group organized soirées to celebrate anniversaries and birthdays, as well as evenings of readings and of song and dance. These were usually attended by between 200 and 400 people, mostly members and their families, including children. Some of the troupe's members received records of Israeli songs from delegates to the Youth Festival, and one member, Marek Moizes, made recordings of these at his place of employment (a tape-recorder factory) and sent them to cities throughout the USSR, including some in Siberia.

A children's choir set up in Vilnius in 1958, also under the auspices of the "collective" for Jewish artistic activity established in Lithuania in 1956, did not fare as well as the drama troupe. Although it was authorized by the Lithuanian SSR party's propaganda department to sing in Russian, Lithuanian and Yiddish, the Vilnius municipal council ordered its disbandment after only one performance on the grounds that studying and singing songs in Yiddish led to the Jews' segregation whereas the USSR was striving for their assimilation.[110]

Another amateur troupe came into being in Daugavpils, Latvia, in the same period and a drama group and choir were set up in Riga in summer 1957. Although a club or "house of culture" was found to house the Riga groups, the cultural secretary of Riga's *gorkom* (party committee) sought to dissuade the four organizers with the line that Jewish culture could be developed only in Birobidzhan[111] and warning them that the party would not tolerate cultural activity in any language other than Russian and Latvian. But the choir came into being, with more than one hundred members beginning rehearsals under Izrail Abramis. The other two hundred applicants who registered for membership had to be turned away because the choir's virtually illegal existence made it necessary for them to rehearse for the first six months in the basement of the shoemakers' collective, and that venue was not large enough for any more. (The four organizers and Abramis did not tell the others that they were operating without party permission out of fear that this would deter members from attending rehearsals.) The choir held its first performance in February 1958 at the Riga Conservatory before a closed audience of one hundred musicians, music professors and critics. Although its high level and the praise that it evoked from the Latvian SSR's leading musicians led to its *de facto* recognition by the authorities, a number of conditions were imposed on its further operation: Jewish songs were not to comprise more than 50 percent of any performance; all programs had to be approved prior to each performance (this was standard procedure); the choir could not be called a Jewish choir, but had to bear the name of the club to which it was officially affiliated; every concert had to open and close with a non-Jewish song; and the compère had to be a non-Jew.

In the course of its existence, the choir gave approximately forty concerts, all of them in large halls and before packed audiences. It performed twice in Vilnius, once in Daugavpils and several times in the nearby tourist center of Dzintari, where Jews from all over the country attended. Its repertoire included traditional Yiddish folk-songs; new Yiddish songs by Soviet Jewish composers including ghetto songs such as Revekka Boiarskaia's "Babii Iar," Sara Feigin's "Ballad for the Warsaw Ghetto Uprising" and Hirsh Glik's "Song of the Partisans"; and some classical pieces. Some of the choir's folk-songs were even broadcast over the local radio.

Having set the choir in motion, its organizers, who had borne the brunt of circumventing the obstacles placed in its path, succeeded in getting permission to start a Yiddish drama group. The group had to be affiliated with a different club than the choir and there could be no cooperation between the two. Plays had to be submitted for censor-ship in Russian translation, and a few seats at every performance had to be provided with earphones so the plays could be heard in Russian and Latvian as well. The group gave eight performances of two plays and was on the verge of producing a third when it was closed down in September 1962, on the grounds that Jewish culture was superfluous and reactionary, obstructing implementation of the general policy of assimilation. The choir followed the drama group into oblivion in March 1963. As David Garber, one of the choir's initiators, has pointed out:

> the existence and abolition of the drama group and choir played an important role in the growth of national consciousness among Latvian Jews. The groups aroused new interest in and love for Jewish culture and encouraged Jews to overcome the fear which Stalinism had implanted in all peoples and to demand the rights guaranteed by Soviet law. They also created a basis on which Jews could meet each other legally, after many years of keeping apart, to talk about matters of Jewish national interest.[112]

Yiddish drama groups existed for short periods in other places. In Leningrad a "musical drama ensemble" directed by Veniamin Khaia-tovskii was set up in 1957. Its terms of reference were to perform plays that depicted Soviet life and had been published in Russian. Although it included among its members old-timers in the Yiddish theater like Zinovii Baev (Kogan), Ester Roitman, Yaacov Klebanov, many of its members had to be taught Yiddish songs in Russian transliteration.

While the Jewish ensemble – unlike that of other nationalities – was not subsidized, its audience was so large that it made a profit. But its members refused to keep any of it for themselves so as not to provide a pretext for the authorities to terminate its activities. Nevertheless, this troupe, too, was eventually closed down, this time on the grounds that it had no permanent place to rehearse or perform, even though it had come second in a competition of Leningrad's amateur troupes only a few months after it was formed. The Leningrad ensemble performed outside Leningrad from time to time, as far away as Kuibyshev in Siberia and Birobidzhan.[113]

There were also troupes in Kishinev and, as of the early 1960s, in Derbent (Dagestan ASSR). The latter, which performed in Judeo-Tat, the language of the Mountain Jews, was at first called the "Inter-Kolkhoz Tat Theater" and from 1966 the "Tat People's Theater." It existed until the end of the sixties and in the seventies was replaced by a Tat song and dance company.[114]

While drama and musical groups were tolerated for shorter or longer periods in various parts of the Soviet Union, other attempts to improve the Jews' cultural situation were never allowed to take off the ground and sometimes resulted in sanctions. In 1957 a group of Leningrad Jews headed by Gedalia Pecherskii wrote to the Minister of Education of the RSFSR and the municipal *ispolkom* (executive committee) asking permission to organize studies of Hebrew and Yiddish and ancient and modern Jewish history and literature; in reply the Hebrew section of Leningrad's Saltykov-Shchedrin Library was closed.[115]

On the other hand, the Kremlin did allow a considerable and well-publicized Yiddish cultural activity in honor of the centenary of the birth of the Yiddish writer Sholom Aleichem in 1959. A selection of Sholom Aleichem's writings appeared in Yiddish, a number of literary evenings and concerts of his works were held throughout the country, and radio and television programs were dedicated to him.[116]

The central event in the celebrations was an evening in Moscow's Kolonnyi Zal under the auspicies of the All-Soviet Writers' Union. Among those on the stage with Secretary of the Union Boris Polevoi, poet Aleksei Surkov and the black American singer Paul Robeson, were several Yiddish writers who had survived the "black years." After selections of his works were read to a delighted audience, Robeson spoke of Sholom Aleichem's defense of poor Jews as the forerunner of Soviet Jewish literature. Robeson – whose appearance was greeted with wild applause – told of his special affection for the Yiddish language, recounting how impressed he had been by the plays of Sholom Aleichem and other Jewish writers that he had attended many years before at the Jewish State Theater. Robeson then went on to praise the high standard of the great actor Mikhoels, who had been killed in 1948, and to tell his audience about the cultural institutions and achievements of the American Jewish community. After these introductory remarks, each of which was applauded as it was translated into Russian, to the evident embarrassment and anger of Polevoi, Robeson sang folk-songs in Yiddish to a spellbound audience. He concluded by singing the Song of the Jewish Partisans, which had been sung in the bunkers and on the barricades of the Warsaw Ghetto by "Jewish heroes" who had "fought a battle which was probably the most courageous of all peoples' wars for independence and honor."

Arie Eliav of the Israeli embassy, who attended this performance, records that he felt "an electric current coursing through the audience" which "froze ... stunned" as one of the world's greatest singers, a man held in high esteem by the Soviet people, talked openly and admiringly of concepts which "every Soviet Jew carried deep in his heart" but were unmentionable in public. When Robeson finished his rendering, "there was a long moment of silence," and then "all of a sudden ... there arose a tremendous wave of applause, and it went on and on, and ... would not end ... All their suffering, pain and humiliation, all their yearnings and longings were put into their clapping hands; and in the rhythmic clapping of thousands of hands, the audience let everyone know what they bore in their hearts and minds."[117]

Within the framework of the Sholom Aleichem centenary, three Soviet artists, including the young singer Nehama Lifshitz, were sent to Paris and Brussels to show the world that the Soviet Union did not discriminate against Yiddish culture.[118] Although four Yiddish books were published in 1959 for the first time since 1948,[119] such books remained generally unobtainable, and approaches to the authorities to persist in the renewal of Yiddish culture were rejected outright on the usual grounds that there was no public for it.

The outright falsity of statements such as this was belied by the crowds that continued to fill Yiddish concerts in the big cities and in towns with large Ashkenazi populations. Even though only 17 percent of the Jewish population gave Yiddish as their mother tongue in the 1959 census and even though many of these had at best only a smattering of the language, Eliav records that young Jews who knew little or no Yiddish nonetheless felt it was their "real mother tongue.''[120] At Yiddish concerts such youngsters relied on older people in the audience to translate what was going on.

Nor did people always attend these performances because of their artistic quality, many of them being unquestionably second or third rate. Indeed, the authorities may have allowed mediocre performers to appear so the audience would be restricted to the elderly and the nostalgic, just as they were freer in permitting Yiddish artists to perform in cities with a smaller and more assimilated Jewish population than in cities such as Kiev, Odessa, Lvov and Minsk.[121] As American Yiddish publicist Ben Zion Goldberg – who had been invited to the USSR to take part in the Sholom Aleichem centennial festivities by virtue of the fact that he was the writer's son-in-law and was known to be sympathetic toward the Soviet Union – pointed out, this was the way to bury Yiddish culture, not to revive it.[122] But here, too, the authorities failed to take the mood of their Jewish citizenry into account. For Jews of all ages and from all walks of life flocked to every performance given for the same reasons that motivated those who attended synagogue:[123] to identify with fellow Jews by sharing a Jewish experience.

Members of the Israeli embassy staff attended these performances in Moscow as faithfully as they attended synagogue. They also tried to schedule their tours to coincide with performances in other cities.[124] For the Israelis knew that their presence at such performances attracted Jews who sought an opportunity to see and possibly speak with representatives of the Jewish state, or to obtain written material on life there.

In the midst of the above, nationally minded Jewish groups continued their activities and new groups were formed in a number of towns. In Moscow, Leningrad and Gorkii, in Kiev, Kharkov and Dnepropetrovsk, in Rostov and Baku, in Riga and Vilnius – to name just a few – small circles were meeting to listen to Israeli radio, discuss events and trends in Israel, and study Hebrew and Jewish history. These informal groups often comprised people of similar social or professional backgrounds. For example, the Leningrad circle for the study of Hebrew that centered around Gedalia Pecherskii and Evsei Dynkin consisted mostly of academics who wanted to learn Hebrew in order to teach it to the next generation.[125] The goal of another Leningrad group formed in the late 1950s was to spread knowledge of Jewish subjects in order to increase Jewish awareness and to study Hebrew themselves to prepare for their eventual *aliya*. To this end, the group disseminated literature received through the Israeli embassy as well as letters from Israel and articles from *Folks-shtime*. Members also began translating a Yiddish book on the Warsaw Ghetto uprising (presumably that of Ber Mark) into Russian and typing up excerpts on Jews from the writings of Maksim Gorky. But this group fell apart when one of its members, Natan Tsirulnikov, was arrested in 1960 for having received materials form the Israeli embassy staff in the proximity of the Moscow Choral Synagogue.[126]

The demand for books for teaching and learning Hebrew kept on growing, as study of the language provided a natural vehicle for institutionalizing nationalist activity. Everywhere Israelis went they were asked for Hebrew dictionaries, grammars and other textbooks, the lack of which restricted efforts to study Hebrew throughout the country.[127] Even in Riga Yitzhak Hayit and David Iofis were teaching Hebrew with almost no teaching aids; since all his Hebrew books had been confiscated in the search that accompanied his arrest in 1951, Iofis taught purely from memory.[128] The only modern Hebrew readily available to those who wanted to keep up their Hebrew, or even study it from scratch by themselves, was *Kol ha'am*, the organ of the Israeli Communist Party. Visitors to Moscow's Lenin Library and Leningrad's Saltykov-Shchedrin Library saw middle-aged readers "consuming the paper" and younger readers poring over it with the help of a dictionary. According to Eliav, the newspaper was read so heavily that it almost crumbled in one's hands.[129]

As earlier, former Prisoners of Zion continued to play a pivotal role in the revival of Zionist activity throughout the USSR. Meir Gelfond, an ex-prisoner himself, has noted that "a national Zionist ideology predominated among the Jewish prisoners in Soviet camps," and now, in the second half of the fifties, "groups of such people who shared a common past, a common ideology, and common hopes for the future, were formed in various Soviet cities." Moreover, the groups they initiated "soon acquired new members from the Jewish youth."[130]

According to Gelfond, such groups arose not only in Moscow, Leningrad, Kiev and Odessa and in the more nationally minded Jewish communities of Georgia, Lithuania and Latvia, but also in settlement cities such as Karaganda, Norilsk, Omsk and Vorkuta – places to which many of the ex-prisoners had been banished or where they had chosen to remain after their release, since they were not allowed to live in Moscow or the capital cities of the Union Republics. Something of the atmosphere that prevailed in the settlement towns of Siberia and Kazakhstan, where ex-prisoners concentrated in large numbers, has been conveyed by Abraham Kaufman, a former Prisoner of Zion, who spent five years in Karaganda after serving an eleven-year sentence in various prisons and camps. In his reminiscences, Kaufman recalls the *seder* on the first night of Passover 1957, at which twenty-two people gathered in a "marrano-like" atmosphere and sat around singing Hebrew songs until 7 a.m. Eleven of those assembled were under twenty-five and the rest, apart from two pensioners, were under forty-five; nine were former prisoners (five for Zionism and Jewish nationalism). Although a number of those present knew Hebrew and spoke it among themselves, Kaufman – who conducted the *seder* from a *haggada* put out in Moscow by Rabbi Shlifer – introduced events from past and present Jewish history about which most of them knew nothing.[131]

Not every member of these groups was ready to commit him- or herself to *aliya* – partly at least because they were not prepared to give serious thought to a contingency that seemed unrealistic. Yet they all wanted to learn Hebrew and Jewish history and to acquire information about Israel with a view to finding out whether the Jewish state might provide a viable alternative if and when the gates were opened to their emigration.[132]

Among printed material received from the Israeli embassy toward the end of the 1950s was *Vestnik Izrailia*, a monthly publication about Israel and world Jewry written specifically in Israel for Jews in the Soviet Union.[133] Private correspondence with relatives and friends in Israel, which had been renewed after Stalin's death, also began to play an increasingly important role in bringing news and succor to nationally minded Soviet Jews.[134]

But materials from outside could hardly remedy the dearth of materials on Judaism, Jewish history and literature which was holding back many who were trying to learn more about the essence of their Jewishness. It was in order to fill this demand that could not otherwise be met that *samizdat* material began appearing in the latter half of the 1950s. Thus, as early as 1956 – three years before the Leningrad group of Tsirulnikov and Rosa Epshtein was putting out materials – Iakov Edelman who had recently returned to Moscow after several years in Vorkuta, disseminated copies of his "A and B." Edelman also translated and distributed the diary of Hanna Senesh, the Palestinian Jewish parachutist originally from Hungary who had been dropped into German-occupied Hungary in 1944; a book on Yosef Trumpeldor, one of the heroes of the Palestinian Jewish *yishuv*; and an article on the Sinai War. Even before he moved from Karaganda to Kalinin near

Moscow in September 1957, Meir Gelfond was distributing these materials in Karaganda along with newspapers and literature that Edelman and Zvi Pregerzon had managed to receive from the Israelis.[135]

Manuscripts smuggled out of the Soviet Union, either through tourists or members of foreign delegations, showed that Soviet Jews, far from being broken, were still producing works of spiritual and literary value. Dora Podolskii of Moscow managed to send the articles she wrote between June 1956 and April 1958 out of the country in this way. Dora was inspired to write about the position of Soviet Jewry by Khrushchev's repeated statements that the silence of Soviet Jews proved there was no Jewish problem in the USSR and attempted to demonstrate otherwise in her articles.

Although a member of the Israeli embassy staff and French journalist and writer Maurice Bitter visited her home, and although her son Boris met with members of the Israeli delegation to the Youth Festival, the Podolskii family tried to operate circumspectly in order to evade unnecessary risk. As distinct from other places, where it mostly sought to nip all contact with Israelis and other Jewish nationalist activity in the bud, the KGB generally permitted Moscow Jews to maintain such contacts for some time before taking steps against them. This might have been to give those engaging in rendezvous with foreigners enough rope to hang themselves, or because the authorities hoped to uncover larger networks of troublemakers.

It was the study of Hebrew that, in a roundabout way, brought the Podolskiis to open their home to outsiders who were interested in Israel. Boris Podolskii had been studying Hebrew with eighty-year-old Grigorii Zilberman. And when Tina Brodetskaia and a friend decided to study the language in 1957, after having befriended two Israeli delegates to the Youth Festival, Rabbi Levin suggested that the two girls approach Zilberman for lessons.[136] After Zilberman put Tina and her friend in touch with the Podolskiis, they began making frequent visits to the Podolskii home, and Dora translated a Yiddish pamphlet she had received from the Israeli embassy entitled "Jewish Communists on the Jewish Question in the Soviet Union" for them and her son.[137] By this time the Podolskiis were already passing on materials they had received to others in Moscow and to relatives in Dnepropetrovsk. Tina and her friend became couriers between Dora and the Israelis, taking the latter Dora's articles and receiving materials in return. On one occasion the Israeli who received an article in the Choral Synagogue told the girls to leave the synagogue as their presence there on an ordinary Sabbath was conspicuous. On another occasion they passed an article to an embassy secretary at the skating rink in Gorkii Park. A third time Tina and her mother received *Elef millim* and other Hebrew texts at a Yiddish concert.

In the fourteen-hour search that preceded the Podolskiis' arrest in April 1958, the KGB found the translation of the Yiddish pamphlet, a book on Jewish history that had been printed in the U.S. (which the Podolskiis had also received from the embassy) and a long Russian article that Dora had just finished, which was a reply to an anti-Israel article that had appeared in *Literaturnaia gazeta*, the prestigious organ of the Writers' Union. Eventually Tina Brodetskaia and her stepfather Evsei Dobrovskii, as well as the eighty-year-old Zilberman, were brought to trial with the Podolskiis; except for Zilberman, all of them were sentenced to terms in hard-labor camps. One of the Dnepropetrovsk relatives who had received Israeli materials from the Podolskiis was also tried and convicted, even though he protested that he had not passed the material on to anyone else. Dora and her husband, Semen, were accused of treason, and the others of anti-Soviet activity, specifically of distributing anti-Soviet literature and participating in an anti-Soviet organization (*organizatsionnaia deiatelnost*, Articles 58–10 and 11 of the RSFSR Criminal Code). As had been the case with the Goberman–Landman group, the apartments and telephones of both the Podolskiis and Dobrovskii-Brodetskiis had been bugged to obtain evidence against them.[138]

The Podolskiis and their colleagues were far from being the only ones accused of Zionist activity in the late 1950s. Early in 1957 Barukh Vaisman and three of his friends – Marek (Meir) Draznin, Hersh Remenik and Iakov Fridman – were arrested in Kiev on the charge of possessing and distributing anti-Soviet materials and conducting other Zionist activity. Draznin was sentenced to ten years' imprisonment, Remenik to eight years and Vaisman and Fridman to five years. Also prior to the repression that followed the Youth Festival, Riga activists Yosef Shnaider and Iurii Kogan had been arrested and charged with listening to and making notes of "anti-Soviet broadcasts" on Kol Yisrael during the Sinai War. Shnaider was further accused of having slandered the Soviet Union and the Party in letters to relatives in Israel. Finally, he was charged with having reproduced photographs of IDF units in his photography shop, and with having kept Yiddish newspapers and newspaper cuttings as well as nationalist, Zionist and anti-Soviet literature – such as the words of *hatikva*, a map of Israel and pictures of Israeli leaders – in his home along with a rifle, bullets and a pistol.

Among others arrested after the Festival was Zolia Katz of Odessa, who – after almost a year of interrogation – was sentenced to eight years' imprisonment on charges of conducting "systematic nationalist propaganda hostile to the Soviet state." In fact, Katz had maintained contact with Israeli sailors whose ships docked in the port of Odessa and had received a prayer book and *talit* (prayer-shawl) along with a copy of the Paris Yiddish newspaper *Undzer vort*, which his accusers described as Zionist and anti-Soviet. He was also accused of passing the newspaper to acquaintances from work and other places along with the Russian-language *Israeli Youth* (brought to the Soviet Union by Israeli delegates to the Youth Festival), which allegedly contained "nationalist, bourgeois and Zionist articles," and a Yiddish record of "nationalist content."

Members of Katz's family remember that the materials he received included picture albums of Israel, a Jewish calendar and records (including one by Israeli singer Yaffa Yarkoni). In addition, Katz was charged with having listened to broadcasts from Israel on a regular basis, propagating their content and praising Israel's "aggressive policy." Following publication of articles in the Soviet press condemning Israeli diplomat Eliyahu Hazan, Katz had also "slandered the Soviet media." Although the KGB insisted that Katz's "counter-revolutionary" activities were aimed at arousing widespread Jewish nationalist sentiment, his family maintain that he shared the materials he received with only five or six other people. However, the fact that he did share out the material explains why the KGB's very thorough search of his home unearthed only a small portion of what he had been given.[139]

David Khavkin, one of the Moscow Jews who had established contact with and received records, souvenirs and other materials from both Israeli delegates to the Youth Festival and the marksmen, was also arrested in 1958. What particularly incensed the authorities was Khavkin's activities connected with Jews from Georgia, whom he supplied with Israeli brochures, records, postcards and souvenirs after receiving their names and addresses from Jews he met in Moscow. It was on one of his trips to the Caucasus that Khavkin was arrested.[140]

Even as far afield as Stalinabad (Dushanbe) a young Jew was sentenced to ten years' imprisonment at the end of the fifties for having collected press cuttings on Israel and urging other Jews to read about the Jewish state.[141] Yet, just as the arrests of July 1955 did not succeed in bringing Zionist activity to a halt, these later arrests failed to dampen nationalist activity. Although the number of arrests in the late 1950s probably exceeded those of the 1970s, which excited the attention of Western public opinion and governments, the movement continued to gather momentum.[142]

In fact, Jewish nationalist activity during the last years of the fifties not only spread but was far more open and intensive than it had been since 1948. The result of this increased activity was that more Jews than ever before began to think of emigration as the only viable alternative to the spiritual genocide being offered them by the Soviet leadership. And their disappointment, frustration and despair were deepening just when opportunities to emigrate – such as the Polish repatriation agreement – seemed to be multiplying. Nor did the demand for cultural rights let up. But, even here, the Jews increasingly demanded expansion of Hebrew rather than Yiddish culture, which meant replacing the traditional vehicle of Russian Jewish culture with the culture of Israel.

Apart from those who managed to repatriate to Poland, thousands of other Soviet Jews now began taking concrete steps to further their own emigration. It is impossible to estimate the numbers of those who sought to reach Poland, whether or not they were entitled to repatriate under the agreement. Nor is there any way of knowing exactly how many Soviet Jews applied to emigrate directly to Israel, both before and after the Sinai War, although on the basis of *vyzovy* sent by relatives in Israel, their number seems to have been considerable.[143] What can be documented, however, is the new atmosphere in the Western regions and Georgia as well as among ex-camp inmates and the younger generation throughout the USSR. As one Western correspondent wrote after visiting the Soviet Union, the secret police had been telling the authorities – both under Stalin and since his death – of the many young Jews who dreamed of reaching Israel.[144] That this worried the Kremlin was made evident by the books and considerable other anti-Israel propaganda that was disseminated during this period in the effort to show Soviet Jews an unattractive Israel.[145] Although articles of this nature had been published since 1951,[146] the material now being aired was much more profuse and spoke in very pointed terms of the evils awaiting would-be emigrants to Israel, especially those from the Soviet Union.

The arrest of Israeli embassy second secretary Eliyahu Hazan in Odessa in September 1957 was certainly further evidence of Moscow's disquietude at its Jewish citizens' display of feelings toward Israel, especially since it was publicized in the Soviet media. Not only did Deputy Foreign Minister Vladimir Semenov inform Israeli Chargé d'Affaires Aviezer Chelouche that Hazan had indulged in "anti-Soviet acitvities" by distributing "anti-Soviet literature," but the Note on Hazan's activities that he handed Chelouche included the charge that Hazan had attempted to enlist a Soviet citizen in these activities.[147]

A "diplomatic source" who had "spent many years behind the Iron Curtain" noted that Moscow's treatment of its Jews was second only to "the Hungarian tragedy" in showing up the Soviet Union for what it really was in the West. The same source also said that, while the Kremlin probably knew that the best solution to its Jewish problem would be to let Jews emigrate, it was undertaking "a vast campaign . . . to destroy Jewish nationalism" by defaming Israel and undermining Soviet Jewry as a people out of fear that letting the Jews emigrate would have unthinkable consequences vis-à-vis the USSR's other minorities.[148] Even Ilya Ehrenburg – one of the Kremlin's Court Jews – was convinced that 100,000 Jews would leave for Israel if the gates were opened. At a private reception in Paris, he admitted that even he did not feel totally assimilated in the Soviet Union because of the antisemitism that still prevailed in that country (as it did "everywhere else in this world").[149] Another Soviet Jew told a communist member of the British delegation to the Youth Festival (who left the party on his return to Britain) that, if they were given permission, half a million Jews would leave "without even waiting to pack their belongings."[150]

But even this estimate was lower than that of most observers, some of whom estimated that over a million Jews would leave if they could. Arie Eliav, who traveled the length and breadth of the USSR during his service in Moscow to meet with Jews from as many communities as possible, estimated that the great majority of the 300,000 Jews of the Western areas and the 200,000 of the Eastern borderlands (Georgian, Mountain and Bukharan Jews) would emigrate to Israel if given the chance, and that considerable numbers of young people would leave from other areas as well.[151] As early as 1957, an American who had visited the Soviet Union reported that almost every Jew over the age of twenty-one with whom he had spoken had expressed the desire to leave for Israel; he was convinced that over a million would emigrate if they could.[152] While I am not contending that great numbers took actual steps toward leaving during the late 1950s, there seems to be no doubt that the idea was becoming more and more embedded in the minds of a considerable percentage of the Soviet Jewish population.[153]

# 8 The early and mid-1960s: the Soviet Jewish national awakening

The trends that emerged in the mid and late 1950s took on dimensions that changed their implications and significance in the decade that followed. Although there might not have been any single occasion as momentous as the 1957 Youth Festival, or any single opportunity to escape the strictures of life in the Soviet Union as great as the repatriation agreement with Poland, there were new and more frequent opportunities for Jews to express themselves. In addition, Soviet domestic circumstances became more conducive to increased Jewish national feeling.

Nationalism, which had remained throughout Soviet history a force of potential social unrest, now became a major factor, indeed almost a fashion, among both Russians and the national minorities. Simultaneously, the combination of de-Stalinization, and the de-ideologization that accompanied Stalin's denunciation, with the apprehensions among certain sections of the establishment regarding the processes set into motion by the renunciation of Stalin's reign of terror, created a climate favorable to the development of dissident movements in general. The two trends served to stimulate the growing Jewish nationalism in that it inevitably fed on similar ideas and ideals and was infected by the general atmosphere.[1] Moreover, the popular antisemitism that was a traditional concomitant of Russian and other nationalist feeling contributed to making Jews more aware of their national identity. For, as the most acculturated national group, they were anathema to the Russians, in that they nonetheless remained "different," and the easiest butt for the anti-Russianism of other national groupings, which viewed them as russifiers.

But the new wave of popular – and official – antisemitism had a backlash effect; some of the USSR's more liberal-minded intelligentsia began to demonstrate open sympathy for the Jews, both in reaction to what they regarded as one of the major banes of Soviet society and as a yardstick of their own humane or humanitarian outlook. Evgenii Evtushenko's poem "Babii Iar," published in 1961, seemed to legitimize Jewish national sentiment. And Ilya Ehrenburg's autobiography, published in the literary journal *Novyi mir* in 1960–61,[2] had a great influence on the Jews as in it this consummate example of the acculturated Soviet Jew had the need to make constant reference to his Jewish origin and identity.

Although the Jewish national movement was distinguished from other dissident movements in that it sought repatriation to a national home outside the USSR rather than any sweeping changes in the Soviet regime, and although repatriation to Israel did not seem out of line with Soviet practice, especially after the Polish repatriation and the departure to their respective homelands of many thousands of Greeks, Germans, Spaniards and others, the Soviet authorities perceived it as a dissident movement. However much at least some of the movement's activists insisted on the fundamental differences between the Jewish and other movements, whether national, democratic or religious, and tried to remain separate from them, this was a subtlety that CPSU ideologists, not to speak of the Soviet security forces, could hardly be expected to appreciate.

Moreover, one of the chief instruments of the Jewish movement, the dissemination of unofficial, uncensored publications known as *samizdat*, was adopted from the general dissident movements.[3] The fact that non-Jewish students and intellectuals were passing around and reading uncensored literature in the 1960s made it all the more natural for Jews, especially the younger generation, to feel that they, too, could do so without the authorities considering their activity a singularly hostile one. Indeed, it was *samizdat* that helped transform sporadic, unorganized Jewish activism into a full-blown movement. Another auxiliary, not unrelated to *samizdat*, was the growing dissemination of the materials provided by the Israeli embassy and Jewish tourists, including reports of Western efforts on behalf of Soviet Jewry. Israeli broadcasts including regular broadcasts in Russian, also helped spread information on Judaism and Israel to increasing numbers of Jewish homes throughout the USSR. These instruments all gave new strength and a more tangible content to the Jewish awakening as one with potential significance for large numbers of Jews who had no previous notion of the meaning or positive connotations of their Jewishness.

When the Soviet authorities again began letting out a few Jews in 1964, news of this development spread throughout the Jewish grapevine, encouraging those who had refrained from submitting applications to leave to do so. Even though the risks involved in applying for a permit remained considerable, once the goal seemed even slightly more attainable, more people were ready to take the chance. Although this interrelationship between the number of exit permits and applications ultimately posed a major dilemma for the Soviet authorities, at this stage it gave the Jewish national movement the momentum and concrete goal that enabled it to become a movement on the practical as well as the theoretical plane.

### Jewish"activists" in the Soviet Union

By the early to mid-sixties the Jewish national movement still had no official – or unofficial – organization, no leaders or institutions and no forum for discussing its content, strategy or tactics. It was a movement born out of need and circumstance. As such, it developed without guidance, without decisions to implement and without discipline or compulsion. Indeed, its very composition and purpose made it the antithesis of Bolshevism. Its sole unit was the primary cell, and its activists (as they came to be known) were those who had the courage and ability to spread the word and to consolidate the movement by establishing contact with other cells, with sympathetic visitors and, above all, with the Israeli embassy. The two latter groupings, in turn, provided written materials and moral encouragement. They also provided the channel through which reports of the Soviet Jewish plight could reach the rest of the world, so that pressure from the outside could reinforce the growing pressure from within.

This period witnessed a change in the groups described in previous chapters. Not only did they grow in both number and membership but they consolidated their ranks in order to prepare for an *aliya* that seemed more possible than ever before. The most active and vocal of these groups were in Moscow and Riga, in both of which cities there were a number of "cells." As before, they still centered largely around ex-camp inmates with their wider connections, greater purposefulness and, often, lesser fear. Some of these, like Zvi Pregerzon, Izrail Mintz, Sergei Morgulis and Meir Kanevskii, belonged to the older generation; others, like David Khavkin, Meir Gelfond, Yosef Shnaider and Yosef Khorol, were still young men in their thirties. No matter their age, however, their common experience and mutual trust provided a solid foundation for activity and cooperation. And the new atmosphere, opportunities and instruments at their disposal provided far more possibilities for effective action than had been conceivable in earlier years.

One important consequence of the large-scale arrests of the late forties and early fifties and of those of the Khrushchev years was precisely this bringing together of people of different ages and backgrounds from all over the Soviet Union. Thus, Zionists from Moscow such as Kanevskii, the Goberman group, the Podolskiis and Khavkin were brought together with others like Zolia Katz of Odessa, Mark Draznin, Barukh Vaisman and Lev Teplitskii of Kiev, Asher Mordekhai Iudelevich of Kharkov, Anatolii Rubin of Minsk and Boris Shperling and Yosef Shnaider of Riga, as well as with Jewish prisoners (some of them Prisoners of Zion) from remote places in Siberia and Central Asia, Georgia and Dagestan.[4]

Those arrested for Zionist activity did not wait for their release to plan for the future. While still in the camps they exchanged addresses, agreed on codes for purposes of correspondence in order to maintain their ties and began cultivating recruits from among political prisoners who had been arrested for non-Jewish dissident activity. The Zionists argued that it was a waste of time and energy for Jews to strive for domestic change, let alone to "sit" for such causes because no matter what regime was in power in the Soviet Union, their position would always remain the same. One of those won over to the Zionist cause, who later became a Jewish activist and participated in the Leningrad hijacking episode, was Eduard Kuznetsov; others were Anatolii Partashnikov and Aleksandr (Alik) Fridman of Kiev.[5]

By the mid-sixties, new groups were also being formed by people in their twenties and thirties, or even late teens. In Riga, for instance, some fifteen young people, among them Boris Druk, his wife Rivka and her brother Yosef Mendelevich, rented an isolated *dacha* (summer house) in a suburb as a meeting place. After discussing the steps necessary to prepare Jews for *aliya*, the group decided that the most important thing was to enrich their knowledge of Judaism and Jewish subjects. They collected membership dues of five rubles per month in order to purchase a second-hand typewriter and whatever old Jewish books they could find at second-hand bookstores. After discovering that there were other clandestine groups in Riga conducting similar activities, they formed ties with them. Among others, they distributed copies of the extracts they had typed out from the books they had acquired, asking the recipients to contribute whatever they could so their work could be continued and expanded.[6]

In Kiev a group of Jews in their thirties was also studying Hebrew and translating articles on Israel, Judaism and antisemitism into Russian. Each member had arrived at the idea of the eternity of the Jewish people in his own way, but they had all been strengthened in this by the military achievements of the Jewish state in 1948 and 1956. One member said his belief in the Jewish people dated back to June 1945, when he was sixteen and heard Shlomo Mikhoels speak at the twentieth anniversary celebration of the Kiev Yiddish State Theater.[7]

In fall 1966 Grigorii (Grisha) Vertlib, Ben-Tsion Tuvin, Gilia (Hillel) Butman, Solomon Dreizner and Aron Shpilberg formed a group in Leningrad with the avowed purpose of fighting assimilation, especially mixed marriages, and studying Hebrew. Their first *ulpan* (Hebrew study group) opened early in 1967 just outside Leningrad, where the group ostensibly went to skate. By spring 1967 this group had grown to fifteen people.[8]

By the middle of the decade, another group, of some twenty students from the University of Sverdlovsk and that town's Technological Institute was studying Hebrew, reading materials obtained from the Israeli embassy by members who traveled to Moscow for the purpose, and holding symposia on Israeli topics. One of the group's members was Eduard (Eitan) Finkelshtain, a well-known activist and refusenik of the movement in the seventies.[9]

In Moscow more and more young people were gathering around older activists such as Zvi Pregerzon, Iakov Edelman and Izrail Mintz, each of whom had his own study group. Edelman's group, of approximately twenty people, met in his apartment weekly where their talk about Israel often grew so lively that his wife feared the neighbors would hear them. He continued to translate books of Jewish interest into Russian, including several chapters of Gideon Hausner's book on the Eichmann trial. Pregerzon and Mintz took their students to Yiddish performances, particularly those of Nehama Lifshitz, who sometimes incorporated Hebrew songs into her program. Mintz's pupils in this period included such famous activists of the 1970s and 1980s as Iosif Begun and Vladimir Slepak. He and Pregerzon both received Israeli literature directly from Israel, Mintz from the Israeli writer Avraham Shlonsky, with whom he corresponded regularly. Among the works they received were those by S. Yizhar, Hanokh Bar-Tov, Binyamin Tammuz, Amos Oz, Shmuel Yosef Agnon and Natan Alterman. Mintz translated some of the writings of Agnon and Aharon Megged into Russian. Throughout this period, too, Pregerzon, his fellow Hebrew writer Zvi Plotkin and others used tourists to smuggle out poems and manuscripts they had written in Hebrew or Yiddish.[10]

Another central figure in Moscow in these years was writer Sergei (Ezra) Morgulis, a veteran Bolshevik who became a Zionist during the eighteen years he spent in prison camps for "Trotskyism" and "Bukharinism." Morgulis began his Zionist activity in the late fifties and continued them until his death in March 1965. His main activity was writing materials for young Soviet Jews, whose need for knowledge of things Jewish he felt most urgently. To this end, he wrote articles and book-length manuscripts, drawing on materials in the Lenin Library, where books of Jewish interest and content were still available to readers, as well as on magazines which he received, often through third parties, from the Israeli embassy. Morgulis was helped in the work of translating and editing by a group of older men who knew Hebrew and Yiddish, among them Mairim Bergman of Moscow and Abram Kaplan of Minsk.[11] A group of students helped him make copies and then distributed them through trusted friends and relatives to student groups in other cities, while Morgulis' friend Meir Kanevskii took materials to more remote places such as Tbilisi, Sukhumi and Baku.

Morgulis' writings included autobiographical articles on his metamorphosis from Marxism-Leninism to Zionism, a history of the Jewish people, a dictionary of Yiddish cultural figures in Russia throughout the generations, a history of the State of Israel and a pamphlet entitled "Hebrew or Yiddish," in which he argued that Israel and Hebrew were the lifeblood of the Jewish people. In a letter he handed to Yiddish writer and poet Avraham Gontar, who was on the staff of *Sovetish heymland*, Morgulis protested the cultural discrimination and deprivation suffered by Soviet Jews and the official disinformation on this issue. He asked whether revolutionary dogma and civic courage did not require party members to criticize forced assimilation as a misinterpretation of communist doctrine. The materials received by Morgulis and his group from the Israeli embassy and those prepared by them for distribution throughout the country became the nucleus of a library that served Jewish activists well into the seventies.

Other Moscow Jews who wrote or copied out Jewish materials included Shmerl Goberman, who engaged in this activity from the time he was released from camp in 1960 until his *aliya* in 1966, and Shmuel Zhidovetskii, who continued working on such materials until he died in 1965.[12] In the early 1960s Grigorii Shapiro of Odessa began what was to become a multi-faceted translation effort of works from Yiddish into Russian in the hope of reaching young and middle-aged people who knew no Yiddish. His translated materials reached Kiev,

Riga and Moscow and even such relatively remote places as Lugansk, Donetsk and Krasnoarmeisk, where he had personal connections. By the middle of the decade Shapiro was translating articles from foreign Yiddish newspapers – *Folks-shtime*, *Naie prese*, *Morgn frayheyt* – his wife typing them up for distribution. He concentrated particularly on news from the Jewish world and on books about Jewish heroism and martyrdom in World War II, for example, Ber Mark's "Warsaw Ghetto Uprising," which had been published by the Soviet Yiddish publishing house Der Emes in 1947.[13]

Another person who must be included in the older generation, although somewhat younger than Morgulis, was Meir Kanevskii, who had been arrested in 1953 for his connections with the Israeli legation. After his release in 1960, he renewed contacts with the Israelis. By the middle of the decade his main activity was distributing materials of Jewish content which he received from the Israelis as well as the writings of Morgulis and his group throughout the USSR. He delivered these materials to Kiev, to those who had "sat" with him in the camps, to Belaia Tserkov, Cherkassy (his home town), Vinnitsa and Odessa (all in the Ukraine); to Vilnius, Baku and the Crimea; and to Tbilisi, Sukhumi and Tskhivali (in Georgia). In the Caucasus he also sold religious articles and Israeli souvenirs (he had particular success with a cigarette lighter that played *Hatikva*) dividing the profits between Morgulis for buying paper and paying the typists and those still in the camps. In addition to sending Prisoners of Zion parcels and written materials, and even bringing *matzot* to the camp in Mordovia in 1963, Kanevskii, like other ex-camp inmates, helped prisoners materially on their release, as they were often penniless.[14]

Two of the most enterprising and fearless activists of the younger generation were Khavkin and Shnaider, both of whom immersed themselves in Zionist activity after their release. The former operated in Odessa until he was able to return to Moscow in 1965. Once back in Moscow, he opened his home to a group that comprised between twenty and forty people, who met there regularly. He supported his activity with funds he received from friends in Georgia. By the time Shnaider returned to Riga that city was becoming a main center for disseminating literature from the Israeli embassy throughout the country and Shnaider quickly became part of this activity. Some of the material he and his friends would mimeograph directly, some they adapted to the needs and tastes of Soviet Jewish readers. Shnaider kept in touch with groups in Vilnius, Leningrad, Kiev and Moscow. Both he and Khavkin told everyone (including the Israelis) who warned them to be more careful that even though they were being followed incessantly, the authorities would never succeed in stopping their activity. Indeed, the two men were among the first activists to be let out when the Soviet authorities decided at the end of the decade to let out the Jewish movement's central figures.[15]

Similar to the Shnaider–Khavkin "network" of ex-camp inmates was the connection between Yosef Khorol, who had moved to Riga from Odessa in 1958, and Gelfond, who received permission to live in Moscow after he married a Muscovite in 1959. Like Shnaider, Khorol and his friends translated, adapted and mimeographed materials, which they then passed on to Gelfond for distribution in Minsk, Kiev and the Urals as well as in Moscow. In 1963 alone Gelfond disseminated some 300 copies each of Bialik's poems, Jabotinsky's *Feuilletons* and *Exodus*, which he received from Khorol.[16]

Other groups in Riga centered around the painter Yosef Kuzskovskii who together with his wife Olga, held open house for hundreds of people on Jewish festivals; David and Miriam Garber, who also held open house for Riga's Jews; Boris Shperling and Boris and Lidiia Slovin, who engaged in preparing and distributing nationalistic materials; and Betar veterans David Varhaftig, Yakov Gurevich, Dov Taubin and Ezra Rusinek, who established contact with a similar group in Vilnius comprising Marek Brudyni, Marek Moizes, Munik Holtzman and his wife. This last group also sent materials to a former colleague from Latvia's pre-Soviet days, Binyamin Tsukerman, who was now in Tomsk, Tsukerman in turn passed on these materials to five or six families in Tomsk and to two students, one of whom sent them on to his home town, Novosibirsk.[17] There were also Habad *hasidim* in Riga who were intent on emigrating to Israel, and meanwhile maintained contact with the Israeli embassy, taught the Hebrew language and Jewish law (*Tora*) and conducted religious ceremonies (circumcisions, Bar Mitzvas, weddings).[18]

While it was mostly these two groups, the pensioners and those in their thirties, who fed the movement, maintained permanent contact with the Israeli embassy and prepared and disseminated materials, the movement's main numerical strength came from those in their twenties, particularly students. It was in this period that young people began to flaunt their Jewish pride by openly wearing chains with the Star of David, which they had either received from tourists or had made by local silversmiths.

The fearlessness of these young men and women was rarely shared by their elders. Far from being daunted by the apprehensiveness that had dominated the lives of their parents who had experienced the traumas of the purges of the 1930s and the repressions of the "Black Years," these youngsters made a conscious decision not to let fear guide their actions. Indeed, their audacity led them to actions unparalleled by the general run of Soviet citizenry. Thus, in 1965 a group of Jewish students addressed an appeal to Prime Minister Kosygin asking him to abolish the *numerus clausus* adopted by universities in Moscow, Leningrad, Kiev and Kharkov, "which are humiliating to us as Soviet citizens and a violation of the sacred rights guaranteed by our Constitution." The appeal was signed by "a group of loyal sons of the Soviet Fatherland of Jewish nationality."[19]

Student activists came not only from large cities but also from the towns and townships of the Ukraine and Belorussia, the Far East, Siberia and the Urals, the Caucasus and Central Asia. And the fact that most of them had grown up in assimilated families and had only found out that there was a separate Jewish history or culture when they began trying to find the meaning of their Jewishness, indicates that in this period, too, the Kremlin's policy of enforced assimilation was having the opposite result. While the majority of them sought to ignore the antisemitism and discrimination they encountered by devoting their time and effort to their studies and profession, a very considerable minority felt the need to do everything possible to recover their dignity as Jews in their own eyes as well as in those of their non-Jewish neighbors.

One Jewish student told a visitor from the West how he and other Soviet Jewish youths viewed their Jewishness and its implications: "Soviet youth – Jewish or non-Jewish" was "in no mood to go questing for ideals. The search today is for self, Jewishness . . . does not develop, as it apparently does in the West, out of endless testing of one's views in debate with other Jews." Although as a child he had not noticed any difference between himself and other children, he began to feel uncomfortable after reading about Yankel with his louse-ridden curls in Gogol's *Taras Bulba*. Yet it was years before he appreciated that he was, "somehow, related to that Yankel." That was when "it dawned on me that there was a choice to make." For him the answer was not "to take the road . . . [of] assimilation . . . a change of name and the masking of racial origin and peculiarities." For, although some had done this successfully, "there came a point when all that I thought was mine to share – Russian culture, language, everything – melted like a mirage, when it was made adequately clear that I had no right to it."

As the student in question explained, it was "no easy task" for young Soviet Jews to seek their own identity. There were no Soviet history books to satisfy their curiosity. He had therefore turned to such "secondary sources" as Lion Feuchtwanger's novels "for a hint of meaning." And, in the wake of the search for books, came "a quest for like-minded people . . . links . . . The desire to emigrate followed naturally. Not just anywhere . . . but to Israel. To find oneself to be no worse off than the Russian Bolshevik building a new society in his own country. It is not a matter of deciding where one's place is, but merely of deciding to be oneself."[20]

The decision made, Jewish students formed their own groups, organized the mass attendance at synagogue on Jewish festivals, went to Yiddish concerts – even though they did not understand the language – listened to and discussed Israeli broadcasts, recorded Hebrew songs and collected books on Jewish subjects. Some of them translated foreign works on Jewish history or Israel into Russian. Sometimes they even took up the battle on an individual basis. Thus in Leningrad in 1960, one such youngster wore an Israeli badge and refused to stand when the prayer for the welfare of the Soviet government was read in the synagogue. Another young man from Minsk, who suffered from antisemitism at his place of work, appealed to the authorities to let him emigrate if they were unwilling or unable to put an end to antisemitism. Called to the police and ordered to leave Minsk for Mogilev as a result of this "outrage," he became the central figure of a new group in that town that gathered every Sunday to listen to Kol Zion lagola.[21]

Many of the activists, young and old, knew that their apartments and telephones were bugged and that they were under constant surveillance. Although there were no large-scale arrests in the 1960s, the authorities did not hesitate to take administrative measures against those who demonstrated their Jewish identity or sympathy for Israel, causing unpleasantness at their places of study and work, and making an occasional arrest apparently to prevent such activities from getting out of hand. Thus, early in the decade (summer 1961) Jewish activists Gedalia Pecherskii and Evsei Dynkin, who had formed a group in Leningrad in the late fifties for the study of Hebrew and Jewish history, had been arrested with the poet Nahum Kahanov of Moscow, presumably to demonstrate the existence of an extensive inter-city network of Jewish activists. Although their trial began in a Leningrad district court, it was transferred elsewhere and held behind closed doors after large numbers of Jews filled the courtroom and courthouse corridors. The three were charged with treason, with maintaining ties with abroad and with foreign representatives within the USSR (both Pecherskii and Dynkin had been in contact with Israeli embassy staff), and with possessing and disseminating anti-Soviet literature. Kahanov was charged, in addition, with writing and disseminating Zionist poems. All three were sentenced to terms in prison: Pecherskii to twelve years, Kahanov to seven and Dynkin, who was over eighty, to four.[22]

In Moscow, too, Jews were charged with anti-Soviet activity and espionage on behalf of Israel, with having in their possession and distributing Zionist materials and maintaining ties with the Israelis. One of these was Volf Rishal, accused in 1961 of organizing Zionist activity in Odessa where he had distributed Israeli newspapers he had received from Israeli diplomats in the Choral Synagogue.[23] Although the Pecherskii trial and verdict, together with the simultaneous expulsion of Israeli diplomat Yakov Sharett, evoked considerable alarm among Leningrad's Jews, on Simhat Tora of that same year more Jews than ever before, especially young people, attended the synagogue. Neither the arrests nor any of the other measures adopted by the authorities deterred the tens of thousands of Jews who had come to the conclusion that only by asserting their Jewishness could they arrive at their desired purpose: emigration to Israel.

At this point we must enlarge on the role that the Israeli embassy in Moscow played in encouraging and aiding the Jewish national awakening during the 1960s. While the embassy did not create the movement, it served as a catalyst and its presence in Moscow was certainly one of the reasons for that city becoming the focus of activity.

Embassy personnel carried on contacts with local Jews – in Moscow and other parts of the country that they visited periodically – if not at personal risk, at least under considerable physical and psychological difficulty. Several of them were the butt of provocations, and, as had happened in 1955, not a few were actually expelled in the early and mid-sixties (for example, Yakov Sharett in 1961, David Gavish in 1966). The Israelis were also the object of an increasingly vehement media campaign accusing them of espionage, subversion and "hooliganism" and of taking undue advantage of their diplomatic status. Time and time again synagogue dignitaries in Moscow and elsewhere shunned them, behaved discourteously toward them and refused to accept the gifts they customarily brought to any synagogue they might be visiting. Worst of all, however, were the persistent efforts to prevent contact between them and other worshippers. The Israelis who served in Moscow in this period had no doubt that this was the doing of the authorities, that the synagogue officials had no choice but to yield to the pressures and constraints to which they were subjected in order to carry on their functions.[24]

All these measures were, however, an indication or confirmation – if such was needed – of the Israelis' popularity among the local Jews and of the concern this was arousing on the part of the authorities. Indeed, the diplomats were keenly aware that, well before the June 1967 war, the Kremlin was looking for pretexts to terminate their presence in the Soviet capital.[25]

Some of the younger activists, who had no way of appreciating the intricacies of the Israelis' status and the tightrope they were walking, did not understand what they viewed as the Israelis' unnecessary caution. For them, not only was the State of Israel recalcitrant in helping them extricate themselves from the USSR, but its official representatives were not exploiting all opportunities to bring them the aid and materials they needed so badly. This view was held, for example, by a group of Rigans who did not, and perhaps could not, appreciate that the Israelis had first of all to look after the diverse needs of the State of Israel and secondly to try and help the entire Soviet Jewish population. This was no simple task given the conditions they had to work in and the fact that the majority of Soviet Jews were largely acculturated and not as committed to *aliya* as, for instance, the Jews of Riga. In fact, the embassy tended to concentrate its very limited human resources on extending a helping hand to precisely that part of Soviet Jewry that was less rooted in its Jewish background.[26]

Given the extremely complex conditions under which it was obliged to work, the Israeli embassy can, on the whole, be credited with considerable achievements in encouraging Jews in Moscow and throughout the length and breadth of the country, as well as in helping those who came to them with specific demands and requests. The very fact that the embassy was present in Moscow, flying the Israeli flag, and that Israeli diplomats attended synagogue services and Jewish performances and concerts regularly was a source of moral support. Furthermore, the materials the Israelis gave out were crucial to the development of the Jewish movement. And, finally, their letting the outside world know about Soviet Jewry's repression helped reassure the latter that they were not alone and isolated.[27]

### Forms of activity

Even though by the early sixties the ultimate purpose of the Jewish national movement was unquestionably *aliya*, the difficulties in attaining what still seemed an intangible objective led the movement to set itself the "intermediate" goal of deepening and broadening Jewish national consciousness, particularly among the young, so that pressure on the Kremlin would mount. And, paradoxically enough, it was the adoption of this *ersatz* goal that helped the movement become a movement proper. At this time the Jews still had no inkling of the potential leverage and nuisance value of the movement for *aliya*. Almost all Jews who felt they had a message within the terms of reference of the secondary target, and who were able to communicate it, found themselves at the center of a group of either their social and professional peers or young people, or of a mixture of both, that was looking for guidance and Jewish content.

The motivation for the search of their Jewish roots was both positive and negative; in the former case it sprang from the desire for self-fulfilment and self-knowledge, and in the latter it was a reaction to popular and government authorized antisemitism and enforced assimilation. Not infrequently, the distinction between them became blurred. Yet, whatever the motivation, sources and methods for learning and conveying the meaning of being Jewish had to be searched for and even created *ex nihilo*. Not only was there no way for young Jews to study any subject of Jewish interest in the course of their education, but, except in the Western territories, even their parents, Jews in their forties and fifties, were mostly unable or unwilling to enlighten their children about their Jewish background.

In this context of a total dearth of Jewish knowledge, listening to Israeli broadcasts became a widespread and popular form of activity. By the early sixties Kol Zion lagola was broadcasting in Russian; by 1964 its broadcasts had become daily; and by the end of our period they covered one and one-half hours per day. Although these broadcasts became the most important source of information on life in Israel and the Jewish world, total reliance on them often gave rise to misunderstandings; Soviet Jews could not always understand all of what they heard, partly because of the difficulties involved in rendering in Russian technical terms pertinent to Israel alone and partly because of fundamental differences between Israel and the USSR. Such basic aspects of Israeli life as freedom of movement or political pluralism remained an enigma to Soviet Jews. Thus, when they heard that someone had left a *kibbutz* they wondered how he had been allowed to do so, for they drew analogies with the *kolkhoz*; and when they heard that David Ben Gurion left the government to become a member of the opposition they could not comprehend how this could happen to Israel's Lenin. Nor could they understand the whys and wherefores of Israel's foreign policy, particularly the establishment of diplomatic relations with West Germany or the necessity for retaliatory measures against the Arab states.

At the same time, Israeli broadcasts about Jewish festivals and Jewish history did provide some of the background material that Soviet Jews needed to understand their heritage. Above all, they provided the Hebrew lessons which, together with Israeli songs, were especially prized by Soviet Jews, who often recorded them on cassettes for future listening and for circulation among those who for one reason or another did not have access to the broadcasts. In the mid-sixties listening to Israeli radio became the most common, most popular and most important means of Jewish education for Soviet Jews. It also provided the framework of activity for most of those seeking to identify as Jews; an unknown number of Jews listened to these broadcasts both individually and in groups, including many who entertained no thoughts of *aliya*. While Yiddish programs from Israel were mostly jammed, the Russian and Hebrew ones could usually be heard without difficulty, as could Yiddish programs from Paris. And even jammed programs began to get through as Jewish technicians and engineers found ways of overcoming both systematic jamming and incidental interference.

Everywhere Israeli diplomats and tourists traveled they found Jews who listened to Israeli broadcasts. And many of those who succeeded in emigrating have testified that these broadcasts were sometimes their only spiritual sustenance. Besides Moscow and Leningrad, Riga and Kaunas, Kishinev and Chernovtsy, where many Jews listened regularly, we have reports of Jews listening in Kiev, Kharkov, Odessa, Dnepropetrovsk, Chernigov, Uman, Donetsk, Yalta, Simferopol and Carpatho-Russia; in Minsk, Gomel and Mogilev; in Rostov, Volgograd, Astrakhan and Nalchik; in Irkutsk, Novosibirsk and Omsk; in Tbilisi, Kutaisi and Sukhumi; in Baku, Derbent and Makhachkala; in Tashkent, Alma-Ata and Dushanbe. Jews from all over the country would phone the Israeli embassy in Moscow requesting more Hebrew and Yiddish songs, more *hazanut* (liturgical music), more news, more background material – in short, more programs. One Jew in Leningrad said that if anyone missed a broadcast, there was always someone to whom he could turn to find out what he had missed. Another, in Moscow, has called the broadcasts the most effective instrument for reaching the youth and nurturing its interest in Israel. And a third has noted that while the older generation used to conceal this activity even from their own children, by the mid-sixties the young people were bringing home equipment that made it possible to hear the broadcasts more clearly, the older family members listening to Yiddish programs, while the younger ones listened to those in Russian or Hebrew.[28]

If the oral word was the movement's daily bread, as it were, the written word brought it long-lasting nourishment and strength. For a book or article which can be read and reread and then discussed with others who have studied it, is generally of more lasting and profound influence than anything heard. There were, at this time, four sources of Jewish books, newspapers and journals; private libraries, sometimes thrown open to fellow Jews[29] and sometimes sold to second-hand bookstores; public libraries (particularly the Lenin Library in Moscow and the Saltykov-Shchedrin Library in Leningrad); the Israeli embassy, which considered providing Soviet Jews with literature of Jewish significance one of its main functions;[30] and Israeli and Western Jewish tourists, who began to supplement the religious articles and literature they brought with secular publications once word of the great hunger for books on all aspects of Jewish life and Israel began to spread. Tourists also helped distribute materials they received from the Israelis in synagogues and other places where they came in contact with Jews whom the Israeli diplomats were unable to reach directly. Some secular literature was also getting through by mail in the early sixties, although the authorities continued to confiscate religious literature.[31]

The most popular works during this period seem to have been *Exodus*, Jabotinsky's *Feuilletons*, books about Israel and the Russian-language Jewish calendar which, as we have seen, comprised a major source of information on Israel, even if, naturally, in résumé.

Those involved in distributing these materials, both local activists and Israeli embassy personnel, had three main problems: their quantity, quality and confiscation by the authorities. Although the Israelis did everything in their power to see that there was enough material, it was difficult to foretell how much to stock, as on principle they only gave out what was asked for. However, although people sometimes had to be disappointed, especially when crowds of Jews came into contact with the Israelis on special occasions, the latter made constant efforts to overcome the problem of quantity. And, on the whole, this did improve over time.[32]

The question of quality was much more complex. A very large proportion of the Soviet Jews who then either comprised the nucleus of the national awakening or were its potential adherents were highly qualified academics or professionals, and even though they were not usually fervent communists, they had naturally been influenced by Marxist-Leninist thinking, concepts and terminology. This meant that the connotations or implications of words used in the West were often not correctly interpreted by them. Thus, in order to be effective, the style and language in which information was couched had to be variegated, intellectually challenging and not tendentious, and, at the same time, suitable to an audience for whom many of the basic economic, socio-political and other terms used in Israel were incomprehensible and that knew virtually nothing about Israeli life. It was not enough to simply translate existing materials into Russian, or simple Hebrew or Yiddish; new materials had to be designed especially for Soviet Jews. This was a tall order, which many in the Israeli establishment were either unable or slow to comprehend due to their parochialism, or unable to handle as a result of what they viewed as more urgent priorities. While diplomats on the spot were sensitive to the problem and felt a direct personal commitment to those Jews who requested materials at considerable risk, as often happens, those at home tended to remain indifferent to their requests.

The third problem – confiscation – was the most frustrating. Even though the Israelis made every effort to ensure that the materials they supplied contained no anti-Soviet extrapolations, and mentioned neither the Soviet regime nor even its Jewish policy, the Soviet authorities waged an unremitting campaign against both the Israelis who distributed this literature and the Soviet Jews who received it. The Israelis were kept under close surveillance throughout the period under discussion in order to deter local Jews from approaching them. And when the latter did succeed in receiving materials, they were often interrogated by the police, who confiscated what they had been given, and warned against further contact.[33] The pace of distribution slowed down from time to time, when it was felt that pressure on the local Jewish community had reached alarming proportions. But it was never stopped completely. For, neither the local activists, for whom this literature was their lifeblood, nor the Israelis, who felt that they should not make decisions for the local Jews, were ready to give up what both perceived as one of their chief activities. They did, however, take steps to reduce the chance of discovery by the KGB and of inveiglement by KGB provocateurs. Tourists, however, were another question. When one of them got taken in for interrogation after being caught handing out materials, the rest of the group with which he traveled was usually deterred from doing the same.

Despite the problems and frustrations, Soviet Jews were becoming increasingly sophisticated in circumventing obstacles, and thanks to the persistence, resourcefulness and courage of an ever-increasing number among them, a considerable amount of material was distributed successfully. This was true not only of the materials received from Israelis and tourists, but also of their own *samizdat* works. Indeed, the role of courier was no less crucial than that of writer or translator.

Two of the main figures in the distribution of materials were Solomon Dolnik, the central figure of the Morgulis group after Sergei Morgulis' death, and Mikhail Margulis, who had returned to Moscow in 1955 after being released from the camps. Margulis brought the works of Sergei Morgulis and Mairim Bergman, together with materials the Morgulis group received from the Israeli embassy, to Yiddish writer Natan Zabara in Kiev and to Aron Merkher in Odessa (with whom he had sat in prison camp), bringing Grigorii Shapiro's translations back from Odessa to Moscow.[34] By 1965 groups in Moscow and Riga were mimeographing everything they received for distribution wherever they had reliable contacts. Young Jews were also passing around copies of Margarita Aliger's poem "Lorelei, a Girl from the Rhine," written in the wake of the Holocaust, Ehrenburg's "Reply to the Poem of M. Aliger" and the replies of Evtushenko, Russian writer Konstantin Simonov and Soviet Jewish children's writer Samuil Marshak to Aleksei Markov's attack on Evtushenko's "Babii Iar."[35]

While the idea of *samizdat* and the tactics of its implementation were borrowed from the general dissident movement, the subject matter of Jewish *samizdat* was entirely different in that it consisted of translations into Russian of Hebrew and Yiddish materials and works of Jewish content that had appeared in other languages, as well as the typing up of Russian-language materials of Jewish interest that were no longer available (such as Jabotinsky's *Feuilletons*). In 1961 a group of students at Moscow State University completed the translation of a French book on Israel's War of Independence, of which they typed up four copies, and began working on a translation of *Exodus*. During this same period, a Leningrad Jew was translating Yehudit Hendel's novel *Rehov hamadregot* (The Street of Steps) from Hebrew, and the daughter of a Jew from Derbent, who was then living in Moscow, was typing articles from *Vestnik Izrailia* and sending them to relatives in Dagestan. Students and others would pass around materials on condition that the recipient agreed to type four more copies of anything he or she was given and to disseminate these further copies among trusted acquaintances.[36]

In 1963 in Riga the group that centered around Boris Slovin was copying excerpts from Jabotinsky and Bialik. It had already put out an abbreviated version of *Exodus*, translated from the German. Indeed, several groups and individuals engaged in translating *Exodus* during the sixties. At the beginning of the decade Mairim Bergman prepared two shortened versions – one of about forty pages, the other perhaps twice that length – using a microfilmed German version in Moscow's Lenin Library.[37] A group of prisoners in a camp in Mordovia translated the work from the original English after one of them, Anatolii Rubin of Minsk, received it from a non-Jewish fellow prisoner. Upon his release from Mordovia in 1963, another inmate, Abram Shifrin, slipped the translation out of camp to Karaganda, where it was retyped before being sent on to Moscow, Leningrad, Kiev and Riga for further duplication.[38]

When Yaacov Gurevich of Riga, who had initiated yet another translation of the book in 1963, received his exit permit early in 1964, his friends continued the work, which was completed in 1965. This group consisted of the typist, a trusted Zionist who worked on the manuscript every night in her home for an entire year; Dov Taubin, who made the translation; Shimon Liborkin, who helped edit it; and Ezra Rusinek, who had been sent a copy in German several years before when he was still in Taganrog and immediately realized the explosiveness of the material, especially for young people. Of the five copies made by this group, two remained in Riga, one went to Binyamin Tsukerman in Tomsk, and two went to Vilnius and Leningrad.[39] Many Soviet Jews have testified to the dramatic effect that the book had on them, people reading it again and again as its content matter was poignantly relevant to the Soviet Jewish experience.[40]

One original document that circulated in *samizdat* in 1962 was a forty-page letter purportedly written to Chairman of the USSR Supreme Soviet Leonid Brezhnev. The letter, written by Mark Blum of Riga, stressed the high level and achievement of Jewish culture, and compared it with that of other national minorities that the Kremlin had encouraged. The "letter" emphasized the need to permit Jews to learn Hebrew, Yiddish and Jewish history. Finally, it pressed for allowing those who felt unable to remain in the USSR to go to Israel. The document reached Jews in Moscow, Leningrad, Odessa and Kremenchug, where it was retyped or xeroxed and given to young Jews, particularly students, to read.[41]

The translation, copying and distribution of materials was expensive as well as risky. Sometimes it was financed by the sale of parcels from relatives abroad and souvenirs from Israel.[42] Engineers among the activists sought inexpensive ways of reproducing materials, including microfilm. And Israeli songs began to be disseminated on tape-recorder or cassettes.[43]

By 1965 *Elef millim*, probably the most popular Hebrew primer, was being mimeographed in the Soviet Union in an effort to meet the ever-growing demand for Hebrew. For, groups in Moscow and Leningrad, Odessa, Kiev and Kishinev, Riga, Vilnius and Kaunas and other towns were now studying Hebrew as an integral part of their activity. The study of Hebrew was given a gigantic boost when Feliks Shapiro's *Hebrew–Russian Dictionary* was published in 1963. Published officially by the regime, it could be purchased, used and retained at home without fear.[44]

One of the main forms of activity that helped crystallize Jewish national consciousness centered around the struggle to have Jewish heroism against Nazi Germany recognized and monuments erected to mark the mass graves of Jews who had fallen victim to the Nazi invaders. Although, at least in the European parts ot the USSR, there can hardly have been a Jewish family that had not lost at least one member in the ghettos, the ranks of the Soviet armed forces or the partisans, the Soviet authorities did nothing to recognize their loss. The seizure by the Israeli secret service of Nazi war criminal Adolf Eichmann in Buenos Aires in May 1960 and his subsequent trial in Jerusalem and execution by the Israelis put paid to the Kremlin's contention that the Soviet Union was the only country continuing the struggle against Nazism and Nazi war criminals. Moreover, the fact that it was Israel that captured Eichmann and brought him to trial increased pride in the Jewish state and underlined its centrality to the entire Jewish people. Finally, and perhaps most important for our study, the Eichmann trial stimulated renewed interest in the Holocaust among the younger, postwar generation as well as those who had managed to survive.[45]

The "rehabilitation" of the Jewish contribution to the war effort was a very important theme in the sustained endeavors of some segments of the Soviet Jewish population to improve the Jews' image in both their own eyes and those of their non-Jewish neighbors. For, although from the mid-fifties on a few sparse references to individual instances of Jewish gallantry and prowess did begin to appear, the Jews as a whole were still not mentioned ］when Soviet nationalities whose sons had been decorated were listed. This, despite the fact that the Jews occupied fifth place among the Heroes of the Soviet Union.[46] It was in this context that a group of six Jewish decorated heroes of World War II submitted a memorandum to the Twenty-second Congress of the CPSU in October 1961, requesting that all privileges granted to other nationalities be restored to Jewish veterans, including recognition of the major role they played in saving "our homeland."[47] (It was also in this context that Grigorii Shapiro in Odessa undertook the translation of materials on Jewish heroism.)

Jews feeling the urgent need to honor their dead and to demonstrate the significance of their sacrifice not only for the Soviet motherland but also for the Jewish people began a persistent struggle to erect a monument at Babii Iar, just outside Kiev, where one of the most horrific Nazi massacres had been carried out on Yom Kippur eve of 1941. It was not by chance that Evtushenko dedicated his poem of protest against Soviet antisemitism to Babii Iar or that his poem was published on the twentieth anniversary of the massacre. Nor was it an accident that a year later Shostakovich based an aria in his Thirteenth Symphony on the poem. For both artists viewed the official blindness toward Jewish martyrdom as one of the manifestations of an antisemitism which they considered one of the most serious drawbacks of the regime. And it was certainly not by chance that, during his encounter with "the creative intelligentsia" in March 1963, Khrushchev singled out "Babii Iar" for attack, or that the authorities eventually succeeded in compelling both poet and composer to soften the impact of their respective works by deleting the most poignant parts.[48]

While Babii Iar was perhaps the best-known scene of mass Jewish murders by the Nazis, Jews in many other towns felt a similar resentment to the refusal to pay even minimal respect to their dead and endeavored to rectify the situation. In Vilnius the local Jewish population tried to obtain funds to erect a fence around the mass graves at Paneriai and to rebuild the monument to the memory of the thousands of Jews who were shot and buried there that had been erected after the war by the Jews of Vilnius with an inscription in Yiddish, destroyed by the authorities in 1952 and replaced by one that made no mention of Jews.[49]

The Jews' resolve to remember their dead was also given expression in memorial prayers recited in the synagogues. None of those who attended services at the Kiev synagogue on Yom Kippur in the 1950s or early 1960s can forget the memorial prayer said for the dead on that day.[50] In the Moscow Choral Synagogue and other synagogues throughout the country, as well as in Israel, the anniversary of the Warsaw Ghetto uprising became the memorial day for victims of the Holocaust.[51] In other places the Sunday between the New Year and the Day of Atonement became Holocaust Remembrance Day. Other opportunities were also seized upon to dwell on the Holocaust and its significance for the survivors, for instance in February 1965, when a meeting was held in the Choral Synagogue to protest the GFR's limitation law regarding Nazi crimes.[52]

The Jews began honoring the mass graves by visiting them in large numbers. In some cities, notably in the Baltic republics, this became a way of demonstrating the Jewish solidarity that the authorities were seeking to eliminate by ignoring the role the Jews had played in the ranks of the Soviet armed forces and the Jewish origin of Nazi victims.[53] Vilnius Jews made regular pilgrimages to Paneriai, where they felt less restrained in speaking both of the great past of Jewish Vilnius as compared with the gloomy present, and of their possible future as Jews in the Jewish state.[54]

The site of the massacre of thirty-eight thousand Jews at Rumbula became a meeting-place for Rigan Jews seeking to express their identity. Unable to ignore the public reaction to the Eichmann trial, the Riga authorities arranged an open-air anti-fascist meeting in October 1962 in the Bikerniki woods, where the Nazis had executed the prisoners of the Riga jail, most of whom were Jews. After hearing the speakers discuss everything but the Jewish aspect of this tragedy, a group of Jews who had attended this meeting decided to mark the spot where the Jews of the Riga ghetto had been exterminated. One of them, David Garber, sought out ex-president of the Riga synagogue Ben-Zion Kaplan, a ghetto survivor who had unearthed materials on Nazi brutalities after the war (for which he was later arrested and sentenced to ten years). The following Sunday the two men, together with Garber's wife Miriam, David Zilberman, Zalman Baron and Mark Blum, went to the Rumbula forest where they established the exact location of the massacre. A week later a group of twenty Jews hung a sign on a fir tree which read: "Here were silenced the voices of 38,000 Jews of Riga on 29–30 November and 8–9 December 1941." Then they sang the "Song of the Partisans" in Yiddish and one of them recited the memorial prayer for the dead.

In April 1963, just before the twentieth anniversary of the Warsaw Ghetto uprising (when a ceremony at Rumbula was attended by some fifty Jews), Baron, Miriam Garber and Blum brought an obelisk-shaped board to the site, in the middle of which was a photograph (by Yosef Shnaider) of Riga artist Yosef Kuzskovskii's picture "On the Last Road." The obelisk, which they placed on the mass grave, was taken care of regularly and remained standing for about eighteen months.

Before this, Garber, Blum and their friends had begun gathering the ashes and remnants of children's shoes that they found on the site, placing them in transparent bags and exhibiting them in Riga. This, together with the permission they received to clean and maintain the site, had a powerful effect on the local Jews, who now began to come to Rumbula in growing numbers.

After the April 1963 memorial meeting it was decided to landscape the site. Every Sunday thereafter Jews came with hoes, rakes, shovels and pails to remove the stones, water the ground and plant flowers, in accordance with an overall design drawn up by Isak Rakhlin, Iakov Vagenheim and Samuil (Bubik) Tsaitlin. By the fall 1963 anniversary of the massacre five of the actual graves that had been located were planted with flowers arranged in the shape of the Star of David and the *menora*. This time 800 people attended the ceremony and news of the event spread to Jews throughout the Soviet Union.

The authorities never officially recognized the ceremonies at Rumbula, despite their allowing the site to be maintained. They decided rather to initiate similar activities at the site of the Salaspils death camp also near Riga; but these officially sanctioned activities never attained the popularity of the Rumbula meetings. Here those at the center of activity were enlisting the help of wider circles – including Jewish managers of large enterprises who sent heavy machinery to the site to speed up the work. It got to the point where so many Jews gathered at Rumbula on Sundays that a special parking lot was set aside for them on the Riga–Moscow highway. One of Latvia's highest-ranking party officials expressed his admiration for the Jews' persistence and solidarity; although the party had spent hundreds of thousands of rubles on commemorating the Salaspils site, he told Isak Rakhlin, it had failed to achieve anything comparable with what "your Jews" had done at Rumbula.

In 1964 the chairman of the *raiispolkom* (the regional executive committee) refused permission to hold the annual memorial meeting, let alone to advertise it in the local press. However, a Rigan Jew, Leonid Rodionov, managed to publish the story of Rumbula in Riga's Latvian newspaper and to send reports of everything taking place there to Jewish communist newspapers in different countries. This, together with the announcement posted in the Riga synagogue, brought 500 Jews to the event, despite rain. It was at this meeting that the seventeen-year-old Yosef Mendelevich read Israeli poet Natan Alterman's "The Silver Tray" in Hebrew and declared that the only lesson that had to be learned from the massacre at Rumbula was: "Our road leads to the Jewish people's historic homeland, the Land of Israel." The meeting, which was immortalized by a photograph of a group singing "Dos shtetl brent" (The shtetl is burning), ended with the entire audience singing the Israeli national anthem.

Some extremist Zionist activists had considered any semi-legal activity, such as that at Rumbula or the organization of the choir and drama groups and even Yiddish concerts, that required approaching the authorities, as "collaboration" and "treachery." They likened those who participated in such activities to the Judenrat in Nazi times, arguing that they merely provided opportunities for the Kremlin to demonstrate to people in the West that Soviet Jews did enjoy privileges. But, after the 1964 meeting at Rumbula, they too favored the activity there as one of the main symbols of the Jewish national movement.

Although they had been unable to deter the thousands of Jews who became involved in the work at Rumbula, the authorities rejected a request by Isak Rakhlin and Samuil Tsaitlin to place a modest slab with a Yiddish inscription "To the Victims of Fascism, 1941" at the site. When permission was eventually granted, it was for an inscription in Latvian, Russian and Yiddish, although even then the authorities made a last-minute attempt to omit the Yiddish. At the pedestal, among the flowers, there was a glass box with six candles lit in memory of the 6 million who perished in the days of "tragedy and heroism."

In this way, Rumbula became a legitimate gathering-place, where thousands of Jews came to hold annual meetings on the anniversaries of the Warsaw Ghetto uprising and the Rumbula massacre. And they came not only from Riga but from Vilnius, Leningrad, Moscow, Kiev, Kharkov, Odessa and even Novosibirsk. No one in Riga or anywhere else in the Soviet Jewish community doubted that these memorials of the Riga Jews were intended as anything but monuments to their struggle for repatriation to their Jewish homeland, a struggle in which the tragedy of the Holocaust played a major role.[55]

The occasional drama group or choir that was allowed to operate, especially in the Baltic republics, was also of considerable significance in reinforcing Jewish national feeling. By 1960 the Vilnius drama group boasted forty-five members, a third of whom were young people, and its membership grew to a hundred during the course of the decade. Together with its affiliated dance company and choir, it had about 180 members by mid-1967. Another drama group, in Kaunas, had between fifty and sixty members – mostly young people – by the middle of the decade and about 120 by the end of our period.[56]

Among others, the performances, and perhaps even more so the rehearsals, of these groups were important socially in that they provided meeting-places and forums for discussing Jewish issues. One of the subjects most vehemently debated by their members was whether they might not be giving Moscow an opportunity to gain political capital in the West, proving as it were the Kremlin's contention that it did permit Jewish cultural activity. While the popularity of the groups, and especially the fact that they attracted so many young people, convinced some of the skeptics of their worth, others continued to be doubtful. Marek Brudnyi was one of the most vocal critics in Vilnius, while in Riga Yosef Shnaider and Yosef Yankelevich joined the choir with the express purpose of breaking it up. Others, notably veteran Zionists, remained aloof from the choirs and drama groups because they were obliged to include Soviet items in an officially recognized Soviet language – Russian, Latvian, Lithuanian or whatever – in all their public performances, and they felt this was an unpardonable concession to the authorities. Indeed, people like editor of *Sovetish heymland* Aron Vergelis did bring foreigners – usually communists or left-wing sympathizers who had reservations about the USSR's Jewish policy – to see the Vilnius ensemble and Riga choir. The members of these troupes, however, tried to make the true situation clear, telling the visitors of the limitations under which they were forced to operate.[57]

There was some contact between the drama groups in different places. The Vilnius people, for instance, met with David Garber and Yosef Yankelevich of Riga to discuss the problems and tactics of their respective groups. And for the tenth anniversary of the Vilnius group people came from all over the country, particularly from other ensembles in places like Kishinev, where Reuven Levin had set up a drama group with the help of Sharfshtein, one of the main figures of the Vilnius group. On one occasion the Vilnius group even succeeded in bringing the entire Kishinev troupe to Vilnius, where the two groups sang and danced together. Just as the Riga choir appeared from time to time in other towns, the Vilnius ensemble appeared twice each in Riga and Leningrad and several times in Minsk, as well as in Kaunas and other places in Lithuania. In the tourist season they went to Palanga on the Baltic and to Druskenniki, a mineral water spa, where they entertained Jewish vacationers from Moscow, Leningrad and elsewhere.

In the early 1960s the Vilnius group introduced Hebrew songs into its performances, first "Hava nagila" and then "Kinneret sheli." Nehama Lifshitz even appeared with this group on several occasions giving it a special boost. One concert that was especially successful was the one on the twentieth anniversary of the Warsaw Ghetto uprising, when the group gave three performances in a hall with a 900-seat capacity. At rehearsals – which were generally attended by many friends of members – Marek Moizes, one of the group's central figures, gave background talks on the Holocaust, allegedly to make their performances more authentic; Moizes even took group members to Paneriai under the same pretext. The entire choir and dance company or groups of their members also performed at Jewish weddings in Vilnius and other cities, thereby broadening the circle with whom they came into contact. Although they tended to steer clear of the synagogue, fearing provocateurs, they always took part in Simhat Tora celebrations.[58]

Attempts to establish similar troupes in other towns were unsuccessful. Iosif Chernobilskii and a group of friends tried to set up a Jewish national theater in Kiev, even trying to collect signatures in the Kiev synagogue for a petition to this effect in February 1966. Although they approached a number of institutions to sponsor such a theater, their request was turned down on the grounds that the lack of a venue and of enough experienced Jewish actors would cause it to operate at a loss.[59]

### Arenas of action

The rules of the cat-and-mouse game played by the Soviet authorities and the Jewish nationalists were not, as we have seen, necessarily laid down by the former, even though both the authority to interpret the law and the force to implement it were at their sole disposal. For the Jews were often able to find ways to circumvent the constraints imposed by the regime.

#### The synagogue

The intricacies of the game were particularly evident in the story of the synagogue, the only relatively permanent framework for Jewish activity in the Soviet Union. We have already touched upon the early stages of the campaign to close down synagogues and the reaction that this provoked in the West. While this measure was not solely or specifically anti-Jewish, in that houses of worship of other religions were also shut down between 1958 and 1964, it struck particularly hard at the Jews, for whom the synagogue was much more than a religious institution. Indeed, the significance of the synagogue as a meeting-place probably only made it a more urgent target in the anti-religious campaign. In any event, by the time the campaign terminated at the end of the Khrushchev period, there were probably between sixty and seventy synagogues in the USSR, approximately half of them in the relatively small communities of Georgia, Dagestan and Central Asia, which accounted for considerably less than 10 percent of the Soviet Jewish population.[60] Many of the small and clandestine *minyanim*, which were usually held in private homes with but few articles of worship, were also closed down in this period. The usual procedure adopted by the authorities was for the police to raid them during services, confiscate all religious articles, threaten the worshippers and order them to cease functioning.[61]

The fear that their synagogues would be closed down was so marked that, as in previous periods, it was not difficult for the authorities to persuade synagogue officials to conduct themselves with due care. They must not, for instance, hire a cantor who was likely to attract people, especially youngsters.[62] They must refrain from collecting or using moneys for any purpose other than the maintenance of the synagogue and religious articles (the entire cost of which was usually borne by the congregation).[63] And there certainly must not be any "nationalist" activity in its precincts. This meant that if Israeli diplomats or foreign tourists attended services, they must be totally isolated from the congregation and prevented from conversing with worshippers. Above all, the congregants must not accept any written materials from them, even of a religious nature. Since the Israelis had no desire to harm the synagogues or their leaders, let alone jeopardize their very existence, the deteriorating situation of the Jewish religion caused them to maintain a low profile and they let their activities be guided by the wishes of the local Jews.

The latter were divided. While some of them seem to have become reconciled to a situation in which the activity of the synagogue was strictly limited to prayer, others held that yielding to the demands of the authorities set a dangerous precedent that would eventually deprive the synagogue and their existence as Jews of content and meaning. This group insisted that they must defy the powers-that-be to the best of their ability. But those who were prepared to converse with outsiders no matter the cost and those opposed to any such contact were usually both in the minority. Most worshippers wavered between letting fear predominate and overcoming it out of an uncontrollable desire to exchange a few words with a visitor.

The few lay officers who saw their task as caring for the needs of their congregants despite the adverse conditions in which they operated were systematically harassed by the authorities. Many of them were replaced by new, more pliant appointees who the authorities believed would be more easily persuaded, for instance, to sign defamatory articles or letters attacking the synagogues.[64] In Moscow and Leningrad, however, the synagogue administration generally included some who were accepted by the congregation and who would listen to its requests. Since these cities are main tourist centers, and their synagogues therefore the focus of world attention, the authorities may have been forced to be more lenient here in an effort to prove that the Jews could worship freely. At the beginning of the decade former president of the Leningrad community Gedalia Pecherskii sent a letter to the Council for the Affairs of Religious Cults, in which he requested that its Leningrad representative be replaced on the grounds that the latter was preventing synagogue elections at a time when the congregants were demanding a change in administration. The event that had particularly aroused the congregants' wrath was the warden's bringing in fifty students to "preserve order" on Passover, on the pretext that a Zionist group was operating against the synagogue's elected leaders and causing disturbances.[65]

The few remaining rabbis were old and frail: Rabbi Lubanov of Leningrad was already ninety when the decade began, and Rabbi Olevskii celebrated his ninetieth birthday in 1963,[66] while Rabbi Levin, who was only in his mid-sixties at the turn of the decade, was a sick man. Although in their hearts these men felt that the synagogue should fulfil all the needs and wishes of the local Jewish community, to activists and outsiders they often appeared unduly acquiescent. Whenever the occasion allowed it, however, their sermons would convey lessons and messages bearing oblique, and sometimes obvious, reference to the Soviet Jewish situation: the need to refrain from internal dissension, from informing, from being swayed by alien civilizations and influences. Thus, they dwelt on the miracles of Hanukka and Purim, the role of the Maccabees as patriots and partisans and the redemption from ancient Egypt. On one Hanukka in Leningrad, Rabbi Lubanov explained that that festival was more important than Purim, because Haman had sought to destroy the Jews physically but the Greeks had threatened them with spiritual extinction. On one Sabbath Rabbi Levin spoke of the sufferings of the Jews in Pharoah's Egypt and the world's apathy and silence, adding that when the redemption finally came about not all " the three million children of Israel" were ready to heed the tidings and to participate in it.[67]

Even when it did not lead to actual closure, the pressure applied, or sanctioned, by the authorities was heavy-handed and unrelenting.[68] Provocations were especially frequent when visitors distributed religious articles or simply left their prayer books or shawls behind. Thus, when Israeli embassy children handed out presents in the Choral Synagogue on Purim in 1960, three people shouted out that this would lead to the synagogue being closed. About a year later two young men interrupted the reading of the *Tora* portion by calling out that one of the Israeli diplomats present in the synagogue was a spy. The people who caused these disturbances were usually strangers in the synagogue, sometimes not even Jews.[69] But, provocations notwithstanding, young people continued to attend services exposing themselves to retaliatory action that included administrative measures at their universities or schools.[70]

In order to prevent contact in the synagogues with Israeli diplomatic personnel and, indeed, with all foreign visitors, the latter were often seated in isolation and warned against talking to worshippers or giving them anything. Wardens sometimes told the Israelis that, in the wake of earlier visits by Israelis, they had been interrogated regarding their conversations with them and the content of the packages they had received for the synagogue and warned against being friendly in the future. These warnings were observed to varying degrees in different places and at different times, depending on circumstances and the attitudes of the individuals concerned.[71]

On the whole, contact between Israelis and local Jews in the synagogues was even more difficult and risky during these years than it had been in the later fifties. Although there were occasional attempts by worshippers to act in blatant defiance of synagogue officials who did not represent their views, most congregants were not prepared to take this risk. While some who spoke with the visitors gave them the official line,[72] others sought ways to show their guests how pleased they were at their coming, for instance by uttering a few words of greeting as they brushed past them. Some still had the courage to wait outside the building after services to converse with the guests or accompany them back to their hotel. In Georgia there would be particularly open demonstrations of Jewish identification and loyalty. And, in Leningrad Evsei Dynkin embarked on such an enthusiastic Zionist tirade on one occasion that Pecherskii himself stopped him.[73]

In Moscow, where members of the Israeli embassy staff attended synagogue every Sabbath, the congregation was divided, some preferring to remain aloof and others doing everything possible to establish and maintain contact. The authorities, for their part, were ever constant in observing whatever went on. Thus, Choral Synagogue warden Mordecai Pineles was replaced in 1960 because he maintained close contact with the Israelis. And when the rabbi and wardens of the smaller Marina Roshcha congregation refused to limit such contacts, similar measures were taken there, even though Moscow's two smaller congregations were relatively more free to express themselves, the pressure applied there being less systematic than in the Choral Synagogue. However, in the atmosphere created by the trials of the Pecherskii group and of Volf Rishal in Moscow, all of whom had been regular synagogue-goers, charges of consorting with the Israelis entailed a very real threat.

In Febraury 1961 there was a general meeting at the Choral Synagogue, attended by a representative of the Council for the Affairs of Religious Cults, at which the Israelis were charged with exploiting the synagogue for disseminating Israeli propaganda. It was clearly in order to restrict contacts that a special loge for embassy officials and other foreign guests was constructed by the time of the fall festivals.[74]

Just prior to the 1962 fall festivals the congregation president read out an announcement that the authorities had summoned the rabbi and administration to tell them that (anonymous) letters had been received accusing them of violating synagogue regulations by allowing Israeli embassy personnel to distribute materials there. Worshippers were asked to cooperate in overcoming these improprieties.[75] On the penultimate Sabbath before Passover in 1963 the same president directed a tirade against all those who asked the Israelis for religious articles as well as against "speculators" who were seeking to "extort" prayer-shawls from the visitors. In this regard, Rabbi Lenin addressed himself in a Sabbath sermon to an article in *Trud*, the trade union newspaper which was often particularly outspoken in its attacks against Israel, about three members of the congregation who had allegedly filled their pockets with whatever they could find when they had been invited to Israeli embassy receptions and "begged" in the synagogue for prayer-shawls, literature and "foreign knick-knacks"; Rabbi Levin called for the cessation of such practices forthwith.[76]

In January 1964 the congregation president attacked the Israelis directly, asserting that they were obstructing the tranquillity of prayers by distributing political materials. At the end of the service Israeli Ambassador Yosef Tekoa, who had walked out for the duration of the talk, was surrounded by worshippers who encouraged the Israelis to continue as usual. In the same year another *Trud* article, this time attacking the embassy for giving out "political literature alien to Soviet people," notably on Simhat Tora, was read out in the synagogue.[77] A few months later Tekoa received a letter signed by members of the administration of the three Moscow synagogues stating that the embassy staff had been asked several times to enable the synagogues to return to being a place for orderly praying and to stop abetting profiteering by distributing prayer-shawls. The letter went on to say that worshippers had asked that embassy personnel be prevented from attending synagogue.[78]

But none of these measures diminished the natural sympathy of the Moscow congregation for the Jewish state and its representatives. When Ambassador Tekoa made his first appearance at the Choral Synagogue in July 1962 the atmosphere was nothing short of festive. The entire congregation rose to its feet as he entered the building and did so again when he was honored with the *maftir* at the end of the *Tora* reading. And as the embassy staff left, at the conclusion of the service, the worshippers arranged themselves in two crowded lines on both sides of the main aisle.[79] When shortly afterwards the steps taken by synagogue officials to minimize the Israelis' status in the eyes of local Jews extended to withholding from them the honor of being called up to the *Tora*, the wardens explained, or insinuated, to congregants who protested the denial of this traditional sign of respect and welcome that this stricture had been forced upon them by the authorities.[80]

Following the death of Israel's second president, Yitzhak Ben-Zvi, in spring 1963, a special memorial service was held in the Choral Synagogue.[81] The Choral Synagogue president who twice denounced the Israelis from the pulpit had to be replaced because his behavior evoked so much criticism among the congregation. And when president of the Marina Roshcha congregation Georgii Lieb addressed the worshippers on the Sabbath preceding Israel's Independence Day in 1965, he spoke about Passover, the First of May and the seventeenth Independence Day of the State of Israel, "which is the state also of the Jews of the USSR and we pray for its welfare and mention Jerusalem in our prayers three times a day." Lieb went on to talk about the heroism of the ghetto fighters, of the Maccabees and of all the uprisings against conquerors and occupiers until the establishment of Israel. He concluded by calling for Jewish solidarity and attacking disputes within congregations and by praying for world peace and peace on the borders of Israel.[82]

The following Sunday, the twentieth anniversary of the victory over

Nazi Germany, a crowd estimated at over a thousand attended the Choral Synagogue. In addition to the usual speeches of praise and thanks to the great Soviet army, which had saved civilization in general and the Jews in particular, the assembly heard a speech by Grigorii Manevich, who had spoken out against the GFR's statute of limitation on Nazi war criminals. "We are all celebrating, justifiably, this historic day of the victory of the Soviet Union, and for all of us this is an unforgettable day," Manevich said, "but let us not forget that in this same month, which is simultaneously the month of May and [the Jewish month of] Iyyar, another historic event of immeasurable importance took place, whose value for us Jews is unlimited. This month marks the regeneration of Israel and the establishment of the State of Israel, to which our own blessed Soviet Union was the first nation to give recognition seventeen years ago." Although the speaker's unexpected deviation was greeted at first with a total hush, as he proceeded to outline the history of the Jewish people from David's victory over Goliath to the horrors the Jews had suffered in Nazi-occupied Europe until the Soviet army liberated them, applause broke out in the crowded hall. Despite the chief warden's indication that his time was up, Manevich continued his discourse, quoting from the poet Judah Halevi and the prophet Ezekiel ("By the rivers of Babylon we sat down and wept as we remembered Zion"). When the warden again tried to interrupt the speaker, the congregation begged him to continue. Manevich ended by calling upon the Soviet Union, "whose loyal sons we are, ready to sacrifice our lives on its behalf at any time," to exhibit once again its friendship toward small peoples who were building their lives anew after suppression and persecution by improving its relations with Israel.[83]

Although *tours de force* such as Manevich's were rare and demanded considerable courage, it must be stressed that they could only take place in the atmosphere of defiance that could be sensed in the Jewish congregation in the face of the Kremlin's attempts to have it eliminate everything not strictly "religious" from its frame of interest.

The Jews' mood of defiance in the USSR's main Jewish cities was highlighted by the crowds that attended synagogue on special occasions and festivals. On the 1963 Day of Atonement the crowd outside the Choral Synagogue was estimated at between 10,000 and 15,000, so many that the street had to be closed to traffic. Excitement reached its peak at the end of the day when the entire congregation proclaimed the traditional concluding declaration, "Next year in Jerusalem!" in unison. The following year, when an estimated 20,000 flocked to the synagogue, even the street could not contain all the worshippers, who were crushed into courtyards and passages between buildings. By 1966 so many young people came to the Choral Synagogue on the eve of the Day of Atonement that a second service was held.[84]

The awe of this day, the occasion of moral stocktaking for all Jews, brought people to the synagogues throughout the country despite the clampdown on religious observance. In 1960 the street outside the Lvov synagogue was packed with Jews from Lvov itself and from the surrounding townships which had no synagogues.[85] In Vilnius the street outside the synagogue was jammed every year with people waiting to utter the final "Next year in Jerusalem!"[86] This declaration was considered so fraught with national content that in Kishinev in 1962 the rabbi announced that it would have to be deleted from the closing service.[87]

Indeed, the authorities sought to oust prayers and phrases referring to Zion and the Land of Israel from the liturgy altogether. Thus, they made this a condition for publishing a second edition of the Peace Prayer Book in the mid-sixties as Rabbi Levin had long sought to do. Naturally Rabbi Levin was unable to accept this interference in the content of the prayers and abandoned the project.[88]

By the end of our period festivals like Passover were also attracting large numbers of those who wished to demonstrate their unity with the Jewish people. Thus, on Passover in 1966 the Choral Synagogue was unable to hold all who came. Moreover, instead of dispersing at the conclusion of the service on the first evening, the crowd stayed to dance and sing Yiddish and Hebrew songs until the early hours. The same occurred on the first evening of Pentecost, when cantor Shteinberg of Tashkent came to Moscow to read the service, and the police had to be called in to disperse the throng. In March 1967 the Choral Synagogue and its environs were the scene of thousands even on the relatively minor festival of Purim. On Passover of that year the number of those attending – including younger people – far exceeded the previous year.[89]

One of the things that helped crystallize this festival as one on which Jewish nationalists focused their dissatisfaction with the regime's obstructionist attitude to the Jewish religion was the ban on *matza* baking, which had been spreading throughout the country since 1957 and reached Moscow in 1962. The proscription affected a large segent of Soviet Jewry since Passover was one of the holidays that many Jews continued somehow to observe.[90] The feeling of deprivation and coercion that it caused led to it becoming a *cause célèbre* among young Soviet Jews, many of whom had probably never eaten, seen or even heard of *matzot*. In 1966–67, when the ban was rescinded as a result of foreign pressure, Jews stood in line for hours, first to hand in their flour (there was no flour in the stores in 1966) and then to receive their *matzot*. Although everyone registering for *matzot* had to give his personal details and must have known that these details would be passed on, those who stood in line included Jews from every walk of life, not only regular synagogue-goers.[91]

The main "happening" in the synagogue, however, continued to take place on Simhat Tora. In 1960 members of the Israeli embassy staff took over the microphone in the Choral Synagogue to lead the singing of Israeli songs, while young people danced and sang in the street outside. In Leningrad that year the thousands who flocked to the synagogue for Simhat Tora removed themselves to the courtyard outside after the president of the congregation announced the end of the service at 9 p.m. The following year the crowd of an estimated 12,000 included students from the conservatory, who played music for the dancing multitude. In 1962 the Leningrad authorities warned the rabbi to prevent a repetition of the events of the previous year. But, although he requested the crowd to disperse at the end of the service, hundreds of young people again remained. The singing and dancing continued in the street until midnight, even after the police took twenty or thirty of them away in their cars.[92]

In 1965 the 25,000 to 30,000 strong crowd at Moscow's Choral Synagogue flowed over into courtyards all along Arkhipova Street. It included, among others, Yosef Shnaider and his group from Riga, who brought along a tape-recorder that played Israeli music recorded from Kol Israel. In 1966 the crowd – 80 percent of them young people – was estimated by local Jews at close to 40,000. When Kol Israel gave the number as 15,000, many of them protested to the Israeli embassy staff. The festivities had been publicized at Moscow State University in a notice headed "Entertainment for the young" and requesting students to prepare their throats for song and their feet for dance. By this time the Israelis no longer had to intitiate the singing and dancing; local youngsters brought their own guitars and accordions, as well as transistor radios that played music straight from Kol Zion lagola. When the lights above the synagogue went out, they lit up the street with torches made from newspapers.[93]

By the mid-sixties Simhat Tora celebrations were being organized by the young in other towns as well. Whereas at the turn of the decade, the festivities in Kiev and Odessa had a solemn and mournful air quite alien to the occasion, because only older people came to synagogue, by 1965–66 youngsters – although not in the same numbers as in Moscow and Leningrad, and not in the same semi-organized fashion – were demonstrating their own Jewish awakening by dancing and singing Hebrew, Yiddish and even Russian songs. In Kharkov, were there was no synagogue, local Jews celebrated by singing Jewish songs in the Intourist cafe![94]

According to Elie Wiesel, the huge participation in Simhat Tora celebrations was proof that the authorities would never succeed in wiping out Judaism or in forcing Jews to assimilate. Even without really knowing what it is, "young Jews want to return to Judaism . . . define themselves as Jews . . . [and] believe in the eternity of the Jewish people."[95]

### Cultural activity

While the synagogues were the only regular meeting place for Jews in towns where they still functioned, many cities and small towns played host to singers and musicians who gave Yiddish concerts and to amateur drama groups and choirs. In the sixties, as in the previous decade, professionals who performed in Yiddish almost invariably drew full houses, whether the soloist or star was Nehama Lifshitz, Zinovii Shulman, Misha (Mikhail) Aleksandrovich, Sidi Tal, Anna Guzik, Emil Hurevits, Veniamin Khaiatovskii or, as of 1964, Emil Kaminka. The social and demonstrative aspects of these occasions were often of greater meaning than the actual songs or recitals. Indeed, a number of the more activist Jews tried to attend every Yiddish performance in their town, at least partly because they knew that Israeli embassy personnel were likely to be there.

The ovations aroused by these concerts were often out of all proportion to their artistic value.[96] And the more popular the artist, the more difficulties the authorities would create. Yiddish artists were pressured to perform more in Russian and other Soviet languages and less in Yiddish and to include more items that reflected "socialist realism" rather than outmoded ideas and experiences. Thus, Anna Guzik and her husband began appearing in the smaller towns of the Ukraine and Moldavia in fall 1960, in concerts that were partly in Russian. And many of the Yiddish artists fulfilled a large proportion of their quota of performances in remote places with relatively small Jewish communities.[97]

The demand for Yiddish performances was such that even a

mediocre theatrical troupe like Vladimir (Binyomin) Shvartser's Moscow Yiddish Drama Ensemble, which was established under official auspices in 1963, was received with enthusiasm. Although it was known that this troupe was probably established only to show the world that Moscow had a Jewish theater again, even nationally minded Jews conceded that the troupe was not an entirely negative phenomenon.[98]

There were also literary evenings at which Yiddish poems or excerpts from stories were read. Some of these marked the anniversaries of the birth or death of writers who had been liquidated. One such evening in 1966 was dedicated to Isak Babel in his home town, Odessa; another, in Moscow, was dedicated to Israeli writer Avraham Shlonsky. Still others were held in honor of Mikhoels, Markish and Kvitko. On the whole, however, these soirées took place in small halls which could only accommodate small audiences.[99]

Among the cultural events which should be mentioned were the odd performance of Sholom Aleichem's plays by non-Jewish actors and theaters which drew large Jewish crowds. When the Kharkov Ukrainian State Theater put on "Tevia the Milkman," with music by Jewish composer Lev Pulver, not even the modifications that the text had undergone prevented the Jewish atmosphere from coming across. And even though the Jewish aspect of the heroine's tragedy was played down in the 1960 student production of "The Diary of Anna Frank," the audiences were largely Jewish.[100] Perhaps most important in this category were the occasional performances of Shostakovich's Thirteenth Symphony, which incorporated Evtushenko's poem "Babii Iar." This composition never failed to draw large numbers of Jewish intelligentsia even after the composer was compelled by the authorities to introduce changes.[101]

American Jewish tenor Jan Peerce made a second visit to the Soviet Union in 1963, giving concerts in Moscow, Leningrad, Tbilisi, Erevan and Baku. His Moscow concert included songs in Hebrew from the Book of Psalms and hasidic songs in Yiddish. The second concert he was to have given in the capital was canceled by the authorities on the pretext that local artists had complained about American performers drawing their audiences away from them. Nor was Peerce – who was originally a cantor – allowed to serve as cantor at the Choral Synagogue on the Sabbath as he had done in 1956.[102]

By the middle of the decade cultural events often turned into demonstrations, yet another sign of new times and of the new atmosphere among young Jews in particular. The youngsters would use the intermissions to sing Israeli songs and dance the *hora* in the foyer, an act of defiance that seems to have been brought to Moscow and other cities from Riga, where the practice began earlier in the decade.[103]

### Israeli events

The number of Israelis that visited the USSR within the framework of international cultural and sport competitions, exhibitions and festivals was supplemented when, in the sixties, bilateral relations began to include cultural exchanges.[104] Just as that major landmark in the Soviet Jewish awakening, the 1957 Youth Festival, had provided a first opportunity for real personal contact with Israeli youth, the tours of Israeli artists and the film festivals and agricultural exhibitions brought new and larger groups of local Jews into touch with the Israelis who visited in the sixties.

An Israeli basketball team that played in Riga in 1961 visited the synagogue on the Sabbath before the match and then walked around the town in small groups to make themselves available to the local Jewish population. While children and young people crowded around them wherever they went, older people were more hesitant and did not begin to approach them until later on in their stay when some of them came to their hotel, and talked, danced and drank with them in the restaurant. As the date of the match neared the excitement grew, as did the numbers of Jews from Leningrad, Vilnius and some of the smaller towns who came to see the Israeli team play. On the day of the game hundreds of Jews lined the streets from the hotel to the stadium, and when the Israelis won, the police were unable to restrain the crowd that mobbed them to congratulate them and ask for souvenirs from Israel. Unquestionably the team's visit and subsequent victory helped improve Israel's image among Jews and non-Jews alike.[105]

The Israeli volleyball team that took part in the European championship in Moscow and Kiev in October 1962 was less successful despite a victory over the Italians, and its games were less well attended. But when the Israelis visited the Kiev synagogue on Simhat Tora, the warden had to warn the enthusiastic congregants that a place of prayer was not intended as a venue for distributing and receiving propaganda material.[106] On the other hand, an Israeli soccer team that took part in a tournament in Odessa the following year attracted large numbers of Jews from that city and from afar.[107]

Two more Israeli basketball teams visited the USSR in 1965, one of them a women's team. Although the authorities used every possible subterfuge to restrict the sale of tickets when this team played in Riga, 80 percent of the spectators were Jewish. They cheered the girls in Hebrew and Yiddish, and when the team won and *Hatikva* was played and the Israeli flag raised, the Jews surged onto the court to embrace them. During the course of the team's visit, young men came to the hotel restaurant to dance with the visitors.[108]

Even more important in stirring Jewish national pride was Israel's participation in the European basketball championship in Moscow early that summer. This time Moscow Jews and those who came from Kiev, Kharkov and Odessa, Kishinev, Riga, Vilnius and Kaunas, Leningrad, Tbilisi, Irkutsk and other cities, had almost two weeks (29 May–10 June) to make contact with the Israelis. And when the Israeli flag was raised and anthem played on the four Israeli victories, the Jews in the crowd exploded with joy.[109]

The tours of Israeli artists, mostly musicians, who performed in the Soviet Union within the framework of cultural exchanges, also became demonstrations of Jewish solidarity and pride. Thus, when Israeli pianist Frederick Portnoi toured the Soviet Union in January 1960, he drew large crowds wherever he appeared. Hundreds stood during his concert in Leningrad and students sat on the stage at the pianist's feet. Israeli diplomat Liova Eliav had a hard time purchasing a ticket to one of the pianist's concerts in Riga, as the ticket offices had been "stormed" as soon as the concerts were advertised and tickets were being sold on the black market. Although every piece that Portnoi played was received enthusiastically, when he played a composition by Israeli composer Paul Ben Haim, who was identified as such in the program, there was thunderous applause, even though the music had no particularly Jewish or Israeli motif and its modern character was unfamiliar to the audience.[110]

The crowds that filled concert halls in Vilnius, Odessa, Kiev, Leningrad and Moscow when Israeli violinist Ivri Gitlis toured the USSR in 1961 applauded ebulliently at every performance. But in notes passed to him during his concerts, they begged him to play Israeli compositions, saying they could hear Bartok and Paganini anytime.[111] And the message was heard back in Israel. Thus, when pianist Pnina Salzman toured Moscow, Leningrad, Riga, Kharkor and Baku a month later, she included pieces by Paul Ben Haim and Menahem Avidom in all her concerts. In Kharkov the demand for tickets was so great that the concert was transferred from a hall of 500 seats to one of 2,000; and even then many were turned away. Except in Baku, where she was guarded too closely, Jews thronged around her at the end of every concert; in Leningrad they even surged onto the stage. In Moscow the applause continued until the lights were turned out, while in Riga crowds of young people singing and dancing the *hora* turned the event into an unbridled nationalist demonstration.[112]

In May 1964 Israeli conductor George Singer gave an entirely Israeli program in Kharkov. Here the crowd included people whose interest in Israel had been aroused after meeting Israelis at the summer resorts of Sochi and Yalta.[113]

Pianist Daniel Barenboim, then twenty-three years old, appeared in Moscow, Leningrad, Vilnius, Zaporozhe, Yalta and Simferopol early in 1965. He, too, included a number of Israeli compositions in his program, notably Menahem Avidom's "Twelve Preludes." Tickets for Barenboim's two Leningrad concerts – which had been widely publicized, even in *Leningradskaia pravda* – were sold out two weeks in advance. Members of the Israeli embassy who attended were told that Israeli artists – "a living link with Israel" – had a tremendous impact on the city's Jews, who were all "nationalistically minded." Lev Kornblit, who attended the concerts of every Israeli artist who visited Leningrad, remembers that Barenboim gave no less than fifteen encores at his second concert there. In Vilnius, where the authorities disallowed any announcement of the event, Barenboim was enthusiastically received by an overwhelmingly Jewish audience, mostly youngsters, many of whom said that they came only because the pianist was Israeli. Young people who attended Barenboim's concert in Simferopol told the Israelis who accompanied him of the encouragement they were receiving from Israeli broadcasts, which they were able to hear without any problems. In Zaporozhe, however, the Jews were afraid to approach the Israelis.[114]

The high point of all the performances by Israelis was the tour of singer Geula Gil, mimic Yaacov (Juki) Arkin and two guitarists in summer 1966. In their three concerts in Moscow, the audience wildly applauded the Israeli and Yiddish songs and all the singer's eight encores were Israeli songs. The throng was so carried away that they joined in the singing of the traditional Hebrew song of greeting *Hevenu shalom aleichem*. Although the exit was so packed with people after her first performance that the artists were hardly able to pass, Geula Gil refused to leave through a side exit. The police were called in for her subsequent performances, but to no avail; they were simply pushed aside by the excited crowd.[115]

In Riga, where she again gave three concerts, tickets were sold out as soon as it was known she was coming, people standing in line all night to purchase them. The audience at the first concert brought hundreds of bouquets, which young people presented to the visitors. One of the guitarists was handed a note from "the united Jewish youth of the Baltic," which, it said, wanted to go to Israel and help make it flourish, so that the Jewish people could become a people like all peoples. The note also asked the Israeli government to demand that Soviet Jews who sought to leave be given exit permits. At the second concert, special guards prevented the spectators from bringing flowers into the 1,500-seat Sports Auditorium where the concerts were held. However, a few managed to smuggle in bouquets and even to present them to the artists. At the end of the evening the artists were whisked away in waiting cars before the crowd had time to gather at the exit.

On the third day, when the auditorium was "packed to the rafters," police reinforcements made certain that the Jews were kept away from the Israelis. The combined frustration and exhilaration of Riga's Jewish youth led to a fracas with the police at the end of the performance. When the Jews surged forward in an attempt to reach the Israelis, a fifteen-year-old girl, Nehama Garber, had a policeman's arm slammed into her chest. Already excited, she slapped his face when she thought she heard him say that not enough Jews had been killed in World War II. The crowd tried to keep the police van into which she was shoved from moving off, shouting "She's only a small girl!" and "The world will know about this. It will know how you treat Jews in Russia. Why don't you let her go? Let us go to Israel." After being told at the police station that slapping a policeman was equivalent to slapping the Soviet state, Nehama was allowed to leave, only to find that a large crowd was waiting to discover what had happened to her. But after a few days she was taken in again, along with her mother, Miriam. Nehama's interrogators tried to make her admit that she had come to the performance with the specific purpose of slapping a policeman and causing a riot. Upon her refusal to confess to what was not true, the interrogators tried to intimidate her by saying that the authorities were aware that her parents had been conducting Zionist activities in their home. (Nehama knew that the apartment and telephone were bugged and that the KGB had searched the family's home three months previously, but had found nothing incriminating.) After several harrowing interrogations, she was brought before a juvenile court and her parents were fined for not giving her a "proper education."[116]

When Geula Gil's group appeared in Vilnius, tickets were sold out even before the announcements were posted, and in the synagogue on the Sabbath before the first concert people told Juki Arkin that the performers were sure to be received enthusiastically because they were Israelis. After what had happened in Riga, there were police inside the hall during the performance, but while this subdued the audience, nothing could hold back the applause when Arkin performed a piece on the Vilnius ghetto and Paneriai (which he had visited). Again the entire audience joined in singing *Hevenu shalom aleichem*.[117]

The Leningrad performance was sold out so far in advance that a second one was added. Again the tickets were sold out before the advertisements were posted and an extra 250 seats were set up to accommodate the demand. Given the mass enthusiasm which these concerts aroused, it is not surprising that the Soviet authorities first postponed and then canceled a visit by the Israeli Philharmonic.[118]

The Kremlin found it more difficult to prevent Israeli participation in international cultural events and scientific conferences. One of the most important of the former were the biennial film festivals, which – since 1959 – provided an unusual opportunity for Jews who knew nothing of Israel and were far removed from any Jewish activity to become acquainted with Israeli landscapes and life. At the 1961 festival, the Israeli films were shown ten times in four different halls, more times than those of any other country. Even so, Jews who came from as far away as Lithuania and Latvia, cities on the shores of the Black and Caspian Seas, the Donbass and Central Asia had to be turned away. The delegation that presented the films and the Israeli diplomats who accompanied them were asked to describe life in Israel, which they were only too ready to do.[119]

The delegation that attended the 1963 film festival included Hanna Rovina, who had been a member of Habima Theater in Moscow in the 1920s, singer Nehama Hendel, producer Yosef Milo, actress Batya Lancett and Director-General of Kol Israel, Hanoch Givton. The standing of the delegation in itself was enough reason for Jews to come. At the first screening of "The Kibbutz" the applause was especially enthusiastic in those places that described and portrayed the construction of kibbutz society, which is based on the principles of equality and socialism. Films on the Holocaust and on the Israeli navy demonstrated the contrast between the destruction of World War II and the rebuilding of Jewish life in the Jewish state. This time the Jewish films were shown to more than 10,000 people from all over the country. On several occasions the police were called in to restore order, and the authorities took counter-measures similar to those imposed at the 1957 Youth Festival. They isolated the Israeli delegation from local Jews, even during the film showings, canceled some of the showings, gave the Israeli films no coverage in the media, and prevented the Israelis from distributing any printed matter whatsoever.[120]

Israel's entries to the 1965 festival included "The Glass Cage," a film on the Eichmann trial (translated into Russian as "Remember"). This time the accompanying delegation comprised actors Misha Asherov and Hulio Hamiel, poetess Dalia Friedlander and Geula Gil. "The Glass Cage" was screened in the main 6,000-seat auditorium, as well as three times in the 1,500-seat "Kosmos" Cinema. One of the main aims of the film was to portray the relations between Israel and West Germany in a truer light than Soviet Jews had received from the local media. The film made a deep impression on the audience, the great majority of whom were Jews. Indeed, all the Israeli films received stormy ovations, as did Geula Gil when she performed in the Gorky Park amphitheater along with representatives of other delegations before a crowd of fifteen thousand.

Although there were difficulties with the screening of some of the films, the Israelis were given some publicity this time. Both *Vecherniaia Moskva* and the festival bulletin carried pictures of Geula Gil and Dalia Friedlander, while those of Ms. Gil and Hulio Hamiel were displayed with those of other famous artists in the window of the Moskva Hotel. In addition, several papers carried articles on "The Glass Cage," paying particular attention to the theme of the world's indifference to the Nazi horrors and to the role of the USSR in defeating Hitler.[121]

Even more important than the film festivals in providing the opportunity for large numbers of Soviet Jews to mingle with Israelis and to demonstrate their pride in Israel's achievements were two international exhibitions, or fairs, to which Israel sent delegations in 1966. At the agricultural exhibition that took place in Moscow in May, the Israeli pavilion became a meeting-place for Jews from all over the Soviet Union, many of them academics and technicians and most of them young.[122] The embassy staff and agricultural delegation were joined by a group of Israelis from several *kibbutzim*, who were visiting Moscow at this time and helped answer questions about Israel's scientific and technological progress. On the day devoted to Israel – each participating country had a special day – Professor Yelan of the Haifa Technion, who headed the Israeli delegation, lectured to a full hall, and at least 2,000 people, approximately one-half of whom had no official invitation, attended the Israeli reception.[123]

The Soviet authorities' response was two-pronged; they intensified their propaganda campaign against Israel and they arrested some of those visiting the exhibition. David Khavkin, one of the people arrested on the exhibition grounds, was held for fifteen days, on the charge of hooliganism and drinking in public. And Solomon Dolnik, one of Moscow's older activists, was arrested immediately after the exhibition and sentenced to five years in prison camp.[124]

Despite such obvious attempts to dampen the Jews' enthusiasm as a *Pravda* announcement on the eve of the opening that Israeli Second Secretary David Gavish had been declared *persona non grata*,[125] the poultry exhibition, which took place in Kiev during August, was no less a success for the Israelis. An estimated 100,000 people visited the Israeli pavilion, the majority of them from Kiev and its surroundings, although many came from far afield, from Moscow, Leningrad and Sverdlovsk, the Baltic republics, Siberia and Central Asia. The twenty thousand that visited the exhibition on Israel's day heard Israeli songs played throughout the grounds.[126]

The last event in which Israelis participated prior to the severance of Soviet–Israeli relations that followed the Six Day War was a food manufacturing and packaging machinery exhibition, held in Moscow in May 1967. On this occasion Israel's Minister of Labor Yigal Allon, who was in the USSR to attend a congress of the International Organization of Social Insurance (the only visit to the USSR by a government minister since 1948), was present on Israel's day. At the reception that day young Soviet Jews sang the "Song of the Palmah," the Israeli army's strike force of which Allon had been commander. Many of those who approached Allon at the reception asked him whether the Israeli government was doing everything in its power to save Soviet Jewry.[127]

### Aliya

The ultimate expression of the Jewish national awakening in the sixties was, of course, application to leave the Soviet Union for the State of Israel. And, on the basis of *vyzovy* sent by relatives in Israel, tens of thousands of Jews must have applied for exit permits in the years between 1960 and 1967.[128] Although the movement lacked even the trimmings of an organization or any recognized leadership, a Soviet Jewish journalist who defected in 1966, Leonid Finkelstein, believed that one-half of the country's Jews were seeking to leave for Israel by the mid-sixties.[129]

Although the drop in exit permits allowing emigration to Israel directly from the Soviet Union – from 753 in 1956 to a mere seven in 1959 – would seem to have been enough to stanch the flow of applications, this was far from the case. Instead of the number of applications for exit permits contracting in accordance with the declining number of those being allowed to leave as had happened in the past, the precedent created by the Polish repatriation agreement of the late 1950s encouraged Jews to keep up the flow of applications. And, slowly, the authorities began approving them again. Between one and two hundred a year were permitted to leave between 1960 and 1962; the number grew to 388 and 539, respectively, in 1963 and 1964; and to the unprecedented heights (except for the period of the Polish repatriation) of 1,444 in 1965, 1,892 in 1966 and 1,162 in the first six months of 1967.[130] Although "informed sources" maintained that this was "only a trickle" compared with the tens of thousands who, in fact, wanted to leave,[131] this jump in the number of Soviet citizens being allowed to join relatives abroad, particularly in Israel, was evidence of a noteworthy new trend.

While statistics for a regional or any other breakdown of these figures are lacking, we can conclude from what appeared in the media about those who emigrated to Israel during this period that a considerable proportion came from the Western borderlands and that, unlike those who emigrated prior to the 1956 Suez Campaign, many were still in the prime of life and some were even children (although this was not the case in the Caucasus or Central Asia, where only invalids and the very old were allowed to leave in the early and mid-sixties). The fact that young people were included among those being allowed to leave instilled a new optimism among the younger generation, further increasing the number of applicants and activists from this age group, including second-generation Soviet citizens from the more acculturated Jewish communities. Foreigners who visited the Soviet Union in the mid or late fifties and returned in the sixties noted that the already considerable desire for *aliya* in the former decade seemed to have grown markedly in the latter one, especially among young people.[132]

Although there were still those who were concentrating their efforts on reducing antisemitism and anti-Jewish discrimination and achieving the right of cultural expression, an increasing number of nationally conscious Soviet Jews had come to the conclusion that a significant concession to Jewish national sentiment was likely or even feasible inside the Soviet Union. As one woman from Kiev put it: after having lived in a ghetto for three years and then spending six months in a Soviet jail (simply for having lived in Nazi-occupied territory), she now wanted to live freely as a Jew and to have Jewish grandchildren to ensure the survival of her people. In the Soviet Union, she was convinced that whether or not things improved for Jews as individuals, those who stayed in the USSR would not remain Jews.[133] The hope of eventually being able to emigrate had now grown to the point where it was giving more and more Soviet Jews the strength and patience to endure and perhaps even escape – at least within themselves – the difficulties and ignominy of their present lives.

Israel's own efforts gave them further hope that the Jewish state represented a practical reality and not just a long-held dream. Israeli broadcasts to Soviet Jewry, visits of embassy officials to Soviet Jewish centers and synagogues as well as of delegations of artists and scientists and sports teams enkindled their imagination. Moreover, Israel had triumphed in its War of Independence against imperialism and heavy odds and had further acquitted itself with distinction in 1956; it had become the refuge of hundreds of thousands of Jews from the Arab countries and – perhaps more important for Soviet Jews – had absorbed tens of thousands of Jews from Eastern Europe in the late 1950s; and finally it could be credited with major achievements in the realm of technology and science. Thus, Israel both represented the only country that could really care for the Jews as a whole (even if individuals with relatives in the U.S., Britain or France might hope that their personal cases would be dealt with by Kennedy, Wilson or de Gaulle) and at the same time fostered the somewhat irrational belief that it had the capability of bringing them from darkness into light.[134] It was this belief that led Soviet Jews first to entreaties not to forget them, then to questions about what Israel was doing on their behalf and, on occasion, to outright protests that the Israeli government and its representatives in the Soviet Union were not doing enough for them.

As in the later years when the emigration movement turned into a large-scale exit, so, too, in the mid-sixties neither the movement as a whole nor the individuals who decided to take practical steps toward leaving the USSR were motivated wholly by the positive impulse created by the Jewish "spark"; the negative fear of antisemitism and its twin, anti-Jewish discrimination, probably played at least as great a role. But the distinction between the two was often blurred, since those whose original incentive might have been anti-Jewish discrimination were frequently swept up in the more positive or formative concepts of the Jewish national awakening.

The urge to do everything possible to go to Israel was all the more remarkable when we consider the difficulties that those who applied to leave the USSR underwent at the hands of the authorities as well as of their employers, the teachers of their children and the Komsomol. While not a few were daunted by these bureaucratic and psychological deterrents, and a few Jews yielded to pressures after having filed applications, requests for *vyzovy* and exit permits continued to grow in the 1960s. Of those who applied for *vyzovy*, some never received them because they had been confiscated by the Soviet security services and others were dissuaded from asking for the necessary documents (the *kharakteristika*) from their places of study or work or even if they did overcome this hurdle, never went to OVIR because they feared that they or their families would suffer recriminations. And many of those who did submit the requisite documentation were refused, usually without being given any reason. There was one more category: Soviet Jewish citizens who allegedly received *vyzovy* from relatives in Israel without having requested them. Although the authorities claimed that the Israeli government was inveigling its citizens to send these affidavits in order to stir up trouble among Soviet Jews, who were "perfectly happy" in the Soviet Union, it is more than likely that those who received these *vyzovy* really belonged to the second category; they had asked for them in a moment of determination and courage, but later denied having taken the initiative out of fear.

Although there is no way of knowing how many people there were in each of the above groups, we do know that the number of affidavits sent from Israel increased to the point where those approved made hardly a dent in the number of exit visas requested and supported with the requisite documents. For, as we have seen, the fact that there were some successful applicants acted as a stimulus for further requests.[135] But, even after Kosygin's December 1966 Paris statement on the unification of families, pressure on would-be emigrants mounted. This included letters and articles in the media, particularly in the local press, directed against specific applicants, people whose names were given, or attributed to disgruntled emigrants to Israel. Indeed, these efforts by OVIR to dissuade and deter applicants were clear proof that the prime minister's promise did not necessarily reflect the unanimous mood of the powers-that-be. Nor could there by any doubt in Jews' minds that this negative attitude would remain purely theoretical. Administrative measures taken against would-be emigrants included dismissal from jobs, with all that that implied economically, socially and administratively in the USSR, where every citizen is under obligation to work. Similarly, they or their children were publicly expelled from the Komsomol and from institutes of higher learning.[136] Finally, there were cases of seemingly arbitrary sadism, of Jews who had received their exit permits being told at the last minute that they could not leave,[137] or of applicants being threatened with confinement in a psychiatric hospital.[138]

It was only the belief that there was some chance of success that induced the average, more or less rational, Soviet citizen to undergo the humiliations and bureaucratic harassment that accompanied requests for exit visas. In addition to the *vyzov* and *kharakteristika*, the would-be emigrant had to bring: his own request to emigrate; a handwritten curriculum vitae; a letter from the superintendent of the house in which he lived confirming his address, together with an order to hand the apartment over to the relevant district committee should he leave; and a four-page questionnaire containing information concerning the composition of his immediate family unit, his place of birth, full details concerning his parents, spouse – who, if he or she was remaining behind, had, like parents, to give a letter of consent to the applicant's departure[139] – children, grandchildren and siblings. He or she also had to submit a notarized birth certificate of every member of the family who sought to leave. If a birth certificate was missing – as was often the case due to the war and other upheavals – they had to bring a substitute document from the relevant court; a copy of the first two pages of his or her identity card; a receipt from Gosbank (the state bank) that the sum needed in order to receive a passport had been deposited; and passport photos. Finally, if the relative abroad had changed his or her name, the applicant had to provide that relative's birth certificate along with a notarized certificate confirming the change.

When an application was refused the applicant would have to wait six months before filing a new one. This often meant that the original affidavit was no longer valid, i.e. that twelve months had gone by since it had been signed by the relative in Israel, in which event the applicant had to acquire not only a new affidavit but also a new set of all the above documents.

To add to the Kafkaesque atmosphere, there were the unknown variables: as the degree of relationship required to validate an affidavit had never been defined, it was never clear beforehand whether a sibling, cousin, uncle or nephew might be acceptable as a signatory.

Thus, while one affidavit would be rejected on the grounds that a sibling was not a close enough relative, another, from a cousin, would be accepted. In this respect, the attitude of the local authorities seems to have played a role, although it never became altogether clear how much was left to them as opposed to the central authorities. For reasons that cannot be ascertained, the authorities in the Baltic republics were, on the whole, the most lenient while those in the Ukraine were more stringent, and those in the Caucasus, as we have seen, allowed only a few older people to emigrate.

The fact that refusals were not explained also meant that applicants had no way of knowing whether there was any sense in lodging a second request or how they could improve their chances if they did. Indeed, the arbitrary nature of the procedure was one of its most discouraging features. There was no way of knowing why one person was allowed to leave and another refused, whether there were quotas for a given year, a given city or region, or for applicants of a certain age or social, educational or professional status. However, when the number of exit permits began growing in 1963, it seemed that the chances were greater in the larger cities of the annexed Western territories.[140]

In the main centers of emigration – Riga, Vilnius, Chernovtsy – there were enough Jews determined to try their luck to result in lines outside the OVIR office.[141] In these towns the enthusiasm with which they awaited exit permits led growing numbers of Jews to start selling their belongings in preparation for *aliya*. By the middle of 1966 considerable numbers of Jews from other parts of the Western territories, such as the Transcarpathian *oblast*, who had little reason to believe their applications would be approved, were taking the risk of applying for exit visas.[142] But nothing characterized the messianic spirit of these years as much as the farewells that local Jews gave those who had received permission to leave. Those still awaiting exit permits accompanied the emigrants to their points of departure, singing and dancing along the way. When Rabbi Avraham Yosef Tverskii of Moscow's Cherkizovo synagogue made *aliya* in late 1963 or early 1964, the farewell given him at the synagogue drew people from as far afield as Siberia.[143] In addition to being festive occasions, these farewells enabled those still awaiting permits to exchange information on how to simplify and speed up the procedure. Would-be emigrants also used the opportunity to ask those leaving to contact their relatives in Israel upon arrival and ask them to send affidavits.

"Refuseniks" had the right of appealing to higher quarters: the minister of the interior or of the preservation of public order; the attorney-general; the Chairman of the Council of Ministers or of the Presidium of the All-Union Supreme Soviet; even the First Secretary himself.[144] While most refuseniks hesitated before taking any step that might expose them to further reprisals, an increasing number resorted to such measures as the years passed. After ten years of requests and refusals, one Jew in Riga burst through a police cordon to hand Kosygin his request to be allowed to join his brother in Israel.[145]

Jews who could not acquire one or more of the requisite documents for an exit visa occasionally also made special appeals to leading figures in the USSR or abroad, for instance, those who had no other hope of leaving at this stage, because they had nobody abroad to send them affidavits. Some of these Jews did try to request exit permits under headings other than the reunification of families. However, one such person who wrote to Kosygin in 1965 that he sought to emigrate to Israel for reasons of religion was told by OVIR that he could not apply without an affidavit. In a period of just over two years, this man wrote almost 700 letters to whomever or whichever local or national institution seemed relevant – without any success.

Another such person, who did receive an exit permit, was Iosif Chernobilskii, a young locksmith from Kiev. After recurrent approaches to Israeli diplomats on their visits to the Ukrainian capital, in fall 1964 he asked an American tourist to see that his appeal for the right to emigrate was publicized when she returned to the U.S.; this was duly done in the Jewish newspaper of her home town, Detroit. Although the author's name was not published in the Detroit paper, the Soviet authorities were able to trace him on the basis of the photostat of his original letter – which was published – because he used the same typewriter for letters he had written in connection with his endeavors to obtain permission for a Jewish theater in Kiev.[146]

Also determined to get to Israel despite his having no relatives there, Iakov (Iasha) Kazakov presented OVIR with a *vyzov* signed by an Israeli embassy official. On 9 June 1967 after OVIR had told him that there was no chance whatsoever for him to emigrate on the basis of this document, he wrote to the USSR Supreme Soviet explaining that he wanted to live in Israel because he was unable in the USSR to receive a Jewish education or to maintain a link with his people. A young man of twenty at the time, Kazakov had learned that he was a Jew at the age of three – from other children. At six, when the Doctors' Plot was publicized, he discovered that being a Jew in the Soviet Union meant being a traitor to the Soviet motherland. Although initially ashamed of his "bad" Jewish identity, as he became older he began frequenting libraries in search of books that would help him find out what being a Jew really meant. Eventually he concluded, merely from reading Soviet propaganda, that if so numerically small a people could be such a grave and powerful enemy of the Soviet Union and had played so significant a role in so many historical events and developments, he wanted to identify fully with this people. Their newly found Jewish identity and their pride at being Jewish led Kazakov and others of his generation to turn instinctively to the Jewish state, whose struggles against great odds, including the Soviet super-power which was arming and supporting its enemies, seemed to personify their own.[147]

Altogether the younger generation was less easily swayed than people in their forties and fifties who were more prone to surrender to harassment and to the frustrations and disappointment involved in applying to leave. It feared the regime less, had less to lose professionally and was more prepared to grapple with the difficulties involved in adjusting to life in Israel. Soviet Jews had already become aware of the efforts being made on their behalf by foreign governments, statesmen and avowed friends of the USSR in other fields.[148] This, together with the fact that a number of emigrants had been allowed to leave after relatives abroad appealed to people like Eleanor Roosevelt, Bertrand Russell, Harold Wilson or Nobel laureates, encouraged others to try this method.[149] Thus, in late 1964 or early 1965, a group of young Rigans contemplated organizing an appeal to American Jewry from Jews in different cities and a variety of professional backgrounds, requesting help in getting to Israel. They were fully prepared to give their personal details (names, addresses, etc.) – at this time still a most unusual, perhaps even an unprecedented step – and eventually to renounce their Soviet citizenship. In addition to exerting pressure on the Soviet authorities, the link with abroad was intended to ensure the Jews in question against arbitrary arrest or other administrative measures.[150] Although many relatives of Soviet Jews had long considered this approach too dangerous, others (probably with the approval of their Soviet kinsmen) felt that approaching Western liberals and governmental bodies offered the best, if not the only, chance of obtaining exit visas, especially for those who had been refused more than once.

One of the refuseniks of the mid-sixties was Moscow Yiddish writer Yosef Kerler. After his request to emigrate had been approved in December 1965, and after he had been dismissed from the Writers'

Union, the permission was rescinded. A major campaign on his behalf was initiated by his relatives in Israel, who wrote to the Soviet leaders, Lord Russell (who also approached Kosygin), U.N. Secretary General U Thant, the Red Cross and Daniel Mayer. In addition, Moshe Decter brought Kerler's case to the attention of playwright Arthur Miller, who wrote a further letter to the Soviet prime minister and to Mikhail Kotov of the Soviet Peace Committee. Kerler himself asked the help of Norwegian Communist Party newspaper correspondent Tore-Jarl Bielenberg, who visited him in his home after hearing of his case from Nehama Lifshitz. Following Kosygin's Paris statement, Kerler also wrote him directly. But all to no avail: in January 1967 the Kerlers received another refusal.[151]

Refusals such as the above notwithstanding, Kosygin's Paris statement, and especially its publication in *Izvestiia* on 5 December 1966, gave new encouragement to those seeking to leave for Israel toward the end of our period. Many who had hitherto hesitated to process their papers felt they could now do so. Indeed, not a few of them went to the OVIR office with the *Izvestiia* cutting in hand. Refuseniks also stepped up new applications on the assumption that Kosygin's statement presaged a change in emigration policy on the part of the Soviet powers-that-be. Yet those applying or re-applying were told by OVIR officials that they had received no instructions regarding the implementation of Kosygin's promise. Or they were told that changes could not be introduced into the reunification-of-families procedure as the process was nearing completion.[152]

In many ways the struggle for *aliya* in the early and mid-sixties paved the way for the large-scale emigration of the post-Six Day War years. Although there was no way of knowing how much of the movement that was being felt in regard to emigration emanated from internal, and how much from external, pressure,[153] the persistence, determination and audacity that developed during these years were apparently beginning to have an effect on the Kremlin. During these years the Jews gained valuable experience in grappling with the difficulties and obstacles being placed in their path. Moreover, many of the ideas and strategies that became regular features of the struggle as it developed during the major *aliya* of the early and mid-seventies were sown and formulated in this earlier period. Finally, not a few of the early leaders of the mass movement of the seventies began their training and preparation in the years under discussion.

### The outbreak of the Six Day War

The final – and broadest – demonstration of Soviet Jewish identification with Israel came with the outbreak of the Six Day War in June 1967. In the weeks that preceded the war Jews throughout the USSR made no effort to conceal their concern for Israel's security. Nor did they contain their exuberance over Israel's subsequent victory. This show of affinity to Israel was the culmination of feelings that had been mounting over the years.

The factors behind this growth in the sympathy for and identity with Israel and the increasing national ferment among Soviet Jewish youth were many and diverse. They ran the gamut from indifference to and alienation from the regime on the part of Soviet youth as a whole, especially among students and intelligentsia, to Israel's capture and trial of Adolf Eichmann, Israeli broadcasts in Russian, the increasing number of Western Jewish and Israeli tourists in the USSR, who helped Soviet Jews become more skeptical about what the Soviet media had to say about Israel, the growing manifestations of antisemitism, and culminating in the Kremlin's political and military support for the Arabs, especially for Egypt's President Nasser who was openly committed to the destruction of the Jewish state. If in 1956 this support had seemed to be primarily anti-Western, since 1964, with the establishment of the PLO and the joint Arab command, that sought to focus Arab unity on the Arab–Israeli conflict, such support could only be interpreted as anti-Israel.[154]

To this must be added the fact that the younger generation of Soviet Jews, who had sparked the movement into prominence, had decided that if they were to remain Jews – which their wholesale rejection by the society around them made inevitable – they were going to be proud ones.[155] To this end many of them were now making a conscious effort to marry among themselves rather than intermarry and to reject the influence of their non-Jewish surroundings.

The Jews' sense of solidarity with Israel deepened in the face of the implied and often explicitly expressed threats posed by the politics and deeds of Arab summitry during 1964–65 and the increasingly serious Arab–Israeli incidents after the neo-Ba'th came to power in Syria in February 1966. Soviet propaganda against Israel – which had in no way undermined Soviet Jewish sympathy for Israel, having, if anything, an opposite effect – was stepped up in the second half of May and early June 1967. For some months the Soviet media had been lashing out at Israel, usually on the pretext of the deteriorating situation between it and Syria.[156] Yet, while Moscow had a definite interest in the leftist neo-Ba'th regime in Damascus, which it saw as a progressive regime with a socialist orientation, there were indications that the severity of the onslaught was motivated by the demonstration of solidarity with Israel on the part of its own Jewish population rather than by international politics. Since they could clearly not admit the interest of their Jews in Israel, Soviet officials had been saying for some time that the main hindrance to improved relations between them and Israel was the latter's interest in Soviet Jewry, which, they insisted, constituted interference in Soviet domestic affairs. There can hardly be any doubt that had Israel been prepared to forgo its commitment to Soviet Jewry, the Kremlin would not have broken diplomatic relations with it in the wake of the Six Day War.

Knowing that the Israeli embassy's days in the Soviet capital were numbered, one member of its staff told a Moscow activist in the latter half of May 1967 that Soviet Jews had to prepare themselves to operate autonomously, without the support and cooperation of Israeli diplomats on the spot.[157]

Thus, nothing the Soviets could write or broadcast against Israel mitigated the anxiety of Soviet Jews as they saw the Jewish state being increasingly threatened by Nasser's entry into the Sinai, the removal of the U.N. force from Gaza and Sharm ash-Shaykh and the closure of the Tiran Straits.[158] In fact, the Soviet propaganda effort only added to their apprehensions. The Jews were glued to their radios, listening to broadcasts from Israel, the BBC, the Voice of America, or whatever else they could pick up, and talked of nothing else.[159] Soviet Jewish anxiety reached its peak on the first day of the war when Radio Moscow broadcast stories of major Arab victories based on information propagated by the Arabs.[160] Many young people awaited members of the Israeli embassy staff at the entrance to the hall where Yiddish singer Anna Guzik was appearing that evening to try and find out what was really happening. When they heard of Israel's successes, they rushed off to spread the news among their friends without waiting to attend the concert.[161]

On the followng Sabbath, the far larger than usual congregation at the Choral Synagogue was astir with exictement. The past week had seen Israel's victory over Egypt and Jordan, including the capture of the Old City of Jerusalem, and, on the previous day the breakthrough to the Golan Heights. On the same day, 10 June, the USSR (and its bloc allies) announced the severance of diplomatic relations with Israel, and within days the Israeli diplomats left the Soviet capital. Until the last moment the embassy received telegrams and phone calls of congratulations and good wishes. As its staff moved off to the airport, and again at the airport itself, they saw Jews waving them farewell.[162]

If the first act of the Soviet Jewish awakening had ended under Stalin, the second terminated with the exit of the Israeli embassy. Yet the story itself showed no sign of coming to an end. On the contrary, however significant a role the Israeli embassy had played since late 1953, when it returned after the first severance of relations, the Jewish movement had developed sufficient momentum to continue the struggle independently, even after the reassuring Israeli presence inside the Soviet Union had been banished.

# Conclusion

The story of the struggle for Soviet Jewish emigration in the years between the establishment of the State of Israel and the June 1967 Six Day War not only sheds light on crucial aspects of Soviet domestic and foreign policy. It also elucidates the peculiar plight of Soviet Jewry, the solidarity of the Jewish people the world over and the Jews' role as a weathervane for general humanitarian values.

Perhaps the first lesson to be drawn from the trends and developments that I have sought to portray and analyze in this work is that the fate of Soviet Jewry is inextricably tied up with events in the Soviet socio-political scene. Thus, to understand the fluctuations in their situation it is essential to bear in mind the needs, aspirations and constraints under which the regime, or leadership, is operating at any given moment. This holds for all periods of Soviet history both prior to the years covered in this study and subsequent to them, down to and including that of Gorbachev's *perestroika*.

Indeed, Soviet Jewish national consciousness was aroused and strengthened by developments on three different planes: (1) the general tendency to emphasize national motifs among the USSR's many ethnic groupings, which resulted from forces as wide-ranging as a general disappointment with Marxist-Leninist theories and dogmas and their application by the Communist Party of the Soviet Union – their sole interpreter in the USSR – and a latent nationalism among both the intelligentsia and the masses of many of these groupings; (2) Jewish developments, such as the Holocaust, which highlighted the tragic result of a long and arduous diaspora existence for all Jews, whether assimilationists or ghetto-dwellers, and the birth of a Jewish state in the Jews' traditional homeland – the antithesis of the Holocaust catastrophe – which beckoned, as it were, on or just beyond the horizon; and (3) the inherent contradiction in the Soviet Union's policy toward its Jews, i.e. the theory of Jewish assimilation, on the one hand, and the practice of antisemitism and discrimination, which prevented most Jews from assimilating even if they so desired, on the other hand.

Our story has shown how the struggle of Soviet Jews to leave the USSR was the inevitable outcome of an awakened national consciousness under conditions that allowed them no national existence within the Soviet Union. Thus, although from time to time certain Jewish groups or individuals believed they could give expression to their national inclinations within the Soviet body politic, especially during the years of de-Stalinization, the illusory nature of such hopes soon showed that emigration to Israel was the only real outlet for Jewish national expression. Although, in the period under discussion, the number of exit visas granted was very small, those who applied to leave were far more numerous, those who contemplated leaving widely thought to comprise up to one-third or even one-half of the entire Soviet Jewish population. Therefore, while the actual struggle to leave the USSR in this period was conducted by only a few thousand, its implications for Soviet Jewry were much broader.

In our period this national enthusiasm and the struggle to leave focused on Israel. For, had the struggle been intended merely as an escape from antisemitism, those unable to assimilate inside the USSR might have been expected to try and leave the Soviet Union for Western countries where they could hope to assimilate successfully. But, since the struggle was designed to find a solution for those who wished to live as Jews, their intensified Jewish awareness drove them to the state where they would automatically become part of a Jewish society. Thus, although it is true that Soviet Jews' national feelings resulted from a mixture of repelling and attracting forces, it would be misleading to ignore their positive motivations, what many of the movement's activists have called the Jewish spark within each individual Jew.

Despite all its drawbacks and problems, which were constantly being emphasized – and exaggerated – in the Soviet media, Israel exercised a fascination for both older Jews who still remembered the Zionist activities of their youth, and younger ones who wanted to participate in the construction of a new society and state. This aspiration was no doubt nurtured by the regime's blatant failure to create the new Soviet nation and society on whose values and virtues they had been brought up since earliest childhood. Therefore, when the USSR began allowing ethnic groupings such as the Poles, Germans, Greeks and Spaniards to repatriate to their national homelands in the post-Stalin period, it seemed logical and realistic for the Jews to strive for their repatriation to their historic homeland.

While at no stage in our period did the Soviet authorities recognize *de jure* the right of Jewish repatriation to Israel, they did allow some Jews to reunite with their families in the new Jewish state and, to some extent, in other countries as well. At first those permitted to leave were almost all elderly people, whose services were no longer required by Soviet society and whose professional and military contribution to Israel would be minimal. (This had significance, among others, vis-à-vis the USSR's Arab allies, who were very sensitive to the likely effects on Israel's military and technological potential of a large-scale Soviet Jewish emigration.) Yet by the end of our period, some younger people as well were being allowed to leave for Israel under the same program, which encouraged others to take steps to prepare themselves for emigration and even to submit applications for exit permits.

While the ordeals and unpleasantnesses suffered by those who registered to leave deterred most Jews from applying, many Jews throughout the country engaged in other "nationalist" activities, which often ended in their arrest and imprisonment. Thus, even after the "black years" of 1948–53, when many thousands of Jews had been arrested and sentenced to long prison terms for "nationalism" and similar "anti-Soviet" activity, Jews were arrested for learning or teaching Hebrew, for receiving Israeli newspapers, Hebrew dictionaries, Jewish calendars and similar materials from the Israeli embassy in Moscow or from tourists or for listening to Israeli broadcasts.

Even though the actual emigration movement was of minor dimensions in this period, and it is therefore extremely difficult to gauge the interrelationship between the pressures applied and the concessions made, there were numerous indications that the Kremlin was reacting to recurrent demonstrations of Soviet Jewish national feeling. There is even reason to believe that, already in the mid-sixties, some Soviet leaders were advocating allowing the departure of Jews who wanted to leave on the basis that not only were they a "disloyal" element, according to the Soviet conception, but also because they were fomenting activity among people of other nationalities, as well as among other Jews. At the same time, since the possibilities and opportunities for expressing their inclinations within the Soviet Union were strictly limited, Soviet Jews were interested in receiving external support for their struggle in the belief that the Kremlin would be more receptive to Western pressures on their behalf.

Although the movement on behalf of Soviet Jewry in the West did not take place in meaningful dimensions until the early to mid-1960s, the first important move in this direction had been taken in reaction to the Doctors' Plot of January 1953. The government of Israel entered the fray early that year by spearheading the mobilization of Jewish and non-Jewish support in the West. Moreover, from the renewal of relations in summer 1953 until the second severance of relations in June 1967, the Israeli legation in the Soviet capital or embassy (as it became in August 1954) provided both moral and material support to Soviet Jews. It became a symbol of major significance by its very existence and the appearance of its personnel at synagogues and Jewish concerts in the major Jewish centers throughout the country. At the same time, the embassy and its personnel played a major role in educating local Jews about Israel and Jewish culture by distributing printed materials that were unobtainable elsewhere. This dissemination of factual material about Israel was in no way different from the activity of other foreign embassies in Moscow – or from that of Soviet embassies in several Western capitals – and every precaution was taken to ensure that the materials in question contained no anti-Soviet allegations. Nevertheless, the Soviet authorities accused the Israeli diplomats who took part in their dissemination of anti-Soviet activity and interference in the USSR's domestic affairs and declared several of them *persona non grata* between 1955 and 1966.

While the Israeli embassy slowed down the pace of its activities from time to time, on the whole it was undeterred by the stringencies under which it operated. For the Israelis were convinced not only of the importance of their task but also of the justification of their behavior from the point of generally accepted norms of diplomatic conduct. In this context, it should be pointed out that, in the wake of World War II, the Jewish people as a whole developed an extra sensitivity to the issue of intercession on behalf of persecuted Jewish communities. Thus, it is in the light of the West's refusal to intercede on behalf of German Jewry in the 1930s, even though it did not deny the threat implicit in Nazi policy toward the Jews, that the Israeli and Western Jewish position vis-à-vis the Soviet Jewish situation in the 1950s and 1960s must be seen.

In its efforts to mobilize Jewish and non-Jewish organizations, individuals and public opinion in the West, the Israeli government was careful to stress the humanitarian nature of its activity on behalf of Soviet Jews. Whether emphasis was on granting the Jews inside the USSR the same cultural and religious rights that were enjoyed by other national minorities, and immunity as individuals from discriminatory measures by the Soviet authorities, or on emigration within the framework of family reunification, the Israelis always strove to clarify that they had no interest in quarrelling with the Soviet regime or entering the cold war. So intent was the Israeli government on severing the Soviet Jewish question from political issues that it remained in the background and did not attempt to challenge Moscow publicly on the issue until the early to mid-1960s.

Although many of those who took up the cudgels on behalf of the Soviet Jewry became interested through other channels, it was the Israelis who provided virtually everyone engaged in the struggle with detailed and updated information on the day-by-day situation of Jews in the USSR. Thus, it was Israel's guiding hand and persistent efforts in cultivating prominent figures and institutions throughout Western Europe, Latin America, Canada, Australia and, above all, the United States, that made the struggle an organized and meaningful one.

Motivated, among others, by the traditional precepts of mutual responsibility among Jews, Jewish leaders, organizations and communities throughout the free world joined the campaign on behalf of Soviet Jewry on a large scale. By the mid-1960s Soviet Jewry had become an issue at the U.N., the U.S. Congress and a number of other parliaments, international political assemblies and associations. It was the focus of attention at professional and intellectual conferences. And it was even brought up in interchanges between Western communist parties and the CPSU, as well as between Western leaders and their Soviet counterparts. The mid-1960s also saw popular demonstrations of support for the struggle that drew thousands in New York and other American cities, as well as the picketing of Soviet embassies and the systematic and ubiquitous harassment of Soviet leaders and lesser officials and representatives.

Although many of those involved in the struggle, particularly those on the left of the political spectrum, began by centering their efforts on improving the lot of Soviet Jews inside the Soviet Union rather than on emigration, by the mid-1960s it was becoming clear to them – as to the Jews inside the USSR – that the Jews had no future in that country even when the regime seemed to be liberalizing. By the end of our period, emigration was an important slogan in the struggle on behalf of Soviet Jewish rights and for some, the central one.

The struggle of the outside world on behalf of Soviet Jewry was being brought into the Soviet Union itself through broadcasts in Hebrew, Yiddish and, above all, Russian, as well as through tourists and delegations from Israel and the West. This demonstration of

Jewish solidarity gave the Soviet Jews the strength and succor to carry on what seemed like an unequal struggle between 2 to 3 million individual Jews – or those among them who dared to challenge the regime without the benefit of any central organization – and the vastly powerful authorities. Indeed, our story, or that part of it with which this volume deals, ends with a great demonstration of solidarity on the part of Soviet Jewry with the Jewish world outside, as personified by the State of Israel. For the concern for the future of Israel that pervaded Soviet Jewry on the eve of the June 1967 war and during the six days that it lasted – when the Jewish state was threatened by Arab armies equipped with sophisticated Soviet weaponry and trained by Soviet military personnel – could not help but bring home to large numbers of the latter where their hearts really lay. While the Six Day War did not give birth to the struggle for *aliya* from the USSR, it did bring that struggle into a new phase, which it is hoped will be the theme of a future volume. It is surely one of the ironies of history that, just as Soviet support for the establishment of the Jewish state in 1948 encouraged the Jews of that country to express their identification with Israel, only twenty years later it was Soviet support of the threat to Israel's continued existence that brought a new generation of Jews to appreciate the need to exchange the Soviet motherland for the Jewish national home. Although there was no longer an Israeli embassy in Moscow, perhaps even because there were no longer official ties between the two countries and Soviet Jews were thrown back on their own resources, their struggle for *aliya* now became more organized, more vociferous and more desperate.

# Notes



### Introduction

1 In the pre-World War II years there had also been Jews who contemplated leaving the USSR, particularly in order to go to Palestine, although large numbers of Jews identified at least at first with the Bolshevik Revolution and the socialist society it sought to construct; yet this was a totally different period and so not one that I shall touch upon here.
2 There seems to be no way of making any reliable estimate of how many people were involved in the Soviet Jewish national movement in the period in question, but several thousand appear to have been involved in some form of Jewish national activity during these years. This number does not even include the great majority of actual emigrants, mostly elderly people seeking to join relatives in Israel.
3 Saturday was until the early 1960s a working day in the USSR.
4 I refrain from using the word Zionist, both because of its pejorative connotations in Soviet jargon and because even those Jews who were conceptually oriented towards the State of Israel could not, of course, be members of any Zionist organization.

### 1 The euphoria of 1948

1 Stalin made his preference for the Great Russians manifest in his famous victory toast of May 1945.
2 A number of minority groupings had been exiled to Siberia, Kazakhstan and Central Asia on charges of collaborating with the German invader and betraying the mother country; see, e.g., Conquest, *The Nation Killers*; Nekrich, *The Punished Peoples*.
3 This statement is based on largely circumstantial evidence for which there is as yet no final research. The accepted estimate is 500,000 Jews in the Soviet armed forces and 200,000 killed; see Shapiro, *Evrei – geroi Sovetskogo Soiuza*, Foreword.
4 The 1939 census had given 3,020,000 Jews, while some 1.9 million inhabited the areas incorporated into Soviet territory in 1939–40, and another 250,000 or so had fled to the Soviet Union from Poland in the wake

of the German invasion of that country. I am grateful for these statistics to Prof. Mordechai Altshuler of the Hebrew University of Jerusalem.

5 Popular antisemitism had been part of the "cultural" tradition of many of the annexed areas and of the entire Ukraine. It was used extensively by the Nazis in occupied areas and in Nazi propaganda to the whole Soviet population in which the Soviet regime was portrayed as inspired and run by Jews.

6 See West, *Struggles*, pp. 33–34; Bernard Turner, "Meyn bagegenish mit Dovid Bergelson un Itzik Fefer in sovetish arbet-lager Bratsk," *Di goldene keyt* (Yid.), 25 (1956), pp. 33–37; and Milovan Djilas in *Borba*, 14 Dec. 1952.

7 The testimony of Soviet Jewish emigrants is crucial and, I believe, conclusive with regard to the growth of Jewish consciousness among Soviet Jews as a result of the war. One witness who experienced life in a wartime ghetto during his early teens has written:

> The war showed that we were hated not only by the Germans but also by the local population. The latter took an active part in the murder of Jews. And now [at the end of the war] they continued to hate us . . . This was the feeling of the youth that survived in the ghetto and of those who returned from evacuation. It was necessary to do something so that this would not happen again. How was this to be accomplished? Only in the [Jews'] historic homeland. After the war we were a different youth. All my contemporaries will confirm this . . . We had no right to forget what we had seen. – Interview with Efraim Volf.

"The war, the destruction of my people . . . the upsurge of antisemitism in the Soviet rear," wrote a second source, "strengthened my Zionist convictions and convinced me that the sole alternative to the annihilation of the Jewish people was the establishment of a Jewish state with a strong army" – memoirs of Gitis Vaismel, PZO Archives. Yet a third source, a senior officer in the Soviet armed forces who came from Minsk, capital of the Belorussian SSR, wrote that his family, who were all killed in the war, could have been saved had it not been for the local authorities – memoirs of Naum Alshanskii, PZO Archives; and cf. interviews with Yosef Khorol of Odessa, Meir Gelfond and Vladimir Levitin.

8 The impact of this contact has not yet been systematically examined, but from the many interviews held with Jews who have since emigrated and from the considerable literature that exists, published and other, there seems little doubt that the Jews of the Western territories had considerable influence on the Jewish national awakening of the postwar period.

9 The first agreements on the exchange of nationals were between the Polish Committee of National Liberation (the first government of the new Polish regime, set up in July 1944) and the governments of the Ukrainian and Belorussian SSRs (9 Sept. 1944) and the Lithuanian SSR (22 Sept. 1944). A repatriation agreement was signed between the Soviet and Polish governments on 6 July 1945.

Repatriation under these agreements officially ended in 1946: almost 250,000 Polish citizens were repatriated in 1945–46. However, between 7,000 and 8,000 were repatriated in 1947 and in 1948 and some 2,600 as late as 1949 – Kersten, *Repatriacija*, p. 229. For further discussion of this repatriation, see Litvak, *Plitim yehudim mipolin*: Ro'i, *Decision Making*, pp. 25–33.

10 This coincided with reports that the communist authorities in Eastern Europe were preventing the departure of Jews to the DP camps in the Western occupation zones of Germany and Austria – e.g., *JC*, 2 May 1947. A British Foreign Office spokesman even pointed out that the USSR and some East European countries "have proved helpful in our efforts to halt illegal immigration [to Palestine] at its source" – *Palestine Post*, 30 Sept. 1947.

11 Hirsh Smolar told the author that he heard from Itzik Fefer, Yiddish writer and member of the Jewish Anti-Fascist Committee (JAFC) presidium, who had been told by no less an authority than Politburo member Lazar Kaganovich, that Stalin himself insisted that Jews be included in the repatriation agreements on the grounds that the Polish Jews had caused all the problems at the Soviet rear during the war, while Gomulka opposed this for fear that the Jews' return might jeopardize the stability of the new regime – interview with Hirsh Smolar. Smolar also said that Kaganovich had maintained contact with the JAFC during the war, when his "pintele Yid" (or Jewishness) was aroused and that the idea of settling Jews returning from the Urals or Central Asia in the Crimea had emanated with Kaganovich – oral reminiscences of H. Smolar at the seventh annual meeting of the Israeli Association of Slavic and East European Studies, Tel Aviv University, 31 May 1984.

12 The constant influx of Polish Jewish refugees into zones where conditions were already difficult could be expected to exacerbate economic hardship and social and ethnic tensions.

13 The U.S. State Department was reportedly informed from Germany that Zionist emigration from Poland to the U.S. zone was Moscow-inspired in the hope that communist agitators would infiltrate into the British zone and exert pressure for immigration to Palestine – *Palestine Post*, 30 Sept. 1947.

   In fact, all three versions contain some truth, which accounts for some of the contradictions that characterized Soviet policy on Jewish emigration from Eastern Europe as a whole and Poland in particular – see Ro'i, *Decision Making*, pp. 25–33. The large numbers of Jews who repatriated from the USSR to Poland in 1945–46 could well have allowed for a significant number to remain in Poland and become active citizens of the new Polish People's Democracy and others to re-emigrate.

14 Gurevitch, "Escape Route."

15 For the *briha*, see Bauer, *Flight and Rescue*; the full story of the *briha* from the USSR, however, remains to be written. For the story of the *briha* from the Soviet Baltic Republics, see Gurevitch, "Escape Route," pp. 101–19, and interviews with Shlomo Gefen, who operated in Vilnius; Hillel (Ilia) Saidin, who operated in Riga; and Pinhas Sheinerberg, who operated in Lvov. For people in Leningrad and Lvov connected with the *briha* who were arrested in later years, see p. 46. For a meeting with someone who

managed to leave the Donbass area in 1945, see West, *Struggles*, pp. 197–99.

16 West, *Struggles*, pp. 191–96.

17 Interview with Lola Reznikov.

18 *FRUS* 1947, vol. 4, pp. 584–85.

19 Alliluyeva, *Letters*, pp. 193 and 196; *Khrushchev Remembers*, pp. 260–64. Some Jews – who had, of course, no direct evidence of Stalin's personal sentiments – saw evidence of a new chauvinist orientation that implied antisemitism in his praise of the Great Russian people at the end of the war – interview with David Khavkin, February 1974.

20 Elbridge Durbrow to Secretary of State George Marshall, 2 Dec. 1947, *FRUS* 1947, vol. 2, pp. 628–30. For Birobidzhan, see p. 22.

21 For the activities of these institutions, see Ro'i, *Decision Making*, ch. 7.

22 Interview with Vladimir Levitin.

23 Interview with Yosef Urman. In addition to Zvi Pregerzon (see n. 53), Urman met in the Lenin Library with a number of Zionists from prewar Poland and Bessarabia. For the dispatch of materials from Palestine to the USSR during the war, see Ro'i, "Soviet Policy in the Middle East."

24 Interviews with Meir Gelfond and Efraim Volf.

25 Interview with Vladimir Levitin. The BBC began broadcasting to the Soviet Union in 1946 and quickly attracted large numbers of listeners from all over the country – Asa Briggs, *The BBC* (Oxford: Oxford University Press, 1985), pp. 225–6 and 313. For poetry by Aliger and its importance for our story, see Averbukh, "Jewish Samizdat at the End of the Forties."

26 For the first Moscow group, see Pregerzon, *Yoman hazikhronot*, pp. 9–10 and 34–35, and unpublished manuscript of Yitzhak Kahanov, written in 1976 after his emigration to Israel, which his daughter, Elima Kahanov-Oliferenko, kindly showed the author; for the second group, see interview with Gitta Landman.

27 Interview with Yosef Urman.

28 West, *Struggles*, p. 37.

29 The Voice of America (VOA) began broadcasting to the Soviet Union in early 1947; for these broadcasts and their impact in the early postwar years, see Inkeles, *Social Change*, chs. 17 and 18. Although there were still no broadcasts from Palestine directed to the USSR, Palestinian radio stations could be picked up in at least the southern parts of the country. In April 1947, a Jew from Odessa wrote to a relative in Palestine: "we listen every evening to all that happens in Palestine" – Haim Kheifets to Yisrael Landres, 14 Apr. 1947. (Kheifets' correspondence with relatives in Israel was kindly shown the author by his daughter, Mrs. Sabina Krakovsky.) Throughout 1948, Kheifets continued to refer to information on Palestine which he heard over the air in letters to his family in that country, especially in his letter of 3 Apr. 1948.

30 The downgrading of Soviet Jewish war heroes and ignoring or concealing of their Jewish origin was already evident in spring 1945 – Ro'i, *Decision Making*, p. 301.

31 Interview with Meir Gelfond.

32 Ibid.

33 For the campaigns against Jewish nationalism and its alter ego, cosmopolitanism, see Ro'i, *Decision Making*, ch. 7, and Pinkus, *Soviet Government*, ch. 4.

34 For a discussion of the Soviet nationalities policy as a whole and the attitude toward the Jews within its framework, see Jacob Miller, "Soviet Theory on the Jews," in Kochan, *Jews in Soviet Russia*, pp. 44–61; for the internal passports recording the nationality of every Soviet citizen over the age of sixteen, see William Korey, "The Legal Position of Soviet Jewry: A Historical Enquiry," ibid., pp. 78–79, and Alec Nove and J. A. Newth, "The Jewish Population: Demographic Trends and Occupational Patterns," ibid., pp. 126–29.

35 See Ro'i, *Decision Making*, ch. 7, especially pp. 315–16; for the situation within the Soviet central leadership at this time, see McCagg, *Stalin Embattled*.

36 GA OR, 1st Special Session, 1st Committee, 51st Meeting, 8 May 1947.

37 For the role of Birobidzhan in this period, see Ro'i, *Decision Making*, ch. 7; *JC*, 18 July and 1 Aug. 1947 and 3 Sept. 1948; and *Folks-shtime*, 8 and 22 Oct. and 11 Nov. 1948.

38 One of these, a lecturer in Alma Ata of Polish origin, was sentenced to six years' imprisonment for preaching Zionism after having told his students, in the wake of Gromyko's appearance at the U.N., that he considered that this signified Soviet acceptance of the need for a Jewish state in Palestine. Another, Iakov Mintsberg of Leningrad, was sentenced to twenty years for Zionism (he was released in 1954). Also arrested, in December 1947, were the physicist Lev Tumerman of the Bauman Physics Institute in Moscow, attached to the USSR Academy of Sciences, and his wife, Lidiia Shatunovskaia. Among the charges brought against the Tumermans was the desire to go to Palestine (although they had taken no steps to implement this desire beyond discussing the possibility in their own circle of friends). They were also accused of receiving secret information from the widow of Pavel Alliluev, with whom Mrs. Tumerman was friendly, and passing it on to Mikhoels, director of the Jewish State Theater and chairman of the JAFC, who in turn allegedly transmitted it to the Americans – Shatunovskaia, *Zhizn v kremle*, and interview with Lev Tumerman.

39 S. Friedman to M. Shertok, 30 Sept. 1948, *Foreign Policy of Israel*, vol. 1, pp. 658–59. According to Marxism-Leninism Jews would naturally and voluntarily assimilate in a society without antisemitism.

40 Author's interview with a former Israeli embassy staff member who talked with a number of erstwhile Prisoners of Zion.

41 For every Jew who threw caution to the winds, there were many who remained afraid and refrained from discussing events in Palestine openly – cf. Avigdor Lezerovich to the author, 19 Feb. 1981.

42 E.g., *Eynikeyt*, 11 and 13 Dec. 1947, 15, 17 and 19 June, 10, 13, 20 and 31 July and 6 Oct. 1948.

43 *Folks-shtime*, 10 Jan. 1948. Hanukka commemorates the rededication of the

Second Temple after the Maccabees defeated the Greek army of Antiochus Epiphanes.

44 *New Times*, 1 Jan. 1948; *Kol Ha'am*, 29 Jan. 1948; R. Moscow in Yiddish for North America, 7 Jan. 1948/SWB I, 12 Jan. 1948; and interview with Yisrael Pinsky. Mikhoels was referring to *Masa'ot Binyamin hashelishi*, which has appeared in English as *The Travels and Adventures of Benjamin the Third* (New York: Schocken, 1968). Lidiia Tumerman-Shatunovskaia has recalled her meeting with Mikhoels on 27 December 1947, at which he expressed concern that the press reports of his recent speech (presumably at the Mendele commemoration) had not included his references to the forthcoming establishment of the Jewish state and his welcoming of the event. She recalls him saying to her: "This is the beginning of the end" – Shatunovskaia, *Zhizn v kremle*, pp. 272–73. Grisha Levinzon, who worked at the Yiddish State Theater, told his childhood friend Haim Rabinovich, who came to congratulate him on the establishment of the State of Israel, that after the partition resolution was passed Mikhoels had taken particular delight in anticipating the presence of an official representative of the Jewish state in Moscow – Haim Rabinovich, unpublished reminiscences, "Otchii dom" (My father's home; Rus.), p. 38, CRDEEJ.

45 The Council was set up during the war to be responsible for liaison with and supervision of all religious creeds other than the Russian Orthodox Church, to fulfil the same functions with which a separate council had been formed.

46 Israeli diplomats who arrived in Moscow the following September found the banners still hanging on the synagogue walls. Significantly, they had been removed by the time of the Jewish New Year some three weeks later – Namir, *Shlihut bemoskva*, pp. 48–49.

47 In May 1948 a Jew came from the provinces to meet his brother who had just been freed from eleven years' imprisonment. They heard of the establishment of the state as they sat in the railway station. Not knowing how to celebrate, they went to the Choral Synagogue, where they found a few elderly Jews studying: they bought food and drink and celebrated with a toast, a *lehaim*, and Jewish melodies. The brothers saw the banner on the eastern wall near the Ark – Rozin, *Mayn veg aheym*, pp. 328–30.

For my reconstruction of both the spontaneous gathering on the Sunday after the state was established and the special service of July 24, I am indebted in particular to the unpublished reminiscences of Yitzhak Kahanov, Mikhlin, *Hagahelet*, pp. 229–30, and the accounts of two eyewitnesses: Eliahu Hoberman – my interview with him and his unpublished memoirs, chapter entitled "Di letzte tekufa" (The last period; Yid.), pp. 28 and 33–34; and Haim Rabinovich, "Otchii dom," pp. 39–41. Rabinovich consistently calls the service a meeting or rally, which was probably its significance for most participants. Rabinovich, an electrical engineer by profession, set up the microphones and put up the banners. After the message to Weizmann was read out, he cried from the gallery "The people of Israel lives!" He used the same slogan when he greeted Golda Meyerson as she made her way from the gallery to introduce herself to Rabbi Shlifer on her first Sabbath in the synagogue. Mrs. Meir later recalled: "When I was in the Moscow synagogue on the New Year, a Jew suddenly cried out: 'The people of Israel lives!' People hushed him, but he repeated the cry" – *Ma'ariv*, 26 June 1972. Apart from the discrepancy regarding the exact occasion, the two stories tally.

48 Interview with Lola Reznikov.

49 Testimony of Yosef Berger-Barzilai, who met Rabbi Feldman in a prison camp, in a lecture at Bar Ilan University, Ramat Gan – *Hatsofe*, 6 June 1963.

50 Interview with Efraim Volf.

51 *JC*, 27 Apr. 1979.

52 Interview with Feige Hofstein, the writer's widow.

53 Interviews with Yosef Urman and Lola Reznikov. Urman, a central figure in the group at the armed forces foreign language school, received the text of the poem from Pregerzon at the Hebrew section of the Lenin Library.

54 West, *Struggles*, p. 43; and interview with Rabbi Mordekhai Hanzin. For the account of a Prisoner of Zion who was told about the establishment of the state by his interrogator in Moscow's Lubianka see A[vraham] Kaufman, "How I learned of the establishment of the State of Israel," *Yalkut magen* (Heb.), 21 (June–August 1961), pp. 42–43.

55 For the Soviet attitude to Israel's War of Independence and military aid to the *yishuv*, see Ro'i, *Decision Making*, ch. 4; also interview with Vitalii Svechinskii.

56 West, *Struggles*, pp. 41–42. The letters of Haim Kheifets, too, were an admixture of concern and elation. Among others, he referred to 1948 as the year of "rebirth and redemption" – H. Kheifets to relatives [unspecified], 3 Apr. and 16 May 1948.

57 *Hamashkif*, 9 Nov. 1948.

58 Azbel, *Autobiography of a Jew*, pp. 60–61.

59 Interview with Benjamin Fein.

60 West, *Struggles*, p. 42.

61 Interview with Meir Gelfond.

62 Tsitsuashvili, "We Wanted to Produce a Large Aliya," pp. 77–78.

63 Interview with Yosef Urman.

64 Interview with Gitta Landman.

65 Interviews with David Levinzon and David Dar.

66 *JC*, 3 Sept. 1948; and testimony of Yehoshua Efman, PZO Archives.

67 *Haboker*, 3 Mar. 1949, according to the testimony of a Jewish member of a Czechoslovak military delegation who attended the trial in Kuibyshev. This officer thought the trial was conducted in Kuibyshev because it is far away from Moscow. (*Haboker* gives the name of the orientalist as Slutskii, but this is almost certainly erroneous.)

68 Ro'i, *Decision Making*, pp. 188 and 200–02; testimony of Gitis Vaismel, PZO Archives – Vaismel sent his request to Peretz Markish at the JAFC; and interview with Esther Lomovskaia, whose husband, Yosef Szmerler, also sent his letter to the JAFC – from Novosibirsk. On his way from the Kiev prison to camp in Vorkuta in 1950, Meir Gelfond passed through Moscow and Gorkii. In the Gorkii prison he met Eduard Sasonkin, formerly

secretary of the editorial board of *Eynikeyt*, who told him that Itzik Fefer asked the party authorities how to deal with the requests when they first appeared and was told to make a list, which duly fell into the hands of the MVD, the Ministry of the Interior, when Fefer and his colleagues were arrested and the JAFC closed down – interview with Meir Gelfond. Sasonkin also told Gelfond of a JAFC reception to have been held in honor of Mrs. Meyerson, which does not seem to have taken place, for Mrs. Meir told the author that she never met any JAFC functionaries – interview with Golda Meir. It should be borne in mind here that the first arrests of JAFC presidium members were made in September 1948, very shortly after the Israeli diplomatic mission arrived in Moscow; David Hofshteyn, for instance, was arrested on 16 September – interview with Feige Hofstein.

69 Hoberman, "Di letzte tekufa" (unpublished memoirs).

70 *JC*, 27 Apr. 1979.

71 Testimony of Haim Gusman, PZO Archives.

72 Interviews with Yisrael Pinsky, Eliahu and Dvora Olstein and David Bitsels; and Maccabee, *Nitsnuts holef batsel*, pp. 97–99.

73 Interviews with Leonid Rutshtain, now Arye Rotem, and David Khavkin.

74 Interviews with Meir Gelfond, Efraim Volf and Lola Reznikov, then Faivilis, who wrote to Ehrenburg asking to be listed among the volunteers seeking to fight in Palestine. Yitzak Kahanov recalls in his reminiscences (p. 19) how his fifteen-year-old daughter, with whom he had never even spoken in Yiddish, let along discussed politics, approached him one day together with a girl friend from Leningrad, to ask how they could get to Israel to take part in the war.

75 Interview with Yaacov Liash.

76 Ben-Horin, *Ma koreh sham*, p. 57.

77 Interview with Efraim Volf. In Israel there were also people who believed that the Kremlin's support for the Jewish state implied a favorable regime, and that what seemed to be its eventual change of policy resulted from Soviet disappointment at Israel's domestic and foreign policies. For the first signs of dissonance and its causes, see Ro'i, *Decision Making*, pp. 198–217, passim, and pp. 273–75.

78 Another source credits Plotkin with also having initiated and organized the special service in Moscow's Choral Synagogue – Z. Plotkin to Haim Shalom Ben-Avram; and reminiscences of Yitzhak Kahanov (pp. 20–24), whom Plotkin told he had organized the service and used the telephone directory to inform Moscow's Jews about it. Plotkin, Pregerzon and Kahanov also wrote to David Ben Gurion in January 1948 expressing their appreciation of his contribution to the redemption of the Jewish people and conveying the good wishes of Soviet Jewry to the *yishuv* – ibid., pp. 1–2 and 15–16.

79 *JC*, 29 Oct. 1948; and interviews with Mikhail Margulis and Vitalii Svechinskii. The third member of the group was Roman Brakman. The three had discussed their plans with some friends with whom they learned some elementary information about Jewish and Zionist history from the Russian-language Jewish Encyclopedia and Simon Dubnow's *History of the Jews*.

80 *JC*, 27 Apr. 1979, and interview with Haim Shperber.

81 Ro'i, *Decision Making*, p. 202.

82 Testimony of Shmuel Ziser, PZO Archives.

83 *Haaretz*, 18 Nov. 1948.

84 Avigdor Lezerovich to Haim Naor, [July] and 5 Sept. 1948, *Behinot*, 8–9 (1979), pp. 295–96. As early as 24 April, Lezerovich had asked whether a representative of the Jewish state was already in Moscow, ibid. Lezerovich's letters were full of allusions to his dream of *aliya*. For the elation with which Jews awaited Mrs. Meyerson, see also interview with David Levinzon. For the anticipation of Mikhoels, who was killed four months before Israel's establishment, of the arrival of official representatives of the Jewish state, see n. 44.

85 *JC*, 29 Oct. 1948.

86 Testimony of Yitzhak Hayit at a symposium on Soviet Jewry, Efal (Israel), 26 Dec. 1984.

87 Interview with Mikhail Margulis.

88 Testimony of Yehoshua Efman, PZO Archives.

89 Interview with Yosef Khorol; see also n. 78.

90 Testimony of Meir Kanevsky, Yad Vashem Archives, Givatayim 3759. The other two synagogues were at Marina Roshcha and Cherkizovo.

91 Interview with Lev Zaltsman.

92 Interview with David Khavkin.

93 Interview with Yosef Neiman.

94 Interview with Meir Gelfond. For the 1948 High Holy Days at the Moscow Synagogue, see Meir, *My Life*, ch. 9; Namir, *Shlihut bemoskva*, pp. 64–67; and Ro'i, *Decision Making*, pp. 193–95.

95 See Ro'i, *Decision Making*, p. 299.

96 A copy of the American official's report was given to the British embassy in Moscow and sent to the Foreign Office on 17 Sept. 1948 – PRO F0371/71645.

97 For the importance of word of mouth in passing on information in the Soviet context, see Thomas Remington, "The Mass Media and Public Communication in the USSR," *The Journal of Politics*, XLIII (1981), pp. 803–17.

98 Interview with Moshe Sneh.

99 Interview with David Levinzon. Zhemchuzhina was in fact sent into exile to Kazakhstan in spring 1949, from which she returned after Stalin's death in 1953.

100 Interview with David Khavkin.

101 E.g., *JP*, 14 June 1954.

102 Several emigrants remember these stories distinctly and believed (and perhaps still believe) in their veracity; see, for example, Lev Zaltsman who "recalls" that fifty-six people – doctors, engineers, professors, etc. – gave Golda a list of Jews who wished to go to Israel, which she in turn handed to Zhemchuzhina and which eventually reached Stalin. The latter's angry reaction ("I didn't know that there were so many enemies under my very nose") was said to have started the anti-cosmopolitan campaign – interview with L. Zaltsman. In what must be seen as an

interesting, and typical, footnote to these stories, a Soviet Jewish emigrant, Lev Navrozov, wrote in *Commentary* (vol. 58, no. 2, August 1974) that upon Stalin's request, Mrs. Meyerson had handed him a list of Jews who would be prepared to participate in the Israeli War of Independence, and that the Jews on the list were arrested and put in camps. In reply to Mrs. Meir's indignant retort to this "serious and shocking allegation" – addressed to *Commentary* editor Norman Podhoretz and published in April 1975 – Navrozov wrote: "Many lists were drawn up in 1948 of Jews who wanted to fight in Israel . . . quite officially and were sometimes even displayed publicly." (The author has heard of no such instances, which does not, however, necessarily disprove the point.) Navrozov agreed that Stalin "knew or could have known all the names on those lists and would have destroyed those listed irrespective of who handed over what to whom, how and when." Navrozov also said he had been "an eyewitness to the events of 1948" and had interviewed "other, even closer eyewitnesses," including an Israeli official who had been on the Israeli legation staff in 1948 and an Israeli editor who discussed these events with Mrs. Meir. Navrozov's reply appeared in the same issue of *Commentary* as Mrs. Meir's letter.

103 This is based on a memorandum composed by the Israeli Foreign Ministry Research Department several years later – S. Leibowitz to the East European Department, Israeli Foreign Ministry, 13 July 1955, ISA/FM/2492/17. I have found nothing on this from the period itself. All the reports from late 1948 to early 1949 relate to discussions of individual cases. Toward the end of 1948 negotiations were said to be under way between the Israeli government and the Soviet legation in Tel Aviv for relatives of Israeli citizens to emigrate (*Palestine Post*, 13 Dec. 1948) but this appears to refer to intercessions on behalf of a very few individuals.

104 I have not been able to discover how many names were on the original list and what its fate was. It is, however, clear from the correspondence between the legation and the Israeli Foreign Ministry (ISA/FM/2502/8), which sent in all eleven such lists to Moscow, that most of them were never passed on to the Soviets because of the latter's totally negative attitude to approaches regarding exit permits for Soviet residents. From a letter from the Israeli Ministry of Immigration to the Foreign Ministry East European Department, dated 3 Oct. 1951, it appears that in just over three years of activity, 701 people in all had been requested by their relatives in Israel – ibid.

105 Shertok's notes on his conversation with Vyshinskii, undated, ISA/FM/2502/8; Namir, *Shlihut bemoskva*, pp. 119–20; *Haaretz*, 17 Dec. 1948.

106 *JC*, 8 Oct. 1948.

107 From the protocol of the reception, 18 Aug. 1948, Labor Party Archives, Bet Berl, File 3–31. For the activities of the Israeli legation in Moscow in its first weeks and months, see Ro'i, *Decision Making*, ch. 5.

108 The Israelis used for this the list of addresses which the Jewish Agency for Palestine had received during World War II for the purpose of sending

printed materials to Jews in the USSR – Namir, *Shlihut bemoskva*, pp. 190–210; Ro'i, *Decision Making*, pp. 204–05.
109  Ibid., pp. 296 and 298; also *JC*, 27 Apr. 1949.
110  Interview with Eliezer Golubov.
111  Testimony of Avraham Shtukarevich upon his arrival in Israel in September 1969. An inmate of one of the Gulag camps recalls how a man named Kanson arrived in camp after having been arrested upon leaving the Israeli mission, on charges of not reporting anti-Soviet activity to which he was privy – Fisher, *Parimakher in gulag*, p. 188.
112  Interview with David Dar.
113  *Pravda*, 21 Sept. 1948.
114  *Folks-shtime*, 15 Oct. 1948.
115  *Folks-shtime*, 15 Nov. 1948.
116  Hoberman, "Di letzte tekufa," p. 29 (unpublished memoirs).
117  Kohler to the U.S. Secretary of State, 19 Mar. 1949. *FRUS* 1949, vol. 5, pp. 597–99.

## 2 Jewish consciousness during the "black years"

1  For the *imperium in imperio* which the prisons and camps comprised in this period, see Wollin and Slusser, *The Soviet Secret Police*, ch. 6.
2  In it all the party secretaries and other leading officials in the city and oblast of Leningrad were replaced, as were Gosplan Chairman and Politburo member Nikolai Voznesenskii and Central Committee Secretary Aleksei Kuznetsov – see Ro'i, *Decision Making*, p. 323, and Conquest, *Power and Policy*, pp. 95–96.
3  For the assault upon nationalist expression and tendencies among minority ethnic groupings in this period, see, e.g., Barghoorn, *Soviet Russian Nationalism* and Tillett, *The Great Friendship*. At the same time, it is worth noting that both in the Western Ukraine and in Lithuania nationalist groups were carrying on a sporadic armed struggle against the regime which was finally quashed only in the 1950s, see, e.g., Bilinsky, *The Second Soviet Republic*, ch. 4.
4  Beriia is one of the most controversial figures in Soviet history and is still awaiting a major, serious research study. For his career and policy and for details of leadership personnel changes in Stalin's last years, see Conquest, *Power and Policy*, chs. 4–8. For the Doctors' Plot, see Ro'i, *Decision Making*, pp. 372–77.
5  See Ro'i, *Decision Making*, pp. 312–17. One of the charges brought against the JAFC was that in 1944 its presidium members had suggested the establishment of a Jewish autonomous region in the Crimea, from which the Tatars had been deported, see ch. 1, n. 11.
6  For the anti-cosmopolitan campaign and its connection with the simultaneous onslaught on Jewish nationalism, including the direct and indirect linkage of some of its victims to a Zionist orientation, see Ro'i, *Decision Making*, chs. 7 and 8. Many Soviet Jewish emigrants have insisted that their

experiences during this period were crucial to the development of their national consciousness, e.g., Butman, *Leningrad–Yerushalayim*, pp. 28–36.

7  From an article entitled "The Soviet Union and its Nationalities" written by Kelly for the *Sunday Times*, PRO/FO 371/106509; and D. Kelly to Sir William Strang, 28 Jan. 1953, ibid.

8  Hoberman, "Di letzte tekufa," pp. 38–39 (unpublished memoirs).

9  Ibid., p. 37.

10  In Moscow David Khavkin avidly read the Russian-language Jewish Encyclopedia that he found in his father's library – interview with D. Khavkin. In a Leningrad bookstore, another young man ran across a copy of V. Jabotinsky's *Feuilletons* in the Russian original which he hastened to purchase – Ben-Horin, *Ma koreh sham*, pp. 29–30.

11  Interview with Meir Gelfond. Not a few of the activitists of the 1960s and 1970s had their first encounter with anti-Jewish discrimination in this period. One of these, Viktor Polskii, who completed his studies in nuclear physics in 1952, like all the other Jewish students at his institute (one-quarter of the graduates), was unable to secure employment until after Stalin's death – Kol Yisrael, 25 Feb. 1985.

12  Quoted in *Lamerhav*, 22 Oct. 1951.

13  In Moscow, Roman Brakman was able to hear Kol Zion lagola – interview with Vitalii Svechinskii; in Riazan, too, there were students who listened to Kol Zion lagola in this period – interview with David Khavkin; so did Jews in Odessa (Namir, *Shlihut bemoskva*, p. 212), in Georgia (Salcman, *Vezakhiti lerehabilitatsia*, p. 219), and in Riga (interview with David Yafit).

14  Binyamin Tsukerman, released from camp but still in exile, in Krasnoiarskii krai in Siberia, bought a radio together with friends in 1950 to listen to the Voice of America and the BBC. By 1952 they were also receiving Israel – interview with B. Tsukerman.

15  Hoberman, "Epilogue," p. 9 (unpublished memoirs).

16  Testimony of Meir Kanevsky, February 1974, Yad Vashem Archives, Givatayim, 3759. Another person who seems to have passed on information on the Soviet Jewish situation was Moisei Chernukhin, see ch. 8, n. 76. For the texts of some of the notes the Israelis received, see Namir, *Shlihut bemoskva*, pp. 350–54.

17  A. Levavi to M. Sharett, 12 June 1950 – ISA/FM/2381/10.

18  Three decrees of 16 May 1941, 30 Sept. 1948 and 15 Jan. 1952, put out of bounds to foreigners resident in the Soviet Union all travel beyond a radius of 40 kilometers (25 miles) from the center of Moscow except for a few parts of the European area of the RSFSR and Georgia. The restrictions included all border areas (Central Asia, the Far East, the southern Caucasus), all ports, except Leningrad and Odessa, and most of the Ukraine – Review of internal developments in the Soviet Union, December 1951–February 1952, PRO/FO 371/100818.

19  See, e.g., Namir, *Shlihut bemoskva*, pp. 204–13.

20  This information is based on the author's conversations with crew members of these ships on several occasions. The Israelis, indeed, hoped that Soviet Jews would enjoy the sight of Israeli oranges in their stores and

markets, but the Soviets seem to have destined the oranges for their elite; in April 1952 *New York Times* Moscow correspondent Harrison Salisbury saw "heaps of Israeli oranges" in Moscow's new Sovetskaia Hotel – Salisbury, *Moscow Journal*, p. 251. Yet the organges that reached Odessa in less than good condition were sold there – interview with Sabina Hefets-Krakovsky.

21 *Novoe vremia*, 21 Aug. and 5 Sept. 1951

22 Pregerzon, *Yoman hazikhronot*, pp. 28–29; and interview with Yosef Khorol.

23 Interview with Gitta Landman.

24 Testimony of Meir Kanevskii, February 1974, Yad Vashem Archives, Givatayim, 3754.

25 Testimony of Haim Gusman, PZO Archives; interviews with Eliezer Golubov and Arye Rotem; and introduction by "Y. Nadav" to Seter, *Halo tish'ali*.

26 One of these was Moshe Shekhter, who had approached the Israelis in 1949 shortly after being liberated from a first period of imprisonment – Dov Satat, Israeli Foreign Ministry East European Department, to Israeli legation, Warsaw, 22 Oct. 1956 (ISA/FM/2502/14).

27 Diary of Gedalia Pecherskii, 10 May and 1 Oct. 1951.

28 Interview with Shlomo Gefen.

29 Interviews with Shlomo Gefen, David Yafit and Binyamin Tsukerman.

30 Interview with Ezra Rusinek.

31 Testimony of Leonid Reznikov, PZO Archives, and interview with Reznikov's wife, Lola, then still Faivilis.

32 Interview with Meir Gelfond.

33 Testimony of Shmuel Ziser, PZO Archives.

34 There were such groups in Saratov, Kuibyshev, Kazan, Sverdlovsk and Ulianovsk. Interviews with Grisha Faigin and Haim Shperber, and Yedidya, "The Study of Hebrew."

35 Author's interviews with Moshe Merhav and Sabina Hefets-Krakovsky. The writers and poets were Irme Druker, Nota Luria, Khono Vainerman and Isak Guberman. Those arrested in the group of older Zionists were the fathers of Mrs. Hefets-Krakovsky, Vitalii (Haim) Kheifets, teacher and educationalist, and of Mr. Merhav, Aron (Archik) Merkher, artist; Naum More-Din, chemistry teacher; two other teachers, Kh. L. (Yehezkel) Tashlitskii and a certain Kit; Pisetskii, an actor at the Odessa Yiddish theater until it was closed in 1949; and Sh. Alik, a tailor who before the war had edited the Yiddish newspaper, *Odeser arbeter*.

36 Interview with Yosef Khorol.

37 Interviews with Sabina Hefets-Krakovsky and Yosef Khorol; reminiscences of Haim Kheifets; and testimony of Nahman More-Din, PZO Archives.

38 Chancery (British embassy, Moscow) to Northern Department (British Foreign Office), 19 Feb. 1953, PRO/FO 371/106576.

39 Interview with a former Prisoner of Zion who has asked to remain anonymous.

40 The indictment against him included his application to leave for Israel to fight in its War of Independence – testimony of Gitis Vaismel, PZO Archives.

41 Interview with Efraim Volf.

42 See, e.g., Medvedev, *T. D. Lysenko*, pp. 128–30. Already in the immediate postwar period CPSU Central Committee Secretary Georgii Malenkov had remarked that 80 percent of the letters arriving in the USSR were for Jews – testimony of Hirsh Smolar at the Israel Association of Slavic and East European Studies, 30 May 1984.

43 These were Articles in the 1926 RSFSR Criminal Code which, with amendments, remained in force until replaced on 1 Jan. 1961 by a new criminal code, ratified by the RSFSR Supreme Soviet in the previous October. For the text of these Articles, see *Ugolovnyi kodeks RSFSR* (The Criminal Code of the RSFSR), Moscow: Gosudarstvennoe izdatelstvo iuridicheskoi literatury, 1950, pp. 36–43.

44 Avigdor Lezerovich to the author, 19 Feb. 1981 and *Behinot*, 8–9, 1979. Among those Lezerovich met in the camps were Kiev Yiddish writer Chayim Loytsker and Odessa Yiddish singer Eliezer Kishko.

45 Interview with David Khavkin.

46 Members of his group had been accustomed to gather in his home to hear the broadcasts, since, as we have seen, only a select few had receivers in the Soviet Union at this time – reminiscences of Haim Gusman, PZO Archives; and interview with Eliezer Golubov.

47 Diary of Gedalia Pecherskii, 22 July 1951.

48 Interview with a former Prisoner of Zion who has asked to remain anonymous.

49 See above, p. 26; testimony of Yosef Berger-Barzilai, *Hastsofe*, 21 June 1963.

50 Testimony of Yehoshua Efman, PZO Archives. Efman, head technologist at a Moscow institute, had been invited to this meeting.

51 Interview with Mikhail Margulis.

52 From the testimony of a Soviet Jewish emigrant who has asked to remain anonymous.

53 Interviews with Meir Gelfond and Yosef Khorol; Pregerzon, *Yoman hazikhronot*, chs. 5 and 6. For the solidarity of national groupings, see Solzhenitsyn, *Gulag Archipelago*, which contains several references to the special relationship among the *zeks* (the camp inmates) of fellow nationals. That stories were rife in the camps in Siberia that special camps were being prepared for the Jews is also recorded in Bartoli, *Als Stalin starb*, p. 161. (This reference and the one in the last note of this chapter were kindly brought to my attention by Dr. Peter Brod of the BBC's East European Division.)

54 By fall 1951 only twenty immigration permits had actually been sent by Israeli citizens to their Soviet relatives, although initially attempts had been made to facilitiate the departure from the Soviet Union of 701 individuals; see ch. 1, n. 104. This was a direct result of the hardships and uncertainties of the Soviet Jewish situation and the desire not to jeopardize the well-being of relatives in the Soviet Union and of the complex, formalistic approach of Soviet officialdom to Israeli intercessions on behalf of Soviet residents – Israeli Foreign Ministry East European Department to Israeli legation in Moscow, 13 Nov. 1951 (ISA/FM/2502/1) and correspondence

between the department and the legation (ISA/FM/2502/8). There seem, in addition, to have been one or two cases of individuals who were able to leave the USSR illegally, for example Leo Blumenfeld of Tallinn who reached Finland in late 1951 or very early 1952 – M. Erel, Israeli legation, Stockholm, to Israeli Foreign Ministry East European Department, 1 Feb. 1952 (ISA/FM/2502/8).

55 The analogy with the Volga Germans and Crimean Tatars was used by Roy Medvedev in "The Middle East Conflict and the Jewish Question in the USSR" (Rus.; May 1970), *Sobranie dokumentov samizdata*, vol. 7, no. 496 (Munich: Radio Liberty, undated). According to Medvedev, barracks were being erected for Jews in parts of Kazakhstan.

Ehrenburg's role in the story was alluded to in his autobiography, *Post-War Years*, pp. 299–300. For his refusal to sign the appeal and the letter he subsequently wrote to Stalin, see Svirskii, *Na lobnom meste*, p. 76, and Goldberg, *Ilya Ehrenburg*, pp. 281–82. The version given in the text is based on Iakov (Yankel) Iakir, who, in turn, heard it from one of Ehrenburg's intimates, Moisei Belinkii.

56 *Allgemeine* (the weekly paper of the GFR Jewish community), XXII (18), 6 May 1977.


### 3  The "thaw," 1953–1956

1 So called after Ilya Ehrenburg's novella, *The Thaw*, on which he started working in fall 1953 "to depict how historical events of tremendous importance affect the lives of people . . . and to impart my feeling about the thaw and my hopes" – Ehrenburg, *Post-War Years*, pp. 322–23.
2 To this day the circumstances that brought about Malenkov's resignation are not clear. Some commentators believe that he initiated the step in the conviction that the time had come for the government apparatus to rule the country, others that he was compelled to resign by his colleagues who did not wish to see the two leading positions – head of the party and the government – in the hands of a single person as they had been under Stalin; see, e.g., Conquest, *Power and Policy*, chs. 9 and 10. (The 19th Party Congress in October 1952 changed the name of the Politburo to Presidium.)
3 See e.g., Charles H. Fairbanks, Jr., "National Cadres as a Force in the Soviet System: The Evidence of Beria's Career, 1949–1953," in Azrael, *Soviet Nationality Policies*, pp. 144–86; and Conquest, *Power and Policy*, ch. 9.
4 The first post-Stalin amnesty was issued on 27 Mar. 1953 marking what has been called "the virtual rejection by the new leadership of a large proportion of the accusations made against Soviet citizens in the previous decades." Among others, this first amnesty proclaimed that those sentenced to up to five years were to be "released from their places of detention" and that "the term of punishment of those convicted to a period of deprivation of freedom for a period of more than five years is to be shortened by one half" – Matthews, *Soviet Government*, pp. 256–57. For the release of political prisoners in the immediate post-Stalin period, see also *Manchester Guardian*, 19 Sept. 1955.

5 On 4 Apr. 1953 *Pravda* announced that the charges brought against the doctors had been annulled, that the doctors had been "fully exonerated of the charges brought against them" and that those responsible for conducting the case had been "arrested and made to answer for their crime."

6 For the text of the Secret Speech, released by the U.S. Department of State in June 1956, see *Khrushchev Remembers*, pp. 559–618; for the motives behind, and analysis of, Khrushchev's de-Stalinization, see *The Anti-Stalin Campaign* and Leonhard, *The Kremlin since Stalin*.

7 In the summer of 1954 the foreign ministers of the Big Four and the Chinese People's Republic met in Geneva to discuss Indochina and the reunification of Korea. In 1955, in addition to further talks at foreign minister level, the first East–West summit since Potsdam took place in that town. For details, see Ulam, *Expansion and Coexistence*, pp. 552–54 and 566–71.

8 See Brzezinski, *The Soviet Bloc*, ch. 8.

9 The author does not contend that Khrushchev ever admitted being antisemitic, but simply that his pronouncements enabled others to reach this conclusion. For, whether the First Secretary's proclivities were the reason for it or not, antisemitism was again showing its head by 1955. For example, Western Jewish sources were reporting that the Soviet press was once again emphasizing the Jewish names of persons charged with crimes against the regime – *JC*, 9 Dec. 1955.

10 *JC*, 10 July 1953 and *JTA*, 5 Feb. 1954.

11 Although a few international events, such as the International Federation of Democratic Women's Conference in November 1949 or the International Economic Conference of April 1952, had brought foreign visitors to Moscow even in Stalin's late years, the Iron Curtain had on the whole been carefully preserved.

12 Article 124 of the 1936 "Stalin Constitution," in force until the 1977 constitution was enacted, stipulated: "Freedom of religious worship and freedom of anti-religious propaganda is recognized for all citizens." – Lane, *Politics and Society*, p. 549.

13 The "Peace Prayer Book" was published in 3,000 copies only, its main purpose being to show that the USSR was not discriminating against its Jews. Despite the considerable publicity given its publication, this sole Jewish prayer book to be published in the Soviet Union since the 1920s did not begin to fill the need for prayer books in synagogues throughout the country. For Rabbi Shlifer's efforts to produce the Peace Prayer Book, see Mikhlin, *Hagahelet*, pp. 156–61. Attempts to put out a second edition of the prayer book by his successor, Rabbi Levin, were systematically frustrated, see p. 317.

14 The *yeshiva* was the first training center for rabbis in the Soviet Union since the 1920s. Its opening, like the publication of the prayer book, was the result of several years of effort on the part of Rabbi Shlifer (Mikhlin, *Hagahelet*, pp. 166–80). The event was certainly one of significance, yet in effect the seminary has not meaningfully altered the Soviet Jewish community's crying need for rabbis and other religious functionaries (ritual slaughterers, cantors, circumcizers). There were never more than twenty

students, many of them elderly men. From time to time the authorities would put a virtual stop to normal teaching activities in the seminary, for example by not renewing the permit to reside in Moscow needed by students who came from outside the capital. In the early years a large proportion of the seminary's students were Georgian Jews who enrolled in order to improve their knowledge of Judaism in preparation for emigration to Israel – interview with Mordekhai Hanzin.

15 For the importance and impact of these concerts, see my article, "Nehama Lifshitz."

16 *New York Herald Tribune*, 21 Aug. 1955.

17 *JTA*, 3 Oct. 1956, quoting *Folks-shtime*.

18 Interviews with Meir Gelfond and Yosef Khorol.

19 For approaches to the Kremlin on this score by Western statesmen and other figures, see ch. 4.

20 *Naye prese*, 12 Oct. 1956. Isakov was one of the USSR's best-known journalists; he had long been connected with *Pravda* and was on the editorial staff of the monthly *International Affairs*. As well as writing his own plays, he had translated the works of Ernest Hemingway, Howard Fast and J. B. Priestley into Russian.

21 *Naye prese*, 15 Oct. 1956.

22 *Al hamishmar*, 23 Aug. 1957; *Di prese* (Buenos Aires), 18 Sept. 1957.

23 Testimony of a member of the Israeli delegation who has asked to remain anonymous.

24 Interview with Marek Moizes. In 1958 a children's choir was also set up under the auspices of the "collective," authorized by the Lithuanian SSR party's propaganda department to sing in Russian, Lithuanian and Yiddish. Yet several days after its first appearance the Vilnius municipal council ordered the choir's dispersal on the grounds that study of and singing in Yiddish led to the Jews' segregation, whereas the USSR was striving for their assimilation. For the Yiddish theater in Vilnius, see also Pinkus, *Soviet Government*, pp. 304–06.

25 Soviet leaders pressed by Western leaders and press representatives insisted consistently that there was no demand for a Jewish theater since the Jews had become integrated into Russian culture; see, e.g., Khrushchev in his conversation with the French socialist delegation that visited the USSR in May 1956, pp. 107–08. For the few concessions actually made in subsequent years – an occasional Yiddish book, as of 1959, and the publication of the Yiddish journal *Sovetish heymland*, see p. 277.

26 That this line emanated from practical rather than theoretical considerations, was made clear in Lenin's "Critical Remarks on the National Question," V. I. Lenin, *Collected Works* (Moscow: Progress, 1964), vol. 21, pp. 43–44.

27 Prior to 1948 the Yiddish writers, approximately 150 in number, had their own union (*ob"edinenie*) within the Union of Soviet Writers – interview with Yosef and Anna Kerler.

28 See, e.g., Danish journalist Erik Seidenfaden in *Manchester Guardian*, 15 Nov. 1955. At the same time, Seidenfaden believed that the majority of

Soviet Jews were probably more concerned with "the security of their own situation" inside the USSR than with realizing "the Zionist creed."

29 This, of course did not apply to Jews who had come to these republics after the war from other parts of the country.

30 Interviews with Gitta Landman and Eliahu Hoberman. Indeed, a considerable part of this chapter is based on my interview with Hoberman and the last two chapters of his unpublished reminiscences which he was kind enough to let me use and to which I have referred in previous chapters, "Di letzte tekufa" and "Epilogue."

31 Eliav, *Between Hammer and Sickle*, pp. 163–64, and Vaisman, *Yoman mahteret ivri*, p. 267.

32 Just occasionally it was also possible to read about the advent of Israeli sports teams, or at least about their scheduled participation in international competitions, in the Soviet press – Vaisman, *Yoman mahteret ivri*, p. 247.

33 For the background of the severance and resumption of relations, see Ro'i, *Decision Making*, pp. 468–74.

34 Hoberman, "Epilogue," p. 10 (unpublished memoirs).

35 Dagan, *Moscow and Jerusalem*, pp. 75–76.

36 The visitor in question was the American Jewish journalist, Chaim Shoshkes; *Davar*, 2 Jan. 1957; and interview with a former member of the Israeli embassy staff.

37 Arie (Liova) Eliav, who served in Moscow from 1958 through 1960, has conveyed something of the atmosphere of the Israelis' encounters with Jews in different parts of the USSR in *Between Hammer and Sickle*, passim, and in *Taba'ot 'edut*.

38 Hoberman, "Epilogue," pp. 10–12 (unpublished memoirs).

39 As early as February 1954 Prime Minister Sharett was told that a special Yiddish-language pamphlet on Israel and an illustrated Jewish calendar were being prepared for Jews in the USSR – Sharett, *Yoman ishi*, vol. 2, p. 350.

40 Vaisman, *Yoman mahteret ivri*, pp. 237–47.

41 Interview with Gitta Landman; Mrs. Landman's son, Pinhas, lived in Dnepropetrovsk after being liberated from prison.

42 Hoberman, "Epilogue," p. 13 (unpublished memoirs). Ilia Saidin of Riga had been active in the *briha* in 1945–46 for which he spent several years in prison camps. Released from camp, but still in exile in the far north (at Salekhard in the Iamalo-Nenetskii okrug), Saidin received a letter from a member of the Israeli embassy whom he had known as a young man in the Zionist movement in Latvia. On his way to Riga in 1955 – every second year he was allowed to travel to his home town for the vacation – he tried to make contact with his old acquaintance. Although unsuccessful in this endeavor, Saidin encountered Goberman at the railway station where his train was due to take him back north. Spotting Goberman's "tail," Saidin rejected the latter's suggestion to stay on in Moscow. Six months later he was called for interrogation and was later brought to Moscow as a witness at Goberman's trial – interview with Eliahu Saidin.

43 In June 1953 the Soviet Ministry of Foreign Affairs advised foreign

embassies that travel restrictions had been lifted for vast areas in the European part of the RSFSR, Ukraine, Belorussia, the Caucasus and Central Asia, although the Urals, border areas and many large Siberian cities remained closed – Salisbury, *Moscow Journal*, pp. 384–85.

44 For stories connected with these trips at the end of the 1950s, see, e.g., Eliav, *Between Hammer and Sickle*, passim.

45 Interview with Shalom Fozailov; see also following note.

46 *JC*, 8 Jan. 1954; interview with Boris Gimelfarb; and Sharett, *Yoman ishi*, vol. 4, p. 959 and vol. 5, p. 350.

47 According to the 1959 census 95.3 percent of the Soviet Jewish population were urban dwellers – Altshuler, *Hakibbutz*, p. 72.

48 Vaisman's manuscript was published in instalments in a number of Israeli and Western Yiddish newspapers and eventually appeared in book form: Yehudi Sovieti Almoni, *El ahai bim'dinat Yisrael* (An Unknown Soviet Jew, To My Brethren in the State of Israel, Heb.; Jerusalem: Kiryat Sefer, 1957), ed. Binyamin Eliav. It was only after Vaisman's death in 1966 that his name was published and his book was reprinted in a fuller edition under the title *Yoman mahteret ivri*, to which reference has already been made. In February 1957, two months before his seventieth birthday, Vaisman was arrested together with other members of his group. He spent three years in camps, where he continued his Zionist activity (see pp. 282 and 289). The charges brought against him, however, did not include composition of the above manuscript, whose authorship the authorities apparently did not discover until after his death.

49 The diaries of Moshe Sharett contain a number of references to reports of members of the Israeli embassy staff on journeys to different parts of the USSR, encounters with large numbers of Jews and the latter's yearning for Israel and excitement at the chance of direct contact with official representatives of the Jewish state – e.g., a report of Moshe and Ida Kehat, June 1955; of Avidar's daughter and son-in-law on returning to Israel after an extensive tour of Belorussia and the Ukraine with the ambassador and his wife, October 1955; of Avidar himself, when Sharett met him in Geneva at the end of the same month and again in February 1956, including a report to the Knesset Foreign Affairs and Security Committee – Sharett, *Yoman ishi*, vol. 3, p. 655; and vol. 5, pp. 1248, 1272, 1348, 1362 and 1373; Shmuel Ben-Tsur, head of the Israeli Foreign Ministry's East European Department, made a similar report on returning from a trip to the USSR where he had visited the Moscow Choral Synagogue together with members of the Israeli embassy staff – ibid., vol. 4, p. 1078.

50 For the significance of the Israeli participation in the Basketball Championship in Moscow for the Jews of the USSR, who, in the words of one of them, all became instant basketball experts, see Vaisman, *Yoman mahteret ivri*, pp. 247–50.

51 *Lamerhav*, 18 July 1956; *Al hamishmar*, 13 and 23 July 1956; Sharett, *Yoman ishi*, vol. 6, p. 1563. The Soviet radio broadcast the return match played in Israel on 31 July, including the playing of *Hatikva*, which was duly heard by Jews throughout the USSR – interview with Yosef Khorol.

52 Interview with Gitta Landman. For Nemirovskaia's precepts, see p. 28.

53 Hoberman, "Epilogue," pp. 91–92 (unpublished memoirs).
54 *Manchester Guardian*, 16 Sept. 1955; see also *New York Herald Tribune* and *Sunday Times*, 30 Oct. 1955, and the translation of the article by Erik Seidenfaden in *Manchester Guardian*, 15 Nov. 1955.
55 Hoberman, "Epilogue," pp. 38, 41–42, 59, 65–67 and 69 (unpublished memoirs).
56 *Haaretz*, 19 Aug. 1955, and see p. 102.
57 For discussions on Jewish issues in one of the camps in Vorkuta, see "Y. Nadav"'s introduction in "D. Seter," *Halo tish'ali* (see following note), pp. 23–26; for celebration of Passover in the same camp, apparently in 1954, see ibid., pp. 30–36.
58 Some of these materials were eventually smuggled out of the Soviet Union and appeared in print in Israel, see pp. 235 and 290. The poems of one Prisoner of Zion, written in Russian, were translated into Hebrew by Israel's leading poets (see Sharett, *Yoman ishi*, vol. 8, pp. 225 and 2279) and appeared under the title *Halo tish'ali*, words taken from the poet Judah Halevi's "Zion, Will You Not Ask After Your Captive Sons?"
59 For the simultaneous strike of 25,000 prisoner-miners in a number of camps in Vorkuta in summer 1953, its organization and suppression, see "Y. Nadav"'s Introduction to *Halo tish'ali*, and Scholmer, *Vorkuta*, ch. 11.
60 "Y. Nadav" has described the September 1953 decision of the Jewish prisoners in his camp to strengthen Jewish groups in other camps whose ranks had been depleted when the authorities discovered that some of their members were on the strike committee, and how he in fact penetrated one such camp. For further information on this period in the camps, see Scholmer, *Vorkuta*; Pregerzon, *Yoman hazikhronot*; and interview with Meir Gelfond. ("Nadav," Scholmer, Pregerzon and Gelfond were all in camps in the Vorkuta complex.)
61 This assumption, made by Hoberman, seems more than reasonable.
62 In the late Stalin period, in their last year of high school, two members of the group had written manifestoes criticizing certain aspects of the regime's policy, including the Jewish one, and disseminated them in the letter-boxes of people with Jewish names, not a few of whom handed over the material to the MVD. By summer 1953 the group was seeking out books of Jewish content in both public and private libraries. Two members, who have since emigrated to Israel, were sentenced to six years' imprisonment for anti-Soviet propaganda and organization; it was in the camps that they first came into contact with convinced Zionists – interview with Naftali Prat (formerly Anatolii Partashnikov) and collective interview with N. Prat, Anatolii (Alik) Feldman, both members of this group, and others.
63 Interviews with David Yafit, Feige, the widow of Yiddish poet David Hofshteyn, Sabina Hefets-Krakovsky, and others.
64 Gelfond, "Illegal Zionist Activity." Gelfond claims that some of these groups were formed as early as 1955. However, while many prisoners were released in 1954 and 1955, my information leads me to believe that this activity did not begin in earnest until the second half of 1956 or 1957.
65 Interview with Meir Gelfond.

66 Interviews with Yosef Khorol and Meir Gelfond. On his return to Odessa, Khorol maintained contact with Pregerzon and later with Gelfond – both in Moscow – who provided him with information on current events in Israel, as well as printed materials which he disseminated among his circle of twenty to thirty people. In Khorol's opinion, each Prisoner of Zion who returned to Odessa had a similar-sized circle of his own.

67 Interviews with Dora and Boris Podolsky.

68 Interview with Marek Moizes.

69 Upon completing their studies in institutes of higher learning, students would be assigned to work in the country's periphery for at least three years.

70 Interview with David Khavkin; for Khavkin's reading material, see ch. 2, n. 10.

71 Interview with Yosef Shnaider. The letter in *Izvestiia* was published on 29 Nov. 1956, see n. 83.

72 Alexander, "Immigration to Israel from the USSR,", pp. 268–335 (see table, p. 9). These figures are not undisputed: e.g., *NYT*, 20 Mar. 1956, quoted Radio Israel as saying that the USSR allowed the emigration of 240 Jews in 1955. As early as mid-December 1953 it was reported that fifteen Jews aged forty to eighty had received permission to emigrate, and that others who had requested permission to leave had been told their applications were being considered – *JC*, 18 Dec. 1953.

73 As we have seen, there had been no emigration under Stalin, except for those repatriated under agreements with the People's Democracies, which had enabled the repatriation of some Jewish citizens of these countries. His successors agreed upon the repatriation of Germans when FRG Chancellor Konrad Adenauer visited the USSR in 1955; Spaniards, mostly people sent to the Soviet Union by the Spanish Republic in the 1930s and their children, began being repatriated by the Soviet government in September 1956 – Korey, *The Soviet Cage*, p. 191.

74 From oral reminiscences by Katriel Katz at an evening dedicated to the study of Soviet-Israeli relations at Tel Aviv University, November 1982.

75 As early as the mid-fifties some commentators were suggesting that not all Jews seeking to emigrate necessarily wanted to go to Israel. *NYT* correspondent Harry Schwartz, who made an extensive tour of the USSR in 1955, reported much antisemitism and anti-Jewish discrimination. While he admitted that Zionism had "apparently not entirely died out," he insisted that the Jews who wanted to leave usually indicated that they were ready to go to any country in the free world that would have them – *JC*, 11 Nov. 1955.

76 Sharett, *Yoman ishi*, vol. 4, p. 1174. The Israeli press, as well as Jewish newspapers in the West, also reported the arrival of Soviet Jewish emigrants during this period; e.g., *JP*, 17 Dec. 1954, 25 Jan., 30 Mar. and 21 Dec. 1955; *JC*, 28 Jan, 18 Feb., 11 Mar. and 20 May 1955, and 6 Jan. 1956.

77 A Jew who had arrived recently from Kiev told this to a public meeting in Ramat Gan late in 1954 – *JP*, 9 Dec. 1954.

78 For how the situation changed regarding leaving through Poland in late 1956, see pp. 252–55.

79 Interview with Yosef Shnaider.

80 See my article "Jewish Emigration and Soviet–Arab Relations."

81 See Ro'i, "Jewish Emigration and Soviet–Arab Relations."

82 The IDF entered the Sinai Peninsula on 25 October and British and French troops landed in the Suez Canal area on 31 October. For Soviet diplomatic activity during the crisis, see Ro'i, *From Encroachment to Involvement*, pp. 182–97.

83 The first such letter, signed by thirty-three public figures, appeared in *Pravda* on 6 Nov. 1956. It stated that "the Jewish citizens of the USSR, together with the entire Soviet people and the whole world demand: hands off Egypt." The letters of the rabbis and other synagogue officials appeared in *Izvestiia* on 28 and 29 Nov. and 14 Dec. 1956. (A few dignitaries seem to have refused to sign, since their names were absent from the list of signatories. One or two may have had their names added by *Pravda* despite their refusal to sign.) As I have stated elsewhere – see my article "The Role of the Synagogue and Religion" – it is easy to condemn the rabbis and other religious dignitaries and much more difficult to understand, let alone condone, their actions; yet, there is no doubt that their position was singularly complex, not to say tragic. In recalling Rabbi Shlifer's visit to the Israeli embassy in Paris for the reception in honor of the foreign delegations who had come to Paris for the unveiling of the Memorial to the Unknown Jewish Martyr, Israel's ambassador to France remembers that in the split second that he found himself standing next to the rabbi, Rabbi Shlifer said to him in Hebrew: "May God give you strength." This was on 31 Oct. 1956 – Jacob Tsur, *Yoman Paris* (An Ambassador's Diary in Paris, 1953–1956, Heb.; Tel Aviv: Om Oved, 1968), pp. 302–03.

84 For Soviet statements – after the cessation of fighting – that they would send volunteers to the Middle East, see Ro'i, *From Encroachment to Involvement*, p. 192. Some people do, in fact, seem to have registered to go to Egypt as volunteers. One of these was a Jew who hoped that once in Egypt he would be able to cross the lines and reach Israel – *Herut*, 8 Sept. 1957.

85 *Haaretz*, 8 Sept. 1957.

86 Interview with Yosef Khorol. Khrushchev himself seemed to be setting the tone; at a speech in Gorkii he got carried away and attacked Ben Gurion and Israel although *a priori* the theme and purport of his speech were supposed to be totally different (the cancellation of a state loan) – interview with Benjamin Fain who was present at the occasion.

87 Members of the Israeli delegation to the 1957 youth festival in Moscow (see pp. 261–68 were amazed at the amount of detail local Jews had about the Sinai War. They heard from several sources how Jews had listened to Israeli broadcasts during the fighting despite the dangers involved; many of them were submitted to surveillance as a result – *Lamerhav*, 25 Sept. 1957.

88 *Herut*, 25 Sept. 1957.

89 E.g., interview with Mordekhai Lapid who was then a nineteen-year-old student called Mark Blum.

90 *Haaretz*, 1 Sept. 1957.

91 E.g., interview with Yosef Khorol. On his return home an Israeli who visited the Soviet Union in the period following the Sinai War reported on the widespread feeling of identity with Israel, pride in its victory and hopes that Israel would not have to withdraw; he also reported on the heavy, oppressive atmosphere surrounding Soviet Jews as a result of their leadership's unequivocally anti-Israel position – Sharett, *Yoman ishi*, vol. 7, p. 2083.

92 *JP*, 14 Feb. 1956. However, another emigrant who went to join relatives in South Africa, believed that only Jews with relatives abroad would wish to leave, that families where all members were still in the USSR would not wish to go, especially in those cases in which younger members were settled and had comfortable positions – *JP*, 14 June 1954. While all such estimates are necessarily inaccurate and problematic, a certain atmosphere could clearly be felt. Not unnaturally, many people would confess intentions of leaving to those who were departing that they would hesitate to express to others who had no desire to leave. Nonetheless, many emigrants were surprised by the number of Jews who came to bid them farewell – e.g., *JP*, 17 Dec. 1954. By the mid-1960s these farewells were an integral component of the *aliya* process (see p. 332).

## 4 The outside world becomes aware of the problem

1 This feeling was especially common among Jews who had come to Palestine from Russia prior to, or shortly after, 1917 and had not forgiven their fellow Jews for having remained behind voluntarily and severed their ties consciously with Zionism and the *yishuv*. Many of the Mapai leadership seem to have shared this view.

2 For a discussion of these problems, see pp. 34–35, and Ro'i, *Decision Making*, pp. 141–49, 198, 204–206 and 344.

3 For the frustration of earlier attempts by the leaders of the *yishuv* and the Zionist movement in the West to discuss Soviet Jewry, especially the problem of Prisoners of Zion, with Soviet representatives, see Ro'i, *"Soviet policy in the Middle East."*

4 Namir, *Shlihut bemoskva*, p. 293.

5 Ibid., pp. 293–95.

6 E.g., *JC*, 8 Oct. 1948, spoke of a 20,000-strong demonstration on the New Year. On 29 October the same paper quoted Jewish repatriates to Poland as saying that the friendly reception accorded Mrs. Meyerson had given Jews the impression that applications to leave for Israel had a greater chance of success.

7 Cf. p. 40 and, in greater detail, Ro'i *Decision Making*, pp. 315–17.

8 A number of Jewish newspapers actually published reports of the arrest of Yiddish writers. On 1 April 1949 the New York *Forverts* reported the arrest of Itzik Fefer, Peretz Markish, Der Nister, Shmuel Halkin and David Bergelson. Further newspaper reports added the names of Moshe Broderzon (*Forverts*, 4 Apr. 1949), Leib Goldberg and Leib Kvitko (*Morgn zhurnal*, 3

May 1949). On 15 April 1949 the Paris socialist Yiddish *Undzer shtime* called on the communist *Naye prese* to confirm or deny these reports. Jewish publicists asked repeatedly for an explanation of these rumors (*Morgn zhurnal*, 6, 9, and 11 May 1949). On 2 June the New York communist *Morgn freyheyt* responded by insisting that those making these inquiries had no right to pry into the USSR's domestic affairs. Yet the paper could "surmise that the Jewish Anti-Fascist Committee [liquidated the previous November] is outdated ... Furthermore, Jewish life in the Soviet Union is undergoing some sort of revision, and before definite decisions and changes are made public, statements cannot be issued."

9 Morris Fine to Louis Bennett, 23 Sept. 1948, AJC files, and interview with Morris Fine. Fine, who headed the AJC Library of Jewish Information in the late 1940s told me that people in the Committee had been concerned by charges of communist and Soviet antisemitism and that there was an urgent desire to dissociate Jews from communism in the public mind. They felt that a sustained scholarly research work showing how Jews were persecuted in the USSR would show the American public that communism was not a haven for Jews. It would also both persuade people that the connection between Jews and communism was not based on reality and give those Jews who did sympathize with the Soviet Union and its ideology grounds for reconsidering their views.

The ultimate product of this effort was Solomon Schwarz's historical survey *Jews in the Soviet Union*. Schwarz was hired to write the book with the guidance of outside scholars (Salo Baron, Nathan Reich, Ian Belinsky). Other scholars added to the AJC staff to ensure the standard of its work on East European Jewry included R. L. Gurland, Bernard D. Weinryb, Joseph Gordon, Will Herberg and Joseph Ofman. Another group coopted to serve as an editorial advisory board comprised Solomon F. Bloom, Philip E. Mosley, Koppel S. Pinson and Avrahm Yarmolinsky – AJC memorandum, "Jews in the Iron Curtain Countries," 1 Feb. 1949.

10 Bezalel Sherman, "The Future of Soviet Jewry," *Jewish Frontier*, February 1951, pp. 5–8.

11 Ro'i, *Decision Making*, p. 344, and *JC*, 4 Jan. 1952.

12 Sh. Eliashiv to A. Vyshinskii, 21 Oct. 1951, ISA/FM/2502/8.

13 *JC*, 15 June 1951. For arms transfers from the Eastern bloc to Israel after 1948, see Uri Bialer, "The Czech–Israeli Arms Deal Revisited," *Journal of Strategic Studies*, VIII, 3 (September 1985), pp. 307–15.

14 *Protocol*, 23rd Zionist Congress, 14–30 Aug. 1951, pp. 247–55.

15 *Divrei haknesset*, vol. 11, p. 1465, 27 Feb. 1952.

16 *NYT* correspondent Dana Adams Schmidt noted in summer 1952 that Israel had followed "a policy of 'nonidentification'" and was still avoiding "outright pro-Western expressions as well as outright anti-Sovietism." He continued that if Israel were to become convinced that emigration from behind the Iron Curtain had been halted, it might adopt a "more forthright" foreign policy – *NYT*, 16 July 1952.

17 *JC*, 14 Dec. 1952 and *JTA*, 16 Jan. 1953.

18 Memorandum by S. Andhil Fineberg, Coordinator, AJC Program on Communism, 12 Dec. 1952, AJC Inventory RG 7–1.

19 Elliot E. Cohen to John Slawson, AJC Executive Vice-President, 12 Dec. 1952, ibid. Among others, AJC executives met with the new U.S. ambassador to the Soviet Union, Charles E. Bohlen, prior to his departure for the USSR in spring 1953, to discuss Soviet antisemitism and possible reactions thereto in the West – Simon Segal to AJC President Jacob Blaustein, 10 Mar. 1953, ibid. Cohen's letter also advocated a major, long-term plan of action and education, mobilizing help from the ADL and eventually also the Jewish Labor Committee as well. This letter must be seen against the background of the highly emotional atmosphere within the American Jewish community, whose sensitivity to Jews being identified with communism had been heightened by the spy case of Julius and Ethel Rosenberg executed after their second appeal was dismissed by the Supreme Court in October 1952.

   A rally was indeed scheduled for Carnegie Hall on 17 March 1953 under the joint auspices of the AJC, ADL, the Committee for Cultural Freedom, the Committee of a Hundred Against Communist Inhumanity, the Amalgamated Clothing Workers of America and the ILGWU – Informal Record of Meeting of Organizational Representatives re March 17 rally, 5 Mar. 1953, ibid. The rally was postponed due to the change in circumstances created by Stalin's death on 5 March, see below.

20 Unsigned memorandum, "AJC program to Combat Soviet Anti-Semitism: Objectives and Themes," 29 Dec. 1952, ibid.

21 *JTA*, 16 Jan. 1953 (SHWD).

22 *NYT*, 19 Jan. 1953.

23 *Divrei haknesset*, vol. 10, 19 Jan. 1953, p. 493.

24 *JTA*, 22 Jan. 1953.

25 *JTA*, 23 Jan. 1953.

26 News Release, undated, AJC Records Center.

27 *JTA*, 23 Jan. 1953.

28 Jacob Blaustein to Nahum Goldmann and Berl Locker, 20 Mar. 1953, AJC Records Center.

29 *JTA*, 23 Jan. 1953.

30 *JTA*, 24 Feb. 1953.

31 *JTA*, 23 Jan. 1953.

32 Ibid.

33 GA OR, 7th Session, 1st Committee, 557th Meeting, 23 Feb. 1953, p. 350.

34 *JTA*, 18 Feb. 1953 (SHWD).

35 *CR*, 83rd Congress, 1st session, vol. 99, part 1, pp. 399–400, part 2, pp. 1441 and 1467–75, and Appendix, pp. 249–50, 369–70, 432–33, 537, 560, 675, 760–61, 784–85 and 839–40. A number of congressmen also asked to have inserted in the *Congressional Record* relevant newspaper articles or resolutions of local Jewish and other organizations, e.g., vol. 99, Appendix, p. 1178, 9 Mar. 1953 and p. 1309, 12 Mar. 1953.

36 *JTA*, 23 Jan. 1953.

37 *CR*, 83rd congress, S. RES. 70, 71 and 84.

38 *CR*, 83rd Congress, 1st session, H. RES. 162, 3 Mar. 1953. (The other two House resolutions were H. RES. 155 and 159.)

39 *CR*, 83rd Congress, 1st session, vol. 99, Appendix, pp. 369–70, 29 Jan. 1953.

40 Texts of some of these protests have been preserved in the AJC Records; see also *JTA*, 23 Jan. 1953. One group of public figures who appealed to President Eisenhower to condemn publicly Soviet persecution of national and religious minority groups included the chairman of the International League for the Rights of Man, Ryan N. Baldwin; the president and executive director of the American Association for the United Nations, Clark M. Eichelberger and William Emerson; the president and executive director of the National Association for the Advancement of Colored People, Arthur S. Spingarn, and Walter White; as well as Eleanor Roosevelt, Mrs. Wendell L. Willkie, former Under-Secretary of State Sumner Welles, and Brigadier–General Telford Taylor, who had been chief U.S. prosecutor at the Nuremburg trials – *NYT*, 20 Feb. (SHWD) and *CR*, 83rd Congress, 1st session, vol. 99, Appendix, pp. 784–85, 20 Feb. 1953.

41 *JTA*, 24 Feb. 1953 (SHWD).

42 Ibid.

43 *JTA*, 26 Feb. 1953.

44 *Evidences*, April 1953. *Evidences* was a French-language magazine published in Paris by the European headquarters of the AJC. The same source had published in its January–February issue the views of a number of leading figures in French intellectual and political life, Jewish and non-Jewish, on the evidence of anti-Jewish discrimination and persecution in the USSR and Eastern Europe (including again Mayer, Malraux and Soustelle, and also Jacques Nantet, chief editor of *Jeune République* and member of the National Committee of Judaeo-Christian Friendship).

45 *JTA*, 24 Feb. 1953 (SHWD).

46 *JTA*, 26 Feb. 1953. The sole opponent of the proposal was the leader of the Left Movement, Dr. Moshe Sneh, who said that such a conference would merely serve to "whip up anti-Jewish propaganda, with consequent danger to the Jews of Eastern Europe" – ibid.

47 *JTA*, 3 Mar. 1953 (SHWD).

48 *JTA*, 6 Mar. 1953 and *NYT*, 9 Mar. 1953.

49 United Jewish Appeal Press Release, undated, AJC Records Center.

50 *NYT*, *JTA*, 3 Apr. 1953.

51 GA OR, 1st Committee, 597th Meeting, 13 Apr. 1953, p. 600, and *JP*, 14 Apr. 1953.

52 *NYT*, 21 Apr. 1953.

53 *JTA*, 22 July 1953.

54 *JTA*, 12 Aug. 1953.

55 World Jewish Congress, Protocol, 3rd Plenary Assembly, 4 Nov. 1953.

56 *Special Report on Treatment of the Jews by the Soviet*, Seventh Interim Report on Hearings before the Select Committee on Communist Aggression, House of Representatives, 83rd Congress, 2nd Session, 22–23 Sept. 1954.

57 *CR*, 84th Congress, 1st Session, vol. 101, Appendix, pp. 1637–38, 10 Mar. 1955.

58 *NYHT*, 16 Apr. 1954; Lehman asked for his speech to be printed in the *Congressional Record*, 83rd Congress, 2nd Session, Appendix, p. 3172, 3 May 1954.

59 *NYT*, 7 Nov. 1954.

60 AJC, Library of Information, 19 Aug. 1955.

61 AJC, Library of Information, 19 Aug. 1955. B'nai B'rith President Philip M. Klutznick also appealed to the president to use his good offices at Geneva to persuade the Soviet government to act in accordance with the above-mentioned proposal of his organization's Board of Governors.

62 Interview with Shaul Avigur.

63 One of those enlisted by Avigur for this activity – toward the end of the fifties – has left us a vivid account of both Avigur's method of mobilizing candidates for Moscow and of the activities involved – Eliav, *Tab'aot 'edut*, pp. 165–67.

64 Aryeh Eshel, head of the Israeli Foreign Ministry East European Department, to the Israeli embassy in Moscow and legations in Eastern Europe, 10 Feb. 1955 (ISA/FM/544/1).

65 The first such meeting took place on 6 Jan. 1954; Y. L. Gideon to East European Department, Israeli Foreign Ministry, 15 Jan. 1954 (ISA/FM/546/7a).

66 A. Eshel to Israeli embassy, Moscow, and legations in Eastern Europe, 10 Feb. 1955 (ISA/FM/544/1).

67 Sharett, *Yoman ishi*, vol. 4, pp. 1122–23.

68 Ibid., vol. 5, p. 1266.

69 Interview with Shaul Avigur, and Sharett, *Yoman ishi*, vol. 5, p. 1139. Those who called for an overt Israeli posture at the head of the protest movement included Shmuel Ben-Tsur, head of the Israeli Foreign Ministry's East European Department; Abe Harman, the same ministry's Deputy Director General for Jewish Affairs; and Haim Yehil, director of the ministry's Information Department.

70 Sharett, *Yoman ishi*, vol. 4, pp. 1122–23.

71 Interview with Binyamin Eliav. Among the manuscripts handled by Eliav were Mikhail Baitalskii's verse, and works of Zvi Pregerzon, Zvi Plotkin and Nahum ben Avraham Kahanov. (For some of the manuscripts, see Sharett, *Yoman ishi*, vol. 7, p. 2047 and vol. 8, pp. 2252 and 2279.) Eliav remained connected with Soviet Jewry both as consul-general in New York in 1960–61 and after his return to Israel, indeed, even following his appointment as director of the Israeli government's information services in 1966.

72 AJC, paper entitled "Demands with regard to Jewish Situation in Communist Countries," 31 Aug. 1955, and paper entitled "Jewish Requests to the Soviet Union," 28 Sept. 1955.

73 Sharett, *Yoman ishi*, vol. 4, pp. 1200–01. Some of this briefing was done by head of the Histadrut Political Department, Reuven Barkatt. For the international links and activities of the Histadrut in these years, see its publications: *Pirke din veheshbon lishnat 1953* (Report for the Year 1953, Heb.). Tel Aviv, January 1955, pp. 173–75; *Have'ida hasheminit shel hahistadrut* (The Eighth Convention of the Histadrut, Heb.), 18–20 Mar. 1956, passim.

74 Sharett, *Yoman ishi*, vol. 4, pp. 1200–01, and vol. 6, p. 1712.

75 The AJC representative in Paris, for example, met prior to the delegation's departure with one of its members, Robert Verdier, former editor of the Socialist Party daily, *Le Populaire*, asking Verdier to raise the Jewish issue with the Soviet leaders and presenting him with a list of questions – unsigned letter to John Slawson, 23 May 1956, AJC Inventory, RG 7–1. See also Sharett, *Yoman ishi*, vol. 4, pp. 1200–01.

76 This question had been prompted by the experience of two delegation members who had visited Kiev, where they had been accosted by a Jewish schoolteacher whose long-due promotion to school inspector had failed to materialize, a non-Jew being preferred. When he lodged a complaint with the party, of which he was a member, he was expelled from its ranks – Stephen W. Pollak to N. Goldmann and E. L. Easterman, 2 July 1956 (CZA, Z6/892).

77 Letter to John Slawson (as in n. 75) and "Khrushchev's Views on Jews and Israel," *American Zionist*, September 1957.

78 From a report submitted by the British CP delegation to the USSR, 12 Jan. 1957, quoted by the AJC to First Deputy Prime Minister Mikoian, 22 Jan. 1959 (see p. 134) – AJC Inventory, RG 7–1, and *CR*, 86th Congress, 2nd Session, vol. 106, part 5, p. 5568, 15 Mar. 1960.

79 Interviews with Prof. Hyman Levy and Binyamin Eliav.

80 Levy, *The Jews and the National Question*, in which Levy sought to give the context of "the strange, almost unexplained, policy which the Soviet Union appears to be pursuing with regard to its Jewish population" (p. 23), and author's interview with Hyman Levy, and sources as in n. 78.

81 *Jews behind the Iron Curtain*, AJC, March 1957, and *New Leader*, 14 Sept. 1959, both quoted from Salsberg's articles on his visit to the USSR that had appeared in the Canadian Yiddish *Vokhnblat* (the *Canadian Jewish Weekly*), the New York *Morgn frayheyt* and *Jewish Life* in the months Oct.–Dec. 1956; also *CR*, 86th Congress, 2nd Session, vol. 106, part 5, p. 5569, 15 March 1960.

82 Communist Yiddish-language papers which took exception to Soviet Jewish policies, particularly on the issue of culture, included, in addition to the Warsaw *Folks-shtime* (see n. 105), *Naye prese* (Paris), *Vokhnblat* (Toronto) and *Tribuna* (Buenos Aires). Even the American communist *Daily Worker* that was not a Jewish paper had criticized Khrushchev on 7 June 1956 for not mentioning Stalin's crimes against Jewish culture in his Secret Speech. For some of the findings of the French CP delegation to the Soviet Union, also in 1956, see pp. 107–08.

83 Interview with Binyamin Eliav.

84 Interview with Binyamin Eliav.

85 Maurice L. Perlzweig to officers of the WJC, 22 June 1955 (CZA Z6/644); and H. J. Berman to the author, 11 Oct. 1984.

86 Memorandum by M. L. Perlzweig, 11 Oct. 1955 (CZA, Z6/644). For Goldmann's intention of visiting the USSR, see also Sharett, *Yoman ishi*, vol. 5, pp. 1260 and 1266; in April 1957 Goldmann, at the suggestion of Aryeh Eshel, head of the Israeli Foreign Ministry East European Department, sought to discuss the Soviet Jewry problem with Marshal Tito – ibid., vol. 7, p. 2113.

87 Interview with Prof. A. Katsh. In the mid-1970s Katsh wrote an article that does not seem to have been published entitled "The Soviet System and the Jews: An Anomaly Wrapped in an Enigma," which he was kind enough to show me. Arsenev's statement is reproduced in this article in the original Russian. For comment on, and a translation of, this statement, see Pinkus, *Soviet Government*, pp. 58 and 59 (document 15). For Katsh's 1956 visit to the USSR, see also Ben-Yosef, *Sefer Avraham Yitzhak Katsh* (Tel Aviv: private edition [1969]), pp. 261–66.

88 *NYHT*, 17 June 1955; *NYT*, 26 June 1955.

89 *Morgn frayheyt*, *JTA*, 30 Sept. 1955. Some days before, on 21 September, *Forverts* had announced that Jewish poet and playwright Moshe Broderzon had been released from a Siberian labor camp and was back in Moscow, and that a report had been received that Yiddish writer Shmuel Halkin had been similarly released and allowed to return to Moscow. Another source told of an encounter with Halkin at a recital by the singer Epelbaum in Lvov – *Jewish Daily Eagle* (Montreal), 20 Sept. 1955.

90 *JTA*, 21 Sept. 1955; *NYT*, 2 Sept. 1955. Held also urged Secretary Dulles to take action on behalf of Soviet Jewry – *JC*, 15 June 1956. For the activities of Held and the Jewish Labor Committee, see pp. 94 and 112; for the rabbinical delegations to the USSR in 1956, see pp. 116–19.

91 Alex L. Easterman, WJC Political Director, and Israel M. Sieff, Chairman of the WJC European Executive, to N. S. Khrushchev and N. A. Bulganin, 25 Apr. 1956; *NYHT*, 27 Apr. 1956.

92 AJC memorandum, 28 May 1956, AJC Inventory, RG 7–1.

93 Seymour J. Lubin to Alan M. Stroock, 26 Sept. 1956, ibid. Kennan, the first U.S. ambassador to the Soviet Union, had written extensively about the USSR.

94 The article, by editor Erik Seidenfaden, appeared in *Information* on 15 October. It was reprinted in the Norwegian and Swedish press and, eventually, also in Britain (*Manchester Guardian*, 15 Nov. 1955).

95 *NYT*, 8 Nov. 1955.

96 *NYT*, 3 Oct. 1955 and 22 Apr. 1956 respectively.

97 One by Chaim Shurer, editor-in-chief of *Davar*, at the National Committee for Labor Israel – *NYT*, 26 Nov. 1955 (Shurer had visited the Soviet Union late in 1954, see p. 115); another at the 31st convention of the Mizrachi Women's Organization of America – *NYT*, 22 Oct. 1956.

98 E.g., *NYT*, 20 Mar. 1956.

99 *NYT*, 2 Apr. 1956. For further rapportage on interest in the U.S. on the Soviet Jewry issue and requests for intervention on behalf of the Soviet Jews, see *NYT*, 29 June and 16 July 1956.

100 *Folks-shtime*, 25 Nov. 1956.

101 *JTA*, 9 Jan. 1956, and *CR*, 84th Congress, 1st Session, vol. 102, Appendix, pp.5495–96 (read in by Congressman Charles C. Digg, Jr., of Michigan).

102 *JC*, 21 and 28 Sept. 1956.

103 Shoshkes' account of his trip appeared in the Israeli daily press on 12 Aug. 1956.

104 *JC*, 16 Mar. 1956; for the original information, see Sharett, *Yoman ishi*, vol. 5, p. 1349.

105 The article, published anonymously on 4 April 1956, was later revealed to have been written by Bunim Heller and Hirsh Smolar of the paper's editorial staff. It caused a great stir at the time as it not only referred to the execution of the Yiddish writers and other figures under Stalin as a fact, but also enumerated a long list of humiliations and sufferings to which Jews had been subjected by the Soviet regime. There had been a whole group of great Yiddish poets, writers and playwrights. But this creative genius had been cut down by "the social plague now known as Beriiaism." (Although Khrushchev and his colleagues customarily blamed Beriia, whom they had executed, for most of the failings which de-Stalinization was supposed to remedy, many of them were not his doing. In fact, Beriia had been associated with some leaders of the Jewish Anti-Fascist Committee.) *Folks-shtime* disclosed that on many occasions Jewish communists had been compelled to "clench their teeth," and had remained silent in the belief that the CPSU would eventually "disentangle this tragic knot." For a translation of the *Folks-shtime* article, see Pinkus, *Soviet Government*, document 74, pp. 211–14.

106 Interview with Binyamin Eliav.

107 *JTA*, 14 May 1956. (The Orthodox rabbis' application had been announced on 12 July 1955 at the RCA's annual convention – AJC Library of Information, 19 Aug. 1955.) Headed by Rabbi David B. Hollander, Honorary President of the RCA, the delegation also comprised Rabbi Gilbert Klaperman, the Council's Vice-President; Rabbi Herschel Schachter, Head of the Council's Israel Commission; and Rabbis Emanuel Rackman and Samuel Adelman, members of the Council Executive Committee. For the rabbis' visit to the USSR and their participation in the service at the Moscow Choral Synagogue, see also my article "The Role of the Synagogue and Religion."

108 Interviews with Rabbis Hollander and Klaperman. In Kutaisi 3,000 Jews waited all night at the airport to greet the rabbis and in Kulashi the entire Jewish community took the day off work in order to welcome them. (When Rabbi Klaperman's Hebrew address in the Tbilisi synagogue was translated by the Hakham, the rabbi realized that the latter was introducing changes to make it more amenable to the authorities.)

109 See, for example, the report on her trip to the USSR – as a member of a British–Soviet Friendship Society delegation in July 1956 – of Councillor Mrs. Seager, Deputy Mayor of Smethwick, who visited the synagogues of Moscow and Leningrad, Riga and Vilnius (where she was probably the first Western visitor for at least a decade). As Mrs. Seager had been briefed by Dr. Stephen Roth of the British Section of the WJC, she knew what to ask and look for in the USSR, and was therefore able to achieve her purpose, despite considerable obstructionism. She, too, was convinced that the Soviets were making a major effort to convince the West of their liberalism vis-à-vis Soviet Jews – Report, unsigned and undated, CZA, Z6/892.

110 Rabbis Kertzer and Golovensky visited only Moscow and Leningrad. Rabbis Israel Mowshowitz, Joseph Miller, Harold H. Gordon, George

B. Lieberman and Jacob B. Grossman went on to Kiev and Odessa as well as a number of communities in Eastern Europe. Rabbi Irving Kosloff, who did not travel with the delegation, visited Minsk, Kharkov and Tbilisi.
111 Interviews with Rabbis David Hollander, Gilbert Klaperman and Herschel Schachter; *Forverts*, 15 Aug. 1956.
112 *The Status of the Jews behind the Iron Curtain*, p. 16.

## 5  The campaign in the West gathers momentum

1 United Nations Human Rights Convention, December 1948, Article 13, para. B.
2 Korey, *The Soviet Cage*, pp. 190–91.
3 Interview with Emanuel Litvinoff; his article, originally prepared for the radio, appeared first in the British *Listener* and later in the U.S.
4 This seemed to tally with the First Secretary's general antisemitism, which implied a desire to be rid of the Jews for, as potential traitors and not intrinsically belonging to Soviet society, they would not wish to participate in the fully communist society that was the CPSU's ultimate goal.
5 Interview with Binyamin Eliav.
6 At a WJC Executive Committee meeting in 1957, which focused on the Soviet Jewish situation, Israel Goldstein of the U.S. said that the WJC wanted the "spark of desire for Jewish communal life and for Jewish culture" which still existed "rekindled," insisting that American Jews were "asking for their fellow-Jews nothing less than Jews wanted to see granted to all men." Israel Sieff of the U.K. said that since 3 million Jews were "in danger of being culturally and spiritually starved to death," the WJC Executive Committee should repeat earlier applications to the Soviet government (one of them presumably the letter to Khrushchev and Bulganin) to send a delegation to Jewish communities in the USSR and that, failing this, the UN be asked "what action should be taken to prevent a traditional culture . . . from being forced to perish."

Shneour Levenberg, also of the U.K., suggested a more minimalist program: a day of solidarity with Soviet Jewry, publication of a White Paper on the Soviet Jewish situation and creation of a special department to deal with the problem of East European Jewry. Rabbi Simon Federbush of the U.S. reverted to the idea of an Emergency World Conference in which "all Jewish parties" would take part – minutes of the WJC Executive Committee, London, 29 April – 2 May 1957, pp. 10–20.

But despite the intensity and broad range of the discussion, the WJC never really rose above the organizational issue. Nor were its persistent diplomatic efforts successful due to its insistence that before anything else a WJC delegation must be invited to the USSR to discuss the issue with the Soviet leaders, which was unacceptable to Moscow. Two resolutions of the WJC's 4th Plenary Assembly held in Stockholm in August 1959 addressed themselves to the Soviet Jewish situation.
7 Korey, "The Right to Leave," pp.10–11.
8 Interview with Binyamin Eliav.

9 Five issues of the *Jewish Observer Newsletter (A Periodical Survey of Events Affecting Jews in the Soviet Bloc)* appeared in 1958–59. The first must have come out very early in 1958 or perhaps even at the end of 1957, and the next four are dated mid-March 1958 through March 1959. The General Introduction to the first number insisted that the newsletter had no intention of serving anti-Soviet or anti-communist propaganda. Nonetheless the section devoted to the Soviet Union described past and current anti-Jewish discrimination, noting that the Soviet authorities had felt compelled to institute a press campaign to try and discourage the upsurge of Jewish nationalism that had taken place in reaction to this discrimination. The four remaining numbers summarized anti-Jewish articles from the Soviet press, refuting parts of Khruschev's interviews with Serge Groussard of *Le Figaro* and a group of American professionals as containing ambiguities and downright untruths. They reported the "singular attention" given by the Soviet media to letters purportedly written by emigrants to Israel (apparently Polish Jews who had benefited from the Soviet–Polish repatriation agreement) besmirching life in Israel. The *Newsletter* also traced how Soviet propaganda and promises concerning Yiddish culture had been replaced by a totally negative attitude.

10 Litvinoff's concern with veracity resulted in his leaving the *Jewish Observer* in April 1959 after the paper was forced to publish a retraction of an unchecked article on Soviet antisemitism.

11 At a public meeting in Paris to mark Israel's Independence Day in May 1960, Deputy Patrice Brocas devoted a considerable part of his speech to the Soviet Jewish situation, quoting extensively from the French edition of the *Newsletter*.

12 Nineteen issues of *Jews in Eastern Europe* had come out by June 1967, I, 1–8; II, 1–5; III, 1–6.

13 *Evrei i evreiskii narod* has appeared consecutively since 1960 and until the time of writing (1987).

14 Interview with Ephraim Tari.

15 Interview with Moshe Decter.

16 Interview with Binyamin Eliav.

17 The article which had appeared in the New York *Daily Worker* on 22 Sept. 1957 was quoted by *New Leader*, 14 Sept. 1959, pp. 11–12.

18 Ibid., pp. 13–19. The Slovès article appeared in the pro-communist American Yiddish-language *Idishe kultur*, Feb. 1959, after the French Communist Party refused to publish it.

19 This section and what follows is based on Joel Cang's report of his visit, submitted to the AJC on 18 Dec. 1959. Cang also published four articles on the Soviet Jewish situation in the *JC*: 23 and 30 Oct., 6 and 13 Nov. 1959. Prior to his trip, at least as early as 1956, Cang had written on Soviet Jewry in the *JC*. Later he published a book, *The Silent Millions*.

20 "Notes on the Jews in the Soviet Union," AJC FAD, October 1961.

21 See, e.g., *Jews in Eastern Europe*, 2 (Nov. 1959), pp. 9–13, and 6 (Dec. 1960), pp. 3–5. The Malakhovka synagogue just outside Moscow was set on fire on the Jewish New Year 1959 and the caretaker's wife lost her life in

the arson; on the evenings before and after, hundreds of leaflets signed by the "Beat the Jews Committee" were posted on buildings in Malakhovka. *JEE* reported that during this period similar leaflets were distributed in Kiev, Kharkov and Vinnitsa, and that windows were smashed in scores of Jewish residences in small towns near Moscow, as well as recurrently in the Choral Synagogue. The Jewish cemetery in the capital was desecrated several times, and hooligans broke into a house in one of the townships near Moscow and beat up Jews who had gathered there for a *minyan*. In August 1960 there was also a blood libel in Dagestan.

22 Ivanov and Sheinis, *Gosudarstvo Izrail*.

23 *CR*, 87th Congress, 2nd Session, vol. 108, Appendix, p. 446, 23 Jan. 1962.

24 *NYHT*, 6 Nov. 1961. For other articles by Evans, see, e.g., "The Kremlin's Persecution of Jews," *Saturday Evening Post*, 16 June 1962 – quoted *CR*, 87th Congress, 2nd Session, vol. 108, Appendix, pp. 4478–79, 19 June 1962.

25 *JC*, 10 Nov. 1961.

26 *Divrei haknesset*, vol. 32, pp. 363–66, 15 Nov. 1961; *JP*, 6 Dec. 1961. For arrests in Moscow in this period, see p. 296; one of Pecherskii's co-defendants was also from Moscow, presumably in order to show the ramifications of the conspiracy against the Soviet state; see pp. 295–96.

27 *NYHT*, 18 Jan. 1962. Others who approached the U.N. included the Religious Zionists of America and the Jewish Labor Committee.

28 E.g., *Trud*, 6 Jan. and 16 Mar. 1961.

29 M. I. Shakhnovich, *Reaktsionnaia sushchnost iudaizma, kratkii ocherk prois-khozhdeniia i klassovoi sushchnosti iudeiskoi religii* (Moscow: USSR Academy of Sciences, 1960).

30 *CR*, 86th Congress, 1st Session, vol. 105, part 11, p. 14470, 28 July 1959.

31 In 1961 and even earlier the Israeli chief rabbinate had sent *matzot* to the USSR for distribution among the Jewish communities – *JC*, 10 Feb. 1961 – while in 1962 a group of American *matza* bakers volunteered to ship a planeload of their product to the Soviet Union in time for the Passover. For protests in Congress and activities in this connection, see, e.g., *CR*, 88th Congress, 1st Session, vol. 109, part 4, pp. 4505–07 and 5045–46, 19 and 25 Mar. 1963, and 2nd Session, vol. 110, part 5, pp. 5719 and 5900, 19 and 23 Mar. 1964.

32 Between July 1961, when the first death sentences were announced, and August 1963, 81 "economic trials" took place in 48 cities. Of the 163 who received death sentences in these trials at least 88 (i.e. 55 percent) were definitely Jewish – *JEE*, II, 4 (Feb. 1964), p. 17.

33 "Principles of Criminal Legislation of the USSR and the Union Republics," approved by the USSR Supreme Soviet, 25 Dec. 1958, Article 22, in Matthews, *Soviet Government*, pp. 269–82.

34 *CR*, 88th Congress, vol. 109, part 4, p. 4507, 19 Mar. 1963.

35 Ibid., pp. 4506–07. The signatories of the appeal to U Thant included Henry Steele Commager, Lewis Gannett, William Ernest Hocking, Martin Luther King, Linus Pauling and Norman Thomas.

36 *JP*, *Al hamishmar*, 29 Jan. 1958. COJO again addressed itself to the Soviet Jewry issue at a meeting in Geneva in 1961 – JC, 25 Aug. 1961.

37 *JC*, 7 and 14 Aug. 1959.
38 *Hakongress hatsioni hakaf hey* (The 25th Zionist Congress; Heb.), 27 Dec. 1960 – 11 Jan. 1961, Stenographic Protocol, Hanhalat Hahistadrut Hatsionit Ha'olamit. Jerusalem, 5721 (1961), p. 700.
39 *JC*, 25 Aug. 1961.
40 *JTA*, 9 Jan. 1961.
41 For Soviet representatives' angry reaction to harassment over Soviet Jewry, see, e.g., Khrushchev's press conference during his September 1959 tour of the U.S. in following section; Secretary to the USSR Supreme Soviet Presidium Mikhail Georgadze was similarly indignant when he was asked at a press conference in Rio de Janeiro why Jews in the Soviet Union were not allowed to be united with families abroad – *JC*, 4 Aug. 1961.
42 The American business community, for example, was exhorted by Moscow to trade with the USSR, while scientists and artists were variously encouraged to participate in the promotion of improved cultural relations.
43 For Eisenhower's discussion with Khrushchev and Herter's with Gromyko, see Assistant Secretary of State Frederick G. Dutton to Senator Javits, 8 Mar. 1962, *CR*, 87th Congress, 2nd Session, vol. 108, part 3, pp. 4104–05, 14 Mar. 1962. Bisgyer (*Challenge and Encounter*, pp. 125–26) reproduces a letter from Assistant to the President, General Wilton B. Parsons, to Label A. Katz published in *NYT*, 12 Oct. 1959, reporting the Eisenhower–Khrushchev conversation. Apparently it took place within the informal part of the talks and therefore was not included in the official protocol. For the Khrushchev visit and his talks with Eisenhower, see also Eisenhower, *White House Years*, pp. 432–48.
44 For Mikoian's statement at a press conference at U.N. headquarters, see *NYT*, 16 Jan. 1959. Khrushchev himself had quoted Chairman of the USSR Supreme Soviet Presidium Kliment Voroshilov as having told the Queen of Belgium, in reply to questioning on Soviet Jewish policy, that his own wife was Jewish; Khrushchev noted that this signified a special attitude since half the members of the CPSU Presidium had Jewish wives – *NYHT*, 22 Apr. 1958.
45 The Presidents' Club became the Presidents' Conference in 1959.
46 See ch. 4 for some of the earlier intercessions on behalf of Soviet Jewry on the part of these organizations. An appeal published by a number of American Jewish organizations on the sixth anniversary of the execution of the Jewish writers asking Moscow to restore the rights of the Jews, including the right of emigration, was handed to Gromyko when he came to New York in August 1958 – *Al hamishmar*, 13 Aug. 1958.
47 Eliezer Greenberg to John Slawson, *Yiddish News Digest*, 2–316, 26 Jan. 1959, specifically *Forverts*, 16 and 20 Jan. 1959, and "Memorandum on the Situation of the Jews in the Soviet Union," submitted to A. Mikoian by the AJC, 22 Jan. 1959. The AJC leaders at this meeting were former Senator Herbert H. Lehman, Honorary Vice-President; Irving M. Engel, President; Jacob Blaustein, Honorary President; and Ralph Friedman, Chairman of the AJC Foreign Affairs Committee. The Jewish Labor Committee also submitted a memorandum to Mikoian, but had been refused an audience,

ibid. For rumors that there was to be a decision for exiling Jews to Birobidzhan at the 21st Party Congress, see also p. 134.

48 H. Winton to S. Segal, 3 and 6 July 1959; Louis B. Heilbronn to AJC President Herbert E. Ehrmann, 8 July 1959; and H. B. Ehrmann to C. Magnin, 13 July 1959 – AJC Inventory RG 7–1.

49 H. Winton to S. Segal, 28 July 1959 – ibid.

50 S. Segal to H. B. Ehrmann, 25 June 1959 – ibid.

51 *JC*, 10 July 1959; *JEE*, 1 (mid-September 1959), pp. 7–10.

52 *JEE*, 2 (Nov. 1959). A similar question by Congress of Industrial Organizations (CIO) leader Walter Reuther – to which Reuther added a further query concerning the reasons for Khrushchev's antagonism to Israel – irritated Khrushchev as was demonstrated by an attack on Reuther in *Trud*, 25 Sept. 1959 (ibid., pp. 16–17). In another conversation with Harry and Alexander Lieb, who had been members of the American War Veterans delegation which visited the USSR in May 1958, Khrushchev reiterated his contention that "the time is not ripe yet" for Jews or other Soviet citizens to be permitted to leave the country, but that the day might come (ibid., p. 17). Addressing a Labor and People's Conference on the fate of Soviet Jews in San Francisco at the time of Khrushchev's visit, President of the American Federation of Labor (AFL) and CIO George Meany accused the Soviet leader of harboring "anti-Semitic prejudices" and maintaining anti-Jewish quotas in education and employment. "Despite Khrushchev's bland denials, the facts of anti-Semitism are clearly established," Meany said (ibid.).

53 Harry Fleishman, AJC National Labor Service, to James B. Carey, 9 Sept. 1959 – AJC Inventory RG 7-1.

54 Bisgyer, *Challenge and Encounter*, pp. 123–26; also *CR*, 87th Congress, 2nd Session, vol. 108, part 3, pp. 4404–07, 14 Mar. 1962; and *JEE*, 2 (Nov. 1959), pp. 19–21.

55 *Newsweek*, 24 Aug. 1959. For discussions among the American Jewish organizations prior to the Khrushchev visit on how to meet with the First Secretary, including contacts with both Soviet and State Department officials, see *JC*, 14, 21 and 28 Aug. 1959. There seems little doubt that disagreements and mutual recriminations within the American Jewish establishment diverted attention from Khrushchev's refusal to meet American Jewish leaders – AJC Press Release, 30 Oct. 1959 and S. Andhil Fineberg, AJC Community Affairs Department, to Area Directors and Executive Assistants, 9 Dec. 1959 (AJC Inventory RG 7–1).

56 AJC, Western Regional Office, *News*, 9 Nov. 1959.

57 AJC *News*, 22 Oct. 1959.

58 *JC*, 16 and 23 Sept. 1960.

59 *JC*, 4 Oct. 1960.

60 *JEE*, II, 1 (Dec. 1962), pp. 59–60; also *CR*, 88th Congress, 1st Session, vol. 109, part 4, 19 Mar. 1963, pp. 4506–07. The statement was signed by Joachim Prinz, Label Katz, Adolph Held, Jewish War Veterans National Commander Theodore Brooks, National Community Relations Advisory Council (NCRAC) Chairman Lewis Weinstein, National Council of Young

Israel President Rabbi David Hill, and President of the New York Board of Rabbis, Rabbi Israel Mowshowitz.

61 AJC FAD memorandum on the situation of the Jews in the Soviet Union, Nov. 1963. Attempts to meet with the Soviet ambassador in Washington had begun in Dec. 1961, when Herbert H. Lehman wrote to Ambassador Menshikov; they were reiterated after Dobrynin replaced Menshikov in March 1962, but all to no avail.

62 Interview with William Korey. Ingles' study, entitled "The Study of Discrimination in Respect of the Right of Everyone to Leave Any Country, Including His Own, and to Return to His Country," was finally published in 1963 after three years of extensive research. For details, see Korey, *The Soviet Cage*, ch. 10. For Korey's own research regarding his report, see ibid., ch. 1. For discussion at the Sub-Commission in January 1961, see pp. 166–67.

63 These included philosopher Karl Jaspers; Bertrand Russell; Albert Schweitzer; violinist Isaac Stern, who had just returned from the USSR; playwright Arthur Miller; Norwegian poet Arnulf Overland; Supreme Court Justice William O. Douglas and Eleanor Roosevelt who, together with Reinhold Niebuhr and Thurgood Marshall of the National Association of Colored People had in May 1960 published an appeal to Khrushchev in which they pointed out that Soviet anti-Jewish discrimination not only contradicted the Soviet Union's own ideology but also the conscience of all to whom the rights of minorities were important; British Labour Party leader Richard Crossman; former French President Vincent Auriol and former Dutch Prime Minister Willem Drees. Some of these – notably Mrs. Roosevelt, Russell and Auriol – signed the conference statement.

64 Ilya Ehrenburg came to Paris in an effort to get the conference canceled and told André Blumel that the purpose of the conference was in fact anti-Soviet; the Soviet embassy in Paris had protested the conference as early as July – *JC*, 22 July 1960, and *Ma'ariv*, 12 and 15 Sept. 1960.

65 I have discussed this piece of Soviet sophistry in my article "Jewish Emigration and Soviet–Arab Relations," p. 215.

66 *Conférence internationale sur la situation des juifs en Union Soviétique* (Paris: Ch. Bernard, undated); also *JEE*, 6 (Dec. 1960). For the continued activity of this forum, see "Conference on the Situation of the Jews in the Soviet Union," July 1961 and Sept. 1963.

67 *New Times*, 4 (Jan. 1961).

68 *Undzer vort*, 10 Oct. and 9 Dec. 1960; *Ma'ariv*, 7 Dec. 1960; *JEE*, 7 (Mar. 1961), pp. 24–25.

69 *Haaretz*, 29 Jan. 1961; *JTA*, 31 Jan. 1961; *JC*, 3 Feb. 1961.

70 *JTA*, 27 Mar. 1961; *JC*, 31 Mar. 1961; *JEE*, 8 (July 1961), pp. 14–20. For Terracini's growing reservations regarding Soviet Jewish policy, see p. 181.

71 *JC*, 27 Oct. and 3 Nov. 1961. Plummer, who had been to the USSR in August, said that Soviet officials told him that the new Yiddish journal *Sovetish heymland* would appear monthly instead of every two months and that he had received "a half-promise that more copies could be published."

72 One American Jewish visitor to the USSR who attended Sabbath services at the Moscow Choral Synagogue has described his lengthy questioning by those Jews who were not afraid. They were particularly anxious to hear about Jewish communities and, above all, about Israel. Although "the tremendous influx of tourists in Moscow during the summer" meant that Western Jews were "no longer a novelty," the questions he was asked "indicated vividly the extent to which they had been denied contact with and information about the Jewish world outside" and "how they had been deliberately misinformed about matters of world interest." One of his questioners, obviously a "plant," sought to impress the tourist that a believing Jew could live as such and teach Judaism to his children, even if he occupied a senior position in society – unpublished article by the tourist in question, Mr. Elihu Bergman, presently of Washington, D.C.

73 Lash, *Eleanor*, pp. 70–71.

74 *Tog-morgn zhurnal*, 28 July 1961.

75 Bisgyer, *Challenge and Encounter*, pp. 136–38.

76 Occasionally a senator or representative indicated that his remarks emanated from an approach by his constituents. Senator Hugh Scott of Pennsylvania, for instance, referred to a resolution of the Philadelphia City and District Committee of the Workmen's Circle, one of the large Jewish fraternal societies, asking him to bring the persecution of Soviet Jews to the attention of both the Congress and the president – *CR*, 87th Congress, 2nd Session, vol. 108, part 6, p. 8140, 10 May 1962.

77 The first of these was a reference by Congressman Michael A. Feighan of Ohio to Chaim Shurer's prediction that "Russian Jews will cease to exist in 10 or 15 years unless the trend is changed inside the Soviet." In the second, Senator Herbert H. Lehman summarized the findings of an AJC fact sheet entitled "The Jews Under Stalin's Successors," which he had inserted *in toto* in the *Record*. And in the third Representative Abraham J. Multer of New York had inserted two articles from the *New York Times* of 9 July 1956, the one by C.L. Sulzberger, "Foreign Affairs – Anti-Semitism Behind the Iron Curtain," and the other by Judd L. Teller, "Plight of Jews in Russia – Hope Expressed that Khrushchev's Statement Portends Freedom" – *CR*, 84th Congress, 2nd Session, vol. 102, Appendix, pp. 557, 2813–15 and 5422–23, 9 Jan., 9 Apr. and 10 July 1956.

78 *CR*, 85th Congress, 2nd Session, vol. 104, Appendix, pp. 3981–82 and 4075–76, 1 and 5 May 1958.

79 *The Soviet Empire: Prison House of Nations and Races, A Study in Genocide, Discrimination and Abuse of Power*, 85th Congress, 2nd Session, Senate, Document no. 122, GPO, Washington, D.C., 1958. The sections on the Jews (pp. 23–25, 58–60 and 69–70) drew heavily on Schwarz, *Jews in the Soviet Union* (see ch. 4, n. 9) and U.S. Congress, Select Committee on Communist Aggression, *Treatment of the Jews under Communism*, Special Report No. 2, 83rd Congress, 2nd Session, GPO, Washington, D.C., 1954.

80 *CR*, 85th Congress, 2nd Session, vol. 104, part 13, pp. 17253–55, 13 Aug. 1958.

81 "Anti-Semitism in the Soviet Union Today," *Facts*, XIII, 3 (Aug.-Sept. 1958).

82 *CR*, 85th Congress, 2nd Session, vol. 104, part 15, pp. 19919–20, 23 Aug. 1958.

83 *CR*, 86th Congress, 1st Session, vol. 105, Appendix, pp. 3375–77, 23 Apr. 1959. The *Izvestiia* article referred to was probably that of 21 Feb. 1959, see Ro'i, "Jewish Emigration and Soviet–Arab Relations," p. 220.

84 *CR*, 86th Congress, 1st Session, vol. 105, part 10, pp. 12527–29, 1 July 1959.

85 *CR*, 86th Congress, 2nd Session, vol. 106, Appendix, pp. 113–14, 11 Jan. 1960.

86 Zvi Gitelman to the author, 5 Aug. 1983, Rabbi R. C. Hertz to the author, 20 Sept. 1983, and *CR*, 86th Congress, 2nd Session, vol. 106, Appendix, p. 491, 19 Jan. 1960. In 1961, Hertz became the second chairman, after Rabbi George Lieberman, of the Committee on Soviet Jewry of the Central Conference of American Rabbis.

87 H. CON. RES. 591, 86th Congress, 2nd Session, 17 Feb. 1960.

88 *CR*, 86th Congress, 2nd Session, vol. 106, part 5, pp. 5561–69, 15 Mar. 1960.

89 *CR*, 86th Congress, 2nd Session, vol. 106, part 5, pp. 5795–97, 16 Mar. 1960.

90 *CR*, 87th Congress, 1st Session, vol. 107, Appendix, pp. 2948–49, 1 May 1961.

91 Ibid., part 10, pp. 13362–63, 25 July 1961.

92 *CR*, 87th Congress, 2nd Session, vol. 108, part 1, pp. 922–31, 25 Jan. 1962.

93 *CR*, 87th Congress, 2nd Session, vol. 108, part 2, 21 Feb. 1962, pp. 2721–22.

94 Ibid., part 2, pp. 2328–30, 15 Feb. 1962.

95 Ibid., p. 2840, 22 Feb. 1962, and H. RES. 550, 22 Feb. 1962.

96 H. CON. RES. 440 and 441, 28 Feb. 1962, and *CR*, 87th Congress, 2nd Session, vol. 108, part 3, p. 3589, 7 Mar. 1962.

97 Ibid., pp. 4104–07, 14 Mar. 1962; cf. also the correspondence between Senator Dodd and the State Department in June–July 1962, *CR*, 88th Congress, 1st Session, vol. 109, part 3, p. 3479, 4 Mar. 1963.

98 *CR*, 87th Congress, 2nd Session, vol. 108, part 4, p. 4648, 21 Mar. 1962.

99 *CR*, 87th Congress, 2nd Session, vol. 108, part 9, pp. 11811–13, 27 June 1962.

100 Ibid., part 10, pp. 14115–16, 19 July 1962.

101 Ibid., p. 13912, 18 July 1962.

102 Ibid., vol. 108, part 11, 2 Aug. 1962, pp. 15403–04; *NYT*, 20 July 1962.

103 American Jewish writer Maurice Hindus, whose native tongue was Russian, came away from the USSR with the conviction that, despite all its talk of assimilation and acculturation, the Kremlin still regarded the Jews as "peculiar people." Indeed, the book he wrote on what he saw during his two visits there includes a chapter entitled "Jew – Russia's Stepson" – Hindus, *House without a Roof*.

104 At a biochemistry congress in Moscow in July 1961 two Jews told Avraham Patchornik of the Weizmann Institute that they listened to Kol Zion lagola; interview with A. Patchornik, who remembers, too, that Jews

congratulated the Israelis on the launching of the spacecraft Shavit 2 of which they had heard from Israeli broadcasts. Another Israeli, Dr. Tova Yeshurun-Berman, who participated in a World Health Organization (WHO) seminar and met Jewish doctors and medical personnel in Kiev, Vinnitsa and the Crimea, found that she had more success in making contact with Jews she met outside her official capacity than with her colleagues. In Vinnitsa a group of Jews who heard that an Israeli had come to their town awaited her at the exit of her hotel to talk about Israel – interview with T. Yeshurun-Berman.

Among the Soviet Jewish emigrants who told me of the importance for Soviet Jewish professionals of encounters with Israeli scientists was Inessa Rubin, widow of the late sinologist Vitalii Rubin. The couple, who made their first contact with Israelis at the 1957 Youth Festival, had lengthy talks with the Israeli delegation to the Orientalist conference in Moscow in August 1960 – interview with I. Rubin.

105 I have been helped in this section by two old hands in broadcasting to the USSR, Victor Grajewski and Aharon Orimian, both of the Israel Broadcasting Authority's External Radio Service.

106 Both tourists and Israeli diplomats received such requests regularly; so, too, did the Israel Broadcasting Authority in Jerusalem. For earlier demands of a similar nature, see pp. 62–63.

197 In Georgia and along the Black Sea coast it was possible to hear not only Kol Zion lagola (on short-wave) but also Israel's internal Kol Israel (on the medium-wave band of a normal radio) – cf. Eliav, *Between Hammer and Sickle*, pp. 163–64. Ezra Rusinek, who was living in Taganrog on the Sea of Azov in the late 1950s and early 1960s, heard Kol Israel regularly – interview with E. Rusinek.

108 Interviews with Binyamin Eliav, Yaacov Yanai and a former member of the Israeli embassy staff, and A. Orimian to the author, 4 and 6 Mar. 1984.

109 Interviews with Y. Yanai and B. Eliav. Yankelevich was supported by Eliav; Director of Kol Zion lagola Avraham Arest, who developed the broadcasts to the USSR with Eliav; Zvi Nezer, Eliav's deputy and successor; and Grajewski, head of the department for broadcasts to the Soviet Union since 1961 – V. Grajewski to the author, 13 Jan. 1985. For the importance of the broadcasts, especially the Russian-language ones, see pp. 298–300.

110 Yedidya, "The Study of Hebrew," and interview with S. Kodesh.

111 One lesson, describing the visit to Israel of a foreign Jew, emphasized that there one can feel oneself "a real Jew" – *JC*, 13 Sept. 1963.

112 I have a number of these calendars in my possession.

113 From time to time the Soviet press had pilloried elderly Jews for earning extra money by copying out calendars by hand. Since people were afraid that they might miss the dates of the Jewish festivals and of the *Yortseyt* (anniversary of the death) of their closest kin, the handwritten calendars giving the Jewish holidays and the Jewish lunar, as well as the Gregorian, months were in great demand. In 1962 and again in 1963, 5,000 Jewish calendars were printed officially and sold for one ruble apiece – *JC*, 10 July 1955, 11 Oct. 1963; *JEE*, II, 4 (Feb. 1964), p. 43.

114 The first issue of *Vestnik Izrailia* appeared in April 1959, the last, no. 37, in January 1963. Its editorial board comprised a number of Israeli public figures, some of whom had long shown interest in the Soviet Jewish cause. One of these was Meir Grossman, head of the Jewish Agency's Information Department and member of the Jewish Agency Executive. Another was journalist Gershon Svet – M. Grossman to G. Svet, 16 and 31 Aug. 1959 (CZA, A239/23).

115 For example, the book that Soviet Jewish journalist Grigorii Plotkin published in 1959 after returning from a trip to Israel entitled *Poezdka v Izrail* (Journey to Israel; Moscow: Literaturnaia gazeta, 1959). The book appeared simultaneously in Russian and Ukrainian; for the articles on which the book was based, see ch. 7, n. 94.

116 The first issue of *Shalom* was dated February–March 1963, the last, no. 19, April 1967.

117 Five numbers of *Ariel* seem to have appeared in Russian between 1962 and 1966.

## 6 The outside world takes up the issue: 1963–1967

1 The poem was published in *Literaturnaia gazeta* in September 1961, the twentieth anniversary of the Babii Iar massacre.

2 *Foreign Affairs*, XLI, 2 (January 1963), pp. 420–30.

3 E.g., Glenn Richter to the author, 6 Sept. 1983.

4 *Pravda*, 1 Mar. 1963; *JEE*, II, 2 (May 1963), pp. 20–24.

5 *JC*, 1 Mar. 1963; *JEE*, II, 2 (May 1963), pp. 24–26. Russell's reply to Khrushchev does not seem to have been published.

6 *JEE*, II, 3 (Sept. 1963), pp. 5–11.

7 The author is grateful to Dr. William Korey and Professor Yoram Dinstein for helping him understand U.N. procedures, especially those relevant to discussion of Soviet Jewry. The following section could not have been written without their guidance.

8 On 19 Nov. 1963, in an address to the Jewish Theological Seminary in New York, Justice Arthur Goldberg of the U.S. Supreme Court called for the establishment of an International Court of Human Rights to enforce essential civil rights under the U.N. Declaration of Human Rights – *JEE*, II, 4 (Feb. 1964), p. 56. Only one relevant limited convention, which the USSR had duly ratified, was in force at the beginning of the decade, the UNESCO Convention against Discrimination in Education, which stipulated "the liberty of parents . . . to choose for their children institutions other than those maintained by the public authorities" – quoted in an AJC FAD working paper, 21 Nov. 1963, part 2, p. 1.

9 E/CN.4/Sub.2/SR.286, 12th Session, 15 Jan. 1960, p. 4. I have not always used quotation marks even when I have reproduced sections of the Sub-Commission's discussions verbatim, since these are summary records which clearly do not quote the exact words of the various speakers.

10 The report was prepared in response to an invitation by the Sub-Commission to governments and NGOs to supply information and com-

ments on the causes of the swastika-daubing incidents in the West of which the first had been in Cologne on Christmas Eve 1959, and was in addition to the CBJO report submitted in October 1960 in connection with the Ingles report (see below) – *New York Post*, 8 Jan. 1961; *JTA*, 31 Jan. 1961; *JEE*, 7 (Mar. 1961), pp. 34–35. For an earlier report by the WJC submitted to the Sub-Commission early in 1958 and calling on the Soviet Union to grant its Jews the same rights as enjoyed by East European Jewish communities, see CZA, A232/88 and *Al hamishmar*, 28 Jan. 1958.

11 For the outcome of the Soviet draft resolution, see E/CN.4/Sub.2/SR.336, 30 Jan. 1961, p. 11.

12 U.N. Secretary General Dag Hammerskjöld had notified member states and NGOs of this projected study in a circular of April 1960.

13 E/CN.4/Sub.2/SR.313, 13th Session, 13 Jan. 1961, pp. 5–7; interview with William Korey; Korey, *The Soviet Cage*; and see p. 138 above. Nixon had written Gromyko on 1 Aug. 1959, just a month prior to Khrushchev's first visit to the U.S.: "In the interest of improving relations between the United States and the Soviet Union, I believe that matters such as this involving principles of nonseparation of families which we both support should not persist as irritants to larger solutions." In reply Gromyko said that requests aimed at permitting Soviet citizens to be reunited with their families in the U.S. "will be considered with proper attention as is always the case in consideration of such affairs." Similar obligations were made in this period by Soviet officials to the Australian government – ibid., p. 190.

14 E/CN.4/Sub.2/SR.366, 14th Session, 25 Jan. 1962, pp. 9–14.

15 Ibid., pp. 6–8.

16 E/CN.4/Sub.2/SR.368, 14th Session, 26 Jan. 1962, p. 5.

17 As a group of experts rather than delegates representing their respective governments, the Sub-Commission altogether habitually refrained from making charges against specific member states.

18 E/CN.4/Sub.2/SR.368, 14th Session, 26 Jan. 1962, p. 7–9.

19 E/CN.4/Sub.2/SR.367, 14th Session, 25 Jan. 1962, p. 12.

20 Interview with Yoram Dinstein.

21 GA OR, 17th Session, 3rd Committee, 1165th Meeting, 29 Oct. 1962, pp. 156–57.

22 GA OR, 17th Session, 3rd Committee, 1170th and 1171st Meetings, 1 and 2 Nov. 1962, pp. 186–87 and 194–95.

23 E/CN.4/Sub.2/SR.381, 15th Session, 15 Jan. 1963, pp. 4–6, and Korey, *The Soviet Cage*, pp. 184–87.

24 E/CN.4/Sub.2/SR.383, 15th Session, 16 Jan. 1963, pp. 5–7.

25 Ibid., pp. 6–9.

26 E/CN.4/Sub.2/SR.384, 15th Session, 17 Jan. 1963, p. 5.

27 E/CN.4/Sub.2/SR.385, 15th Session, 18 Jan. 1963, pp. 7–8 and 11–12.

28 Ivanov had said that any violation of religious freedom in the USSR or of the right to leave the country without discrimination was punishable by law.

29 E/CN.4/Sub.2/SR.386, 15th Session, 18 Jan. 1963, pp. 3, 5 and 11.

30 E/CN.4/Sub.2/SR.389, 15th Session, 22 Jan. 1963, pp. 4–5.

31 E/CN.4/Sub.2/SR.395, 15th Session, 25 Jan. 1963, p. 3.
32 *Haboker*, 27 Jan. 1963.
33 E/CN.4/Sub.2/SR.396, 15th Session, 25 Jan. 1963, pp. 8–9.
34 GA OR, 18th Session, 3rd Committee, 1241st Meeting, 24 Oct. 1963, pp. 151–52 and 154.
35 E/CN.4/Sub.2/SR.416, 16th Session, 20 Jan. 1964, pp. 7–10.
36 E/CN.4/Sub.2/SR.421, 16th Session, 23 Jan. 1964.
37 Commission on Human Rights, 20th Session, 807th Meeting, E/CN.4/SR.807, 12 Mar. 1964, pp. 5–12. The Soviet Deputy Permanent Representative to the U.N., Platon Morozov, refuting charges of Soviet antisemitism, cited the large number of Jews represented on "central and local bodies," among "scientific workers," in the free professions and in the ranks of recipients of academic degrees – E/CN.4/SR.808, 12 Mar. 1964, pp. 10–12.
38 Economic and Social Council, 35th Session, 1249th Meeting, 8 Apr. 1963, p. 48.
39 Economic and Social Council, 37th Session, 1338th Meeting, 30 July 1964, pp. 168–71.
40 The book, published in 1963 by the Ukrainian Academy of Sciences, included, in addition to crude attacks on the Jewish religion and those who practiced it, numerous Sturmer-like illustrations.
41 E/CN.4/Sub.2/SR.434, 12 Jan. 1965, pp. 3–9.
42 E/CN.4/Sub.2/SR.438, 16th Session, 14 Jan. 1965, pp. 8–9.
43 Commission on Human Rights, 21st Session, 819th Meeting, 24 Mar. 1965, E/CN.4/SR.819, pp. 8–10; *JC*, 2 Apr. 1965. Cohn noted that while a new edition of the Russian Orthodox version of the Bible had been printed in 1957 and a Protestant one in 1958, and three editions of the Qur'an had been produced between 1958 and 1962, permission had not been given for publishing the Hebrew Bible. He also pointed out that whereas Jews were unable to have contact with co-religionists abroad, the nationwide Baptist federation was affiliated to the World Council of Baptists, while Muslims were allowed to send and receive delegations and make the pilgrimage to Mecca. For the situation of religion in the Soviet Union in the period in question, see Richard Marshall, *Aspects of Religion in the USSR, 1917–1967* (Chicago: Chicago University Press, 1971).
44 GA OR, 20th Session, 3rd Committee, 1312th Meeting, 20 Oct. 1965, pp. 115–19. On 17 October the U.S. and Brazil had suggested the condemnation of antisemitism as a form of racism. The USSR at first proposed to substitute Nazism and neo-Nazism for antisemitism and then came forward with the idea of bracketing the four: Zionism, antisemitism, Nazism and neo-Nazism. But immediately afterwards the Soviets suggested to the Americans that both their proposals be retracted, thus making clear that their proposals had been intended to negate and neutralize that of the U.S. and Brazil.
45 GA OR, 21st Session, 3rd Committee, 1391st Meeting, 12 Oct. 1966, pp. 84–85, 87–88 and 92.
46 GA OR, 21st Session, 1428th Plenary Meeting, 4 Oct. 1966, p. 13. Ambassador Comay made further mention of the Soviet Jews' cultural deprivation

and the religious discrimination against them in the same session, at the discussion of the Draft International Covenants on Human Rights – 1495th Plenary Meeting, 16 Dec. 1966, p. 4.

47 E/CN.4/Sub.2/SR.503, 18th Session, 19 Jan. 1967, pp. 4–5. At the following meeting Zeltner replied to Nasinovskii's accusation that his statement had been a tissue of lies by pointing out that he had merely quoted from documents placed before the Sub-Commission – E/CN.4/Sub.2/SR.504, 19 Jan. 1967, p. 9.

48 Commission on Human Rights, 23rd Session, 928th Meeting, 15 Mar. 1967, pp. 6–7, and *New York Times*, 16 Mar. and 1 May 1967.

49 *JC*, 13 and 20 Sept. 1963, and *JEE*, II, 4 (Feb. 1964), p. 59.

50 *JEE*, III, 1 (Nov. 1964), pp. 81–86, and 6 (May 1967), p. 131.

51 *JC*, 13 May 1966.

52 *Anti-Semitism in the Soviet Union, A Socialist International Report* [1970].

53 *JEE*, III, 6 (May 1967), pp. 132–33. The ICFTU, which had a membership of over 60 million, had submitted a memorandum to ECOSOC as early as April 1963 declaring that "a distinct and unmistakable pattern of hostility toward Jews" was evident in the USSR – ibid., II, 3 (Sept. 1963), p. 76.

54 *Cleveland Jewish News*, 24 June 1966.

55 "Monthly Chronicle of Soviet Jewish Affairs," *Focus on Soviet Jewry*, Feb. 1966, and ibid., June–July 1966, p. 8.

56 *Di prese* (Buenos Aires), 22 Sept. 1966. In his introduction, too, Terracini admitted that it was difficult to find a valid explanation for the discriminatory policies toward the Jews "still practised in the Soviet Union – *JC*, 16 Sept. 1966. For comment on the book, *Gli ebrei nell' URSS: a cura di 'Nuovo Argumenti'* (Milan: Garzanti edition, 1966), see *Radio Free Europe (RFE) Research*, "On Soviet Anti-Semitism and Non-Ruling Parties," 30 Aug. 1967. For Terracini's first public appearance on the Soviet Jewish issue, in 1961, in which he had sought to defend Soviet Jewish policy, see p. 143.

57 *JC*, 14 Jan. 1966; *JEE*, III, 5 (Oct. 1966), pp. 51–52.

58 Quoted in *JEE*, III, 5 (Oct. 1966), pp. 52–57; *JC*, 8 July 1966.

59 *Soviet Jewry – A Reply to I. Liebler*.

60 *France nouvelle*, 5 May 1964, cited by Fejto, *The French Communist Party*, p. 159. Despite the party's official reticence, it was reported that at its Seventeenth Congress in May 1964, a number of PCF leaders raised the Soviet Jewish issue before Suslov and Ponomarev, but were met with such a sharp reaction that the subject was dropped.

   For approaches to the PCF leadership, specifically Assistant General Secretary Waldeck Rochet, but also Politburo members Roger Garandy, Henri Krasucky and Raymond Guyot, see Armand Kaplan, Executive Director of the WJC Paris office, to R. Garandy, 6 Feb. 1964, and to N. Goldmann, 9 Apr. 1965, CZA, Z6/2066.

61 For intercession on behalf of a Soviet Yiddish writer by the Norwegian communist organ *Friheten*'s Moscow correspondent, see p. 335.

62 *Political Affairs*, 18 Aug. 1966; nevertheless, in a report in Feb. 1967 on the visit to the USSR of party leader Gus Hall, the same journal defended Soviet Jewish policy.

63 *Daily Worker*, 28 Feb. 1967; *NYT*, 1 Mar. 1967.

64 *JC*, 7 May 1965; *Israelitisches Wochenblatt* (Zurich), 21 May 1965; *JEE*, III, 4 (June 1966), p. 98; J. I. Linton to N. Goldmann, 2 Apr. 1965 (CZA, Z2/2066); *The Council of Europe*. For activity in the British parliament, see pp. 225–26; for discussion on Soviet Jewry in the parliaments of Norway and the Netherlands, see pp. 226–27.

65 *Journal of the International Commission of Jurists*, V, 1–2 (Summer 1964), pp. 3–47.

66 For the nine occasions on which Javits spoke on the Soviet Jewish situation in the First Session of the Eighty-eighth Congress, see *CR*, 88th Congress, 1st Session, vol. 109, part 1, pp. 772–74, 22 Jan. 1963, part 4, pp. 4505–07 and 5405, 19 and 25 Mar. 1963, part 8, pp. 10029–30, 4 June 1963, part 10, pp. 12856–57, 18 July 1963, part 11, p. 15423, 20 Aug. 1963, part 13, pp. 17710–11 and 17966–69, 23 and 25 Sept. 1963, and Appendix, pp. 7417–18. For Keating's eight intercessions, see ibid., part 1, pp. 664–68, 21 Jan. 1963, part 9, pp. 12058–59, 2 July 1963, part 10, pp. 13196–98, 24 July 1963, part 12, p. 15848, 26 Aug. 1963, part 13, p. 17966, 23 Sept. 1963, part 15, pp. 19652–53, 16 Oct. 1963, part 16, pp. 21722–23, 13 Nov. 1963, and part 18, p. 23216, 4 Dec. 1963. For Scott's appearances, see ibid., part 1, p. 768, 22 Jan. 1963 and Appendix, p. 2903, 9 May 1963 (Scott also brought to the U.S. Senate a resolution of the Pennsylvanian Senate demanding action by the State Department and the U.S. U.N. mission). For Dodd, see ibid., part 3, p. 3479, 4 Mar. 1963. For Ribicoff, see ibid., part 13, pp. 17960–69, 25 Sept. 1963 and part 15, p. 20099, 22 Oct. 1963.

67 Farbstein submitted H. CON. RES. 69 and 70, see below. For Farbstein, see also *CR*, 88th Congress, 1st Session, vol. 109, Appendix, p. 6968, 7 Nov. 1963; and for Halpern, see ibid., p. 3429, 28 May 1963.

68 Ibid., vol. 109, part 16, pp. 21722–23, 13 Nov. 1963.

69 E.g., ibid., Appendix, p. 1410, 14 Mar. 1963.

70 *Haboker*, 31 Jan. 1963.

71 H. CON. RES. 70 and 78, 31 Jan. and 4 Feb. 1963.

72 *CR*, 88th Congress, 1st Session, vol. 109, part 13, pp. 17710–11, 23 Sept. 1963.

73 S. RES. 204 and *CR*, 88th Congress, 1st Session, vol. 109, part 13, pp. 17690–96, 25 Sept. 1963. The proposed resolution led to a *New York Herald Tribune* editorial (3 Oct. 1963) which said the execution of Jews in the USSR provided grounds for accusing it of genocide.

74 *JC*, 27 Sept. 1963.

75 *CR*, 88th Congress, 1st Session, vol. 109, part 14, pp. 19006–08 and 19283–84, 8 and 10 Oct. 1963, part 16, pp. 21180–93, 6 Nov. 1963, and Appendix, pp. 6392–93 and 7086, 14 Oct. and 13 Nov. 1963.

76 Ibid., vol. 109, part 15, pp. 19652–53, 16 Oct. 1963.

77 GA OR, 18th Session, 1209th Meeting, pp. 4–7, 20 Sept. 1963. The president had also told the Assembly that he hoped that, just as the U.S. was working to right its wrongs, "other multiracial societies will meet these standards of fairness and justice." He pointed out that "since human rights

are indivisible," the U.N. "cannot stand aside when these rights are abused and neglected by any Member State." Another indirect assault on the Soviets was made by Assistant Secretary of State for Educational and Cultural Affairs Lucius Battle, when he charged UNESCO with distributing a booklet misrepresenting the Soviet Jewish situation and having the audacity to call it *Equality of Rights Between Races and Nationalities in the U.S.S.R.* In particular, he took exception to a statement concerning the Jews' "voluntary assimilation" – *JP*, 8 May 1963.

78 *JC*, 1 Nov. 1963; *CR*, 88th Congress, 1st Session, vol. 109, part 16, pp. 2188–89, 6 Nov. 1963; *JEE*, II, 4 (Feb. 1964), p. 57. Already in August, on returning from a trip to the USSR, Harriman had revealed that the U.S. government was seeking to influence Moscow to allow Soviet Jews to leave the country, but doubted whether it could achieve anything in this direction – *Haaretz*, 8 Aug. 1963.

79 I am grateful to Mr. Myer Feldman for providing me with much of the information on this section – his letter to me of 27 Feb. 1984. Justice Goldberg, too, told me that he first spoke to Kennedy about Soviet Jewry when he was still Secretary of Labor – interview with A. Goldberg – but it is possible that Goldberg's dates are not precise. (In any case, I have found no corroborating evidence for this assertion.) On the intercession of Goldberg, Javits and Ribicoff with Kennedy and Rusk, and on subsequent developments, see *Ma'ariv*, 27 Dec. 1963, and Lawrence, *Three Million More?*, pp. 169–75.

80 *Ma'ariv*, 27 Dec. 1963; Lawrence, *Three Million More?*, pp. 169–75.

81 19 Aug. 1964, Washington, D.C. – the text of the statement was kindly supplied to me by Senator Ribicoff.

82 *CR*, 88th Congress, 2nd Session, vol. 110.

83 *CR*, 88th Congress, 2nd Session, vol. 110, part 3, pp. 3745–46, 26 Feb. 1964.

84 Quoted in letter from Robert E. Lee, Acting Assistant Secretary for Congressional Relations, to Representative Seymour Halpern, 6 Nov. 1964 – *CR*, 89th Congress, 1st Session, vol. 111, part 1, pp. 147–48, 6 Jan. 1965.

85 Ibid.

86 *American Examiner*, 13 Apr. 1967.

87 *CR*, 88th Congress, 2nd Session, vol. 110, part 17, p. 22694, 23 Sept. 1964.

88 U.S. Information Agency Director Carl T. Rowan had written to Fulbright to this effect in March and Assistant Secretary of State Frederick G. Dutton followed suit in April.

89 *CR*, 88th Congress, 2nd Session, vol. 110, part 17, pp. 22775–82, 24 Sept. 1964.

90 Ibid., part 18, pp. 23520–21, 2 Oct. 1964; *JTA*, 6 Oct. 1964.

91 *CR*, 89th Congress, 1st Session, vol. 111, part 1, pp. 146–48, 6 Jan. 1965, and Acting Assistant Secretary Lee to Representative Halpern as in n. 84 above.

92 Ibid., vol. 111, part 2, pp. 922 and 1804–05, 19 Jan. and 2 Feb. 1965.

93 S. CON. RES. 17, passed in the House 21 June 1965 (see immediately below).

94 E.g., a *Washington Post* editorial, 18 Jan. 1965.

95 *NYT*, 16 Apr. 1965.

96 *NYT*, 4 Dec. 1966 quoted in *JEE*, II, 6 (May 1967), pp. 126–27.

97 *CR*, 90th Congress, 1st Session, vol. 113, part 8, pp. 10502–04, 24 Apr. 1967.

98 Heschel's September speech was sent to 2,000 Conservative rabbis, many of whom used it as the basis for their Yom Kippur sermons.

99 AJC FAD memorandum, "The Situation of the Jews in the Soviet Union," 21 Nov. 1963.

100 *CR*, 88th Congress, 2nd Session, vol. 110, part 6, pp. 7164–66, 7 Apr. 1964.

101 Ibid., part 5, pp. 6899–6906, 6 Apr. 1964.

102 Ibid., pp. 7103–07, 6 Apr. 1964.

103 Ibid., part 6, pp. 7599–7600, 10 Apr. 1964.

104 Ibid., pp. 7165–66, 7 Apr. 1964.

105 Appelbaum, "U.S. Jews' Reaction." The AJCSJ chairmanship and physical location were rotated every six months until 1966, when it found a permanent abode at the main offices of NCRAC.

106 Ibid., pp. 23–24.

107 Appelbaum, "U.S. Jews' Reaction," pp. 25–26, quoting *NYT*, 16 July 1965; Rabbi Emmanuel Jacobovits to J. Birnbaum, 3 Feb. 1965, SSSJ Archives; Orbach, *The American Movement*, p. 24. Goldmann was supported by the leading officials of the WJC (Perlzweig, Armand Kaplan in Paris, Mark Turkow in Buenos Aires), Joachim Prinz of the American Jewish Congress, Yehuda Hellman, Secretary of the Presidents' Conference, and Rose Halperin and others of the Jewish Agency Executive, American Branch – interview with B. Eliav.

108 Memorandum on the conference by S. Andhil Fineberg, 15 Apr. 1964, AJC Inventory RG 7-1.

109 Jerry Goodman to Simon Segal, 11 Dec. 1964, AJC Inventory RG 7-1.

110 Minutes of AJCSJ meeting, 2 Mar. 1965, CZA, Z6/2066.

111 From text of speech in AJC Inventory RG 7-1; *Tog-morgn zhurnal*, 3 June 1965; *Haaretz*, 4 June 1965; *Jewish Chronicle* (Pittsburgh, Pa.), 11 June 1965.

112 *Haaretz*, 4 June 1965.

113 *New York Times*, 2 June 1965.

114 AJCSJ statement, 27 July 1965, AJC Inventory RG 7-1.

115 *CR*, 89th Congress, 1st Session, vol. 111, part 18, pp. 24436–38, 24909–10 and 24738, 20 and 22 Sept. 1965, and *Washington Post*, 20 Sept. 1965.

116 E.g., speech of Representative Lester Wolff at Roslyn, Long Island, on 22 Feb. 1967 – *CR*, 90th Congress, 1st Session, vol. 113, part 7, pp. 8505–06, 5 Apr. 1967.

117 *Soviet Jewry Today*, an interim report issued by the AJCSJ, New York, quoted in *CR*, 89th Congress, 1st Session, vol. 111, Appendix, p. 5341, 21 Sept. 1965, and 2nd Session, vol. 112, part 1, pp. 1145–49, 26 Jan. 1966.

118 *CR*, 89th Congress, 2nd Session, vol. 112, Appendix, pp. 2177–78, 21 Apr. 1966; A Declaration of Rights for Soviet Jewry, 18 Apr. 1966, AJC Inventory RG 7-1.

119 *Cleveland Jewish News*, 22 Apr. 1966.

120 *NYT*, 18 Apr. 1966. The conference also heard an analysis of the Soviet Jewish situation by Professor Eric Goldhagen, Director of the Institute for East European Affairs at Brandeis University.
121 *NYT*, 17 Apr. 1966.
122 Albert D. Chernin to NCRAC membership, 20 Sept. 1966 – AJC Inventory RG 7-1.
123 Statement on meeting between Walt Rostow and Leaders of 25 Member Organizations of AJCSJ, 19 Sept. 1966; opening remarks of Aaron Goldman, Lafayette Park, 19 Sept. 1966; A. Chernin to NCRAC membership, 20 Sept. 1966, AJC Inventory RG 7-1; and *NYT*, 20 Sept. 1966.
124 A. Chernin to NCRAC membership, 12 Oct. 1966, AJC Inventory RG 7-1.
125 *JEE*, III, 6 (May 1967), p. 126.
126 When asked by me to explain their interest both Senator Javits and Justice Goldberg, for instance, began by noting that their forebears had come from Russia – interviews with J. Javits and A. Goldberg. Referring to Kosygin's announcement regarding family reunification, a Jewish Federation Council of Greater Los Angeles pointed out that "national agencies, including the United HIAS Service and the American Jewish Conference on Soviet Jewry, are urging all their constituent member organizations to join in an intensive program to interpret to American Jews the procedures for search of relatives and reunion." The circular, dated 1 June 1967, was signed by Council President Victor M. Carter.
127 Glenn J. Richter to the author, 6 Sept. 1983.
128 *CR*, 88th Congress, 1st Session, vol. 109, part 15, p. 20099, 22 Oct. 1963; *JC*, 18 Oct. 1963; *JEE*, II, 4 (Feb. 1964), pp. 51–54; and interview with M. Decter. The standing committee, which bore the name The Conference on the Status of Soviet Jews, later coopted A. Philip Randolph, Bayard Rustin and scientist Eugene Rabinowitz, a left-wing liberal who was much concerned with nuclear disarmament and was prominent in the anti-Vietnam movement. Several months after the conference, Arthur Miller published an article "On Obliterating the Jews" (*New Leader*, 16 Mar. 1964), in which he clarified the context and rationale of his own concern and explained why he was convinced that antisemitism existed in the USSR.
129 *World Journal Tribune*, 4 Dec. 1966; *JEE*, III, 6 (May 1967), pp. 125–26; and interview with M. Decter.
130 *American Examiner*, 13 Apr. 1967.
131 Quoted in *CR*, 88th Congress, 1st Session, vol. 109, part 4, p. 4506, 19 Mar. 1963.
132 *NYT*, 7 Dec. 1962, quoted in *CR*, 88th Congress, 1st Session, vol. 109, part 1, pp. 772–73, 22 Jan. 1963 and Appendix, pp. 317–18, 28 Jan. 1963.
133 *JEE*, III, 1 (Nov. 1964), p. 93.
134 *Cleveland Jewish News*, 24 June 1966.
135 Rabbi Daniel Litt to Rabbi Robert A. Rothman, 31 Mar. 1964. I am grateful to Dr. Louis (Lou) Rosenblum of Cleveland for having allowed me to use the archives of the Cleveland Council on Soviet Anti-Semitism (as the Committee became in 1965), which include a wealth of private correspon-

dence and newspaper cuttings, notably from local Jewish and non-Jewish newspapers, as well as the Council's own publications. (The archives, previously in Rosenblum's private possession, have meanwhile been transferred to the Jewish Archives of the Western Reserve Historical Society, Cleveland, Ohio.)

136 Appelbaum, "U.S. Jews' Reaction," p. 23.

137 *Plain Dealer*, 11 Oct. and 9 and 27 Nov. 1963; *Cleveland Press*, 24 Oct. 1963.

138 Interview with L. Rosenblum.

139 L. Rosenblum to Louis Nemzer, 17 May 1965.

140 The circular, dated 27 Oct. 1963, is in the archives of the Cleveland Council.

141 The Chairman and four Co-Chairmen of the Cleveland Committee to N. S. Khrushchev, 2 Apr. 1964.

142 The telegram, dated 12 Oct. 1963, is in the archives of the Cleveland Council.

143 A copy of this circular of 17 Mar. 1965 is in the Cleveland Council archives.

144 *Spotlight*, 1 (Nov. 1965).

145 The meeting had been arranged by Congressman Robert Sweeney (D. – Ohio); *Plain Dealer*, 29 Nov. 1963, 9 May 1965 and 31 Mar. 1966.

146 H. Caron to Lynn Gershman, 22 Dec. 1963.

147 L. Gershman to H. Caron, 28 Dec. 1963.

148 Rabbi D. Litt to Rabbi R. A. Rothman, 31 Mar. 1964.

149 Appelbaum, "U.S. Jews' Reaction," p. 23; and Brafman and Schimmel, *Trade for Freedom*, pp. 23–24. Morris Brafman was head of the League.

150 Cf. Orbach, *The American Movement*, p. 4.

151 J. Birnbaum and David Disenhouse to D. Dubinsky, 2 Sept. 1964, SSSJ archives. I wish to take the opportunity to express my gratitude to Jacob Birnbaum and Glenn Richter for their cooperation in helping me understand the beginnings of SSSJ as well as its activities and goals in these early years.

152 Interview with J. Birnbaum.

153 The first such booklet entitled *Save Soviet Jewry Handbook* was dated July 1965. Further *Program Handbooks* were put out annually thereafter.

154 Interview with J. Birnbaum.

155 J. Birnbaum to the Chairman, Platform Committee, Democratic Party and to John M. Bailey, Democratic National Committee, 27 July 1964; Congressman Farbstein's secretary, Barbara Merne, to J. Birnbaum, undated; and J. Birnbaum to L. Farbstein and Emanuel Celler, 2 Aug. 1964 – SSSJ Archives. For the request to this effect of Senator Ribicoff, see p. 189.

156 K. B. Keating to J. Birnbaum, 12 June 1964; J. K. Javits to J. Birnbaum, 13 June 1964; J. Birnbaum and D. Disenhouse to D. Dubinsky, 2 Sept. 1964; *Jewish Press*, 16 Oct. 1964 – SSSJ Archives; *NYHT*, 19 Oct. 1964.

157 *NYT*, 5 Apr. 1965; *Save Soviet Jewry Handbook* (Summer 1965), pp. 26–27.

158 *NYT*, 20 Dec. 1965; *Focus on Soviet Jewry* (Apr. 1966).

159 *NYT*, 30 Apr. and 1 May 1967.

160 *NYT*, 1 May 1967. A previous full-page advertisement published in the same paper on the eve of the vigil under the title "Justice for Russian

Jewry", with an impressive list of sponsors, was put out under the official auspices of the Center for Russian Jewry, a publicity framework for the SSSJ. It ended with a call to the White House "to leave no doubt in the minds of the Kremlin that its policies in regard to Soviet Jews are repugnant to millions of Americans"; to the Kremlin to give its Jews "equal rights," to combat "antisemitic elements" and to "facilitate" the reunion of families; to the U.N. to "see this tragedy as one of the great moral challenges of our time" and to place it "high on the agenda for human rights"; and to Americans "secure in their own freedom, to give our cause their active support." And finally it declared: "Let the Jews of the Soviet Union take heart! They are no longer forgotten."

161 Orbach, *The American Movement*, pp. 31–32.

162 Appelbaum, "The U.S. Jews' Reaction," p. 25; Friedberg, "Defending Soviet Jews."

163 S. Andhil Fineberg, AJC Community Relations Consultant, to Senator Keating, 15 Apr. 1964, reprinted in an AJC memorandum entitled "The American League for Russian Jews."

164 N. Levanon to J. Birnbaum, 30 June 1967, SSSJ archives; also Orbach, *The American Movement*, p. 33.

165 E.g., Orbach, *The American Movement*, p. 31. The American Jewish press sporadically reported lectures given by Meir Rosenne before local Jewish meetings on the situation of Soviet Jewry.

166 *Ma'ariv*, 17 July 1964.

167 *JEE*, III, 1 (Nov. 1964), p. 95.

168 Ibid., p. 94.

169 Ibid., III, 4 (June 1966), pp. 91–92.

170 *JC*, 2 Apr. 1965; *JEE*, III, 4 (June 1966), p. 92.

171 *JC*, 14 Jan., 1 Apr. and 13 May 1966; *JEE*, III, 4 (June 1966), p. 82.

172 *JEE*, III, 5 (Oct. 1966), pp. 29–30. A stencil report of the students' conversation at the Soviet embassy was kindly supplied me by Mr. Gordon Hausmann who headed the delegation and organized the demonstration.

173 The documentation for Australian Jewish and non-Jewish activity on behalf of Soviet Jews, including the resolutions of 5 March 1962 and of the ECAJ annual meeting of 14–15 Nov. 1964, and the three pamphlets – Liebler, *Soviet Jewry and Human Rights; Soviet Jewry. A Reply to I. Liebler*; and *Soviet Jewry and the Australian Communist Party* – have been kindly supplied to the author by the office of the ECAJ.

174 *JEE*, III, 1 (Nov. 1964), p. 95.

175 Ibid., III, 6 (May 1967), p. 133. For the Australian U.N. representative's condemnation of Soviet anti-Jewish discrimination at the U.N. General Assembly Third Committee – on 12 Oct. 1966 – see p. 176.

176 ECAJ, Minutes of the Annual Meeting, Melbourne, 14–15 Nov. 1964; Verbatim transcript of I. Liebler's speech, WJC meeting, Strasbourg, 14 July 1965; ECAJ circular, 14 Feb. 1967.

177 *Davar*, 16 Jan. 1963.

178 *Le Monde, Figaro*, 28 Apr. 1965.

179  *JEE*, II, 4 (Feb. 1964), p. 56.

180  *JC*, 27 May 1966.

181  *JEE*, III, I (Nov. 1964), pp. 95–96.

182  For the picketing of Soviet embassies by Jewish students in a number of European capitals, see p. 214.

183  *JC*, 25 Oct. 1963.

184  *JC*, 22 and 29 Nov. 1963.

185  *JC*, 21 May 1965.

186  *Focus on Soviet Jewry*, Feb. 1966 ("Monthly Chronicle of Soviet Jewish Affairs").

187  *Jewish Observer*, 18 June 1965.

188  *JEE*, III, 6 (May 1967), p. 131.

189  *JC*, 3, 10 and 17 Feb. 1967.

190  *JC*, 17 Feb. 1967.

191  *JEE*, II, 4 (Feb. 1964), p. 53, and III, 2 (May 1965), p. 81, and 5 (Oct. 1966), pp. 65–66. In reply to criticism by two young speakers, the heads of the Canadian Jewish Congress admitted that they had hitherto not done enough and would increase their efforts. (A first Canadian Jewish Congress resolution on Soviet Jewry, in summer 1963, had omitted any mention of the reunification of families, although at its Eastern Region Conference in December 1963 it included this as well.)

192  *JEE*, II, 4 (Feb. 1964), p. 60.

193  Ibid., III, 6 (May 1967), p. 132.

194  Ibid., p. 127.

195  *JC*, 20 Sept. 1963.

196  Ibid., 11 Oct. 1963; *Yalkut magen*, 28–29 (Dec. 1963), pp. 16–18.

197  *Stampa, Corriere della Sera*, 20 Jan. 1966; *Popolo*, 21 Jan. 1966; *JP*, 6 Feb. 1966; *Haaretz*, 15 Mar. 1966.

198  *JC*, 20 Sept. 1963; *JP*, 2 Oct. 1963. The invitations to the conference were co-signed by novelist Romulo Gallegos, former President of Venezuela, and messages were received from Argentinian President-Elect Arturo Illia, the ex-President of Brazil, Juscelino Kubitschek de Oliveira, of Mexico, Emilio Portes Gil, and of Colombia, Eduardo Santos, and the American writer Waldo Frank. The conference was given wide coverage in the Brazilian press.

199  *JEE*, III, 4 (June 1966), pp. 92–94.

200  *Di prese*, 27 Apr. 1966.

201  *Focus on Soviet Jewry*, May 1966.

202  *JC*, 20 May 1966.

203  *JEE*, III, 6 (May 1967), pp. 131–32.

204  *Combat*, 30 Oct. 1964; *JEE*, III, 2 (May 1965), p. 82.

205  *JC*, 30 Apr. 1965. The conference's organizing committee included the three Scandinavians who had helped produce the Socialist International Study Group Report in 1964: Alvar Alsterdal, John Sannes and Mogens Pihl – *JEE*, III, 4 (June 1966), p. 89.

206  Russell also sent letters and telegrams to the October 1964 meeting in Paris – in which he stressed the Left's "moral responsibility for protesting

against the intolerable persecution which the total picture of Soviet treatment of the Jews conveys" so that it not be left to advocates or protagonists of the cold war; to the organizers of a student meeting devoted to Soviet Jewry at McGill University in Montreal in early 1966; to the WUJS, in support of its efforts to publicize the facts about Soviet Jews; and to the New York Ad Hoc Commission on the Rights of Soviet Jews in March 1966 – *JEE*, III, 2 (May 1965), p. 82 and 4 (June 1966), pp. 82–84 and 87–89. For activity by other left-wing intellectuals, see, for instance, a letter to *The Times* (London) published on 26 June 1966, which was signed by thirty-three British intellectuals and public figures, including Kingsley Amis, editor of the *Statesman and Nation*; former ambassador to Moscow William Hayter; and Max Hayward.

207 A Soviet parliamentary delegation that had visited Canada headed by Deputy Chairman of the Council of Ministers Dmitrii Polianskii had also been accosted with the question of Soviet Jewry. A *Toronto Telegram* editorial addressed to the delegation maintained that antisemitism was as perplexing to Canadians as it was to "progressive Soviet citizens" (the reference was clearly to Evtushenko, Shostakovich and so on) and was an "obstacle to understanding between Canada and the USSR" – *JEE*, III, 5 (Oct. 1966), p. 65.

208 *JEE*, III, 1 (Nov. 1964), pp. 96–98; Karl Berman to the author, 22 July 1985.

209 *JEE*, III, 2 (May 1965), pp. 82–83.

210 *Ma'ariv*, 15 Dec. 1963.

211 *JEE*, III, 2 (May 1965), pp. 84–85, and 4 (June 1966), p. 99.

212 *JTA*, 9 Apr. 1964.

213 *Hansard*, vol. 716, col. 16, 12 July 1965, and vol. 722, cols. 415–16, 21 Dec. 1965. In July the question was put by David Webster, M.P. for Weston-super-Mare.

214 *Hansard*, vol. 732, cols. 8–9, and vol. 741, cols. 118–19; *JEE*, III, 5 (Oct. 1966), p. 61.

215 *Focus on Soviet Jewry*, June/July 1966, pp. 1–2, including a list of the first 171 signatories and the exchange in the House of Commons.

216 *JP*, 6 Feb. 1966; *JEE*, III, 4 (June 1966), p. 99. The issue had been raised in parliament by Liberal Deputy Cornelis Berkhouwer, and he was supported by C. L. Patijn and C. Goedhart (Labor) and Anthony E. M. Duynstee and Peter A. Blaisse (Roman Catholic).

217 *JC*, 15 Apr. 1966; *JEE*, III, 4 (June 1966), pp. 98–99. The question was also raised in the Irish Dáil in July 1965 – *JP*, 6 Feb. 1966.

218 *JC*, 1, 8 and 15 Nov. 1963.

219 In some cases the fact of their intercessions has, at least, become known. For de Gaulle's unsuccessful attempt to discuss its Jews with the Soviet leadership, for representations made to Foreign Minister Maurice Couve de Murville by French Jewish leaders and for the memorandum presented to the latter by the French Jewish community, see *Focus on Soviet Jewry*, June/July 1966.

220 *JEE*, III, 4 (June 1966), p. 93.

221 *Davar*, 3 Dec. 1963; *JEE*, III, 1 (Nov. 1964), pp. 93–94.

222 This was revealed on 30 Nov. 1965 by Under-Secretary for External Affairs Marcel Cadieux together with the hope that this was "likely to reinforce the tendency towards some relaxation in Soviet treatment of the Jewish community which had come about recently" – *JEE*, III, 4 (June 1966), p. 100.

223 *JEE*, III, 5 (Oct. 1966), p. 66.

224 Interview with Yoram Dinstein.

225 E.g., ECOSOC, Document 819, 24 Mar. 1965. See also pp. 176–77, and the Soviet attempt – in the debate on the international convention on the limitation of all forms of racial discrimination – to link Zionism with antisemitism, fascism and racism as ideologies that should be condemned by the U.N., see p. 176.

226 Certain fringe groups, however, were concerned by the Soviet counter-attack. Thus, the Israel–USSR Friendship Society issued a pamphlet on Soviet Jewry in November 1963 which cautioned that the Soviet government could not remain indifferent to the anti-Soviet campaign being conducted in Israel in connection with anti-Jewish discrimination in the USSR in which Israeli officials were taking an active part – *Haaretz*, 3 Dec. 1963.

227 For the improvement in Soviet–Arab relations as of 1964, following a temporary ebb, and for the context of both trends, see Ro'i, *From Encroachment to Involvement*, pp. 367–400.

228 Ambassador Dmitrii Chuvakhin raised the point at his first meeting with Foreign Minister Golda Meir in January 1965, and returned to the theme in April when he told her: "You know well what stands in the way of an improvement of our relations with you. It is the problem of Soviet Jews and of your activities on this subject, especially in international forums. If you change your policy on this point and if you stop provoking us, an improvement in relations will follow." When Chairman of the USSR Supreme Soviet Nikolai Podgornyi received Israel's new ambassador, Katriel Katz, in March 1966 he, too, pointed out that: "Declarations about the desire to improve relations are not sufficient if, at the same time, in your Parliament and from members of your government, we also hear declarations harmful to the Soviet Union, for instance, regarding the so-called Jewish problem." Dagan, *Moscow and Jerusalem*, pp. 145, 163–64 and 170–71.

229 For Gromyko's 14 May 1947 speech at the 1st Special Session of the U.N. General Assembly, see Ro'i, *From Encroachment to Involvement*, pp. 38–41. Soviet insensitivity, if not actual antagonism, to manifestations of national solidarity was not restricted to Jews. When Khrushchev visited the United Arab Republic in 1964 he had a verbal clash with Iraqi President 'Abd as-Salam 'Arif on this very issue – ibid., pp. 379–83.

230 *Divrei haknesset*, vol. 38, pp. 1336 and 1339–41, 4 Mar. 1963; *Haaretz*, 5 Mar. 1963; *Herut*, 8 Mar. 1963.

231 *Haboker*, 1 July 1963; *Herut*, 16 Dec. 1963.

232 *JC*, 27 Sept. 1963; *Haboker*, 6 Sept. 1964; *Haaretz*, 9 Sept. 1964.

233 *Davar*, 17 July 1964; *Hatsofe*, 19 July 1964.

234  *Davar*, 26 July 1964.

235  Eshkol had addressed himself to the question in the Knesset on 23 Oct. 1963 and 27 July and 19 Oct. 1964.

236  *Divrei haknesset*, vol. 42, pp. 1221–23, 10 Feb. 1965. For the previous occasion – in 1961 – when the issue was transferred from the Knesset plenary to the Committee, see p. 129.

237  Tenth Conference of Mapai, 16–19 Feb. 1965, Resolutions, Labor Party Archives, Bet Berl, File 21–10.

238  *Davar, Ma'ariv*, 20 May 1965; *Idishe tsaytung* (*El Diario Israelita* – Buenos Aires), 21 May 1965.

239  *Herut*, 29 June 1965. Already at its previous, fifth, convention in 1955 Magen had called upon world Jewry "not to forget the plight of our brethren in the Soviet Union" and to press the Soviet authorities to release all Jews arrested for Zionist activities and to allow Jews to emigrate – *JP*, 17 Mar. 1955; *JTA*, 18 Mar. 1955.

240  For Goldmann's position see *JC*, 20 Sept. 1963; *NYHT*, 11 June 1965; *'Al hamishmar, Yedi'ot aharonot*, 24 June 1965, and p. 197.

241  Interview with B. Eliav. Those who met with Goldmann included, in addition to Shaul Avigur and Binyamin Eliav, Prime Minister Eshkol, Deputy Prime Minister Abba Eban, Foreign Minister Meir and Jewish Agency Chairman Moshe Sharett and Treasurer Louis Arieh Pinkus.

242  *Divrei haknesset*, vol. 44, p. 348, 12 Jan. 1966.

243  *JC*, 5 Aug. 1966. Foreign Minister Meir also referred to the Soviet Jewish problem in her Israel Independence Day address in London's Albert Hall in April 1966, where her audience included House of Commons leader Herbert Bowden and Shadow Cabinet Minister Quentin Hogg – *JC*, 29 Apr. 1966.

244  *Davar*, 9 Dec. 1966.

245  *Yedi'ot aharonot*, 17 Feb. 1967; *JEE*, 6 (May 1967), p. 134.

246  Interview with B. Eliav. In preparation for Soviet Jewry Week Director-General of the Ministry of Education and Culture Yaacov Sarid instructed schools to hold discussions and special classes on the history of Soviet Jewry. The events of the week itself included an exhibition of photographs, documents and press cuttings on Soviet Jewry, which opened in Jerusalem and was later transferred to Tel Aviv. The week ended with a public discussion in which M.K. Gideon Hausner, Prof. Aryeh Tartakower and Jewish Agency Director-General Moshe Rivlin took part. At the end of March a non-party Students' Committee was set up at the Hebrew University of Jerusalem that was to become the focus of activity of an informational nature concerning Soviet Jewry. For the materials smuggled out of the USSR, see also ch. 3, n. 58 and p. 281.

247  As the 1960s drew to a close, and even more so in the 1970s, this manipulation, as it were, by the Israelis of the American Jewish establishment became a major bone of contention in the American Soviet Jewry movement.

248  In 1962, for example, the consul at the Soviet embassy in Tel Aviv signed no less than 1,000 entry visas to the USSR from Israel alone – *Yedi'ot aharonot*, 11 Mar. 1963.

249 For the visits of Shoshkes, see interview with B. Eliav; Shoshkes was editor of the Paris Yiddish *Undzer vort*. For that of Goldberg, see Goldberg, "Travels in the Soviet Union" and *Focus on Soviet Jewry*, Sept. 1966; for his 1959 visit, see p. 278.

250 Feuer, "The Soviet Jews." For Feuer's discussion of Soviet antisemitism at the USSR Institute of Philosophy, see Lewis S. Feuer, "Meeting the Philosophers," *Survey*, 51 (Apr. 1969), pp. 10–23, and *JEE*, III, 4 (Feb. 1966), pp. 6–11.

251 *Tog-morgn zhurnal*, 14 Oct. 1964.

252 Weiss, "The Plight of the Jews."

253 For the ease with which the casual tourist could fail to break through the barriers created by the Soviet authorities to prevent outsiders from discovering facts about the Soviet Jewish situation, see Weiss, "The Plight of the Jews."

254 *JC*, 11 Oct. 1963. Indeed, some Jews refrained not only from inviting foreign relatives to their homes, but even from meeting them in their home towns, preferring to see them in Moscow or in a holiday resort.

255 *Davar*, 28 Apr. 1963; *Ma'ariv*, 28 June 1963; Wiesel, *The Jews of Silence*, pp. 17–18; Dagoni, *Betsipornei hakagebe*, p. 16; Lawrence, *Three Million More?*, pp. 31–32.

256 E.g., *Yedi'ot aharonot*, 7 June 1963; "A Report from the Jewish Information Service," Feb. 1964, AJC FAD 1; Hollander, "Russia Through a Woman's Eyes." (Mrs. Hollander, the wife of Rabbi David Hollander, accompanied him on his fourth visit to the Soviet Union in 1965 in order to meet relatives there.)

257 *Yedi'ot aharonot*, 4 Jan. and 26 Feb. 1963.

258 *Al hamishmar*, 29 Nov. 1963.

259 *Hatsofe*, 16 Oct. 1963.

260 *JP*, 5 June 1963; *Kol ha'am*, 7 June 1963.

261 E.g., *Davar*, 1 Feb., 20 Dec. 1963.

262 *Tog-morgn zhurnal*, 14 Oct. 1964.

263 *Hatsofe*, 1 Mar. 1963. Jewish friends had also asked him to send them Bibles and Hebrew primers.

264 *Al hamishmar*, 22 Feb. 1963.

265 The letter is produced in full in Lawrence, *Three Million More?*, pp. 194–96.

266 *NYT*, 26 and 27 July 1965; *Washington Post*, 27 July 1965; and Poupko, "Mission to Soviet Jewry." Upon his return to the U.S. in 1964, Rabbi Poupko lectured on Soviet Jewry to audiences across the country and told of some of his experiences in *Jewish Life*, XXXII (Spring 1965), pp. 29–36 and in *In shotn fun kremlin*, pp. 15–43, an edited compilation of the articles he wrote on his 1964, 1965 and 1967 visits, which had been published in North American, Israeli, West European, South African and Australian newspapers, particularly in *Tog-morgn zhurnal*.

267 *Jewish Exponent*, 19 Oct. 1964; *NYT*, 30 Nov. 1964.

268 *American Examiner*, 19 Aug. 1965.

269 *JC*, 19 Nov. 1965.

270 Poupko, *In shotn fun kremlin*, pp. 107–217; *JC*, 10 and 24 June and 1 July 1967.

271 Wiesel, *The Jews of Silence*, passim. Ben Zion Goldberg wrote similarly about his experience when he visited the Kiev synagogue. Although the warden pleaded with them to go home and the rabbi detained Goldberg in the hope that they would leave, coming outside Goldberg found many of the congregants waiting lined up in two rows for him to pass between. "Not a word was said – they only looked at me. And I looked back and said Good Sabbath. The eyes of these Jews pursue me and demand that I write about them" – Goldberg, "Travels in the Soviet Union," p. 319.

272 Upon the delegation's return, Mrs. Jacobson called on the USSR to let its Jews create an organized community existence, participate in Jewish meetings abroad and visit relatives in other countries, including Israel – *Di prese* (Buenos Aires), 28 Oct. 1966. Many members of the Hadassah delegation became active on behalf of Soviet Jewry as a result of their visit.

273 Interview with A. Chernin.

274 E.g., *Moskovskaia pravda*, 28 June 1963.

275 *NYT*, 6 Oct. 1963.

276 *Ma'ariv*, 28 June and 1 July 1963. The story of the tourist, Yehuda Kogan, is the theme of Dagoni, *Betsipornei hakagebe*.

277 *Trud*, 21 Aug. 1963, told of the expulsion of an Israeli tourist who had sought to "brainwash" Soviet Jewish citizens concerning the situation of the Jews in Israel.

278 *CR*, 89th Congress, 1st Session, vol. 111, part 2, p. 2454, 9 Feb. 1965.

279 *JEE*, III, 1 (Nov. 1964), pp. 98–99.

280 Arriving in Paris in April 1964 in the midst of the consternation aroused by the Kichko book, Aleksei Adzhubei, Khrushchev's son-in-law and editor of *Izvestiia*, expressed "surprise" at the number of questions put to him on the Soviet Jewish situation; about one-half of a forty-minute interview he gave to Radio Europe One was taken up with the Jewish question – *JEE*, II, 5 (July 1964), pp. 34–60.

281 *JEE*, II, 4 (Feb. 1964), p. 61.

282 E.g., the Soviet embassy in Mexico City sought to undermine both the conference of Mexican intellectuals in April 1966 and the Latin American intellectuals' symposium held in Mexico City in May – *JC*, 20 May 1966 and *JEE*, III, 5 (Oct. 1966), p. 61. The Mexican Left joined in the efforts to have the latter canceled.

283 *Literaturnaia gazeta* – quoted by *Davar*, 13 Oct. 1963; *JEE*, II, 4 (Feb. 1964), p. 61.

284 This may however, have simply been a function of the change of leadership in October 1964 which brought about a general remittance in the severe anti-religious campaign of Khrushchev's last years that had led to the closing of houses of worship of different religions.

285 Rabbi Gavrilov was sentenced to be shot for speculating in gold and foreign currency; as a result of the considerable foreign agitation aroused by the death sentence in a host of countries (see, e.g., *JC*, 27 Sept. and 1 Nov. 1963; *JEE*, II, 4 (Feb. 1964), p. 57) the Soviet authorities commuted the sentence to fifteen years' imprisonment in January 1964 – ibid., p. 18.

286 *JC*, 14 May 1965.
287 *Soviet Weekly*, 4 June 1966.
288 *JC*, 1 July 1966; *JEE*, III, 5 (Oct. 1966), p. 27.
289 Ibid., III, 6 (May 1967), pp. 14–17.
290 The words "all possible" were deleted in the version designed for the Soviet public.
291 *JC*, 9 Dec. 1966.
292 The statement, signed by Rabbi Israel Miller, was released on 7 Dec. 1966 – AJC FAD 1.
293 *NYT*, 6 Dec. 1966. Canada had a considerable Ukrainian population.
294 *NYT*, 9 Dec. 1966. For figures regarding Israel, see table on p. 9.
295 *JEE*, III, 6 (May 1967), pp. 3–6.
296 *Guardian*, 9 Feb. 1967.

## 7  A first breakthrough: November 1956–December 1959

1 For the student unrest, demonstrations and atmosphere of protest toward the end of 1956, see McLean and Vickery, *The Year of Protest* and Lichtheim and Laqueur, *The Soviet Cultural Scene*. See also Breslauer, *Khrushchev and Brezhnev*, pp. 57–58. For the Secret Speech, see p. 56.
2 Breslauer, *Khrushchev and Brezhnev*, pp. 7–8.
3 See p. 81. This step did not have serious repercussions for the average Soviet Jew. The granting of emigration permits to individuals who had close relatives in Israel prior to October 1956 had not been accompanied by any official declaration, and outside the Western territories those Jews who knew of it through the Jewish grapevine or Kol Zion lagola broadcasts entertained little hope regarding their own chances at least in the foreseeable, short-term future. Consequently, the termination of this policy, which was likewise in no way indicated to the public, dashed the hopes of relatively few people.
4 For the early, 1944–45, agreements, see p. 17. For something of the atmosphere that surrounded the repatriation of the second half of the 1950s, see Salcman, *Vezakhiti lerehabilitatsia*, ch. 25.
5 See Khrushchev's statement to a group of American progressives, pp. 257–58 below.
6 For statistics of emigration to Israel from Eastern Europe in general and from Poland in particular, see *Israel Government Yearbooks*.
7 *NYT*, 17 May 1956.
8 The political changes that were shaking Poland as it took the path of de-Stalinization and the mounting antisemitism in the country are ancillary to our main theme. Suffice it to note that this was a component of both an irredentist nationalism and an upsurge of anti-Stalinism, many of Poland's leading Stalinists having been Jews. (The two leading Jewish figures, Jakob Berman and Hilary Minc, departed the political scene in 1956.)
9 *JC*, 29 June and 6 and 13 July 1956. Replying to pressure on the part of the Arab League, Cyrankiewicz stressed again in September that Poland was opposed to mass emigration, which might be open to mistaken interpretations – *Ma'ariv*, 19 Sept. 1956.
10 *JP*, 5 Aug. 1956, quoting *Tog-morgn zhurnal*.

11 In 1957, for instance, of Poland's 148,472 emigrants, 90,317 went to the GFR and 23,636 to the GDR, out of an estimated German population of 160,000. In the same year 30,331 left for Israel – out of a Jewish population that was thought to be about 50,000 – including several thousand Polish Jews who had repatriated from the USSR (see below) – *Die Welt*, 3 Aug. 1957; *Folks-shtime*, 28 Jan. 1958, quoting PAP, 25 Jan. 1958.

12 The vast majority of Poles returning to Poland came from the Soviet Union, but some did come from the Western countries as well. Out of a total of 33,000 repatriates in 1956, only 3,000 came from capitalist countries – E. A. Berthoud, British ambassador in Warsaw, to Foreign Secretary Selwyn Lloyd, 18 Feb. 1957 (PRO/FO 371/12882). According to Berthoud, "there can be few Polish families who are not involved" in the issue of Polish repatriation from the USSR and Gomulka was tackling the matter "no doubt with an eye on the popularity of the new regime" (Gomulka had returned to power the previous fall). The widespread anxiety as to the "fate and future" of Poles remaining in the Soviet Union "increased the natural Polish dislike and mistrust of the Russians" so that a repatriation agreement was an essential ingredient in "the interests of the firm Polish–Soviet friendship which Gomulka is trying so hard to instil in his country as the price of increased independence" in domestic affairs.

13 *Davar, Lamerhav*, 5 July 1956, quoting *Tog-morgn zhurnal*, 4 July 1956; *JC*, 20 July 1956.

14 A number of them later reverted to their former position. For the shift in the latter half of 1956 and the reversal, see *Folks-shtime*, 13 Nov. 1956 and 9 Apr. 1959; *Al hamishmar*, 13 Dec. 1956 and 4 Jan. 1957; *Lamerhav*, 25 Dec. 1956; and *JC*, 5 Dec. 1958.

15 *Al hamishmar*, 3 Mar. 1957; *NYT*, 23 June 1957; *Yedi'ot aharonot*, 29 Sept. 1957; *Ma'ariv*, 19 Nov. 1957.

16 Brzezinski, *The Soviet Bloc*, p. 293n., quoting *Po prostu*, 23–30 Dec. 1956.

17 See the joint communiqué published on the termination of Gomulka's visit to Moscow – *Pravda*, 19 Nov. 1956. For the Polish October, see Brzezinski, *The Soviet Bloc*. ch. 11.

18 *Pravda* published the document in full on 26 Mar. 1957.

19 The rumors of an impending agreement that had been rife prior to the October crisis included details that were not far removed from its final version. *Jerusalem Post* reported on 12 Sept. 1956 that, according to an "independent news agency" (Mid-European Press), the USSR would be repatriating some 20,000 Jews within the coming year, most of them from the Lvov and Vilnius regions, and some who would be released for that purpose from prisons and labor camps.

20 For the mood among Polish Jews in the USSR at this time, their outlook on the issues that determined their decision to leave and their attempts to repatriate, see interviews with Yosef Guri, Pesah and Masha Polak, and Esther Lomovskaia. Mrs. Lomovskaia also kindly provided photostats of the correspondence that her late husband, Jozef Szmerler, conducted with the relevant Soviet and Polish authorities in his (unsuccessful) attempt to repatriate to Poland.

21 The pressure of Polish opinion at home and that of Poles abroad were

indeed a major influence on the Polish leadership in insisting on repatriation.

22 I am grateful for these ideas to two leading Polish Jewish emigrants to Israel: Prof. Leon Boim, who was Dean of the Law Faculty at Wroclaw University until his emigration in March 1957 and a member of both the regional committee of the Polish Communist Party (PUWP) and the Idisher Kulturgezelshaftlekher Farband in Polen (the Polish Jewish Cultural-Social Association), had been present at the party's eighth plenum which returned Gomulka to power in October 1956; and Hirsh Smolar, who was editor-in-chief of the Warsaw Yiddish *Folks-shtime* – interviews with L. Boim and H. Smolar.

23 Interview with a former member of the Israeli embassy staff in Warsaw.

24 *JP*, 18 Mar. 1957, quoting *NYT*, 17 Mar. 1957. Nonetheless, it has been suggested that the Idisher Kulturgezelshaftlekher Farband may have influenced the Polish authorities to try to keep the Jews in Poland, although this seems far-fetched since the Farband had declined to the point where it lacked the power to be of influence. (It is beyond the scope of this work to discuss in detail either the inclinations of the Farband or its political capacity.)

25 *NYT*, 15 Mar. 1957.

26 One of the consequences of the slowdown was that the Jews awaiting emigration to Israel who had previously been billeted in or around Warsaw were now sent to Lower Silesia – an area that had been the center of marked antisemitism – together with the mass of non-Jewish repatriates – *JC*, 30 Aug., 11 Oct., 8 Nov. and 13 Dec. 1957.

27 *The Times*, 4 Jan. 1958. In this context of Soviet obstructionism we must also see the warnings repatriates were given by Soviet officials about the antisemitism that awaited them in Poland.

28 *JP*, 18 Mar. 1957.

29 *Hadassah News Press Release*, 4 Apr. 1958.

30 As early as December 1956, the Polish ambassador in Paris, Stanislas Gajewski, said that between 300,000 and 500,000 Poles would shortly be repatriated to Poland and that at least 10 percent of these repatriates would probably be Jewish – *JC*, 28 Dec. 1956.

31 Yosef Shnaider of Riga, who contemplated marrying a Polish citizen in order to reach Poland, gave up the idea because he had already applied to emigrate to Israel and it was impossible to do both – interview with Y. Shnaider.

32 *NYT*, 27 July 1957. The group had been organized by the Committee for Promoting Enduring Peace. Two members, the Quaker Jerome Davis and General Hugh Hester, published accounts of their conversations with Soviet leaders in *Daily Worker*, 15 Aug. 1957, and *JC*, 23 Aug. 1957; see also *National Jewish Monthly*, March 1962.

33 *National Jewish Monthly*, March 1962.

34 See Ro'i, "Jewish Emigration and Soviet–Arab Relations."

35 *NYT*, 27 July 1957.

36 Jozef Szmerler, for instance, submitted all the requisite documents for himself, his wife and their son. He was eventually informed that his

request had been refused, but with no reason why. Later he was told that they could not leave since his wife's parents, who lived in the same apartment, did not intend accompanying them. A further lengthy correspondence ensued with no change in the stand of the authorities. Finally Szmerler became ill and died in Novosibirsk at the age of forty-two – interview with E. Lomovskaia. Similarly, when Yiddish writer Yosef Kerler, whose wife had indeed been a Polish citizen in 1939, requested permission to repatriate to Poland, only Mrs. Kerler was granted permission though the agreement stated that spouses of Polish citizens would be allowed to accompany them – interview with Yosef and Anna Kerler.

37 Harry Bronstein of the U.S., for instance, has recorded that he "organized" such documents for Jews in this period – *Nedelia* (Rus.; Tel Aviv), 24 June 1979. Yosef Urman, a Prisoner of Zion who was released from camp in June 1956 and had never been a Polish citizen, was sent documents from Poland by a fellow Prisoner of Zion who had indeed been a Polish citizen, come from the Polish territories and reached Poland; but Urman was unable to obtain the required corroboration in his place of residence and so was unable to use the documents – interview with Y. Urman.

38 Interview with Marek Moizes.

39 Interviews with M. Gelfond and Y. Khorol. A detailed account of one attempt to "repatriate" with the help of a fictitious Polish wife has been given by Branover, *Vozvrashchenie*, pp. 200–08. When fraud was uncovered, the Soviet Jewish "spouse" had to bear the consequences. One such person, Isak Levitan, was imprisoned after his Polish "wife" admitted that the marriage had been one of convenience – interview with I. Levitan.

40 Netzer, "Jewish Emigration."

41 Among the eight currency speculators brought to trial in Vilnius in early 1962 was a young widow whose "attempt to flee the USSR by marrying an elderly foreigner" had been foiled by the latter's sudden death. Her name, the Soviet press pointed out, was Zismanovich and she had a sister in Miami Beach. Another member of the group was Basya Reznitskii, who had three sisters in the U.S. and a brother in Israel – *Trud*, 16 Jan. 1962. For the "economic crimes," see pp. 130–31.

42 Thus, a handful of repatriates who continued to Israel and subsequently asked to return to the USSR were welcomed there with open arms, and their stories of the hardships of life in Israel were broadcast, televised and printed in the Soviet media. These cases served as proof of Khrushchev's seemingly Delphic assertion: on the one hand, Soviet Jews did not want to emigrate to Israel; on the other hand, the Soviet authorities received "many letters from Jews in Israel, applying for permission to return from Israel to their native land, the Soviet Union" – Ro'i, "Jewish Emigration and Soviet–Arab Relations," p. 215, quoting *Pravda*, 9 July 1960. The fact that these returnees not only were allowed to reenter the Soviet Union, but also had their stories published there, would seem to indicate that at least some of those who returned had been "planted" among the emigrants by the Soviets in the first place.

43 The previous Festivals – which were held biennially – took place in Prague

(1947), Budapest (1949), Berlin (1951), Bucharest (1953) and Warsaw (1955). The WFDY had been set up in 1945.

44 Although from the point of view of the Festival's organizers the Israelis formed a single delegation, in fact it comprised two distinct groups of about 100 each. One delegation represented the Israeli Communist Party and the other the three Zionist socialist parties (Mapam, Ahdut ha'avoda and Mapai), mostly from the *kibbutzim*. The Soviet Jews made a clear distinction between the two delegations, many of them shunning the communists, who wore a different emblem (already in 1955 in Warsaw they had not worn the *menora*, Israel's emblem) – *NYT*, 22 Sept. 1957. Nonetheless, the real situation of Soviet Jews came as such a shock to some members of the Banki (Bnei noar komunisti yisraeli) delegation that they left the party – interview with Zeev Otic; *JP*, 29 Aug. 1957. For the communist delegation and its behavior in Moscow, see, for example, *Haaretz*, 6 Sept. 1957.

45 In fact, although the hand that was accustomed to arrest was restrained for the duration of the Festival, the eye that was accustomed to keep watch was as vigilant as ever, so that many people paid later for their relative permissiveness and lack of circumspection. One source has recorded that a companion was appointed for every participant in the Festival, students being mobilized to report to the authorities on everything connected with the guest they were assigned to watch and especially encounters with Soviet citizens – Salcman, *Vezakhiti lerehabilitatsia*, pp. 230–1. Certainly, the Israelis felt they were under constant, undisguised surveillance – *Ma'ariv*, 22 Sept. 1957.

46 According to the official Soviet estimate, 30,000 foreigners participated in the Festival – *Komsomolskaia pravda*, 18 Aug. 1957.

47 For something of the atmosphere that pervaded the encounter between representatives of Soviet youth and their counterparts from the free world, see *JP*, 15 Aug. 1957; *She'arim* (Jerusalem), 18 Aug. 1957.

48 According to the British ambassador in Moscow: "While a great effort was made to impress the merits of the Soviet system" on all the delegations, who were royally entertained, "the organisers' chief targets were the delegations of the colonial and underdeveloped countries" – D. P. Reilly to S. Lloyd, 9 Oct. 1957 (PRO/FO 371/128976). A special Soviet–Arab friendship evening was held under the auspices of the Soviet Peace Committee – *Davar*, 1 Aug. 1957. For the marked attention given to the Omanis, the Jordanians and the Egyptians at the Festival opening ceremony, see *Davar*, 29 Aug. 1957; for the attitude to the Arabs in Moscow, see also *Ha'olam hazeh*, 4 Sept. 1957.

49 In their broadcasts of the opening ceremony the Soviet media skipped the Israeli entrance into the stadium entirely. Nonetheless it was possible to discern that the applause which greeted the Israelis (identifiable despite the omission because the delegations marched into the stadium in alphabetical order) was considerably louder than that welcoming other delegations – *Davar*, 29 July 1957.

50 David Khavkin had returned to Moscow from Alma-Ata, prior to the

conclusion of his assignment there, in order to meet the Israeli delegation. Deciding that a phone call to the Festival organizing committee entailed no risk, he called several times to find out the day and hour of the Israelis' arrival, but was unable to elicit any information – interview with D. Khavkin. Anatolii Rubin of Minsk, who reached the capital a week before the opening of the Festival, was similarly unsuccessful in obtaining information about the Israelis' anticipated arrival – interview with A. Rubin.

51 When the train did stop at a station, the Israelis performed folk dances on the platform to the accompaniment of Israeli music and some of them were able to talk to Jews and distribute souvenirs and pamphlets – *Ma'ariv*, 16 Aug. 1957; *Davar*, 9 Sept. 1957. In Kiev the square outside the station was packed with people unable to break through the police barrier that prevented them from making contact with the Israelis – *Yedi'ot aharonot*, 30 Aug. 1957.

52 Interviews with D. Khavkin and A. Rubin.

53 *Ma'ariv*, 4 Aug. 1957; *Haaretz*, 20 Aug. 1957.

54 *Ma'ariv*, 13 Aug. 1957; *Idisher zhurnal* (Toronto), 15 Aug. 1957. Upon his return to Cairo from the Soviet Union in early September of that year, Soviet Ambassador Evgenii Kiselev said that the Israeli delegation had included spies assigned the task of harming the Arab delegations and falsifying the meaning of the Festival. "Therefore, the Soviet authorities decided to expel the Israeli delegation" – *Al hamishmar*, 8 Sept. 1957.

55 *L'information d'Israel* (Tel Aviv), 14 Aug. 1957; *Idisher zhurnal*, 22 Aug. 1957. The departure of the Israeli delegation was followed by a virulent attack upon it, among others for trying to create a link with Soviet Jewry.

56 *Idishe prese* (Rio de Janeiro), 9 Aug. 1957; *JC*, 9 Aug. 1957; *Lamerhav*, 22 Aug. 1957. The Israeli material included a pamphlet in Russian entitled *A Letter from Israel: The Story of a Native-Born Citizen of Israel*, written specifically for the purpose by Israeli writer Aharon Megged. In a letter to the Keren Hayesod directorium after their return, the leaders of the delegation wrote that the 15,000 flower postcards presented to the delegation by Keren Hayesod had been distributed by the delegation to Jews at the railway stations in Ungenyi, Tiraspol, Kishinev, and indeed all along the route to Moscow. In the capital itself they were given to Jews from Leningrad, Kaunas, Kiev, Odessa and other places. These postcards had been received with great enthusiasm until the distribution of printed material was stopped. The letter, dated 21 Oct. 1957, was kindly shown me by David Sorek who participated in the delegation and preserved materials relating to the Festival, including a number of letters he received in its wake from a girl in Moscow.

57 *Lamerhav*, 20 Aug. 1957; *Al hamishmar*, 28 Aug. 1957.

58 *Pravda*, 29 July 1957.

59 *Al hamishmar*, 16 Aug. 1957; *Devar hashavu'a*, 29 Aug. 1957.

60 *Lamerhav*, 6 Sept. 1957.

61 Ibid.; *Al hamishmar, Yedi'ot aharonot*, 30 Aug. 1957; *Haaretz*, 8 Sept. 1957; *Davar*, 13 Sept. 1957; Carl Alpert, "My People from the Depths," *Hadassah*

*Newsletter*, Oct. 1957. One Georgian Jew bore a tatoo: "If I forget thee, O Jerusalem . . . ," *Devar hashavu'a*, 29 Aug. 1957.

62 For the texts of some of these notes and cards, see the album put out by the Festival delegation (Tel Aviv, undated).

63 *NYHT*, *Haaretz*, *Ma'ariv*, 4 Aug. 1957; *Ma'ariv*, 11 Aug. 1957.

64 *Davar*, 16 Sept. 1957.

65 *Ma'ariv*, 4 Aug. 1957; *Davar*, 5 Aug. 1957; *Herut*, 25 Aug. 1957; *Al hamishmar*, 26 Aug. 1957; Rubin, *Magafayim humim*, p. 85. A Jewish visitor to the USSR in 1959 found out that the change of venue of at least one Israeli performance had been decided upon in advance. A woman instructed to mix with the crowds, overhear conversations and report on them knew about it at least a week in advance – Goldberg, *The Jewish Problem*, p. 164.

66 *Davar*, 25 Aug. 1957; *Devar hashavu'a*, 29 Aug. 1957.

67 Frustrated by his attempt to welcome the Israelis on their arrival (see n. 50 above), David Khavkin was determined to meet them as soon as possible. He and at least one other Jew were actually able to infiltrate into the center of the stadium prior to the opening ceremony and had ample opportunity there to make their acquaintance and also to find out the address at which they were staying. From then on he spent virtually the entire time of their stay with the Israelis (see also n. 73 below) – interview with D. Khavkin.

68 *Lamerhav*, 20 Aug. 1957; *Yedi'ot aharonot*, 30 Aug. 1957; *Al hamishmar*, 1 Sept. 1957.

69 *Ma'ariv*, 30 Aug. 1957.

70 These included David Khavkin and Anatolii Rubin, both arrested in 1958 after long months of surveillance. They had received Israeli material, Khavkin a calendar, two records and a number of postcards, Rubin "books, pamphlets, dictionaries and souvenirs to take back to Minsk." Rubin had been closely watched ever since he met with the Israelis, and by the time of his arrest the KGB had three large files of incriminating evidence against him. Microphones had been installed in his home and a hotel conversation between him and an elderly American Jewish couple on a visit to their birthplace near Minsk had been recorded as well – interviews with D. Khavkin and A. Rubin; Rubin, "Moi put v Izrail" (My Road to Israel – Rus.; unpublished typescript), pp. 74–77, and *Magafayim humim*, pp. 83–88; and Schroeter, *The Last Exodus*, p. 275.

71 At the border town of Ungenyi, their first station in the Soviet Union, delegation members noticed that all the souvenirs a girl and her mother had received were taken from their bags – *Devar hashavu'a*, 29 Aug. 1957.

72 *Haaretz*, *She'arim*, 1 Sept. 1957; *Al hamishmar*, 2 Sept. 1957.

73 David Khavin hosted a number of Israelis, some of them several times. Khavkin invited other local Jews on these occasions – interview with D. Khavkin. For a very moving account of one delegation member's visit to the home of an elderly Jewish couple, see Shoham, *Pegishot bemoskva*, pp. 24–27. Within a few days of the Festival's opening the badge was selling in Moscow for fifty rubles – *Yedi'ot aharonot*, 30 Aug. 1957.

74 *Haaretz*, 30 Aug. 1957; *Hadassah Newsletter* (Oct. 1957).

75 *Herut*, 8 Sept. 1957. Only two weeks after the Festival ended Komsomol Central Committee Secretary Aleksandr Shelepin was writing that "Soviet youth cannot entirely agree with what some of the youth delegations from capitalist countries displayed at the Festival" and calling upon Soviet youth "to fight against the infiltration of these ideologies, moral views and customs which harm us" – *Komsomolskaia pravda*, 18 Aug. 1957.

76 One Soviet Jew wrote: "The only thing of which I have become aware (unfortunately, too late) is that I am a Jew. In recent years many Jews have been reborn as Jews." In a faltering Yiddish that had not been used for years, the writer asked many specific questions about Israel and about how it manages to survive in such a small area ("They say here that a bullet from the Arab side of the border passes through your entire country"). "And these," the author concluded, "are not all my questions. I could fill a whole book with them" – *Davar*, 30 July 1957.

77 *Ma'ariv*, 29 Aug. 1957; *Yedi'ot aharonot*, 6 Sept. 1957. See also p. 285.

78 *Lamerhav*, 8 Sept. 1957; *Al hamishmar*, 13 and 25 Sept. 1957.

79 For the identification of Soviet Jewish youth with Israel, see, for example, *Lamerhav*, 15 Sept. 1957; for the fervor of their questions and answers, see *Lamerhav*, 6 Sept. 1957.

80 *Al hamishmar*, 30 Aug. 1957; Carl Alpert, "My People from the Depths," *Hadassah Newsletter*, Oct. 1957; Shoham, *Pegishot bemoskva*, pp. 28 and 30; and see below, p. 279.

81 For other meetings with young Jews, see *Davar*, 13 Sept. 1957.

82 A twelve-year-old girl from Vilnius requested a souvenir in fluent Hebrew; another Jew, also from Vilnius, told of how he and his friends listened to Israeli broadcasts, adding: "We will make *aliya* as soon as they allow it. Wait for us" – *Yedi'ot aharonot*, 29 Aug. 1957.

83 *Haaretz*, 8 Sept. 1957. Others entertained similar illusions – *Haaretz*, 20 Aug. 1957; *Yedi'ot aharonot* and *Devar hashavu'a*, 29 Aug. 1957; *Al hamishmar*, 30 Aug. 1957.

84 *Yedi'ot aharonot*, 29 Aug. 1957; *Haaretz*, 1 Sept. 1957; *Christian Science Monitor*, 17 Sept. 1957; interview with Y. Urman, who traveled from Chernovtsy for the Festival; Shoham, *Pegishot bemoskva*, p. 28.

85 *Davar*, 13 Sept. 1957.

86 Interview with Tina Brodetskaia.

87 *Haaretz*, 30 Aug. 1957.

88 Those who met the Israelis included a number of academics from universities and research institutes – interview with Inessa Rubin.

89 Goldberg, *The Jewish Problem*, p. 166.

90 One of these was Tina Brodetskaia – interview with T. Brodetskaia.

91 Khavkin, for example, received more material from the Israeli marksmen (see p. 269) than he had from the delegation to the Festival – interview with D. Khavkin.

92 One of these was a sixteen-year-old schoolgirl from Moscow who corresponded with David Sorek of Kibbutz Nir Yitzhak (see n. 56 above) for two years.

93 *NYHT*, 10 Sept. 1957. The article went on to say that the world must

prepare to "marshal its moral forces" in anticipation of the "retaliatory measures" the Kremlin must be expected to plan.

94 Soviet Ambassador Aleksandr Abramov had informed the Israelis as early as August 1955 that his government was ready for mutual tourism (Sharett, *Yoman ishi*, vol. 4, p. 119), yet the numbers were still minimal. As late as fall 1959 a group of Israeli tourists was told by Intourist officials that the USSR was not interested in tourists from Israel. Certainly, Israel was not encouraged to stimulate Soviet tourism to Israel after a group of Soviet Jewish tourists published virulently anti-Israeli articles in summer 1958 – *Literaturnaia gazeta*, 26 and 30 Aug. 1958 and *Vecherniaia Moskva*, 8 Aug. 1958.

95 A member of the architects' delegation, Y. Ben-Sira, reported on returning to Israel that Jews had come from all over the Soviet Union to see the Israeli exhibits, some of them spoke Hebrew, and some had brought their children with them – *Yalkut magen*, 10 (July–Oct. 1958), p. 15.

96 *Al hamishmar*, 2 Oct. 1958; *Yalkut magen*, 10 (July–Oct. 1958), p. 15.

97 See pp. 116–19.

98 The other two members were also Jews: war veteran Lieutenant-General David Dragunskii and writer Aleksandr Chakovskii. For Rabbi Shlifer's visit to the Israeli embassy in Paris on 31 Oct. 1956, see ch. 3, n. 83, and Mikhlin, *Hagahelet*, pp. 260–66.

99 For this campaign, see Bourdeaux, *Religious Ferment*, pp. 12–16; Bociurkiw, "Church–State Relations," pp. 96–99; and Bociurkiw, "De-Stalinization and Religion."

100 For measures taken against the Jewish religion during this period, see Rothenberg, "Jewish Religion," pp. 176–85; for reactions in the West to these measures, see pp. 130–31. Since there were no data anywhere – except presumably at the Council for the Affairs of Religious Cults – as to where synagogues existed and where they did not, there was often no way of knowing when a synagogue was closed down unless an Israeli diplomat or Western Jewish tourist happened to visit that community and meet local Jews.

101 See, for example, Eliav, *Between Hammer and Sickle*, pp. 54–59.

102 Other religious denominations in the Soviet Union had recourse to similar unofficial prayer-houses or prayer-meetings for dearth of officially sanctioned houses of worship.

103 For my description of the relationship between the Israeli embassy staff and the synagogue officials, I am grateful to a number of former Israeli diplomats who were kind enough to let me interview them on their experiences in the USSR. Of those who served in the period covered by this chapter I should like to make mention of Ambassador Yosef Avidar and his wife Yemima (1955–58), Ambassador Arye Harel (1959–62), Avraham Agmon (1956–58) and Arie (Liova) Eliav (1958–60).

104 E.g., Mikhlin, *Hagahelet*, pp. 290–92.

105 Since travel was impossible in the USSR without specific permission to stop off at each place in one's itinerary, all foreigners, including diplomats, submitted their travel programs to the relevant authorities, who, if the trip was ratified, informed the local authorities.

106 For instance, the story of the fire at the synagogue in Malakhovka, just outside Moscow, in which the sexton's wife met her death, was quickly spread abroad, see ch. 5, n. 21.

107 For Yom Kippur and Simhat Tora in this period, see *JEE*, 2 (Nov. 1959), p. 23; Eliav, *Between Hammer and Sickle*, pp. 73–79; Hindus, *House without a Roof*, p. 324; Shashar, *Yisraeli bemoskva*. Shashar and two other Israelis spent the 1959 fall festival season in the Soviet Union. For Yom Kippur they were in Riga (ibid., pp. 56–60), for the first days of Succot (the Feast of Tabernacles) in Moscow (ibid., pp. 101–03), and for Simhat Tora in Odessa (ibid., pp. 160–63). For Yom Kippur in Moscow, Kiev, Leningrad and Lvov in 1958, see *Yalkut magen*, 10 (July–Oct. 1958), pp. 14–15. On the eve of Simhat Tora, apparently in 1959, the Leningrad group of Natan Tsirulnikov and Rosa Epshtein spread the word in the city's institutions of higher learning that the following day was a Jewish holiday – interview with Shoshana Zusman-Epstein. The same year Shlomo Gefen came from Lithuania to Leningrad for Simhat Tora and was astounded at what he saw there in the synagogue – interview with S. Gefen.

108 Interview with D. Khavkin.

109 Eliav gives examples of visits to non-Ashkenazi communities and of the distinctly more Jewish character of their existence; see *Between Hammer and Sickle*, pp. 71 (in Baku) and 147–73 passim.

110 Interview with Marek Moizes.

111 To be more precise, the *gorkom* secretary said that Jews could only have Yiddish culture in their own territory. When the organizers retorted: "Where, in Israel?" the secretary said, "No, Birobidzhan" – interview with David Garber.

112 Garber, "Choir and Drama in Riga," p. 44 and interview with D. Garber. The other initiators of the choir were Shimon Khlavin, Yosef Mirskii and Meir Ragulskii.

113 *Yalkut magen*, 10 (July–Oct. 1958), p. 49; *Morgn frayheyt*, 27 Oct. 1959; and interview with Asher Blank. While *Morgn frayheyt* talked of a membership of sixty, Blank records that there were between twenty and thirty members.

114 I am indebted for this information to Prof. Mordechai Altshuler of the Hebrew University, Jerusalem; see also Zand, "Notes."

115 Diaries of G. Pecherskii and interview with S. Zusman-Epstein, who was one of the signatories of these letters. The reply of the RSFSR Ministry of Education and the letter to the Chairman of the Leningrad City Executive Committee are reproduced in Pinkus, *Soviet Government*, pp. 302–3.

116 See Goldberg, *The Jewish Problem*, p. 4. The selection of Sholom Aleichem's writings, *Oisgevelte verk*, was published in Moscow by Melukhe ferlag fun kunstlerisher literatur; see below.

117 Eliav, *Between Hammer and Sickle*, pp. 40–43.

118 See my article, "Nehama Lifshitz."

119 See Shmeruk, "Hapirsumim beyidish," p. 67.

120 One young man stated specifically: "the fact that I do not know it is

neither my fault nor the fault of my parents" – Eliav, *Between Hammer and Sickle*, p. 14.

121  Thus, for instance, while Nehama Lifshitz was allowed to appear in the first three of these cities in 1959, later these, too, were removed from her itinerary; Minsk had been excluded from the start. See Ro'i, "Nehama Lifshitz."

122  *Al hamishmar*, 3 July 1959.

123  They were not, however, as we have noted, necessarily the same Jews. For members of the intelligentsia, who never went near a synagogue, did not balk at going to a Yiddish concert.

124  Nehama Lifshitz, for instance, kept the embassy informed of her schedule with this end in view; see Ro'i, "Nehama Lifshitz."

125  On this group, see also p. 276 above.

126  For this group, see also n. 107 above; Yedidya, "The Study of Hebrew;" and interview with S. Zusman-Epstein. According to Tsirulnikov's widow her husband was not yet thinking of *aliya*; however, she does remember that he received material from the Israelis, including *Vestnik Izrailia* (see p. 158), and that when he called her from Moscow to tell her he was being followed she rushed off to warn Gilia (Hillel) Butman, later one of the people involved in the Leningrad hijacking episode, who was a member of the group – interview with Rahel Tsirulnikov.

127  E.g., the Israeli delegation to the Youth Festival, see p. 266.

128  Aware that he was under constant surveillance as a former Prisoner of Zion, Iofis was careful to refrain from any public activity after he returned from Vorkuta in September 1955. He did, however, continue to meet with trustworthy friends in private homes from time to time and to teach Hebrew to his son and anyone else who wanted to learn the language – interview with D. Yafit.

129  Eliav, *Between Hammer and Sickle*, pp. 96–71. Eliav also tells of a Jewish father's effort to obtain materials with which to teach both himself and his young daughter Hebrew directly from Israel – ibid. Another person who began studying Hebrew with the aid of a dictionary and a textbook from Israel was the Moscow girl who corresponded with one of the Israeli delegates to the Youth Festival; cf. n. 56 above.

130  Gelfond, "Illegal Zionist Activity."

131  Kaufman, *Lagernyi vrach*, pp. 376–78. For the Karaganda group, see also pp. 76–77. Another ex-Prisoner of Zion who set up a group in the late 1950s was Yosef Urman in Chernovtsy – interview with Y. Urman.

132  Many interviewees have stated that the Jews' attitude to *aliya* was in many ways a function of their understanding of the feasibility of its implementation. Nonetheless, the marksmen's delegation which visited the USSR in summer 1958 was asked several times about the veracity of details which appeared in the Soviet media concerning hunger, unemployment and difficult living conditions in Israel – *Yalkut magen*, 10 (July–Oct. 1958), p. 42.

133  For details, see p. 158.

134 As we have already seen, a number of Soviet Jews began corresponding with members of the Israeli delegation to the Youth Festival.

135 Interview with M. Gelfond. Unfortunately, Gelfond could supply me with no information whatever on the content of "A and B" beyond its title which he remembered clearly; nor was I able to glean any further information on this from other interviewees.

136 Tina says she went to Rabbi Levin in 1956, but this is clearly a mistake, since she says it was after the Festival; and Rabbi Levin only became rabbi in Moscow in 1957.

137 Two such pamphlets were published in Tel Aviv under the name *Yidishe komunisten vegn der yidn-frage in Ratnfarband*, one in 1957 and the other in 1958. The first, presumably the one Dora Podolskii translated, contained the reflections of J. B. Salsberg on his two visits to the Soviet Union, published in the New York *Morgn frayheyt* between 30 Oct. and 26 Dec. 1956; *Folks-shtime*'s open letter to Leonid Ilichev, head of the Press Department at the Soviet Foreign Ministry, of 3 Nov. 1956 protesting his denial of anti-Jewish discrimination and repression in the USSR and his condemnation of the *Folks-shtime* article disclosing the death and disappearance of Soviet Jewish writers and public figures under Stalin (for details, see pp. 115–16 and Pinkus, *Soviet Government*, pp. 59–61 and 512–13, nn. 69 and 77); an appeal to Chairman of the Council of Ministers Nikolai Bulganin and Chairman of the Presidium of the USSR Supreme Soviet, Kliment Voroshilov, for the revival of Soviet Jewish cultural life, published in *Morgn frayheyt* on 4 Nov. 1956; and a *Morgn frayheyt* editorial of 16 Dec. 1956 on the national and Jewish question in the Soviet Union. For the reaction of Jewish communists in the West to the situation of Soviet Jewry, see pp. 109–10 and pp. 181–82.

138 The description of the group's activities is based on interviews with Dora and Boris Podolsky.

139 Interviews with Y. Shnaider and Katz's widow Sarah and daughter Lilia Abergil, who remember, too, that despite the protracted interrogation, the KGB was unable to discover the identity of Katz's "accomplices." For the Hazan incident, see below.

140 Interview with D. Khavkin. Others arrested in 1958 included Anatoli Rubin of Minsk (see nn. 50 and 70 above) and Boris Shperling of Riga (interview with B. Shperling).

141 This information I received from a Soviet Jewish emigrant who has asked to remain anonymous; I have been unable to discover the name of the Jew from Dushanbe.

142 Gelfond, "Illegal Zionist Activity," p. 39.

143 Israeli Foreign Minister Golda Meir told the Knesset in summer 1960 (see p. 140) that Israeli residents had sent 9,236 applications for reunification to relatives in the USSR over the past five years, each application relating to a family unit – *Divrei haknesset*, vol. 29, 8 Aug. 1960, pp. 2101–02.

144 *Ma'ariv*, 14 Nov. 1958.

145 The books were Plotkin's *Poezdka v Izrail* (see ch. 5, n. 115) and Ivanov and

Sheinis, *Gosudarstvo Izrail*. For anti-Israel newspaper articles of this period, see, e.g., *Komsomolskaia pravda*, 15 Oct. 1957, which published what purported to be letters from Soviet Jews who had gone to Israel, "letters full of sorrow and suffering" telling friends and relatives of their "bitter disappointment" and regret at having gone to Israel. The radio was also mobilized in this effort, see, e.g., Radio Kiev, 17 Dec. 1958, as quoted by *Near East Report*, 15 Jan. 1959.

146 For a first major anti-Israel article clearly intended for Soviet Jews, see p. 45.

147 *Pravda*, 9 Sept. 1957. A further article in the same paper on 23 Sept. 1957, accusing Israel of resorting to the black market and underworld methods in the conduct of its diplomacy, was also an indirect reference to the Hazan incident. See also *NYHT*, 10 Sept. 1957, and *NYT*, 22 and 23 Sept. 1957. For Hazan's interrogation by the KGB and the attempt of the Soviets to enlist him for espionage activity, see Sharett, *Yoman ishi*, vol. 8, p. 2307.

148 *Christian Science Monitor*, 30 Oct. 1958.

149 *NYHT*, 30 May 1959.

150 *JC*, 30 Sept. 1957.

151 Eliav, *Between Hammer and Sickle*, pp. 213–16.

152 *Jewish Advocate* (Boston), 5 Sept. 1957. The tourist in question, George S. Abrams, was a young Harvard law graduate. A similar estimate was made by American Jewish jurist Samuel Leibowitz who visited the Soviet Union in 1958 – *Undzer veg*, Nov. 1958. And Rabbi David Hollander, who had headed the 1956 delegation of Orthodox rabbis from the U.S., said that Soviet Jews would flock to Israel when the gates were opened – *JTA*, 3 Aug. 1960. For further speculations on this issue, see Hindus, *House without a Roof*, pp. 321–23. Hindus, who was in the USSR in 1958 and again in 1960, writes that "Jews in Moscow and Leningrad estimate that at least 500,000 Soviet Jews would emigrate to Israel were they permitted to do so."

153 Even in this period, some Jews contemplated leaving illegally, not simply by marrying someone who had been a Polish citizen in 1939, but by finding gaps in the frontier. One of them, David Romm, visited Yosef Khorol in Odessa in late 1958 to investigate the possibility of leaving through the city's port. Khorol, who had worked in the port for a short period in 1947 and knew how strict the passenger control was on every boat, told Romm that he would be better off committing suicide – interview with Y. Khorol.

## 8 The early and mid-1960s: the Soviet Jewish national awakening

1 The indigenous, non-Jewish population of the Baltic republics, for instance, was particularly permeated with nationalist feeling, even entertaining the irrational belief that somehow they would one day live again in free and independent states. For the Baltic republics and their various national movements, see, e.g., Katz, *Major Soviet Nationalities*, part 2.

2 "Liudi, gody, zhizn" (People, Years, Life), *Novyi mir*, 8 (1960), pp. 24–60, and 1 (1961), pp. 91–152.

3 For more on this traditional form of Russian oppositional activity and its development in the late fifties and early sixties (*Syntax, Phoenix, Sphinxes*), see Howard Biddulph, "Protest Strategies of the Soviet Intellectual Opposition," and Gayle Durham Hollander, "Political Communication and Dissent in the Soviet Union," in Tokes, *Dissent in the USSR*. For an anthology of general dissident literature, see Meerson-Aksenov and Shragin, *Russian 'Samizdat.'*

4 Interviews with Y. Shnaider and D. Khavkin.

5 Interviews with Y. Shnaider, D. Khavkin and Naftali Prat.

6 Reminiscences of Y. Mendelevich, *Ma'ariv*, 2 and 3 March 1981, and Mendelevich, *Mivtza' hatuna*, pp. 20 and 25–26. While still in secondary school, Mendelevich had discovered that, like his own family, some of his classmates talked about *aliya* at home. Thereafter these schoolboys met in a quiet corner of the school courtyard to discuss problems connected with *aliya*.

7 Interview with a former member of the Israeli embassy staff. Among others, the group protested the statements that were being made by Nahum Goldmann (see p. 197), insisting that harassment and pressure on the part of world opinion would indeed improve the Soviet Jewish situation. For Mikhoels' appearance in Kiev, see West, *Struggles* pp. 213–16.

8 Yedidya, "The Study of Hebrew," and Butman, *Leningrad–Ierusalim*, pp. 85–86 and 170.

9 Interview with E. Finkelstein.

10 For the activities of Mintz during the years in question, see Aharoni, *Shlonsky: Mikhtavim* and interview with Y. Mintz; for the activities of Pregerzon, see, among others, Yehuda Slutsky, "Zvi Pregerzon," *Behinot*, 6 (1975), pp. 82–102; for those of Edelman, see interview with M. Gelfond. For Hebrew and Yiddish manuscripts smuggled out of the USSR, see also ch. 3, n. 58 and p. 235.

11 Among those who received materials prepared by Morgulis and his group was Anatolii Rubin of Minsk after his release from camp in December 1964 – interview with A. Rubin. For Morgulis and his group and what they wrote, translated and edited, see Lazaris, *Evrei i dissidenty*, pp. 88–93. Bergman's translations included a shortened version of *Exodus* (see p. 303); Ber Mark's book on the Warsaw Ghetto uprising; biographical material on Chaim Weizmann; and a speech by Ben Gurion on the occasion of the Sinai War entitled "David Against Goliath."

For Kaplan and his activity, see *Libi bemizrah*, a collection of Kaplan's letters to his family in Israel, with a foreword by his sister, Sara Kafri. After emigrating to Israel, Solomon Dolnik, who was a member of this group, wrote Mrs. Kafri: "I first met him [Kaplan] in 1960. The awareness that we must act to deepen Jewish sentiment . . . brought us together . . . We were unable to stand idly by and not act for the good of our people . . . We were able to acquire Hebrew newspapers and journals from Israel, which we used to explain the situation there. The State of Israel gave us courage, enthusiasm, and encouragement in our struggle." When Kaplan's sister visited him in 1961, he showed her the notes he made from Kol Zion lagola broadcasts and told her how he improved his knowledge of Hebrew by reading whatever he could find in that language, often with the help of a dictionary, and then distributed materials based on what he had read – ibid., pp. 9–12.

12 Interview with a former member of the Israeli embassy staff.

13 Interview with G. Shapiro. In the mid-sixties, Shapiro also began collecting materials from Russian-language sources that enabled him in later years to publish his *Evrei – geroi Sovetskogo Soiuza* (Jewish Heroes of the Soviet Union, Rus.; Tel Aviv, 1984). Ber Mark's *Der ofshtand fun varshaver geto* appeared in English as *Uprising of the Warsaw Ghetto* (New York: Schocken, 1975). In addition to the edition put out by Der Emes, two further Yiddish editions appeared in Warsaw by Idisz Buch, in 1955 and 1963.

14 Interview with M. Kanevsky and testimony of M. Kanevsky, Yad Vashem, Givatayim, 3579.

15 Interviews with D. Khavkin and Y. Shnaider. For the mimeographing and dissemination of materials, see also Isaiy Averbuch, "Jewish Samizdat and the Means of Its Preparation," *Behinot*, 8–9 (1979), pp. 61–62.

16 Interview with M. Gelfond.

17 Interviews with E. Rusinek, B. Tsukerman, B. Shperling, B. and L. Slovin, D. and M. Garber, M. Lapid and D. Yafit; see also Zilberman, *Iosif Kuzkovskii*, pp. 37–57.

18 Interview with Y. Branover. Although Branover had grown up in a family that did not observe the precepts of Judaism, by the early 1960s he was beginning to observe the Sabbath and eat kosher. In 1964 he joined the Habad movement.

19 *Focus on Soviet Jewry* (Jan. 1966), p. 1. The appeal referred to Article 121 of the 1936 "Stalin" Constitution that was still in force, which spoke of the right of citizens to education, including "instruction in schools in their native language," and to Article 123, which specified: "Equality of rights of citizens of the USSR, irrespective of their nationality or race, in all spheres of economic, government, cultural, political and other social activity, is an indefeasible law. Any direct or indirect restriction of the rights of, or conversely, the establishment of any direct or indirect privileges for, citizens on account of their race or nationality, as well as any advocacy of racial or national exclusiveness or hatred and contempt, are punishable by law" – Lane, *Politics and Society*, p. 549.

20 *JC*, 14 Jan. 1966.

21 Interview with a former member of the Israeli embassy staff.

22 *JC*, 10 Nov. 1961; *Leningradskaia pravda*, 11 Nov. 1961; and interview with Shoshana Zusman-Epstein. Reporting the sentence, *Leningradskaia pravda* stated that the accused had been found guilty of violating Articles 64 (a) and 70 (b) of the RSFSR Criminal Code, and had maintained contacts with members of a foreign embassy of a capitalist state, who had several times visited Leningrad "for this purpose." The accused, moreover, had reg-

ularly supplied these diplomats with information used abroad to cause damage to the USSR, and had received anti-Soviet literature from them that they had distributed. Not surprisingly, *Leningradskaia pravda* made no mention of the petitions the accused had sent to the Soviet leadership for permission to study Hebrew. For Western rapportage on, and reaction, to the Leningrad trial of Oct. 1961, see p. 129; for the complaints Pecherskii sent the authorities, see Pinkus, *Soviet Government*, pp. 302–03, concerning adult education in Hebrew and Yiddish and Jewish history and literature (cf. also p. 276); p. 325, concerning the unlawful activities of the militia; and p. 328, concerning certain synagogue worshippers. Pinkus also published two documents on the trial (ibid., pp. 225–26).

23 Interview with Zeev Rishal, and *JC*, 17 Nov. 1961.

24 See, for example, Eliav, *Tab'aot shahar*, p. 306; for similar manifestations in earlier periods, see pp. 64–65 and 270–71.

25 See, for example, lecture by Katriel Katz, Israeli ambassador in Moscow from 1965 to 1967, at the inauguration ceremony of the Dr. Irene Halmos Endowment Fund for Research in Soviet–Israeli Relations Toward Peace, Jaffee Center for Strategic Studies at Tel Aviv University, 30 Oct. 1983.

26 This criticism was voiced by a number of activists in Riga, notably those who centered around Boris and Lidiia Slovin – Schroeter, *The Last Exodus*, pp. 70–71; for a different view, held by other Rigans, see n. 32 below.

27 Numerous Western tourists have told of the significance that the Israeli embassy had for Soviet Jewry; see, e.g., p. 239. So, too, have many Soviet emigrants to Israel in interviews and personal reminiscences.

28 All sources corroborate the immense popularity of the Israeli broadcasts and the intense interest in them.

29 Yosef Koritskii of Moscow claimed that more than sixty persons came to his home to read a certain issue of *Shalom*.

30 By the early 1960s Russian-language materials provided by the embassy included *Vestnik Izrailia* and *Shalom*, which were designed especially for Soviet Jewry; and *Ariel*, a cultural journal that appeared in Israel and was translated into Russian (see p. 158). The embassy also supplied an occasional copy, usually in a foreign language, of *Exodus*, or other books that were specifically requested, as well as religious literature, children's books, Hebrew dictionaries and grammars and newspapers.

31 We have already noted that Izrail Mintz received materials regularly from Avraham Shlonsky after he returned to Moscow in 1963; see p. 290.

32 One local activist says that the Israelis did as much as was humanly possible in the circumstances. True, they might receive *Exodus* in English, German or Yiddish instead of in Russian, which was what they needed, and the Israelis might not be able to supply as many copies of *Vestnik Izrailia* and *Shalom* as could be profitably used, but the latter never failed to bring some materials wherever they appeared. Given the variety of the demand and the number of people involved, this in itself was a feat – interview with Y. Shnaider.

33 In Chernovtsy children who had been given badges by members of the

Israeli embassy were compelled to hand them over to the KGB and to sign a statement admitting that they had received anti-Soviet materials – interview with Yosef Urman. Mrs. Sabina Heifets-Krakovsky has kindly shown me protocols of searches conducted by the KGB in the home of her parents and in her own office, where she had concealed two books – Pevsner's Russian–Hebrew dictionary and a geography book of Israel – that her father, Haim Heifets, had recently been given.

34  Interview with M. Margulis; Margulis was one of three young men who had been arrested in 1950 after trying to cross the border into Turkey in 1949, see p. 46. For the development of Jewish *samizdat* in the 1960s, see Hoffman, "Jewish Samizdat."

35  Interview with Mordekhai Lapid.

36  Interview with a former member of the Israeli embassy staff.

37  Interview with M. Margulis.

38  Anatolii Rubin, "Moi put v Izrail" (My Road to Israel; Rus., unpublished, CRDEEJ, pp. 142–43, and *Magafayim humim*, pp. 151–52; Shifrin, *Hamemad harevi'i*, chs. 37 and 38; and interview with Boris and Leah Slovin.

39  Interview with E. Rusinek. Gurevich had received the book in German translation from a Swedish tourist, Anna Rock, in 1961 – interview with A. Rock. It was a sign of the conditions under which these groups operated that Rusinek did not find out that Slovin's group had put out a shortened version of *Exodus* until after his own group's translation was finished; nor did he know that Liborkin was helping Taubin. Another Moscow group that translated the full text from the English original divided the work up among its four members – Viktor Polskii, Vladimir Prestin, David Drabkin and Leonid Lefkovskii – some of whom seem to have sub-contracted their portion to other trusted friends. They put out five or six typewritten copies of this edition, at least one of which went to Leningrad, and then produced "a second edition" – interview with V. Polsky.

40  Shifrin, *Hamemad harevi'i*, and Hoffman, "Jewish Samizdat."

41  Interview with M. Lapid. In 1962 as well Lapid – then still Mark Blum – made five copies of a booklet entitled "A Collection of Selected Poems on Jewish Themes," which included most of the items then doing the rounds in Jewish circles (excerpts from Aliger's poem, the replies to Markov's attack on "Babii Iar"), a number of poems by well-known Jewish and non-Jewish poets and a few that he had written himself under various pseudonyms. The booklet was kindly shown me by Lapid.

42  We have seen that Meir Kanevskii was selling such souvenirs in the Caucasus to finance the *samizdat* activity of Sergei Morgulis and his group.

43  As early as 1960 the group around Liborkin in Riga was taping songs from an Israeli record – interview with E. Rusinek; in the early 1960s Taubin recorded songs for Tsukerman in Tomsk on reels supplied by the latter – interview with B. Tsukerman; the songs that Geula Gil sang in her performances in the USSR in 1966 (see pp. 323–25 below) were also taped and distributed – interviews with D. Khavkin and Yitzhak Kogan of Leningrad. One Jew who apparently also recorded Geula Gil's songs was Iosif Begun – Gilbert, *The Jews of Hope*. For the beginnings of *magnitizdat*,

tape-recordings of uncensored songs and broadcasts, see Gene Sosin, "Magnitizdat: Uncensored Songs in Dissent," in Tokes, *Dissent in the USSR*, pp. 276–309.

44 True, Hebrew was taught in a few institutions – including Moscow State University, where it was taught by former Habima actor Abram Rubinshtain, first as Shapiro's assistant and then as his successor – yet it was very difficult for a Jew to be accepted for these courses, which were designed for civil servants. This therefore did not legitimize the study of Hebrew in the way that the publication of the dictionary did. For further details, see Yedidya, "The Study of Hebrew."

45 For the main themes of Soviet media coverage of Eichmann's capture, trial and execution, see *JEE*, 5 (Aug. 1960), pp. 3–4, and 8 (July 1961), pp. 14–19.

46 Leneman, *La tragédie des juifs*, pp. 220 and 222; for further details, see Pinkus, *Soviet Government*, pp. 400–01 and 423–25.

47 *JC*, 17 Nov. 1961.

48 When the municipal authorities in Kiev finally decided in 1965 to erect a monument at Babii Iar, the announcement stated that it was to be a monument to "the victims of Nazism," omitting to specify their Jewish origin; see *Pravda*, 10 Sept. 1965. *Sovetish heymland* tried to amend this by referring to the planned monument as one to the victims of the Nazis, Ukrainians, Russians and Jews, but this was clearly meant to mislead. For when over 200 drawings and some thirty, large-scale plans for the monument were exhibited at the Ukrainian Architects' Club in Kiev, a group of local Jews protested that there were no inscriptions in Yiddish. Indeed, a Jewish architect who submitted a plan with a Yiddish inscription was requested to "withdraw it." A special tribunal judged the projects, but the ultimate approval was to be given in Moscow – *Focus on Soviet Jewry* (Feb. 1966), p. 3. When the monument was eventually erected – in 1976 – there was not even a hint of the Jewish origin of the majority of the victims. For the story behind the decision to erect a monument at Babii Iar, and the involvement of the Soviet intelligentsia in this issue, see Pinkus, *Soviet Government*, pp. 96–99, 114–26 and 435–38.

49 *JC*, 28 Aug. 1959, and Schwarz, *Evrei v Sovetskom Soiuze*, p. 253. When a Jewess in Rovno asked the local party secretary why no monument had been erected to the memory of the Jews who had perished there during the Nazi occupation, she was told that this was because the Jews had gone to their death like lambs – interview with a former member of the Israeli embassy staff.

50 See pp. 69–70 above.

51 In 1966 nearly the entire Jewish community of Tallinn was reported to have attended the first meeting commemorating the heroes of the Warsaw Ghetto in that town. Those who participated included a large number of students and several hundred boys and girls – *Focus on Soviet Jewry* (May 1966).

52 Among the speakers were Grigorii Manevich, who linked the crimes of the Nazis with the persecutions the Jews had endured throughout the centuries, and Mordecai Hanzin, who gave a fiery speech on the tragedy of the

Jewish people in the last generation. For the text of Manevich's speech, see Manevich, *Izbrannye rechi*, pp. 69–80.

53 In 1965 Masha Rolnikaite was allowed to publish her memoirs of the Vilnius ghetto under the title *Ia dolzhna rasskazat* (I must tell), first in the journal *Zvezda*, 2 and 3 (1965) and then in a separate volume (Moscow: Politizdat, 1965). This was clearly a concession on the part of the authorities, who may have seen in Rolnikaite a Soviet Anna Frank. In her story she speaks of Paneriai "where the bloody actions were carried out – mass killings of the Jewish population," of "secret partisan organizations" and "armed opposition to the fascists" in the ghetto, which helped refute the legend of the Jews going meekly to their death and was therefore of special value to the Jews. Rolnikaite's memoirs were reviewed in *Novyi mir* 4 (1965), pp. 249–50. Another, similar concession was the publication by *Druzhba narodov*, 8 (1965) of Yitzhak (Isak) Meras' novel, "Vechnyi shakh" (Stalemate with Death, Rus.; originally published in Lithuanian in 1963 and put out in book form in Moscow by Khudozhostvennaia literatura, 1966). The novel dealt with the suffering of the Jews in the ghettoes during World War II and their fight against the Nazis. (*Druzhba narodov* habitually translated into Russian literary works published in the languages of the USSR's national minorities.)

54 Interview with M. Moizes. The Jews of Kaunas also gathered periodically at Fort Nine to talk about Israel. Although they would come in hundreds on the anniversary of the massacre there, they were, however, unable to organize a special ceremony because of constant surveillance – interview with Yehezkel Polarevich.

55 The symbolic connection between the Holocaust and the national rebirth was highlighted by a color picture near one of the mass graves portraying a *menora* whose pedestal was made of roots twisted around, and tied with, barbed wire, but which nonetheless shone with bright flames that grew into large branches bearing green leaves. My story of Rumbula is based primarily on Mordecai Lapid, "The Memorial at Rumbula," *Jewish Frontier*, XXVIII, 6 (June 1971), pp. 11–19, supplemented by a Hebrew version of the same story – M. Perah, "Ha'mitingim' berumbula" (The Meetings at Rumbula), *Yalkut moreshet*, 13, pp. 5–16 (Mark Blum, who, in Israel became Mordecai Lapid, used the pen-name M. Perah); by an interview with David Garber, and an article by Garber in *Nasha strana* (Tel Aviv), 26 April 1979; and by the reminiscences of Y. Mendelevich, *Ma'ariv*, 2 March 1981.

56 Interviews with Valerii Gorelik and M. Moizes.

57 Interviews with Y. Shnaider, D. Yafit and M. Moizes. On one occasion, when Pesah Novik, editor of the New York Communist *Morgn frayheyt*, visited Riga, Shnaider met him at the airport and sought to show him that there was in fact no Jewish culture, and that he and others were being systematically hoodwinked by the Soviets.

There is a discrepancy between the version of David Garber, who insists that the authorities put an end to the choir's activities and existence in 1963, and that of Yosef Shnaider, who contends that it was he and Iudelevich who broke it up. Presumably what happened was that the authorities became aware of the internal disagreements that rent the choir, and this made it easier for them to close it down.

58 *JC*, 31 March 1967, and interview with Marek Moizes.

59 *JEE*, III, 6 (May 1967), p. 67; Schroeter, *The Last Exodus*, p. 39.

60 *Focus on Soviet Jewry* (April 1966), p. 1 gives a list published by the Center of Contemporary Jewish Studies, Brandeis University, which identified sixty-two synagogues throughout the entire country. The Soviets themselves gave the figure of 450 synagogues to the United Nations as late as 1959, although Rabbi Shlifer had indicated in 1956 that there were just over one hundred functioning synagogues in the entire country. At the end of the anti-religious campaign, the Soviets were maintaining that there were over ninety synagogues, again unquestionably an exaggerated figure, as quite a number were undoubtedly closed down during the years 1957–64 – Joshua Rothenberg, *The Jewish Religion in the Soviet Union* (New York: Ktav, 1971), pp. 45–46.

61 Eliav, *Between Hammer and Sickle* pp. 48–49. Even cemeteries, which as we have seen sometimes served as venues for the local Jewish population, were either simply closed down or used for construction and development sites without new lots being allocated to the community. Eliav writes (ibid., pp. 64–65): "Thousands visit the cemeteries at Riga and Vilna, Kishinev and Minsk, Moscow and Leningrad, and other places. Anyone who has not been present at such a scene has not witnessed the full tragedy of a community which, splintered and scattered, seeks desparately for some way to come together and uses even its dead as a means whereby it can unify itself." For references to the function of cemeteries, see also my article, "The Role of the Synagogue and Religion."

62 The authorities insisted that "the synagogue is no place for Soviet youngsters." In Tashkent, for example, Jews under thirty were reported to have been specifically forbidden to go to synagogue in this period – *JC*, 14 Jan. 1966.

63 Interview with Rabbi M. Hanzin. Here and there synagogues nonetheless retained a charity or mutual aid fund and the existence of poor-boxes in synagogues and the misappropriation, as it were, of the moneys collected in them were occasionally the topic of media attacks on the synagogues, e.g. Trofim Kichko's article, "What Do Jewish Ethics Teach?", *Voiovnichii ateist*, 12 (1962), pp. 37–41.

64 In Riga, the chairman of the congregation (one Zilberman) was deposed in fall 1960; so too was Rabbi Natan-Neta Olevskii in Moscow's Marina Roshcha synagogue although he continued to function as rabbi. The latter synagogues's new administration included Georgii Lieb as assistant chairman, one of the most controversial figures of Moscow's synagogue life who soon became the synagogue's chairman. In 1961 synagogue officers were replaced in Vilnius, Minsk, Kiev, Kishinev and Tashkent – *JC*, 1 Dec. 1961 and interview with a former member of the Israeli embassy staff. For Lieb, see also p. 315 and n. 82.

65 The synagogues' administrative councils continued throughout our period

to be subjected to purges. In 1966 Haim Ochs, one of the wardens of Moscow's small Cherkizovo synagogue, was removed from office in an attempt to introduce more reliable elements – *Focus on Soviet Jewry* (June–July 1966), p. 1. So too was Rabbi Shlomo Shapiro, rabbi and chairman of the Ashkenazi community in Dushanbe – *JEE*, III, 5 (Oct. 1966), p. 37. For continuing warnings to synagogue officials to prevent contact between local worshippers and foreign visitors and the receipt by the former of written materials, see *Focus on Soviet Jewry* (Aug. 1966).

66  The celebration of Rabbi Olevskii's birthday, which coincided with the 35th anniversary of the Marina Roshcha synagogue where he officiated, was widely publicized by Novosti abroad, but not within the USSR – *JEE*, II, 5 (Feb. 1964), p. 43. Among other details, Novosti mentioned the presence of Israeli diplomats and the reading out of telegrams from other congregations – *Al hamishmar*, 25 Oct. 1963.

67  Interviews with former members of the Israeli embassy staff.

68  In January 1960 the Riga synagogue was broken into and a fire started; in the Moscow Choral Synagogue stones would periodically be hurled into the building during services, windows being broken and worshippers frightened; in 1964 a fire broke out in one of the rooms in the building and religious articles, including Scrolls of the Law, were burned. In Minsk in the same year the roof of the synagogue was removed, without any forewarning, in the middle of prayers – *JEE*, passim.

69  Interviews with former members of the Israeli embassy staff.

70  According to reports between thirty and fifty students seen at synagogues in Moscow and Leningrad on Jewish festivals in the mid-1960s were warned by the heads of Komsomol cells at their universities that if they did not desist from such "undesirable" practices, their permits to live and study in these cities would be taken from them – *Focus on Soviet Jewry* (May 1966), p. 5, and (June–July 1966), pp. 3–4.

71  Thus, on a visit to Tbilisi in 1960 one embassy official was prevented from making any contact with worshippers in the Georgian synagogue, but was under no constraint whatever in the Ashkenazi one – interview with a former member of the Israeli embassy staff.

72  In Odessa, when two Israeli diplomats sought to give *matzot* to the synagogue in 1965, on the grounds that their baking was prohibited in the USSR, they were not only told that this was untrue, they were also attacked for Israel's sale of weapons to the GFR and for its alleged failure to protest Bonn's intention to apply the statute of limitation to the prosecution of war criminals. (Two hundred Odessan Jews were said to have signed a protest against the German statute of limitation – *JC*, 16 April 1965.)

73  This and some of the ensuing sections are based on interviews with former members of the Israeli embassy staff. See also Doron, *Betatspit uve'imut*, pp. 246–47. Doron, who was Israeli ambassador in Bucharest, visited the Soviet Union for the Feast of Tabernacles in 1965.

74  When Ambassador Harel protested, Rabbi Levin replied that this was intended as a sign of honor – *JC*, 15 Sept. 1961. The loge was retained for this purpose until the end of our period.

75 Another allegation related to Jews from Georgia who were said to be using the synagogue as a cover for financial malpractices. The authorities clearly could not view kindly the attendance at the Moscow synagogue of Jews from other parts of the country – many of whom undoubtedly came in order to see the Israelis – as this countered their policy of discouraging connections between Jews from different cities; see also my article, "The Role of the Synagogue and Religion."

76 The article appeared on 9 June 1963. One of the three, Moisei Chernukhin, had been dismissed from the *dvadtsatka*, among others because he had told a foreigner in 1949 about the Jews' position in the USSR (or, according to the *Trud* version, had told "cock-and-bull stories about living conditions in our country") which had been used to initiate "a hostile campaign against the Soviet Union."

77 The article appeared on 11 March 1964.

78 Copies of the letter were sent to the Council for the Affairs of Religious Cults, Israel's two chief rabbis and *Morgn frayheyt*. These protests continued until the end of our period. On 30 May 1967 Rabbi Levin sent a letter to Israeli Chief Rabbi Yitzhak Nissim averring that members of the Israeli embassy staff had behaved improperly in the synagogue and taken advantage of their attendance at prayers to violate Soviet laws. Rabbi Nissim was asked to tell Ambassador Katriel Katz to desist from these activities as disturbing the sanctity of the Sabbath – *Ma'ariv*, 19 July 1967, quoting *Izvestiia*.

79 The writer Yizhar Smilansky, who visited the USSR in summer 1962 as a member of the Israeli delegation to the World Peace Congress, witnessed a similar scene in the synagogue. Smilansky was deeply impressed by the silent contact created between the congregation and the Israeli diplomats despite their physical separation, and by the worshippers' constant gazing at the Israelis in the hope, as it were, of drawing some sort of inspiration from their very appearance. On this Sabbath, too, the entire congregation rose to its feet as the diplomats entered, and at the end of the service arranged itself in two columns for the guests to walk between, shaking hands and greeting them with a "Shabbat shalom" – Y. Smilansky, "Impressions of a Visit in the Soviet Union" (Heb.), *Hapo'el hatsa'ir*, XXXIII (21 Aug. 1962), pp. 4–7.

80 When Ambassador Tekoa's wife bore a son, the synagogue officials, headed by the rabbi, were hesitant about honoring him with the *maftir*, the most prestigious honor. Upon the insistence of congregation secretary Mordecai Hanzin, however, they went to a senior official of the Council for the Affairs of Religious Cults to obtain the requisite permission – interview with Rabbi Hanzin.

81 *Al hamishmar*, 2 May 1963; see also my article, "The Role of the Synagogue and Religion."

82 Interview with a former member of the Israeli embassy staff. Despite this speech Lieb was well known for consistently misleading tourists about the true situation of the Jews in the Soviet Union – *JEE*, II, 5 (Feb. 1964), p. 43.

83 *Haaretz*, 4 June 1964; also *Israelitisches Wochenblatt*, 21 May 1965. The version

of Manevich's speech given in his collected speeches (*Izbrannye rechi*, pp. 81–90) differs considerably from what he seems to have actually said; presumably he was carried away by his own oratory. The text he had prepared pointed out that although Soviet Jews found much that was incomprehensible in Israeli policy and things "with which we disagree and even protest against . . . we are glad at the successes of the Jewish state and experience its worries and anxieties." The written text insisted on the need for Soviet Jews to have their own culture and to fulfil their obligations both to the martyrs of World War II and to "the present and future generations," by punishing war criminals, setting up fitting memorials to the victims of the ghettos and participating in the struggle for peace. The "believing Jews" of the Soviet Union, the text concluded, "see no irreconcilable contradictions between the teachings of Judaism and the tasks of the construction of the Communist society."

84 Interview with a tourist to the USSR who has asked to remain anonymous.

85 The Lvov synagogue was closed down in fall 1962, after a particularly vicious campaign in the local media against the Jewish religion as a whole and the Lvov synagogue in particular. An Israeli embassy official had attended the synagogue on the New Year, just prior to its closure, when the warden announced that the visitors would have to take the gift they had brought the synagogue – religious articles for the festivals – back to Moscow. For a previous visit by Israelis to the Lvov synagogue, see p. 271; for the closing of the synagogue in Lvov and the propaganda campaign that accompanied it, see Eliav, *Between Hammer and Sickle*, pp. 54–58.

86 Interview with Shlomo Gefen. Gefen, who lived in Druskenniki from 1957 to 1963, travelled to Vilnius or other towns for the Jewish festivals in order to be able to refrain from working on these days.

87 For earlier examples of a decree prohibiting this particular prayer, see my article, "The Role of the Synagogue and Religion."

88 Interview with Rabbi M. Hanzin. Hanzin translated the Aramaic portions of the liturgy into Russian so the authorities could check their content prior to discussion of a possible second edition.

89 *JC*, 8 April 1966 and 28 April 1967, and *Brooklyn Jewish Press*, 7 April 1967.

90 See, e.g., Wiesel, *The Jews of Silence*, p. 23, and Ro'i, "The Festival of Passover."

91 *Focus on Soviet Jewry* (March 1966), p. 2.

92 In 1960 some thirty young people were arrested in Moscow on the night of Simhat Tora and interrogated until morning: what had brought them to the synagogue? were they believers or members of some religious organization? what were their ties to the embassy?

93 *Herut*, 10 Dec. 1965; Wiesel, *The Jews of Silence*, pp. 104–16, and my article, "The Role of the Synagogue and Religion," as well as interviews with former members of the Israeli embassy staff. For the practice of spreading information about approaching Jewish holidays and Simhat Tora in particular, see also ch. 7, n. 107.

94 Wiesel, *The Jews of Silence*, chs. 5 and 6, and my article, "The Role of the Synagogue and Religion."

 95 Wiesel, *The Jews of Silence*, p. 92.
 96 *NYT* correspondent Theodore Shabad reported the "continuing avid interest of Soviet Jewry in Yiddish culture despite the apparent coolness of the authorities," as evidenced by "the sellout audience" of fifteen hundred who "jammed" the House of Culture of Railroad Workers "to give an enthusiastic reception" to Sidi Tal's "rather mediocre provincial variety show." Shabad noted that the audience included "a surprising number of young couples and even some children" as well as several persons who were "unusually well dressed," apparently from "high income groups" – *New Leader*, XLVI (7 Jan. 1963), p. 7.
 97 Early in the decade the singer Zinovii Shulman was asked to stop performing in Yiddish, while Anna Guzik was reported to have said that she hardly had the strength left for the war of attrition which she had to fight for every Yiddish piece or song.
 98 This troupe was one of those that performed in the Moscow Municipal Hall on the occasion of the fiftieth anniversary of the death of Sholom Aleichem in 1966. Upon Shvartser's recital of the lines "vos mir zenen, zenen mir, ober yidn zenen mir" ("whatever we are, we are, but we are Jews"), the whole audience broke into applause – *Focus on Soviet Jewry* (May 1966), p. 3.
 99 See, e.g., my article, "Nehama Lifshitz."
100 "The Diary of Anna Frank" had appeared in Russian that year (Moscow: Inostrannaia literatura) with an introduction by Ilya Ehrenburg.
101 Michel Tatu, then correspondent of *Le Monde* in Moscow, noted that "the most prominent living Soviet composer," Dmitrii Shostakovich, had "refused to disavow his 'Thirteenth Symphony' . . . performed for the first time despite the official boycott, on 18 December [1962], the very day after the celebrated discussion", i.e. Khrushchev's first encounter with "the creative intelligentisa" – *Power in the Kremlin*, p. 303. See also Pinkus, *Soviet Government*, pp. 98–99 and p. 488, n. 62. An American student who was in Leningrad for White Nights in 1966 and who has asked to remain anonymous, attended six Shostakovich concerts in honor of the composer's sixtieth birthday. At the last concert, which was the first performance in Leningrad of the Thirteenth Symphony, the audience began calling for Evtushenko, who was in the audience (Shostakovich was in hospital recovering from a heart attack). The Jews, who comprised an estimated 85 percent of the audience, treated the poet like a god and only agreed to disperse when he asked them to do so. (An announcement that the fire department demanded their departure had had no effect.)
102 *Al hamishmar*, 29 July 1963.
103 Interviews with T. Brodetskaia, D. Khavkin and E. Finkelstein.
104 For Soviet–Israeli cultural relations, see Dagan, *Moscow and Jerusalem*, passim, and Govrin, "Israel–Soviet Relations."
105 Jews later told a Canadian rabbi of their excitement when the Israeli team played a Red Army team in Riga and how there were 15,000 applications for the stadium's 1,200 seats – *JEE*, 8 (July, 1961), p. 42.
106 *Davar*, 31 Oct. 1962.

107  *Al hamishmar*, 29 Nov. 1963.

108  Mendelevich, *Mivtza' hatuna*, pp. 25–26; Schroeter, *The Last Exodus*, p. 70.

109  Interviews with M. Margulis and Tanhum Cohen-Mintz who captained the Israeli team. Margulis took special pleasure in noting how the Russians among the audience lowered their heads when the Israeli team scored points. (He also remembers seeing an Israeli football team being defeated 0 : 5, which he called "a real tragedy.") For the excitement at one of the games in which the Israelis defeated their rivals, see Doron, *Betatspit uve'imut*, pp. 229–30.

110  Eliav, *Between Hammer and Sickle*, pp. 146–47.

111  *Al hamishmar*, 5 Nov. 1963.

112  *JC*, 22 Nov. 1963, and interviews with D.Iofis, who attended Salzman's concert in Riga, where he even exchanged a few words with Ambassador Tekoa and his children who were sitting nearby, and with Lev Kornblit, who attended both her concerts in Leningrad.

113  Interview with a former member of the Israeli embassy staff who accompanied Singer on his tour.

114  Interviews with L. Kornblit and former members of the Israeli embassy staff.

115  *Ma'ariv*, 4 July 1966. Ms. Gil's Moscow and perhaps also Leningrad concerts were taped on cassettes; see n. 43 above.

116  Sonia Rita Dnitz, "Nehama Comes to Israel," *Israel Magazine*, III, 4 (April 1971); interview with David and Miriam Garber; and Mendelevich, *Mivtza hatuna*, pp. 26–28. Three other people who had been involved in the same incident, Avigail Katz, Maksim Kushlin and Mark Blum, were arrested, tried on 30 Aug.–2 Sept. 1966 and sentenced to prison terms. Blum (now Lapid) has kindly shown me the text of the verdict.

117  *Ma'ariv*, 17 July 1966; and interview with S. Gefen. Goskontsert, the Soviet organization that sponsored the tour, demanded that the piece on Paneriai be removed from subsequent concerts on the grounds that it had not been included in the original program.

118  Soviet diplomats were reported to have expressed concern over the orchestra's impending visit, as local Jews had been asking for details of performances for some time before the final cancellation (which came after two postponements) – *Focus on Soviet Jewry* (Oct. 1966), and interview with M. Margulis.

119  *Yalkut magen*, 21 (June–Aug. 1961), p. 26. The program included films on Degania (the first kibbutz) and on turning Lake Hula (a swamp in northern Israel) into arable land.

120  *Al hamishmar*, 16 and 30 July 1963, and interview with Boris Gimelfarb who came to the festival from Odessa.

121  Interview with David Khavkin, who came from Odessa for the festival and sent photographs of the Israeli stand and exhibits to friends throughout the USSR.

122  Embassy personnel estimated that 90 percent of the 150,000 who visited the pavilion were Jews.

123  Among the young Soviet Jews who sang Israeli songs at the reception

were Yosef Shnaider and other Riga activists; interviews with former members of the Israeli embassy staff and with Y. Shnaider; *Focus on Soviet Jewry*; *Davar*, 24 Feb. 1967, and *Yalkut magen* 41 (March 1967), pp. 19–21. *Focus on Soviet Jewry* describes how Jewish visitors to the Israeli pavilion were detained, interrogated and ordered to give up whatever gifts they had received.

124 *Izvestiia*, 24 Feb. 1967; *JEE*, III, 6 (May 1967), pp. 20–22; and interviews with D. Khavkin and S. Dolnik. Dolnik's arrest was accompanied by searches in the homes of other activists, particularly of members of the group of which he was a central figure, e.g., that of Abram Kaplan in Minsk, where all materials pertaining to Israel and Jewish topics were confiscated – *Libi bemizrah*, pp. 11–12 and 24.

125 *Pravda*, 14 Aug. 1966.

126 Interviews with M. Kanevskii and E. Finkelstein, both of whom visited the poultry exhibition (the former from Moscow, the latter from Sverdlovsk).

127 For the exhibition, see *JP*, 19 May 1967, and interviews with Gitta Landman and Y. Shnaider, both of whom visited the Israeli pavilion, the former together with Moisei Brodskii, who had been arrested with her in 1955, and Shnaider with Anatolii Feldman of Kiev with whom he had been in prison camp, and Grisha Faigin, another Riga activist. For information on Allon's visit to the USSR, see *JP*, 8, 9, 11, 17 and 25 May 1967, and interview with Tova Yeshurun-Berman, who participated in the same delegation as Allon.

128 Golda Meir had, as we have seen, spoken of 9,236 *vyzovy* sent up to summer 1960.

129 *JC*, 26 Aug. 1966; *NYT*, 1 Jan. 1967.

130 See table, p. 9. Interestingly, there was a parallel growth in the reunification of families from other Soviet national minorities and from among Soviet citizens who were nationals of other countries or had relatives there:

|             | in 1964 | in 1965 |
| ----------- | ------- | ------- |
| Germans     | 200     | 500     |
| Greeks      | 800     | 2,000   |
| Armenians   | 133     | 287     |
| Canadians   | 95      | 172     |
| Australians | 30      | 80      |

131 *Chicago Sentinel*, 29 Sept. 1966.

132 E.g. Prof. Abraham Katsh.

133 Goldberg, "Travels in the Soviet Union," pp. 9–10.

134 On Passover in 1966, for instance, a twelve-year-old boy told an Israeli tourist attending services at the Riga synagogue: "I know that people are

looking at me and that when I get back to school tomorrow there will be trouble. But I don't care. Save us! Get us out of here!" – interview with a former member of the Israeli embassy staff.

135 Many Moscow Jews, for instance, who learned through the Jewish grapevine that Liova Rubashov, nephew of Israeli President Zalman Shazar, and his family had been allowed to leave, immediately applied for exit visas; 250 people were said to have been so encouraged – *Focus on Soviet Jewry* (Jan. 1966).

136 The daughter of a would-be emigrant from Moscow was expelled from Moscow State University in 1966 just two weeks before graduation. She was also told that she would be obliged to pay a sum of 10,000 rubles, the cost of the education which the Soviet state had given her. Jews applying to universities were sometimes asked outright: why should we have to prepare doctors, engineers and teachers for Israel? In Chernovtsy, one Komsomol member whose parents had applied to leave was compelled to "confess" publicly that he was a traitor and enemy of the Soviet people – *JC*, 10 June 1966; *JEE*, III, 5 (Oct. 1966), p. 26. *Focus on Soviet Jewry* (Jan. 1966), p. 2, reported the case of a Kiev boy who was told that he would be thrown out of the Komsomol unless his parents withdrew their application to emigrate, and of a Kharkov boy who was asked to sign a paper promising to "persuade" his parents not to commit the "shameful act" of leaving the USSR. *New York Times* told on 1 Jan. 1967 of teachers compelling young children to promise that their names would be erased from the applications of their parents; see also *JC*, 27 Jan. 1967.

137 This happened to Yiddish writer Yosef Kerler and his wife – interview with Yosef and Anna Kerler.

138 Confinement of dissidents in psychiatric institutions, which became common practice in the 1970s, had been used in the early Bolshevik period – indeed, even in pre-revolutionary times – as well as under Stalin and Khrushchev; see Frederick C. Barghoorn, "The Post-Khrushchev Campaign to Suppress Dissent: Perspectives, Strategies and Techniques of Repression," n. 153, in Tokes, *Dissent in the USSR*; Robert M. Slusser, "Historic and Democratic Opposition," ibid., p. 340; Reddaway, *Uncensored Russia*, p. 232; Medvedev and Medvedev, *A Question of Madness*, p. 198; Hosking; *A History of the Soviet Union*, p. 343.

139 Sometimes elderly parents would be persuaded to withhold such consent, without which even grown-up children could not receive exit permits, since Soviet law states that a citizen is responsible for his parents in their old age. This stipulation had been specified in the 1918 and 1926 Family Codes – Madison, *Social Welfare in the Soviet Union*. In recent years it has become further institutionalized through its inclusion in the Constitution of the USSR, 1977, Article 66.

140 For a description of the obstacles a would-be applicant had to overcome and the "invidious" position in which he found himself as a result of the very processing of his application, see *Focus on Soviet Jewry* (April 1966), p. 5.

141 This was especially true after Kosygin's Paris statement.

142  Interview with Shmuel Gottesman. A number of Jews left for Israel in this period from Mukachevo, Uzhgorod and Khust, including families with children; a few also emigrated from this area to the U.S. to be reunited with family there.

143  Rabbi Tverskii, who had served a long prison term, was known as a man of uncompromising character and was very popular – interview with Rabbi M. Hanzin.

144  Or, as he was called as of October 1964, the secretary-general.

145  The American Yiddishist Ben Zion Goldberg encountered a woman on a park bench in Kiev who wanted to leave for Israel with her husband and sixteen-year-old daughter (see n. 133 above). After receiving four affidavits from her brother in Israel, and four refusals, she wrote to Khrushchev – Goldberg, "Travels in the Soviet Union," pp. 9–10. The Rigan was Boris Krechmar – interview with Ezra Rusinek.

146  Only in Palestine, Chernobilskii wrote in his appeal, had the purity, the pride and the life of the Jewish nation been preserved. And now that Israel existed no government practicing genuine freedom had the right "to forbid people of the Jewish nation to emigrate to their republic," just as Armenians were allowed to emigrate from other countries to their native land. For such a refusal contradicted "the principles of democracy and socialism" – *Detroit Jewish News*, 23 Oct. 1964. Chernobilskii was arrested in late summer 1966, but subsequently released and granted permission to emigrate with his wife and son in early spring 1967 – *JC*, 13 Jan. 1967; *JEE*, III, 5 (May 1967), pp. 75–79; and Schroeter, *The Last Exodus*, pp. 38–39.

147  For the story of Iasha Kazakov, see Cohen, *Ehad shehefer et hademama*.

148  Thus, the Jews of Minsk attributed to them their receiving a building that could serve as a synagogue after the closing of the city's sole synagogue. Lord Russell had received letters from Jews in the wake of the publication of his correspondence with Khrushchev, some of which attested to the favorable conditions in which Soviet Jews lived and denied discrimination, while others expressed their gratitude for his interest and intervention on their behalf. The moral encouragement that Soviet Jews derived from such support explains their resentment at the position adopted by Nahum Goldmann.

149  One person who was allowed to leave apparently as a result of the direct intervention of Eleanor Roosevelt was Rabbi Haim Meir Kahane of Chernovtsy – interview with Rabbi Kahane. Mr. William Emerson of the Franklin D. Roosevelt Library has kindly supplied me with a copy of Mrs. Roosevelt's appeal to Khrushchev on behalf of Rabbi Kahane.

150  Interview with Boris and Leah Slovin. These ideas, of which nothing came at the time, were, of course, accepted strategy in the 1970s.

151  Interview with Yosef and Anna Kerler.

152  *JC*, 6 Jan. 1967.

153  This is still a moot and much disputed point today, both as far as the period in question and later periods are concerned. For my own personal opinion, see Conclusion.

154 Soviet aid to Nasser was also unpopular among wide circles in the general Soviet public, which viewed it as diverting badly needed resources from the Soviet population whose living standards were still very low. For repercussions of these views among the Soviet leadership, see Ro'i, *From Encroachment to Involvement*, p. 459. For details concerning Arab endeavors to attain unity in the mid-sixties, see, e.g., Malcolm Kerr, *The Arab Cold War 1958–1967*, 2nd ed. (London: Oxford University Press, 1967).

155 Thus, by the early 1960s it was not uncommon for Jewish youngsters to hit back at antisemitic outbursts – both vocally and physically. Even before this there had been rare instances of this. Shlomo Gefen, for instance, then in Syktyvkar in the Komi ASSR, advised his fourteen-year-old daughter Yael as early as 1956 to strike at her tormentors when they taunted her for her Jewishness and for having a Hebrew name. When she did so, indeed, the mocking ceased – interview with S. Gefen.

156 See, e.g. Ro'i, *From Encroachment to Involvement*, documents 89 and 93; for the USSR's growing commitment to the neo-Ba'th regime of Salah Jadid, see ibid., document 91, and *Noveishaia istoriia arabskikh stran (1917–1966)* (Modern History of the Arab Countries (1917–1966), Rus.; Moscow: Nauka, 1968), pp. 88–93.

157 Interview with Meir Gelfond.

158 One young Jewess, a librarian in Odessa, long troubled by the USSR's Jewish policy, began in the mid-sixties "to think more and more of Israel." In a letter she published several years later, Raiza Palatnik wrote: "The prelude to the Six Day War shocked me to my very roots. It seemed to me that the whole world looked on apathetically while well-equipped armies prepared to finish Hitler's work, to annihilate the small Jewish state of 2,500,000, to erase from the face of the earth the State of Israel reborn after 2,000 years. On the eve of the war ... while [Soviet UN Ambassador Nikolai] Fedorenko was cynically declaring in the UN, 'Don't over-dramatize the event', I was close to nervous exhaustion. I wanted to shout to humanity, 'Help!'" – quoted in Cohen, *Let My People Go!*, p. 71. One of the members of the Israeli delegation which included Yigal Allon, that visited the USSR in May 1967, has also testified that the crisis in Israel and the vicious anti-Israel propaganda in the Soviet media merely increased the enthusiasm of the Jews who sought out the Israelis everywhere – interview with Dr. Tova Yeshurun-Berman.

159 Interview with David Khavkin.

160 See, for example, *Middle East Record*, 1967 (Jerusalem: Israel Universities Press, 1971), p. 232.

161 Anna Guzik's husband, Mikhail Chaikovskii, who usually introduced the program, spoke this time of the role of the artist in giving encouragement in times of national duress, when the soul was in anguish. At the end of the evening, he said that the concert was Anna Guzik's contribution to the Jewish people's war effort – interview with former members of the Israeli embassy staff.

162 Interviews with former members of the Israeli embassy staff and with Eitan Finkelstein.

# Bibliography


PRIMARY SOURCES

Aharoni, Aryeh (ed.), *Avraham Shlonsky: Mikhtavim Iiyehudim bivrit hamoatsot* (Letters to Jews in the Soviet Union; Heb.). Tel Aviv: Sifriyat poalim, undated.

*The Anti-Stalin Campaign and International Communism: A Selection of Documents.* New York: Columbia University, 1957.

*Conférence internationale sur la situation des juifs en Union Soviétique.* Paris: Ch. Bernard, undated.

*The Council of Europe on the Jews of the Soviet Union.* London: World Jewish Congress, July 1965.

*Foreign Relations of the United States 1947* . . . Washington, D.C.: Government Printing Office, 1971 . . .

*Libi bemizrah. Igrot ketanot migalut brit hamoatsot leahot bezion* (My Heart Lies in the East. Small Letters from the Soviet Diaspora to a Sister in Zion; Heb.). Kfar Yehoshua: Family Publication, 1972.

Liebler, Isi, *Soviet Jewry and Human Rights.* Victoria: A Human Rights Research Publication, 1965.

Manevich, Grigorii, *Izbrannye rechi* (Selected Speeches; Rus.). Jerusalem: Shamir, 1976.

Matthews, Mervyn (ed.), *Soviet Government. A Selection of Official Documents on Internal Policy.* London: Jonathan Cape, 1974.

Meerson-Aksenov, Michael, and Shragin, Boris (eds.), *The Political, Social and Religious Thought of Russian 'Samizdat' – An Anthology.* Belmont, Mass.: Nordland, 1977.

*Parliamentary Debates (Hansard), House of Commons Official Report*, Fifth Series. London: Her Majesty's Stationery Office.

Salisbury, Harrison, *Moscow Journal.* Chicago: University of Chicago, 1961.

Sharett, Moshe, *Yoman ishi* (Personal Diary; Heb.). Tel Aviv: Sifriyat Ma'ariv, 1978.

*Soviet Jewry. A Reply to I. Liebler.* Sydney: Current Book Distributors, 1965.

*Soviet Jewry and the Australian Communist Party* . . . *Documents.* Victoria: A Human Rights Research Publication, 1966.

*State of Israel. Documents on the Foreign Policy of Israel*, vol. 1, 14 May–30 September 1948 . . . Jerusalem: Government Printer, 1981 . . .

United Nations Assembly Official Records.

## SECONDARY SOURCES

**Books and monographs**

Alliluyeva, Svetlana, *Letters to a Friend*. London: Hutchinson, 1967.

Altshuler, Mordechai, *Hakibbutz hayehudi bivrit hamoatsot beyamenu* (Soviet Jewry Today; Heb.). Jerusalem: Magnes, 1979.

Azbel, Mark, *Autobiography of a Jew*.

Azrael, Jeremy (ed.), *Soviet Nationality Policies and Practices*. Chicago: Chicago University Press, 1979.

Azbel, Mark, *Autobiography of a Jew*.

Barghoorn, Frederick C., *Soviet Russian Nationalism*. New York: Oxford University Press, 1956.

Bauer, Yehuda, *Flight and Rescue: Brichah*. New York: Random House, 1970.

Ben-Horin (pseudonym), *Ma koreh sham* (What's Going On There; Heb.). Tel Aviv: Am Oved, 1970.

Bilinsky, Yaroslav, *The Second Soviet Republic: The Ukraine after World War II*. New Brunswick, N.J.: Rutgers University Press, 1964.

Bisgyer, Maurice, *Challenge and Encounter*. New York: Crown Publishers, 1967.

Bortoli, Georges, *Als Stalin starb, Kult und Wirklichkeit* (When Stalin Died, Cult and Reality; Ger.). Stuttgart: Seewald Verlag, 1974.

Bourdeaux, Michael, *Religious Ferment in Russia*. London: Macmillan, 1968.

Brafman, Morris, and Schimmel, David, *Trade for Freedom*. New York: Shengold, 1975.

Branover, Herman, *Vozvrashchenie* (The Return; Rus.). New York: Free Press, 1977.

Breslauer, George W., *Khrushchev and Brezhnev as Leaders: Building authority in Soviet Politics*. London: George Allen and Unwin, 1982.

Brzezinski, Zbigniew K., *The Soviet Bloc*. Cambridge, Mass.: Harvard University Press, 4th Printing, 1971.

Butman, Hillel, *Leningrad–Yerushalayim vehanaya aruka beineihem* (Leningrad–Jerusalem and a Long Stopover in Between; Heb.). Tel Aviv: Hakibbutz hameuhad, 1981. (Also published in Russian: *Leningrad–Ierusalim s dolgoi peresadkoi*. Jerusalem: Biblioteka Aliya, 1981.)

Cang, Joel, *The Silent Millions*. London: Rapp and Whiting, 1969.

Cohen, Geula (ed.), *Ehad shehefer et hademama* (One Who Broke the Silence; Heb.). Jerusalem: Bernard Deutsch, 1970.

Cohen, Richard, *Let My People Go!* New York: Popular Library, 1971.

Conquest, Robert, *Power and Policy in the U.S.S.R.* New York: Harper & Row, 1967.

*The Nation Killers: The Soviet Deportation of Nationalities*. London: Macmillan, 1970.

Crankshaw, Edward (ed.) *Khrushchev Remembers*. London: André Deutsch, 1971.

Dagan, Avigdor, *Moscow and Jerusalem*. London: Abelard-Schuman, 1970.

Dagoni, Noah, *Betsipornei hakagebe* (In the Claws of the KGB; Heb.). Tel Aviv: Israeli Ministry of Defence, 1984.

Doron, Eliezer, *Betatspit uve'imut* (Observation and Confrontation; Heb.). Jerusalem: Mabat, 1978.

Ehrenburg, Ilya, *Men, Years, Life*, vol. 6, *Post-War Years, 1945–54*. London: MacGibbon & Kee, 1966.

Eisenhower, Dwight D., *The White House Years: Waging Peace, 1956–1961*. New York: Doubleday, 1965.

Eliav, Arie L., *Between Hammer and Sickle*. New York: Signet Books, 1969.
 *Taba'ot 'edut* (Rings of Faith; Heb.). Tel Aviv: Am Oved, 1983.
 *Taba'ot shahar* (Rings of Dawn; Heb.). Tel Aviv: Am Oved, 1984.

Fejto, François, *The French Communist Party and the Crisis of International Communism*. Boston: MIT, 1967.

Fischer, Lipa, *Parimakher in gulag* (Barber in Gulag; Yid.). Tel Aviv: Hamenorah, 1977.

Gilbert, Martin, *The Jews of Hope*. London: Macmillan, 1984.

Goldberg, Anatol, *Ilya Ehrenburg: Writing, Politics and the Art of Survival*. London: Weidenfeld and Nicolson, 1984.

Goldberg, Ben Zion, *The Jewish Problem in the Soviet Union*. New York: Crown Publishers, 1961.

Hayward, Max, and Fletcher, William C. (eds.), *Religion in the Soviet State*. New York: Praeger, 1969.

Hindus, Maurice, *House without a Roof*. New York: Doubleday, 1961.

Hosking, Geoffrey, *A History of the Soviet Union*. London: Fontana and Collins, 1985.

Inkeles, Alex, *Social Change in Soviet Russia*. Cambridge, Mass.: Harvard University Press, 1968.

Ivanov, Konstantin, and Sheinis, Zinovii, *Gosudarstvo Izrail, ego polozhenie i politika* (The State of Israel, Its Situation and Policy; Rus.). Moscow: Izd. politicheskoi literatury, 1958.

Katz, Zev, Rogers, Rosemarie, and Harned, Frederic (eds.), *Handbook of Major Soviet Nationalities*. New York: Free Press, 1975.

Kaufman, Abram I., *Lagernyi vrach* (Camp Doctor; Rus.). Tel Aviv: Am Oved, 1973.

Kersten, Krystyna, *Repatriacija ludnosci polskij po II wojnie swiatowej* (The Repatriation of the Polish Population after World War II; Pol.). Wroclaw: Ossolinskich, 1974.

Kochan, Lionel (ed.), *The Jews in Soviet Russia since 1917*. London: Oxford University Press, 1970.

Korey, William, *The Soviet Cage*. New York: Viking Press, 1973.

Lane, David, *Politics and Society in the USSR*. London: Martin Robertson, 2nd ed., 1978.

Lash, Joseph P., *Eleanor; The Years Alone*. New York: W. W. Norton, 1972.

Lawrence, Gunther, *Three Million More?* New York: Doubleday, 1970.

Lazaris, Vladimir, *Evrei i dissidenty* (Jews and Dissidents; Rus.). Tel Aviv: Effect, 1981.

Leneman, Léon, *La tragédie des juifs en U.R.S.S.* Paris: Desclée de Brouwer, 1959.

Leonhard, Wolfgang, *The Kremlin since Stalin*. New York: Praeger, 1962.

Levy, Hyman, *Jews and the National Question*. London: Hillway, 1958 (Revised American edition; New York: Cameron Associates, 1959).

Lichtheim, George, and Laqueur, Walter (eds.), *The Soviet Cultural Scene 1956–1957*. New York: Atlantic Books, 1958.

Litvak, Yosef, *Plitim yehudim mipolin bivrit hamoatsot, 1939–1946* (Jewish Refugees from Poland in the Soviet Union, 1939–1946; Heb.). Tel Aviv: The Institute for Contemporary Jewry at the Hebrew University, Jerusalem; Hakibbutz Hameuhad; Bet Lohamei Hagetaot, 1988.

Maccabee, Nechemiah, *Nitsnuts holef batsel* (A Sparkle Passes in the Shadow; Heb.). Tel Aviv: Or Am, 1981.

Madison, Bernice, *Social Welfare in the Soviet Union*. Stanford, Calif.: Stanford University Press, 1968.

Markish, Esther, *Lahazor miderekh aruka* (Return from a Long Trip; Heb.). Tel Aviv: Hakibbutz Hameuhad, 1977.

McCagg, William O. Jr., *Stalin Embattled 1943–1948*. Detroit: Wayne State University, 1978.

McLean, Hugh, and Vickery, Walter N. (eds.), *The Year of Protest 1956*. Westport, Conn.: Greenwood Press, 1961.

Medvedev, Zhores, *The Rise and Fall of T.D. Lysenko*. New York: Columbia University Press, 1969.

Medvedev, Zhores, and Medvedev, Roy, *A Question of Madness*. New York: A. A. Knopf, 1971.

Meir, Golda, *My Life*. Jerusalem and Tel Aviv: Steimatsky, 1975.

Mendelevich, Yosef, *Mivtza' hatuna* (Operation "Wedding"; Heb.). Jerusalem: Keter, 1985.

Mikhlin, Imanuel, *Hagahelet*. Jerusalem: Shamir, 1986.

Namir, Mordecai, *Shlihut bemoskva* (Heb.; Eng. title: Israeli Mission to Moscow). Tel Aviv: Am Oved, 1971.

Neishtat, Mordekhai, *Yehudei Gruzia* (The Jews of Georgia; Heb.). Tel Aviv: Am Oved, 1970.

Nekrich, Aleksandr, *The Punished Peoples*. New York: W. W. Norton [*c.* 1978].

Orbach, William W., *The American Movement to Aid Soviet Jews*. Amherst: University of Massachusetts Press, 1979.

Pinkus, Benjamin, *The Soviet Government and the Jews 1948–1967*. Cambridge: Cambridge University Press, 1984.

Poupko, Bernard A., *In shotn fun kremlin* (In the Shadow of the Kremlin; Yid.). New York: Ferlag Einikeit, 1968.

Pregerzon, Zvi, *Yoman hazikhronot* (Diary of Memoirs; Heb.). Tel Aviv: Am Oved, 1976.

Prital, David (ed.), *In Search of Self*. Jerusalem: Mount Scopus Publications, 1982.

Reddaway, Peter (ed.), *Uncensored Russia: The Human Rights Movement in the Soviet Union*. London: Jonathan Cape, 1972.

Ro'i, Yaacov, *Soviet Decision Making in Practice. The USSR and Israel 1947–1954*. New Brunswick, N.J: Transaction, 1980.

    *From Encroachment to Involvement*. New York and Jerusalem: John Wiley and Israel Universities Press, 1974.

Ro'i, Yaacov, and Beker, Avi (eds.), *Jewish Culture and Identity in the Soviet Union*. New York: New York University Press, forthcoming.

Rozin, Aharon, *Mayn veg aheym* (My Way Home; Yid.). Tel Aviv: Yiddish Culture Association, 1981.

Rubin, Anatoli, *Magafayim humim, magafayim adumim* (Brown Boots, Red Boots; Heb.). Tel Aviv: Dvir, 1977.

Salcman, Mojshe, *Vezakhiti lerehabilitatsia* (And They Rehabilitated Me; Heb.). Tel Aviv: Israel Books, 1974.

Scholmer, Joseph, *Vorkuta*. New York: Henry Holt, 1955.

Schroeter, Leonard, *The Last Exodus*. New York: Universe Books, 1974.

Schwarz, Solomon, *The Jews in the Soviet Union*. Syracuse, N.Y.: Syracuse University Press, 1951.

Seter, D. (pseudonym), *Halo tish'ali* (Will You Not Ask? Songs of Zion from the Soviet Union; Heb.). Tel Aviv: Am Oved and Biblioteka Aliya, 1975.

Shapiro, Gershon, *Evrei – geroi Sovetskogo Soiuza* (Jewish Heroes of the Soviet Union; Rus.). Tel Aviv: private ed., 1982.

Shashar, Michael, *Yisraeli bemoskva* (Israeli in Moscow; Heb.). Jerusalem: Kiryat Sepher, 1961.

Shatunovskaia, Lidiia, *Zhizn v kremle* (Life in the Kremlin; Rus.). New York: Chalidze Publications, 1982.

Shifrin, Avraham, *Hamemad harevi'i* (The Fourth Dimension; Heb.). Tel Aviv: Ma'oz, 1976.

Shoham, Natan, *Pegishot bemoskva, 1957* (Meetings in Moscow, 1957; Heb.). Merhavia: Sifriyat Hapoalim, 1957.

Solzhenitsyn, Alexander, *The Gulag Archipelago*. New York: Harper & Row, 1973.

Svirskii, Grigorii, *Na lobnom meste: literatura nravstvennogo soprotivleniia (1946–1976)* (At the Place of Execution: The Literature of Moral Resistance, 1946–1976; Rus.). London: Novaia literaturnaia biblioteka, 1979.

Tatu, Michel, *Power in the Kremlin*. New York: Viking Press, 1969.

Tillett, Lowell, *The Great Friendship: Soviet Historians on the Non-Russian Nationalities*. Durham: University of North Carolina Press, 1969.

Tokes, Rudolf L. (ed.), *Dissent in the USSR*. Baltimore and London: Johns Hopkins, 1975.

Ulam, Adam, *Expansion and Coexistence*. New York: Praeger, 1968.

Vaisman, Barukh, *Yoman mahteret ivri* (Hebrew Underground Diary; Heb.). Ramat Gan: Massada, 1973.

West, Benjamin, *Struggles of a Generation*. Tel Aviv: Massada, 1959.

Wiesel, Elie, *The Jews of Silence*. London: Valentine and Mitchell, 1969.

Wollin, Simon, and Slusser, Richard M., *The Soviet Secret Police*. London: Macmillan, 1957.

Zilberman, David, *Iosif Kuzkovskii* (Rus.). Tel Aviv: Kariv, 1975.


**Articles and chapters in books**

Alexander, Z., "Immigration to Israel from the USSR," *Israel Yearbook on Human Rights*, VII (1977), pp. 268–335.

Appelbaum Paul S., "U.S. Jews' Reaction to Soviet 'Anti-Zionism'," *Patterns of Prejudice*, XII, 2 (March–April 1978), pp. 21–32.

Averbuch, Isaiy, "Jewish Samizdat and the Means of Its Preparation," *Behinot* (Heb.), 8–9 (1978), pp. 52–67.

Averbukh, Yeshayahu, "Jewish Samizdat at the End of the Forties: Margarita Aliger's Poem 'Your Victory'," in Ro'i and Beker, *Jewish Culture and Identity*.

Bociurkiw, Bohdan R., "De-Stalinization and Religion in the USSR," *International Relations*, XX, 3 (Summer 1965), pp. 312–330.

"Church–State Relations in the USSR," in Hayward and Fletcher, *Religion in the Soviet State*.

Feuer, Lewis, "The Soviet Jews: Resistance to Planned Culturocide," *Judaism*, XIII, 1 (Winter 1964), pp. 90–100.

Friedberg, Maurice, "Defending Soviet Jews: Placards or Memoranda?" *Midstream*, XI, 3 (Sept. 1965), pp. 59–64.

Garber, David, "Choir and Drama in Riga," *Soviet Jewish Affairs*, 1 (1974), pp. 39–44.

Gelfond, Meir, "Illegal Zionist Activity in the Soviet Union in the 1950s– 1960s," in Prital, *In Search of Self*.

Goldberg, Ben Zion, "Travels in the Soviet Union," *Midstream*, XII, 9 (Nov. 1966), pp. 3–19.

Govrin, Yosef, "Israel–Soviet Relations 1964–1966," Research Paper, No. 29, The Soviet and East European Research Center, The Hebrew University of Jerusalem, 1978.

Gurevitch, Baruch, "On the Underground 'Escape Route' in Lithuania and Latvia in 1946," *Shvut* (Heb.), 10 (1984), pp. 101–119.

Hoffman, Stefani, "Jewish Samizdat and the Rise of Jewish National Consciousness in the Soviet Union," in Ro'i and Beker, *Jewish Culture and Identity*.

Hollander, Fay, "Russia Through a Woman's Eyes," *Jewish Life*, XXXIII, 2 (Nov.–Dec. 1965), pp. 25–34.

Korey, William, "The 'Right to Leave' for Soviet Jews," *Soviet Jewish Affairs*, 1 (June 1971), pp. 5–12.

Netzer, Zvi, "Jewish Emigration from the USSR in 1981–82," *Soviet Jewish Affairs*, XII, 3 (Nov. 1982), pp. 3–17.

Poupko, Bernard A., "Mission to Soviet Jewry," *Jewish Life*, XXXIII (Sept.–Oct. 1965), pp. 8–25.

Ro'i, Yaacov, "The Festival of Passover versus the Soviet Regime," *Bar-Ilan, Annual of Bar-Ilan University. Studies in Judaica and the Humanities*, XXIV–XXV (1989), pp. 173–195.

"Jewish Emigration and Soviet–Arab Relations, 1954–67," in Kedourie, Elie, and Haim, Sylvia G. (eds.), *Zionism and Arabism in Palestine and Israel*. London: Frank Cass, 1982.

"Nehama Lifshitz – Symbol of the Jewish National Awakening," in Ro'i and Beker, *Jewish Culture and Identity*.

"The Role of the Synagogue and Religion in the Jewish National Awakening," in Ro'i and Beker, *Jewish Culture and Identity*.

"Soviet Policy in the Middle East: The Case of Palestine during World War II," *Cahiers du monde russe et soviétique*, XV, 3–4 (July–Dec. 1974), pp. 373–408.

Rothenberg, Joshua, "Jewish Religion in the Soviet Union," in Kochan, *Jews in Soviet Russia*.

Shmeruk, Kh., "Hapirsumim beyidish bivrit hamoatsot 1917–1960" (Publications in Yiddish in the Soviet Union, 1917–1960; Heb.), in Shmeruk, Kh. (ed.), *Pirsumim yehudiim bivrit hamoatsot 1917–1960* (Jewish Publications in the Soviet Union, 1917–1960; Heb.). Jerusalem: Historical Society of Israel, 1961.

Slutsky, Yehuda, "Zvi Pregerzon," *Behinot* (Heb.), 6 (1975), pp. 88–102.

Tsitsuashvili, Gershon, "We Wanted to Produce a Large Aliya," in Prital, *In Search of Self*.

Weiss, David, "The Plight of the Jews in the Soviet Union. A Culture in Torment," *Dissent*, XIII, 4 (July–Aug. 1966), pp. 447–464.

Yedidya, Vera, "The Struggle for the Study of Hebrew," in Ro'i and Beker, *Jewish Culture and Identity*.

Zand, Michael, "Notes on the Culture of the Non-Ashkenazi Jewish Communities under Soviet Rule," in Ro'i and Beker, *Jewish Culture and Identity*.

# Index

## Soviet and East European Studies

# Soviet and East European Studies